Contemporary Issues in Adolescent Development

Contemporary Issues in Adolescent Development

John Janeway Conger
University of Colorado School of Medicine

HARPER & ROW, PUBLISHERS

New York, Evanston, San Francisco, London

To the Memory of
John D. Benjamin, Mark Rudnick, and René Spitz

Sponsoring Editor: George A. Middendorf
Project Editor: David Nickol
Designer: Scott Chelius
Cover Designer: Rita Naughton
Production Supervisor: Will C. Jomarron

CONTEMPORARY ISSUES IN ADOLESCENT DEVELOPMENT

Library of Congress Cataloging in Publication Data

Conger, John Janeway, comp.
Contemporary issues in adolescent development.

1. Adolescence—Addresses, essays, lectures.
2. Adolescent psychology—Addresses, essays, lectures.
3. Youth—Sexual behavior—Addresses, essays, lectures.
I. Title.
HQ796.C77   301.43'15   74–14345
ISBN 0-06-041363-8

contents

53/23

preface

The primary aim of this book is to explore, through selected studies, issues of contemporary concern in the field of adolescent development. In some instances this involves taking a fresh look at long-standing problems, such as the effects of physical or cognitive growth on personality development and functioning during adolescence. In other instances, however, the problems themselves are, if not entirely new, at least very different in the forms in which they are currently manifested. Exploring such issues (e.g., changing sex roles, newer forms of alienation, changing sexual values and behavior) requires an examination not only of these phenomena themselves and their effects on adolescents, but also of the social conditions that helped to bring them about.

Today's adolescents are coming to maturity in a rapidly changing, complex, conflict-ridden society, and it is my strong conviction that any attempt to provide a sophisticated, meaningful view of contemporary adolescent development must include an appreciation of current social change. As will become apparent in the course of the book, the adolescent's development—psychological, social, even cognitive and physical—is significantly influenced by changes in such social institutions as the family, schools, and the world of work, as well as by the conflicts and divisions taking place in society generally. It should not be surprising, therefore, that the articles selected for inclusion are drawn from a wide variety of sources—psychological and psychiatric, sociological, biological, even philosophical and literary.

It has become somewhat of a cliché to say that these are "the best of times and the worst of times." Nevertheless, the fact remains that adolescents today face problems in establishing a secure sense of personal identity, in developing a stable value system, and in choosing a direction for their lives, which are much more complex than was the case in more static, less ambiguous social eras. At the same time, the very ambiguity of the current social climate and the variety of choices in interpersonal relationships, social involvement, and work that are open to the adolescent potentially provide unique opportunities for personal growth and development. Whether the individual adolescent will be able to take advantage of these opportunities or will instead be overwhelmed by the complexity of the attendant problems will depend largely on prior and continuing patterns of parent-child relationships, the degree of support provided by peers and interested adults, and the kinds of commitments that a thus far reluctant society is willing to make to the welfare of its most valuable resource—its young people.

The readership to which the book is addressed includes students in developmental psychology, sociology, education, child and adolescent psychiatry, pediatrics, and adolescent medicine and nursing. The book can be used either as a supplement to textbooks in these fields or in its own right. It is also intended to be of use to graduate students and established professionals in these various fields, as well as to others interested in the problems of adolescence during these troubled and challenging times.

I would like to express my deep appreciation to the authors of the various studies contained in the book, and to their publishers, for permission to include their work. Whatever merit the book may have is obviously due to their wholehearted cooperation and encouragement. I would also like to thank my friend and frequent collaborator, Paul Henry Mussen, for his helpfulness in reviewing the introductions to the various parts of this book. Finally, I would like to express my continuing gratitude to my longtime friend and secretary, Dorothy R. Townsend, for her invaluable assistance in putting this book together. Without her help in tracking down articles, obtaining permissions, deciphering my illegible hieroglyphics, and typing the manuscript—all in her usual calm, pleasant, and intelligent way—there would have been no book.

J. J. C.

one

psychological aspects of adolescent growth and development

part one

Many adults have long since forgotten how acutely aware the average adolescent is of the physical and physiological changes that accompany puberty. Yet such intense awareness is hardly surprising. One of the major tasks of the adolescent period is the development of a sense of identity, of who one is as a person. A sense of identity, in turn, requires being able to perceive the self as separate from others (despite ties to them); it also requires a feeling of "wholeness," that is, a feeling of self-consistency not only in the sense of internal consistency at a particular moment but over time. One needs to feel that although he is not precisely the same today as he was yesterday, he is at least very similar to, and has meaningful links with, the person he was yesterday.

However, the adolescent (particularly the younger adolescent) is faced with rapid increases in height, changing bodily dimensions, and the objective and subjective changes related to sexual maturation. Obviously, all of these developments challenge the adolescent's feeling of self-consistency, and he needs time to integrate them into a gradually emerging sense of positive, self-confident ego identity.

This problem is not made easier by the shift toward a greater dependence on peers and a reduced dependence on parents that occur during this same period. Like any marginal group concerned about where it presently stands and, more importantly, where it is headed, the adolescent peer group often tends to overemphasize conformity to group norms, not only in social behavior, but in appearance and abilities; it also tends to be critical, sometimes highly critical, of apparent deviations. Although there have been some hopeful signs recently of a greater tolerance of diversity among some groups of young people, deviance in rate of development and physical appearance can still be an agonizing experience for many adolescents.

As Paul Henry Mussen and Mary Cover Jones demonstrate in the first article in this part, the problem is likely to be greater for boys who mature late than for those who mature early. The latter may have a number of problems not faced by boys who mature at an average rate (e.g., being expected, because of their more mature appearance, to behave in a more adult manner or to possess a higher level of skills than other same-aged peers). But at least the early maturer is already developing in the direction ultimately expected of and by all males.

In contrast, the late maturer may wonder when, if ever, he will catch up physically and sexually with his more mature peers. And he may tend to be treated longer as "a little boy." It is thus not too surprising that Mussen and Jones found late maturers to be more "immoderate" in their behavior, more tense and eager in manner, more talkative, more restless, and more involved in attention-getting behavior. What is more dramatic is that initial differences between early and late maturers still tended to be reflected in behavior many years later.

As Margaret Siler Faust shows in the second article, differences between early- and late-maturing girls, while generally not as great as for boys (perhaps because of more rigid sex-typed social pressures on boys for "manly" development), are more complicated and tend to vary with age. She found that at the sixth-grade level early maturation (as determined by age of menarche) tended to be a social handicap, but by the eighth and ninth grades, early maturers were viewed more favorably by their peers. As Faust points out, such discontinuities can place considerable psychological strain on the girl, particularly the late maturer who may be favored initially by her peers only to be, in a sense, left behind a year or two later.

As noted at the outset, the physiological changes associated with puberty, including marked hormonal changes, may produce direct effects not only on outwardly observable development but also on the adolescent's subjective feelings and motivations, providing at times a feeling of "strangeness" about one's own reactions. A variety of investigations have found a significantly higher level of physical aggressiveness and sexual pressures among adolescent boys than among their female peers, and it has been hypothesized that this may be related to much higher rates of testosterone (male hormone) production among adolescent males. Harold Persky, Keith D. Smith, and Gopal K. Basu found that the production rate of testosterone was highly correlated with psychological measures of hostility and aggression in younger (but not older) males.[1] It appears that a higher rate of testosterone production may lead to increased aggressive behavior, but it is also possible that the relationship between these two variables is a two-way street: Some recent animal research indicates that male primates show a decrease in testosterone levels when deprived of a dominant role with females and other males.

Among girls, as the ingenious study by Melville Ivey Boufford and Judith M. Bardwick (the third reading) demonstrates, hormonal fluctuations in the course of the menstrual cycle may produce significant and predictable fluctuations in mood. Anxiety, for example, tends to be higher during the premenstrual stage than during ovulation, which is more likely to be characterized by feelings of satisfaction and success.

As we shall see in later parts of this book, many other factors play an important role in determining the kind of adult an adolescent will become—the particular personality characteristics, the abilities and skills, and the degree of personal satisfaction, self-reliance, and social effectiveness he or she will manifest. In many instances the kind of parents an adolescent has, the peers he interacts with, and the social institutions to which he is exposed will prove crucial. But humans are biological as well as social beings and will inevitably reflect, either directly or indirectly, the influences of biological factors in their development.

---

[1] H. Persky, K. D. Smith, and G. K. Basu, Relation of Psychologic Measures of Aggression and Hostility to Testosterone Production in Man. *Psychomatic Medicine,* 1971, *33,* 265–277.

Self-conceptions, motivations, and interpersonal attitudes of late- and early-maturing boys

Paul Henry Mussen   Mary Cover Jones
University of California, Berkeley

While intensive case studies show that personal and social adjustment during adolescence may be profoundly influenced by rate of physical maturation, there is a scarcity of systematic data on the relationship between the adolescent's physical status and his underlying motivations, self-conceptions, and interpersonal attitudes. There is, however, a small body of evidence which demonstrates that greater physical maturity is associated with greater maturity of interest among girls (*10*) and that early-maturing boys differ from their late-maturing peers in both overt behavior and reputational status. In one study (*8*) in which a staff of trained observers assessed a large group of adolescents on a number of personality variables, boys who were consistently retarded in physical development were rated lower than those who were consistently accelerated in physical attractiveness, grooming, and matter-of-factness; and higher in sociability, social initiative (often of a childish, attention-getting sort), and eagerness. Reputation Test (*11*) data indicated that classmates regarded the late-maturing boys as more attention-getting, more restless, more bossy, less grown-up and less good-looking than those who were physically accelerated.

On the basis of these findings, it may be inferred that adult and peer attitudes toward the adolescent, as well as their treatment and acceptance of him, are related to his physical status. This means that the sociopsychological environment to which late-maturers are subjected—and consequently the social learning situations they encounter—may be significantly different from that of their early-maturing peers. As a consequence, according to the ratings summarized above, they acquire different patterns of overt social behavior. It seems reasonable to hypothesize that groups differing in physical status will also differ in more covert aspects of behavior and personality.

Indirect evidence relevant to this hypothesis comes from an investiga-

Reprinted from Child Development, 1957, 28, 243–256. Copyright © 1957 by The Society for Research in Child Development, Inc. By permission.

tion of the long-term consequences of physical acceleration or retardation during adolescence. Jones (6) found that group differences in physique had practically disappeared by the time her early- and late-maturing subjects reached their early thirties. Nevertheless, young adults who had been physically retarded adolescents differed from those who had been accelerated in several important psychological characteristics. In general, it appeared that the adult subjects could be described much as they had been during adolescence. Thus, those who had been early-maturers scored higher on the good impression, socialization, dominance, self-control (low score on impulsivity), and responsibility scales of the California Psychological Inventory, while those who had been slow in maturing scored higher on the flexibility scale. On the Edwards Personal Preference Schedule, early-maturers scored significantly higher on the dominance scale, while the late-maturing were high in succorance. Jones concludes that the early-maturing "present a consistently favorable personality picture with regard to . . . important social variables" (6). Moreover, there was some evidence that these men had attained more stable vocational adjustments than those who had been late in maturing. These group differences in later adjustment suggest that the sociopsychological atmosphere in which the adolescent lives may have profound immediate and enduring effects on his personality structure as well as on his overt behavior.

The present study was designed to investigate the relationship between maturational status and certain important covert aspects of personality during late adolescence. Personality structure was assessed by means of the Thematic Apperception Test (TAT) which seems to be the most appropriate and sensitive instrument for this purpose. More specifically, on the basis of the literature reviewed above and other general works on the psychology of adolescence (1, 4, 5), we formulated and tested a series of propositions relating to differences between the physically retarded and accelerated in self-conceptions, underlying motivations, and basic interpersonal attitudes. These variables were translated into TAT categories—needs (*n*), Press (*p*), and descriptions (defined briefly in Table 1)—and the scores of early- and late-maturers in each of these categories were compared. The propositions and the rationale underlying them, together with the TAT variables involved, follow.

1. In view of their obvious physical retardation, relatively unfavorable reputations and disadvantageous competitive position in many activities, the late-maturing boys are more likely to have feelings of inadequacy. Hence, more boys in this group than in the early-maturing group are likely to have negative self-conceptions (TAT category: *negative characteristics*).

2. The adolescent in our culture generally desires some independence and adult status. This may be the source of a major problem for the late-maturer, however, since he is often regarded and treated as a small boy by adults and peers and is not likely to be granted independence as early as physically accelerated boys. Therefore, it may be anticipated that more late- than early-maturers regard adults, particularly their parents, as dominating, forcing them to do things they don't want to or preventing them from doing things they want to do (high scores in *p Dominance*). Moreover, the parental treatment these boys experience and parental refusal to grant them independent status may be interpreted as personal

Table 1
**Number of Early- and Late-Maturers Scoring High in
TAT Variables**

TAT Variable	Definition of Variable	High Early-Maturers	High Late-Maturers	Chi-Square Value	P
Proposition 1					
Negative characteristics	H is described in negative terms (e.g., imbecile, weakling, fanatic)	5	13	6.80	<.01
Proposition 2					
p Dominance 1	H forced by parents to do something he doesn't want to do	4	8	1.73	.09
p Dominance 2	H prevented by parents from doing something he wants to do	6	8	.31	>.30
p Dominance 3	Total instance of H's being forced by parents to do something and/or prevented from doing something	7	11	1.46	.11
p Rejection	H rejected, scorned, or disapproved of by parents or authorities	5	11	3.69	.03
Proposition 3					
n Aggression 1	H is aggressive in physical, asocial way	8	3	3.88	.02
n Aggression 2	H is mad at someone, argues	7	4	1.52	.10
n Aggression 3	Total of all H's aggressive actions	11	8	1.26	.10
n Autonomy 1	H leaves home	7	10	.75	.20
n Autonomy 2	H disobeys or defies parents	7	11	1.46	.11
n Autonomy 3	Total of instances in which hero leaves and/or defies his parents	3	9	4.16	.02
Proposition 4					
n Affiliation 1	H establishes good relations with his parents	8	8	.00	>.50
n Affiliation 2	H falls in love, has a romance, marries	9	14	2.66	.05

Table 1   *(Continued)*

TAT Variable	Definition of Variable	High Early-Maturers	High Late-Maturers	Chi-Square Value	P
n Affiliation 3	Total instance in which H establishes and/or maintains friendly relations	8	12	1.46	.11
Proposition 5					
n Succorance	H feels helpless, seeks aid or sympathy	7	12	2.43	.06
p Nurturance 1	H is helped, encouraged, or given something by parents	5	8	.93	.18
p Nurturance 2	H is helped, encouraged, or given something by someone else (not parents)	8	14	3.88	.02
Proposition 6					
n Achievement	H attempts to attain a high goal or to do something creditable	9	10	.02	> .50
n Recognition	H seeks fame and/or high prestige status	9	8	.28	> .30
Proposition 7					
Denial of feeling	H states that picture elicits no thoughts or feelings	9	5	2.43	.06

rejection. Hence we predicted that more late-maturing boys would score high in *p Rejection.*

3. These feelings of being dominated and rejected may result in attitudes of rebellion against the family and in feelings of hostility. We therefore expected that more of the late-maturing group would reveal strong aggressive needs (high scores in *n Aggression*) and desires to escape from (*n Autonomy*—leaving parents), or to defy, the family (*n Autonomy*—defying parents).

4. On the basis of the data indicating that slow-maturers showed a great deal of social interest (although often of an immature kind), we hypothesized that more members of this, than of the early-maturing group would reveal strong interests in friendly, intimate interpersonal relationships (high scores in *n Affiliation*).

5. Assuming that, as Jones and Bayley (*8*) suggest, the social initiative and attention-getting devices of the late-maturers are of a compensatory

nature, we would expect this group to be basically dependent and to have strong needs for support from others. These should be manifest by higher scores in TAT *n Succorance* and *p Nurturance*. The latter may be considered a more indirect measure of dependence, a kind of wish-fulfilling view of the world as helpful and friendly.

6. The early-maturer, being regarded and treated as more adult, is more likely to become self-confident, and to acquire high status goals. For these reasons, we predicted that more of the physically accelerated would give evidence of high achievement goals (high scores in *n Achievement*) and concern with personal recognition (high scores in *n Recognition*).

7. Late-maturing boys in our culture probably face more problems of personal adjustment than do their early-maturing peers. As a result of this, they may become more aware of their problems, and, as the high degree of flexibility of young adults who had been retarded in maturing suggests, more insightful. Hence we predicted that they would be more willing and able than early-maturers to face their own feelings and emotions (low score in the TAT variable *denial of feeling*).

In summary, we attempted to test seven propositions related to difference in the personalities of early- and late-maturing boys. It was hypothesized that more late-maturers would score high in variables relating to negative self-conceptions, dependence, aggression, affiliation, rebelliousness, and feelings of being dominated and rejected. More early-maturers, on the other hand, were expected to reveal strong achievement and recognition needs, feelings of personal success, and tendencies toward denial of feelings.

PROCEDURE

The thirty-three 17-year-old male subjects of this investigation were members of the Adolescent Growth Study which included a normal sample of boys in an urban public school system (3). The subjects of the present investigation represented two contrasting groups, selected on the basis of their physical maturity status: 16 of them had been among the most consistently accelerated throughout the adolescent period; the other 17 had been among the most consistently retarded.[1] All of them took the Thematic Apperception Test, which provides the basic data of this study, at age 17.

The TAT consisted of 18 pictures: nine from the Murray set which is now standard (cards, 1, 5, 6, 7BM, 10, 11, 14, 15, 17); five pictures from the set generally used in 1938 when these data were collected (a man

---

[1] The present sample includes 27 of Jones and Bayley's (8) 32 subjects (the 16 most consistently retarded and 16 most consistently accelerated boys in the study). The other five boys had not taken the TAT at age 17. The six subjects who were in the present study but not in Jones and Bayley's study are the three "runners-up" from each end of the physical maturity distribution, i.e., the three who were closest to the 16 most accelerated cases and the three cases next to the 16 most retarded.

and woman seated on a park bench; a bearded old man writing in an open book; a thin, sullen, young man standing behind a well-dressed older man; a tea table and two chairs; an abstract drawing of two bearded men); and four designed especially for this investigation (the nave of a large church; a madonna and child; a dramatic view of mountains; a boy gazing at a cross which is wreathed in clouds).

The tests were administered individually. Each card was projected on a screen while the subject told a story which was recorded verbatim. Standard instructions were given for the Murray cards, and subjects were asked to describe the feelings elicited by the other four pictures. Most of the stories were brief, consisting of only one or two sentences.

As we noted earlier, each of the personality variables involved in the seven propositions was translated into a TAT scoring category. The scoring scheme involved counting the relevant needs, press, and descriptions of the heroes of the stories, the assumption being that the storyteller has identified with the hero: the hero's needs are the same as the boy's; the press that impinge upon the hero are the ones that affect the boy telling the story. A total of 20 needs, press, and descriptive categories, each defined as specifically as possible, was developed in the analysis of the protocols. A score for each subject for each TAT category was derived by counting the number of stories in which it appeared. A list of the categories used, together with brief descriptions of them, is found in Table 1.

To test the reliability of this analysis, one of the authors (PM) and another psychologist[2] independently scored 15 complete protocols (300 stories). The percentage of interrater agreement was 90, computed by the usual formula (number of agreements divided by number of agreements plus number of disagreements).

In order to eliminate bias, the scoring used in the present study was done "blind," that is, independent of knowledge of the subject's maturational status.

RESULTS

Frequency distributions of the scores of all subjects were made for all the TAT variables. Each distribution was then dichotomized at the point which most nearly enabled the placing of half of the 33 subjects above, and half of them below, the dividing point. Subjects having scores above this point were considered high in this particular variable; those with scores below this point were considered low in this variable. Chi-square tests were used to test the seven propositions, i.e., to ascertain whether or not high scores in certain TAT variables were in fact more characteristic of one group (late- or early-maturers) than of the other.

Table 1 lists the TAT variables, the number of late- and early-maturers with high scores in the variable, the chi-square value obtained and the

[2] We are indebted to Dr. Virginia B. Ware for her participation in this aspect of the study.

level of significance. It should be noted that the hypotheses tested were one-sided hypotheses, while the chi-square value is in terms of a two-sided hypothesis. When chi-square has only one degree of freedom, the square root of chi-square has a distribution which is the right hand half of a normal distribution. In order to test a one-sided hypothesis, the chi-square test must be converted into the equivalent value in terms of a unit normal deviate (2). The levels of significance reported in Table 1 were evaluated in these terms.

Table 1 shows that, as had been predicted, more late-maturing than early-maturing boys revealed feelings of inadequacy and negative self-concepts, i.e., scored high in the TAT variable *negative characteristics.* Hence proposition 1 was confirmed. This finding is consistent with the frequently made clinical observation that retardation in physical maturation may be an important source of personal maladjustment and attitudes of inferiority.

Proposition 2 stated that more late-maturers regard their parents as highly dominating and rejecting. The evidence summarized in Table 1 substantially supported this proposition. While the difference was not statistically significant, more late- than early-maturers scored high in *p Dominance by parents* (total). There was a marked difference between the groups in the variable which involves parental domination by forcing the child to do something he does not want to do (*p Dominance by parents, forcing*). However, examination of the data with respect to the variable *p Dominance by parents* (*prevention*) makes it necessary to reject that part of the proposition which maintains that late-maturers are more likely to view their parents as highly restrictive of their activities.

That aspect of proposition 2 which deals with feelings of rejection was confirmed by our data. Compared with the early-maturing group a significantly greater proportion of the late-maturers told stories in which the hero was rejected by parents or authority figures. These feelings of rejection may stem from different sources. In some cases, the parents' behavior may make it clear that they are disappointed in their physically retarded son whom they regard as immature. The boy, perceiving this attitude, may interpret it as rejection. In other cases, parental reluctance to allow the late-maturing boy to establish his independence may lead to considerable tension in the family and the boy's feelings of rejection may simply reflect the ongoing parent-child conflict.

It is possible that earlier in their teens, soon after the physical changes of adolescence became apparent, many of the early-maturing boys also experienced conflicts with their parents, arising from difficulties in establishing their independence or in handling emerging heterosexual interests. At that time they too may have felt dominated or rejected. However, by the age of 17, when these data were collected, these boys were ordinarily treated as adults and granted more freedom. Hence, they were more likely to have resolved many of their conflicts with their parents and to feel accepted and independent.

The hypothesis (part of proposition 3) that more late-maturers would be highly aggressive was rejected on the basis of the evidence given in Table 1. In fact, the differences between the two groups on all the TAT aggression variables were in the opposite direction from the prediction.

High scores in the variables relating to aggression of the most overt and violent type were significantly more frequent among the early-maturers, and more members of this group also scored high in measures of milder (verbal) aggression and of total aggression. While late-maturers may experience more problems of adjustment and greater frustrations than their early-maturing peers, they apparently do not manifest greater aggressive motivation. It may be that their own feelings of inadequacy or fears of retaliation and punishment for aggression inhibit their expression of hostile feelings, even in fantasy. On the other hand, the early-maturers who feel more secure personally, and recognize their own relatively advantageous physical and social status, may feel freer to express their aggressive needs. Since aggression is a culturally stereotyped masculine trait, it seems possible that the physically accelerated, being accepted as mature and identifying readily with adult males, are more likely to acquire this characteristic. In any case, the finding that early-maturers express higher aggressive motivation during late adolescence seems consistent with Jones' finding that, as young adults, they score high on the dominance scale of the Edwards Personal Preference test (6). Perhaps the relatively strong aggressive motivation of the early-maturer, or the mature sex-role identification it may imply, serves as a basis for the development of later qualities of leadership and persuasiveness (7).

As Table 1 indicates, the other aspect of proposition 3 was confirmed: a significantly greater proportion of late- than of early-maturers displayed strong motivations to escape from, or defy, their parents. These may be essentially aggressive reactions, stemming from feelings of parental domination and rejection, or they may reflect the late-maturers' awareness of their strife with their parents whom they perceive as blocking their drives for independence. These strong needs for escape and defiance may also be considered evidence of a generally immature way of handling parent-child conflicts. Perhaps, by the age of 17, the early-maturers have already resolved many of their conflicts with their families and/or have learned to handle these in less rebellious and in more direct and mature ways.

Proposition 4 stated that, compared with their early-maturing peers, more late-maturers would manifest strong needs for establishing close social contacts with others. While there was some confirmatory evidence, the results were not clear-cut. When all affiliative needs were considered together (score for *n Affiliation—total*), the group differences were in the predicted direction, but not statistically significant. Examination of the protocols revealed that almost all instances of affiliation concerned either parents or the opposite sex; there were very few stories involving close, friendly associations between like-sexed peers. The two major types of affiliation were scored separately. As Table 1 shows, late-maturers did not differ from early-maturers with respect to need for affiliation with parents, but a significantly greater proportion of the former group displayed strong motivation for heterosexual affiliation.

In view of the late-maturers' strong feelings of inadequacy and dependent needs (see below), it is surprising that a greater proportion of this group did not exhibit strong needs to establish and maintain close bonds with their parents. This may be due to the late-maturers' more intense conflicts with their parents at this age (17 years), their fears of being rejected and dominated by them, and their generally defiant attitudes which prevent them from admitting, even in fantasy, their strong underlying needs to form close contacts with them.

The significant difference between groups in *n Affiliation* (*love, romance, marriage*) is subject to several possible interpretations. For one thing, this category may refer to general needs to establish close relations with others (with peers or adults other than parents) and not merely to desire for contact with the opposite sex. The set of stimulus cards may not have been adequate to elicit responses indicative of more general affiliative needs; hence, these were expressed through responses in the heterosexual affiliation category. If this is true, proposition 4 was confirmed, and the late-maturers' high scores in this variable indicate their greater general interest in establishing and maintaining friendly relationships.

It is also possible that the late-maturers' strong affiliative needs are actually directed only toward members of the opposite sex, i.e., that *n Affiliation* (*love, romance, marriage*) measures specifically heterosexual interests. Assuming that this is true, there is another plausible explanation for the discovered difference. As we saw earlier, the late-maturer may be afraid to admit that he desires close associations with his parents. He may also feel that his immaturity and poor reputational status prevent him from establishing successful social relationships with like-sexed peers. Hence, he may "displace" his affiliative needs to members of the opposite sex, who in his fantasies, may seem more responsive.

A third possible explanation of the difference is based on Jones and Bayley's findings that the late-maturers show less overt interest in girls and are regarded as less good-looking (*8*). From these data, it may be inferred that the physically retarded probably do not have successful and rewarding experiences with girls. Hence their heightened need for affiliation with the opposite sex, expressed in the TAT, may reflect their attempts to satisfy in fantasy needs which they cannot satisfy adequately in reality.

The data were generally supportive of proposition 5 which stated that late-maturers are likely to have strong underlying dependent needs. A higher proportion of this group than of their early-maturing peers scored high in *n Succorance,* the difference between the two groups approaching statistical significance ($p = .06$). Furthermore, high scores in the category involving receiving help and support from others (not including parents) (*p Nurturance—nonparents*)—an indirect measure of dependent needs— were significantly more characteristic of the physically retarded than of the physically accelerated. In view of the late-maturers' attitudes toward their parents, discussed above, it is not surprising to find that perceptions of parents as kindly and supportive (high scores in *p Nurturance-parents*) were not significantly more common in this group than in the early-maturing group.

On the basis of the data involving the TAT variables *n Achievement* and *n Recognition,* we rejected proposition 6 which stated that more early-maturers would be self-confident and have high needs for achievement and personal recognition. In our culture there is strong pressure to develop needs for achievement and personal recognition, and, according to our results, these needs and feelings may become intense regardless of—or perhaps in spite of—the child's maturational status, feelings of personal adequacy, dependency, and adjustment to parents.

Two interesting incidental findings from the TAT data seem to be consistent with the proposition that more early- than late-maturers are likely to be self-confident. Seven boys in this sample of 33 adolescents told stories in which the hero was helpful or kind to someone else (*n Nurturance*). Of this group, six were early-maturers, while only one was a late-maturer ($\chi^2 = 2.09$, $p = .07$). Insofar as *n Nurturance* may be a measure of the storyteller's own feelings that he can accept an active, mature role, more of the accelerated group feel self-assured with respect to having attained mature status.

The other incidental finding which seems to support proposition 6 is based on responses only to card 1 of the Murray series which depicts a young boy contemplating a violin which rests on a table in front of him. Eight of the subjects spoke of the boy (the hero) as a prodigy or a genius. Of these, seven were early-maturers; only one was physically retarded ($\chi^2 = 5.25$, $p = .01$). If the attribution of this prestige status and accomplishment to the hero reflects the subject's own feeling that he has been an achiever, it follows that more of the physically accelerated have positive self-concepts. In view of the small number of cases involved, both of these findings must be considered tentative, but they do offer some evidence in support of proposition 6.

Proposition 7, which stated that relatively few of the physically retarded boys are unwilling or unable to face their own feelings and emotions, received some support from the TAT data summarized in Table 1. A smaller proportion of the members of this group than of the physically accelerated group specifically denied that the pictures evoked any feelings or emotions (e.g., "It doesn't make me think of anything"). While this variable may not adequately measure *denial of feeling* as a major defense mechanism, this result seems to indicate that late-maturers are more sensitive to their own feelings and more ready to admit and face them openly. Since these qualities are basic to the development of psychological insight, it may be inferred that late-maturers, as a group, are more likely to become insightful individuals.

DISCUSSION

The results of the study support the general hypothesis that, in our culture, the boy whose physical development is retarded is exposed to a sociopsychological environment which may have adverse effects on his personality development. Apparently, being in a disadvantageous competitive position in athletic activities, as well as being regarded and treated as immature by others, may lead to negative self-conceptions, heightened feelings of rejection by others, prolonged dependent needs, and rebellious attitudes toward parents. Hence, the physically retarded boy is more likely than his early-maturing peer to be personally and socially maladjusted during late adolescence. Moreover, some of his attitudes are likely to interfere with the process of identification with his parents, which is generally based on perceptions of them as warm and accepting (9). This, in turn, may inhibit or delay the acquisition of mature characteristics and attitudes which are ordinarily established through identification with parents. Fortunately for the late-maturers' subsequent adjustments, they seem more willing and able to face their feelings and emotions. This may be a result of their awareness of others' attitudes toward their immaturity or their feelings of personal inadequacy and dependency.

The physically accelerated boys, on the other hand, are likely to experience environmental circumstances which are much more conducive to good psychological adjustment. Hence, their psychological picture, as reflected in their TAT stories, is much more favorable. By the time they were 17, relatively few early-maturers harbored strong feelings of inadequacy, perceived themselves as rejected or dominated by parents or authorities, or felt rebellious toward their families. As a group, they appeared to have acquired more self-confidence and had probably made stronger identifications with mature adults. Hence, they perceived themselves as more mature individuals, less dependent and in need of help, and more capable of playing an adult male role in interpersonal relationships.

These findings assume additional, probably greater, importance when they are considered in the light of Jones' findings on the early adult (age 33) adjustments of boys who had been retarded or accelerated in physical maturing (6). It should be recalled that by this age physical differences between the two groups had practically disappeared. Certain important psychological differences were noted, however, and these were consistent with the differences at age 17, reported in the present study. For example, the responses of the early-maturing group to two paper-and-pencil tests revealed that, as young adults, they were more dominant, more able to make a good impression, and more likely to be turned to for advice and reassurance; more self-controlled; and more willing and able to carry social responsibility. In short, they present a general picture of psychological maturity. Moreover, more of the early-maturers seemed to have made successful vocational adjustments. In contrast to this, when the late-maturers became adults, they tended to be highly dependent individuals who could be described, on the basis of their test responses, as tending to be rebellious, touchy, impulsive, self-indulgent, and insightful. Most of these characteristics are indicative of poor adjustment and psychological immaturity. Fewer of this group had made good vocational adjustments.

The striking correspondence between the two descriptions of the groups, derived from different kinds of tests and collected at widely separated periods of time, lends further support to Jones' conclusion that "the adolescent handicaps and advantages associated with late- or early-maturing appear to carry over into adulthood to some extent" (6). It seems clear that many attributes of adolescent personality (patterns of motivation, self-conceptions, and attitudes toward others) characteristic of late- and early-maturing boys are relatively stable and durable rather than situational and transitory. This may be attributable to the fact that in our culture adolescence is generally a critical and difficult period of adjustment. Within a relatively brief interval of time, the child must work out numerous complex and vitally important personal problems, e.g., adaptation to his changed biological and social status, establishment of independence, vocational adjustment. In dealing with these problems, he may acquire new behaviors and personality attributes which have broad ramifications, not only on his current adjustment, but also on his subsequent development. If the adolescent can cope with his problems without too much inner stress and turmoil, his self-esteem, feelings of adequacy, and consequently his subsequent adjustment, are likely to be enhanced. On the other hand, if his problems induce great tension and anxiety, he is likely to feel frustrated and inadequate, and, if these feelings are maintained, to adjust less satisfactorily as an adult.

Obviously, the adolescents' success or failure, as well as ease or tension, in handling his problems will be determined to a large degree by the sociopsychological forces to which he is subjected during this time, and these, as we have seen, may be significantly related to his rate of maturation. Thus, physical status during adolescence—mediated through the sociopsychological environment—may exert profound and lasting influences on personality. For this reason, many aspects of the adult's behavior and personality seem consistent with his adolescent adjustments, attitudes and motivations.

Insofar as our results permit generalization, they suggest that some important aspects of motivation, such as needs for achievement and personal recognition, are not significantly affected by maturational status. It may be that among subjects whose achievements are strongly encouraged and rewarded from very early childhood, the need to achieve becomes powerful and resistant to change even in the face of feelings of helplessness and inadequacy. The latter may inhibit the achievement-oriented overt behavior of some late-maturers, but the underlying motivation to achieve seems as strong in this group as it is among the physically accelerated.

In conclusion, it should be noted that, although rate of maturing and associated factors may affect personality development, the relationship between physical status and psychological characteristics is by no means simple. A vast number of complex, interacting factors, including rate of maturation, determine each adolescent's unique personality structure. Hence, in any specific instance, the *group* findings of the present study may not be directly applicable, for other physical, psychological, or social factors may attenuate the effects of late- or early-maturing. For example, an adolescent boy who is fundamentally secure and has warm, accepting parents and generally rewarding social relationships may not develop strong feelings of inadequacy even if he matures slowly. Analogously, the early-maturing boy who has deep feelings of insecurity, for whatever reasons, will probably not gain self-confidence simply because he matures early. In summary, in understanding any individual case, generalizations based on the data of the present study must be particularized in the light of the individual's past history and present circumstances.

SUMMARY

The present investigation was designed to test seven propositions concerning the relationship between rate of physical maturation and important aspects of personality structure, specifically, self-conceptions, underlying motivations, and basic interpersonal attitudes. The TAT protocols of thirty-three 17-year-old boys—16 who had been consistently physically accelerated throughout adolescence and 17 who had been consistently retarded—were analyzed according to a scoring schema involving 20 needs, press, and descriptive categories. The scores of early- and late-maturers in each of the categories were compared.

An earlier study (*8*) demonstrated that late-maturing boys are more likely than their early-maturing peers to encounter a generally unfavorable sociopsychological environment. Analysis of the data of the present study indicates that this situation may have adverse effects on the personalities of the physically retarded. These boys are more likely to have negative self-conceptions, feelings of inadequacy, strong feelings of being rejected and dominated, prolonged dependency needs, and rebellious attitudes toward parents. In contrast, the early-maturing boys present a much more favorable psychological picture during adolescence. Relatively few of them felt inadequate, rejected, dominated, or rebellious toward their families. More of them appeared to be self-confident, independent, and capable of playing an adult role in interpersonal relationships. Early- and late-maturing groups did not differ significantly from each other in needs for achievement or personal recognition.

These findings make it clear that rate of physical maturing may affect personality development in crucially important ways. However, it is important to note that in any particular case, the effects of early- or late-maturing may be significantly modified by the individual's psychological history and present circumstances.

REFERENCES

1. Farnham, M. L. *The adolescent.* New York: Harper & Row, 1951.
2. Fisher, R. A. *Statistical methods for research workers.* (7th ed.) Oliver & Boyd, 1938.
3. Jones, H. E. Observational methods in the study of individual development. *J. consult. Psychol.,* 1940, *4:* 234–238.
4. Jones, H. E. *Development in adolescence: approaches to the study of the individual.* Appleton-Century-Crofts, 1943.
5. Jones, H. E. Adolescence in our society. In Anniversary Papers of the Community Service Society of New York, *The family in a democratic society.* Columbia Univ. Press, 1949. Pp. 70–82.
6. Jones, M. C. The later careers of boys who were early- or late-maturing. *Child Develpm.,* 1957, *28:* 113–128.
7. Jones, M. C. A study of socialization patterns at the high school level. *J. genet. Psychol.,* 1959, *93:* 87–111.
8. Jones, M. C., & Bayley, N. Physical maturing among boys as related to behavior. *J. educ. Psychol.,* 1950, *41:* 129–148.
9. Payne, D. E., & Mussen, P. H. Parent-child relations and father identification among adolescent boys. *J. abnorm. soc. Psychol.,* 1956, *52:* 358–362.
10. Stone, C. P., & Barker, R. G. The attitudes and interests of premenarcheal and postmenarcheal girls. *J. genet. Psychol.,* 1939, *54:* 27–71.
11. Tryon, C. M. Evaluations of adolescent personality by adolescents. *Monogr. Soc. Res. Child Develpm.,* 1939, 4(4).

developmental maturity as a determinant in prestige of adolescent girls

Margaret Siler Faust
Scripps College

The factors involved in gaining and maintaining prestige during adolescence are still obscure, despite the numerous investigations which have sought to define them. Of the physical characteristics which have been studied in relation to prestige, level of maturity consistently has been found to be significant for boys (6, 8, 10). It has been clearly established that early-maturing boys command an advantage in social relations, not only during adolescence (2, 10), but in the later years of life, as well (13). The gains in strength and physical ability which accompany puberty (6, 7, 15) provide an advantage for the early-maturing boy in at least one important avenue for gaining prestige, i.e., athletics (6, 17, 18).

For girls, however, the relation between developmental maturity and prestige is less evident and has not been clearly established. While early maturing provides no obvious prestige-gaining advantage for girls (such as competence in athletics brings for boys), it seems reasonable to expect that the rate and timing of physical changes at adolescence would have significant concomitants in the behavior and reputations of adolescent girls (4, 16). One means of determining whether early puberty, with its concomitants, is advantageous or deleterious to the social status of girls would be to analyze Guess Who reputations of adolescent girls in terms of the girls' level of physical development during adolescence.

It is the purpose of the present research to determine for girls whether developmental maturity is a determinant in prestige during adolescence. The study is an extension of Tryon's *Evaluations of Adolescent Personality by Adolescents* (17), in which she noted differences between 12-year-old and 15-year-old boys and girls in their evaluation of traits with respect to prestige. In the present study of adolescent girls four consecutive grades have been included in the analysis in order to see more clearly the relationship between developmental maturity and the evaluations of prestige and other traits during this phase of adolescence. The period from the sixth to the ninth grades is generally a time of rapid physical changes for girls, and it might be expected that developmental differences among girls would be systematically associated with certain trait scores

Reprinted from Child Development, 1960, 31, 173–184. Copyright © 1960 by The Society for Research in Child Development, Inc. By permission.

of the Guess Who test. Some traits or reputations might be ascribed characteristically to the more mature rather than to the less mature girls. On the other hand, it is possible that, as the level of maturity of the girls changes from one grade to the next, their evaluations of traits and of developmental maturity may undergo progressive changes as well. In order to see more clearly the changing relationship between developmental maturity and the reputations of adolescent girls, the present analysis is undertaken for each grade separately. This may help to clarify the meaning which early and late development has for girls at various times during the adolescent period.

SUBJECTS

The subjects were 731 girls enrolled in the sixth, seventh, eighth, and ninth grades in a suburban school community.[1] Girls in the three upper grades attended junior high school, while the sixth graders attended various elementary schools, all of which were within the junior high school attendance area. The population represents roughly 96 per cent of the girls enrolled in the classes selected for the study.

PROCEDURE

The test used in this investigation was a duplication of the Guess Who test which Tryon (17) employed, with the addition of the following pair of items, which were designed to measure prestige:

Here is someone whom everyone thinks a lot of, who influences the group. What he (or she) says or does is important to the group.
Here is someone whom no one thinks much of; what he (or she) says or does matters little to the group.

The Guess Who test, comprised of 21 pairs of trait descriptions, was administered in the natural classroom setting to both boys and girls, although only the scores of the girls were analyzed for the present purpose.

Following Tryon's procedure, the sixth graders were instructed to mention on the test anyone within their classroom, while in the three junior high school grades the pupils were instructed to mention anyone within their whole grade.[2]

SCORING THE GUESS WHO TEST

For every girl the number of mentions received on the positive and the negative item of each trait pair was summed algebraically, following

[1] The author is deeply grateful to Supt. Norman O. Tallman and to school principals Messrs. Wood, Post, Niedermeyer, and Wise of the Montebello (California) Unified School District for their cooperation in this research.
[2] See Faust (3) for detailed description of administration, tabulation, and scoring procedures.

Tryon's procedure. A score of zero was assigned to anyone who was mentioned on neither item of a trait pair or who received an equal number of positive and negative mentions. Self-mentions were excluded.

For the sixth grade girls each score was expressed as a proportion of the number of mentions received relative to the number of possible mentions (girls in the class). This gave scores which were comparable among the seven sixth grade classes, which varied considerably in size.

SCORING DEVELOPMENTAL MATURITY

Developmental maturity was assessed by means of menarcheal age scores, the data for which were obtained by the school nurses for the sixth grade girls and by the women's physical education staff for the three junior high school grades. The data were obtained at a time when the girls were in a health class or physical education class separate from the boys, and when it would seem very natural for the staff to obtain such developmental data.

Subsequently, the girls were classified into four developmental groups. Girls who had not reached menarche were considered "Prepuberal," while girls who had reached menarche within a year of the time of testing were classified "Puberal." Girls who had reached menarche more than one year and less than three years prior to the testing were called "Postpuberal." All others were considered "Late Adolescent." The distribution of girls in each developmental group is given in Table 1 for the four grades.

Table 1
Classification into Developmental Groups

Grade	Prepuberal	Puberal	Postpuberal	Late Adolescent	Total
Sixth	96	29	5	0	130
Seventh	66	99	53	3	221
Eighth	17	45	104	27	193
Ninth	4	16	106	61	187
Total	183	189	268	91	731

ANALYSIS OF DATA

Pearson product-moment correlations between *prestige* and each of the other Guess Who traits were computed for each of the four grades separately, and the findings are presented in Table 2. The close correspondence between Tryon's prestige-lending traits and the traits yielding the highest correlations with *prestige* by the present method is discussed elsewhere (3).

Before testing whether Guess Who scores were a function of develop-

Table 2
**Correlations Between Prestige and Other Guess Who Traits
Within Each Grade**

	Sixth N = 130	Seventh N = 221	Eighth N = 193	Ninth N = 187
Restless	−.42**	−.31**	−.15*	−.12
Talkative	−.01	.08	.15*	.05
Active-Games	.18*	.27**	.42**	.34**
Humor-Jokes	.23**	.34**	.29**	.35**
Friendly	.68**	.73**	.68**	.68**
Leader	.48**	.46**	.67**	.63**
Fights	−.27**	−.15**	−.10	−.05
Assured-Class	.43**	.33**	.55**	.34**
Daring	.47**	.39**	.41**	.50**
Tidy	.57**	.48**	.48**	.35**
Older Friends	.20*	.17*	.27**	.05
Humor-Self	.35**	.35**	.75**	.59**
Grown-up	.33**	.25**	.19**	.20**
Attention-getting	−.23**	−.09	−.18*	−.33**
Assured-Adults	.57**	.41**	.45**	.48**
Popular	.68**	.80**	.93**	.82**
Happy	.43**	.62**	.67**	.58**
Good-looking	.65**	.42**	.42**	.54**
Enthusiastic	.65**	.56**	.67**	.61**
Bossy	.15	−.01	−.03	−.12

* Significant at .05 level.
** Significant at .01 level.

mental maturity, it was necessary to ascertain whether the various developmental groups within each grade were of comparable CA. Analysis of variance revealed that, at each grade, the developmentally more mature girls were significantly older than the less mature girls. Therefore, it became necessary to determine whether CA differences within a grade were related to Guess Who test scores. Twenty-one correlations between CA and Guess Who scores were computed for each grade. Of these 84 correlations, only one reached significance at the .05 level of confidence, and one is fewer than would be expected on a chance basis alone! Therefore it was unnecessary to use a covariance method of holding CA constant while analyzing the effect of developmental maturity upon Guess Who scores, since CA differences within a grade were found to be unrelated to trait scores. Thereupon, an analysis of variance (12, p. 261 ff.) was conducted for each grade to determine whether any given trait was more closely associated with one level of development than with another. Some developmental groups in certain grades were not large enough to warrant their inclusion in the statistical analysis (*see* Table 1). Table 3 shows the mean scores of developmental groups on the Guess Who items upon

Table 3
**Average Score for Individuals on Items Which Differentiated
Significantly Among the Developmental Groups**

	Prepuberal	Puberal	Postpuberal	Late Adolescent	p
Grown-up					
Sixth	0.1	4.3	*	*	.05
Seventh	−1.1	0.4	1.2	*	.001
Eighth	−2.0	−1.1	0.5	2.2	.001
Ninth	*	−0.8	0.2	0.8	.01
Older Friends					
Seventh	0.0	0.8	1.4	*	.001
Eighth	−0.2	0.4	0.9	2.6	.001
Daring					
Ninth	*	−0.2	0.7	0.6	.01

* Group not large enough to be included in the analysis.

which significant differences among the developmental groups were revealed by this analysis.

RESULTS

At every grade the more mature girls received progressively higher mean scores on the item *grown-up* than did their less mature classmates. Similarly, on the item *older friends* consistent differences among the developmental groups were observed at each grade, although only in the seventh and eighth grades did the differences reach statistical significance. While CA differences within a grade were unrelated to trait scores, developmental differences significantly affected the opinions which girls had of their peers on these traits.

On the other hand, the differences among developmental groups on the trait *daring* reached the .01 level in the ninth grade only. Since the differences on the trait *daring* were significant only in this grade and since they do not reflect a consistent trend in mean scores for the developmental groups, it is difficult to determine whether or not the differences might have resulted from chance alone.

Differences in mean scores among developmental groups were not great enough to reach significance on the other traits. However, the differences in mean scores for developmental groups on many of the items followed a consistent pattern within each grade. A consideration of the mean scores of developmental groups on the prestige-lending traits alone (*see* Table 2) suggests that level of development had some effect upon Guess Who evaluations. Considering only the item *prestige* and the items correlated significantly with *prestige,* it is apparent that one developmental group at each grade received more than a chance allotment of high scores on these favorable traits. At each grade the developmental group which received the highest mean score on *prestige* tended to receive high scores also on the items which correlated positively with *prestige* and to receive low scores on the items which were negatively correlated with *prestige* for that grade.

By means of the binomial test it was determined that at each grade one developmental group was attributed more of the prestige-related traits than was a likely occurrence on the basis of chance (*see* Table 4). For the three junior high school grades the most mature groups consistently received the highest mean scores on *prestige* and on items significantly correlated with it, such as *popular, friendly,* and *assured-adults.* While girls in the later stages of development were favored during the junior high school years, this was not the case for the sixth grade girls. Instead, the least mature girls, the prepuberal group, received favorable scores on most of the desirable traits in the sixth grade.

Table 4

Distribution of Favorable Scores on Prestige-Lending Traits for Developmental Groups in Each Grade

Grade	No. of Traits Significantly Correlated with Prestige	Prepuberal	Puberal	Postpuberal	Late Adolescent	p
Sixth	18	15	3	*	*	.003
Seventh	17	4	$3\frac{1}{2}$	$9\frac{1}{2}$	*	.035
Eighth	18	1	3	1	13	.00003
Ninth	15	*	$1\frac{1}{2}$	$5\frac{1}{2}$	8	.05

Note. When two developmental groups received the same high mean score, each was given credit for one-half.
* Group not large enough to be included in the analysis.

In the sixth grade a prepuberal girl is developmentally "in phase" with the majority of her classmates, and being at the prepuberal stage of development seems to be an asset in prestige in sixth grade. However, in the seventh grade the average girl is in the puberal group (*see* Table 1); yet the prestige-lending traits are most frequently ascribed to the postpuberal girls. In both eighth and ninth grades, when the average girl is in the postpuberal group, the desirable traits are most frequently ascribed to girls in the late adolescent group (four to six years beyond menarche).

DISCUSSION

A girl's level of physical maturity is not the only determinant in her scores on the Guess Who items, but, together with associated emotional, social, sexual, and personality changes, level of maturity does contribute significantly to the reputation which a girl has in her social group. Although puberal development contributes only a small amount of variance to the Guess Who trait scores, it does seem to contribute enough to give slight but consistent direction to the mean trait scores.

Adolescents' awareness of developmental differences is clearly revealed in their evaluations on certain Guess Who traits. While CA bore no significant relation to scores on the items *grown-up* and *older friends,* at every grade the more mature girls received progressively higher mean scores than did their less mature classmates on these items. Thus, developmental differences were more significant than CA differences in affecting these scores. It is evident that the more mature girls are taller, on the average (14), and that they appear more "grown-up" in terms of secondary sex characteristics (5). These associated factors of development may be the basis for the girls' evaluations on the trait *grown-up.* The possible relation of developmental maturity to the scores on *older friends* is likewise evident. For the more mature girls to seek out comparably mature girl friends of a higher grade in school is reasonable and is consistent with Jones' finding (9) that level of maturity is a factor in friendship selection. In addition, level of development is related to maturity of interests and activities (16), and common interests are known to be important in establishing friendships (1). The evaluations on the trait *older friends* may indicate, on the other hand, that the more mature girls are judged as having boy friends in a higher grade in school. Since the boys of a given grade mature later than the girls, the girls of advanced physical maturity may find satisfaction of their heterosexual interest in dating older boys. However, by ninth grade, associating with older friends is no longer judged as being prestige-lending ($r = .05$). Perhaps, as the discrepancy in physical maturity between boys and girls diminishes, the prestige-lending nature of dating older boys is concomitantly reduced to insignificance.

According to Jones and Bayley (10), the traits *grown-up* and *older friends* were two of the Guess Who items upon which the early- and the late-maturing boys received significantly different scores. Consistently on six testings throughout the adolescent period the group of late-maturing boys were seen as less "grown-up" and less likely to have "older friends" than were the early-maturing boys. These findings correspond with those found here among the girls: *grown-up* and *older friends* were characteristic of the more mature girls at each grade.

Although the scores of physically immature boys and girls are similar on these two traits, their scores on the other Guess Who traits show a marked sex difference. Jones and Bayley (10) report that the late-maturing boys received above average scores on *attention getting, restless, assured-class,* and *talkative,* while the evidence from the present study is that the less mature girls *in junior high school* were characterized by the traits *non-attention getting, quiet,* and *avoids fights.* According to Jones and Bayley, boys seem to defend themselves against the anxieties of late development by compensation for inferiority, expressed in attention-getting mannerisms. However, for girls the defense against immature physical status in junior high school seems to be more of a withdrawal and an attempt to be inconspicuous in the group. Both of these patterns seem to represent a perseveration of certain components of the respective, sex-appropriate, preadolescent pattern, which was prestige-lending for neither boys nor girls at this level.

The findings of this study suggest that for girls level of development is a factor in the assignment of traits during adolescence. Although the single trait *prestige* is not significantly associated with level of physical maturity, the high scores on this item are consistent with the pattern of high scores on the other desirable traits; i.e., one developmental group at each grade received more of the favorable scores than would be expected on a chance basis. When all of the prestige-lending traits of a given grade are considered as a whole. It appears that prestige is more likely to surround those in the sixth grade who are developmentally "in phase" (prepuberal), whereas during the junior high school years being ahead of the group developmentally seems to be an advantage. While prepuberal status may be hazardous for girls in junior high school, it is not considered "immature" nor undesirable in sixth grade. A prepuberal girl in sixth grade is developmentally "in phase" with the great majority of her classmates, while a prepuberal girl in ninth grade is a "developmental isolate." A girl's level of physical maturity is not only relative to the development of others in the class, but it is seen against a background of developmental differences within the whole school. Being at the prepuberal level of development seems to lend different qualities to the composite picture of an individual in elementary school than it does to one in the junior high school grades.

Although the evaluations of traits in relation to *prestige* were much the same for sixth and for seventh grade girls (rho = .90), the actual traits were attributed to a developmentally different group of girls. In the one year from sixth to seventh grade, the prestige-lending qualities shift from the prepuberal to the postpuberal girls, a developmental difference of two to three years. Moreover, in the eighth and ninth grades it is the late adolescent group, girls from four to six years beyond menarche, who are at the favored developmental level. This discontinuity between rate of developmental change and rate of change in prestige-lending evaluations suggests that a girl who is prepuberal in sixth grade cannot remain in the favored developmental position in junior high school, because her level of maturity cannot keep pace with the *rate* at which peer evaluations change with respect to developmental maturity.

This discontinuity suggests that for girls neither physical acceleration nor physical retardation is consistently advantageous. It is not until the junior high school years that the early-maturing girl "comes into her own" and reaps the benefit of her accelerated development. Until that time her precocious development is somewhat detrimental to her social status. The adjustments which inevitably must be made to losses and gains in status during the adolescent period (18) may be partly a function of this discontinuity in the relationship between developmental maturity and prestige during the adolescent period. Tryon alluded to this discontinuity and its significance when she described Case 29 (17), a girl who commanded prestige at 12 years of age, but who at age 14 or 15 was still developmentally immature. Tryon noted that in the ninth grade "she is now one of the very few little girls; she seemed like a child in the midst of adults with a group of girls; tended to avoid large mixed groups of boys and girls and their activities" (p. 64). The emotional hazard of losing status during adolescence because of relative physical immaturity is not infrequently noted in case studies and observed in child guidance clinics. Contrariwise, as the findings of this study suggest, precocious physical maturity may possess its hazards, particularly in the period before entrance to junior high school.

After the transition to junior high school, girls begin to ascribe prestige to classmates who have been physically mature for a longer period of time and to girls whose interests and activities are undoubtedly more advanced. Perhaps these more mature girls satisfy a requirement for prestige in the group because of their "advanced standing" with respect to the new developmental tasks which the less mature girls are facing.

The significance of the present research is in its clarification of the changing relationship between developmental maturity and social prestige during adolescence. The findings of this study do not support Jones' assertion that "the very early maturing girl . . . is in many respects in a disadvantageous position" (8). From an unpublished study arising from the Adolescent Growth Study, Jones states that *"when we compared them* (italics the writer's) . . . we found that the early-maturing (girls) were below average in prestige, sociability, and leadership; below average in popularity; below average in cheerfulness, poise, and expressiveness." Perhaps the discrepancy between the present study and the one which Jones reports lies in the phrase "when we compared them," for it is apparent that the present findings for *sixth* grade girls are not unlike the H. Jones quotation. However, the present findings indicate that early-maturing is indeed advantageous in all three junior high school grades. By junior high school accelerated development has taken on a prestige-lending connotation. The favorable position of the early-developing girl is generally consistent with other of the California Growth Study findings, although not with the citation above of H. Jones. M. C. Jones and Mussen (11) report: "Although the differences were not consistent in all categories, the early-maturing girls tended to score more favorably than the slow-maturing on 'total adjustment,' and also on family adjustment and feelings of personal adequacy. These data from the self-report inventory seem to be generally consistent with the findings from the TAT" (p. 497).

The findings of the present research point out the complex nature of variables which interact in producing a girl's reputation during adolescence. The data support the hypothesis by Jones and Mussen (11) that early and late development may mean different things at different times during adolescence. The discontinuity between rate of change in evaluations of prestige and rate of physical changes during adolescence means that, for girls, accelerated development is not a sustained asset throughout the adolescent period, as it is for boys. Accelerated development for girls is somewhat detrimental to prestige status before the junior high school years, while it places a girl in a very favorable social position throughout the junior high school years.

SUMMARY

The purpose of the present study was to ascertain for girls whether level of physical maturity is a determinant in prestige during adolescence. Tryon's Guess Who test, including an additional pair of items designed to measure prestige, was administered to 731 girls in the sixth, seventh, eighth, and ninth grades. Correlations between prestige and the other 20 traits were computed for each grade separately, and the correlations were tested for significance.

Level of physical maturity was assessed by means of menarcheal age scores, which were obtained by the school nurses for the sixth grade girls and by the women's physical education staff for the three junior high school grades. On the basis of the menarcheal age data girls at each grade were classified into four developmental groups.

In order to determine whether CA differences within a grade were related to Guess Who scores, correlations between CA and each of the 21 Guess Who traits were computed for each grade. No significant relation was found between CA differences within a grade and Guess Who trait scores.

An analysis of variance based upon developmental groups revealed that the developmentally more mature girls at each grade received significantly higher scores on the items *grown-up* and *older friends* than did their less mature classmates. Differences in mean scores among developmental groups were not great enough to reach significance on the other traits. However, one developmental group at each grade received the highest scores on more of the prestige-related traits than would be expected on the basis of chance. By means of the binomial test, it was determined that *prestige* and the significant prestige-related traits were more frequently ascribed to sixth grade girls who were developmentally "in phase" (prepuberal), while in all three junior high school grades girls who were physically accelerated and were in the most mature developmental groups received more of the favorable reputation scores. Thus, for girls precocious physical development tends to be a detriment in prestige status during sixth grade, while it tends to become a decided asset during the three succeeding years.

The findings indicate that the level of development is not a single factor in determining a girl's status in the group, but it is an important part of a composite of factors in creating a girl's reputation during adolescence. A discrepancy between rate of developmental change and rate of change in prestige-lending evaluations during adolescence was noted and was interpreted in terms of the different meaning which early and late development have for girls at different times during adolescence. After the transition to junior high school, the more favorable reputation scores were ascribed to the physically accelerated girls.

REFERENCES

1. Bonney, M. E. A sociometric study of the relationship of some factors to mutual friendships in the elementary, secondary, and college levels. *Sociometry,* 1946, *9:* 21–47.
2. Bower, P. A. The relation of physical, mental, and personality factors to popularity in adolescent boys. Unpublished doctoral dissertation, Univ. of California, Berkeley, 1941.

3. Faust, Margaret S. Developmental maturity as a determinant in prestige of adolescent girls. Unpublished doctoral dissertation, Stanford Univer., 1957.
4. Frank, L. K. Personality development in adolescent girls. *Monogr. Soc. Res. Child Develpm.,* 1953, *16:* No. 53.
5. Greulich, W. W. Physical changes in adolescence. *Yearb. nat. Soc. Stud. Educ.,* 1944, *43(1):* 8–32.
6. Jones, H. E. *Development in adolescence.* New York: Appleton-Century-Crofts, 1943.
7. Jones, H. E. *Motor performance and growth.* Berkeley: Univer. of California Press, 1949.
8. Jones, H. E. Adolescence in our society. In *The family in a democratic society: anniversary papers of The Community Service Society of New York.* New York: Columbia Univer. Press, 1949. Pp. 70–82.
9. Jones, Mary C. Adolescent friendships. *Amer. Psychologist,* 1948, *3:* 352. (Abstract)
10. Jones, Mary C., & Bayley, Nancy. Physical maturing among boys as related to behavior. *J. educ. Psychol.,* 1950, *41:* 129–148.
11. Jones, Mary C., & Mussen, P. H. Self-conceptions, motivations, and interpersonal attitudes of early- and late-maturing girls. *Child Develpm.,* 1958, *29:* 491–501.
12. McNemar, Q. *Psychological statistics.* New York: Wiley, 1955.
13. Mussen, P. H., & Jones, Mary C. Self-conceptions, motivations, and interpersonal attitudes of late- and early-maturing boys. *Child Develpm.,* 1957, *28:* 243–256.
14. Shuttleworth, F. K. Sexual maturation and physical growth of girls age six to nineteen. *Monogr. Soc. Res. Child Develpm.,* 1937, *2:* No. 5.
15. Stolz, H. R., & Stolz, Lois M. *Somatic development of adolescent boys.* New York: Macmillan, 1951.
16. Stone, C. P., & Barker, R. G. The attitudes and interests of premenarcheal and postmenarcheal girls. *J. gent. Psychol.,* 1939, *54:* 27–71.
17. Tryon, Caroline. Evaluations of adolescent personality by adolescents. *Monogr. Soc. Res. Child Develpm.,* 1939, *4:* No. 23.
18. Tryon, Caroline. The adolescent peer culture. *Yearb. nat. Soc. Study Educ.,* 1944, *43(l):* 217–239.

patterns of affective fluctuation in the menstrual cycle

Melville Ivey Boufford   **Judith M. Bardwick**
University of Michigan

Twenty-six female college students aged 19–22 were tested for differences in anxiety level during the menstrual cycle. Ss were asked to talk for 5 min. on "any memorable life experience." These verbal samples were recorded at ovulation and 2–3 days preceding the onset of menses during 2 complete menstrual cycles for each S. The samples were scored according to Gottschalk's (1961) Verbal Anxiety Scale (VAS) for Death, Mutilation, Separation, Guilt, Shame, and Diffuse Anxiety. The verbal samples were also examined for thematic variations.

The sensitivity of the VAS was confirmed, as it revealed consistent and significant variations in anxiety level between ovu'ation and premenstrual samples for each S. The premenstrual anxiety level was found to be significantly higher (p < 0.0005) than that at ovulation over all Ss. Additional findings showed consistent themes of hostility and depression as well as themes of noncoping during the premenstrual phase of the menstrual cycle. In spite of individual differences between Ss, these findings indicate significant and predictable affective fluctuations during the menstrual cycle which correlate with endocrine changes. Qualitative data on "premenstrual syndrome" and psychosomatic aspects of premenstrual symptoms were also presented.

Because its periodic functioning is central to the female physically as well as psychologically, the reproductive system offers an ideal system for the physical expression of attitudes and emotions. There have been many studies on the psychodynamic characteristics of women who suffer such reproductive dysfunctions as infertility,[9,13] habitual abortion,[8,10,15] pseudocyesis,[7] and severe difficulties during pregnancy.[16] These studies were concentrated on psychological affects and their influence on physiology.

In 1942 Benedek and Rubenstein[4] did pioneer work in examining affects from another perspective, that of physiological influences on psychology. In studying the effects of endocrine changes upon psychological affects, they found that female psychiatric patients demonstrated striking and consistent psychodynamic manifestations related to particular hormonal phases of the menstrual cycle. They found passive-receptive tendencies

Reprinted from Psychosomatic Medicine, 1968, 30, 336–345. Copyright © 1968 by the American Psychosomatic Society: By permission.

to be correlated with progesterone production, and active heterosexual strivings with estrogen production. Benedek, in a later paper,[3] further characterized the premenstrual phase of the menstrual cycle as being high in feelings of fear about mutilation and death, sexual fantasies, anxiety, and depression. At ovulation she found almost no evidence of anxiety-related themes.

Shainess[11] found the low estrogen and progesterone phase just preceding menstruation to be generally associated with a yearning for love, feeling of helplessness, anxiety, and defensive hostility. Sutherland and Stewart[14] noted that premenstrual depression and irritability were associated with a wide range of unpleasant physical symptoms. These studies tend to confirm the hypothesis of psychosomatic interaction as a basis for affective changes evidenced in the menstrual cycle.

Psychosomatic studies of emotion need an easily administered psychological test that provides comprehensive and immediate measurement of the affect associated with a given physiological state. After Gottschalk *et al.*[5] conducted extensive studies of validity and reliability, Gottschalk's Verbal Anxiety Scale (VAS) seemed to offer a valuable method for handling this problem. Based on a content analysis of free-association verbal samples, this scale serves as a measure of preconscious and conscious anxiety manifested by the subject at the time of testing. The scale reliably differentiates between different populations on the basis of the anxiety being measured.[5]

Gottschalk *et al.*[6] used the VAS to measure affective changes in 5 subjects during the menstrual cycle. They reported that their results were not statistically significant across *Ss,* and attributed this result to the small size of the sample. Their data did suggest, however, a tendency for transient decreases in levels of anxiety and hostility during ovulation.

A purpose of the present study was to replicate the work of Gottschalk *et al.*[6] with normal subjects, using a larger sample, in an effort to obtain statistically significant results. Whereas in other previous research, selected neurotic and psychotic *Ss* were frequently used, the use of a normal population might show more universal applicability of findings indicating affective change during the menstrual cycle. With experimental controls and a larger sample of normal girls, we hope to find significant results that demonstrate the overwhelming and normal impact of physiological change upon emotions.

On the basis of the preceding considerations, the following hypotheses were evolved. The difference in anxiety level between ovulation and premenstruation ought to be consistent for each individual *S*. Since it was hypothesized that the change in anxiety level would be a function of endocrine changes, the changes in anxiety level were expected to be consistent for all *Ss*. It was also predicted that the anxiety level for all *Ss* during premenstruation would be significantly higher than at ovulation.

METHOD

SUBJECTS

The *Ss* were 26 female college students 19–22 years of age. Twenty-two were members of 1 living unit, and 4 were members of another. All members of the first house volunteered, but 9 had to be dropped because of irregular cycles, absence during the testing period due to spring vacation, use of oral contraceptives, or other purely pragmatic problems. There seemed to be no reason to suspect a bias in this volunteer population.

PROCEDURE

Menstrual Data. The *Ss* were asked to volunteer for participation in a "study of the menstrual cycle" and were given no indication as to any expected affective fluctuations. They were told that participation would involve four 10-min. interviews, 1 at ovulation and 1 premenstrually for 2 complete menstrual cycles. The interviews were to be arranged at their convenience. A cooperative group effort was encouraged, and because *E* was a member of the house from which the majority of the *Ss* came, participation was encouraged and supported. Volunteers were asked to write down the date of onset of their most recent menstrual period and the approximate length of the cycle. Since many were uncertain, their participation began at the onset of their next period.

Because of the number of subjects and the voluntary nature of their participation, basal body temperature (low point preceding a rise in temperature indicating ovulation) was recorded for only 3 or 4 days preceding the scheduled ovulation of each girl as determined by the available menstrual history. This measure, coupled with verbal descriptions of ovulation symptoms and the observed onset of menses, was felt to give a fairly reliable estimate of the time of ovulation. Each girl was interviewed 4 times, twice premenstrually and twice at ovulation. Ovulation, when estrogen levels are highest, was determined by basal body temperature and menstrual history; for the majority of cases, this was 14–16 days following the onset of menses. The premenstrual interviews were conducted 2–3 days before scheduled menstruation, when both progesterone and estrogen levels are low.

Interview. At each session, the *S* was interviewed privately, at her convenience. She was asked to speak for 5 min. into a tape recorder about "any memorable life experience." After the 5-min. session, a general questionnaire, asking about any current problems or worries and about her physical health at that time, was administered. This was done to detect any sources of external stress that might contaminate the results. Following the 5-min. verbal sample at the first premenstrual interview, a detailed questionnaire on menstrual history was administered (for content see Table 3).

Scoring. The verbal samples were transcribed verbatim from the tapes. Two judges independently scored the typescripts using Gottschalk's analysis technique for the VAS.[10] Judges scored the samples clause by clause for indications of: (1) Death Anxiety, (2) Mutilation Anxiety, (3) Separation Anxiety, (4) Guilt Anxiety, (5) Shame Anxiety, and (6) Diffuse Anxiety. Under each of these categories, reference to the self (except as agent) received a score of 3; to animate others, 2; and to inanimate others, 1 (except in Categories 4, 5, and 6); denial was scored as 1. The total anxiety score for each sample is obtained by summing all items. To control for differences in verbal output in the 5-min. periods, the total score is divided by the number of words in the sample and then multiplied by 100. The square root of this final raw total anxiety score is used for all statistical comparisons.

While *E* was one judge, the other examiner trained in this technique had no knowledge of the *Ss* or of the particular menstrual phase corresponding to each sample. The tests were scored at random and the particular menstrual phase was not recorded on the typed sample. The use of code numbers prevented any knowledge of the particular *S* giving the sample. The interjudge correlation was .81, showing good scoring reliabil-

Table 1

Mean Combined Anxiety Scores for 26 Female Ss at Ovulation and Premenstruation over 2 Complete Menstrual Cycles

S (No.)	Mean Combined Ovulation Scores	Mean Combined Premenstrual Scores	Premenstrual Minus Ovulation Score	Rank
1	1.10	1.90	+0.80	18
2	0.77	1.85	+1.08	22
3	1.30	1.35	+0.05	1
4	1.15	1.75	+0.60	12
5	1.29	2.75	+1.46	25
6	1.20	2.20	+1.00	19.5
7	1.70	2.40	+0.70	15.5
8	1.90	1.30	−0.60	12
9	1.60	1.50	−0.10	2
10	1.40	0.83	−0.57	10
11	0.90	1.45	+0.55	9
12	1.45	2.80	+1.35	24
13	1.05	1.50	+0.45	6
14	0.84	2.45	+1.61	26
15	1.70	2.70	+1.00	19.5
16	1.29	0.97	−0.32	5
17	1.65	1.13	−0.52	8
18	3.10	3.30	+0.20	3
19	1.75	2.40	+0.65	14
20	2.70	2.95	+0.25	4
21	0.90	1.65	+0.75	17
22	1.43	2.55	+1.12	23
23	2.90	3.60	+0.70	15.5
24	0.85	1.90	+1.05	21
25	1.60	2.20	+0.60	12
26	1.30	1.80	+0.50	7

Gottschalk's Verbal Anxiety Scale was used, and scores were taken from 5-m n. free-association verbal samples.

Table 2
Anxiety Scores for 26 Female Ss Arranged in Order of Sampling

Ss (No.)	Sample 1	Sample 2	Sample 3	Sample 4
1	O_1 1.8	PM_1 3.3	O_2 0.42	PM_2 0.52
2	O_1 0.24	PM_1 2.7	O_2 1.3	PM_2 1.0
3	O_1 1.5	PM_1 1.0	O_2 1.1	PM_2 1.7
4	O_1 1.2	PM_1 1.7	O_2 1.1	PM_2 1.8
5	O_1 2.3	PM_1 2.4	O_2 0.28	PM_2 3.1
6	O_1 1.1	PM_1 2.2	O_2 1.3	PM_2 2.1
7	PM_1 2.2	O_1 2.1	PM_2 2.6	O_2 1.4
8	O_1 2.0	PM_1 1.4	O_2 1.8	PM_2 1.2
9	O_1 1.5	PM_1 1.5	O_2 1.7	PM_2 1.5
10	PM_1 0.26	O_1 1.8	PM_2 1.4	O_2 1.0
11	O_1 1.5	PM_1 1.2	O_2 0.3	PM_2 1.7
12	O_1 1.6	PM_1 2.2	O_2 1.3	PM_2 1.4
13	PM_1 1.4	O_1 1.1	PM_2 1.6	O_2 1.0
14	PM_1 2.1	O_1 1.6	PM_2 2.8	O_2 0.08
15	PM_1 2.3	O_1 1.9	PM_2 3.0	O_2 1.5
16	O_1 2.3	PM_1 1.7	O_2 0.28	PM_2 0.24
17	O_1 1.3	PM_1 1.3	O_2 1.0	PM_2 0.95
18	O_1 3.4	PM_1 3.9	O_2 2.8	PM_2 2.7
19	PM_1 1.9	O_1 1.7	PM_2 2.7	O_2 1.8
20	O_1 3.3	PM_1 3.0	O_2 2.1	PM_2 2.9
21	O_1 0.9	PM_1 1.2	O_2 0.9	PM_2 2.1
22	O_1 1.9	PM_1 1.7	O_2 0.95	PM_2 3.4
23	O_1 3.6	PM_1 2.8	O_2 2.2	PM_2 4.2
24	PM_1 1.6	O_1 0.8	PM_2 2.2	O_2 0.9
25	O_1 1.6	PM_1 1.6	O_2 1.6	PM_2 2.8
26	O_1 1.2	PM_1 1.8	O_2 1.5	PM_2 1.7

O indicates ovulation; PM, premenstruation.

ity. In addition, Dr. Gottschalk was kind enough to check one-third of our score samples and reported good consistency with his scoring.

Although hostility and depression are not included in Gottschalk's VAS, we also made a simple tabulation of the number of statements of hostility and depression in each 5-min. sample because these seemed to be recurrent affects. In addition, a general analysis of each sample was made to determine the most salient themes. Information from the menstrual history questionnaire was qualitatively evaluated.

RESULTS

The Wilcoxen test for 2 matched samples was used to compare the mean premenstrual anxiety scores with the mean anxiety scores for all subjects at ovulation. The premenstrual anxiety scores were found to be

Table 3
Anxiety Categories at Ovulation and Premenstruation

Ss (No.)	Death Anxiety d	Rank	Mutilation Anxiety d	Rank	Separation Anxiety d	Rank	Guilt Anxiety d	Rank	Shame Anxiety d	Rank	Diffuse Anxiety d	Rank
1	+ 2	+ 5	+22	+17	−11	−20	+5	+19.5	− 1	− 3.5	− 1	− 3.5
2	0		+13	+16	+ 3	+10.5	+1	+ 4.5	− 1	− 3.5	+ 6	+19.5
3	0		− 2	− 8.5	+ 1	+ 2	−5	−19.5	+ 3	+10.5	+ 1	+ 3.5
4	− 1	− 2.5	0		− 2	− 5.5	−3	−14.5	+ 9	+22	+ 5	+18
5	+ 8	+11	+ 1	+ 4	+10	+19	+3	+14.5	0		+ 1	+ 3.5
6	0		0		0		+1	+ 4.5	+ 4	+14	+ 4	+17
7	+ 4	+ 8	+ 1	+ 4	0		+3	+14.5	0		+ 3	+14
8	0		+ 1	+ 4	0		0		− 6	−20	−11	−23
9	0		0		+ 3	+10.5	−1	− 4.5	− 1	− 3.5	+ 3	+14
10	0		+ 1	+ 4	− 3	−10.5	−1	− 4.5	+ 2	+ 8	− 2	− 9
11	+ 1	+ 2.5	+ 1	+ 4	+ 3	+10.5	−2	−10	0		+ 2	+ 9
12	+ 3	+ 6.5	0		0		−1	− 4.5	− 1	− 3.5	+ 3	+14
13	0		0		+ 4	+14.5	−1	− 4.5	− 1	− 3.5	+ 2	+ 9
14	+ 5	+ 9	0		− 1	− 2	0		+ 4	+14	+15	+24
15	+ 6	+10	+ 4	+11.5	+ 2	+ 5.5	−3	−14.5	+ 8	+21	+ 6	+19.5
16	0		+ 1	+ 4	− 8	−18	−1	− 4.5	− 5	−18	− 1	− 3.5
17	0		− 4	−11.5	+ 3	+10.5	+1	+ 4.5	− 2	− 8	+ 2	+ 9
18	+11	+12.5	+ 2	+ 8.5	− 4	−14.5	+7	+22	− 3	−10.5	− 3	−14
19	− 3	− 6.5	− 7	−15	+24	+21	−3	−19.5	+ 4	+14	+ 2	+ 9
20	0		− 3	−10	+ 2	+ 5.5	−2	−10	− 4	−14	+ 7	+21
21	0		0		+ 5	+16	+3	+14.5	+ 2	+ 8	+ 1	+ 3.5
22	+11	+12.5	+ 1	+ 4	+ 1	+ 2	+2	+10	− 5	−18	+ 8	+22
23	0		0		+ 6	+17	0		+15	+23	0	
24	− 1	− 2.5	+ 6	+14	+ 3	+10.5	0		+ 4	+14	+ 3	+14
25	+ 1	+ 2.5	+ 5	+13	+ 2	+ 5.5	+5	+19.5	+ 1	+ 3.5	0	
26	0		0		0		−3	−14.5	+ 5	+18	− 1	− 3.5
	T = 11.5		T = 45		T = 70.5		T = 104.5		T = 88		T = 49.5	
	N = 13		N = 15		N = 21		N = 22		N = 23		N = 24	
	z = 2.36		z = 1.49		z = 1.56		z = 0.715		z = 1.52		z = 2.87	
	p < 0.02		p = 0.14		p = 0.12		p = 0.50		p = 0.13		p < 0.01	

d indicates the number of statements at premenstruation minus number of statements at ovulation; N, the number of Ss contributing in this anxiety category.

significantly higher at the .0005 level than those at ovulation (Table 1). The same test revealed no significant differences between the anxiety levels of the same cycle phase during the 2 different cycles.

When the sample scores were arranged in the order in which they were taken there was no evidence for a serial effect. We found no systematic increase or decrease in the anxiety scores from the first to the fourth sample (Table 2).

Because we were pressed for time, we were unable to prolong the experiment for the additional month which would have permitted a balanced design in which half of the Ss began participation at ovulation and half at premenstruation. Seven Ss began at premenstruation; they were Ss 7, 10, 13, 14, 15, 19, and 24. There is no systematic difference between these scores and those of the remaining Ss.

Using the Wilcoxen test (2-tailed approximation for small samples where N < 25) for those Ss contributing to each category,[12] highly significant differences were noted in the categories of death and diffuse anxiety.

The ovulation and premenstrual anxiety scores were tabulated over all *Ss,* and the frequency of each type of anxiety at the 2 cycle phases was compared. The premenstrual Death Anxiety score was significantly higher than that at ovulation, (p < 0.02) as was the Diffuse Anxiety score (p < 0.01). Separation Anxiety, Multilation Anxiety and Shame Anxiety were higher premenstrually—at the .14, .12, and .13 levels respectively—while Guilt Anxiety remained fairly constant over the 2 phases of the menstrual cycle (Table 3).

DISCUSSION

The statistical analysis lends strong support to the hypotheses. Every *S* was consistent when her mean anxiety levels, premenstrually and at ovulation, were compared. This was true for the 21 *Ss* whose anxiety level was higher at premenstruation as well as for the 5 *Ss* whose anxiety level was higher at ovulation. There was considerable variability in a *S's* response, largely due to the sensitivity of the measure to changes in situational anxiety.[5] Nevertheless, when the mean anxiety levels for all *Ss* were combined, the comparison between the premenstrual and ovulation anxiety levels showed the anxiety level at premenstruation to be significantly higher at the .0005 level.

Five of the 26 *Ss* showed a higher level of anxiety at ovulation. One of these *Ss* had a mean difference of only .10 between her mean ovulation and premenstruation scores. For 3 of the other 4 *Ss,* an examination of their ovulation questionnaires on "current situation" revealed that they all expressed more than the usual anxiety over some environmental factor at the time of the ovulation test sessions. Their concerns at that time ranged from the attempted suicide of a friend to the prospect of facing a great deal of make-up school work due to illness.

The presence of a lower level of anxiety at ovulation compared with that at premenstruation in 21 of these subjects confirmed Gottschalk's findings,[6] which had indicated a transient decrease in anxiety at ovulation. The fact that a higher level of premenstrual anxiety (significant at the .01 level) was present in this sample was consistent with other research.[3,6,11]

When the specific types of anxiety were examined, higher premenstrual incidence of Death, Mutilation, and Separation Anxiety in this normal population confirmed earlier findings of Benedek[4] with psychiatric patients. In the present study, as in Benedek's, the premenstrual phase was characterized by fear of mutilation and body damage. Also confirmed was Shainess' observation[11] of an increase at premenstruation in yearning for love, anxiety about being separated from love, and a feeling of helplessness in dealing with the situation.

A tabulation of the instances of hostility outward and the few instances of hostility inward (depression) suggested a trend towards higher premenstrual hostility as noted by Gottschalk[6] Shainess,[11] and Benedek,[3] as well as some tendency towards premenstrual depression (Sutherland and Stewart[14]). The inclusion of hostility and depression themes with those from the anxiety scale would increase the already significant differences between the affects expressed premenstrually and those seen at ovulation.

When the verbal samples were examined, consistently recurring themes unique to the hormonal phases were found. A constantly recurring theme at ovulation was a self-satisfaction over success or the ability to cope with a situation:

> . . . so I was elected chairman./ I had to establish with them the fact/ that I knew/ what I was doing./ I remember one particularly problematic meeting,/ and afterwards, L. came up to me and said/ "you really handled the meeting well."/ In the end it came out the sort of thing/ that really bolstered my confidence in myself./

Contrast this with a sample from the same girl premenstrually during the same cycle:

> They had to teach me how to water ski./ I was so clumsy/ it was really embarrassing/ 'cause it was kind of like saying to yourself/ you can't do it/ and the people were about to lose patience with me./

This type of thematic adequacy-inadequacy dichotomy appeared repeatedly in different forms, and while inadequacy could be scored in terms of separation and shame anxiety, the coping theme might have remained unrecognized without a clinical evaluation. Concern with coping was, however, a consistent theme and may be similar to Benedek's description of active striving at ovulation versus passive reception at premenstruation.[3]

Another theme which was not scorable on the anxiety scale, but which occurred often, was hostility. The incidence of hostility was much greater premenstrually than at ovulation:

> . . . talk about my brother and his wife./ I hated her./ I just couldn't stand her./ I couldn't stand her mother./ I used to do terrible things to separate them./

This hostile, sexually anxious, and incestuous verbal sample is in striking contrast to the sample from the ovulatory phase of the same cycle for the same girl:

> . . . talk about my trip to Europe./ It was just the greatest summer of my life./ We met all kinds of terrific people/ everywhere we went/ and just the most terrific things happened./

Thematic consistencies were also evident in the samples scorable by the anxiety scale. For example, in the following sample from another girl, a theme of Death Anxiety was evident at premenstruation:

> I'll tell you about the death of my poor dog M./ . . . oh, another memorable event, my grandparents died in a plane crash./ This was my first contact with death/ and it was very traumatic for me/ . . . Then my grandfather died/ and I was very close to him./

In contrast, the sample at ovulation for the same girl:

> Well, we just went to Jamaica/ and it was fantastic/ the island is so lush and green/ and the a . . . water is so blue/ the place is so fertile/ and the natives are just so friendly./

Finally, the following was a clear example of premenstrual Mutilation Anxiety which provided a strong contrast with a very peaceful, contented ovulation narrative for still another girl during 1 menstrual cycle:

> . . . came around the curve and did a double flip and landed upside down./ I remember the car coming down on my hand and slicing it right open/ and all this blood was all over the place./ Later they thought/ it was broken/ cause every time I touched the finger it felt/ like a nail was going through my hand./

At ovulation:

> We took our skis and packed them on top of the car/ and then we took off for up North./ We used to go for long walks in the snow/ and it was just really great, really quiet and peaceful./

These examples illustrate the pronounced and consistent variation between premenstrual and ovulatory anxiety levels in our normal subjects, both as measured by the anxiety scale and by independent thematic analysis.

In spite of the neutral explanation to *Ss* that this experiment aimed at investigating the menstrual cycle, it was felt that any possible contaminating knowledge or intuition by some *Ss* as to the expected mood swings should be ascertained. At the conclusion of the experiment, *Ss* were asked to write what they felt the aim of the experiment has been. Most *Ss* assumed we were studying moods, but in their evaluations did not mention specific affects such as anxiety, depression, or hostility, or expected mood changes. This result was encouraging, though future use of the scale might be better disguised if verbal samples were taken in conjunction with a cognitive task, seeming to place the experimental emphasis on the latter.

There was one unexpected experimental control. One *S* was interviewed on Day 14 of her menstrual cycle for an ovulatory sample. The sample was highly anxious, yielding a score of 2.8, significantly higher than her previous score of 1.4 at ovulation. Thematically there were references to death, mutilation, and separation. The next day, she began to menstruate, 2 weeks early.

The qualitative evaluation of the menstrual history questionnaire revealed several additional findings of interest. When asked if they experienced any symptoms before their periods by which they could tell they were about to menstruate, all girls reported at least 1 symptom. The average number of symptoms reported was 6. The percentage of girls reporting particular symptoms (Table 4) provided an interesting portrait of the "premenstrual syndrome" for girls of this age (compare Sutherland and Stewart,[4] 1965).

Table 4
Premenstrual Syndrome

Symptoms	(%)*
Diarrhea	12
Constipation	12
Headaches	15
Breast swelling	73
Backaches	41
Nausea	26
Change in sleeping habits	34
	(12 less, 22 more)
Stomach swelling	65
Change in eating habits	46
	(20 less, 26 more)
Irritability	65
Physical sensitivity	40
Spotting	7
Weight gain	40
Dream about sex	12
Feel sexy with boyfriend	31
Cramps	42
Skin eruptions	40
Depression	12

N = 26
* Percentage of population reporting a given symptom.

It was suspected that those girls who had received childhood gratification from the sick role (i.e., maternal attention, special privilege) might exhibit a greater number of premenstrual symptoms. As expected, those girls who experienced fewer than the average 6 symptoms reported little gratification from the sick role as a child. Those girls reporting more than 8 symptoms, however, indicated either extreme gratification from the sick role or, at the other extreme, expressed bitterness at being neglected during childhood illnesses. Thus, we see the use of the reproductive system as an arena for the physical acting out of psychological conflicts.[1,2] The girls who received extreme gratification from childhood illness in the form of extra love and attention continued to seek this source of gratification with premenstrual symptoms. Those who were neglected when ill as children seemed to be reacting to this neglect by demanding that attention be paid to their premenstrual physical difficulties. This seems to be an example of the classic psychosomatic etiology—the defensive function of the physical (conversion) symptom in preserving psychological balance in a socially acceptable way.

Although one might expect strong individual differences in reaction, the Anxiety Scale and thematic analysis revealed consistent and significant mood swings unique to a particular menstrual phase. A conclusion which seems warranted is that these physical, especially endocrine, changes so influence psychological behavior that, in spite of personality differences, even in normal subjects, psychological behavior becomes predictable on the basis of menstrual cycle phase. Our results, coupled with those of Gottschalk, Benedek, and Shainess have obvious, but nonetheless exceedingly important pragmatic implications. The menstrual cycle exercises gross influences on female behavior. That females may cope or not cope, test anxious, hostile, or depressive, appear healthy or neurotic on psychological tests, is due as much to menstrual cycle phase as to core psychological characteristics.

SUMMARY

Twenty-six female college students, ages 19–22, being tested for differences in anxiety level during the menstrual cycle, were asked to talk for 5 min. on "any memorable life experience." These verbal samples, which were recorded at ovulation and 2–3 days preceding the onset of menses during 2 complete menstrual cycles for each S, were scored according to Gottschalk's Verbal Anxiety Scale (VAS) for Death, Mutilation, Separation, Guilt, Shame, and Diffuse Anxiety. The verbal samples were also examined for thematic variations.

The sensitivity of the VAS was confirmed, as it revealed consistent and significant variations in anxiety level between ovulation and premenstrual samples for each S. The premenstrual anxiety level was found to be significantly higher ($p < 0.0005$) than that at ovulation over all Ss. Additional findings showed consistent themes of hostility and depression as well as themes of noncoping during the premenstrual phase of the menstrual cycle. In spite of individual differences between Ss, these findings indicate significant and predictable affective fluctuations during the menstrual cycle which correlate with endocrine changes. Qualitative data on "premenstrual syndrome" and psychosomatic aspects of premenstrual symptoms were also presented.

REFERENCES

1. Bardwick, J. M. The need for individual assessment of Ss in psychosomatic research. *Psychol Rep 21:* 81, 1967.
2. Bardwick, J. M. Psychosomatic relations in women. Unpublished data, 1967.
3. Benedek, T. "Sexual functions in women and their disturbance." In *American Handbook of Psychiatry* (Vol. I), by Arieti, S., Ed. Basic Books, New York, 1959.
4. Benedek, T., and Rubenstein, B. *The Sexual Cycle in Women: The Relation Between Ovarian Function and Psychodynamic Processes.* Washington, D.C., National Research Council, 1942.
5. Gottschalk, L. A., Springer, K. J., and Gleser, G. C. "Experiments with a method of assessing the variations in intensity of certain psychological states occurring during two psychotherapeutic in-

terviews." In *Comparative Psycholinguistic Analysis of Two Psychotherapeutic Interviews,* by Gottschalk, L. A., Ed. Internat. Univ. Press, New York, 1961.

6. Gottschalk, L. A., Kaplan, S., Gleser, G. C., and Winget, C. M. Variations in magnitude of emotion: A method applied to anxiety and hostility during phases of the menstrual cycle. *Psychosom Med 23:* 300, 1962.

7. Greaves, D. C., Green, P. E., and West, L. J. Psychodynamic and psychophysiological aspects of pseudocyesis. *Psychosom Med 22:* 24, 1960.

8. Grimm, E. Psychological investigation of habitual abortion. *Psychosom Med 24:* 369, 1962.

9. Peberdy, G. R. "The psychiatry of infertility." In *Studies in Fertility.* Blackwell Scientific Publishers. Oxford: Medical Press, 1958, 239, 703.

10. Seward, G. H. The question of psychophysiologic infertility: Some negative answers. *Psychosom Med 22:* 24, 1960.

11. Shainess, N. A re-evaluation of some aspects of femininity through a study of menstruation: A preliminary report. *Compr Psychiat 2:* 20, 1961.

12. Siegel, S. *Nonparametric Statistics.* McGraw-Hill, New York, 1956, p. 75.

13. Stone, A., Sandler, B., and Ward, M. E. Factors responsible for pregnancy in 500 infertility cases. *Fertil Steril 7:* 1, 1956.

14. Sutherland, H., and Stewart, I. A critical analysis of the premenstrual syndrome. *Lancet 1:* 1180, 1965.

15. Weil, E. J., and Tupper, G. Personality, life situation, and communication: A study of habitual abortion. *Psychosom Med 22:* 448, 1960.

16. Zuckerman, M., Nurnberger, J., Gardner, S., Vandiver, J., Barrett, B., and den Breeijen, A. Psychological correlates of somatic complaints in pregnancy and difficulty in childbirth. *J Consult Psychol 27:* 4, 324, 1963.

two

cognitive development and personality

part two

The dramatic progress in physical and physiological development that occurs during the adolescent years is accompanied by equally impressive gains—both quantitative and qualitative—in cognitive development. Indeed, it is during adolescence that many kinds of mental ability, especially those least dependent on experience, approach their peak. Not only is the adolescent able to master cognitive tasks that in middle childhood he was able to perform only with great difficulty, if at all; he is also able to think about problems in entirely new ways.

In particular he becomes capable, to varying degrees, of what Jean Piaget calls "formal operational thought"—the ability to think abstractly and entertain hypotheses or theoretical propositions that depart from immediately observable events. In contrast to the child, who for the most part is preoccupied with concrete, here-and-now problems, the adolescent is able "not only to grasp the immediate state of things but also the possible state they might or could assume."[1] Furthermore, he is able to conceptualize his own thought, "to take his mental constructions as objects and reason about them."[2]

The implications of these changes are many. It is obvious that without the capacity for engaging in formal operations, the adolescent would be unable to deal with many complex educational and vocational demands. It would be impossible, for example, to master such academic subjects as calculus or the use of metaphors in poetry without a high level of abstract thinking.

What is less apparent, however, is that many of the personality and behavioral characteristics frequently encountered among adolescents— relentless criticism of parental values and existing social, political, and religious systems, a more self-conscious introspective and analytical approach to the self, even the use of such sophisticated defense mechanisms as intellectualization and asceticism[3]—are all dependent on the capacity to think abstractly and to erect and explore hypotheses, much in the manner of a scientist.

In the first article in this part, David Elkind discusses in detail some of the more salient psychological manifestations of the development of formal operational thinking: *adolescent egocentrism* (which he views as resulting from a failure to differentiate between the concerns of others and those of the self) and two related phenomena, the construction of an *imaginary audience* and a *personal fable*. These phenomena do much to explain why the adolescent is likely to feel that others are more preoc-

---

[1] D. Elkind, Cognitive Development in Adolescence. In J. F. Adams (Ed.), *Understanding Adolescence*. Boston: Allyn & Bacon, 1968, p. 152.

[2] D. Elkind, Egocentrism in Adolescence. *Child Development,* 1967, *38,* 1099.

[3] A. Freud, *The Ego and the Mechanisms of Defense.* New York: International Universities Press, 1946.

cupied with his appearance and behavior than may actually be the case and that his feelings and thoughts—his joys as well as his moments of despair—are somehow special and unique.

The level and complexity of the adolescent's political thinking, his value systems, and his conceptions of morality are also influenced to a significant extent by his level of cognitive development. In the second article Joseph Adelson and Robert P. O'Neil demonstrate, in an ingenious series of experiments, how the adolescent's political thinking becomes progressively more abstract, better structured, more flexible, and more creative—and less authoritarian, rigid, and simplistic—as cognitive development shifts in the direction of formal operations. As will become evident in our consideration of the work of Lawrence Kohlberg and Carol Gilligan and of Erik Erikson in Part Ten, the adolescent's level of moral development and, indeed, his need for and capacity to achieve a sense of identity are also closely related to his level of cognitive development.

In the third article, George Scarlett provides a touching individual example of the way in which one adolescent's cognitive development is reflected in her whole view of herself and her world. The diary of Anne Frank provides us with an intimate glimpse into the thinking of a courageous, sensitive, intelligent, and articulate—but also very human, fallible, and vulnerable—young girl struggling toward maturity. Many traditional characteristics of adolescent thinking are illustrated in Anne's account of her feelings and reactions to life, even though the existence she and her family were required to live (in hiding from the Nazis) was in many ways abnormal and unusually stressful. There were her contradictory feelings; her shifts from thoughtful and mature to childlike and impulsive behaviors and back again; her efforts to achieve independence from her parents; her impatience with what she viewed as adult inconsistencies and hypocrisy; her occasional feelings of loneliness, self-criticism, and isolation. Most striking in Anne's thinking, however, was her concern for justice: "We see here not a childlike respect for authority and constraint but a concern for mutual respect between individuals and, most important, a sense of autonomy in the area of morality." As Scarlett observes, one is reminded of Piaget's statement, "Authority as such cannot be the source of justice, because the development of justice presupposes autonomy."[4]

---

[4] J. Piaget, *The Moral Judgment of the Child.* Transl. M. Gabain. New York: Free Press, 1965, p. 319.

egocentrism in adolescence

David Elkind
University of Rochester

Within the Piagetian theory of intellectual growth, the concept of ego-centrism generally refers to a lack of differentiation in some area of sub-ject-object interaction (Piaget, 1962). At each stage of mental develop-ment, this lack of differentiation takes a unique form and is manifested in a unique set of behaviors. The transition from one form of egocentrism to another takes place in a dialectic fashion such that the mental struc-tures which free the child from a lower form of egocentrism are the same structures which ensnare him in a higher form of egocentrism. From the developmental point of view, therefore, egocentrism can be regarded as a negative by-product of any emergent mental system in the sense that it corresponds to the fresh cognitive problems engendered by that system.

Although in recent years Piaget has focused his attention more on the positive than on the negative products of mental structures, egocentrism continues to be of interest because of its relation to the affective aspects of child thought and behavior. Indeed, it is possible that the study of ego-centrism may provide a bridge between the study of cognitive structure, on the one hand, and the exploration of personality dynamics, on the other (Cowan, 1966; Gourevitch & Feffer, 1962). The purpose of the present paper is to describe, in greater detail than Inhelder and Piaget (1958), what seems to me to be the nature of egocentrism in adolescence and some of its behavioral and experiential correlates. Before doing that, how-ever, it might be well to set the stage for the discussion with a brief review of the forms of egocentrism which precede this mode of thought in adolescence.

FORMS OF EGOCENTRISM IN INFANCY AND CHILDHOOD

In presenting the childhood forms of egocentrism, it is useful to treat each of Piaget's major stages as if it were primarily concerned with resolv-ing one major cognitive task. The egocentrism of a particular stage can then be described with reference to this special problem of cognition.

Preparation of this paper was supported in part by grant No. 6881 from the Office of Education.

It must be stressed, however, that while the cognitive task characteristic of a particular stage seems to attract the major share of the child's mental energies, it is not the only cognitive problem with which the child is attempting to cope. In mental development there are major battles and minor skirmishes, and if I here ignore the lesser engagements it is for purposes of economy of presentation rather than because I assume that such engagements are insignificant.

SENSORI-MOTOR EGOCENTRISM (0–2 YEARS)

The major cognitive task of infancy might be regarded as *the conquest of the object.* In the early months of life, the infant deals with objects as if their existence were dependent upon their being present in immediate perception (Charlesworth, 1966; Piaget, 1954). The egocentrism of this stage corresponds, therefore, to a lack of differentiation between the object and the sense impressions occasioned by it. Toward the end of the first year, however, the infant begins to seek the object even when it is hidden, and thus shows that he can now differentiate between the object and the "experience of the object." This breakdown of egocentrism with respect to objects is brought about by mental representation of the absent object.[1] An internal representation of the absent object is the earliest manifestation of the symbolic function which develops gradually during the second year of life and whose activities dominate the next stage of mental growth.

PRE-OPERATIONAL EGOCENTRISM (2–6 YEARS)

During the preschool period, the child's major cognitive task can be regarded as *the conquest of the symbol.* It is during the preschool period that the symbolic function becomes fully active, as evidenced by the rapid growth in the acquisition and utilization of language, by the appearance of symbolic play, and by the first reports of dreams. Yet this new capacity for representation, which loosed the infant from his egocentrism with respect to objects, now ensnares the preschool children in a new egocentrism with regard to symbols. At the beginning of this period, the child fails to differentiate between words and their referents (Piaget, 1952b) and between his self-created play and dream symbols and reality (Kohlberg, 1966; Piaget, 1951). Children at this stage believe that the name inheres in the thing and that an object cannot have more than one name (Elkind, 1961a, 1962, 1963).

The egocentrism of this period is particularly evident in children's linguistic behavior. When explaining a piece of apparatus to another child, for example, the youngster at this stage uses many indefinite terms and leaves out important information (Piaget, 1952b). Although this observation

---

[1] It is characteristic of the dialectic of mental growth that the capacity to represent internally the absent object also enables the infant to cognize the object as externally existent.

is sometimes explained by saying that the child fails to take the other person's point of view, it can also be explained by saying that the child assumes words carry much more information than they actually do. This results from his belief that even the indefinite "thing" somehow conveys the properties of the object which it is used to represent. In short, the egocentrism of this period consists in a lack of clear differentiation between symbols and their referents.

Toward the end of the pre-operational period, the differentiation between symbols and their referents is gradually brought about by the emergence of concrete operations (internalized actions which are roughly comparable in their activity to the elementary operations of arithmetic). One consequence of concrete operational thought is that it enables the child to deal with two elements, properties, or relations at the same time. A child with concrete operations can, for example, take account of both the height and width of a glass of colored liquid and recognize that, when the liquid is poured into a differently shaped container, the changes in height and width of the liquid compensate one another so that the total quantity of liquid is conserved (Elkind, 1961b; Piaget, 1952a). This ability, to hold two dimensions in mind at the same time, also enables the child to hold both symbol and referent in mind simultaneously, and thus distinguish between them. Concrete operations are, therefore, instrumental in overcoming the egocentrism of the preoperational stage.

CONCRETE OPERATIONAL EGOCENTRISM (7–11 YEARS)

With the emergence of concrete operations, the major cognitive task of the school-age child becomes that of *mastering classes, relations, and quantities.* While the preschool child forms global notions of classes, relations, and quantities, such notions are imprecise and cannot be combined one with the other. The child with concrete operations, on the other hand, can nest classes, seriate relations, and conserve quantities. In addition, concrete operations enable the school-age child to perform elementary syllogistic reasoning and to formulate hypotheses and explanations about concrete matters. This system of concrete operations, however, which lifts the school-age child to new heights of thought, nonetheless lowers him to new depths of egocentrism.

Operations are essentially mental tools whose products, series, class hierarchies, conservations, etc., are not directly derived from experience. At this stage, however, the child nonetheless regards these mental products as being on a par with perceptual phenomena. It is the inability to differentiate clearly between mental constructions and perceptual givens which constitutes the egocentrism of the school-age child. An example may help to clarify the form which egocentrism takes during the concrete operational stage.

In a study reported by Peel (1960), children and adolescents were read a passage about Stonehenge and then asked questions about it. One of the questions had to do with whether Stonehenge was a place for religious worship or a fort. The children (ages 7–10) answered the question with flat statements, as if they were stating a fact. When they were given evidence that contradicted their statements, they rationalized the evidence to make it conform with their initial position. Adolescents, on the other hand, phrased their replies in probabilistic terms and supported their judgments with material gleaned from the passage. Similar differences between children and adolescents have been found by Elkind (1966) and Weir (1964).

What these studies show is that, when a child constructs a hypothesis or formulates a strategy, he assumes that this product is imposed by the data rather than derived from his own mental activity. When his position is challenged, he does not change his stance but, on the contrary, reinterprets the data to fit with his assumption. This observation, however, raises a puzzling question. Why, if the child regards both his thought products and the givens of perception as coming from the environment, does he nonetheless give preference to his own mental constructions? The answer probably lies in the fact that the child's mental constructions are the product of reasoning, and hence are experienced as imbued with a (logical) necessity. This "felt" necessity is absent when the child experiences the products of perception. It is not surprising, then, that the child should give priority to what seems permanent and necessary in perception (the products of his own thought, such as conservation) rather than to what seems transitory and arbitrary in perception (products of environmental stimulation). Only in adolescence do young people differentiate between their own mental constructions and the givens of perception. For the child, there are no problems of epistemology.

Toward the end of childhood, the emergence of formal operational thought (which is analogous to propositional logic) gradually frees the child from his egocentrism with respect to his own mental constructions. As Inhelder and Piaget (1958) have shown, formal operational thought enables the young person to deal with all of the possible combinations and permutations of elements within a given set. Provided with four differently colored pieces of plastic, for example, the adolescent can work out all the possible combinations of colors by taking the pieces one, two, three and four, and none, at a time. Children, on the other hand, cannot formulate these combinations in any systematic way. The ability to conceptualize all of the possible combinations in a system allows the adolescent to construct contrary-to-fact hypotheses and to reason about such propositions "as if" they were true. The adolescent, for example, can accept the statement, "Let's suppose coal is white," whereas the child would reply, "But coal is black." This ability to formulate contrary-to-fact hypotheses is crucial to the overcoming of the egocentrism of the concrete operational period. Through the formulation of such contrary-to-fact hypotheses, the young person discovers the arbitrariness of his own mental constructions and learns to differentiate them from perceptual reality.

ADOLESCENT EGOCENTRISM

From the strictly cognitive point of view (as opposed to the psychoanalytic point of view as represented by Blos [1962] and A. Freud [1946] or the ego psychological point of view as represented by Erikson [1959]), the major task of early adolescence can be regarded as having to do with *the conquest of thought.* Formal operations not only permit the young person to construct all the possibilities in a system and construct contrary-to-fact propositions (Inhelder & Piaget, 1958); they also enable him to conceptualize his own thought, to take his mental constructions as objects and reason about them. Only at about the ages of 11–12, for example, do children spontaneously introduce concepts of belief, intelligence, and faith into their definitions of their religious denomination (Elkind, 1961a; 1962; 1963). Once more, however, this new mental system which frees the young person from the egocentrism of childhood entangles him in a new form of egocentrism characteristic of adolescence.

Formal operational thought not only enables the adolescent to concep-tualize his thought, it also permits him to conceptualize the thought of other people. It is this capacity to take account of other people's thought, however, which is the crux of adolescent egocentrism. This egocentrism emerges because, while the adolescent can now cognize the thoughts of others, he fails to differentiate between the objects toward which the thoughts of others are directed and those which are the focus of his own concern. Now, it is well known that the young adolescent, because of the physiological metamorphosis he is undergoing, is primarily concerned with himself. Accordingly, since he fails to differentiate between what others are thinking about and his own mental preoccupations, he assumes that other people are as obsessed with his behavior and appearance as he is himself. *It is this belief that others are preoccupied with his appear-ance and behavior that constitutes the egocentrism of the adolescent.*

One consequence of adolescent egocentrism is that, in actual or im-pending social situations, the young person anticipates the reactions of other people to himself. These anticipations, however, are based on the premise that others are as admiring or as critical of him as he is of him-self. In a sense, then, the adolescent is continually constructing, or react-ing to, *an imaginary audience.* It is an audience because the adolescent believes that he will be the focus of attention; and it is imaginary because, in actual social situations, this is not usually the case (unless he contrives to make it so). The construction of imaginary audiences would seem to account, in part at least, for a wide variety of typical adolescent behaviors and experiences.

The imaginary audience, for example, probably plays a role in the self-consciousness which is so characteristic of early adolescence. When the young person is feeling critical of himself, he anticipates that the audi-ence—of which he is necessarily a part—will be critical too. And, since the audience is his own construction and privy to his own knowledge of himself, it knows just what to look for in the way of cosmetic and behav-ioral sensitivities. The adolescent's wish for privacy and his reluctance to reveal himself may, to some extent, be a reaction to the feeling of being under the constant critical scrutiny of other people. The notion of an imaginary audience also helps to explain the observation that the affect which most concerns adolescents is not guilt but, rather, shame, that is, the reaction to an audience (Lynd, 1961).

While the adolescent is often self-critical, he is frequently self-admiring too. At such times, the audience takes on the same affective coloration. A good deal of adolescent boorishness, loudness, and faddish dress is probably provoked, partially in any case, by a failure to differentiate between what the young person believes to be attractive and what others admire. It is for this reason that the young person frequently fails to understand why adults disapprove of the way he dresses and behaves. The same sort of egocentrism is often seen in behavior directed toward the opposite sex. The boy who stands in front of the mirror for 2 hours combing his hair is probably imagining the swooning reactions he will produce in the girls. Likewise, the girl applying her makeup is more likely than not imagining the admiring glances that will come her way. When these young people actually meet, each is more concerned with being the observed than with being the observer. Gatherings of young adolescents are unique in the sense that each young person is simultaneously an actor to himself and an audience to others.

One of the most common admiring audience constructions, in the adolescent, is the anticipation of how others will react to his own demise. A certain bittersweet pleasure is derived from anticipating the belated recognition by others of his positive qualities. As often happens with such universal fantasies, the imaginary anticipation of one's own demise has been realized in fiction. Below, for example, is the passage in *Tom Sawyer* where Tom sneaks back to his home, after having run away with Joe and Huck, to discover that he and his friends are thought to have been drowned:

> But this memory was too much for the old lady, and she broke entirely down. Tom was snuffling, now, himself—and more in pity of himself than anybody else. He could hear Mary crying and putting in a kindly word for him from time to time. He began to have a nobler opinion of himself than ever before. Still, he was sufficiently touched by his aunt's grief to long to rush out from under the bed and overwhelm her with joy—and the theatrical gorgeousness of the thing appealed strongly to his nature too—but he resisted and lay still.

Corresponding to the imaginary audience is another mental construction which is its complement. While the adolescent fails to differentiate the concerns of his own thought from those of others, he at the same time overdifferentiates his feelings. Perhaps because he believes he is of importance to so many people, the imaginary audience, he comes to regard himself, and particularly his feelings, as something special and unique. Only he can suffer with such agonized intensity, or experience such exquisite rapture. How many parents have been confronted with the typically adolescent phrase, "But you don't know how it feels. . . ." The emotional torments undergone by Goethe's young Werther and by Salinger's Holden Caulfield exemplify the adolescent's belief in the uniqueness of his own emotional experience. At a somewhat different level, this belief in personal uniqueness becomes a conviction that he will not die, that death will happen to others but not to him. This complex of beliefs in the uniqueness of his feelings and of his immortality might be called a *personal fable,* a story which he tells himself and which is not true.

Evidences of the personal fable are particularly prominent in adolescent diaries. Such diaries are often written for posterity in the conviction that the young person's experiences, crushes, and frustrations are of universal significance and importance. Another kind of evidence for the personal fable during this period is the tendency to confide in a personal God. The search for privacy and the belief in personal uniqueness leads to the establishment of an I-Thou relationship with God as a personal confident to whom one no longer looks for gifts but rather for guidance and support (Long, Elkind, & Spilka, 1967).

The concepts of an imaginary audience and a personal fable have proved useful, at least to the writer, in the understanding and treatment of troubled adolescents. The imaginary audience, for example, seems often to play a role in middle-class delinquency (Elkind, 1967). As a case in point, one young man took $1,000 from a golf tournament purse, hid the money, and then promptly revealed himself. It turned out that much of the motivation for this act was derived from the anticipated response of "the audience" to the guttiness of his action. In a similar vein, many young girls become pregnant because, in part at least, their personal fable convinces them that pregnancy will happen to others but never to them and so they need not take precautions. Such examples could be multiplied but will perhaps suffice to illustrate how adolescent egocentrism, as manifested in the imaginary audience and in the personal fable, can help provide a rationale for some adolescent behavior. These concepts can, moreover, be utilized in the treatment of adolescent offenders. It is often helpful to these young people if they can learn to differentiate between the real and the imaginary audience, which often boils down to a discrimination between the real and the imaginary parents.

THE PASSING OF ADOLESCENT EGOCENTRISM

After the appearance of formal operational thought, no new mental systems develop and the mental structures of adolescence must serve for the rest of the life span. The egocentrism of early adolescence nonetheless tends to diminish by the age of 15 or 16, the age at which formal operations become firmly established. What appears to happen is that the imaginary audience, which is primarily an anticipatory audience, is progressively modified in the direction of the reactions of the real audience. In a way, the imaginary audience can be regarded as hypothesis—or better, as a series of hypotheses—which the young person tests against reality. As a consequence of this testing, he gradually comes to recognize the difference between his own preoccupations and the interests and concerns of others.

The personal fable, on the other hand, is probably overcome (although probably never in its entirety) by the gradual establishment of what Erikson (1959) has called "intimacy." Once the young person sees himself in a more realistic light as a function of having adjusted his imaginary audience to the real one, he can establish true rather than self-interested interpersonal relations. Once relations of mutuality are established and confidences are shared, the young person discovers that others have feelings similar to his own and have suffered and been enraptured in the same way.

Adolescent egocentrism is thus overcome by a twofold transformation. On the cognitive plane, it is overcome by the gradual differentiation between his own preoccupations and the thoughts of others; while on the plane of affectivity, it is overcome by a gradual integration of the feelings of others with his own emotions.

SUMMARY AND CONCLUSIONS

In this paper I have tried to describe the forms which egocentrism takes and the mechanisms by which it is overcome, in the course of mental development. In infancy, egocentrism corresponds to the impression that objects are identical with the perception of them, and this form of egocentrism is overcome with the appearance of representation. During the preschool period, egocentrism appears in the guise of a belief that symbols contain the same information as is provided by the objects which they represent. With the emergence of concrete operations, the child is able to discriminate between symbol and referent, and so overcome this type of egocentrism. The egocentrism of the school-age period can be characterized as the belief that one's own mental constructions correspond to a superior form of perceptual reality. With the advent of formal operations and the ability to construct contrary-to-fact hypotheses, this kind of egocentrism is dissolved because the young person can now recognize the arbitrariness of his own mental constructions. Finally, during early adolescence, egocentrism appears as the belief that the thoughts of others are directed toward the self. This variety of egocentrism is overcome as a consequence of the conflict between the reactions which the young person anticipates and those which actually occur.

Although egocentrism corresponds to a negative product of mental growth, its usefulness would seem to lie in the light which it throws upon the affective reactions characteristic of any particular stage of mental development. In this paper I have dealt primarily with the affective reactions associated with the egocentrism of adolescence. Much of the material, particularly the discussion of the *imaginary audience* and the *personal fable* is speculative in the sense that it is based as much upon my clinical experience with young people as it is upon research data. These constructs are offered, not as the final word on adolescent egocentrism, but rather to illustrate how the cognitive structures peculiar to a particular level of development can be related to the affective experience and behavior characteristic of that stage. Although I have here only considered the correspondence between mental structure and affect in adolescence, it is possible that similar correspondences can be found at the earlier levels of development as well. A consideration of egocentrism, then, would seem to be a useful starting point for any attempt to reconcile cognitive structure and the dynamics of personality.

REFERENCES

Blos, P. *On adolescence.* New York: Free Press, 1962.

Charlesworth, W. R. Development of the object concept in infancy: methodological study. *American Psychologist,* 1966, *21:* 623. (Abstract)

Cowan, P. A. Cognitive egocentrism and social interaction in children. *American Psychologist,* 1966, *21:* 623. (Abstract)

Elkind, D. The child's conception of his religious denomination, I: The Jewish child. *Journal of genetic Psychology,* 1961, *99:* 209–225. (a)

Elkind, D. The development of quantitative thinking. *Journal of genetic Psychology,* 1961, *98:* 37–46. (b)

Elkind, D. The child's conception of his religious denomination, II: The Catholic child. *Journal of genetic Psychology,* 1962, *101:* 185–193.

Elkind, D. The child's conception of his religious denomination, III: The Protestant child. *Journal of genetic Psychology,* 1963, *103:* 291–304.

Elkind, D. Conceptual orientation shifts in children and adolescents. *Child Development,* 1966, *37:* 493–498.

Elkind, D. Middle-class delinquency. *Mental Hygiene,* 1967, *51:* 80–84.

Erikson, E. H. Identity and the life cycle. *Psychological issues.* Vol. 1, No. 1, New York: International Universities Press, 1959.

Freud, Anna. *The ego and the mechanisms of defense.* New York International Universities Press, 1946.

Gourevitch, Vivian, & Feffer, M. H. A study of motivational development. *Journal of genetic Psychology,* 1962, *100:* 361–375.

Inhelder, Barbel, & Piaget, J. *The growth of logical thinking from childhood to adolescence.* New York: Basic Books, 1958.

Kohlberg, L. Cognitive stages and preschool education. *Human Development,* 1966, *9:* 5–17.

Long, Diane, Elkind, D., & Spilka, B. The child's conception of prayer. *Journal for the scientific Study of Religion,* 1967, *6:* 101–109.

Lynd, Helen M. *On shame and the search for identity.* New York: Science Editions, 1961.

Peel, E. A. *The pupil's thinking.* London: Oldhourne, 1960.

Piaget, J. *The child's conception of the world.* London: Routledge & Kegan Paul, 1951.

Piaget, J. *The child's conception of number.* New York: Humanities Press, 1952. (a)

Piaget, J. *The language and thought of the child.* London: Routledge & Kegan Paul, 1952. (b)

Piaget, J. *The construction of reality in the child.* New York: Basic Books, 1954.

Piaget, J. *Comments on Vygotsky's critical remarks concerning "The language and thought of the child" and "Judgment and reasoning in the child."* Cambridge, Mass.: M. I. T. Press, 1962.

Weir, M. W. Development changes in problem solving strategies. *Psychological Review,* 1964, *71:* 473–490.

growth of political ideas in adolescence: the sense of community

Joseph Adelson
University of Michigan

Robert P. O'Neil
Allen Park Veterans Administration Hospital, Michigan

During adolescence the youngster gropes, stumbles, and leaps towards political understanding. Prior to these years the child's sense of the political order is erratic and incomplete—a curious array of sentiments and dogmas, personalized ideas, randomly remembered names and party labels, half-understood platitudes. By the time adolescence has come to an end, the child's mind, much of the time, moves easily within and among the categories of political discourse. The aim of our research was to achieve some grasp of how this transition is made.

We were interested in political ideas or concepts—in political philosophy—rather than political loyalties per se. Only during the last few years has research begun to appear on this topic. Earlier research on political socialization, so ably summarized by Hyman (1959), concentrated on the acquisition of affiliations and attitudes. More recently, political scientists and some psychologists have explored developmental trends in political knowledge and concepts, especially during childhood and the early years of adolescence; the studies of Greenstein (1965) and of Easton and Hess (1961, 1962) are particularly apposite.

Our early, informal conversations with adolescents suggested the importance of keeping our inquiry at some distance from current political issues; otherwise the underlying structure of the political is obscured by the clichés and catchphrases of partisan politics. To this end, we devised an interview schedule springing from the following premise: Imagine that a thousand men and women, dissatisfied with the way things are going in their country, decide to purchase and move to an island in the Pacific; once there, they must devise laws and modes of government.

The research was supported by grants to the first author from the H. H. Rackham Faculty Research Fund of the University of Michigan and from the Social Science Research Council. It constituted a portion of the second author's doctoral dissertation submitted to the University of Michigan.

Reprinted from the Journal of Personality and Social Psychology, 1966, 4, 295–306. Copyright © 1966 by the American Psychological Association. Reprinted by permission.

Having established this premise, the interview schedule continued by offering questions on a number of hypothetical issues. For example, the subject was asked to choose among several forms of government and to argue the merits and difficulties of each. Proposed laws were suggested to him; he was asked to weigh their advantages and liabilities and answer arguments from opposing positions. The interview leaned heavily on dilemma items, wherein traditional issues in political theory are actualized in specific instances of political conflict, with the subject asked to choose and justify a solution. The content of our inquiry ranged widely to include, among others, the following topics: the scope and limits of political authority, the reciprocal obligations of citizens and state, utopian views of man and society, conceptions of law and justice, the nature of the political process.

This paper reports our findings on the development, in adolescence, of *the sense of community*. The term is deliberately comprehensive, for we mean to encompass not only government in its organized forms, but also the social and political collectivity more generally, as in "society" or "the people." This concept is of course central to the structure of political thought; few if any issues in political theory do not advert, however tacitly, to some conception of the community. Hence the quality of that conception, whether dim, incomplete, and primitive, or clear, complex, and articulated, cannot fail to dominate or temper the child's formulation of all things political.

The very ubiquity of the concept determined our strategy in exploring it. We felt that the dimensions of community would emerge indirectly, in the course of inquiry focused elsewhere. Our pretesting had taught us that direct questions on such large and solemn issues, though at times very useful, tended to evoke simple incoherence from the cognitively unready, and schoolboy stock responses from the facile. We also learned that (whatever the ostensible topic) most of our questions informed us of the child's view of the social order, not only through what he is prepared to tell us, but also through what he does not know, knows falsely, cannot state, fumbles in stating, or takes for granted. Consequently we approached this topic through a survey of questions from several different areas of the schedule, chosen to illuminate different sides of the sense of community.

METHOD

SAMPLE

The sample was comprised of 120 youngsters, equally divided by sex, with 30 subjects at each of 4 age-grade levels—fifth grade (average age, 10.9), seventh (12.6), ninth (14.7), and twelfth (17.7). The sample was further divided by intelligence: At each grade level, two thirds of the subjects were of average intelligence (95–110) and one third of superior intelligence (125 and over), as measured by the California Test of Mental Maturity. Table 1 shows the distribution by grade, intelligence, and sex. For

Table 1
Distribution of Sample by Grade, Sex, and Intelligence

	Boys		Girls	
	Average IQ	*Superior IQ*	*Average IQ*	*Superior IQ*
5th grade: *N*	10	5	10	5
Mean IQ	106.1	127.8	105.1	128.4
7th grade: *N*	10	5	10	5
Mean IQ	104.1	140.0	104.5	134.4
9th grade: *N*	10	5	10	5
Mean IQ	106.6	133.2	105.1	134.0
12th grade: *N*	10	5	10	5
Mean IQ	106.1	140.8	103.8	134.8

each grade, school records were used to establish a pool of subjects meeting our criteria for age, sex, and IQ; within each of the subgroups so selected, names were chosen randomly until the desired sample size was achieved. Children more than 6 months older or younger than the average for their grade were excluded, as were two otherwise eligible subjects reported by their counselor to have a history of severe psychological disturbance.

This paper will report findings by age alone (to the next nearest age) and without regard to sex or intelligence. We were unable to discover sex differences nor—to our continuing surprise—differences associated with intelligence. The brighter children were certainly more fluent, and there is some reason to feel that they use a drier, more impersonal, more intellectualized approach in dealing with certain questions, but up to this time we have not found that they attain political concepts earlier than subjects of average intelligence.

The interviews were taken in Ann Arbor, Michigan. We were able to use schools representative of the community, in the sense that they do not draw students from socioeconomically extreme neighborhoods. The children of average IQ were preponderantly lower-middle and working class in background; those of high intelligence were largely from professional and managerial families. Academic families made up 13% of the sample, concentrated in the high IQ group; 5% of the "average" children and somewhat over one quarter of the "brights" had fathers with a professional connection to the University of Michigan. In these respects—socioeconomic status and parental education—the sample, which combined both IQ groups, was by no means representative of the American adolescent population at large. Yet our inability to find differences between the IQ groups, who derive from sharply different social milieux, makes us hesitate to assume that social status is closely associated with the growth of political ideas as we have measured them, or that the findings deviate markedly from what we would find in other middle-class suburbs.

INTERVIEW

The aims, scope, and form of the interview schedule have already been described. In developing the schedule we were most concerned to find a tone and level of discourse sufficiently simple to allow our youngest subjects to understand and respond to the problems posed, yet sufficiently advanced to keep our older interviewees challenged and engaged. Another aim was to strike a balance between the focused interview—to ease scoring—and a looser, more discursive approach—to allow a greater depth of inquiry and spontaneity of response. Our interviewers were permitted, once they had covered the basic questions of a topic, to explore it more thoroughly.

The interviews were conducted at the school. There were six interviewers, all with at least some graduate training in clinical psychology. The interviews were tape-recorded and transcribed verbatim. Those conducted with younger subjects were completed in about 1 hour, with older subjects in about 1½ hours.

RELIABILITY

In order to appraise the lower limits of reliability, only the more difficult items were examined, those in which responses were complex or ambiguous. For five items of this type, intercoder reliabilities ranged from .79 to .84.

RESULTS

When we examine the interviews of 11-year-olds, we are immediately struck by the common, pervasive incapacity to speak from a coherent view of the political order. Looking more closely, we find that this failure has two clear sources: First, these children are, in Piaget's sense, egocentric, in that they cannot transcend a purely personal approach to matters which require a sociocentric perspective. Second, they treat political issues in a concrete fashion and cannot manage the requisite abstractness of attitude. These tendencies, singly and together, dominate the discourse of the interview, so much so that a few sample sentences can often distinguish 11-year-old protocols from those given by only slightly older children.

The following are some interview excerpts to illustrate the differences: These are chosen randomly from the interviews of 11- and 13-year-old boys of average intelligence. They have been asked: "What is the purpose of government?"

11A. To handle the state or whatever it is so it won't get out of hand, because if it gets out of hand you might have to . . . people might get mad or something.

11B. Well . . . buildings, they have to look over buildings that would be . . . um, that wouldn't be any use of the land if they had crops on it or something like that. And when they have highways the government would have to inspect it, certain details. I guess that's about all.

11C. So everything won't go wrong in the country. They want to have a government because they respect him and they think he's a good man.

Now the 13-year-olds:

13A. So the people have rights and freedom of speech. Also so the civilization will balance.

13B. To keep law and order and talk to the people to make new ideas.

13C. Well, I think it is to keep the country happy or keep it going properly. If you didn't have it, then it would just be chaos with stealing and things like this. It runs the country better and more efficiently.

These extracts are sufficiently representative to direct us to some of the major developmental patterns in adolescent thinking on politics.

PERSONALISM

Under *personalism* we include two related tendencies: first, the child's disposition to treat institutions and social processes upon the model of persons and personal relationships; second, his inability to achieve a sociocentric orientation, that is, his failure to understand that political decisions have social as well as personal consequences, and that the political realm encompasses not merely the individual citizen, but the community as a whole.

1. "Government," "community," "society" are abstract ideas; they connote those invisible networks of obligation and purpose which link people to each other in organized social interaction. These concepts are beyond the effective reach of 11-year-olds; in failing to grasp them they fall back to persons and actions of persons, which are the nearest equivalent of the intangible agencies and ephemeral processes they are trying to imagine. Hence, Subject 11A seems to glimpse that an abstract answer is needed, tries to find it, then despairs and retreats to the personalized "people might get mad or something." A more extreme example is found in 11C's statement, which refers to government as a "he," apparently confusing it with "governor." Gross personalizations of "government" and similar terms are not uncommon at 11 and diminish markedly after that. We counted the number of times the personal pronouns "he" and "she" were used in three questions dealing with government. There were instances involving six subjects among the 11-year-olds (or 20% of the sample) and none among 13-year-olds. (The most striking example is the following sentence by an 11: "Well, I don't think she should forbid it, but if they, if he did, well most people would want to put up an argument about it.")

Although personalizations as bald as these diminish sharply after 11, more subtle or tacit ones continue well into adolescence (and in all likelihood, into adulthood)—the use of "they," for example, when "it" is appropriate. It is our impression that we see a revival of personalization among older subjects under two conditions: when the topic being discussed is too advanced or difficult for the youngster to follow or when it exposes an area of ignorance or uncertainty, and when the subject's beliefs and resentments are engaged to the point of passion or bitterness. In both these cases the emergence of affects (anxiety, anger) seems to produce a momentary cognitive regression, expressing itself in a loss of abstractness and a reversion to personalized modes of discourse.

2. The second side of personalism is the failure to attain a sociocentric perspective. The preadolescent subject does not usually appraise political events in the light of their collective consequences. Since he finds it hard to conceive the social order as a whole, he is frequently unable to understand those actions which aim to serve communal ends and so tends to interpret them parochially, as serving only the needs of individuals. We have an illustration of this in the data given in Table 2. Table 2 reports the answers to the following item: "Another law was suggested which required all children to be vaccinated against smallpox and polio. What would be the purpose of that law?"

A substantial majority—about three quarters—of the 11-year-olds see the law serving an individual end—personal protection from disease. By 13 there has been a decisive shift in emphasis, these children stressing the protection of the community. At 15 and after, an understanding of the wider purposes of vaccination has become nearly universal.

PARTS AND WHOLES

Another reflection of the concreteness of younger adolescents can be found in their tendency to treat the total functioning of institutions in terms of specific, discrete activities. If we return to the interview excerpts, we find a good example in the answer given by Subject 11B on the purpose of government. He can do no more than mention some specific governmental functions, in this case, the inspecting of buildings and highways. This answer exemplifies a pattern we find frequently among our younger subjects, one which appears in many content areas. Adolescents only gradually perceive institutions (and their processes) as wholes; until they can imagine the institution abstractly, as a total idea, they are limited to the concrete and the visible.

Table 3 is one of several which demonstrates this. The subjects were asked the purpose of the income tax. The responses were coded to distin-

Table 2
Purpose of Vaccination

	Age			
	11	*13*	*15*	*18*
Social consequences (prevention of epidemics, etc.)	.23	.67	1.00	.90
Individual consequences (prevention of individual illness)	.70	.33	.00	.10

Note. $\chi^2(3) = 46.53$, $p < .001$. In this table and all that follow $N = 30$ for each age group. When proportions in a column do not total 1.00, certain responses are not included in the response categories shown. When proportions total more than 1.00, responses have been included in more than one category of the table. The p level refers to the total table except when asterisks indicate significance levels for a designated row.

Table 3
Purpose of Income Tax

	Age			
	11	*13*	*15*	*18*
General support of government	.23	.33	.47	1.00*
Specific services only	.23	.17	.23	.00
Do not know	.53	.50	.30	.00

Note. *p* level refers to row designated by asterisk.
* $\chi^2(3) = 9.54$, $p < .05$.

guish those who answered in terms of general government support from those who mentioned only specific government services. (In most cases the services referred to are both local and visible—police, firefighting, etc.) We observe that the percentage of those referring to the government in a general sense rises slowly and steadily; all of the high school seniors do so.

NEGATIVES AND POSITIVES

Before we leave this set of interview excerpts, we want to note one more important difference between the 11- and 13-year-olds. Two of the former emphasize the negative or coercive functions of government ("To handle the state . . . so it won't get out of hand"; "So everything won't go wrong . . ."). The 13-year-olds, on the other hand, stress the positive functions of the government—keeping the country happy or working properly. This difference is so important and extensive that we will treat it in depth in a later publication, but it should be discussed at least briefly here. Younger subjects adhere to a Hobbesian view of political man: The citizenry is seen as willful and potentially dangerous, and society, therefore, as rightfully, needfully coercive and authoritarian. Although this view of the political never quite loses its appeal for a certain proportion of individuals at all ages, it nevertheless diminishes both in frequency and centrality, to be replaced, in time, by more complex views of political arrangements, views which stress the administrative sides of government (keeping the machinery oiled and in repair) or which emphasize melioristic ends (enhancing the human condition).

THE FUTURE

The adolescent years see a considerable extension of time perspective. On the one hand, a sense of history emerges, as the youngster is able to link past and present and to understand the present as having been influenced or determined by the past. On the other, the child begins to imagine the future and, what may be more important, to ponder alternative futures. Thus the present is connected to the future not merely because the future unfolds from the present, but also because the future is *tractable;* its shape depends upon choices made in the present.

This idea of the future asserts itself with increasing effect as the child advances through adolescence. In making political judgments, the youngster can anticipate the consequences of a choice taken here and now for the long-range future of the community and can weigh the probable effects of alternative choices on the future. The community is now seen to be temporal, that is, as an organism which persists beyond the life of its current members; thus judgments in the present must take into account the needs of the young and of the unborn. Further, the adolescent becomes able to envision not only the communal future, but himself (and others) in possible statuses in that future as well.

The items which most clearly expose the changing meaning of the future are those dealing with education. When we reflect on it, this is not surprising: Education is the public enterprise which most directly links the generations to each other; it is the communal activity through which one generation orients another toward the future. Several questions of public policy toward education were asked; in the answers to each the needs of the communal future weigh more heavily with increasing age. One item runs: "Some people suggested a law which would require children to go to school until they were sixteen years old. What would be the purpose of such a law?" One type of answer to this question was coded "Continuity of community"; these responses stress the community's need to sustain and perpetuate itself by educating a new generation of citizens and leaders. Typical answers were: "So children will grow up to be leaders," and "To educate people so they can carry on the government." Looking at this answer alone (analysis of the entire table would carry us beyond this topic), we find the following distribution by age (see Table 4).

Another item later in the interview poses this problem: "The people who did not have children thought it was unfair they would have to pay taxes to support the school system. What do you think of that argument?" Again the same category, which stresses the community's continuity and its future needs, rises sharply with age as shown in Table 5.

Finally, we want to examine another education item in some detail, since it offers a more complex view of the sense of the future in adolescent political thought, allowing us to observe changes in the child's view

Table 4
Purpose of Minimum Education Law

	Age			
	11	*13*	*15*	*18*
Continuity of community	.00	.27	.33	.43

Note. $\chi^2(3) = 11.95$, $p < .01$.

Table 5
Should People Without Children Pay School Taxes?

	Age			
	11	*13*	*15*	*18*
Continuity of community	.10	.10	.47	.60

Note. $\chi^2(3) = 18.61$, $p < .001$.

Table 6
Should Son be Required to Attend School Though Father Wants Him to Enter Business?

	Age			
	11	*13*	*15*	*18*
Yes, education needed to function in community	.00	.23	.43	.77***
Yes, education good in itself	.03	.23	.20	.27
Yes, education needed in business	.40	.47	.23	.13
Yes, prevents parental coercion	.57	.47	.43	.23

Note. *p* level refers to row designated by asterisk.
*** $\chi^2(3) = 25.54$, $p < .001$.

of the personal future. The question was the last of a series on the minimum education law. After the subject was asked to discuss its purpose (see above), he was asked whether he supports it. Almost all of our subjects did. He was then asked: "Suppose you have a parent who says 'My son is going to go into my business anyway and he doesn't need much schooling for that.' Do you think his son should be required to go to school anyway? Why?"

Table 6 shows that as children advance into adolescence, they stress increasingly the communal function of education. Younger subjects respond more to the father's arbitrariness or to the economic consequences of the father's position. They are less likely to grasp the more remote, more general effects of a curtailed education—that it hinders the attainment of citizenship. Representative answers by 11-year-olds were: "Well, maybe he wants some other desire and if he does maybe his father is forcing him"; and ". . . let's say he doesn't like the business and maybe he'd want to start something new." These children stress the practical and familial aspects of the issue.

Older subjects, those 15 and 18, all but ignored both the struggle with the father and the purely pragmatic advantages of remaining in school. They discoursed, sometimes eloquently, on the child's need to know about society as a whole, to function as a citizen; and to understand the perspectives of others. Here is how one 18-year-old put it:

> . . . a person should have a perspective and know a little bit about as much as he can rather than just one thing throughout his whole life and anything of others, because he'd have to know different things about different aspects of life and education and just how things are in order to get along with them, because if not then they'd be prejudiced toward their own feelings and what *they* wanted and they wouldn't be able to understand any people's needs.

Older subjects see education as the opportunity to become *cosmopolitan,* to transcend the insularities of job and kinship. For the older adolescent, leaving school early endangers the future in two ways. On the personal side, it threatens one's capacity to assume the perspective of the other and to attain an adequate breadth of outlook; thus, it imperils one's future place in the community. On the societal side, it endangers the integrity of the social order itself, by depriving the community of a cosmopolitan citizenry.

CLAIMS OF THE COMMUNITY

We have already seen that as adolescence advances the youngster is increasingly sensitive to the fact of community and its claims upon the citizen. What are the limits of these claims, the limits of political authority? To what point, and under what conditions can the state, acting in the common good, trespass upon the autonomy of the citizen? When do the community's demands violate the privacy and liberty of the individual? The clash of these principles—individual freedom versus the public welfare and safety—is one of the enduring themes of Western political theory. Many, perhaps most, discussions in political life in one way or another turn on this issue; indeed, the fact that these principles are so often used purely rhetorically (as when the cant of liberty or of the public good is employed to mask pecuniary and other motives) testifies to their salience in our political thinking.

A number of questions in the interview touched upon this topic tangentially, and some were designed to approach it directly. In these latter we asked the subject to adjudicate and comment upon a conflict between public and private interests, each of these supported by a general political principle—usually the individual's right to be free of compulsion, on the one hand, and the common good, on the other. We tried to find issues which would be tangled enough to engage the most complex modes of political reasoning. A major effort in this direction was made through a series of three connected questions on eminent domain. The series began with this question:

> Here is another problem the Council faced. They decided to build a road to connect one side of the island to the other. For the most part they had no trouble buying the land on which to build the road, but one man refused to sell his land to the government. He was offered a fair price for his land but he refused, saying that he didn't want to move, that he was attached to his

land, and that the Council could buy another piece of land and change the direction of the road. Many people thought he was selfish, but others thought he was in the right. What do you think?

Somewhat to our surprise, there are no strong developmental patterns visible, though we do see a moderate tendency (not significant statistically, however) for the younger subjects to side with the landowner (see Table 7). The next question in the series sharpened the issue somewhat between the Council and the reluctant landowner:

The Council met and after long discussion voted that if the landowner would not agree to give up his land for the road, he should be forced to, because the rights of all the people on the island were more important than his. Do you think this was a fair decision?

The phrasing of the second question does not alter the objective facts of the conflict; yet Table 8 shows decisive shifts in position. It is hard

Table 7
Which Party Is Right in Eminent-Domain Conflict?

	Age			
	11	*13*	*15*	*18*
Individual should sell; community needs come first	.30	.20	.30	.40
Detour should be made; individual rights come first	.60	.47	.27	.37
Emphasis on social responsibility; individual should be appealed to, but not forced	.10	.17	.17	.07
Ambivalence; individual is right in some ways, wrong in others	.00	.13	.27	.17

Table 8
Should Landowner Be Forced To Sell His Land?

	Age			
	11	*13*	*15*	*18*
Yes, rights of others come first	.40	.37	.63	.70
No, individual rights come first	.57	.50	.33	.07**
No, social responsibility should suffice	.03	.10	.00	.23

Note. *p* levels refers to row designated by asterisk.
** $\chi^2(3) = 12.17$, $p < .01$.

to be sure why: perhaps because the second question states that the Council has considered the matter at length, perhaps because the Council's decision is justified by advancing the idea of "the people's rights." Whatever the reason, we now see a marked polarization of attitude. The younger subjects—those 11 and 13—continue to side with the landowner; those 15 and 18 almost completely abandon him, although about one quarter of the latter want to avoid coercion and suggest an appeal to his sense of social responsibility.

The final question in the series tightened the screws:

> The landowner was very sure that he was right. He said that the law was unjust and he would not obey it. He had a shotgun and would shoot anyone who tried to make him get off his land. He seemed to mean business. What should the government do?

The landowner's threat startled some of the subjects, though in very different ways depending on age, as Table 9 shows: The younger subjects in these cases did not quite know what to do about it and suggested that he be mollified at all costs; the older subjects, if they were taken aback, were amused or disdainful, saw him as a lunatic or a hothead, and rather matter-of-factly suggested force or guile to deal with him. Nevertheless, this question did not produce any essential change in position for the sample as a whole. Those older subjects who had hoped to appeal to the landowner's social conscience despaired of this and sided with the Council. Otherwise, the earlier pattern persisted, the two younger groups continuing to support the citizen, the older ones favoring the government, and overwhelmingly so among the oldest subjects.

These findings seem to confirm the idea that older adolescents are more responsive to communal than to individual needs. Yet it would be incorrect to infer that these subjects favor the community willy-nilly. A close look at the interview protocols suggests that older adolescents choose differently because they reason differently.

Most younger children—those 13 and below—can offer no justification for their choices. Either they are content with a simple statement of preference, for example: "I think he was in the right"; or they do no more than paraphrase the question: "Well, there is really two sides to it. One is

Table 9
What Should Government Do If Landowner Threatens Violence?

	Age			
	11	*13*	*15*	*18*
Detour	.60	.63	.37	.10
Government coercion justified	.23	.27	.57	.83

Note. $\chi^2(3) = 29.21$, $p < .001$.

that he is attached and he shouldn't give it up, but again he should give it up for the country." These youngsters do not or cannot rationalize their decisions, neither through appeal to a determining principle, nor through a comparative analysis of each side's position. If there is an internal argument going on within the mind of the 11- or 13-year-old, he is unable to make it public; instead, he seems to choose by an intuitive ethical leap, averring that one or the other position is "fair," "in the right," or "selfish." He usually favors the landowner, because his side of the matter is concrete, personal, psychologically immediate, while the Council's position hinges on an idea of the public welfare which is too remote and abstract for these youngsters to absorb. Even those few children who try to reason from knowledge or experience more often than not flounder and end in confusion. A 13-year-old:

> Like this girl in my class. Her uncle had a huge house in——, and they tore it down and they put the new city hall there. I think they should have moved it to another place. I think they should have torn it down like they did, because they had a law that if there was something paid for, then they should give that man a different price. But then I would force him out, but I don't know how I'd do it.

What we miss in these interviews are two styles of reasoning which begin to make their appearance in 15-year-olds: first, the capacity to reason consequentially, to trace out the long-range implications of various courses of action; second, a readiness to deduce specific choices from general principles. The following excerpt from a 15-year-old's interview illustrates both of these approaches:

> Well, maybe he owned only a little land if he was a farmer and even if they did give him a fair price maybe all the land was already bought on the island that was good for farming or something and he couldn't get another start in life if he did buy it. Then maybe in a sense he was selfish because if they had to buy other land and change the direction of the road why of course then maybe they'd raise taxes on things so they could get more money cause it would cost more to change directions from what they already have planned. [Fair to force him off?] Yes, really, just because one person doesn't want to sell his land that don't mean that, well the other 999 or the rest of the people on the island should go without this road because of one.

In the first part of the statement, the subject utilizes a cost-effectiveness approach; he estimates the costs (economic, social, moral) of one decision against another. He begins by examining the effects on the landowner. Can he obtain equivalent land elsewhere? He then considers the long-range economic consequences for the community. Will the purchase of other land be more expensive and thus entail a tax increase? Though he does not go on to solve these implicit equations—he could hardly do so, since he does not have sufficient information—he does state the variables he deems necessary to solve them.

The second common strategy at this age, seen in the last part of the statement, is to imply or formulate a general principle, usually ethico-political in nature, which subsumes the instance. Most adolescents using this approach will for this item advert to the community's total welfare, but some of our older adolescents suggest some other governing principle—the sanctity of property rights or the individual's right to privacy and autonomy. In either instance, the style of reasoning is the same; a general principle is sought which contains the specific issue.

Once a principle is accepted, the youngster attempts to apply it consistently. If the principle is valid, it should fall with equal weight on all; consequently, exceptions are resisted:

> I think that the man should be forced to move with a good sum of money because I imagine it would be the people, it said the rights of the whole, the whole government and the whole community, why should one man change the whole idea?

And to the question of the landowner's threatening violence: "They shouldn't let him have his own way, because he would be an example. Other people would think that if they used his way, they could do what they wanted to." Even a child who bitterly opposes the Council's position on this issue agrees that once a policy has been established, exceptions should be resisted:

> Well, if the government is going to back down when he offers armed resistance, it will offer ideas to people who don't like, say, the medical idea [see below]. They'll just haul out a shotgun if you come to study them. The government should go through with the action.

THE FORCE OF PRINCIPLE

Once principles and ideals are firmly established, the child's approach to political discourse is decisively altered. When he ponders a political choice, he takes into account not only *personal* consequences (What will this mean, practically speaking, for the individuals involved?) and pragmatic *social* consequences (What effect will this have on the community at large?), but also its consequences in the realm of *value* (Does this law or decision enhance or endanger such ideals as liberty, justice, and so on?). There is of course no sharp distinction among these types of consequences; values are contained, however tacitly, in the most "practical" of decisions. Nevertheless, these ideals, once they develop, have a life, an autonomy of their own. We reasoned that as the adolescent grew older, political principles and ideals would be increasingly significant, and indeed would loom large enough to overcome the appeal of personal and social utility in the narrow sense.

To test this belief we wanted an item which would pit a "good" against a "value." We devised a question proposing a law which, while achieving a personal and communal good, would at the same time violate a political ideal—in this case, the value of personal autonomy. The item ran: "One [proposed law] was a suggestion that men over 45 be required to have a yearly medical checkup. What do you think of that suggestion?" The answer was to be probed if necessary: "Would you be in favor of that? Why (or why not)?" Table 10 shows the distribution of responses.

Table 10
Should Men over 45 Be Required To Have a Yearly Checkup?

	Age			
	11	13	15	18
Yes, otherwise they would not do it	.50	.07	.00	.03***
Yes, good for person and/or community	.50	.80	.70	.60
No infringement on liberties	.00	.13	.27	.37**

Note. p level refers to rows designated by asterisk.
** $\chi^2(3) = 11.95$, $p < .01$.
*** $\chi^2(3) = 33.10$, $p < .001$.

The findings are interesting on several counts, aside from offering testimony on the degree to which good health is viewed as a summum bonum. The 11-year-olds, here as elsewhere, interpret the issue along familial and authoritarian lines. The government is seen in loco parentis; its function is to make its citizens do the sensible things they would otherwise neglect to do. But our primary interest is in the steady growth of opposition to the proposal. The basis for opposition, though it is phrased variously, is that the government has no business exercising compulsion in this domain. These youngsters look past the utilitarian appeal of the law and sense its conflict with a value that the question itself does not state. These data, then, offer some support to our suggestion that older adolescents can more easily bring abstract principles to bear in the appraisal of political issues. Strictly speaking, the findings are not definitive, for we cannot infer that all of those supporting the law do so without respect to principle. Some of the older adolescents do, in fact, recognize the conflict implicit in the question, but argue that the public and personal benefits are so clear as to override the issue of personal liberties. But there are very few signs of this among the younger subjects. Even when pressed, as they were in a following question, they cannot grasp the meaning and significance of the conflict; they see only the tangible good.

DISCUSSION

These findings suggest that the adolescent's sense of community is determined not by a single factor, but by the interaction of several related developmental parameters. We should now be in a position to consider what some of these are.

1. *The decline of authoritarianism.* Younger subjects are more likely to approve of coercion in public affairs. Themselves subject to the authority of adults, they more readily accept the fact of hierarchy. They find it hard to imagine that authority may be irrational, presumptuous, or whimsical; thus they bend easily to the collective will.

2. With advancing age there is an increasing grasp of the *nature and*

needs of the community. As the youngster begins to understand the structure and functioning of the social order as a whole, he begins to understand too the specific social institutions within it and their relations to the whole. He comes to comprehend the autonomy of institutions, their need to remain viable, to sustain and enhance themselves. Thus the demands of the social order and its constituent institutions, as well as the needs of the public, become matters to be appraised in formulating political choices.

3. *The absorption of knowledge and consensus.* This paper has taken for granted, and hence neglected, the adolescent's increasing knowingness. The adolescent years see a vast growth in the acquisition of political information, in which we include not only knowledge in the ordinary substantive sense, but also the apprehension of consensus, a feeling for the common and prevailing ways of looking at political issues. The child acquires these from formal teaching, as well as through a heightened cathexis of the political, which in turn reflects the generally amplified interest in the adult world. Thus, quite apart from the growth of cognitive capacity, the older adolescent's views are more "mature" in that they reflect internalization of adult perspectives.

4. We must remember that it is not enough to be exposed to mature knowledge and opinion; their absorption in turn depends on the growth of *cognitive capacities.* Some of the younger subjects knew the fact of eminent domain, knew it to be an accepted practice, yet, unable to grasp the principles involved, could not apply their knowledge effectively to the question. This paper has stressed the growth of those cognitive capacities which underlie the particular intellectual achievements of the period: the adolescent's increasing ability to weigh the relative consequences of actions, the attainment of deductive reasoning. The achievement of these capacities—the leap to "formal operations," in Piaget's term— allows him to escape that compulsion toward the immediate, the tangible, the narrowly pragamatic which so limits the political discourse of younger adolescents.

5. In turn the growth of cognitive capacity allows *the birth of ideology.* Ideology may not be quite the right word here, for it suggests a degree of coherence and articulation that few of our subjects, even the oldest and brightest, come close to achieving. Nevertheless there is an impressive difference between the younger and older adolescents in the orderliness and internal consistency of their political perspectives. What passes for ideology in the younger respondents is a raggle-taggle array of sentiments: "People ought to be nice to each other"; "There are a lot of wise guys around, so you have to have strict laws." In time these sentiments may mature (or harden) into ideologies or ideological dispositions, but they are still too erratic, too inconsistent. They are not yet principled or generalized and so tend to be self-contradictory, or loosely held and hence easily abandoned. When younger subjects are cross-questioned, however gently, they are ready to reverse themselves even on issues they seem to feel strongly about. When older subjects are challenged, however sharply, they refute, debate, and counterchallenge. In some part their resistance to easy change reflects a greater degree of poise and their greater experience in colloquy and argument, but it also bespeaks the

fact that their views are more firmly founded. The older adolescents, most conspicuously those at 18, aim for an inner concordance of political belief.

These then are the variables our study has suggested as directing the growth of political concepts. We must not lean too heavily on any one of them: The development of political thought is not simply or even largely a function of cognitive maturation or of increased knowledge or of the growth of ideology when these are taken alone. This paper has stressed the cognitive parameters because they seem to be so influential at the younger ages. The early adolescent's political thought is constrained by personalized, concrete, present-oriented modes of approach. Once these limits are transcended, the adolescent is open to influence by knowledge, by the absorption of consensus, and by the principles he adopts from others or develops on his own.

A DEVELOPMENTAL SYNOPSIS

We are now in a position to summarize the developmental patterns which have emerged in this study. It is our impression that the most substantial advance is to be found in the period between 11 and 13 years, where we discern a marked shift in the cognitive basis of political discourse. Our observations support the Inhelder and Piaget (1958) findings on a change from concrete to formal operations at this stage. To overstate the case somewhat, we might say that the *11-year-old* has not achieved the capacity for formal operations. His thinking is concrete, egocentric, tied to the present; he is unable to envision long-range social consequences; he cannot comfortably reason from premises; he has not attained hypothetico-deductive modes of analysis. The 13-year-old has achieved these capacities some (much?) of the time, but is unable to display them with any consistent effectiveness. The *13-year-olds* seem to be the most labile of our subjects. Depending on the item, they may respond like those older or younger than themselves. In a sense they are on the threshold of mature modes of reasoning, just holding on, and capable of slipping back easily. Their answers are the most difficult to code, since they often involve an uneasy mixture of the concrete and the formal.

The *15-year-old* has an assured grasp of formal thought. He neither hesitates nor falters in dealing with the abstract; when he seems to falter, it is more likely due to a lack of information or from a weakness in knowing and using general principles. His failures are likely to be in content and in fluency, rather than in abstract quality per se. Taking our data as a whole we usually find only moderate differences between 15 and 18. We do find concepts that appear suddenly between 11 and 13, and between 13 and 15, but only rarely do we find an idea substantially represented at 18 which is not also available to a fair number of 15-year-olds.

The *18-year-old* is, in other words, the 15-year-old, only more so. He knows more; he speaks from a more extended apperceptive mass; he is more facile; he can elaborate his ideas more fluently. Above all, he is more philosophical, more ideological in his perspective on the political order. At times he is consciously, deliberately an ideologue. He holds forth.

REFERENCES

Easton, D., & Hess, R. D. Youth and the political system. In S. M. Lipset & L. Lowenthal (Eds.), *Culture and social character.* New York: Free Press of Glencoe, 1961. Pp. 226–251.

Easton, D., & Hess, R. D. The child's political world. *Midwest Journal of Political Science,* 1967, *6:* 229–246.

Greenstein, F. *Children and politics.* New Haven: Yale University Press, 1965.

Hyman, H. H. *Political socialization.* Glencoe, Ill: Free Press, 1959.

Inhelder, B., & Piaget, J. *The growth of logical thinking from childhood to adolescence.* New York: Basic Books, 1958.

adolescent thinking and the diary of Anne Frank

George Scarlett
Clark University

The diary of Anne Frank affords one a rare glimpse into the thoughts of an adolescent. And one of the most striking features of Anne's thinking is her tremendous concern for justice and being treated as an equal. Much has been written about the affective development of the adolescent, and more recently the cognitive studies of adolescence have described adolescent egocentrism and the adolescent's task of taking up adult roles. Anne's diary displays the themes and forms common to adolescent thinking, but it is this concern for justice that is perhaps the most striking feature of the book.[1a]

> "For in its innermost depths youth is lonelier than old age." I read this saying in some book and I've always remembered, and found it to be true. Is it true then that grownups have a more difficult time here than we do? No. I know it isn't. Older people have formed their opinions about everything, and don't waver before they act. It's twice as hard for us young ones to hold our ground, and maintain our opinions, in a time when all ideas are being shattered and destroyed, when people are showing their worst side, and do not know whether to believe in truth and right and God.*

Anne wrote the above passage after two years in hiding and just three weeks before she and her family were discovered by the Grüne Polizie. When, therefore, she speaks of "a time when all ideals are being shattered," she is referring to the condition of war. But her words may also be interpreted as describing the condition of adolescence.

First of all, Anne states that adults have formed their opinions and, by implication, that adolescents are only in the process of doing so. This development of opinions is part of the adolescent's primary task—the formation of an adult role.

Anne received her diary before she and her family were forced to go

* From *Anne Frank: The Diary of a Young Girl*. Copyright 1952 by Otto H. Frank. All quotations by permission of Doubleday & Company, Inc., New York, and Vallentine Mitchell & Company, Ltd., London.

Reprinted from The Psychoanalytic Review, Vol. 58, No. 2, 1971, through the courtesy of the Editors and the Publisher, National Psychological Association for Psychoanalysis, New York, N.Y.

into hiding because they were Jews. They hid in the back part of an office building, and Anne describes the packing scene prior to their flight:[1b]

> The first thing I put in was this diary. . . . I put in the craziest things with the idea that we were going into hiding. But I'm sorry, memories meant more to me than dresses.

Like the first message, we may interpret the above in two ways. One way is to take Anne literally and note that she cherishes the memories of her past more than dresses. The second is that Anne places more value on thoughts than on things. The supremacy of 'mind over matter' is directly connected with Anne's major concern for constructing her own role as an adult; it is only because she values thought in itself that she is also concerned with using her powers of thinking to solve the problem of working out an adult role. And the value which is placed upon thought at this time in her life is in turn related to newly acquired abilities to reflect, i.e., to think about one's thoughts and to analyze one's actions.

The situation at the beginning of adolescence is this: the young adolescent, while cherishing thought, at the same time divorces himself from many of the practical concerns that were his as a child. For example, Anne Frank at fourteen describes herself when still in school as a superficial being, meaning that the younger Anne was more concerned with the practical than with reflection. But what we see as distinctly adolescent about Anne's thinking is that she is so centered in the primary problem of constructing an adult role that she is far less concerned with reflection as a means of governing actions than is the adult. That is to say, Anne's thought is far more separated from her activity than it was when she was younger, but it is still tied more to herself than is the thinking of most adults. In common sense terms, Anne probably thinks a great deal more about herself than do most adults. Paradoxically, this reflecting upon oneself, this egocentric thought, is relatively unreflective, for in reflecting we mean to reproduce in thought what exists in fact.

One of the most striking concerns in Anne's thinking is her concern for justice. We see here not a childlike respect for authority and constraint but a concern for mutual respect between individuals and, most important, a sense of autonomy in the area of morality. She writes: "It isn't the fear of God but the upholding of one's own honor and conscience [that matters]. . . ."[1c] One is reminded of Piaget's statement, "Authority as such cannot be the source of justice, because the development of justice presupposes autonomy."[3]

As an example of Anne's new sense of justice, take Anne's observation of Mrs. Van Daan, a middle-aged woman, who with her husband and sixteen-year-old son, joined the Franks in hiding:[1d]

> Mrs. Van Daan is unbearable. I get nothing but "blow-ups" from her for my continuous chatter. . . . This is the latest: she doesn't want to wash up the pans if there is a fragment left. . . . After the next meal Margot [Anne's older sister] sometimes has about seven pans to wash up and Madame says: "Well, Margot, you have got a lot to do!"

No longer does Anne treat adults with the unilateral respect accorded them when she was a child. Anne's new abilities to reflect and her concern for taking up an adult role lead her to insist (at least in thought) upon equality with adults. She judges adults as she would judge her peers except that she is perhaps more sympathetic toward the latter.

Anne's 'new morality' is truly a loss of innocence in regard to her relationship to adults. The fact that she no longer regards them as the tree of the knowledge of good and evil stimulates a kind of prophetic rage at the realization that what was once thought to be divine is only the product of human beings, only an idol worshiped by ignorant men. And so, like a great many adolescents, she sometimes judges them more harshly than they probably deserve. For instance,[1e]

> Why do grownups quarrel so easily, so much, and over the most idiotic things? . . . I'm simply amazed again and again over their awful manners and especially . . . stupidity. . . .

One other example of Anne's new emphasis on cooperation as the basis for interpersonal relations is found in her record of an argument between herself and a dentist by the name of Dussel who had joined the Franks and Van Daans several months after the Franks first went into hiding. He and Anne shared a room. Anne was fond of reading and asked Mr. Dussel if she might use the desk in their room for a few hours each week. Mr. Dussel very unwisely refused on the grounds that he needed the desk for his work which he felt was more important than the work of a school girl. Anne replied:[1f]

> When you first came here we arranged that this room should be for both of us; if we were to divide it fairly, you would have the morning and I all the afternoon! But I don't even ask that much, and I think that my two afternoons are perfectly reasonable.

Anne eventually got her own way.

The subtlety in Anne's morality is nowhere better shown than in her regard for the intentions of people and not just the consequences of their actions. Furthermore, Anne's new powers of thought enable her to concentrate more clearly on the dependence of a person upon his situation. Therefore, Anne's sense of justice is not the childlike concern for the letter of the law but rather for its spirit as manifest in her concern for intentions and for equity. Regarding the suffering of her own family and other Jews, Anne writes, "It is not the Dutch people's fault that we are having such a miserable time."[1g] And later on, towards the end of the war when some of the non-Jewish Dutch were turning against the Jews, Anne writes:[1h]

> . . . I can't understand that the Dutch, who are such a good, honest, upright people, should judge us like this, we, the most pitiful of all people of the whole world.

That is to say, it is inequitable to persecute the Jews since they are more handicapped than other groups and deserve pity because of their situation.

Perhaps the most obvious consequence of the adolescent's 'new morality' is the temporary rift that it encourages between parent and child. One reason for this is stated by Anne in the following passage:[i]

> My treatment varies so much. One day Anne is so sensible and is allowed to know everything; and the next day I hear that Anne is just a silly little goat who doesn't know anything at all and imagines that she's learned a wonderful lot from books. . . . Oh, so many things bubble up inside me as I lie in bed, having to put up with people I'm fed up with, who always misinterpret my intentions.

Anne is therefore concerned by the inconsistent treatment she gets from adults as well as their not understanding her intentions.

There is a difficult problem facing every parent of a young adolescent that the adolescent cannot appreciate. If we look at the few references Anne makes concerning her own *actions,* we see that they are often impulsive and sometimes indistinguishable from the actions of a child. As she herself puts it, ". . . they haven't given me the name 'little bundle of contradictions' all for nothing!"[j] The principle contradiction here is between Anne's actions and her thoughts. But this contradiction between childlike actions and an adultlike insistence upon being treated as an equal exists and fosters estrangement only because of Anne's adolescent egocentrism, her inability to see herself as adults see her. Adolescence is perhaps the most morally conscious age group and an age which insists that its intentions be understood. It is therefore ironic that the adolescent is at the same time relatively ignorant of the intentions and perspectives of others.

A parent who does not respect the adolescent's mind is asking for trouble. For example, after Anne and her sister Margot had been quarreling, Anne's father stopped the two and apparently gave a judgment in favor of Margot. Anne wrote afterwards, "It so happened I was neither offended nor cross, just miserable. It wasn't right of Daddy to judge without knowing what the squabble was about. . . ."[k] Anne was "miserable" not because she thought herself to be totally on the side of justice but because she felt she deserved a fair trial in which she was judged by a peer. Instead she was often treated as follows:[l]

> How is it that Daddy was never any support to me in my struggle, why did he completely miss the mark when he wanted to offer me a helping hand? Daddy tried the wrong methods, he always talked to me as a child who was going through difficult phases. . . . I didn't want to hear about "symptoms of your age," or "other girls," or "it wears off by itself."

Anne's concern for justice and being treated as an equal is manifest even more in her relationship with her mother than with her father. Even though both Mr. and Mrs. Frank treated Anne as a child, it is probable that Anne's mother, like most mothers, was more obvious in her treatment. Anne writes, "Mummy sometimes treats me just like a baby, which I can't bear."[1m] And the fact that Anne was a girl increased the chances for more friction between mother and daughter than between father and daughter. Reasons for this have too often been limited to the competition between mother and daughter for the father's love. It seems more feasible, however, to place the major emphasis on the fact that an adolescent girl's real mother often stands in opposition to the ideal mother she hopes herself to be someday. And if (as it seems to be in Anne's case) there are in fact many similarities between mother and daughter, the daughter will become all the more upset and mad at being like her imperfect mother. Anne writes:[1n]

> In spite of all my theories, and however much trouble I take, each day I miss having a real mother who understands me. That is why with everything I do and write I think of the "Mumsie" that I want to be for my children later on. . . . To give me the feeling of calling Mummy something which sounds like "Mumsie," I often call her "Mum": the incomplete "Mumsie," as it were, whom I would so love to honor with the extra "ie" and yet who does not realize it.

This passage also reveals Anne's ability to use language in an adult but autistic (i.e., noncommunicable, wish-fulfilling thought) manner. Anne's use of language accomplishes the double task of withholding love without communicating her dissatisfaction to her mother.

It may be a characteristic of adolescent thinking to place particular emphasis on a specific instance of "injustice" occurring near the beginning of adolescence and to cherish the memory of this instance. I have heard too many people relate what to them were crucial experiences of "injustice" around the beginning of adolescence to think this is mere coincidence. Anne writes:[1o]

> One thing, which perhaps may seem rather fatuous, I have never forgiven her. It was on a day I had to go to the dentist. Mummy and Margot were going to come with me and agreed that I should take my bicycle. When we had finished at the dentist, and were outside again, Margot and Mummy told me that they were going into town to look at something or buy something, I don't remember exactly what. I wanted to go too, but I was not allowed to, as I had my bicycle with me. Tears of rage sprang into my eyes, and Mummy and Margot began laughing at me. . . . It is queer that the wound that Mummy made then still burns, when I think of how angry I was that afternoon.

What is significant about this incident is that on the surface it does not appear to warrant much attention, but that in reality it was extremely important to Anne because she was being treated as a child at a time when she was beginning to realize she was someone different from a child, someone who deserved to be treated as the equal to an adult.

In general, we may describe Anne's new moral code as a distinction between what is and what ought to be. A child rarely makes this distinction, and if he does, it is for different reasons than those of the adolescent. To make such a distinction is not a child's way of thinking, for it generally signifies thinking in terms of possibilities or hypotheses as opposed to thinking solely in terms of what is at hand. The adolescent's 'new morality' is symptomatic of his ability to think that the world does not have to exist the way it does and has existed. Furthermore, the adolescent's concern for what ought to be is part of his concern for what will be.

The future-oriented aspects of adolescent thinking are significant in another respect, for the adolescent's show of altruism and concern for what ought to be is never divorced from his own ambitions. That is to say, appearing at various times in an adolescent's discourses on injustice is the insinuation that the speaker or writer of such discourses may be just the person to actualize the ideals and goals being discussed. This is perhaps no better illustrated than in the motivation of an adolescent to better his predecessors. Anne writes:[1p]

> I am becoming still more independent of my parents; young as I am, I face life with more courage than Mummy; my feeling for justice is immovable, and truer than hers. I know what I want, I have a goal, an opinion, I have a religion, and love. Let me be myself and then I am satisfied. I know that I'm a woman, a woman with inward strength and plenty of courage.
>
> If God lets me live, I shall attain more than Mummy ever has done. I shall not remain insignificant, I shall work in the world and for mankind.

Again we note that like so many characteristics of adolescent thinking, the blending of altruism and ambition as shown here is part of Anne's concern for constructing an adult role in society.

Furthermore, the previous example serves as another illustration of adolescent egocentrism and the 'new morality.' Egocentrism is here manifested by the fact that Mrs. Frank was most likely not the failure Anne depicts her as being. This is suggested by the fact that in all her writings, Anne criticizes her mother for primarily two things: treating Anne as if she were a child and criticizing her. As said before, treating a young adolescent as a child is quite normal for mothers. And as for criticizing Anne, Anne's actions were in all probability often asking for some sort of criticism, for Anne states that Mrs. Frank did not treat Margot in the same manner—indicating that Mrs. Frank was not an indiscriminant criticizer. It was likely the manner in which her mother criticized her rather than the content which Anne most disliked. Therefore, the two things which Anne dislikes about her relationship with her mother are quite interrelated.

The aspect of Anne's thinking which has been described as a blend of altruism and ambition is related in a curious way to another aspect of adolescent thinking and behavior, namely, the occasional discovery of the fragility of personal theories and resulting self-castigation. This always occurs through some kind of social intercourse and differs from an adult's discovering his own mistake in that there is a great deal more self-castigation. The reason for this adolescent reaction has in large part to do with an adolescent's chronic appeal to ideas rather than experiences when presenting an opinion. Furthermore, the 'mind over matter' approach to thinking can satisfy some of the ego needs of an individual who is concerned about her being equal to adults. It is a "let's-pretend-I'm-an-adult" world which operates in peace until someone intervenes to point out discrepancies. Anne once wrote a letter to her parents expressing her feelings about how unjustly she was treated and how she felt she deserved to be treated as someone older than they were treating her. Anne's father was saddened by the letter and told Anne that he thought she was being a bit harsh. Anne writes:[14]

> Oh, I have failed miserably; this is certainly the worst thing I've ever done in my life. . . . No, Anne, you still have a tremendous lot to learn, begin by doing that first, instead of looking down on others and accusing them.

Her words reveal that she has a vague notion about the motivation behind many of her moral judgments. Her reaction is not that of an adult who says, "Yes, I was wrong. I hope I won't make the same mistake again." Anne's reaction is, ". . . you still have a tremendous lot to learn. . . ." She therefore seems to be orienting more toward the empirical. In brief, the relative absence of appealing to the concrete is understandable in the light of her concern for constructing a role in society, and this concern when demonstrated in something like a diary is in part a compensation which allows for the self-assertion and imitation of adult models in thought that prove so difficult for the adolescent to realize in action.

The fact that Anne often chooses to express her wishes and concerns in writing is another characteristic of her behavior which is not childlike. The speech of the very young child serves a relatively minor role in the regulation of his thoughts and actions. Speech in the very young child more often merely accompanies his actions. Around the age of six or seven, a child develops the ability to use inner speech as a means for regulating his activity, but this speech is limited in its being oriented toward the concrete situation the child is in at a given time. Only with the advent of adolescence do we find inner speech playing a greater role in the life of the individual than vocal speech, and by the time of adolescence it is far more difficult to make a distinction between thought and speech than it was in childhood. Although the written word is not identical with inner speech, it is closely allied with it.

Furthermore, we may note that Anne sometimes found it easier to write letters to those living in the same house than to speak with them directly. There seem to be several reasons for this. First, unlike the child, Anne is more concerned with communicating intentions and unsure feelings as opposed to the childish motivation to communicate observations of the activity of the moment or the past. Second, because she lacks the security of either not caring about or not being sure of her place in society, Anne finds it far more difficult to communicate verbally than to communicate in writing. To communicate verbally lays one open to criticism, criticism which a young adolescent is often ill equipped to handle. Furthermore, in writing one can ponder over words whereas speaking often brings out unintended or ill-formed thoughts, thoughts which lead to misinterpretation, one of the things an adolescent most fears. As Anne puts it:[15]

> I'm not a baby or a spoiled darling any more, to be laughed at, whatever she does. I have my own views, plans, and ideas, though I can't put them into words yet. Oh, so many things bubble up inside me as I lie in bed, having to put up with people I'm fed up with, who always misinterpret my intentions.

What we find in adolescent thinking is a realization that there is a gulf between personal understanding and spoken explanation, and it is sometimes easier to retreat into a diary or a letter than to risk failing while attempting to bridge that gulf.

Another aspect of Anne's language which differs from the language of the child is the use of abbreviated language that is quite clear in communicating an intended thought. The child's abbreviated language is unintended and most often difficult to understand. But take the following example of Anne's abbreviated language: "It is drizzly weather, the stove smells, the food lies heavily on everybody's tummy, causing thunderous noises on all sides! The war at a standstill, morale rotten."[18] The meaning of Anne's account is clear, and furthermore, the omission of the word *is* on two occasions adds a poetic touch to the account. The description has its own rhythm and gives one the feeling of something that was once moving rapidly but is now grinding to a halt. In other words, unlike the child's abbreviated language, Anne's omissions sometimes *add* meaning and facilitate communication.

One way of describing the poetic sense manifest in Anne's abbreviated language is that, unlike the child, Anne is able to appreciate the *form* of something while ignoring its content. In the area of morality we noted that her criticisms of elders seemed to be directed as much at the content of the adult's sentences as at the way in which these sentences were said. A child is also sensitive to attitudes hiding behind words, but this sensitivity is only on the intuitive, not the conceptual level. Another example of this ability to appreciate form is brought out in the following criticism Anne made about a book: "I can't drag myself away from a book called *The Knock at the Door* by Ina Boudier-Bahkar. The story of the family is exceptionally well written."[1c] A child might say the book was interesting or very realistic, but it is unlikely he would say "well written." And this interest in form is itself related to the adolescent orientation toward the abstract, toward thinking instead of toward acting.

Adolescent love has received a great deal of attention from many writers concerned with adolescent thinking. And the majority of these writers seem to place considerable emphasis on puberty as the great event marking the beginning of adolescence. But there is more to love than biology, and as Piaget and Inhelder point out, ". . . what distinguishes an adolescent in love from a child in love is that the former generally complicates his feelings by constructing a romance or by referring to social or even literary ideals of all sorts."[2] Furthermore, adolescent love is characteristically a search for extrafamilial relationships which will satisfy the need to be understood and accepted *as an equal*.

The diary is itself taken by Anne to be a friend. She writes:[1u]

> I hope I shall be able to confide in you completely, as I have never been able to do in anyone before, and I hope that you will be a great support and comfort to me.

What Anne sees in her diary and what she sees in her peers is the possibility of creating a bond of affection and satisfaction of certain ego needs not being met within her own family. Again, concerning the reason for starting a diary, Anne writes:[1v]

. . . as I don't intend to show this cardboard-covered notebook, bearing the proud name of "diary," to anyone, unless I find a real friend, boy or girl, probably nobody cares. And now I come to the root of the matter, the reason for starting a diary: it is that I have no such real friend.

But even a diary is insufficient in meeting an adolescent's needs. Lucky for Anne, the Van Daans had a son, Peter, to whom she could turn. She writes: "I have longed so much and for so long, I am so lonely, and now I have found consolation [with Peter]."[1w] The intensity of feeling shown here is the factor underlying Anne's claim that she has been lonely for "so long," and it is typical of the adolescent in love to consider even a month or two unbearably long.

Nowhere in the diary is love for love's sake and the construction of a romance brought out more clearly than when she compares Peter Van Daan to her pre-war boyfriend, Peter Wessel. She writes, "Peter Wessel and Peter Van Daan have grown into one Peter, who is beloved and good, and for whom I long desperately."[1x]

Anne's feelings about love are also related to her concern for constructing an adult role. This is especially clear in her concern over sex-appropriate behavior and what it means to be a woman. She writes, ". . . I ponder far more over Peter than Daddy. I know very well that I conquered him instead of he conquering me."[1y] . . . "I like it much better if he explains something to me than when I have to teach him; I would really adore him to be my superior in almost everything."[1z] At another time she is pleased for acting in a way that fits the image of the supportive wife. Concerning a pre-war boy friend, she writes, "I seem to act as a stimulant to keep him awake. You see we all have our uses, and queer ones too at times!"[1aa]

And perhaps the cognitive aspects of adolescent love shed some light on the oft-noted "homosexual" phase many adolescents seem to go through prior to their intense motivation to have relations with the opposite sex. Anne writes:[1bb]

> After I came here, when I was just fourteen, I began to think about myself sooner than most girls, and to know that I am a "person." Sometimes, when I lie in bed at night, I have a terrible desire to feel my breasts and to listen to the quiet rhythmic beat of my heart. . . . I already had these kinds of feelings subconsciously before I came here, because I remember that once when I slept with a girl friend I had a strong desire to kiss her, and that I did so. I could not help being terribly inquisitive over her body, for she had always kept it hidden from me. . . . I go into ecstasies every time I see the naked figure of a woman. . . . It strikes me as so wonderful and exquisite that I have difficulty in stopping the tears rolling down my cheeks. If only I had a girl friend!

Can we explain the meaning of this passage by referring only to puberty? Our answer is that if we think of puberty in terms of its relation to the adolescent's concern for constructing an adult role, then it seems puberty serves primarily as a reinforcement of this concern. That is to say, the pride and curiosity in one's own sexual development is based upon the fact that such development means a closer approximation of what it is to be an adult. And likewise, the fear that such development stimulates is in part a fear of how to use and think about what has developed, or in other words, how to be an adult in the realm of action and thought as well as in the realm of the physical.

As a conclusion to this analysis of the cognitive aspects of Anne's diary, I would like to return to the 'mind over matter' theme brought out earlier in this discussion. As Piaget has pointed out, adolescent thinking and formal operational thinking in general is not so much a series of specific behaviors, but rather a generalized *orientation*. That is, presented with any problem, it is not unlike the adolescent to *think through* possible solutions. Furthermore, the adolescent is capable of varying (in thought) a single factor (all other things being equal) so as to arrive at solutions systematically rather than by chance. As an example of this ability to think systematically, take the following event that took place while Anne was still in school. Because of her continually talking while in class, Anne was made to write a composition entitled, "A Chatterbox."[1cc]

> I thought and thought and then, suddenly having an idea, filled my allotted sides [of paper] and felt completely satisfied. My arguments were that talking is a feminine characteristic and that I would do my best to keep it under control, but I should never be cured, for my mother talked as much as I, probably more, and what can one do about inherited qualities.

In other words, Anne demonstrates her ability to reason formally by structuring relationships and by humorously fabricating a relationship between talking in class and inherited qualities.

As a postscript to this analysis, I think it appropriate to draw some implications from what has been said concerning the nature of adolescent thinking. First of all, this discussion has been limited primarily to the cognitive aspects of adolescent behavior. But where emotional and personality factors have been discussed, it is hoped that these are regarded in the light of the ability to think formally. Furthermore, in regard to the 'rift' between adolescent and parents, I think that an awareness that an adolescent is capable of thinking on a more sophisticated level than most adults believe, and an awareness that adolescents are extremely concerned with what it means to be a mature human being, and an awareness that adolescents are extremely concerned with justice, says something to anyone puzzling over how to react to student violence and race relations, topics which are of such importance to us at this time. For the adolescent-parent relationship can serve as a model for understanding the effects of a status differential, where at least one member of the relationship is unhappy over the inequality. Finally, from the two major concerns brought out in Anne's thinking it would seem reasonable to ask ourselves if our society is addressing itself to these concerns enough so as to meet the needs of the adolescent population.

REFERENCES

1. Frank, A. *The Diary of a Young Girl*. Transl. B. M. Mooyart. New York: Doubleday, Modern Library, 1952. pp. (a) 278; (b) 24; (c) 270; (d) 38;

(e) 43; (f) 99; (g) 18; (h) 253; (i) 57; (j) 280; (k) 55; (l) 187; (m) 201; (n) 137; (o) 142; (p) 222; (q) 241; (r) 24; (s) 135; (t) 82; (u) 9; (v) 12; (w) 232; (x) 174; (y) 277; (z) 205; (aa) 19; (bb) 143; (cc) 17.

2. Piaget, J. and B. Inhelder. *The Growth of Logical Thinking from Childhood to Adolescense.* Transl. A. Parsons and S. Milgram. New York: Basic Books, 1961. p. 336.

3. Piaget, J. *The Moral Judgment of the Child.* Transl. M. Gabain. New York: Free Press, 1965. p. 319.

three

adolescence, the family, and society

part three

All adolescents are confronted with the need to adjust to the physical, physiological, and cognitive changes that accompany puberty and later maturation. As we shall see in some detail in later parts of this book, all adolescents must also meet a number of other developmental demands: achievement of independence, establishment of workable relationships with same- and opposite-sex peers and adults, preparation for a vocation, and development of a philosophy of life—a view of the world and a set of guiding moral beliefs and standards that, however simple and basic, are "nonnegotiable."

Although these social demands are common to all adolescents, the forms they take and the ease or difficulty of meeting them satisfactorily will vary from one society to another and from one time period to another. In our own time, the difficulties of the adolescent period have been significantly increased by changes in the nature of the family and its relations with other social institutions; by deep divisions and conflicts among adults in our society, which are reflected in their attitudes and behaviors toward adolescents and in the reactions of adolescents to adult authority; and by an ever-accelerating rate of social change.

In the first article in this part, John Janeway Conger points out that increasing urbanization and geographic mobility have tended to weaken the stability and interdependence of communities, have impaired communication between the family and other social and political institutions, and have decreased the size of the family itself from the extended family of an earlier day to today's relatively isolated nuclear family. In addition, recent years have witnessed the rise of "youth culture," an increasing age segregation throughout society, and a decline of adult authority. The result has been that today's parents and their children have grown up in markedly different worlds and, consequently, the problems of communication between them—and between adults and adolescents generally—have been magnified. However, while these rapid social changes have tended to increase the so-called generation gap, current popular notions about the size of this gap are vastly exaggerated. While parents and adolescents do differ in a number of their values and attitudes, there are also many commonalities and the *average* adolescent basically likes, respects, and enjoys the company of his parents.

Conger also notes, that despite romantic notions to the contrary, parents still play a crucial role in aiding or hindering the adolescent's development of competence, independence, and self-esteem. In today's complex, ever-changing world, both authoritarian, autocratic parents and negligent, laissez-faire parents hinder their child's optimal development, whereas flexible and democratic, but authoritative, parents foster it.

In the second article, E. James Anthony takes note of society's recent obsessive preoccupation with adolescents and youth and the conflicting, stereotyped, irrational forms this obsession frequently assumes. For both broad social and individual psychodynamic reasons, adolescents are variously viewed as "the enemy within" or the potential saviors of the world; as victimizers or victims; as sexually threatening or objects of envy; as maladjusted or simply going through normal developmental struggles; as dependent children or embryonic adults. As Anthony views it, the danger is not only that adults may use irrational, overly simplistic stereotypes in dealing with adolescents, but that adolescents in turn will respond to such stereotypes with behaviors that seem to confirm them—resulting in "self-fulfilling prophesies."

He emphasizes the need for parents and clinicians to avoid irrational stereotypes as much as possible and to respond to adolescents "on a person-to-person basis" with objectivity and self-assurance, empathy and sympathy. If dealt with in this manner most adolescents will emerge into adulthood, not free of all conflicts and problems, but on reasonably good terms with themselves and others and capable of meeting the demands and inevitable frustrations of living.

In the third article, Julius Zellermayer and Joseph Marcus review the effects on adolescent development of a novel pattern of child rearing that differs in a number of important respects from both the extended family of an earlier day and today's nuclear family. In the Israeli kibbutzim, children and adolescents have contact—often daily contact—with their own parents and develop warm emotional ties to them. But they live and develop among peers of both sexes, and primary adult responsibility for child rearing lies outside the family.

There are definite expectations regarding the young person's responsibilities to his peers and the kibbutzim as a whole at various ages. Further, there is an avoidance of what Erikson refers to as the "psychosocial moratorium" characteristic of later adolescence among many middle- and upper-class Western adolescents. Under these circumstances, Zellermayer and Marcus find, many of the adolescent problems that may develop in isolated nuclear-family settings are avoided or minimized. Relations with parents, while close, are less ambivalent, stormy, and "overdetermined"; independence-dependence conflicts are fewer; and the transfer of emotional attachments to others, including peers, proceeds more smoothly and with less emotional upheaval. "Identity crises" appear to be minimal or nonexistent and there is a general focus on "reality," self-assertion, mastery, and social commitment to the larger community.

Obviously, there may be alternative societal paths to successful adolescent development. But it appears clear that in a society characterized by rapid social change, ever-new demands, and declining authority of many traditional social institutions, much greater emphasis needs to be placed on finding ways to decrease age segregation and the isolation of nuclear-family parents and their children; to increase communication and understanding among children, adolescents, and adults of all ages; to reduce societal polarization and restore a sense of morality and social commitment; and to encourage flexibility, competence, self-esteem, and a unifying sense of purpose in children and adolescents.

a world they never knew: the family and social change

John Janeway Conger
University of Colorado School of Medicine

There can be little doubt that the present century has been one of fundamental, in some respects even radical change for our society. Increasing urbanization and geographic mobility have been altering the face of the country and the nature of its social institutions, including the family, at a rather astonishing rate. In 1900, nearly two out of every three persons in America lived in a rural area, either on farms or in small towns. Today that figure has declined by half, to only about one person in three.[1] Significantly, the greatest population shift has been away from the traditional "heartland of America"—the central Midwest and South—and toward the burgeoning metropolitan areas along the east and west coasts and the southern shores of the Great Lakes.[2] Even for those already living in such urban areas, however, mobility has not ceased.

Incredible as it may sound, in the last decade more than half of all families in the United States have moved every five years.[3] All population groups have been affected, from the nomadic corporate executive at one end of the socioeconomic spectrum, for whom "the price of position and social mobility includes a willingness to be geographically mobile,"[4] to the hundreds of thousands of agricultural workers—black, brown, and white—who have been forced off the land by increasing agricultural automation and restricted land use into urban slums with which they are ill-prepared to cope.

These changes have tended to weaken the stability and interdependence of communities, impair communication between the family and other social and political institutions, and shrink the size of the family (and its sources of both material and psychological support) from the extended family of an earlier day to today's relatively isolated nuclear family. All of these changes have made the family's burdens greater and increased still further the difficulties of child rearing.

Furthermore, because of the rapidity of the rate of change, today's adolescents and their parents have grown up in markedly different worlds. As the sociologist Kingsley Davis observed more than thirty years ago,

Excerpted from a longer article, and reprinted by permission of Daedalus, Journal of the American Academy of Arts and Sciences, Boston, Massachusetts. "Twelve to Sixteen: Early Adolescence," Fall 1971, 100, 1105–1138.

and as Kenneth Keniston has emphasized again recently,[5] when the developmental experiences that shape our personalities and the social changes that must be confronted vary markedly from adults to young people, from parents to their children, generational differences in cultural values and outlook—even in knowledge—tend to be magnified. In short, as current jargon has it, the greater the rate of social change, the larger the generation gap may be expected to be. Thus, to the extent that today's parents look only to their own experience as adolescents for expectations about their children's probable adolescent behavior, or for guidance in understanding their needs, outlooks, and goals, they are almost bound to encounter frustration, bewilderment, or disappointment.

A WORLD THEY NEVER KNEW

The parent of today's young adolescent is most likely to have been born in the early 1930's and to have entered adolescence in the middle 1940's. Thus most of his preadolescent development took place in the, at least relatively, simpler era that preceded World War II. True, the lingering shadow of the Great Depression may have hung over his family, but by and large it was still a smaller, more intimate, and in many ways a more predictable world—at least for the broad middle class.

Although the nation's flight to the metropolitan centers and their suburban satellites, like that of lemmings to the sea, was already under way, nearly half of all Americans still lived on farms and in the traditional small towns that are enshrined in American mythology and the paintings of Norman Rockwell.[6] Even in our larger cities, we still had neighborhoods. Consequently, many of today's parents grew up in informal, often daily association, not only with members of their immediate family, but also with other relatives of all ages, who, if they did not live in the same household, could often be found down the street or around the corner. As Urie Bronfenbrenner has observed:

> Everybody in the neighborhood minded your business. . . . If you walked on the railroad trestle, the phone would ring at your house, and your parents would know what you had done before you got back home. People on the street would tell you to button your jacket, and ask why you were not in church last Sunday. Sometimes you liked it and sometimes you didn't—but at least people *cared.*
>
> You also had the run of the neighborhood. You were allowed to play in the park. You could go into any store, whether you bought anything or not. They would let you go out back where you could watch them unpack the cartons, and hope that one would break. At the lumberyard, they let you pick up the good scraps of wood.[7]

It is this older, less rapidly changing world that many of today's parents seem to be recalling when they talk of the world their own adolescent children face. In a recent study by Daniel Offer of normal, largely middle-class, midwestern adolescent boys, parents were asked to describe their own early years:

Most of the parents, particularly fathers, said their families had been affected by the Depression, were less affluent, harder working. Nearly all said their sons had more things, more knowledge, more opportunities—and they were glad of that. But there was a strong hint, as these parents talked, that their sons were not better off, despite the things and opportunities. The suggestion was that one *should* have to work hard for rewards, that it all should not come as easily as to today's young. There was some nostalgia, too, as expressed by one father: "I grew up in the Depression and everybody worked to keep the family going. We were a large and closely knit family. I had a good time." Or this from another father: "In my day the world was small and there was more mystery to things—there were still kids—you know."[8]

The great social issues that today bombard our senses and confuse and divide us as a people—war, racial and socioeconomic injustice, simultaneous growth and destruction of our cities, pollution of the environment—had not yet exploded on the national consciousness, although obviously below the surface the seeds were being sown. But the exhaustibility of our resources was not yet so evident, and ever-increasing technology could still be equated with progress.

Even though the late middle-childhood or early adolescent years of these parents were overshadowed by World War II, at least it was a war, probably the last one, that the country as a whole believed in and identified with. Soldiers and sailors were everybody's heroes, and not merely, as now, the unfortunate victims of a new kind of Russian roulette in an otherwise "business as usual" society. When the nation's adults began to pick up the pieces again in the aftermath of that war, it was primarily with a passion to restore their own childhood and adolescent conceptions of "normality." This was the familiar era of the "split-level" and the "silent generation," with its single-minded devotion to home, family, and security. This was the atmosphere in which many of today's parents completed their own adolescence and crystallized their values and expectations. In many ways, it may be said that today's adolescents have grown up with the consequences.

Born in the late 1950's, today's adolescents have been nursed on the uneasy peace that followed the Korean war and weaned on a diet of increasing social malaise, discord, and divisiveness. By the time they entered school, we had plunged into the hectic decade of the 1960's—initially with the dream that accelerated technology would bring unprecedented progress in the "war against poverty," in education, in civil rights, in the salvation of our cities, in peace, and in an ever increasing prosperity for all. What was to have been a new era, however, turned instead into what Andrew Hacker has called the Age of Rubbish, characterized by violence, separatism, and a rudderless morality. In short, to a virtually unprecedented degree, today's adolescents have been exposed to an adult society deeply divided within itself.

Decline of Adult Authority. One of the inevitable and most important consequences in the minds of today's young has been a decline in adult authority. In an earlier generation in this country, and in other less fragmented and less rapidly changing cultures, adolescents have been able to view adult society as at least relatively homogeneous. While adolescents may have felt that "they"—the adults—were misguided, compromising, apathetic, or just plain wrong, nevertheless, there was an identifiable, reasonably self-confident, confrontable "they." Parents, particularly the father, could be viewed with considerable justification as the adult society's resident ambassadors in the family court. As such, parents derived authority and wisdom—implied or real—from their position as representatives of the adult power structure and could serve as sympathetic guides to its mysteries and as effective models for success in gaining entry into it.

A majority of today's adolescents in this country are denied such coherent perceptions. At least from middle-childhood on, they have been exposed to increasingly bitter divisions among prestigeful adults on almost every front, from the broadest social issues to the most intimate questions of personal standards and morality. Even to the limited extent that adolescents have been able to view adult society as speaking with one voice and planning a unified attack on society's mounting problems, the evidence of its capacity to achieve success has not been overly reassuring. Consequently, the "authority" of the adult culture is compromised in the eyes of many adolescents, and with it the authority derived by parents from their position as family representatives of this culture.

As will become evident, all of this is not to say that parents can no longer serve as effective role models for their children. But it does suggest that their authority may no longer be derived simply from their status as representatives of a unified adult society, as would be the case in more static, more homogeneous cultures. It must come more from their own individual strengths and resources, or at most from their position as representatives of only a limited segment of adult society. This, of course, does not make the task of the parent any easier, for he too is confronted with "a world I never made," despite some adolescents' rather naive and occasionally arrogant assertions to the contrary.

At any rate, the older assertion that "father (that is, adult society) knows best" is likely to be met—not merely for psychodynamic, but for increasingly reality-based reasons as well—with the adolescent response of "who's kidding whom?"

The Rise of "Youth Culture." A related difference between the worlds in which parents and their adolescent sons and daughters have developed lies in the increasingly prominent role of "youth culture" and its potential effects on younger adolescents. In a day when at least a majority of young people went to work at seventeen or eighteen after graduation from high school, we were faced with two fairly discernible groups, adolescents in the traditional sense, and adults (including young adults). Currently, increasing visibility has been assumed by a third group, variously identifiable as "post-adolescents" or, more simply, "youth." With greater numbers of these young people in our society than ever before,[9] and with more and more of them denied access to full adult status for longer and longer periods of time (whether as college or graduate students in the case of the advantaged, or as rootless unemployed or underemployed in the case of the disadvantaged), the size of this group has grown, along with its visibility, definability, seeming cohesiveness, and social impact upon both adults and young adolescents.

As a consequence, young adolescents are currently exposed, not only to age-mate peers and to an older adult society, but also to a widely publicized older youth culture, a culture which is frequently viewed as in conflict with these other groups for the loyalty and emulation of young adolescents. The situation is further complicated by the fact that this youth culture as perceived by young adolescents (and to a large extent also by adults) often bears little resemblance to the actual behavior, attitudes, and value systems of the average post-adolescent or youth.[10] What the young adolescent perceives is, of course, influenced in part by personal observation of the post-adolescent generation. But it is also influenced to a significant degree by the popular sterotypes of this group which have been created and sustained by the mass media, and by commercial interests eager to tap what is by all odds the most affluent generation of young people in history. (Some of the recent rock festivals provide particularly distasteful examples of highly commercialized and cynical exploitation of young people under the guise of encouraging "love," "freedom," and independence of "materialistic" values.)

Because of such illusory but powerful stereotypes, some young adolescents may be led to view their youthful elders as more influential, more homogeneous, and more active in a wide variety of behaviors (for example, sexual activities, preoccupation with drugs, revolt against "the system") than is actually the case for many of them. Thus, the possibility arises that a young adolescent may think he is merely emulating older youth when, in fact, he is actually going beyond them, and leaping into life styles and behaviors that older youth themselves may not be prepared to follow. While the available evidence[11] indicates that the average young adolescent has not risen to such lures, more vulnerable minorities clearly have done so.

Age Segregation. Accompanying the growth of an older adolescent youth culture has been a reduction in the extent of interaction among age groups, both within the family and in the community. In the words of a task force of the recent White House Conference on Children, children and adolescents are currently

> deprived not only of parents but of people in general. A host of factors conspire to isolate the young from the rest of society. The fragmentation of the extended family, the separation of residential and business areas, the disappearance of neighborhoods, zoning ordinances, occupational mobility, child labor laws, the abolishment of the apprentice system, consolidated schools, television, separate patterns of social life for different age groups, the working mother, the delegation of child care to specialists—all these manifestations of progress operate to decrease opportunity and incentive for meaningful contact between children and persons older, or younger, than themselves.[12]

Herbert Wright and his associates at the University of Kansas have recently compared the daily life of children still growing up in a small town environment with that of the far greater number living in metropolitan areas. Among the principal differences that they found was that "unlike their urban and suburban age-mates, children in a small town become well acquainted with a substantially greater number of adults in different walks of life, and are more likely to be participants in the adult settings which they enter.[13] This may be one reason why relatively few of today's adolescents follow in the occupational footsteps of their fathers. A survey by James Coleman has revealed that 23 per cent of high school boys in small towns, as contrasted with only 9.8 per cent of boys in city and suburban schools, planned to enter their fathers' occupations.[14] Indeed, under conditions of life in many of today's cities and suburbs, the adolescent may never have seen anybody actually performing the type of work he is considering upon completion of his education. In social activities, too, this same trend toward age segregation may be observed: "Whereas invitations used to be extended to entire families, with *all* the Smiths visiting *all* the Joneses, nowadays every social event has its segregated equivalent for every age group down to the toddlers. The children's hour has become the cocktail hour. While the adults take their drinks upstairs, the children have their 'juice time' in the rumpus room downstairs."[15]

Members of the White House Conference task force found this situation increasingly disturbing:

> The young cannot pull themselves up by their own bootstraps. It is primarily through observing, playing, and working with others older and younger than himself that a child discovers both what he can do and who he can become— that he develops both his ability and his identity. It is primarily through exposure and interaction with adults and children of different ages that a child [or adolescent] acquires new interests and skills and learns the meaning of tolerance, cooperation, and compassion. Hence to relegate children to a world of their own is to deprive them of their humanity. . . . Yet, this is what is happening in America today.[16]

CONSEQUENCES OF SOCIAL CHANGE

There can be little doubt that recent and continuing changes in the nature of the family and in its relations to society, and the rate of these changes, have increased the stresses confronting today's nuclear family. But have they also, as is so widely asserted, produced a virtually unbridgeable generation gap between today's average parents and their adolescent sons and daughters? Has the contemporary nuclear family become obsolete? And have parents become irrelevant as models for their children's psychological and social development? . . .

DIMENSIONS OF THE GENERATION GAP

The avid follower of the mass media's instant sociology might easily conclude that there is not merely a universal generation gap between today's parents and their adolescent sons and daughters, but an abyss. What are the facts, insofar as we can ascertain them at the present time?

The best answer appears to be that there *is* a generation gap between the average parent of today and his adolescent young, but that this gap is neither as wide nor as totally new as we have been led to expect, nor is it qualitatively very similar to popular stereotypes. In recent representative national surveys[17] of both younger and older adolescents and of their parents, approximately two out of three young people and seven out of ten parents expressed the view that a gap exists but that it has been exaggerated. Only about one young person in four, and a like percentage of their parents, felt that there was a large gap, while only a small minority of both groups (about one in twenty) felt that there was no gap. Intensive investigations of more limited samples have yielded similar findings.[18]

Popular notions that a state of cold or hot war exists between today's average parents and their own adolescent young, that the average adolescent disapproves of the way he has been reared, that he views his parents as unhappy, frustrated people who have "sold out" their basic values to the establishment, and that he is uncomfortable in their presence and unable to communicate with them also received little support. When asked to describe their present relationships with their parents, a majority of both younger and older adolescents (57 per cent) stated that they got along fine with their parents and enjoyed their company. Approximately one in three said that they were fond of their parents but had trouble communicating with them. Only a small minority (4 per cent) stated that they did not enjoy spending time with their parents. Interestingly, among the one-third who felt they had trouble communicating, only 18 per cent expressed the view that it was their parents' fault; 6 per cent said it was their own fault; and an overwhelming majority (74 per cent) said it was "both our faults." Furthermore, when asked if they felt their upbringing had been "too strict, too permissive, or about right," over 80 per cent felt that it had been about right.

Nor does the average adolescent view his parents as unhappy, frustrated souls who have "sold out." Three out of four adolescents fifteen and older expressed the belief that their father "has been happy in his work." Four out of five stated that their parents had "lived up to their own ideals." In addition, approximately three out of four adolescents, both younger and older ones, stated that they were in general agreement with their parents' ideals. Indeed, a variety of studies indicate that in many areas the values of a majority of today's adolescents are surprisingly unsurprising.

Current Trends in Adolescent Values. While significant and probably growing minorities of contemporary adolescents have become profoundly disillusioned and "turned off' by a society that they view variously as unjust, cruel, violent, hypocritical, superficial, impersonal, overly competitive, or immoral, the average adolescent still shares many traditional values with his parents. Thus, a substantial majority of today's adolescents and their parents subscribe to such beliefs as the following: competition encourages excellence; the right to private property is sacred; depending on how much character a person has, he can pretty well control what happens to him; society needs some legally based authority in order to avoid chaos; and compromise is essential to progress. Approximately two out of three contemporary adolescents express the view that hard work leads to success, and that success is worth striving for.[19]

While many adolescents speak of their opposition to "materialistic values," paradoxically they seem to accept readily this generation's relative affluence. Seventy-six per cent of a national sample of adolescents regarded shopping as "one of the experiences I most enjoy."[20] It would appear more accurate to say that many contemporary adolescents are finding that materialistic goals are insufficient to produce a sense of personal fulfillment, rather than to say that adolescents generally are opposed to material values.

Although the average adolescent has retained many traditional values, he is not overly impressed with the current state of society and its principal institutions.[21] For example, only 22 per cent of adolescents have a "great deal" of confidence in the government's ability to solve the problems of the 1970's, 54 per cent have "some confidence, but not a lot," and 22 per cent have "hardly any" confidence. A substantial majority believe that most of our social institutions, including big business, the military, political parties, and the mass media, including television, are in need of at least moderate reform. It should be noted, however, that only a portion of this skepticism reflects a generation gap. Although the young are more critical of these institutions than their parents, adults have also shown an attitude shift recently in the direction of greater skepticism.

Nevertheless, generational differences do exist, even for the average adolescent and his parents, both in their current views and also in comparisons of the views of today's adolescents and those of their parents when they were the same age. Although only a small minority, especially of younger adolescents, are militant activists on social or political issues, most do appear to have a greater concern than their parents did at the same ages, or do now, with such issues as socioeconomic discrimination and racial prejudice. Thus, for example, adolescents are far more willing than their parents to have increased school integration and to have blacks or other minority group members as neighbors.[22] Interestingly, in their attitudes they seem to be reflecting flexibility, tolerance, and lack of prejudice, as much as or more than crusading zeal.

This attitude of relative tolerance, of a greater willingness to let others (except possibly parents) "do their own thing," pervades much of adolescent thinking—younger and older alike. It is accompanied by a relatively high value placed on open, honest, and "meaningful" interpersonal relationships with others. Thus, while they are more tolerant than their parents of premarital sexual relationships in which love and commitment are present, they appear generally opposed to promiscuity, not only in principle, but for the most part in behavior. They are far more convinced than their parents of the importance of sex education in their high schools, and believe that it should be taught in coeducational classes. Three out of four believe that though a double standard of sexual behavior still exists, it is wrong.[23]

Most are interested in job success as conventionally defined, but they are, at least relatively, less concerned with achieving status and recognition by society in their future jobs than earlier generations were, and more concerned with finding work that is "meaningful" and enjoyable and in which they can have pride.[24] Three out of four say they would not work for a company that causes substantial pollution, and four out of five say they could not accept easily a job in which they were treated impersonally. A majority believe that "business is overly concerned with profits and not with public responsibility."[25] In our junior and senior high schools, today's abler, better informed students are far more concerned than their parents with student participation in policy-making and with innovation and "relevance" in curricula; in contrast, their parents are more concerned with maintenance of discipline and the development of orderly routines of study.[26]

Two other characteristics of current adolescents deserve brief mention, although they are difficult to document. Despite their often impressive intellectual capability, many adolescents today appear less knowledgeable about the past and less convinced that there are lessons to be learned from it. They are more inclined to view the future as either unpredictable, or at best full of options that need not be explored yet. Relatively, though only relatively, they do appear to be more of a "now" generation.

In a related vein, it is essential to realize that while both parents and adolescents are confronted with the irrational and chaotic forces increasingly abroad, and our apparent inability to control them effectively, many parents are still able—with their own childhood experiences as a frame of reference—to view this unhappy state of affairs as a deviation from a subjective conception of "normality." In contrast, their children for the most part have no such frame of reference. While they may have found elements of stability within their homes, the uncertainties of the world outside its walls are not new for them—not a deviation from prior expectancies. They are in fact normal, for to these young people these uncertainties have, in greater or less measure, always existed. In a survey by Louis Harris for *Newsweek,* a nationwide sample of adolescents age thirteen to seventeen described the world they live in as "warlike," "impersonal," "competitive," and "fast moving" and fraught with constant change.[27]

This important difference between the perspectives of parents and their adolescent sons and daughters may help to explain some current adolescent preoccupations that puzzle or alarm many parents. While parents frequently cling nostalgically to the symbols of a simpler, more rational past, the "now" generation looks for ways of living in the present, for finding meaning in uncertainty and irrationality. They look for meaning in seeming meaninglessness—"happenings," elaborate "put-ons" in dress and manner, distortions of "reality" in light shows and movies, the current preoccupation with astrology and, in some older adolescents, with Eastern religions.[28]

Finally, and perhaps most significantly, today's adolescents reveal a pervasive need for a world in which there is more true friendship and love. Indeed, no other values are as strongly and consistently held. Nine out of ten contemporary adolescents—whether younger or older, affluent or disadvantaged, conservative, middle-of-the-road, liberal, or revolutionary—are in agreement about the importance of these values (although they may differ widely in many of their other beliefs). They consistently find these values in short supply. Less than one in five adolescents agrees strongly that "most people will go out of their way to help someone else," or that they "can be depended on to come through in a pinch."[29]

In brief, the average contemporary adolescent appears to be relatively more ready than his more self-conscious predecessors of earlier generations to put into practice a philosophy of "live and let live" and of pragmatic idealism. More than earlier generations, he appears to be a sophisticated and critical exponent of the art of the possible—not illusioned, but not disillusioned either. With considerable justification, James A. Wechsler, editor of the *New York Post,* has termed today's adolescents a generation of "flaming moderates."[30] Whether this will continue to be the case, or whether the size of the profoundly disenchanted minority will continue to grow, is still an open question.

How can we reconcile these rather wide discrepancies, not only between the apparent facts and popular stereotypes about the size and nature of the so-called generation gap, but also between what we might expect theoretically, on the basis of the nature and rate of social change? I think we can look to at least five factors that should be considered, but which tend frequently to be overlooked:

1. Many current pronouncements about the generation gap are based on faulty analysis and inappropriate conclusions. They derive largely from comparing nonrepresentative samples of adults with equally nonrepresentative samples of young people. Both the popular media and a number of social scientists as well have tended to picture adolescents, whether favorably or unfavorably, in terms of the manifest characteristics of visible, controversial, sometimes highly articulate minorities: high school and junior high school activists, minority group militants, hippies and "teeny boppers," even, at times, hard drug users and delinquents. Particular attention has focused on a counterculture of elite, affluent, urban upper-middle-class adolescents of all ages, especially on the east and west coasts.[31] In contrast, although the statistical and semantic justification is doubtful, to say the least, adults have been most commonly characterized recently as members of a "silent majority" of "middle Americans."

In fact, however, as David Riesman has recently noted, a number of current so-called generational conflicts could better be described as class conflicts—between a minority of relatively affluent middle-to-upper-middle-class adolescents whose families have long been secure in their social and economic status and a minority of working-class adults who have only recently, and sometimes rather tenuously, gotten hold of the lower rungs of the middle-class ladder.[32] Similar observations could be made regarding some other so-called generational conflicts that actually more closely reflect ethnic and other divisions.

Such simplistic adolescent-adult comparisons ignore the fact that ours has long been a heterogeneous society, rather than simply a "melting pot," both for adults and adolescents, and it appears to be becoming ever more so. Any number of recent investigations[33] make clear that the variations among important subgroups of adolescents are at least as great, and frequently greater than those between the average adult and the average adolescent, whether in the areas of political and social values, sexual attitudes and behavior, patterns of drug use, or educational and vocational goals.

2. Popular stereotypes also tend to confuse and confound comparisons between adults and adolescents generally with those between individual parents and their own adolescent sons and daughters, despite the fact that these may differ significantly. Thus in one recent study,[34] while two-thirds of adolescents fifteen years of age and older replied "yes" to the

question, "Do your parents approve of your values and ideals?" a majority of these same adolescents responded negatively to the question, "Do they approve of the way *your generation* expresses their ideals?" Adolescents also tended to be more critical, generally in rather stereotyped terms, of the "older generation" taken as a whole than of their own parents.

When adults were asked what they disliked about today's adolescents as a group, the most frequently mentioned complaints involved: a lack of respect for authority, undisciplined behavior, lack of ambition or motivation, overindulgence and overpermissiveness by parents and others, lack of responsibility, lack of manners, "too smug and self-assured," and, interestingly, "lack of dialogue with elders." Similarly, when young people were asked about their parents' generation, the most commonly cited complaints were that they were "too set in their ways" and that there was a lack of communication ("they won't listen to us").[35] Furthermore, as Keniston and others have shown,[36] in a number of instances adolescents may come into conflict with the values of some adult authority figures in their society precisely because those values conflict with values the young person has acquired from, and shares with, his parents.

3. There is also a widespread tendency to confuse generational differences that may be truly new, either in kind or in magnitude, with those that have traditionally separated parents and children—if for no other reason than that successive generations occupy differing positions in the life cycle. The adolescent who is just becoming aware of the insistent stirring of sexual impulses will inevitably differ from the middle-aged adult who perceives their urgency waning. Adolescents need ways to consume their energy; adults look for ways to conserve it. Young people are concerned about where they are going; adults are concerned about where they have been. Adults, having personally experienced the many partial victories and defeats and the inevitable compromises of living, tend to be tempered in their enthusiasms and cautious in their moral judgments. Young people, in contrast, tend to be impatient, impulsive, and given at times to imperious moral judgments that allow little room for shades of grey. They are more likely to move rapidly from the heights of profound joy to the valley of despair. Adults must worry more about their children; adolescents must worry more about themselves. The psychological defense mechanisms of adolescents are in flux and only partially effective; those of adults tend, like arteries, to harden with age.

Consider the following brief quotation:

> The young are prone to desire and ready to carry any desire they may have formed into action. Of bodily desires it is the sexual to which they are the most disposed to give way, and in regard to sexual desire they exercise no self-restraint. They are changeful too, and fickle in their desires, which are as transitory as they are vehement. . . . They are passionate, irascible, and apt to be carried away by their impulses. . . . They have high aspirations; for they have never yet been humiliated by the experience of life, but are unacquainted with the limiting force of circumstances. . . . Again, in their actions they prefer honor to expediency. . . . If the young commit a fault, it is always on the side of excess and exaggeration. . . . They regard themselves as omniscient and are positive in their assertions; this is, in fact, the reason of their carrying everything too far.[37]

While this description might easily have been taken from John Aldridge's recent popular book, *In the Country of the Young,* the fact is that it was written by Aristotle over 2,300 years ago. Obviously, *all* aspects of the so-called generation gap are simply not that new.

4. Even some of the more sophisticated formulations of generational conflict have tended, I believe, to underemphasize the potential of parents, as well as adolescents, to change with changing times. It has recently been observed, although systematic data are lacking, that adults who are currently the parents of adolescents are more likely to be sympathetic and "understanding," not only toward their own children, but toward adolescents generally. At any rate, it is clear that many of today's parents have undertaken an "agonizing reappraisal" of a number of their own attitudes and beliefs in the face of social change—not infrequently as a consequence of exposure to the concerns of their own adolescent sons and daughters.

5. Finally, there is a widespread tendency to overlook the possibility that parents and adolescents may be able to differ in some of their values and modes of behavior and still remain capable of mutual understanding and respect.

As should already be evident, none of this is to say that there are not a significant and probably growing number of adolescents, younger and older alike, for whom the gap between themselves and their parents is not only wide, but in some cases virtually unbridgeable. It is simply to say that they do not *presently* represent a majority of contemporary adolescents. Whether the ranks of the disenchanted minority will continue to grow will depend in large measure on the steps taken by parents and by the leaders of our society to stem the decline of a sense of community among young people and adults alike, and to restore a sense of genuine moral and social concern.

CONTINUED RELEVANCE OF PARENTAL MODELS— FACT OR FICTION?

It has also become increasingly fashionable lately in some circles to assert that because of the nature and rate of recent social change, parents have become largely irrelevant as models or guides to their adolescent young's current and future development. Indeed, some social critics, such as David Cooper, the British psychiatrist and author of *Death of the Family,*[38] have gone so far as to proclaim that the family has become, not simply irrelevant to the needs of children and adolescents, but a malignant force that acts only to frustrate the fulfillment of these needs.

A more moderate position has been assumed recently by Margaret Mead and others.[39] Mead's essential argument is that in earlier and more stable cultural eras—which she terms "postfigurative" and which are most dramatically exemplified by some relatively static preliterate societies— children and adolescents could realistically look to their parents and other adults for guidance because these adults were, in fact, the best, most experienced guides to the social and vocational roles that the younger generation would eventually assume.

In the more recent past, characterized by a moderate rate of social change and a culture termed by Mead as "cofigurative," the young had to look more to their peers and less to parents and other adults for clues to successful adaptation.

> In . . . cofigurative cultures the elders are still dominant in the sense that they set the style and define the limits within which cofiguration is expressed in the behavior of the young. . . . But at the same time, where there is a shared expectation that members of a generation will model their behavior on that of their contemporaries, especially their adolescent age mates, and that their behavior will differ from that of parents and grandparents, each individual, as he successfully embodies a new style, becomes to some extent a model for others of his generation.[40]

But in view of the extremely rapid rate of change that our young currently face, and that they will continue to face in the world of tomorrow, Mead finds both the postfigurative and the cofigurative models inadequate. Instead, she sees a "prefigurative" culture developing—one in which "it will be the child and not the parent or grandparent that represents what is to come. . . . As I see it, children today face a future that is so deeply unknown that it cannot be handled, as we are currently attempting to do, as a generation change with cofiguration within a stable, elder-controlled and parentally modeled culture in which many postfigurative elements are incorporated."[41]

For Mead, all of those, including today's parents, who grew up before World War II are pioneers, immigrants in an unexplored land—the "country of the young." In this new terrain, the young person will have to chart his own paths, without significant assistance from either parents *or* peers. Under such circumstances, about all that parents can provide—and contrary to some popular misconceptions of Mead's message, she considers them of vital importance—are love and trust.

While I would agree that contemporary parents can learn, and indeed need to learn, much from their adolescent young about adaptation to inevitable change, there is little or no evidence to support the notion that the converse is not equally the case. A background of love and trust are, as Erik Erikson asserts, fundamental.[42] Without them, the child's chances of becoming a reasonably happy, effective, contributing adult, of developing a positive self-image and a sense of his own identity, are seriously impaired, as clinical experience and any number of more systematic investigations make abundantly clear.

But, as will also become evident, the role that parental models play in fostering or hindering the child's and adolescent's psychological development, and preparing him to meet the challenges of emerging adulthood, extends far beyond these essential ingredients.

Parent-Child Relationships and the Developmental Tasks of Adolescence. What often tends to be lost sight of amid the polemics of the generation gap and our—often legitimate—concerns about the nature and rate of current social change is that while the rapidity of change increases the difficulties of adolescent adaptation for both parent and child, the basic developmental tasks which the adolescent must master if he is to become a competent, autonomous, responsive, and responsible adult still remain.[43] The period between puberty and nominal adulthood may be relatively short (as in the case of the blue-collar youth who may be employed, married, and a parent at nineteen) or relatively long (as in the case of the upper-middle-class youth who may still be involved in his education, unmarried, and largely dependent on his parents at twenty-five). It may also, depending on cultural and familial circumstances, be relatively simple or complex.

Nevertheless, adolescence still involves the accomplishment of a number of critically important developmental tasks: adjustment to the physical changes of puberty and later adolescent growth and to the flood of new subjective impulses brought on by genital maturity; the development of independence from parents or other caretakers; the establishment of effective social and working relationships with same- and opposite-sex peers, preparation for a vocation; and, withal, the development of a system of values and a sense of identity—some kind of personal answer to the age-old question, "Who am I?"

The fact that in today's rapidly changing world these tasks may be more complex, and that both parent and child have fewer consistent blueprints to guide them in their accomplishment, does not fundamentally alter the situation. Sexual and social roles of men and women may change, as indeed they are changing today; the responsibilities and privileges associated with independence may change; the difficulties of projecting the vocational needs of the future may increase; and the kind of personal and social identity that will be viable in both today's and tomorrow's world may alter. But regardless of the particular forms assumed, each remains a critical and indispensable task of adolescent development.

Despite romantic or hostile assertions to the contrary, the single most important external influence in aiding or hindering the average adolescent (particularly the young adolescent) in the accomplishment of these tasks—at least in today's relatively isolated nuclear family—are his parents. The real question, then, is not whether parental models are any longer important; rather, it is what kinds of parental models are necessary and appropriate in preparing contemporary adolescents to cope with the largely unpredictable world of tomorrow.

Models of Parent-Child Interaction. In the case of adolescents, this question obviously involves the effects, not simply of current parental models and patterns of parent-child interaction, but a long history of prior ones, extending back to early childhood. Whether parents are loving or rejecting; calm or anxious; involved or uninvolved; rigid or flexible; controlling, guiding, but encouraging of autonomy or laissez-faire—all have been found, singly and in combination, to influence the child's subsequent behavior and adjustment.[44] For example, the child who is subjected to covertly hostile, restrictive parental child-rearing practices is likely to internalize his angry feelings (as in the case of many neurotic children and adolescents); in contrast, the child who is reared under hostile but lax conditions is more likely to act out his resentment (as in the case of many delinquents).

The behavior of the child whose parents are high on the dimension of love (warmth) may also vary, depending on coexisting conditions. Thus, children reared in warm but restrictive (as opposed to autonomy-encouraging) homes are likely to be more dependent and conforming; less aggressive, dominant, and competitive with peers; less friendly; less creative; and more hostile in their fantasies. In contrast, those reared in homes where parental love is evident though not cloying, and where the child is given considerable age-appropriate autonomy, are likely to emerge as more active, outgoing, socially assertive, and independent, as well as friendly, creative, and lacking in hostility toward others or self. While such children may also tend to be somewhat disobedient, disrespectful, and rebellious on occasion, these behaviors appear to manifest themselves largely because of feelings of security and lack of severe punitive response from parents, and to be "more easily turned on and off in response to reinforcing conditions,"[45] rather than reflecting chronic anger and frustration, or uncontrollable expressions of deep-seated but dammed-up feelings of hostility.

In short, it appears clear that the heritage of parent-child relationships that the young person carries into adolescence will affect the relative ease with which he adjusts to the changed roles and new demands of this period. The overprotected child, who may have achieved a workable modus vivendi within the circumscribed confines of the family during middle-childhood, may find coping with the demands of others for independence and self-reliance during adolescence extremely difficult to handle. Similarly, the overindulged child as he approaches adolescence may find the society's unwillingness to provide a like degree of indulgence frustrating. The child of hostile parents may until adolescence have controlled his counterhostility reasonably well, only to lose this control under conditions of increased stress, conflict, and opportunities for acting-out behavior that accompany adolescence.

Furthermore, the appropriateness of particular patterns of prior and current parental behavior may vary markedly with cultural conditions and with the speed of social change. Thus, the child reared in Mead's postfigurative culture, where change is slow and the requisite skills and patterns of living demanded by the culture are handed down from one generation to another essentially intact, is in a very different position from, for example, an upper-middle-class child in American society in 1971. Whereas authoritarian and even autocratic parental models may serve reasonably adequately in the former instance, where conformity and diligence are more important to the adolescent than creativity, curiosity, and independence, they do not serve very well in a rapidly changing culture, where the parent can often neither predict nor control the types of challenges his adolescent young will face.

Much nonsense has been written recently by anxious or angry adults, asserting that all dissent among today's young can be blamed on their "permissive" upbringing, with Dr. Benjamin Spock usually perceived as the omnipotent, all-pervasive villain of the piece.[46] Aside from the inherent absurdity of attributing all dissent either to permissiveness or to Dr. Spock as its alleged agent, a case can certainly be made independently about the unwisdom of unrestricted permissiveness.

One needs, however, to be careful about what is meant by permissive-

$5 3/23$

ness. Does it mean indulgence, intimidation of parents by children, a laissez-faire parental attitude, or simple neglect? In this connection, Urie Bronfenbrenner makes the interesting point that many studies originally interpreted as indicating a universal trend toward permissiveness in child rearing in this country since World War II could as well be interpreted as indicating a progressive decrease in "recent decades in the amount of contact between American parents and their children."[47]

Or does the term "permissiveness," at least as employed by some authoritarian adults, really refer to the encouragement of autonomy and of adolescent participation in decision-making, albeit under parental guidance and ultimate authority? The presumed alternative to so-called permissiveness in the minds of many vociferous critics seems to be a return to an authoritarian or autocratic model, which might (or might not) have prepared an adolescent for some simpler, postfigurative era, but certainly not for today's unpredictable world, where change and readiness for change are the name of the game. In effect, what these latter-day Miniver Cheevys seem to be crying out against is not so much the changing behavior of the players as the changing rules of the game itself. Adolescents in tomorrow's world will require discipline (ultimately self-discipline), but they will also require independence, self-reliance, adaptability, creativity, and the ability to distinguish between assertiveness and hostility, not to mention a sense of humor. And these characteristics are fostered . . . neither by permissiveness or parental neglect, nor by autocratic or authoritarian child-rearing methods. . . .*

REFERENCES

1. *The American Almanac for 1971* (*The Statistical Abstract of the United States,* 91st ed.) (New York: Grosset and Dunlap, 1971).
2. Lawrence A. Mayer, "New Questions about the U.S. Population," *Fortune* (February 1971), pp. 82–85. Source: U.S. Census, 1970.
3. Hans Sebald, *Adolescence: A Sociological Analysis* (New York: Appleton-Century Crofts, 1968). See also Charles W. Hobart, "Commitment, Value Conflict and the Future of the American Family," *Marriage and Family Living,* 25 (1963), 406.
4. Sebald, *Adolescence.*
5. Kingsley Davis, "The Sociology of Parent-Youth Conflict," *American Sociological Review,* 5 (1940), 523–536; Kenneth Keniston, *The Uncommitted: Alienated Youth in American Society* (New York: Dell, 1960). See also Vern L. Bengston, "The Generation Gap: A Review and Typology of Social-Psychological Perspectives," *Youth and Society,* 2 (1970), 7–32.
6. *American Almanac.*

---

* See Part IV of this book ("Parental Models and the Development of Independence") for a discussion of parental patterns associated with the development of adolescent competence, adaptability, and independence.—Ed.

7. Urie Bronfenbrenner, *Two Worlds of Childhood: U.S. and U.S.S.R.* (New York: Russell Sage Foundation, 1970), p. 96.

8. Daniel Offer, *The Psychological World of the Teenager: A Study of Normal Adolescent Boys* (New York: Basic Books, 1969), p. 64.

9. Mayer, "New Questions about the U.S. Population."

10. For example, see Daniel Yankelovich, *Generations Apart* (New York: Columbia Broadcasting System, 1969); Louis Harris, "Change, Yes—Upheaval, No," *Life*, 70 (January 8, 1971), 22–27; and Elizabeth Douvan and Joseph Adelson, *The Adolescent Experience* (New York: John Wiley, 1966).

11. Harris, "Change." See also Paul Henry Mussen, John Janeway Conger, and Jerome Kagan, *Child Development and Personality*, 3d ed. (New York: Harper and Row, 1969).

12. *Children and Parents: Together in the World,* Report of Forum 15, 1970 White House Conference on Children (Washington, D.C.: Superintendent of Documents, 1971).

13. Herbert Wright and others, "Children's Behavior in Communities Differing in Size" (unpublished manuscript, Department of Psychology, University of Kansas, 1969), cited in Bronfenbrenner, *Two Worlds of Childhood.*

14. James S. Coleman, *The Adolescent Society* (New York: Free Press, 1963), p. 7.

15. Bronfenbrenner, *Two Worlds of Childhood,* p. 100.

16. *Children and Parents.*

17. For example, see Harris, "Change," and Yankelovich, *Generations Apart.*

18. Offer, *The Psychological World of the Teenager;* Douvan and Adelson, *The Adolescent Experience;* Mussen, Conger, and Kagan, *Child Development.*

19. Harris, "Change."

20. Louis Harris, "The Teen-Agers," *Newsweek* (March 21, 1966), pp. 57–72.

21. Harris, "Change." See also Mussen, Conger, and Kagan, *Child Development,* and Yankelovich, *Generations Apart.*

22. L. Harris and others, "What People Think About Their High Schools," *Life* (May 16, 1969), p. 32. See also Mussen, Conger, and Kagan, *Child Development.*

23. Ira L. Reiss, "The Scaling of Sexual Permissiveness," *Journal of Marriage and the Family* (1964), pp. 188–199; Morton Hunt, "Special Sex Education Survey," *Seventeen* (July 1970), pp. 95ff; Harris, "Change"; Vance Packard, *The Sexual Wilderness: The Contemporary Upheaval in Male-Female Relationships* (New York: David McKay, 1968); Bernard Rosenberg and Joseph Bensman, "Sexual Patterns in Three Ethnic Subcultures of an American Underclass," *Annals of the American Academy of Political and Social Sciences,* 376 (1968), 61–75.

24. Harris, "Change."

25. Yankelovich, *Generations Apart.*

26. Harris, "What People Think." See also Charles E. Silberman, *Crisis in the Classroom: The Remaking of American Education* (New York: Random House, 1970).

27. Harris, "The Teenagers."

28. Mark Gerzon, *The Whole World Is Watching* (New York: Paperback Library, 1970); Naomi Feigelson, *The Underground Revolution* (New York: Funk and Wagnalls, 1970); Lewis Yablonsky, *The Hippie Trip* (New York: Pegasus, 1968).

29. Yankelovich, *Generations Apart.*

30. Mussen, Conger, and Kagan, *Child Development.*

31. For example, see Theodore Roszak, *The Making of a Counter Culture* (New York: Doubleday Anchor Books, 1969); Joel Fort, *The Pleasure Seekers: The Drug Crisis, Youth, and Society* (New York: Grove Press, 1969); Gerzon, *The Whole World Is Watching;* Yablonsky, *The Hippie Trip;* Feigelson, *The Underground Revolution.*

32. T. George Harris, "The Young are Captives of Each Other: A Conversation with David Riesman," *Psychology Today* (October 1969), 28ff.

33. See, for example, Richard Scammon and Ben J. Wattenberg, *The Real Majority* (New York: Coward-McCann, 1970); Richard S. Blum and others, *Society and Drugs* (San Francisco: Jossey-Bass, 1969); Mussen, Conger, and Kagan, *Child Development;* Adelson, "What Generation Gap?" Packard, *The Sexual Wilderness;* Rosenberg and Bensman, "Sexual Patterns."

34. Harris, "Changes."

35. George H. Gallup, Jr., and John O. Davis, III, "Gallup Poll," *Denver Post,* May 26, 1969, and Harris, "What People Think." An apparent failure to distinguish clearly between parent-child and youth-adult conflicts is seen in Lewis S. Feuer, *The Conflict of Generations* (New York: Basic Books, 1969).

36. Kenneth Keniston, *Young Radicals: Notes on Committed Youth* (New York: Harcourt, Brace, and World, 1968); Edward E. Sampson, Harold A. Korn, and others. *Student Activism and Protest* (San Francisco: Jossey-Bass, 1970).

37. *Rhetoric of Aristotle,* cited in Norman Kiell, *The Universal Experience of Adolescence* (Boston: Beacon Press, 1964), pp. 18–19. For comparisons, see Otto Fenichel, *The Psychoanalytic Theory of Neurosis* (New York: Norton, 1945) and John W. Aldridge, *In the Country of the Young* (New York: Harper and Row, Perennial Library, 1971).

38. David Cooper, *Death of the Family* (New York: Pantheon, 1970).

39. Margaret Mead, *Culture and Commitment: A Study of the Generation Gap* (New York: Doubleday, 1970).

40. *Ibid.,* pp. 32–33.

41. *Ibid.,* pp. 62, 88.

42. Erik H. Erikson, *Childhood and Society,* 2d ed. (New York: W. W. Norton, 1963). See also E. James Anthony and Therese Benedek, *Parenthood: Its Psychology and Psychopathology* (Boston: Little, Brown, 1971).

43. Joan Aldous, *The Family Development Approach to Family Analysis* (prepublication manuscript, Family Study Center, University of Minnesota, 1967), chap. 4.

44. For comprehensive reviews, see Wesley C. Becker, "Consequences of Different Kinds of Parental Discipline," in Martin L. Hoffman and Lois Wladis Hoffman, eds., *Review of Child Development Research*

(New York: Russell Sage Foundation, 1964). See also Mussen, Conger, and Kagan, *Child Development,* esp. chaps. 12, 14, and 15; Lois Meek Stoltz, *Influences on Parent Behavior* (Stanford, Calif.: Stanford University Press, 1967); and Earl S. Schaefer, "A Configurational Analysis of Children's Reports of Parent Behavior," *Journal of Consulting Psychology,* 29 (1965), 552–557.

45. Becker, "Consequences of Different Kinds of Parental Discipline," p. 197.
46. Matt Clark and Jean Seligmann, "Bringing up Baby: Is Dr. Spock to Blame?" *Newsweek* (September 23, 1968), pp. 68–72; and Benjamin Spock, "Don't Blame Me!" *Look* (January 26, 1971), pp. 37–38.
47. Bronfenbrenner, *Two Worlds of Childhood,* p. 98.

the reactions of adults to adolescents and their behavior

E. James Anthony
Washington University School of Medicine

A QUESTION OF STEREOTYPES

"In recent years," remarks a contemporary psychologist (Adelson, 1964), "the adolescent has come to weigh oppressively on the American consciousness," and to occupy "a peculiarly intense place in American thought and feeling." This was in contrast to earlier times when he was generally regarded with tolerant condescension as a simple-minded character living "outside the world of adult happenings" and inhabiting "an Eden of pre-responsibility." Now, he had "invaded the adult world" in two antithetical stereotyped forms. In one, he was the *victimizer,* "leather-jacketed, cruel, sinister, and amoral," the carrier of society's sadistic and sexual projections, replacing the gangster and Negro in this role. In the other, he was pictured as the *victim,* passive and powerless in the face of adult corruption that sought to exploit his gullibility.

These were not the only adolescent stereotypes available to the adult population, but they presented an element of ruthlessness and sadism that resonated disturbingly in the minds of the older group and were seized upon as shibboleths in the ongoing "conflict of the generations." So powerful have been these over-simplified preconceptions and so resistant to rebuttal by opposing facts that they have made their influence felt even within the family circle, causing parents to respond to their adolescent children as if they were embodiments of negative ideas rather than real people.

To compound the mischief even further, the stereotypes have also functioned as mirrors held up to the adolescent by society reflecting an image of himself that the adolescent gradually comes to regard as authentic and according to which he shapes his behavior. In this way, he completes the circle of expectation. The adult is convinced of the validity of his stereotypes since the predicted behavior does in fact occur; the adolescent is convinced that he is simply doing what everyone is expecting him

Reprinted from Excerpta Medica International Congress Series No. 108, Proceedings of the VIth International Congress of the International Association for Child Psychiatry and Allied Professions, pp. 46–59. Edinburgh, July 24–29, 1966. By permission of the Excerpta Medica Foundation.

to do; and society at large is convinced that it has a problem on its hands by the daily news of incidents chronicled luridly by its reporters.

The response of any individual adult to any given adolescent may therefore be dictated by a collusion of three factors: a collective reaction as represented by the stereotype, an idiosyncratic reaction based on the personalities and experiences involved and the "transference" reaction in which pre-existing factors from an earlier phase of life exert an influence unbeknown to the participants on their attitudes, affects and actions, often to the detriment of the relationship. There is probably no human transaction in which any of these occurs uncontaminated by the presence of the other two and the situation to a large extent determines which one predominates. As a general rule, the more negative the relationship, the less operative is the person-to-person response and the more conspicuous the stereotypic and irrational, unconscious modes of transacting.

In the next section follow various contemporary polarities of stereotypic thinking in their nascent form unmodified by personal considerations. The adolescent will be seen as victimizer and victim, as dangerous and endangered, as sexually rampant requiring restraint and as sexually inadequate needing encouragement, as emotionally maladjusted crying out for treatment and as emotionally free emitting a breath of fresh therapeutic air onto stale adult conflicts, as an enviable object to be cut down and as a repository of the adult's unfulfilled ambitions to be built up, as a redundant family member to be extruded with as much haste as decency will permit and as a lost object to be mourned in passing. Both adult and adolescent oscillate between these extreme images, and when the pair are not in phase, the resulting interaction may occasion a high degree of perplexity with the bewilderment evident in the inconsistent and confused communications that then flow between the participants.

The inherently dichotomous nature of the stereotype is reflected in the good or bad images created. The behavior of the adolescent is more of a continuum with the reactions distributed along a Gaussian curve, the extreme manifestations occurring with lesser frequency. However, because they tend to gain greater publicity, the impression is created that they are the statistically expectable modes of teenage behavior. The "headline intelligence" characteristic of the public mind has come to consider adolescence and delinquency as synonymous, interchangeable labels. The clinician does little to correct this misconception, since he himself is constantly confronted with extreme reactions and may eventually be led to regard them as typical rather than atypical and infrequent. The "good" adolescent, although representing perhaps three quarters of the adolescent population, is so effectively camouflaged by his conformity to the standards of a given culture, that he is scarcely credited with existence. Instead of victim or victimizer, his role with respect to the adult has a special and satisfying quality to it that was not present in his dependent status as a child and will not be present in his ultimate status as an adult. In large measure, it can be viewed as a learning experience in which the adolescent is constantly practicing the adult role under the experienced tutelage of a friendly and encouraging adult. The relationship is regarded as basically helpful and trustworthy, even if a little avuncular and out of date. Since this chapter is directed mainly towards clinicians, it must be understood that the clinical viewpoint, with its more pathological emphasis, will be salient. Since the stereotypic reaction and the vicious misunderstanding it engenders is felt to make a major contribution to pathology, the two factors, the clinical and the stereotypic, will be interwoven in the account that follows.

THE STEREOTYPIC REACTION TO THE ADOLESCENT AS A DANGEROUS AND ENDANGERED OBJECT

The image of the "victimizer," slowly, relentlessly, and ruthlessly stalking the terrified adult, calls attention to a surprising metamorphosis in the life of the individual through which the weak and helpless child is transformed into a potent and menacing figure that can now threaten the adult on whom he once depended for his security and sustenance. Every period of human history has accorded recognition to the potential dangerousness of this transitional period and complex procedures have been instituted to control the situation. In the Darwinian and later Freudian speculation on the "primal horde," the threat to the father with the supervention of adolescence ended with the killing and eating of the father. It was never clear in the theory to what extent such a termination was inevitable and "natural," but one would expect that when the primal hordes banded together in the form of communities, the fathers would begin to legislate in favor of their own survival, perhaps resorting to the extrusion of the adolescent male as a first resort and then eventually subduing him by means of institutional techniques. In this context, it is interesting to note that adolescent male monkeys when caged with a typical monkey family—father, three or four wives, and one or two adolescent females helping to care for a few infants—are often slain by the father at the onset of puberty.

The later institutional methods of dealing with the same problem, by means of initiation rites, secret adult societies and prolonged apprenticeships, were generally effective in subduing any revolutionary trends present in the adolescent and in suppressing any inordinate wishes he might entertain for possession of the women, the work and the food of the adults.

There is another side to the adult's reaction other than this preoccupation with the dangerousness of the adolescent. It takes the form of marked concern for the safety of the younger person and may express itself in practical measures to safeguard him against premature exposure to the physical and emotional stresses of the adult world. The minor is protected legally against exploitation by the unscrupulous adult and may react to the protection as "over-protection" regarding the prohibitions imposed as ways of thwarting his normal and necessary drives. He is quick to detect the hostility behind the solicitude, and he is often inclined to react to the former rather than to the latter component of the adult's ambivalence.

The same mixture of intention is present in the reactions of primitives. In many parts of the world, girls are suspended between earth and sky, inside a dark, airless and filthy contraption at the time of their first menstruation not only because there is a fear that they will blight the crops, blunt the weapons, sour the milk, and cause cattle to miscarry, but also because they themselves, if exposed to light, may suffer from sores, grow blind, or shrivel up into skeletons. The precautions taken, therefore, to isolate and insulate them are activated as much by concern for their safety as for the safety of the adults (Frazer, 1949).

As far as institutional measures go, the more advanced societies appear to ignore adolescence almost as completely as the primitives recognize it, but the sense of danger still remains. In the words of one anthropologist: "We prescribe no ritual; the girl continues on a round of school or work, but she is constantly confronted by a mysterious apprehensiveness in her parents and guardians. . . . The society in which she lives has all the tensity of a room full of people who expect the latest arrival to throw a bomb" (Mead, 1930).

Psychotherapists, confronted by the adolescent, have put forward as many reasons and rationalizations as parents and adults in general for treating the adolescent with special care and caution or not treating him at all. They have argued cogently in favor of treatment but by other therapists and in other institutions. Many have concluded, on the basis of sound reason, that it is better to leave adolescents psychotherapeutically alone during adolescence because of their well-known proclivity to act out and drop out. The vivid metaphors they have coined possess a strong deterrent quality. "One cannot analyze an adolescent in the middle phase," says one prominent author; "It is like running next to an express train" (Freud, 1958). Another likens adolescence to "an active volcanic process with continuous eruptions taking place, preventing the crust from solidifying" (Geleerd, 1957). Once the psychotherapist gets it into his head that he has to deal with a bomb that might explode or a volcano that might erupt or an express train that will outpace him, he will approach the treatment situation with very mixed feelings. If one adds to this array of stereotypes the reputation that even the mildest adolescents have for resorting to slight delinquencies at the least provocation, then the psychotherapist's reason for bypassing adolescence is easier to understand if not to condone. The teenage patients that do come to therapy and remain in therapy are generally severe passive character disorders that are developmentally preadolescent in their make-up. They behave with the cooperativeness of the average adult and child patient, but they remain largely untouched by the therapeutic process.

Within the last decade, these various considerations plus a growing sense of responsibility towards a neglected group, have led clinicians to conclude that adolescents are best dealt with by psychiatrists who, whatever their major affiliations are, wish to deal with adolescents. There are child psychiatrists as well as adult psychiatrists who have a "built-in" flair for resonating sympathetically and empathizing deeply with the "in-between" situation. This gives them a sufficiency of comfort and confidence in coping with even tempestuous teenagers and dampens down the fluctuations between the cautious and the carefree. Adolescents are especially sensitive to the "phony" attitudes and mannerisms of adults who are not too sure whether to talk "down" or "up" or "on the level" with them and are liable to exploit this uncertainty to the full by taking up provocative counter-positions.

THE STEREOTYPIC RESPONSE TO THE ADOLESCENT AS A SEXUAL OBJECT

Even in these pseudo-sophisticated days, when information on infantile sexuality can be purchased in every drug store and vivid accounts of pre-pubertal, heterosexual activities have been reported in the press, the emergence of biological sexual maturity in children invariably seems to take the family off guard as if it were completely unprepared for this natural and long expected event. It would appear that early manifestations of the sexual impulse are in some way disregarded or depreciated as "child's play" and therefore not to be taken too seriously. With the development of the secondary sexual characteristics and the occurrence of seminal emissions and menstrual flow, the family becomes uneasily aware of the new sexual object in its midst. Its response varies from family to family. In some, the succession of pubertal events may be shared by the family members as in the manner of other achievements, whereas in others, it is hushed up and confined to the privacy of the bedroom and bathroom.

Parental reactions to puberty are closely correlated with the extent to which sexuality has found a comfortable acceptance in the household as gauged by the affectionate demonstrations between the members and the level of accurate biological knowledge possessed by the children. There are parents who regard it as the consummation of their own psychosexual development, rounding off the cycle of the generations. There are others who are pruriently intrigued by the shy and groping sexuality of the novitiate and obtain vicarious enjoyment in stimulating its appearance and mocking its ineptness. A third group of parents, with a high degree of sexual repression, may react with dismay and displeasure at the slightest display of erotic feeling. The frigid woman, psychosexually infantile, not only insists on maintaining an asexual status for herself but also for her children (Stekel, 1930). She is blind to the pubertal indices and repulsed by any form of adult heterosexuality. On the other hand, she is not greatly perturbed when the adolescent displays homosexual tendencies, symptoms indicating oral and anal fixations or incestuous concerns. The hostile reactions to maturity contrast with the overflow of pathological tenderness occasioned by immaturity, so that the children are caught up in a vortex of changing attitudes and behavior that bewilder them even more than the biological events taking place in them. Unable to accept her own femininity, the frigid woman is inevitably led to sabotage the sexual development of her adolescent daughter. As long as the little girl is a "neuter," the mother remains on good terms with her, but with puberty, a dynamic conflict comes into focus and a fierce hostility takes hold of the mother. She cannot and will not allow her daughter to become a woman and the resulting conflict around the sexual identity in the daughter reactivates her own identity problem. It is difficult for any child to develop beyond the neurotic inhibitions of its parents, but nowhere is this truer than in the development of sexual identity.

The transition from "asexual" child to sexual adolescent may not only put the parent's psychosexual maturity to the test, but also tax her relationship with the child. "The very individual towards whom the parent was able to show overt signs of love during childhood has now become a sexually stimulating and taboo object. As a result the parent must mobilize defenses to handle the anxiety provoked by his own incestuous fantasy" (Bell, 1961).

Another effect of adolescence on the adult is the reactivation of their own adolescent struggles with overt autoerotic, homosexual and oedipal conflicts with the development of what amounts to an adolescent decompensation in retrospect. Not infrequently, this upsurge of suppressed adolescent feeling may drive the parent into psychotherapy. A given family may therefore have two crises occurring concomitantly—the crisis of adolescence in the child and a reactivated adolescent crisis in his parent.

These roused sexual impulses may confine themselves to the realm of psychopathology, but a breakthrough into everyday life is not so uncommon especially in homes where there is a general degradation of living conditions as a result of economic privations, alcoholism, and mental illness. A weak incest barrier may give way under these circumstances and a spate of miscarriages and pregnancies may result. In one survey at an obstetrical hospital, it was calculated that at least one third of the illegitimate pregnancies were the products of incestuous union mainly with the father. It is surprising that the figure is not even greater when one takes into account the prevalence of "Lolita" fantasies in middle-aged men with adolescent daughters, as revealed in psychotherapy. It is also characteristic of fathers who have near-incestuous relationships with their daughters to react to any adult heterosexual interests on the part of the girls with prudish indignation.

The ambivalence noted in the parent's response to the adolescent as a dangerous object is equally true of the present consideration. An analysis of transactions between parents and adolescents around a covertly sexual conflict can illustrate how both sides play out their conscious and unconscious roles in response to wishes and fears that are implied but seldom verbalized. At one level, the parent may react with justifiable anxiety in keeping with his cultural standards and the adolescent, in turn, may behave in a way appropriate to the codes prevalent in the peer group. Underlying this reaction, there may be another less conscious one in which the parent may be provoking the adolescent to act out some of his own urgent repressed fantasies, at the same time punishing him for attempting to do so. The child may be dimly aware of this unconscious manipulation and may respond to the conflicting communications of the two levels with a double-bind communication of his own. For example, he may deny that he has done anything bad, indignant at the suspicion, and at the same time, he may "blow up" the experience and make a sexual mountain out of an ignominious mole hill. On still another level, the parent may be reacting to a deep dissatisfaction with his own sexual lot in life and envious that his child is getting something whilst he is being deprived. The adolescent, in his turn, may react with anger because he is being accused of engaging in activities the like of which he has often desired but cannot bring to pass because of his own inhibitions or the inhibitions of his partner. Under these circumstances, both parents and child may feel that his biological drives are setting up an insuperable barrier between them (Spiegel, 1957).

The sexual rivalry appearing in the family at this time can have disruptive effects on marriage. An attractive daughter may become a serious rival to a mother who has been thwarting her husband for many years. The father begins to take notice of his daughter and finds reasons for taking her out in place of her mother. He may also begin to respond to other "dates" in a jealously hostile manner, either sulkily ignoring their existence or else referring to them in terms of scathing criticism. (One young girl amusingly referred to her father as suffering from an attack of "oedipops.")

The mother-daughter rivalry has its most extreme expression within the setting of the "menopausal-menarche" syndrome, when the mother's waning reproductive life is confronted with the flowering sexuality of the girl. The interaction stirs up considerable anxiety and depression in both and the nagging relationship of prepuberty is transformed into an open warfare in which the Geneva conventions are abandoned.

The reactions of adults to the sexual pressures produced by their adolescent children may run the gamut of sexual psychopathology from the autoerotic to heterosexual "acting out" so that unfaithfulness may enter the marriage for the first time. There is no doubt that the sexuality of the adolescent is a stimulus for the sexuality of the parent. This is well demonstrated again in the primitive situation when the adolescent is initiated into sexual life and the adult seizes upon the occasion to be openly sexual. "The use of obscene language, expressions of desire for prohibited sexual relationships, public mention of the sexual act and its mechanics, immodest exposure and hip movements—all these ordinarily shocking acts are expected and performed by women leading the novices back from the initiation ceremony" (LeVine, 1963).

In psychotherapy with adolescents, the countertransference feelings may become erotic and disturbing, especially when the therapeutic alliance is a heterosexual one. The incest barrier is not as strong in the transference relationship as it is in real life, and the adolescent can be as seductive and charming as with the parents. The therapist has techniques for dealing with children and with adults, but he is often at a loss to know what to do therapeutically with the adolescent. For want of anything better, he may simply combine the child and adult approach or move from one to the other. He may find himself defeated whatever his approach. When, for example, he treats the adolescent girl with the open friendliness he reserves for his child patients, she may react disconcertingly like a mature woman, so that his innocent maneuvers take on the guise of seduction; and when he retreats to the adult position and keeps her at a distance, she melts away leaving behind a little girl who cannot understand why she may not be loved in the old way.

The therapist may also find himself reacting as indignantly as the parents to reports of sexual misdemeanors and even adopting a strategy of moral expediency. He may warn against boys who proceed beyond "third base" and confront the defiant patients with threats of pregnancy and venereal disease in the name of the reality principle. Such difficulties have led many to conclude that adolescents should be treated by therapists of their own sex. When this happens, the situation is different but no less disturbing. The blatant homosexuality of the adolescent under conditions of treatment may evoke countertransference responses in the therapist that may take the form of outright rejection.

THE STEREOTYPIC RESPONSE TO THE ADOLESCENT AS A MALADJUSTED INDIVIDUAL

In one of the many current portraits of the adolescent, the author refers to "a fluent, loose-jointed restlessness alternating with catatonic repose" (Denny, 1965). A puzzled teacher likened the experience of his contact with adolescents to a ride on the big dipper, "sometimes you are up and sometimes you are down, but you never knew for certain when the next swing was coming." The adult in our Western culture has apparently learned to expect a state of acute disequilibrium and anticipates the "storm and stress" in his adolescent child as he once anticipated the negativism of his two year old. The expectation has seemingly been incorporated into the literature of psychological development and it may take methodical research and many years of endeavor to remove it from the text books. There is, however, growing anthropological and sociological support for the concept that society gets the type of adolescent it expects and deserves, and this is true of even those members who come into daily contact with the ordinary teenager. In a recent poll of teachers, for example, more than 80% of them subscribed to the opinion that adolescence was a phase of "great emotional disturbance," and more than half of them believed that the child at this time underwent a complete personality change (Denny, 1965).

It is not surprising, from what we said earlier on, that adolescents themselves begin to share this opinion and to assume that their mood swings and waywardness are signs of incipient insanity. The referral to the psychiatrist may help to confirm this inner apprehension and it is at this age that the fear of the psychiatrist is at its greatest. It is at this age that the altered body image, the alienation of parts of the psychic structure, and the intense masturbatory conflicts all give rise to the same terrible speculation with the panic stricken reaction: "I'm not nuts. I don't need a nut doctor."

The immature, unstable parent, like the sexually inhibited one, helps to aggravate these feelings of inner looseness and uncoordination. In fact, the unstable parent may respond to the increased pressures introduced by adolescence by regressing into helplessness himself and may invite and obtain a protective, solicitous almost therapeutic response from the adolescent. This "reversal of generations" which can be looked upon as a natural development of life when the parent figures shift into the helplessness of old age, is sometimes prematurely in evidence at this early stage. In his "therapeutic" role the adolescent may be burdened with many of the adjustment problems of the parent. "At last I've got someone to talk to. I've never been able to say this to anyone else. I have never been able to tell anyone what a sexual brute your father really was. Now that you know all about sex, you can realize what I have been through with him, etc., etc."

Adolescent feelings persisting in the parents do not always work negatively for the adolescent child. They can and do often lead to greater sympathy, empathy and understanding. The parent with a better recollection of his own adolescent difficulties can use this constructively in dealing with his child and, in so doing, may be able to help himself. The capacity to identify with the adolescent will permit the parent to handle the usual type of adolescent problem with a lighter touch. They may react, as one author puts it, with "a felt nostalgia for the youthful exuberance, fresh love impulses, and a sneaking adoption of the rebellion" (Miller, 1962). This "ectopic youthfulness" enhances the sensitivity of the individual in relationship to younger individuals.

The fluctuations characteristic of adolescence demand flexibility on the part of the parent, the changing mood and manners calling constantly for changing attitudes and behavior towards them. It is not easy for even the average parent to shift comfortably in rhythm with these emotional swings since he is so often left completely in the dark as to what has occasioned them. For example, a transient depression may reflect an intercurrent scholastic or vocational difficulty, a setback in a love affair, a nostalgia for the lost world of childhood and its love objects or an upsurge of guilt from a reactivation of unconscious sexual and aggressive urges leading to a hostile retreat from the world. On the other hand, it may be no more than a phase of introspection as the adolescent stops to take stock of himself. The same variety of causes may underlie states of happiness, and it is therefore not surprising at all that the psychologically untutored parents, however devoted, may find themselves exasperated by the unpredictable nature of the affect (Jacobson, 1961).

The therapist, like the parent, has his own special problems in fitting himself and the adolescent into the same therapeutic situation. What disturbs him, as it disturbs the parent, is the "unsettled state" of the adolescent ego and the sheer intensity of the libidinal and aggressive impulses. He may show a similar sensitivity to the swings in object relationships. The adolescent's continued need to experiment with his object world, cathecting and decathecting without too much rhyme or reason can interfere in the therapeutic situation with the establishment of a stable transference state that can proceed to a workable transference neurosis. In fact, the therapist is treated in the same "transitional" way as the other objects in the adolescent's life, and the countertransference of the therapist may take the form of inner resentment at the "fickleness" of the patient as he struggles to break away from the reactivated infantile tie.

A great many therapists find it highly uncomfortable to treat children during the earlier phase of adolescence when they neither play nor talk nor look to a friendly adult for help, but seem merely bent on escape. The patient is bored and restless, may yawn openly in response to a well-thought out interpretation, and, when the therapist attempts to focus on the relationship, they will counter with a description of their passionate involvements at school and elsewhere. The therapist finds himself put on the shelf with a hundred other objects currently competing for the adolescent's attention. He will be irritated, and parents will readily recognize and sympathize with the essence of his irritation. "Most of the young adolescents I have seen consider all adults their natural enemies. If they say anything at all, they will barely state a complaint, and then defiantly wait for you to magically do something about it. I have never found any way to handle this, and the only children of this age I have treated are those who started with me at an early age or were quite immature . . . a great deal of environmental manipulation is usually required, and as soon as external pressures are relieved, the patient tends to drop out of treatment" (Personal communication, 1962).

The high drop-out rate in psychotherapy has given the adolescent a bad name in therapeutic circles and therapists are wary of taking them on for any form of intensive treatment. The main complaint is that they do not seem to form a stable working relationship, but this is like saying that the seasons vary throughout the year and that you cannot depend on having warm days and blue skies for picnics in the middle of March. It is in "the nature of things." Once the therapist has accepted the fluctuating responses and the irregular attendance as a "natural" part of the general variability of the period, he can settle down to incorporating them into his technical approach, even to the extent of regularizing anticipated breaks from treatment.

THE STEREOTYPIC RESPONSE TO THE ADOLESCENT AS AN OBJECT OF ENVY

It is clear that "psychologically speaking" the adolescent is on his way up when the caretaking adults are on their way down. This basic anabolic-catabolic distinction understandably provokes in the adult envy for the adolescent's youthful vigor with all its freedom, freshness and joyful foolishness. The envy may show itself in a contrast derision at the simplicity and awkwardness of the younger person and at his lack of experience in worldly matters. At its worst, it can take the form of highly sadistic measures disguised in the form of initiation rites and rituals.

A frequent cause of disturbances in the family is the narcissistic parent in competition with the adolescent of the same sex. He has long been better at doing most things than his son and he can hardly conceive that the latter is now overtaking him. At this point, the better-adjusted parent will retire gracefully from the scene, acknowledging the new state of affairs, whilst his immature counterpart will attempt strenuously to outdo his rival in every activity even to the point of a coronary attack, as occurred in one case recently when a father undertook to beat his teenage son in ten different athletic events and was rushed to hospital at the end of the eighth.

The envious response to the biological events of puberty may take a variety of forms. A woman analyst (Chadwich, 1932) has discussed the sadistic manifestations of the mother in her treatment of the girl at her first menstrual period: "We should reflect that many mothers do their best to keep young and to deny, even to themselves, the fact that they are growing older and find an adolescent daughter an uncomfortable reminder of what they are striving to forget or to hide from others. It often happens that the first menstruation may coincide with the mother's menopause, and this will greatly magnify her reactions."

In primitive communities, the attack on the pubertal child is institutionalized and, therefore, more open. An anthropologist offers this description of the reaction of the mothers to the removal of the clitoris at a ceremony for female initiation: "As soon as the piece of flesh has dropped to the ground, the crowd of women begin trilling loudly, gaily screaming and shouting, and in some cases dancing individually" (LeVine, 1963).

The conflict of the generations is therefore directed in some part at keeping upcoming youth with all his enthusiasm, his drive, his developing skills and knowledge, his relatively open mind, and his colossal capacity for assimilating new ways and new ideas from overthrowing the "establishment" and upsetting the adult roles. Initiation rites help to keep him in his place, and so do qualifying examinations (Stengel, 1941). The examiner may regard the examination as a means of "getting his own back on his father" or, of getting his own children to "toe the line" and do exactly what they are told. The hostility of some examiners on these occasions has passed into the student folklore, but it does lead to a great deal of impotent counterhostility on the part of the students. It is interesting to recall that following examinations during the Middle Ages, the candidate was required to take an oath that he would not "take vengeance on the examiner."

The mechanisms of envy in the adult frequently feed on the differences between the child's experience of life and what the parent himself had to go through as a child. "I never had a car at your age, and I don't see why you should. You get more allowance in a week than I got in a year. I had to work my way through high school, but you go to a private one." The feelings are exacerbated by grandparents, once so hard on the parents and now so intent apparently on "spoiling" the adolescent grandchild.

One way the parents have developed in dealing with these scarifying feelings of envy is by identifying with the newcomer and making his future narcissistically their own. He can then carry the parent's unrealized ambitions and aspirations and the energies are thus harnessed to pushing the adolescent up rather than keeping him down, although the process may generate as much conflict and resentment in the younger person.

The complex cluster of emotions involved in this particular adult reaction—the hatred, the ambivalence, the sadomasochism, the envy and jealousy, the resentment, the reproachfulness, and, most difficult for the adolescent to endure, the dramatized martyrdom—is usually not so manifest in the workings of the therapeutic alliance, especially if the therapist has undergone some treatment himself. Nevertheless, there are certain transient manifestations of envy that crop up from time to time in the course of treatment and stem from a "comparison of lots." In one instance, a therapist found himself becoming increasingly angry with an adolescent boy whom he had been treating for some years. On carrying out a little self-analysis, he found himself deeply envious of the boy's progress as a patient and unable to derive any satisfaction whatsoever from the excellent outcome. He not only felt that the boy was getting much more out of the treatment situation than he himself ever did, but moreover he had to wait until well into adult life for his help. He recalls struggling hopelessly and despairingly with his adolescent predicament to the point of contemplating suicide, and now he was confronted with this rich child who obtained it as he needed it. Having undone the severe inhibition impeding his patient, he had watched the unfolding of a delicate and tender adolescent romance which had filled him with pain at the thought that he himself had never and would never experience such young love. At that time of life, he had been racked with unfulfilled desires for which masturbation and fantasy were no compensation. He even envied the good relationship that the boy had established with his parents which was again so unlike his own experience. At the time that he had felt his first angry countertransference response, his patient had been given a Thunderbird by his father and had taken his girl for a trip through the countryside. In his self-analysis, this immediately evoked one of his adolescent fantasies. His father had suddenly broken through the barrier of their bad relationship and had presented him with a motorcycle. Full of a new confidence, he was riding through the countryside and encountered a young hitchhiker. He picked her up and they passed an idyllic day in the country.

The deep clash lay between the unfulfilled adolescent fantasy of the therapist and the consummations achieved by the patient, resulting in an overpowering surge of envy that almost brought the treatment to a premature ending.

THE STEREOTYPIC REACTION TO ADOLESCENTS AS LOST OBJECTS

Many writers have commented on the depression that invades the earlier part of adolescence when the children are decathecting their childhood objects. The children lose their parents, but the parents also begin to lose their children, and it is this depression that may evolve into a serious clinical melancholia. The parents experience a sense of emptiness about the home and an absence of goals that had motivated them so strongly and consistently throughout the childhood of their children.

The attempt to recapture the vanishing object can be strenuous. With every artifice at their command, certain parents will attempt to close the doors and raise the drawbridges and dig deep moats to keep their burgeoning offspring in, for they cannot bring themselves to realize that the loss entailed is almost as inevitable as death and almost as irreversible. They may offer themselves as apparently new objects, disguised as adolescent playmates but the adolescent readily detects the old object in the new and struggles to escape even more strenuously. They may attempt to keep pace with the young and wear themselves out in so doing, or, at least for a while they may successfully deny entrance to any new object.

It may take some time to discover that gaining new objects and losing old ones go hand in hand in the course of normal adolescent development and that their only chance of preventing the escape of the adolescent is to set about systematically enslaving the child from his earliest years, so that by the time he reaches adolescence, the incestuous enthralment is complete. This is the type of child who never seems to enter adolescence. Childhood is prolonged indefinitely and the parent certainly has possession of the child. However, the ambivalence involved in the fixation is so severe, and the pathological developments of the child so extreme, that the conservation is associated with little real happiness for the parent.

A surer way of retaining some part at least of the lost child is by helping the process of separation and individuation to its completion and culmination in the adult child. A new relationship then becomes possible in which two adults, linked by mutual happy memories find to their surprise (not knowing the strength of the identification processes) that they have many interests in common and discover a new mature pleasure in each other as people. This pleasure is no longer derived from the old anaclitic model but depends on the rediscovery of the child as an adult object, the parent having gracefully relinquished the child at the start of adolescence.

The problem for the therapist is also a major one and, unless resolved, can result in one form of interminable treatment. Termination may become a crucial problem for the therapist with patients of all ages but particularly so at adolescence, when it may reactivate separation difficulties experienced by the therapist during his own adolescence. This is, once again, a countertransference issue. As previously affirmed, it is part of normal development for the adolescent to wish to break away from the regressive treatment relationship, and it is in the nature of the countertransference based on parental identification that the therapist can constantly find rational reasons why it is always too early to do so. There is an inevitable struggle between these two opposing forces, culminating in the guilty escape of the patient and in an angry depression, often masked, in the therapist. It may take several incomplete terminations for the patient finally to end his treatment and for the therapist to feel satisfied that it was really the right moment. Some of this termination anxiety may go underground to be reactivated, as in a recent instance, when a former adolescent patient sent her therapist a wedding invitation which promptly precipitated a depression in him.

STEREOTYPIC REACTIONS OF SOCIETY TO THE ADOLESCENT

There are recent indications that an organized teenage subculture is undergoing rapid development in the United States and that the products of this culture are producing mixed reactions in the adult population. Books and articles give a good indication of the way in which adult opinion is consolidating around the adolescent problem. The literature seems fairly evenly divided between those who are for the adolescent and say so and those who are against, but find it difficult to express their hostility directly. A few sentences will convey the flavor of this latter attitude. "Teenage, like birth and death is inevitable. It is nothing to be ashamed of. Nor is it a badge of special distinction worthy of a continuous birthday party . . . we are not against teenagers nor are we particularly for them. It would be dishonest for us to claim that some of our best friends are teenagers . . . we are not writing this book to declare war on teenagers . . . what worries us is not the greater freedom of youth but rather the abdication of the rights and privileges of the adults for the convenience of the immature . . . the pages which follow are not intended as a declaration of war . . . we do not want to be cantankerous. . . ." (Morrow, 1962).

There is some feeling on the opposite side for the "vanishing" adolescent (Friedenberg, 1959). The adult's response to adolescent activity is recognized as being more influenced by the adult's own unconscious needs and tensions than by what the adolescent is actually doing. It is noted how often the adolescent personality generates a major conflict in the adult, characterized by much anxiety and hostility (usually disguised as concern) and giving rise to a whole complex of feelings, attitudes and influential, unconscious trends. The author feels that the primary response is invariably to adolescent sexuality but that the total reaction is then maintained by the irrational vigor of the adult's libidinal energy. He thinks that adults are threatened firstly by the fear that adolescents will grow out of control situations, and secondly, by the fear of aging with concomitant envy of a life not yet squandered. The adolescents themselves react to the adult's reactions and act out the rituals imposed by an anxious culture.

The advice offered to teenagers in special newspaper columns sounds as if it all comes from the same fashionable textbook. The counselors oscillate between the stereotypic response to adolescents as victims and victimizers. For example, parents may be told to view their teenager's hostility without any reaction other than sympathy and understanding. The permissiveness, accorded currently to early childhood, is merely pushed up one notch into adolescence. Having been pals, rather than parents during childhood, they now become a mixture of part-time providers and part-time social workers.

In a different column or in the same column, at a different time, they may be advised, instead, to stand firm, set limits, forbid excesses, practice a little old-fashioned discipline, and never to leave teenagers of opposite sexes unchaperoned. There is a growing feeling that adults have made life too exciting for the adolescent and that the "sorcerer's apprentice" has got out of hand. The treatment for this is by no means certain except to devise legitimate sublimations. All in all, the parent is being forced as usual into the dilemma of doing too much or too little, of giving too much or too little, and his resulting uncertainty is recognized and exploited by the adolescent.

The commercial groups have discovered the teenager and are lyrical about their latest customer. In his comments on advertising and marketing to young people, a well-known advertiser has this to say: "Just look at youth; no established pattern; no backlog of items—youth is the greatest growing force in the community. It has definitely been established that because he is open minded and desires to learn, he is often the first to accept new and forward-looking products" (Gilbert, 1957). The adolescent of commerce is, therefore, seen not only as a grand spender on his own account, but also as a pied piper who sets the style and the trends for adult society to follow. The switch of major interest to the adolescent and a subtle cultivation of his narcissism, his age-specific anxieties, his wish for acceptance and his struggling sexual consciousness are fully exploited in thousands of advertisements in newspapers and journals.

The interest is not without good foundations. In her study of "The Upbeat Generation" with regard to influence and affluence, the author has estimated that teenagers are now spending up to $10,000,000,000 a year and that companies are bypassing parental preferences to study the fond likes and dislikes of the younger group (Cox, 1962). One adult response to this found expression in a pathetic newspaper article entitled "The Displaced Generation" in which the author laments "the glories of the past" when adults were adults and teenagers were still just children. Nowadays, the distinction between the adult and adolescent, he complains, has become as narrow and nebulous as the distinction between male and female.

REACTION TO THE ADOLESCENT AS AN OBJECT OF RESEARCH

As indicated in previous sections, therapists have been passing through a crisis with respect to how the adolescent should be treated, at what stage of adolescence this should occur and by whom the treatment should be carried out. The research worker, too, has specific problems when investigating the adolescent. In the past, research in this area has been relatively sparse owing to the fact that the developmental phase was poorly described and lacked guiding constructs that would help to raise meaningful questions. When the concept of identity formation was first introduced as a specific problem of adolescence, research gained a new impetus. Work began to be done on the developmental features that fit into the sense of identity and the pathological factors that interfere with its formation. However, this in itself is not sufficient to sustain any large-scale research program.

The impression derived from surveying the total field of investigation directed to this stage of life is that researchers are still staying away from it as much as therapists and are often as confused in their approach as the therapist. It was found that research techniques that appeared suitable for use in childhood or during adulthood failed to elicit meaningful data during adolescence. In a recent longitudinal study conducted in the United States, researchers had shown an interest in extracting something more from the developmental scene than simple physical and psychological measures of difference. Until puberty they had managed to satisfactorily elaborate hypotheses and procedures that threw light on the adapting and coping processes of the child. When they reached adolescence, the research and the researchers underwent a strange crisis that reflected itself in many disturbing and disrupting meetings between the investigators. They betrayed uncertainty as to how to approach the adolescent as a research object, being convinced that their previous strategies could no longer apply to this new situation. They could not agree among themselves as to what they wanted to investigate or how they wanted to investigate, and many were in favor of bypassing the adolescent phase, leaving it "silent," and postponing their research activity until early adulthood. Those who looked at this particular research crisis from the outside felt that a number of complex issues were involved and that the catastrophic reaction of the participants mirrored not only the usual uncertainty of the adult with respect to adolescence but also an unconscious resistance against reactivating the basic adolescent conflicts. Some of the investigators, who had been very much at home with the child, felt "disoriented" when confronted with the adolescent.

'THE "GOOD" REACTION TO ADOLESCENCE

Normality, in psychology and psychiatry is a concept difficult to define in operational terms. One can point to the fact that the majority of adolescents seem to come through adolescence and develop into average adults with average reactions as an indication that things cannot be as bad as they look under a closer clinical scrutiny. Although we might be dissatisfied with the finished products and aware that many of them will eventually find their way into mental hospitals, divorce courts, coroner's courts, prisons and homes for alcoholics and addicts, the larger group who achieve statistically average lives must have been subjected to "good enough" reactions.

The "good" reaction or "good enough" reaction is one in which the stereotypic response is minimal or absent, the adult responding on a person-to-person basis. It is a reaction which is relatively free from the irrational influence of "transference," so that once again, the adult responds not in terms of the there-and-then but of the here-and-now. The third ingredient to a "good" reaction is the element of empathy and sympathy originating in a satisfactory adolescent experience; not satisfactory in the sense of being free from conflict, but satisfactory in the sense of having gone some distance towards making these conflicts conscious and resolving them. The acceptance of the once adolescent provides a sounding board to test out all future reactions for adolescent consumption.

Much the same applies to the therapist, whose "good" reactions are also intimately bound up with his experiences of childhood and adolescence. His special hazard is the "Pygmalion" fantasy, which besets all therapists but especially those who treat teenagers. These may feel a strong urge to mold the soft, pliable substance of adolescence into a form reminiscent of the therapist's, the theme song being "why can't the patient be more like us." The therapist, who is not in love with his own personality, can offer the adolescent the opportunity to emerge from the struggles of the transitional period with an identity that he himself can respect and, above all, with an identity that he can call his own.

REFERENCES

Adelson, J. (1964): The mystique of adolescence, *Psychiatry, 27:1.*
Bell, A. (1961).: *The Role of Parents in Adolescence,* Edited by Lorand, S. and Schneer, Hoeber, New York.
Chadwick, M. (1932): *The Psychological Effects of Menstruation, Nervous and Mental Diseases,* New York.
Cox, C. (1962): *The Upbeat Generation,* Prentice Hall, New York.
Denny, T., Feldhausen, J. and Condon, C. (1965): Anxiety, divergent thinking, and achievement, *Journal of Educational Psychology, 56/1:* 40.
Frazer, J. (1949): *The Golden Bough,* Abridged edition, Macmillan, London.
Freud, A. (1958): *Adolescence, Psychoanalytic Study of the Child, 13:* 255. International Universities Press, New York.
Friedenberg, E. J. (1959): *The Vanishing Adolescent,* Beacon Hill, Boston.

Geleerd, E. R. (1957): Some aspects of psychoanalytic technique in adolescents, *Psychoanal. Stud. Child, 12,* 263, International Universities Press, New York.

Gilbert, E. (1957): *Advertising and Marketing to Young People,* Printers Inc., New York.

Jacobson, E. (1961): Adolescent moods and the remodelling of the psychic structure, *Psychoanal. Stud. Child, 16:* 164, International Universities Press, New York.

LeVine, R. A. and Le Vine, B. B. (1963): Nyansongo: A Gussi community in Kenya. In: *Six Cultures,* p. 15. Edited by Whiting, B. B., John Wiley and Sons, New York.

Mead, M. (1930): Adolescence in primitive and modern society. In: *The New Generation,* p. 169. Edited by Calverton, V. F. and Schmalhausen, S. Macaulay Co., New York.

Miller, E. (1962): Individual and social approach to the study of adolescence, *Brit. J. Med. Psychol., 35:* 211.

Morrow, C. and Morrow, F. (1962): *Teenage Tyranny,* Hechinger, New York.

Personal Communication, (1962).

Spiegel, J. P. (1957): Interpersonal influences within the family, *Group Processes, Transactions of the Third Conference, 23,* Edited by Schaffner, B. The Josiah Macy Foundation, New York.

Stekel, W. (1930): Frigidity in mothers. In: *The New Generation,* p. 24, Edited by Calverton, V. F. and Schmalhausen, S; Macaulay Co., New York.

Stengel, E. (1941): In: Three cases of anxiety and failure in examinations, J. D. Sutherland. *Brit. J. Med. Psychol., 19:* 73.

kibbutz adolescence: relevance to personality development theory

Joseph Marcus
Julius Zellermayer
Hadassah Medical School
Jerusalem Mental Health Center

INTRODUCTION

In recent years, interest in adolescence as a life period and as a developmental phase has increased considerably. The duration of adolescence has been extended beyond the former traditional limit of 18 years of age, when the young adult had to accept the duties and the privileges of responsible citizenship. It has been claimed that modern technological societies require longer developmental preparation on the part of the adolescent and that the acquisition of more advanced vocational abilities and societal adaptabilities demands a prolongation of learning and role experimentation during a rather extended "psychological moratorium" (Erikson, 1959). Manifestations of adolescent and young adult turmoil and rebellion not only have become more widespread but also have gained scientific sanctification, being increasingly valued as developmental necessities without which individual maturity cannot easily be reached.

However, some doubts have recently been expressed: Is adolescence in our time really and essentially different from what it was in the past? Is the "turmoil" of our present age different from the storm and stress ("Sturm und Drang") of the past? Is it really necessary to have a "psychological moratorium" and could not that moratorium have its detrimental effects together with its advantages? Is adolescent turmoil a developmental necessity and can maturity be achieved only through a turbulent passage through this phase? Is there only one royal road to maturity? If not, what are the sociocultural or individual constituents that determine or co-determine the course of the process and the eventual developmental outcome?

RELEVANCE OF FIELD APPROACH

Adolescents in our time appear to have become a distinct subpopulation with a culture of their own. They display similarities in behavior, atti-

Reprinted from the *Journal of Youth and Adolescence*, 1972, 1, 143–153. Copyright © 1972 by the Plenum Publishing Corporation.

tudes, and values across many national boundaries. However, generalizations would be misleading. Dissimilarities exist in different societies which apparently derive from the respective prevalent culture patterns, value orientations, family structures, and educational principles and practices.

To account for both the similarities and the dissimilarities, adolescents (as well as children) have to be studied in their sociocultural context. Whatever the weight of genetic predisposition for personality development, the impact of the societal matrix cannot be disregarded. The necessity of a field approach, therefore, seems obvious. This statement should not be misinterpreted as advocacy of an extreme environmentalism but as a recognition of the fact that childhood (adolescence) and society are one complex interlocking whole and that it is of major theoretical and practical concern to disentangle—if possible—the respective determinants. The Israeli kibbutzim provide us with an appropriate society in which to attempt such an analysis of component determinants. In this society, the total field is discernable and observable. Adolescence (as well as childhood) in the kibbutz has an institutionalized character. Development as a whole is goal-directed, and meanings and values are ascribed to individual and collective behaviors. One can hope that understanding the interrelation of this "field" and of adolescence outcome may contribute to our knowledge of some of the basic issues of adolescence that have become of such great social significance.

DESCRIPTION OF THE KIBBUTZ

Kibbutz society has been described in a number of publications by Spiro (1965, 1963), Rabin (1965), Jarus *et al.* (1970), Talmon-Graber (1970), and Marcus (1971). At the present time they comprise some 260 villages with a population of close to 130,000 persons. Schematically, we may define the kibbutz as a completely collective society, in which all property is owned by the collective and all decisions are made in general settings of the whole community. Such decisions may not only be economic ones, but also social and very individual ones (such as permitting one to study, etc.). Membership is voluntary and there is deep dedication to the socialist philosophy of a democratic nonexploitive commune. All share equally in common economic fortunes and facilities, including dormitory rooms, medical units, separate children's houses, and school. Significant deviation from these basic doctrines and practices has been strongly opposed through the 60 years of kibbutz existence, in spite of the many dynamic changes that have occurred in the realities of kibbutz life.

From the beginning the kibbutz has adhered to the principle of collective education based upon the rearing of children within their own peer groups from birth, alongside their participation in family life with their parents and siblings. To live and grow up inside a framework of biological and psychological siblingship, and to progress through successive and complementary group settings from birth to adulthood, have been the aims and ethics of the kibbutz. It was their a priori conviction that optimal developmental outcome could best be guaranteed by structuring the individual's passage through predetermined phases of biopsychological development and his progressive entrance into and separation from age-appropriate group settings. They were not unaware that developmental and behavioral difficulties, as well as outright psychopathologies may emerge, in spite of the planned developmental process, and that these would require educational and psychotherapeutic intervention. Therapeutic services of their own were therefore founded. However, to become a *homo novus,* oriented toward and rooted in a highly ethical socialist community, not as a group-conformist but as a fully individuated person, a continuous group life experience was needed. Kibbutz education was therefore designed to provide this experience in a consistent way.

EDUCATIONAL MODEL AND THE SOCIOCULTURAL MATRIX

With this general orientation in mind, let us now briefly describe the adolescent "condition" in the kibbutz and the adolescents themselves. Adolescence in the kibbutz extends from the beginning of puberty to the age of 18, when both boys and girls enter the army. During this adolescent period they live in their "Youth Society." This is the age-appropriate version of their collective existence, the final stage in a sequence of group settings: the "infants house" from birth to 18 months, the "toddlers house" (two to three years), nursery kindergarten (three to four years), junior kindergarten (four to five years), transitional kindergarten (five to seven years), and the primary school house. The adolescents live separately from their parents and are responsible for certain independent social institutions, learning thereby to manage their affairs in a spirit of democracy and self-government. They enjoy and play an integral role in kibbutz society and are called upon to contribute to its welfare. In addition to studying, they also participate in the economic life of the kibbutz, doing daily productive work in the agricultural, industrial, and service branches. They are looked upon as the hope of the future and thus sense their own worth and positive role in the continuation of the society. Thus they have ample opportunity to feel independent and yet part of the adult world at the same time. They know that they live in a nonaffluent community, where commodities are not abundant. The economic ups and downs of their collective is for them a distinct experience in which they have to share with knowledge and responsibility.

The adolescents of both sexes live together in the same house (sometimes in the same room) in groups of up to 20 members. There is a closeness of the sexes, but also a rather strong moral code which clearly limits actual sexual intimacy. Erotic attachments are permitted, but it is understood that youth under 18 should abstain from sexual intercourse. Even after that age they are advised not to indulge in irresponsible sexual behavior; fluctuating sexual attachments encounter moral indignation and free love is taboo.

In recent years, nonpromiscuous pairing has become increasingly accepted from the ages of 16 to 17, but it most often involves members of other groups and other social frameworks. This kind of exogamous orientation is a result of a kind of sibling taboo generated by the extreme closeness of members of the same group during their whole childhood. These attitudes do not overlook the strong sexual urges flooding the youngster.

But it is the educator's conviction that it is necessary to achieve control and mastery by channeling drives into constructive work, sports, studying, etc. This attitude extends to premarital heterosexual contact which is accepted for a short period, and expected to lead to marriage. Extramarital relations are not easily tolerated as they may lead to break-up of families. Such family dissolution is avoided, in spite of the wide provision of collective rearing of children. This is a clear expression of the moral conviction of kibbutz society that the interests of children require that parents stay together. This sexual code is reinforced by a consistent framework of recommended behaviors and roles of the two sexes into which the adolescents are expected to project themselves. Although the sexes are equal in the legal and civic sense, male-female relations are increasingly conceptualized in terms of functional complementarity. It is expected that women have a function as mothers and homemakers. As was customary in traditional society, the role of the man is seen to be in the area of instrumentality, that of the woman in the area of emotions.

Femininity is not devaluated at present as it was in the pioneer period. Women are permitted and encouraged to be physically attractive. There is a clear trend toward promoting the respective roles and identities of boys and girls, discouraging the diffusion of identity that characterized kibbutz society in its early historical period that is so prevalent in adolescence and adult culture in many parts of the western world today.

Thus, we are dealing, by and large, with a sociocultural field in which: the basic principles, values, and life partners are shared by the community as a whole; there exists a social contract with mutual and well-defined commitments; and there exists a dominant reality to which the adolescents are expected to adapt and which they will have to continue in their adult roles as the responsible next generation.

DEVELOPMENTAL OUTCOME

What is the overall schematic result of this educational and experiential framework? At the end of the adolescent phase, kibbutz youth are generally a healthy and constructive group. They participate fully in kibbutz society, and outside it. They succeed in institutions of higher learning, in various and often dangerous army roles, show initiative, high sense of duty, pragmatism, improvization, and lack of sentimentality. At the same time, they demonstrate comradeship, high moral commitments, and human sensitivity. As young adults they embark on a variety of careers and are well represented among the country's professional soldiers, artists, and writers and, in recent years, scientists. Psychopathology is not markedly different from what we find among comparable groups outside the kibbutz. Delinquency and drug use have been rare, homosexuality is nearly unknown in those born and raised from early childhood in this system. There is, on the whole, normal heterosexual development (Antanovsky *et al.,* 1969; Rabin, 1965), although in some youth the close intimacy between the sexes during adolescence coupled with a relatively puritanical sexual code may have contributed to a strengthening of sexual repression and some difficulties later when engaging in more intimate erotic and sexual relations (Nagler, 1970). They easily communicate with others in mixed groups of kibbutz and city youth as, e.g., in institutions of higher learning and in the army. When suffering from the various psychopathological conditions, the well-known universal conflicts are uncovered in psychotherapy as well as the same reactions and sensitivities to strains and stresses found in their non-kibbutz peers. Clearly the kibbutz is not a panacea, an all-healing remedy. Genetic dispositions, temperamental incompatabilities between the child and his caretakers, intercurrent diseases and their consequences, and other vicissitudes of life contribute here, as elsewhere, to behavioral and clinical conditions and to a variety of personality types defying any sterotypal description (Spiro, 1965; Rabin, 1965; Bettelheim, 1969).

Surprisingly, specific personality traits truly "typical" of kibbutz youth could not be delineated (Antanovsky *et al.,* 1969) on a variety of personality tests (Barron Ego Strength Test, Byrne Repression-Sensitization Scale, Rokeach Dogmatism Scale, Edwards Personal Preference Schedule).

A distribution similar to that found in city high school graduates who were selected for army officer's training was found, with a tendency toward high ego strength, low degree of dogmatism, and good heterosexual development. There were, however, indications that they scored significantly higher than city youths in sociometric tests and had a better articulated, more differentiated, field-independent perceptual style in tests of perceptual articulation (Preale *et al.,* 1970; Witkin *et al.,* 1962). This is suggestive, according to the authors, of their possessing an identity distinctly independent of the social environment. They differed markedly from city youth in their relative noninvolvement in adolescent turmoil rebellion, which enabled them to enter more or less smoothly into adult society, whether in their home kibbutz or in new collective settlements in whose establishment they often take a very decisive part.

It is remarkable that after three years' army service, during which time they had numerous opportunities to learn various new skills and consider many options for their future, about 85% return to and are absorbed in the kibbutz, establish families, etc. This is a personal decision without which they cannot become full members of their collective. Very often the new settlements are established in noncultivated, desert, and borderline areas, where the youth repeat the hard pioneering experiences of the parent generation. Undoubtedly this creates strains and disappointments for the home kibbutz which has to face and comply with the loss of some of the young generation. But on the part of the young generation, this may express their desire for independence and creativity away from the overpowering figures of their parents. It may mask, in a constructive way, their rebellion. But even in that case it attests to a very strong identification with the system and identical motivations, and reflects their deep conviction about the merits of their system and its "culture."

RECAPITULATION OF THE MAIN POINTS AND ISSUES

Before discussing the theoretical and practical implications of the presented data, let us briefly recapitulate the main points:

(A) Adolescence in the kibbutz proceeds inside a structured social setting; it is the last, concluding phase of peer group living, preceded by similarly structured settings in early and middle childhood; it is terminated officially at the age of 18, at which time the young boy and girl are supposed to have finished the essential part of their adolescent maturation and to be in possession of their respective *nuclear social and sexual identity;* they are expected to reach this maturational level without major emotional upheavals and only moderate intergenerational estrangement, guaranteeing thereby a more or less uncomplicated and smooth continuation of their society and culture.

(B) These aims seem on the whole to have been realized. As a human group these adolescents compare favorably with other control groups. The absence of homosexuality and major delinquency is remarkable and may merit our special consideration.

DISCUSSION

Let us now ask: Are these fortuitous occurrences, or are they natural outgrowths of the system, of the educational methods employed? And, if they are not accidental, which of the various factors would deserve closer attention and be credited with significance?

First let us state that we do not consider adolescence outcome to be independent of preadolescent development. As a matter of fact, we are convinced, on the basis of clinical experience, that the *previous phases of development,* in infancy, early childhood, and latency are of *decisive nature.* Mostly what we encounter in clinical practice as adolescent disorders are a continuation, intensification, or reemergence of past psychopathology, although with different phase-appropriate and phase-determined symptomatologies. It is obvious that during adolescence new and specific challenges have to be mastered in the problem areas of sexuality and identity.

However, when a relatively efficient coping apparatus has been established in the preadolescent period, adolescence may not be more than a transitional normative crisis (Erikson, 1959), which most youngsters will pass without undue difficulties. What, therefore, are the necessary prerequisites for efficient coping with the normative crisis of adolescence?

There is general agreement that the challenges facing the youngster at this time are: coping with and mastering the enormous increase of his aggressive and sexual drives; liberating himself from his emotional ties with his parents; transferring his former libidinal attachments from intrafamilial objects to heterosexual objects; finding his place in society, in which he will not anymore be an object of care, but a responsible subject with rights and obligations. These are formidable tasks and to master them he must (a) mobilize adaptational (coping) mechanisms—most of which he learned and acquired in his preceding developmental struggles—and (b) be helped by society, its institutions, and its code of recommended and prohibited behaviors, which point to directions and goals.

In earlier papers (Zellermayer and Marcus, 1971, 1972) we reviewed the preparatory childhood phases; we were impressed that the two basic features of (a) supplementary caretaking by mother, father, and caretaker and (b) the continuous socialization inside the peer group from birth on were of special significance. What has been termed "multiple mothering" reinstituted somehow the childhood situation of the former extended household in which the biological parents play a central but not an exclusive role. *To be parented appears to be crucial, but it must not be by the biological parents.* As a consequence of this early childhood constellation, a less-cathected relationship seems to develop between a child and his parents, though the emotional ties remain close. However, as a consequence of this kind of relationship, self-assertion and transfer of emotions to other objects during the adolescence phase seem to proceed with less ambivalence, conflict, and emotional upheaval. Growing up within the peer groups seemed to be instrumental in developing capacities of social interaction, acceptance of social control, and a sense of group identity. These constituents of growing up, on the one hand, and the real accomplishments, on the other, led us to the conclusion that the kibbutz is an effective environment capable of preparing the child entering puberty to deal with the new challenges facing him.

In terms of field approach, we have to face the following crucial issues: Is it advantageous to belong to a structured society in order to achieve a successful passage through this normative crisis? Is it advantageous to be exposed to a behavioral code which defines general roles and more specifically sex roles? Is it best to live and grow up in conditions of non-relativity of moral and social standards? And, finally, is it correct to limit the adolescent phase to its traditional 12- to 18-year period? Proponents of the "extended adolescence" concept argue that preparation for living and functioning in a highly technological, rapidly changing, and mobile society with constantly fluctuating values and styles requires many cognitive and behavioral skills that require an extended period during which to develop. Therefore adolescent experimentation with many roles before reaching final role destination is seen by them as being necessary and even commendable. This implies that maturation does not take place until then.

But we wonder whether, in our modern theorizing about adolescence, we have not put ourselves into a trap from which we cannot easily be extricated. By proposing new and far-reaching objectives, which cannot be realized in a limited period, one is forced to extend adolescence. Then by extending it, one subsequently has to introduce additional objectives. We would suggest leaving the dividing line at 18 to 19 years, in order to avoid diffusion between adolescence and adulthood. The needs and potentials are not the same before and after 18. Adult life only begins at this time, and the adolescent should, hopefully, be equipped with the necessary psychic instrumentalities to embark upon it successfully. It is not realistic to expect him to have reached "identity" at that time. At the most, an initial nuclear identity orientation may have been initiated. This may become consolidated during a subsequent and prolonged developmental process. In order to achieve such nuclear developmental achievements, society must provide youth with a framework. During this preparatory phase for adulthood, the adolescent cannot afford limitless experimentation. The primary objective at this stage is mastery of the new drives that endanger the relative ego stability reached at the end of latency, and society must come to his aid. For the majority of adolescents, being left to their own devices at this specific time may be disastrous and may undermine their precarious equilibrium. Blos' assessment (1962) of society's role deserves to be emphasized: "Social institutions in their effect on the individual aim at the elaboration of attitudes and character traits, at the selective responsiveness to social stimuli and value systems which restrict reactions to a circumscribed scope. . . . It seems of intrinsic significance that modern democratic capitalistic society does not offer youth any status confirmation, no initiation rites for consecration. Adolescents left to their own devices will spontaneously form competitive organizations within their own ranks. Gangs, cliques . . . set themselves against each other. . . . The vacuum of uninstitutionalized adolescents in western society thus allows on the one hand a high degree of personality differentiation and individuation, since there are no obligatory models, but on the other hand . . . facilitates deviate and pathological development." This is a clear warning. We would fully agree with Blos on this crucial issue and only emphasize that it concerns *the traditional period of adolescence from 12 to 18.* Since time immemorial, society intervened actively in the adolescent's formation. It is only in our time that it has begun to escape from its responsibility.

We would object to this attitude for theoretical and practical reasons. Thus we would assume that limiting adolescence to its traditional length and structuring it with the help of society may have the important implication of counteracting "adolescent turmoil." If we declare turmoil to be a development "necessity," we may thereby contribute to its occurrence. As a matter of fact, there is no evidence whatsoever that healthy maturation fails to take place without "turmoil." Grinker's "homoclites" (Grinker *et al.,* 1962) and Offer's normal adolescents (1969) clearly disprove such an assumption. Both authors have described smooth passage of adolescent development without intervening "crisis" in their American populations. Their adolescents resolve their problems by action and with little introspective rumination and smoothly project themselves into adult roles. They manifest a great capacity for interpersonal relations and identification with adults. They remind us in many respects of the kibbutz adolescents in their task orientation, goal directedness and interpersonal relatedness. Their focuses are on "reality," self-assertion, mastery, and social commitment. They seek to become adults and not to remain in prolonged, semidependent "psychological moratoria." They strive to establish themselves by adjusting to a common system of basic values. They do not feel and do not judge themselves as conformists by entering into the "establishment" that holds out a fair degree of hope that their aspirations will be fulfilled (Ruesch, 1967).

Taking all this into consideration, we have to state that kibbutz adolescents are, after all, not such an exception to the rule. There still remain differences which deserve theoretical consideration, such as nonoccurrence of homosexuality in their society and some other phenomena, but these we must leave for future discussion in another context. But what they represent is one of many varieties of adolescence, resulting from the constituents of the specific field to which they are exposed. They demonstrate dissimilarities to other adolescents, insofar as the total field is radically different. They demonstrate similarities when similar field conditions prevail.

SUMMARY

The process of adolescence in the Israeli kibbutzim was reviewed. The lack of adolescent turmoil, on the one hand, and the overall positive developmental outcome, on the other, stimulated our interest in regard to the influence of the total sociocultural field with its child-care principles and its value orientations on the formation of personality, behavioral patterns, and maturational achievements.

Among the factors most influential in contributing to the positive outcome were (a) the growing up in an environment in which regular transfer among caretaking adults is methodically practiced; (b) growth through successive stages of socialization within the peer group; (c) participation as an adolescent in a structural, goal-oriented individual and group program.

It was our impression that, as a result of these factors, basic trust is promoted, oedipal attachments become less intense, social responsibility and interpersonal relations are enhanced, and feelings of alienation from the social matrix are prevented. Adolescent turmoil under these conditions seems to become less necessary for growth of independence and individuality. Acquisition of adult roles and functions seems to proceed with less struggle, due to the provision by society of socially recommended and prohibited behaviors.

The issue of the duration of the period of adolescence was discussed and it was suggested that to limit it to its former traditional length may contribute to adolescent consolidation and prevent unnecessary role diffusion inherent in the prolonged psychosocial moratorium.

What has been said above summarizes on a descriptive level the cumulative experiences and observations of the authors and other clinicians and educators, combined with those research data which are available to date. As the focus of our discussion was "adolescence and society," we have not attempted in this paper to make an analysis of individual psychological development. This latter issue as well as other problems must be left for future elaboration and detailed research.

REFERENCES

Antanovsky, A., Marcus, J., and Katz, J. (1969). An investigation of leadership qualities of kibbutz-raised young men, Tech. Report, European Research Office, U.S.A. Project No. DAJ3768-0765.

Bettelheim, B. (1969). *The Children of the Dream.* Collier-Macmillan Ltd., London.

Blos, P. (1962). *On Adolescence.* The Free Press of Glencoe (Macmillan), New York, pp. 204–205.

Erikson, E. H. (1959). Identity and the life cycle. *Psychol. Issues 1(1):* 110–121; Monograph 1, International Universities Press, Inc., New York.

Grinker, R. R., Sr., Grinker, R. R., Jr., and Timberlake, J. (1962). A study of mentally healthy young males (homoclites). *A.M.A. Arch. Gen. Psychiat. 6:* 405–453.

Jarus, A., Marcus, J., Oren, J., Rapaport, Ch. (eds.) (1970). The child and his family in the kibbutz. In *Children and Families in Israel,* Gordon and Breach, New York, pp. 235–328.

Marcus, J. (1971). Early child development in kibbutz group care. *Early Child Development and Care 1(1):* 67–98.

Nagler, L. (1970). The child and his family in the kibbutz—mental health. In Jarus, A., Marcus, J., Oren, J., and Rapaport, Ch. (eds.), *Children and Families in Israel,* Gordon and Breach, New York, pp. 300–328.

Offer, D. (1969). *The Psychological World of the Teen-Ager.* Basic Books, Inc., New York and London.

Preale, S., Amir, Y., and Sharon, S. (1970). Perceptual articulation and task effectiveness in several Israeli sub-cultures. *J. Personal. Soc. Psychol. 15:* 180–195.

Rabin, A. J. (1965). *Growing Up in the Kibbutz.* Springer, New York.

Ruesch, J. (1967). Social communication. In *Comprehensive Textbook of Psychiatry,* Freedman, A. M., and Kaplan, H. J. (eds.), The Williams & Wilkins Co., Baltimore, p. 189.

Spiro, M. E. (1963). *Kibbutz, Venture in Utopia.* Schocken Books, New York.

Spiro, M. E. (1965). *Children of the Kibbutz.* N.Y. Schocken Paper Book, New York, 2nd ed.

Talmon-Graber, Y. (1970). *The Kibbutz.* Magnes Press-Hebrew University, Jerusalem.

Witkin, H. A., Dyk, R. B., Faterson, H. F., Goodenough, D. R., and Karp, S. A. (1962). *Psychological Differentiation.* John Wiley, New York.

Zellermayer, J. and Marcus, J. (1971). L'adolescence dans les kibboutz d'Israel. Confrontations Psychiatriques No. 7-1971, Psychopathologie de l'Adolescence, pp. 261–292.

Zellermayer, J., and Marcus, J. (1972). Towards a reclarification of some issues of child development theory in light of kibbutz experience. In Arieti, S. (ed.), *The World Biennial of Psychiatry and Psychotherapy,* Vol. II, Basic Books, New York and London.

four

parental models and the development of independence

part four

The development of independence is central to any discussion of the tasks of adolescence, not only in its own right, but also because of its intimate relationship to the accomplishment of other tasks. The adolescent who is unable to resolve the conflict between continuing dependency and the newer demands (and privileges) of independence in the direction of greater independence will encounter difficulties in many other areas as well. Without the achievement of separation and autonomy, the adolescent can hardly be expected to achieve mature heterosexual and peer relationships, confident pursuit of a vocation, or a clearly defined sense of his or her own identity.

The relative ease or difficulty of establishing independence depends in considerable measure on prior and continuing parent-child relationships. But what kinds of relationships foster the development of independence? Much confusion has resulted from recent societal polemics; all dissent demonstrated by young people is being blamed on a "permissive" upbringing, and a "return" to a "no nonsense" authoritarian or autocratic model of parental behavior is being advocated. The implication is that the permissive and the authoritarian/autocratic models are the only existing alternatives.

However, as Diana Baumrind points out in the first article in this part, that is not the case. Furthermore, in her view, neither authoritarian parental control nor permissive noncontrol fosters the optimal development of children and, especially, adolescents. "Demands which cannot be met or no demands, suppression of conflict or sidestepping of conflict, refusal to help or too much help, unrealistically high or low standards, all may curb or understimulate the child so that he fails to achieve the knowledge and experience which could realistically reduce his dependence upon the outside world." According to Baumrind, the idea that authoritarianism and permissiveness represent the only alternative models of child rearing stems from a failure to distinguish clearly between authoritarianism and "authoritativeness." The authoritative parent, unlike the authoritarian or autocratic parent, values and encourages the development of autonomous self-will; but unlike the permissive or neglectful parent, he or she also values disciplined behavior and the assumption or responsibility. Whereas the distinction between authoritarian and authoritative parental behaviors is important in the case of children, it assumes special importance in the case of adolescents because they are capable of assuming increasingly greater responsibility for their own behavior and need to do so if they are to become mature, self-reliant adults.

In the second article, Glen H. Elder, Jr., provides empirical support for the advantages to adolescents of authoritative (or what he calls "democratic") parental models, as opposed to autocratic or permissive models. Furthermore, results of the study he describes demonstrate that, within each model, parents who try to make the exercise of parental power "legitimate" in their children's eyes through the use of frequent explanations of their conduct are more likely to facilitate optimal development. Adolescents who perceived their parents as democratic (i.e., allowing the adolescent to contribute freely to discussion of issues relevant to his behavior and to participate in decision-making, but with ultimate responsibility retained by the parents), and as providing frequent explanations, were generally most likely to want to be like the parents and to comply with the parents' wishes; *they were also* likely to be self-confident and independent (although permissive parents, *if they provided frequent explanations,* were also likely to foster confidence and independence). In contrast, children of autocratic parents were least likely to display confidence and independence. Ironically, the children of autocratic parents who felt no need for parental explanations were least likely to be motivated to comply with parental wishes.

In the third article, Denise Kandel and Gerald S. Lesser compare the nature of parent-adolescent interactions in the United States and Denmark. Contrary to some popular impressions, they found that both American and Danish adolescents manifested generally positive relationships with their parents. American parents, however, were more likely to display authoritarian, nonexplaining parental behaviors and were likely to treat their adolescents as children longer than Danish parents. Danish adolescents, in turn, were more likely to have "a strong subjective sense of their independence." In both countries feelings of independence were enhanced when parents were democratic, provided explanations for their rules, and actively engaged their children in the decision-making process.

The democratic (or authoritative) child-rearing model as defined in these studies, providing as it does for perceptions of parental fairness, feelings of personal security, and the development of *both* responsibi'ity and increasing autonomy, is especially important in a turbulent period of rapid social change. In times such as the present the need for adult autonomy is at a premium; there are few clear-cut social guidelines, so responsibi'ity must come largely from within; and the opportunities for generational conflict, hostility, and alienation are legion.

authoritarian vs. authoritative parental control

Diana Baumrind
University of California, Berkeley

Social protest against our political institutions, national policy, and cultural mores is so vigorous in its expression, and fundamental in its rejection of constituted authority, that it should provoke a thoughtful inquiry not only into the issues raised, but also into the conditions which legitimate authority and into those which render authority illegitimate or ineffectual.

Three years ago I wrote an article entitled *Effects of Authoritative Parental Control on Child Behavior* (2). In that article I contrasted three modes of parental control—permissive, authoritarian, and authoritative—in order to show that relevant arguments against the use of authoritarian parental control did not apply to authoritative parental control. I shall repeat some of those arguments because I think they are still cogent.

However, the analysis which I made at that time is most relevant to what Dubin and Dubin (5) call the Authority Inception Period which ends at about 6 years. It deals very little with the conditions which legitimate authority in late childhood and adolescence, a matter of considerable social importance today. I will use the feminine gender to refer to the parent and the masculine gender to refer to the child.

There are a number of arguments[1] against the use of certain disciplinary techniques which are made in support of permissive childrearing which I would like to discuss briefly after defining the *permissive parent*.

As I understand the values of the permissive parent, she attempts to behave in a nonpunitive, acceptant, and affirmative manner toward the child's impulse, desires, and actions. She consults with him about policy decisions and gives explanations for family rules. She makes few demands for household responsibility and orderly behavior. She presents

---

[1] For a more detailed treatment of the validity of such arguments, see (2).

This is a revised version of a talk delivered at San Jose State College Workshop, Conflict and Adolescence, June 21, 1968, San Jose, Calif. This talk was in part supported by research grant HD0228 from the National Institute of Child Health and Development.

Reprinted from Adolescence, 1968, 3, 255–272. By permission of the author and Libra Publishers, Inc.

herself to the child as a resource for him to use as he wishes, not as an active agent responsible for shaping or altering his ongoing or future behavior. She allows the child to regulate his own activities as much as possible, avoids the exercise of control, and does not encourage him to obey externally defined standards. She attempts to use reason but not overt power to accomplish her ends.

The alternative to adult control, according to Neill, is to permit the child to be self-regulated, free of restraint, and unconcerned about expression of impulse or the effects of his carelessness.

To quote Neill:

> *Self-regulation means the right of a baby to live freely, without outside authority in things psychic and somatic.* It means that the baby feeds when it is hungry; that it becomes clean in habits only when it wants to; that it is never stormed at nor spanked; that it is always loved and protected (14, p. 105, italics Neill's).
>
> *I believe that to impose anything by authority is wrong. The child should not do anything until he comes to the opinion—that it should be done* (14, p. 114, italics Neill's).
>
> Every child has the right to wear clothes of such a kind that it does not matter a brass farthing if they get messy or not (14, p. 115).
>
> Furniture to a child is practically nonexistent. So at Summerhill we buy old car seats and old bus seats. And in a month or two they look like wrecks. Every now and again at mealtime, some youngster waiting for his second helping will while away the time by twisting his fork almost into knots (14, p. 138).
>
> Really, any man or woman who tries to give children freedom should be a millionaire, for it is not fair that the natural carelessness of children should always be in conflict with the economic factor (14, p. 139).

Arguments given against the use of certain disciplinary techniques:

1. It has been argued by clinically trained advocates of permissive childrearing, such as Lawrence Frank (7) or the early Spock, that *punishment has inevitable negative side effects, and is an ineffective means of controlling behavior.* However, the experimental or clinical evidence for this contention is by no means convincing. Clinical studies have tended to confuse punitive, rejecting attitudes in parents with the effects of punishment *per se* and to attribute the known negative effects of punitive and rejecting attitudes to the use of aversive stimuli, i.e., punishment, as well. Severe, unjust, and ill-timed punishment administered by an unloving parent is probably harmful as well as ineffective. However, there are some theoretical grounds to suppose that the milder forms of punishment, unlike traumatic rejection or beatings may have, like other forthright uses of power, beneficial side effects, such as the following:

a. more rapid re-establishment of affectional involvement on both sides following emotional release;

b. high resistance to similar deviation by siblings who vicariously experience punishment;

c. emulation of the aggressive parent resulting in prosocial assertive behavior;

d. lessening of guilt reactions to transgression; and

e. an increased ability of the child to endure punishment in the service of a desired end.

In addition, the proposition that punishment is an *ineffective* means of controlling human behavior may indeed be a "legend" as Solomon (20) and Walters, Parke, & Crane (21) suggest. Under conditions prevailing in the home setting, punishment may be quite effective in helping to accomplish particular objectives.

2. Another argument against the exercise of parental control is *that close supervision, high demands, and other manifestations of parental authority provoke rebelliousness* in children.

In fact, Bandura and Walter (1), Glueck and Glueck (9), and McCord, McCord, and Howard (12) found that higher demands were made by the parents of the least hostile or delinquent children. Finney (6) found that, while parental rigidity was associated with covert hostility in children, firm control was associated with conscience development.

In my own study of middle class parents of preschool children (3, 4), those parents who demanded that their children be orderly and assume household responsibilities provided more enriched and orderly surroundings, and involved themselves more conscientiously with their welfare. Perhaps that is why such demands were viewed by the child as reasonable, and did not tend to provoke rebellion.

A distinction must be made between the effects on the child of unjust, restrictive, subjective authority, when compared to rational, warm, and issue-oriented authority. There is considerable evidence that arbitrary authority but not rational authority is associated in the child with negative affect, disaffiliativeness, and rebelliousness.

3. A third argument against the imposition of authority is that *firm parental control generates passivity and dependence.* However, Hoffman's (11) results indicate that parental assertiveness, and submissiveness in the child are negatively correlated. Sears' (18) findings on early socialization and later aggression suggest that high punishment for aggression, like "reactive unqualified power assertion," does not lead to submissive behavior. My own results were that parents of the most self-reliant and approach-oriented group of children were rated highest in firm control and reactive power assertion.

4. It has been argued in support of permissive childrearing that *permissiveness frees the child from the presence and authority of the parent.* However, rather than having no effect upon him, the noninterference of an adult who is present when the child is misbehaving seems to signify approval of his behavior, not neutrality, and actually tends to increase rather than leave unaffected the incidence of that behavior. For example, Siegel and Kohn (19) demonstrated that the presence of a permissive adult increased the incidence of aggression shown by nursery school boys to somewhat younger boys. To quote Siegel and Kohn:

Two-thirds of the Ss in the adult-present sessions were more aggressive in the second than in the first session, and all the Ss in the adult-absent sessions were less aggressive in the second than in the first session. This finding is in confirmation of the hypothesis which was drawn from a consideration of the nature and the effects of adult permissiveness with children, and of the nature of young children's controls for aggression (19, pp. 140–141).

5. It has also been argued that *controlling parents are motivated by the Authoritarian Personality Syndrome.* Fromm used the term authoritarian personality to refer to the syndrome in which enactment of the role of inhibiting authority characterizes the individual's interpersonal relations in order to defensively protect a weak ego from any possible assault.

While parents motivated by the authoritarian personality syndrome are controlling, it does not follow that the converse is true. Some subgroups of controlling parents permit high autonomy in many areas of the child's life. Lois Hoffman et al. (10) described a subgroup of parents who were perceived by their children as both coercive and permissive of high autonomy.

I found that, whereas the parents of relatively alienated preschool children tended to use inhibiting control, the parents of exceptionally mature children exerted even firmer control, used reason to explain their directives, and encouraged independent expression. This latter group of parents certainly did not exhibit the authoritarian personality syndrome. They were open and receptive although highly authoritative in their requirement for compliance. Thus, several investigators have identified subgroups of controlling parents who are not restrictive of children's autonomy or motivated by the authoritarian personality syndrome and have shown that children react differently to inhibiting and rational control.

It seems likely that:

Authoritarian control and permissive noncontrol may both shield the child from the opportunity to engage in vigorous interaction with people. Demands which cannot be met or no demands, suppression of conflict or sidestepping of conflict, refusal to help or too much help, unrealistically high or low standards, all may curb or understimulate the child so that he fails to achieve the knowledge and experience which could realistically reduce his dependence upon the outside world. The authoritarian and the permissive parent may both create, in different ways, a climate in which the child is not desensitized to the anxiety associated with nonconformity. Both models minimize dissent, the former by suppression and the latter by diversion or indulgence. To learn how to dissent, the child may need a strongly held position from which to diverge and then be allowed under some circumstances to pay the price for nonconformity by being punished. Spirited give and take within the home, if accompanied by respect and warmth, may teach the child how to express aggression in self-serving and prosocial causes and to accept the partially unpleasant consequences of such actions (2, p. 904).

AUTHORITARIAN VS. AUTHORITATIVE

I would like to *contrast the prototypic authoritarian parent with the prototypic authoritative parent.*

The *authoritarian parent* as she is generally described in the literature attempts to shape, control, and evaluate the behavior and attitudes of

the child in accordance with a set standard of conduct, usually an absolute standard, theologically motivated and formulated by a higher authority. She values obedience as a virtue and favors punitive, forceful measures to curb self-will at points where the child's actions or beliefs conflict
with what she thinks is right conduct. She believes in inculcating such
instrumental values as respect of authority, respect for work and respect
for the preservation of order and traditional structure. She does not encourage verbal give or take, believing that the child should accept her
word for what is right.

The *authoritative parent* as she appears in my studies also attempts
to direct the child's activities but in a rational, issue-oriented manner.
She encourages verbal give and take, and shares with the child the reasoning behind her policy. She values both expressive and instrumental attributes, both autonomous self-will and disciplined conformity. Therefore, she
exerts firm control at points of parent-child divergence, but does not hem
the child in with restrictions. She recognizes her own special rights as
an adult, but also the child's individual interest and special ways. The
authoritative parent affirms the child's present qualities, but also sets standards for future conduct. She uses reason as well as power to achieve
her objectives. She does not base her decisions on group consensus or
the individual child's desires; but also, does not regard herself as infalli-
ble or divinely inspired.

Some quotations from Rambusch, in describing the Montessori method,
illustrate the way in which authoritative control is used to resolve the
antithesis between pleasure and duty, and between freedom and
responsibility.

The discipline resides in three areas in a Montessori classroom: It resides in
the environment itself which is controlled; in the teacher herself who is controlled and is ready to assume an authoritarian role if it is necessary; and from
the very beginning it resides in the children. It is a three-way arrangement,
as opposed to certain types of American education in which all of the authority
is vested in the teacher, or where, in the caricature of permissive education,
all of the authority is vested in the children.

When a child has finished his work he is free to put it away, he is free
to initiate new work or, in certain instances, he is free to not work. But he
is not free to disturb or destroy what others are doing. If the day is arranged
in such a way that at a certain time the teacher must demand of the children
that they arbitrarily finish what they are doing—if it is lunchtime, or recess or
whatever—the child must accommodate himself to the demand of the group.
It is largely a question of balance. In a Montessori class the teacher does not
delude herself into believing that her manipulation of the children represents
their consensus of what they would like to do. If she is manipulating them
insofar as she is determining arbitrarily that this must be done at this time,
she is cognizant of what she is doing, which the child may or may not be.

The importance of the responsibility in selecting matter for the child to learn
is placed in the hands of those adults who are aware of what the culture will
demand of the child and who are able to "program" learning in such a way
that what is suitable for the child's age and stage of development is also learn-
able and pleasurable to him. Both Dewey and Montessori feel that interest and
discipline are connected and not opposed. Dewey himself decried unrestrained
freedom of action in speech, in manners, and lack of manners. He was, in

fact, critical of all those progressive schools that carried the thing they call freedom nearly to the point of anarchy (17, p. 63).

The body of findings which I reviewed in the article cited, and certainly the results of my own research, support the position that authoritative control can achieve responsible conformity with group standards without loss of individual autonomy or self-assertiveness.

As Dubin and Dubin (5) point out, by the imposition of parental authority, the child in his first six years learns to express his social individuality, within the confines of what the culture will accept. He finds that there are ranges of acceptable behavior in most situations of action. By having orderly experiences with available behavioral choices, the child learns to distinguish between conforming and deviant behavior. Later when he is capable of moral judgments, he may choose to engage in deviant behavior, but he will do so prepared to endure the punishment which may follow. Hopefully he will have learned the value to him of authoritative behavior and know how to play the role behavior which is reciprocal. He will also have had his parent as a model for the role of a rational authority, a role he can himself assume at a later age.

USE OF POWER IN CHILDHOOD AND ADOLESCENCE

I believe then that the imposition of authority even against the child's will is useful to the child during the Authority Inception Period. During those early years exercise of power is a legitimate right of the parents. Indeed, power serves to legitimate authority in the mind of the child.

During childhood, power is asymmetrical in the family unit. That is, the parent's ability to exercise control over the child and to restrict his autonomy exceeds that of the child, in reciprocal interaction with his parent. The parent by virtue of her physical size, experience, and control over the sources of supply can, in most instances where there is a divergence, carry out her wishes despite the resistance of the child, and the child cannot do likewise. Parents vary of course in the extent to which they acknowledge the asymmetry of their power, or are effectively able to use power.

The major way in which parents exercise power is by manipulating the stimuli which affect the child—rewarding with positive reinforcers and punishing with aversive stimuli. The main factor which makes a parent a successful reinforcing agent or an attractive model for her child to imitate is her effective power to give the child what he needs—i.e., her control over resources which the child desires, and her willingness and ability to provide the child with these resources in such a manner and at such a time that the child will be most gratified. Both morally and practically, gratification of the child's needs is a precondition for the effective imposition of parental authority.

Piaget's analysis of the development of the idea of justice (15) suggests that the child's organization of a moral order is based upon power in the early years. In the mind of the young child, power legitimates the parent's right to exercise authority. The parent's ability to gratify the child and to withhold gratification legitimates her authority. The child has not yet reached the level of cognitive development where he can legitimate authority, or object to its imposition, on a principles basis.

The parent can accelerate the child's cognitive development both by requiring the child to accommodate at the top limit of his ability to do so, and by using reason to support her directives. Even though the specific reason may not be understood by the child, he learns that authority must ultimately be legitimated on a principled basis. By using reason, the authoritative parent teaches the child to seek the reasons behind directives and eventually to exercise his option either to conform, or to deviate and to cope with the consequences. Reason does not really legitimate authority for the young child, in the same way as power does, or in the same way as it will at adolescence.

Punishment has an informational role for the parent and the child. By setting a price on negatively sanctioned behavior, both the parent and the child can determine how important it is to the child that he perform an act which he knows will be punished at a given level of intensity. When a child repeats an act knowingly for which he has been punished moderately severely, the parent has grounds to question the legitimacy of her rejection of that act. Punishment and other manifestations of power then are an important part of the feedback which advance the parent's understanding of the child and his level of cognitive and moral development.

By early adolescence, however, power cannot and should not be used to legitimate authority. The young person is now capable of formal operational thought. He can formulate principles of choice by which to judge his own actions and the actions of others. He has the conceptual ability to be critical even though he may lack the wisdom to moderate his criticism. He can see clearly many alternatives to parental directives; and the parent must be prepared to defend rationally, as she would to an adult, a directive with which the adolescent disagrees. Moreover, the asymmetry of power which characterizes childhood no longer exists at adolescence. The adolescent cannot be forced physically to obey over any period of time.

When a young child refuses to obey, his parent can persist until he does obey, giving him a reason based upon a principle which he may not understand, or a reason based upon the asymmetry of power, which he is sure to understand. She can say, "you must do it because I say so"; and the child will accept such a parental maneuver as legitimate even if he continues to have objections on hedonistic grounds, because he is not yet capable of principled objections.

An adolescent, on the other hand, is capable of principled objections. When an adolescent refuses to do as his parent wishes, it is more congruent with his construction of reality for the parent simply to ask him "Why not?" Through the dialogue which ensues, the parent may learn that her directive was unjust; or the adolescent may learn that his parent's directive could be legitimated. In any case, a head-on confrontation is avoided. While head-on confrontation serves to strengthen authority in the Authority Inception Period, it undermines authority during adolescence.

This does not mean that the parent relinquishes her authoritative role. It does mean that she enacts her role in a different way, one suited to the level of development of the older child. She makes limited use of power to settle parent-child divergences, and then primarily to guard her personal interests or to break a stalemate when the adolescent's objection is based, not on principle, but on pique. The adolescent can understand and be held to a contractual agreement. The adolescent, egocentric as he is, can recognize the egocentric needs of parents. More often than is admitted, a parent-child divergence involves a simple conflict of interests. The parent requires quiet and the young person wants to play loud music; if the adolescent were to come in late, his parent would lose sleep; if the working parent is to rest after dinner, the children must do the dishes. Children recognize the legitimacy of demands based on personal rights, provided that parents represent the matter as it is, and the balance of giving is well in favor of the children, as indeed it must be if parents are to have any special rights.

The authority of the parent at adolescence stands or falls on the parent's past performance, and what she is at present, in relation to what the adolescent needs her to be. The adolescent needs a parent who has something to say that is worth listening to, and who is fully receptive to what he has to say. The adolescent needs to have someone to argue with in order to develop his own position. His parents can play this role of friendly adversary. The adolescent needs a strongly stated thesis to relate his own thinking to. A convincing antithesis requires a well-formulated thesis. The authoritative parent can state and defend her own thesis vigorously, and yet not limit the freedom of the adolescent to express and argue for his antithesis. The parent must not expect the resultant synthesis to be merely a restatement of her own thesis. By receiving the antithesis presented to her by her adolescent, the parent gains knowledge of that with which she is authorized to deal.

Receptivity does not mean listening in order to achieve conformity after talk. It does mean that an antithetical position which may threaten the stability of the system is encouraged to interact with that system. Only in that way can the system continue to perform its function. A system which cannot absorb dissent cannot survive. Revolutionary fervor is nourished by the refusal of constituted authority to receive antithesis, to be renewed by dissent. If constituted authority were as successful in absorbing dissent as Marcuse thinks it is, there would be no basis for the revolutionary fervor he advocates.

Under normal conditions, adolescents do not rebel against all authority by any means. They differentiate quite accurately between authoritarian and authoritative parental control. Pikas (16), in his survey of 656 Swedish adolescents, showed that significant differences occurred in their acceptance of parental authority, depending upon the reason for the directive. Authority which was based on rational concern for the child's welfare was accepted well by the child, while authority which was based on the adult's desire to dominate or exploit the child was rejected. The former, which he calls rational authority, is similar to "authoritative control," and the latter, which he calls inhibiting authority, is similar to "authoritarian control," as these terms are used in this discussion. Pikas' results are supported by Middleton and Snell (13) who found that parental discipline regarded by the child as either very strict or very permissive was associated with lack of closeness between parent and child and with rebellion against the parents' political viewpoints.

THE MAJOR CHALLENGE TO AUTHORITY TODAY

The major challenge to authority today is not that the young have no respect for authority, but that they have little reason to have respect for authority. Both youth and their parents are disaffected with their social institutions—with their schools, churches and their government. The mythology of affluence has been exploded. The credibility gap on issues of poverty and war has made extension of trust unfeasible, and open rebellion morally feasible. It is very difficult today for constituted authorities, even rational authorities, to have respect for themselves. Rational authorities have cause to question the legitimacy of their authority. Until relatively recently, parents could believe that by maintaining order with the family, they were upholding a higher order to which they too submitted—this higher order was defined by religious mandate, cultural tradition, or national way. Think of the basis upon which Susannah Wesley, mother of the founder of Methodism, legitimated her authority in the 18th century. These are her words:

> As self-will is the root of all sin and misery, so whatever cherishes this in children insures their after-wretchedness and irreligion; whatever checks and mortifies it promotes their future happiness and piety. This is still more evident, if we further consider, that religion is nothing else than doing the will of God, and not our own: that the one grand impediment to our temporal and eternal happiness being this self-will, no indulgences of it can be trivial, no denial unprofitable. Heaven or hell depends on this alone. So that the parent who studies to subdue it in his child, works together with God in the renewing and saving a soul. The parent who indulges it does the devil's work, makes religion impracticable, salvation unattainable; and does all that in him lies to damn his child, soul and body forever (8, pp. 30–31).

Since the impediment to temporal and eternal happiness was thought to be self-will, the parent behaved in authoritarian ways because she cared for the child, not because she was weak or punitive.

While Mrs. Wesley believed that the mores of her society were divinely inspired, many parents not only know these mores are not divinely inspired, but find them in no sense inspirational. Concerning our social structure, many parents agree with their adolescents, when they in the words of Mario Savio find the operation of the machines so odious and vile as to require of them that they put their bodies on the gears and upon the wheels and upon the levers to prevent these wheels from working at all. To be more specific, these parents share the moral outrage of their adolescents at the atrocities of the Vietnam war, and the gross inequities in distribution of wealth in this country. Maintenance of structure and order is high in the hierarchy of values of authoritative parents, as we have defined these parents. What are they to do, they ask, when maintenance of structure and order conflicts with a higher value, such as killing to no just purpose. These parents feel responsible for the sins of their generation, and their faith in their own expertness is shaken. Their faith in the value of obedience, and in the possibility of constructive nonconformity is shaken. We have said that authoritative control can achieve responsible conformity with group standards without loss of individual autonomy and self-assertiveness. Conformity with group standards, if this means support of the Vietnam war, does not seem responsible to many parents today. How are they to rear their children to conform responsibly if they do not believe that it is responsible to conform? How are they to rear their children to constructively dissent if they do not believe that constructive dissent will be received by constituted authority?

In summary, I examined the criticisms directed by advocates of permissiveness against parental control and showed that to the extent that these criticisms were valid, in early childhood they were relevant to authoritarian control and not authoritative control. I contrasted the conditions and processes which legitimate authority in childhood with those which legitimate authority in adolescence. In particular, I argued that the imposition of authority by use of power is legitimate in childhood and not in adolescence, because the level of cognitive and moral development of the adolescent is such as to require that he be bound by social contract and moral principles rather than by power. Lastly, I discussed what I felt to be the fundamental challenge to authority today.

In closing, I would like to say that an increasingly larger segment of today's youth are rejecting the alternatives offered by established authority, not because they are rebellious neurotics, but because these alternatives are not morally acceptable. If their dissent is not received, and the system to which they object is not radically altered, we who are in a position of authority can expect to be confronted with what Marcuse calls the Great Refusal. We will be faced with an absolute rejection of the society and its institutions by many of our brightest and most competent youth. That absolute rejection will negate the distinction between rational and arbitrary authority, between authoritative and authoritarian adult control. If we cannot fully receive the message from the most dissenting of our youth, we may be faced with the complete withdrawal of legitimacy from rational as well as arbitrary authority by the very youth upon whom we count for cultural continuity.

REFERENCES

1. Bandura, A., & Walters, R. H. *Adolescent Aggression.* New York: Ronald, 1959.
2. Baumrind, D. "Effects of Authoritative Parental Control on Child Behavior," *Child Development,* 1966, *37–4:* 887–907.
3. Baumrind, D. "Child Care Practices Anteceding Three Patterns of Preschool Behavior," *Genetic Psychology Monographs,* 1967, *75:* 43–88.
4. Baumrind, D., & Black, A. E. "Socialization Practices Associated with Dimensions of Competence in Preschool Boys and Girls," *Child Development,* 1967, *38-2:* 291–327.

5. Dubin, E. R., & Dubin, R. The Authority Inception Period in Socialization," *Child Development,* 1964, *34:* 885–898.
6. Finney, J. C. Some Maternal Influences on Children's Personality and Character," *Genetic Psychology Monographs,* 1961, *63:* 199–278.
7. Frank, L. K. "Freedom for the Personality." *Psychiatry,* 140, *3:* 341–349.
8. Gesell, A. *The Guidance of Mental Growth in Infant and Child,* New York: Macmillan, 1930.
9. Glueck, S., & Glueck, E. *Unraveling Juvenile Delinquency.* New York: Commonwealth Fund, 1950.
10. Hoffman, L., Rosen, S., & Lippitt, R. "Parental Coerciveness, Child Autonomy, and Child's Role at School," *Sociometry,* 1960, *23:* 15–22.
11. Hoffman, M. L. "Power Assertion by The Parent and its Impact on the Child," *Child Development,* 1960, *31:* 129–143.
12. McCord, J., & Howard, A. "Familial Correlates of Aggression in Nondelinquent Male Children," *J. Abnorm. Soc. Psychol.,* 1961, *62:* 79–93.
13. Middleton, R., & Snell, P. "Political Expression of Adolescent Rebellion," *Amer. J. Sociol.,* 1963, *68:* 527–535.
14. Neill, A. S. *Summerhill.* New York: Hart, 1964.
15. Piaget, J. *The Moral Judgment of the Child.* New York: Free Press, 1965.
16. Pikas, A. "Children's Attitudes Toward Rational Versus Inhibiting Parental Authority," *J. Abnorm. Soc. Psychol.,* 1961, *62:* 315–321.
17. Rambusch, N. M. *Learning How to Learn: An American Approach to Montessori.* Baltimore: Helicon, 1962.
18. Sears, R. R. "Relation of Early Socialization Experiences to Aggression in Middle Childhood," *J. Abnorm. Soc. Psychol.,* 1961, *63:* 466–492.
19. Siegel, A. E., & Kohn, L. G. "Permissiveness, Permission, and Aggression: The Effects of Adult Presence or Absence on Aggression in Children's play," *Child Development,* 1959, *30:* 131–141.
20. Solomon, R. L. "Punishment," *Amer. Psychologist,* 1964, *19:* 239–253.
21. Walters, R. H., Parke, R. D., & Cane, V. A. "Timing of Punishment and Observation of Consequences to Others as Determinants of Response Inhibition," *J. Exp. Child Psychol.,* 1965, *2:* 10–30.

parental power legitimation and its effect on the adolescent

Glen H. Elder, Jr.
University of North Carolina

When a child requests a reason or explanation concerning a particular restriction, at least two responses are open to the parent. On the one hand, the parent may fulfill the request and demand compliance; on the other, the parent may ignore the child's inquiry. From the child's perspective, this is essentially the difference between the expression of legitimate and coercive power.

The results of small group research suggest the following inferences: adolescents who perceive their parents as asserting coercive rather than legitimate power over them should be less highly attracted to their parents,[1] and less likely to conform to rules of conduct in the absence of parental surveillance,[2] than other adolescents. Research reveals that adolescents have less favorable attitudes toward coercive than legitimate

---

This investigation is partially based on the author's doctoral research which is part of the Adolescent Study directed by Dr. Charles E. Bowerman, Department of Sociology and Anthropology, University of North Carolina. The Adolescent Study is supported by Public Health Service research grant M-s045 from the National Institute of Mental Health. The writing of this report was made possible by a post-doctoral fellowship from the National Institute of Mental Health during 1961–1962. I am very much indebted to Dr. Bowerman for his guidance as dissertation advisor and to Drs. Richard Simpson and Harry Crockett for their invaluable evaluations and criticisms of early drafts of this research report.

[1] Bertram H. Raven and John R. P. French, Jr., "Group Support, Legitimate Power and Social Influence," *Journal of Personality,* 26 (December, 1958), pp. 400–409; John R. P. French, Jr., H. William Morrison, and George Levinger, "Coercive Power and Forces Affecting Conformity," *Journal of Abnormal and Social Psychology,* 61 (January, 1960), pp. 93–101.

[2] Bertram H. Raven and John R. P. French, Jr., "Legitimate Power, Coercive Power, and Observability in Social Influence," *Sociometry,* 21 (June, 1958), pp. 83–97.

power,[3] and that coercive power expression by mothers promotes the development of hostility and power needs among children of nursery school age.[4] These findings suggest that the legitimation of power by parents leads to a strengthening of affective relations between parents and the adolescent, and tends to encourage behavioral conformity to parental rules.

The effects of legitimate and coercive parental power on adolescents are less clear when the legitimacy of different levels of parental power is considered. Since the effects of different levels of power on adolescent affection for parents vary substantially, it follows that the effects of legitimate and coercive power may also differ by the level of parental power.[5] For instance, the autocratic parent who, as a rule, does legitimize his demands and restrictions by explaining them, is apt to evoke different kinds of reactions from adolescents than is the permissive parent who offers frequent explanations. Similarly, infrequent explanations at these two levels of power are apt to have different effects on adolescent behavior. Building upon experimental and survey findings regarding the differential effects of legitimate and coercive power, this research is concerned with determining how such effects, as revealed in adolescent behavior and reactions to parents, vary in relation to three levels of parental power.

In an earlier study, seven types of parent-adolescent interdependence in the child rearing relationship were delineated.[6] Five of these structures are condensed in this research to measure high, moderate and low parental power.

Autocratic. The parent does not allow the adolescent to express his views on subjects regarding his behavior nor permit him to regulate his own behavior in any way.

Democratic. The adolescent is encouraged to participate in discussing issues relevant to his behavior although the final decision is always made or approved by the parent.

Permissive. The adolescent has more influence in making decisions

---

[3] Anatol Pikas, "Children's Attitudes toward Rational Versus Inhibiting Parental Authority," *Journal of Abnormal and Social Psychology,* 62 (March, 1961), pp. 315–321.

[4] Martin L. Hoffman, "Power Assertion by the Parent and Its Impact Upon the Child," *Child Development,* 31 (March, 1960), pp. 129–143.

[5] Adolescents with highly dominant parents in contrast to democratic parents were much more likely to feel unwanted by their parents, to be low on affectional orientation toward parents, and to consider their child rearing policy to be unreasonable. See Glen H. Elder, Jr., "Structural Variations in the Child Rearing Relationship," *Sociometry,* 25 (September, 1962), pp. 241–62; and *Family Structure and the Transmission of Values and Norms in the Process of Child Rearing,* unpublished Ph.D. Dissertation, University of North Carolina, 1961, Chapters IX and X.

[6] Elder, "Structural Variations in the Child Rearing Relationship," *op. cit.*

which concern him than does his parent. The laissez-faire and ignoring types of interdependence are included in this level of power.

The effects of frequent and infrequent explanations of rules of conduct at the three levels of parental power will be examined on (1) the attractiveness of parents—the desire of adolescents to be like or model their parents; (2) compliance with parental requests—conformity to parental wishes regarding peer associations; and (3) autonomy—adolescent independence in decision making and feelings of self-confidence in personal goals and standards of behavior. First, however, the relationship between parental explanations and level of parental power will be investigated. Let us state some general expectations concerning each of the dependent variables (as well as parental explanation) in the order in which they are considered in the subsequent analysis.

HYPOTHESES

A parent may shrug off a child's inquiry by heatedly exclaiming, "You do it, I don't need to explain," or, in contrast, meet the request with an explanation which seems reasonable.[7] Autocratic parents totally exclude their children from participating in the formulation of decisions which concern them while the children of democratic and permissive parents have much more freedom in self-direction. These differences lead us to predict that *the frequency of explanation is inversely related to parental power.*

Since research indicates that positive sentiment toward a power agent increases as the perceived legitimacy of his power increases, it is likely that modeling is positively related to the frequency of parental explanations.[8] However, this relationship is apt to vary by level of parental power, since a recent study shows affection toward parents to be related to parental power in a curvilinear manner.[9] Adolescents of autocratic and permissive parents tended to be low on affection. From these results we hypothe-

---

[7] The legitimation of rules of conduct was consistently a major function of parental explanations in an earlier exploratory study of a number of child rearing variables. In lengthy focused interviews with 60 ninth and twelfth grade adolescents who represented the extremes in social adjustment and in social class status, we found that the control wielded by parents who explained their rules was in practically all cases viewed as right and reasonable. As one youth put it, "They explain why it's right and it's right, that's all." Very few youths who received frequent explanations could think of times when "false or made up" explanations were offered. The rarity of this practice may be due to the fact that pseudo-reasons seldom fooled or satisfied these adolescents. One girl revealed that she "just tossed them back" at her parents. For the most part, the data from this study indicate that frequent explanations of rules and demands definitely tended to make the regulations seem right in the eyes of adolescents.

[8] For example, see Raven and French, "Group Support, Legitimate Power, and Social Influence," *op. cit.*

[9] Elder, "Structural Variations in the Child Rearing Relationship," *op. cit.*

size that *modeling is most common among adolescents with democratic parents who frequently provide explanations for their rules.* Miller and Swanson found that parental explanations were strongly associated with resistance to temptation in their sample of adolescent boys.[10] While explanations may be directly related to obedience, it is apparent that this relationship is likely to vary substantially by level of power. For instance, we know that autocratic and permissive parents are apt to be less accepting and supportive than the democratic parent[11] and that parental warmth is instrumental in facilitating the adoption of parental standards.[12] Hence, we predict that *conformity to parental rules is most typical of adolescents with democratic parents who frequently provide explanations.*

The possible effects of non-explaining parents on the autonomy of the child are considerable. According to Hoffman, the arbitrary, threatening nature of rules and demands left unexplained ("unqualified power assertion," in his terminology) requires from a child the "unconditional surrender of his own interests and involvements," tends to "frustrate his momentary need for task completion," and "constitutes an assault on his autonomy as well."[13] Miller and Swanson labelled a mother who does not explain requests as *arbitrary.*

> If she is arbitrary, he must obey without understanding. His world soon consists of high fences bounding many little spaces from which he can escape only by risking her disapproval. In new situations he cannot afford the risk of arriving at his own judgments. Because he often does not understand the purposes of his mother's regulations, he cannot tell whether she will condemn the actions he takes on his own initiative. He can be sure only that following directions, whether or not they make sense, is the best way to keep out of trouble and win approval.[14]

The non-explaining parent is thus apt to undermine the self-confidence of the adolescent in his ability to make his own decisions as well as

---

[10] Miller and Swanson found that boys who received explanations of parental requests were more likely to write stories in which heroes resist temptation than were boys of parents who seldom offered explanations. Daniel R. Miller and Guy E. Swanson, *Inner Conflict and Defense,* New York: Holt-Dryden & Co., 1960, p. 172. Reasoning with the child, which is another method of making parental regulations seem reasonable and legitimate, is highly related to the development of conscience. See Robert Sears, Eleanor Maccoby, and Harry Levin, *Patterns of Child Rearing,* New York: Row Peterson & Co., 1957, p. 393.

[11] Elder, *Family Structure and the Transmission of Values and Norms in the Process of Child Rearing, op. cit.,* Chapter XI.

[12] See, for example, Paul Mussen and Luther Distler, "Masculinity, Identification, and Father-Son Relationships," *Journal of Abnormal and Social Psychology,* 59 (November, 1959), pp. 350–356.

[13] Martin L. Hoffman, "Power Assertion by the Parent and Its Impact upon the Child," *op. cit.,* pp. 131–132.

[14] Miller and Swanson, *op. cit.,* p. 80.

weaken his desire for such independence. While adolescent autonomy may be positively related to the parental practice of explaining rules and requests, it is likely to be inversely related to parental power. By definition, the autocratic type of parent-child interdependence severely limits opportunities for adolescents to acquire wisdom and confidence in independent decision making. Assuming that adolescent autonomy is positively related to the frequency of parental explanations and is negatively related to parental power, we hypothesize that *autonomy is most common among adolescents of permissive parents who explain their requests and is least characteristic of autocratically reared adolescents who seldom receive explanations concerning rules of conduct.*

METHOD

The data for this investigation were obtained from a larger project on adolescence in the Institute for Research in Social Science at the University of North Carolina. This larger study is concerned with determining the affectional, associational, and value orientations of adolescents in grades seven through twelve. Slightly more than half of these respondents were obtained from public schools in central North Carolina, and the rest from both public and parochial school systems in central Ohio. The data were collected in April and May, 1960, with a structured questionnaire administered by teachers in the classroom. The data for this present study were obtained from a 40 per cent sample of the seventh through ninth grade students and 60 per cent of the tenth through twelfth graders, randomly drawn from the 19,200 white adolescents from unbroken homes.

The frequency of parental explanation is measured by two five-response category items which are similar in wording except for the referent.

> When you don't know why your (mother/father) makes a particular decision or has certain rules for you to follow, will (she/he) explain the reason?
>
> Unexplained power expression (low legitimation) (1) Never, (2) Once in a while, (3) Sometimes
> Explained power expression (high legitimation) (4) Usually, (5) Yes, always

The seven types of parent-adolescent interdependence are measured by two seven-response category items, one referring to mother and the other to father. The three levels of parental power are measured by response categories (1) autocratic, (3) democratic, and (5, 6, and 7) permissive, to the following question.

> In general, how are most decisions made between you and your (mother/father)?
>
> AUTOCRATIC
> 1. My (mother/father) just tells me what to do.
>
> DEMOCRATIC
> 3. I have considerable opportunity to make my own decisions, but my (mother/father) has the final word.

PERMISSIVE
5. I can make my own decision but my (mother/father) would like for me to consider (her/his) opinion.
6. I can do what I want regardless of what my (mother/father) thinks.
7. My (mother/father) doesn't care what I do.

PARENTAL POWER AND THE FREQUENCY OF EXPLANATIONS

Differences between autocratic, democratic, and permissive parents are examined with age, sex, and social class of the adolescent controlled (Table 1).[15] The data reveal that democratic and permissive parents are from two to four times as likely to explain their rules and expectations frequently than are autocratic parents.[16] Democratic parents are slightly more likely to explain than are permissive mothers and fathers. These differences are most evident among middle class parents. Generally, class differences are greatest among autocratic mothers and democratic and permissive parents; lower class autocratic mothers and middle class democratic or permissive mothers and fathers are more likely to explain their rules and policy. Mothers are more likely to explain frequently to younger than older adolescents and to girls rather than boys. Age and sex differences are inconsistent for fathers.[17]

Within each age, sex, and class sub-group frequent explanations are least common among autocratic parents and are most common among democratic parents. In most categories, more than 70 per cent of democratic and permissive parents frequently provide reasons for their actions

---

[15] Younger and older adolescents are those in grades seven through nine and ten through twelve, respectively. Adolescents and their families were placed in middle and lower class categories by assigning the youths' fathers' occupations to occupational categories employed by the U.S. Bureau of the Census. "Clerical and kindred workers" and above were classified as middle class. "Farmers, farm managers, and farm laborers" were treated as unclassified. The sample is largely urban.

[16] Nonetheless, the reasonableness of the autocratic parent's child-rearing policy is strongly enhanced when explanations are frequently provided. The evaluations of two groups of autocratically reared adolescents were compared with respect to the fairness of their parents' child rearing policy. One group frequently received explanations when requested and perceived greater freedom in decision making during the past two years, whereas the other group of adolescents was low on both parental explanations and decision-making freedom. The former group of adolescents was more than twice as likely as the latter youths to consider their parents to be usually or more often fair (for older males toward their fathers, 68.7 versus 30.3 per cent). See Elder, *Family Structure and the Transmission of Values and Norms in the Process of Child Rearing*, pp. 637–643.

[17] Tests of significance have not been employed in the evaluation of results due to the nature and size of our sample and to our interest in the general pattern of relationships.

Table 1
Frequent Parental Explanations by Autocratic, Democratic, and Permissive Parents: Age, Sex, and Social Class Controlled

		Frequent Parental Explanations: Per Cent of Adolescents							
		Older Males		Older Females		Younger Males		Younger Females	
Parent	Level of Parental Power	*Middle Class*	*Lower Class*	*Middle Class*	*Lower Class*	*Middle Class*	*Lower Class*	*Middle Class*	*Lower Class*
Mother	Autocratic	(18) 31.6	(35) 42.7	(10) 16.7	(19) 22.5	(25) 31.2	(62) 43.4	(16) 36.4	(50) 37.9
	Democratic	(232) 75.6	(239) 73.8	(243) 79.2	(250) 76.2	(266) 82.1	(218) 72.9	(276) 87.3	(262) 74.6
	Permissive	(190) 73.1	(208) 70.3	(215) 84.0	(228) 76.0	(121) 74.7	(118) 63.4	(144) 79.1	(144) 76.6
Father	Autocratic	(23) 18.7	(36) 19.5	(32) 23.4	(38) 19.0	(39) 34.2	(78) 36.3	(31) 29.8	(64) 27.2
	Democratic	(224) 74.7	(217) 73.8	(285) 79.2	(187) 73.6	(250) 81.7	(176) 64.7	(253) 83.5	(197) 71.4
	Permissive	(130) 75.6	(139) 63.8	(143) 72.2	(168) 70.6	(85) 65.4	(96) 66.7	(108) 72.0	(109) 63.4

when asked to do so, whereas this is true for generally less than 40 per cent of the autocratic parents. Thus autocratic parents are inclined to resist explaining their rules and thereby impose coercive controls and demands.

THE DESIRE TO MODEL

As a measure of the attractiveness of parents, we asked the following question with respect to each parent: "Would you like to be the kind of person your (mother/father) is?" The five responses to this item ranged from "Yes, completely," to "Not at all." The responses, "Yes, completely," "In most ways," and "In many ways," are considered as indicating the desire to model, i.e., to be like mother and/or father. This item taps the degree to which the adolescent values the attributes and behavior of a parent and is not restricted to sex-appropriate behavior.

In accord with our hypothesis, modeling is most typical of democratically reared adolescents who often receive explanations.[18] Non-explaining

---

[18] Both the types of parent-adolescent interdependence and the frequency of parental explanations vary in relation to social class. Given a certain level of parental power along with high or low power legitimation, the effects as manifest in adolescent behavior appear similar among middle and lower class youths. The principal variation by social class is in the contrasting distribution of middle and lower class parents by these two variables.

Table 2
**Levels of Parental Power and Frequency of Explanations
in Relation to Desire of Adolescents to Model Their
Parents: Age and Sex Controlled**

| | | Per Cent of Adolescents Who Would Like To Be the Kind of Person Their Mothers/Fathers Are in Many, Most, or All Ways | | | | | |
| | | Autocratic | | Democratic | | Permissive | |
Parent	Age and Sex	Freq.	Infreq.	Freq.	Infreq.	Freq.	Infreq.
Mother	OM	(41) 77.4	(38) 45.2	(391) 83.4	(100) 62.5	(283) 71.5	(74) 48.1
	YM	(69) 81.1	(66) 48.9	(418) 86.7	(91) 65.5	(136) 57.6	(36) 32.4
	OF	(22) 88.0	(30) 29.7	(499) 93.4	(107) 70.8	(392) 88.2	(68) 59.6
	YF	(57) 85.0	(61) 56.0	(512) 95.0	(90) 69.2	(266) 92.4	(53) 64.6
Father	OM	(42) 71.2	(113) 45.7	(405) 91.8	(119) 76.8	(220) 82.4	(57) 47.5
	YM	(92) 80.0	(123) 58.0	(399) 94.8	(118) 78.7	(164) 90.6	(63) 68.5
	OF	(81) 62.8	(141) 42.0	(243) 78.4	(54) 43.9	(340) 89.9	(58) 64.4
	YF	(43) 45.3	(55) 22.7	(291) 64.1	(50) 39.7	(24) 57.4	(33) 31.1
		Mean Per Cent					
Mother	Boys	79.3	47.0	85.1	63.0	64.6	40.3
	Girls	86.5	42.9	94.2	70.0	90.3	62.1
Father	Boys	75.6	51.9	93.3	77.8	86.5	58.0
	Girls	54.1	32.4	71.3	41.8	73.7	47.8
		Mean Per Cent Difference Between Freq. and Infreq. Explanations					
Mother		38.0		23.2		26.3	
Father		22.7		22.5		27.2	

autocratic and permissive parents are least apt to be modeled. Boys are generally more apt to model their fathers and girls their mothers, regardless of level of power and frequency of explanation.

Explaining parents are in all instances more likely to be modeled than are parents who seldom explain. By removing the control on age and sex and computing mean percentage differences between the proportions of youths who desire to model explaining and non-explaining mothers and fathers by each level of power, we find little variation in the differences—five of the six mean percentage differences fall between 22.5 and 27.2 per cent. Thus, adolescent attraction to parents is increased to a similar degree at most levels of parental power by the frequent explanation of rules.

Democratically reared adolescents are more likely to model their mothers and/or fathers than are adolescents of either autocratic or permissive parents who are comparable in frequency of explanation. Since the democratic type of interdependence facilitates greater parent *and* adolescent involvement in decision making concerning the adolescent than the other two types, this result appears to support the Meadian conception of role learning through interaction.[19] The greater the parent-adolescent interaction, the greater the likelihood that the adolescent will desire to be like his parent. This probability of role imitation seems enhanced considerably when the parent, in addition to frequently interacting with the child, frequently explains the reasons for restrictions and demands which may not be understood.

COMPLIANCE WITH PARENTAL RULES

The economic and educational changes in American society have fostered the emergence of what Coleman describes as adolescent subcultures ". . . with values and activities quite distinct from those of the adult society."[20] The significant effects of peers upon an adolescent's values, academic motivation, and achievement is convincingly documented by the findings of Coleman's study. A stringent test of the degree to which an adolescent would comply with parental rules and requests might be represented by a situation in which his parents objected strongly to some of his friends. The way in which these cross-pressures are resolved—in favor of parents or peers—would reflect the salience of each group relative to the youth's behavior and indicate to some extent the nature of the youth's system of values and moral standards. As an occasion of parent-peer conflict, the following question was asked: "If your parents were to object strongly to some of the friends you had, would you: (1) Stop going with them, (2) See them less, (3) See them secretly, (4) Keep going with them openly?" The first two responses indicate a measure of compliance with parental wishes; the last two represent resolution in favor of peers.

Similar to the results on the modeling of parents, compliance is most common among adolescents with democratic parents who explain their

---

[19] See Orville G. Brim, Jr., "Family Structure and Sex Role Learning by Children: A Further Analysis of Helen Koch's Data," *Sociometry*, 21 (March, 1958), pp. 1–16; and "Personality Development as Role Learning," in I. Iscoe and H. Stevenson (eds.), *Personality Development in Children*, Austin, Texas: University of Texas Press, 1960.

[20] James S. Coleman, "The Adolescent Subculture and Academic Achievement," *American Journal of Sociology*, 65 (January, 1960), p. 337.

Table 3
**Levels of Parental Power and Frequency of Explanations
as Related to Adolescent Compliance with Parental Wishes:
Sex of Adolescent Controlled**

| | | | | Per Cent of Adolescents Who in Response to Strong Parental Objections to Some of Their Friends Would: | | |
| | | | | | | |

Sex	Level of Parental Power	Parental Explanations	N	Stop Going with Them or See Them Less	See Them Secretly or Openly	Total Per Cent
	Autocratic	Freq.	85	70.6	29.4	100
		Infreq.	123	35.0	65.0	100
Boys	Democratic	Freq.	604	74.2	25.8	100
		Infreq.	110	60.9	39.1	100
	Permissive	Freq.	341	66.0	34.0	100
		Infreq.	100	44.0	66.0	100
	Autocratic	Freq.	54	79.6	20.4	100
		Infreq.	107	43.0	57.0	100
Girls	Democratic	Freq.	626	85.0	15.0	100
		Infreq.	84	77.4	22.6	100
	Permissive	Freq.	385	79.8	21.2	100
		Infreq.	75	53.3	46.7	100

rules frequently (Table 3).[21] However, variations in the likelihood of compliance by level of power are pronounced only under conditions of infrequent explanations. Hence, the frequency of parental explanations seems to be more crucial in inducing conformity than level of power. This suggests that level of power may be a more significant factor in regulating observable behavior, while the rationalization of rules by explanations is strongly related to the child's adoption of parental rules. Although no meaningful variations in these results were observed by age, girls are in all instances more likely to claim that they would obey their parents than are boys.

Variations in the frequency of parental explanation have relatively little effect on the likelihood of adolescents' conforming in democratically structured relationships. Presumably an authority structure of this kind engenders mutuality of respect, understanding and trust and reduces the

---

[21] Since compliance to parental wishes and autonomy represent aspects of a child's behavior, it is essential to analyze simultaneously the joint effects of maternal and paternal power and explanations. In order to do this and yet have sufficient cases for analysis, we are forced to limit the analysis to parents who correspond in both level of power and in frequency of explanations.

necessity for explanatory efforts. It appears that as structural asymmetry increases in parent-child relations toward either autocratic control or permissiveness, obedience to parental rules becomes increasingly contingent on explanatory efforts by parents. In addition to the factor of parental affection and explanations, extreme asymmetry in the structure of the child-rearing relationship may be associated with general communication failures in the transmission of rules and values. Under such conditions parents may simply say little and rigorously control their children or detach themselves completely in child rearing.

AUTONOMY

One indication of an adolescent's ability to direct his own behavior is the degree to which he feels confident that his ideas and opinions about what he should do and believe are right and best for him. A youth who expresses confidence in his own values, goals, and awareness of rules is presumably more capable of operating effectively on his own. A second aspect concerns the degree of adolescent self-reliance in problem solving and decision making. When faced with a really important decision about himself and his future, the adolescent who seeks ideas and information from others but makes up his own mind exhibits a high degree of autonomy in problem solving. Two items which measured these two aspects of autonomy were dichotomized and the responses were cross-tabulated to provide four empirical types of dependence-independence; adolescents who have or lack confidence in their own ideas, values, and goals may either be relatively dependent or independent in decision making.

An analysis of the three levels of power and the frequency of parental explanation in relation to these four types of dependence and independence behavior is shown in Table 4. The results partially confirm our hypotheses. As predicted, autonomy (both confident and independent) is most typical of adolescents with parents who are both permissive *and* frequent explainers. On the other hand, we find that youths who seldom receive explanations are least apt to exhibit autonomy, and this result does not vary by level of power.

An examination of variations in the two aspects of autonomy reveals that adolescents with autocratic parents who explain are more apt to feel *self-confident and dependent* in decision making than are children of autocratic parents who seldom explain (a difference of 17.1%), and are more likely to express confidence in their adequacy for self-direction, whether dependent or independent in decision making (a mean difference of 7.5%). There is practically no percentage difference between the proportions of self-confident and independent youths with explaining and non-explaining parents at this level of power. Thus, among adolescents with autocratic parents, those who receive frequent explanations are most likely to report a dependent type of self-confidence in their ideas and values. As the power of parents decreases, explanations have a different effect on adolescent autonomy; they seem to foster a sense of self-confidence and independence in their children.

About fifteen percent of the adolescents with parents who are both autocratic and non-explaining report that they lack confidence in their

Table 4
Levels of Parental Power and Frequency of Explanations in Relation to Types of Adolescent Dependence- Independence Behavior

Level of Parental Power	Parental Explana- tions	N	Lack of Confidence		Confidence		Total Per Cent
			De- pendent	Inde- pendent	De- pendent	Inde- pendent	
Autocratic	Ferq.	139	27.3	6.5	37.4	28.8	100
	Infreq.	231	34.2	14.7	20.3	30.3	100
Democratic	Ferq.	1233	10.5	6.7	37.6	45.2	100
	Infreq.	194	22.7	9.8	35.6	31.9	100
Permissive	Freq.	729	13.2	7.2	29.8	49.8	100
	Infreq.	177	28.2	13.6	24.9	33.3	100

Above columns spanned by: Types of Adolescent Dependence- Independence Behavior[a]

[a] The degree of self-confidence in personal ideas and values was measured by the following item: How confident are you that your own ideas and opinions about what you should do and believe are right and best for you? [Lack of confidence] (1) Not at all confident, (2) Not very confident, (3) I'm a little confident. [Confidence] (4) I'm quite confident, (5) I'm completely confident.

Self-reliance in problem-solving and decision making was measured by the following item: When you have a really important decision to make, about yourself and your future, do you make it on your own, or do you like to get help on it? [Dependent] (1) I'd rather let some one else decide for me, (2) I depend a lot upon other people's advice. (3) I like to get some help. [Independent] (4) Get other ideas then make up my own mind, (5) Make up my own mind without any help.

ideas yet prefer to make important decisions on their own. It is plausible that these adolescents feel the need to depend on their parents but find them rejecting and unsympathetic concerning their problems. Hence they function independently in decision making but do so reluctantly. When age and sex were introduced simultaneously as controls, variations by age were observed; younger adolescents were inclined throughout to be less confident and more dependent. However, this age difference did not appreciably alter the above results.

The application of behavior controls which are seldom explained and hence not understood is likely to appear very arbitrary and unpredictable. Under such circumstances, there is apt to be little security for a child in interaction with a powerful parent.[22] Among adolescents who seldom

[22] An adolescent's feeling of security might be expressed in terms of a power ratio in which his perception of the magnitude of his own power *plus* all friendly or supportive power he can count upon from other sources is in the numerator,

receive explanations of parental requests, autonomy shows a curvilinear relation to level of power. Youths with democratic parents are more likely than adolescents with autocratic or permissive parents to express confidence in and preference for governing themselves. Infrequent explanation is more negatively related to adolescent autonomy on the autocratic than on the permissive level of power.

The effects of parental explanations on adolescent autonomy vary considerably by level of power. Although frequent explanations of rules tend to make them more meaningful and acceptable, they do not encourage autonomy unless accompanied by moderate or low parental power. Freedom to experiment in self-direction and to learn by assuming the responsibilities of decision making appear to be necessary experiences for children to desire and feel confident in self-government. Given this allowance of behavioral freedom, frequent parental explanation of requests and regulations seems to increase markedly the likelihood of adolescent self-confidence and independence in decision making.[23] While autonomy is less probable among youths who seldom receive explanations, it is most common under these conditions among adolescents with democratic parents.

The implications of these results seem particularly relevant to academic motivation and aspiration. If the explanation of autocratic control seems to amplify feelings of dependency in decision making, is this type of power assertion related to low adolescent educational goals and to low aspirations regarding the attainment of these goals? Since a restrictive autocratic regime in child rearing does not encourage a strong achievement orientation,[24] it is probable that frequent explanations on this level of power induce acceptance of such power and heighten passivity and indifference toward scholastic achievement. On the other hand, frequent explanations of rules along with some freedom in self-government are likely to augment a youth's desire to achieve scholastically by giving him a sense of emotional security, by providing him with opportunities to operate on his own, and by strengthening his self-confidence with respect to his ability to be independent.

An examination of data bearing on these possibilities revealed that the frequency of explanations was positively related to adolescent commitment to completing high school and to a desire to go to college if the opportunity were provided, on each level of power. A comparison of the proportions of college-oriented boys in the "explaining" and "non-ex-

---

and with the adolescent's perception of the magnitude of all hostile power that may be used against him in the denominator. See Dorwin Cartwright, "Emotional Dimensions of Group Life," in *Feelings and Emotions,* Martin L. Reynert (ed.), New York: McGraw-Hill Book Co., Inc., 1950, pp. 441–442.

[23] Cf. Lois W. Hoffman, Sidney Rosen and Ronald Lippitt, "Parental Coerciveness, Child Autonomy and Child's Role at School," *Sociometry,* 23 (March, 1960), pp. 15–22, especially p. 20.

[24] See Bernard C. Rosen and R. D'Andrade, "The Psychosocial Origins of Achievement Motivation," *Sociometry,* 22 (September, 1959), pp. 185–218; and Fred L. Strodtbeck, "Family Interaction, Values and Achievement," Chapter V in *Talent and Society,* David McClelland (ed.), New York: D. Van Nostrand, 1958.

plaining" categories by level of power revealed the following percentage differences: 7.1, autocratic; 19.0, democratic; and 15.1, permissive. These differences are similar in each of the four age and sex groups. Thus, it appears that the scholastic impetus provided by autocratic parents, compared to that provided by democratic and permissive parents, is not heightened appreciably by frequent explanations. As in its effects on adolescent autonomy, the level of parental power appears to be the crucial factor.

The relationship between level of power and educational goals and aspirations is curvilinear in form with the frequency of explanations controlled. This relationship is illustrated by the percentage of college-oriented boys who frequently receive explanations from their parents; the respective percentages from autocratic to permissive are 57.1, 78.8 and 69.6. Similar results were obtained for girls. Adolescents with democratic and explaining parents are thus most likely to have high educational goals.

About one-half of the boys and girls in grades seven through nine who have autocratic parents who seldom explain are not sure that they will finish high school. The implications of this result seem relevant to the drop-out problem, particularly in view of findings concerning the character of a group of drop-outs from Chicago schools. In a three year treatment study of 105 drop-outs, Lichter *et al.* found that, "about two-thirds of the boys and one-half of the girls were dependent children who were unwilling to assume any self-responsibility. The boys generally expressed their dependency in open helplessness and the girls by angry demands for gratification."[25]

These findings suggest that the effects of variations in the legitimacy of parental power are altered considerably by level of power. We have observed that explanation on the democratic level has an entirely different effect on adolescent autonomy and educational aspirations than it has on the autocratic level. In comparison, the effects of frequent explanations on adolescent desire to model and obey parents vary much less by level of power. Given infrequent explanations of rules and requests, adolescent modeling and compliance tend to decrease sharply as parental power increases.

By assuming that frequent explanations are an indication of a high degree of parental warmth and that level of power is an indication of both parental warmth and the degree of adolescent freedom in decision making, we are able to see why a child's autonomy in decision making and his educational goals are strongly contingent upon the type of parent-adolescent interdependence. Moderate or low parental power appears to be essential in fostering ambitions and effectiveness outside of the family. With opportunities to develop an instrumental orientation, frequent explanations operate as a positive reinforcement.

Since parental attractiveness and obedience to parental rules have been shown to be heavily dependent on the warmth of parents, it is understandable that the effects of explanation are much greater than the effects

---

[25] Solomon Lichter, Elsie Rapien, Francis Seibert and Morris Sklansky, *The Dropouts,* Glencoe, Illinois: The Free Press, 1962, p. 249.

of level of power on these two variables. Thus, while adolescents who receive frequent explanations from autocratic parents are inclined to model their parents and to obey them, they are most likely to be dependent on them in decision making and to be indifferent concerning school and college. In conclusion, parental explanation is related to a strong parent orientation, while the level of parental power determines whether the child is over-protected and over-controlled.

SUMMARY

The frequency of parental explanations, employed as a measure of the degree of power legitimation, was analyzed in relation to adolescent desire to model parents, obedience to parental rules, and autonomy in decision making on three levels of parental power. Previous research on the effects of legitimate versus coercive power has generally overlooked the significance and potential modifying effects of levels of power. Data for this investigation were obtained from a structured questionnaire administered to white adolescents who lived with both parents in the states of Ohio and North Carolina.

We find that adolescents are more likely to model their parents and to associate with parent-approved peers if their parents explain their rules frequently when asked to do so. The attractiveness of parents as models is less among autocratic and permissive parents than among democratic parents regardless of the frequency of explanations. Variations in compliance by level of power are evident only when explanations are seldom explained—here we find that adolescents with democratic parents are most apt to abide by parental objections to some of their friends.

With the exception of autocratic parents and their adolescents, we find similar results with respect to adolescent autonomy. Generally, adolescents with democratic or permissive parents are much more likely to be confident in their ideas and opinions and to be independent in decision making if their parents explain their rules often than if they do not explain. However, frequent explanations on the autocratic level of power were more related to dependency, which may or may not be of a self-confident type. Infrequent explanations by autocratic parents were related to both low confidence and independence in decision making. Thus, the legitimizing of parental dominance has the effect of making this power more acceptable, and, in doing so, heightens dependency needs as well as self-confidence.

The implications of these results were explored for scholastic motivation and college aspirations. The strongest commitment to high school graduation and to obtaining a college education was evident under conditions of frequent explanations and moderate or low parental power. The effects of level of power appeared to be stronger than the effects of parental explanation.

In summary, the effects of parental explanations on adolescent behavior are generally modified by the level of parental power—whether the parent is autocratic, democratic, or permissive. Thus, any appraisal of the relationship between parental power legitimation and adolescent adjustment and development should include the effects of variations in parental power.

parent-adolescent relationships and adolescent independence in the United States and Denmark

Gerald S. Lesser
Denise Kandel
Harvard University

This paper examines patterns of interactions between adolescents and their parents in two cultures, the United States and Denmark. We focus in particular on factors within the family which promote the development of independence, clearly the major task facing both adolescents and parents during the adolescent period.

The data come from a larger study concerned with the internal structure and relative influence of families and peer groups in the United States and Denmark.

METHOD

A. SAMPLE

In the spring and summer of 1965, data were collected from all students in three high schools in the United States (N = 2,327) and 12 secondary schools in Denmark (N = 1,552) through the use of structured questionnaires. In addition, the students' mothers were asked to complete self-

Based on a paper presented at the Groves Conference, Boston, Massachusetts, April, 1968. The research and analyses reported herein were supported through the Cooperative Research Program of the Office of Education (Project #2139, OE-4-10-069) and by the Harvard University Center for Research and Development in Educational Differences (Office of Education Contract OE-5-10-239). We would like to thank the Bureau of Applied Social Research, Columbia University, for providing technical assistance with the processing of the data.

Reprinted from the Journal of Marriage and the Family, 1969, 31, 348–358. By permission of the National Council on Family Relations.

administered, structured mailed questionnaires containing many questions identical to those included in the students' instrument: 70 per cent of the mothers in the United States and 75 per cent in Denmark returned their questionnaires.[1] The findings to be discussed in this chapter are based on data from students of matched adolescent-mother pairs from intact families;[2] there are 1,141 such pairs in the American sample and 977 in the Danish.[3] The proportion of boys in these pairs is 51 per cent in the United States and 48 per cent in Denmark.

The samples in this study were not selected to be representative of the total adolescent population in each country, but rather to include schools in different ecological settings, such as rural and urban. While an attempt was made to match Danish and American schools on that basis, differences appear in the demographic characteristics of the American and Danish families sampled.[4] The American families are larger than the Danish ones. Because of differences in the secondary school system of the two countries, the Danish students in the sample are slightly younger than the Americans. The median age of the Americans is 16 years as compared to 15 years for the Danes. There are also large differences in the occupational distribution of the two samples. The Danish sample contains a much larger proportion of farmers (24 per cent) and managers

---

[1] An analysis of possible response bias among respondent and non-respondent mothers was carried out by comparing the answers from students whose parents replied and of those whose parents did not reply. Overall, the group of responding mothers does not differ from non-responding mothers on the variables we studied: socio-demographic characteristics and family patterns. However, most previous studies of respondent bias in mail questionnaires have found that non-respondents are of lower socioeconomic background than respondents (Mildred Parten, *Surveys, Polls and Samples,* New York: Harper & Bros., 1950; Leo G. Reeder, "Mailed Questionnaires in Longitudinal Health Studies: The Problem of Maintaining and Maximizing Response," *Journal of Health and Human Behavior,* 1 (1960), pp. 123–129; Claire Selltiz *et al., Research Methods in Social Relations,* New York: Holt-Dryden, 1959; Edward A. Suchman and Boyd McCandless, "Who Answers Questionnaires," *Journal of Applied Psychology,* 24 (1940), pp. 445–455). An exception has been reported in the family literature. F. Ivan Nye, "Marital Interaction," pp. 263–281, in *The Employed Mother in America,* ed. by F. Ivan Nye and Lois W. Hoffman, Chicago: Rand McNally & Co., 1963, reports similar response rates to a mailed questionnaire among middle- and lower-class mothers.

[2] The proportion of presently married mothers (intact families) is slightly higher in Denmark (90 per cent) than in the United States (83 per cent).

[3] The patterns of family life reported by adolescents from intact families in the total sample and the more restricted sample of matched adolescent-mother pairs are identical. The decision to restrict the analysis to a sample of adolescents from intact families with a respondent mother was motivated by the requirements of the analysis reported in this paper as well as those of the overall study. We were interested in (1) the father's as well as the mother's role in the family, (2) comparing the adolescents' and the mothers' reports of the same family events, (3) analyzing concordance in values between mother and child and the effects of family patterns on transmission of values from parent to child.

[4] Kandel *et al., op. cit.*

and officials (28 per cent) and smaller proportion of skilled (15 per cent) and unskilled workers (20 per cent) than the American sample where these groups amount to two per cent, 11 per cent, 36 per cent, and 34 per cent, respectively.

We were concerned, therefore, that the differences in family patterns observed between the Danish and American samples might reflect structural or occupational characteristics[5] of each sample rather than true cultural differences. However, we examined the effect of each of these factors, and in particular father's occupation, on the patterns of family interaction to be described below and found no significant or consistent differences among the different occupational groups in the two countries.[6] Therefore, while the cross-cultural comparisons to be presented do not control for father's occupation, this probably does not affect the cross-cultural differences that appear.

Overall, in both countries, the patterns of family life reported by the

---

[5] For a review of existing American studies on the effect of size on family functioning, see John A. Clausen and Judith R. Williams, "Sociological Correlates of Child Behavior," in *Child Psychology*, ed. by Harold W. Stevenson, Chicago: Yearbook of the National Society for the Study of Education, 1963, pp. 62–107; and John A. Clausen et al., *Family Size and Birth Order as Influences upon Socialization and Personality: Bibliography and Abstracts*, mimeographed, July 1965. Glen H. Elder and Charles E. Bowerman, "Family Structure and Child-Rearing Patterns: The Effect of Family Size and Sex Composition," *American Sociological Review*, 28 (1963), pp. 891–905, report a very slight tendency for parents who have three or more children living at home to be more authoritarian than parents with fewer children. A large number of American studies have reported on the differences between the middle and the lower class on child-rearing attitudes, parental values, and family power structure. See for instance Robert Blood and Donald Wolfe, *Husbands and Wives*, Glencoe, Illinois: Free Press, 1960; Urie Bronfenbrenner, "Socialization and Social Class Through Time and Space," in *Readings in Social Psychology*, ed. by Eleanor Maccoby, Theodore Newcomb, and Eugene Hartley, New York: Henry Holt and Company, 1961, pp. 400–425; Melvin L. Kohn, "Social Class and Parental Values," *American Journal of Sociology*, 64 (1959), pp. 337–351; Melvin L. Kohn, "Social Class and the Exercise of Parental Authority," *American Sociological Review*, 24 (1959), pp. 352–366; Donald G. McKinley, *Social Class and Family Life*, New York: The Free Press, 1964; Leonard I. Pearlin and Melvin L. Kohn, "Social Class, Occupation, and Parental Values: A Cross-National Study," *American Sociological Review*, 31 (1966), pp. 466–479; and William H. Sewell, "Some Recent Developments in Socialization Theory and Research," *Annals of the American Academy of Political and Social Sciences*, 349 (1963), pp. 163–181. Glen H. Elder, "Structural Variations in the Child-Rearing Relationship," *Sociometry*, 25 (1962), pp. 241–262, however reports only very slight differences between middle-class and lower-class parents in the amount of control they exercise over their adolescent children.

[6] The unexpectedness of these results led us to reexamine closely some of the findings presented by previous investigators. It would seem that some well-accepted conclusions are not substantiated clearly by the data which are presented in evidence. For instance, the table which is used by Blood and Wolfe (*op. cit.*, Table 8, p. 33) to demonstrate the direct relationship between social class and husband's authority in the family shows a *curvilinear* rather than a linear relationship.

mothers are similar to those reported by the adolescents. This paper is based upon the adolescents' answers.

B. QUESTIONNAIRES

Data from respondents were collected through self-administered structured questionnaires. The topics included, among others, adolescents' values and attitudes and patterns of family interaction. Identical forms of the questionnaire were used in both countries.[7]

Great care was taken to insure that the questions asked, which had been developed in the United States, would be relevant in Denmark. In the effort to establish conceptual as well as linguistic equivalence of the questionnaire items, the pretesting of instruments combined back translation[8] with both individual and group field interviewing in the following sequence:

1. The original questionnaires were translated into Danish; then another translator independently translated this Danish version back into English (back translation).

2. Original and retranslated English versions were then compared and discrepancies clarified and corrected.

3. A second Danish version was then pretested in interviews with individual adolescents, with probes used to assess the meaning of the questions to them.

4. Based upon this pretest information, the Danish questionnaire was again revised and then back translated into English and then once again into Danish.

5. Field interviewing in small groups constituted the next trial phase.

6. A final back translation was performed.

In these successive cycles of translation, back translation, individual field testing, back translation, group field testing, and additional translation, the back translation steps attempted to reach linguistic equivalence, while the interspersed field interviewing attempted to approach conceptual equivalence in the meaning of the questions.

RESULTS

The analysis that follows is divided into three sections and examines the following points: (1) the distribution of patterns of parent-adolescent interaction in the United States and Denmark, (2) the independence which adolescents experience in both countries, and (3) the association between family patterns and feelings of independence.

---

[7] For more details, see Kandel *et al., op. cit.*

[8] Irwin Deutscher, "Language and Human Conduct: Some Problems of Comparability in Cross-Cultural and Interpersonal Contexts," in *Institutions and the Person,* ed. by Howard Becker, Blanche Geer, David Riesman, and Robert Weiss, Chicago: Aldine, 1968.

1. PATTERNS OF PARENT-ADOLESCENT INTERACTION IN THE UNITED STATES AND DENMARK

A. Parental Authority. As an index of parental power structure, patterns of decision-making between parent and adolescent were used. These patterns were measured by two five-response category items, one for the mother and one for the father. These items were modified from Bowerman and Elder, and Elder.[9]

Three types of power were defined:

> Authoritarian: The parent makes all decisions relevant to the adolescent.
> Democratic: Decisions are made jointly by the child and his parent.
> Permissive: The adolescent has more influence in making decisions than his parent.

Striking differences exist between Danish and American families in the distribution of these patterns of parental authority. Some of these differences have been discussed elsewhere[10] and they will only be reviewed briefly here.

In both countries, the father relates in a more authoritarian manner to his children than the mother.[11] However, the Danes report democratic and equalitarian patterns between parents and adolecents to a much greater extent than the Americans.[12] The relative predominance of one pattern of parental authority over the other in the two countries is illustrated even more vividly when one considers simultaneously the authority patterns of mother and father in the same family. The predominant family combination in Denmark is the joint democratic (41 per cent); the predominant American pattern is the joint authoritarian (32 per cent).[13]

Consistent with their more autocratic control, American parents insist on many more specific rules than do the Danes. Respondents were presented with a list of eight rules and asked to check which ones the parents had for their teen-age children in the family: 55 per cent of the American adolescents indicate that their parents have three or more rules for them as compared to only 29 per cent of the Danes.

---

[9] Charles E. Bowerman and Glen H. Elder, "Variations in Adolescent Perception of Family Power Structure," *American Sociological Review*, 29 (1964), pp. 551–567; Elder, *op. cit.*

[10] Denise B. Kandel and Gerald S. Lesser, "Parental Relationships of Adolescents in the United States and Denmark," *Transactions of the 6th World Congress of Sociology*, 4, Louvain: Editions Nauwelaerts, 1968.

[11] The greater authoritarianism of the adolescent's father as compared to the mother is also reported by Elder (*op. cit.*) for the United States.

[12] Bowerman and Elder's (*op. cit.*, "Variations in Adolescent Perception of Family Power Structure") measure of type of authority included seven decision-making alternatives which were combined differently than the five alternatives of the present study. If one collapses the Bowerman-Elder categories to produce our categories, the Bowerman-Elder sample contains an even smaller proportion of truly democratic families than the present American one.

[13] Kandel and Lesser, *op. cit.*

The differences in prevalence of the democratic pattern in both countries do not explain the differences in number of rules. While the number of rules in a family is directly related to the amount of power which parents exercise toward their children in the decision-making process, the cross-cultural differences in number of rules persist even when type of power is held constant. Within each pattern, Danish mothers and fathers have fewer rules for their children than the Americans. (Data are not presented.)

B. Communication Between Parents and Adolescents. Danish parents and their adolescents also communicate with each other more extensively than do American parents and their children. Danish parents provide more explanations for their decisions and rules than the American parents (see Table 1). (In both countries, fathers provide fewer explanations than mothers.) In addition, Danish adolescents are more likely than Americans to discuss their personal problems with their parents (Table 1).

Although a strong relationship exists between type of parental authority and the frequency of parental explanations for rules, the cross-cultural differences in frequency of explanations are reduced only slightly when type of parental authority is controlled for. Within each pattern, the Danish parent is more likely to provide explanations than the American. (Data are not presented.)

C. Other Patterns. With respect to the other patterns investigated—reliance, affective behavior, and modeling—in both countries adolescents have close relationships with their parents. However, the Danes are somewhat less likely than the Americans to rely upon the mother for advice; they are also less close to the mother and less likely than the Americans to want to be the kind of person the mother is. By contrast, they are closer to the father and are more likely than the Americans to rely upon the father for advice, to enjoy doing things with him, and to want to be the kind of person he is (Table 1).

It is against the background of the Danish data that the relative importance of the mother in the American family assumes its full significance.[14]

2. ADOLESCENT INDEPENDENCE

A. When Are Rules Instituted? American and Danish parents differ not only with respect to the number of rules they insist upon, but also with

---

[14] In this discussion of cross-cultural differences, within-family differences which result from the sex of the child have been purposely ignored. The same general cross-cultural differences appear among both boys and girls, and the same intra-family variations appear in both countries. Overall, one can observe in both countries a somewhat warmer and more intimate contact between children and parents of the same sex than of the opposite sex. The differences in many instances are small. Furthermore, while girls are consistently closer to their mothers than to their fathers, boys are not always closer to their fathers than to their mothers.

Table 1
Adolescent's Perceptions of Patterns of Interaction with Mother and Father, by Country

Family Pattern	Interaction with Mother United States	Interaction with Mother Den-mark	Interaction with Father United States	Interaction with Father Den-mark	Cross-Cultural Differences Mother	Cross-Cultural Differences Father
Parental Authority						
Authoritarian	43	15	53	31	.001	.001
Democratic	40	61	29	48		
Permissive	17	24	18	21		
Total N	(983)	(950)	(955)	(936)		
Communication						
Per cent of Adolescents						
Who feel that parent "always"						
explains her (his) decisions	30	43	21	33	.001	.001
Total N	(973)	(937)	(954)	(930)		
Who talk over "most" or "all"						
their problems with parent	41	52	23	26	.001	.001
Total N	(970)	(946)	(952)	(938)		
Reliance						
Per cent of Adolescents						
Who depend "very much" or						
"quite a bit" on parent for						
advice and guidance	59	54	43	50	.05	.05
Total N	(825)	(852)	(827)	(846)		
Affective Relations						
Closeness to parent						
Extremely close	33	22	21	19	.001	.001
Quite close	30	35	29	36		
Moderately close	26	30	27	31		
Not close	11	13	23	14		
Total N	(967)	(944)	(935)	(936)		
Per cent of Adolescents						
Who enjoy doing "many"						
things with parent	35	35	34	43	ns	.001
Total N	(971)	(941)	(953)	(941)		
Modeling						
Wanting to be like parent in						
Most ways	42	30	36	36	.001	.001
Many ways	21	40	21	38		
Few ways	37	30	43	26		
Total N	(968)	(941)	(937)	(935)		

*Significance of differences *between* countries for each pattern, as measured by Chi-square.

Table 2
Adolescent's Behavior and Existence of Rule in Family, by Country

	United States		Denmark	
	Does Rule Exist about Time on TV?		**Does Rule Exist about Time on TV?**	
Adolescent Behavior: Per Cent	*Yes*	*No*	*Yes*	*No*
Watching TV 1 hour or less	41%	27%**	39%	66%**
Total N	(157)	(746)	(89)	(828)
	about time on homework?		about time on homework?	
Spending 2 hours or more on homework	26	19**	39	48
Total N	(291)	(604)	(234)	(632)
	against going steady?		against going steady?	
Not going steady	70	59*	48	63*
Total N	(140)	(559)	(84)	(564)

* Differences within each country significant at .05 (Chi-square test).
** Differences within each country significant at .001 (Chi-square test).

respect to the conditions under which they apply these rules. The patterns of socialization of adolescents by their parents—the need for rules and the specific ways in which rules function—appear to be completely the opposite in the United States and Denmark. For three areas for which the adolescent has been asked about parental rules, information is also available about the adolescent's corresponding behavior. These areas are television watching, number of hours on homework, and going steady.

The relationship between rule and behavior appears in Table 2. For each area, it has been assumed that the following behaviors on the part of the adolescent represent the kind of behavior which parents try to enforce with their rule: watching television as little as possible (one hour or less), doing homework for two hours or more, and not going steady. The association between rules and (assumed) preferred behavior operates in opposite directions in the two countries. In the United States the proportion of adolescents showing the behavior favored by parents is *highest* when the parents have a *specific* rule about it. In Denmark it is *highest* when there is *no* rule. For instance, the proportion of adolescents watching TV for one hour or less every day in the United States is 41 per cent when the parents have a rule about number of hours spent watching television as against only 27 per cent when they have no rule. In Denmark the corresponding percentages are 39 and 66. Similar differences appear with respect to the other two areas.

Those associations throw some light on the functioning of the family in the United States and Denmark. The data suggest the existence of two different patterns of adolescent socialization in the two countries: external constraints in the United States versus internalized norms in Denmark. In the United States, parents apparently need to enforce specific rules in order to insure that the adolescent does what is expected of him. If there are no rules, the adolescent is likely to engage in the disapproved behavior. In Denmark the adolescents appear to have internalized their parents' wishes and to behave in the approved fashion without any further external constraints. Rules are instituted in those cases in which Danish adolescents do not yet do what is expected of them. Thus, the Danish adolescent appears better able to act in a self-governing and independent fashion than the American.

These findings suggest also that the different socialization patterns during adolescence may be a consequence of different socialization practices during childhood. We would suggest that the American parent fails to limit the behavior of the child adequately so as to lead him to acquire some self-discipline early in life, while the Danish parent exercises greater control in childhood leading to greater self-direction in adolescence. If the speculation is correct, there would thus be early permissiveness and later constraint in the United States versus early control and later independence in Denmark. Data are not currently available to test these hypotheses. But the early permissiveness of American parents has been amply documented in existing American parent-child studies and has been one of the aspects of American life most frequently commented upon by foreigners.[15] No data are available about early child-rearing practices in Denmark.

B. The Independence of Danish Adolescents. A series of additional findings provide evidence that the Danish adolescent is not only treated more like an adult by his parents but also that he feels *subjectively* more independent from his parents than does the American.

The feeling of independence from parents expresses itself in a variety of ways. For example, in case of a conflict with parents, Danes are more likely than the Americans to act according to their own rather than their parents' wishes. When asked what they would do if their parents were to object to their friends, more Danes than Americans say they would continue to see these friends (Table 3). More Danish than American adolescents also believe (1) that they hold opinions different from their parents' and (2) are granted the freedom from both parents which they, the adolescents, think they should have[16] (Table 3). Similarly, about twice as many Americans as Danes believe that their parents should treat them more like an adult than they do at present (Table 3). The last two items are very highly correlated: students who experience freedom are less

---

[15] Geoffrey Gorer, *The American People,* New York: W. W. Norton & Company, 1948.
[16] The exact text of the question is: "Do your parents give you as much freedom as you think you *should* have?" Responses are: yes, both do; mother does; father does; neither does.

Table 3

Feelings of Independence from Parents, by Country

Per Cent of Adolescents	United States	Denmark
Who would continue to see friends openly when parents objected to friends	44	53
Total N	(1,030)	(943)
Who feel that their opinions are different from those of their parents	42	61
Total N	(822)	(883)
Who feel they get enough freedom from both parents	63	78
Total N	(829)	(860)
Who feel their parents should treat them more like adults	59	32
Total N	(703)	(686)

Differences between countries for total sample for each variable significant at p < .001 level (Chi-square test).

likely to wish their parents would treat them more like adults. However, among American adolescents who feel they get enough freedom, almost half feel it is given to them in such a way that nevertheless they do not feel they are being treated as adults. (Data are not presented.)

It can be argued that the adolescent's satisfaction with the degree of freedom granted to him by his parents depends as much upon his *subjective* definition of how much freedom is enough freedom as upon the *actual* amount of liberty granted him. The American adolescent's relative dissatisfaction with the amount of freedom granted him by his parents could reflect greater absolute demands on his part as compared to the Danes. However, the data indicate that the subjective feeling of freedom is based upon reality. The smaller the number of rules, the stronger the feeling of satisfaction with the amount of freedom granted by parents[17] (Table 4). The satisfaction expressed by the child therefore appears to be an accurate indicator of the independence with which he is being raised. Greater freedom and independence are being granted the adolescent in Denmark than in the United States.

That American parents treat their children as children for a longer period of time than the Danes becomes even more apparent when one examines adolescents of different ages. In both countries, as adolescents grow older, the number of rules decreases and the proportion of adolescents experiencing adequate freedom increases. But the American adoles-

---

[17] The same findings obtain on the mother's report of number of rules in the family.

Table 4
Feelings of Independence by Number of Rules and Country

	United States			Denmark		
	Number of Rules			**Number of Rules**		
Per Cent of Adolescents	0–1	2–3	4 & over	0–1	2–3	4 & over
Who feel that both parents have given them enough freedom	75	63	56	88	71	63
Total N	(197)	(338)	(281)	(423)	(301)	(127)
Who feel that parents should treat them more like adults	48	55	67	27	39	37
Total N	(174)	(278)	(241)	(347)	(242)	(92)

Chi-square differences within countries significant at .01.

Table 5
Independence by Age and Country

	United States					Denmark				
	Age					**Age**				
Per Cent of Adolescents	14	15	16	17	18	14	15	16	17	18
Who report* 0–1 rules	11%	22%	21%	27%	32%	42%	40%	53%	55%	58%
Total N	(35)	(143)	(247)	(303)	(175)	(12)	(292)	(297)	(245)	(72)
Who feel that both parents give them enough freedom**	49	59	54	66	78	66	78	75	82	86
Total N	(35)	(131)	(223)	(282)	(155)	(12)	(275)	(275)	(225)	(73)
Who say parents should treat them more like adults†	72	56	56	59	59	67	35	32	31	18
Total N	(29)	(117)	(183)	(232)	(139)	(9)	(213)	(212)	(191)	(61)

* United States tau-beta = −.082, p < .01; Denmark, tau-beta = −.160, p < .01.
** United States Chi-square p < .001; Denmark, Chi-square ns.
† United States tau-beta = −.002, ns; Denmark, tau-beta = .083, p < .05.

Table 6
**Feelings of Independence by Joint Parental Authority
Pattern and Country**

Per Cent of Adolescents	United States Joint Parental Authority			Denmark Joint Parental Authority		
	Authoritarian	*Democratic*	*Permissive*	*Authoritarian*	*Democratic*	*Permissive*
Who feel both parents give them enough freedom	58	82	68	60	88	78
Total N	(239)	(164)	(76)	(83)	(345)	(120)
Who feel parents should treat them more like adults	63	44	64	46	21	39
Total N	(201)	(133)	(63)	(59)	(276)	(105)

Chi-square differences within countries significant at .001.

cent is still subject to more rules at the age of 18 than the Dane at 14 years (Table 5). The proportion of adolescents satisfied with the amount of freedom granted them by both parents is at the same level among the 14-year-old Danes as among the 17-year-old Americans (Table 5); and while at 18 years of age 59 per cent of Americans say that their parents should treat them more like adults than they presently do, only 18 per cent of Danes feel this way (Table 5). Furthermore, the proportion of children desiring more adult status remains at a constant level in the United States at ages 15 through 18, while in Denmark this proportion decreases consistently with age.

Thus, the pattern of adolescent socialization seems to be different in the United States and Denmark, the Danish adolescents experiencing an increasing degree of independence through his teens while the American appears to remain at a stationary and less emancipated level.

3. FAMILY PATTERNS AND INDEPENDENCE

In both countries, feelings of independence from parents are associated with certain family patterns. It was noted earlier that the fewer the rules in the family, the greater the feelings of independence experienced by adolescents (Table 4). However, permissiveness in decision-making, as such, does not lead to most intense feelings of being granted independence. As shown in Table 6, most freedom and most satisfaction with adult status granted by parents are experienced by children of democratic mothers and fathers who engage their children actively in the decision-

Table 7
Feelings of Independence by Joint Parental Explanations
for Rules and Country

	United States Joint Frequency of Explanations*			Denmark Joint Frequency of Explanations*		
Per Cent of Adolescents	Both Parents High	One High One Low	Both Parents Low	Both Parents High	One High One Low	Both Parents Low
Who feel both parents give them enough freedom	79	57	50	85	70	63
Total N	(300)	(293)	(224)	(558)	(176)	(107)
Who feel parents should treat them more like adults	47	51	68	26	40	54
Total N	(249)	(180)	(186)	(447)	(147)	(80)

* Frequency of parental explanations was defined as follows: high: parents explain "usually" or "always"; low: parents explain "sometimes," "once in a while," or "never."
Chi-square differences within countries significant at .001.

making process.[18] Similarly, the adolescents' subjective feelings of independence are enhanced when parents provide many explanations for their rules and decisions (Table 7).[19]

---

[18] Since the independence questions asked about parents in general, the joint mother and father authority pattern was considered. It was noted earlier that while feelings of being granted sufficient freedom and of being treated as an adult are highly interrelated, they are not identical. Table 6 shows this clearly. While the permissive authority pattern leads to greater feelings of freedom than the authoritarian pattern, both patterns lead to the same degree of dissatisfaction with the adult status granted by parents. This suggests that the permissive pattern is often interpreted by the child as an expression of disinterest and disengagement on the part of his parent (for other supporting data, see Kandel *et al., op. cit.*).

[19] We investigated feelings of independence while controlling simultaneously for parental authority and frequency of explanations. The findings do not support Elder's conclusion that autonomy in adolescents is highest among those with parents who are both permissive and high explainers (Glen H. Elder, "Parental Power Legitimation and Its Effects on the Adolescent," *Sociometry*, 26 (1963), pp. 50–65). In the present sample, most independence is experienced by children of democratic

Table 8
Patterns of Interaction with Mother by Country and Freedom from Mother

| | Gets Enough Freedom from Mother* | | | |
| | United States | | Denmark | |
Per Cent of Adolescents	*Yes*	*No*	*Yes*	*No*
Who talk over most problems with mother	48	19	54	32
Who depend very much upon mother for advice	28	9	20	8
Who enjoy doing many things with mother	43	15	37	24
Who feel extremely close to mother	37	16	26	5
Who want to be like mother	50	18	34	16
Total N	(616)	(201)	(733)	(116)

* Answers to question "Do your parents give you as much freedom as you think you *should* have?" were combined into the following two categories: yes = yes both do, mother does; no = father does, neither does.

All Chi-square differences within each country significant at .001.

The patterns of parent-adolescent interaction which are associated with feelings of independence were noted above to be more characteristic of Danish families than of the American. However, the cross-cultural differences in the frequency of these family patterns do not account entirely for the cross-cultural difference in adolescents' feelings of independence, especially with respect to feeling that one is being granted adequate adult status. With respect to feelings of freedom, Table 6 shows that when type of parental authority is held constant, cross-cultural differences have completely disappeared among the authoritarian families and are very much reduced in the other two patterns. When frequency of parental explanations is held constant, cross-cultural differences in feeling of freedom are reduced only when parents provide frequent explanations (Table 7). And even when they are subject to the same number of rules, more Danes than Americans are satisfied with the amount of freedom granted them.

The cross-cultural differences in satisfaction with adult status granted by parents are not much affected when family patterns are held constant, except for frequency of parental explanations.

parents who are high explainers. These differences may result from differences in the definitions of parental authority in the two studies. However, we find, as Elder, that at each level of power, frequent explanations enhance the feeling of independence of the adolescent.

The family patterns examined so far pertain to the parents' interactions toward their children. As regards the child's interaction with his parents, in both countries, the feeling of being granted adequate independence from parents is associated with positive interactions with parents. Far from leading to estrangement from parents, the enhanced feeling of independence is associated with closeness to parents and positive feelings toward them. Thus, many of the adolescents in the sample are able to develop a sense of autonomy while maintaining close relationships with their parents.[20]

Students who feel they get enough freedom from their parents are more likely to feel extremely close to them, to enjoy doing many things with them, to talk most problems over with them, to depend upon their parents for advice, to want to be like their parents in many ways. Illustrative data for mother appear in Table 8. Similar results obtain for father, but the supporting data are not presented.

Table 9 illustrates the strong positive association that exists between the adolescents' satisfaction with the freedom granted them by their parents and their attitudes toward their parents. In both countries, adolescents who experience sufficient freedom less frequently see their parents as old-fashioned, less frequently report that it is harder to get along with them than it used to be, or report conflicts[21] with their mother or their father than adolescents who yearn for greater freedom.

It is clear that in contrast to the strong cross-cultural differences observed in the distribution of family patterns, the relationship of family patterns to other variables follows *identical* trends in both the United States and Denmark. The fact that some cross-cultural differences in feelings of independence still persist when relevant family patterns are held constant shows that adolescents and their families exist within a larger social and cultural context which exercises its influence beyond that of the family itself.

DISCUSSION AND CONCLUSION

Contrary to the commonly held belief that adolescents are estranged from their parents, the present data suggest that in the United States and Denmark adolescents are close to their parents,[22] in particular to their mothers.

---

[20] Elizabeth B. Murphey, Earle Silber, George V. Coelho, David A. Hamburg, and Irwin Greenberg, "Development of Autonomy and Parent-Child Interaction in Late Adolescence," *American Journal of Orthopsychiatry,* 33 (1963), pp. 643–652.

[21] The item about conflicts is based on an open-ended question which asked the adolescent to list the kinds of things about which he had experienced most conflicts and disagreements with each of his parents over the past year.

[22] A recently completed study, based on a representative sample of American adolescents, now provides supporting evidence for this conclusion (IRS National Survey of Youth, 1967, A Report to Participants).

Table 9

Attitudes Toward Parents by Country and Freedom from Parents

| | Freedom from Parents | | | | | | | |
| | United States | | | | Denmark | | | |
Per Cent of Adolescents	Both Enough	Yes Mother	Yes Father	Neither Enough	Both Enough	Yes Mother	Yes Father	Neither Enough
Who say it is harder for them to get along with their parents	29	32	55	53**	26	41	49	44**
Who feel that their parents are old-fashioned	17	33	32	55**	14	36	28	56**
Who mention one or more specific conflicts with mother during the past year	68	74	81	81*	57	62	78	86**
Who mention one or more specific conflicts with father during the past year	59	69	70	67*	42	71	48	78**
Total N	(520)	(99)	(47)	(154)	(668)	(66)	(53)	(64)

* Differences within each country significant at .05 (Chi-square test).
** Differences within each country significant at .001 (Chi-square test).

Five general areas of interaction were examined: authority, communication, reliance, affective behavior, and modeling.

The patterns reported by adolescents in the two countries differ most dramatically in the areas of parental authority and communication. Families where the parent alone makes decisions have been characterized as "authoritarian"; where both parent and child decide jointly, as "democratic"; and where the child alone decides, as "permissive." The authoritarian pattern is the one most frequently observed in the United States, whether the practice of mothers alone, of fathers alone, or of the two jointly are considered. The authoritarian pattern is infrequent in Denmark, and the modal family pattern is the democratic. American families have more rules and provide fewer explanations for their rules and decisions than do Danish families. Danish adolescents are more likely than the Americans to discuss their problems with their parents. The prominence of the mother in the American family is revealed in the cross-cultural distribution of adolescent dependence for advice on his mother, closeness to her, and desire to be the same kind of person she is.

A most striking cross-cultural difference appears around the issue of independence. Danish adolescents have a strong subjective sense of their independence from parental influence: they feel more frequently than the Americans that they would disregard their parents' wishes about not seeing friends, that their opinions are different from those of their parents, that they are being treated like adults by their parents and get sufficient freedom from their parents.[23] Furthermore, in contrast to the Danes, American adolescents appear unable to behave according to their parents' wishes unless their parents have clear and specific rules for them. These findings, thus, do not support the widespread belief that American adolescents act independently and are encouraged by their parents to be independent at an earlier age than Europeans.[24]

In both countries, feelings of independence are enhanced when parents have few rules, when they provide explanations for their rules, and when they are democratic and engage the child actively in the decision-making process. Furthermore, feelings of independence from parents in both countries, far from leading to rebelliousness, are associated with closeness to parents and positive attitudes toward them.

Thus, while the two countries are characterized by different distributions of family patterns, the interrelationships among these patterns and the consequences for adolescent socialization follow similar trends in

---

[23] This independence may express itself in a variety of ways, including the sexual sphere. For example, Harold T. Christensen and George R. Carpenter, "Value-Behavior Discrepancies Regarding Premarital Coitus," *American Sociological Review,* 27 (1962), pp. 66–74, found a greater permissiveness in attitudes and behaviors regarding premarital sexual intimacy among university students in Denmark than in the United States.

[24] Lenore Boehm, "The Development of Independence: A Comparative Study," *Child Development,* 28 (1957), pp. 85–92, Lawrence Wylie, "Youth in France and the United States," *Daedalus,* 91 (1962), pp. 198–215.

both countries.[25] For example, the implications of authority structure for independence are the same in the United States and Denmark. Parental authority, which is defined along a continuum involving the child's participation in the decision-making process, is related in a curvilinear fashion to the feeling of independence. Children with democratic parents experience most freedom. Similarly, Devereaux and his collaborators[26] found differences in socialization practices of parents in England, Germany, and the United States, but great uniformities in the interrelationships among different variables within each country. These cross-cultural data suggest that, while socialization practices of families in the Western world differ somewhat, the consequences of particular practice for the child are similar within each culture.

The overall similarity in the interrelationships among variables in both countries should not conceal the possibility that differences in the distribution of the items and the preponderance of particular patterns in one culture as compared to the other may lead to great differences in adolescent behavior in the two countries. For example, extrapolations from Elder's[27] findings suggest that the greater prevalence of the democratic authority pattern in combination with the more frequent explanations of rules in Denmark than in the United States may have particular implications for the issue of adolescent independence. Danish adolescents would not only be more independent than the Americans, but they would also experience a more complete type of autonomy vis-à-vis their parents. The combination of authoritarian parental authority and frequent explanations, which is common in the American situation, would indeed lead to feelings of dependency.

An inescapable conclusion from these results is that in the United States, parents treat their adolescents as children longer than in Denmark. Danish adolescents are expected to be self-governing; American adolescents are not. One can speculate about conditions in the two countries which lead to these differences in family structure. For example, children in the United States remain in school longer than in Denmark. They are not expected to make adult decisions as quickly as the Danes. Yet, at the same time American children have more money and experience greater pressure to spend in adult ways than the Danes. Having delayed the adulthood training—that is, teaching the children self-discipline—the parents are faced in the United States with adolescents who are in fact more dependent on them psychologically yet have the greater economic

---

[25] This finding provides confirmatory evidence for Bronfenbrenner's theoretical concept of "optimal level" in the influence of parental behavior upon the child (Urie Bronfenbrenner, "Toward a Theoretical Model for the Analysis of Parent-Child Relationships in a Social Context," in *Parental Attitudes and Child Behavior,* ed. by John Glidewell, Springfield, Illinois: Charles C Thomas, 1961, pp. 90–109).

[26] Edward C. Devereaux, *Socialization in Cross-Cultural Perspective: A Comparative Study of England, Germany, and the United States,* paper presented at the 9th International Seminar on Family Research, Tokyo, Japan, September 1965.

[27] Elder, *op. cit.,* "Parental Power Legitimation and Its Effects on the Adolescent."

opportunity to do things independently. We would suggest that children in the United States are subject to a delayed socialization pattern, both in terms of autonomy from parental control as an adolescent and perhaps discipline as an earlier child. We would speculate that, as young children, Danes are subject to stronger discipline than the Americans. If this were indeed true, the discipline exercised at an early age would create a child who as an adolescent is far more disciplined and one to whom, as a consequence, the parent can afford to give freedom.

sex differences and
sex roles

part five

With the growth of the women's movement and a greater emphasis on individual self-expression generally (as well as the development of more sophisticated measurement techniques), there has been a renewed research interest in the area of sex differences and, where differences are found, the reasons for them. Some investigators have focused primarily on biological factors (e.g., the effects of sex-linked hormonal output on neurophysiological structure and functioning—see pp. 2–3, 28–39); others have concentrated their attention on environmental influences (e.g., differences in the way boys and girls are likely to be treated by parents, even in infancy, and differences in sex-role expectations for males and females on the part of society generally). It seems clear—even on the basis of the limited amount of research to date—that both genetic-maturational *and* social experience variables may play a role in the development of sex differences, sometimes in complex interaction. But this is not the critical question. What we most need to know, and what we are only beginning to explore systematically, is the *relative* importance of biologically determined and experiential influences on specific, traditionally sex-linked, personality characteristics and behaviors under varying conditions.

That this is a complex and still little understood matter is well illustrated in the first study in this part, by Norma Feshbach and Gittelle Sones. It is frequently asserted that male adolescents are more aggressive than females, and attempts have been made to seek explanations either in hormonal differences (e.g., higher testosterone production in males) or differential patterns of reward in child rearing. But what is meant by *aggression* and how is it manifested? Feshbach and Sones explored sex differences in the reactions of adolescent male and female pairs of friends to a same-sexed newcomer. It was found that female friendship pairs displayed more negative, rejecting attitudes toward a same-sex stranger than pairs of male friends. As these investigators note, the issue then became one of whether these sex differences "are a reflection of differences in hostility." While possible alternative explanations are not ruled out, their tentative conclusion is that at least in terms of this sort of *indirect aggression* (as distinguished, say, from physical assault), adolescent girls behaved more aggressively than males; this supports an earlier finding with much younger children. Clearly, caution in drawing ready conclusions, either about the nature and extent of sex differences or about their etiology, is indicated at the present stage of our knowledge. Nevertheless, substantive progress in this difficult field is beginning to be made.

In the second article, Matina Horner explores some of the subtle psychological conflicts that have traditionally played a role in limiting achievement-striving among white, college-educated young women and some of the stereotyped societal pressures and expectations that may help to account for them. Horner found that many of her subjects, particularly those most capable of and interested in achievement, were motivated to "avoid success" because they anticipated that it would lead to negative consequences, including fear of social rejection, loss of affiliative ties, and doubts about one's femininity or "normality." At the heart of this paradox was a socially conditioned concern that femininity and competitive achievement do not mix, that competition—especially with men—leads to the loss of a feminine image not only in the view of others but, more critically, in one's own eyes as well. As a result, many young women lowered or abandoned their initially high vocational goals during the course of college or switched to more traditionally feminine occupational goals. Those who retained highly demanding, nontraditional aims tended to have boyfriends or husbands who strongly approved these aims. Even here, however, potential concern about competition was usually ameliorated by a conviction on the young woman's part that there was no danger of exceeding the boyfriend's accomplishments because of his presumed superior intelligence or special talents.

The anxiety created by violating traditional social stereotypes is not confined to adolescent girls and women, however. In a related study, Horner and her colleagues also found a relatively high "fear of success" among young black males. Whereas among the white, middle-class females the anxiety stemmed largely from violating traditional sex stereotypes, in young black males it apparently involved violating long-standing, discrimination-based racial stereotypes.

Also of related interest, in a 1968 investigation of male and female college students in a large midwestern university, Horner found a significantly higher incidence of the "motive to avoid success" on the part of females. However, in a recent, continuing replication of this study by Lois Hoffman at the same institution, no such sex difference has been found.[1] While female avoidance of success-striving has remained at its former level (65 per cent), there has been a marked increase in the incidence of success avoidance among males, canceling out the previously obtained sex difference. Nevertheless, significant differences have remained *in the psychological factors underlying success avoidance.* While for female subjects fear of rejection and affiliative loss still predominate, among males the primary determinant is apparently a growing conviction that while a moderate investment in work is reasonable and appropriate, striving for maximum success is simply not worth the candle. Perhaps in the future a greater similarity between increased numbers of males and females will develop, with more women seeking to combine marriage and long-term careers and more men seeking a closer balance between vocational concerns and family involvement.

The fact that traditional sex-role stereotypes have been a major determinant of the perceived conflict between femininity and achievement on the part of significant numbers of young women leads logically to the following question: Is such sex-role stereotyping reduced by the presence of a maternal model who herself successfully combines the roles of wife and mother with an external career?

---

[1] L. W. Hoffman, The Professional Woman as Mother. Paper presented at the Conference on Successful Women in the Sciences, New York Academy of Sciences, New York, N.Y., May 11–13, 1972.

In the study described in the third reading, Susan R. Vogel and her colleagues investigated the effects of maternal employment on the sex-role perceptions of college students. They found that sons and daughters whose parents have both been employed outside the home perceived "significantly smaller differences between masculine and feminine sex roles than do students whose fathers have worked and whose mothers have remained home, unemployed." Among sons and daughters of working mothers, greater *competence* (traditionally viewed as a positive "masculine" characteristic) was attributed to females, while greater *warmth-expressiveness* (traditionally a positive "feminine" characteristic) was attributed to males. Inasmuch as allowing for a more equitable and flexible distribution of both kinds of traits in both sexes appears to facilitate personal growth, improved communication and understanding between the sexes, and a more constructive and less destructive social order (given the conditions of modern life), the results of this study appear encouraging. They indicate that rigid, extreme, and self-limiting sex-role stereotypes are not immutable.

At the same time, it is important to avoid the danger of imposing new sets of stereotypes—even some "ideal" *androgynous* balance—on all boys and girls, men and women. The ultimate aim of any process of socialization, in our view, should be to permit each adolescent to develop his or her *unique* potential as a human being, consistent with the rights of others. As Anne Anastasi observed nearly twenty years ago, "The overlapping in all psychological characteristics is such that we need to consider men and women as individuals. . . ."[2]

---

[2] A. Anastasi, *Differential Psychology.* New York: Macmillan, 1958, pp. 497–498.

Sex differences in adolescent reactions toward newcomers

Gittelle Sones

Norma Feshbach
University of California, Los Angeles

The aim of this study is to investigate sex differences in indirect expressions of aggression among adolescent girls and boys. The literature for sex differences in children's aggression indicates that while boys are generally more aggressive than girls, under some circumstances, girls may manifest more aggression than boys (Maccoby, 1966). The direction of sex differences in aggression appears to be closely related to the mode of aggressive response. Greater aggression among girls than boys seems to be associated with verbal aggression (Jersild & Markey, 1935; Muste & Sharpe, 1947), with prosocial aggression (Sears, 1961), and, more broadly, with indirect expressions of aggression (Feshbach, 1969).

Sex differences in adult aggression have also been shown to vary with the measure of aggression employed (Bennett & Cohen, 1959; Kagan & Moss, 1961; Sarason, 1965). It is evident from studies with older children and adults that girls have more anxiety over aggression than boys (Berkowitz, 1964; Buss & Brock, 1963; Consentino & Heilbrun, 1964; Rothaus & Worchel, 1964; Sears, 1961; Wyer, Weatherley, & Terrell, 1965). Thus, it seems reasonable to assume that the direction of a sex difference yielded by a particular aggressive response measure depends not only upon differences in aggressive motivation but also upon the degree to which that response elicits anxiety, and upon the sex typing of the response.

The great range of behaviors that are subsumed under the rubric of aggression further complicates the derivation of generalizations concerning sex differences in aggression. It is an empirical question as to whether such diverse behaviors as a physical attack, a critical re-

---

This article is based on the master's thesis of the second author conducted under the direction of the first author, at the University of California, Los Angeles.

Appreciation is expressed to the participating schools and the League of Cooperating Schools.

mark, a humiliating action, and an unfriendly gesture are all functionally similar. If aggression is conceptualized, as in psychoanalytic theory and as in the frustration-aggression model of Dollard et al. (Dollard, Doob, Miller, Mowrer, & Sears, 1939), as a motivated sequence of behavior, the goal of which is to inflict pain, then there are clearly many methods, indirect and direct, by which this goal can be achieved. The tendency of girls to manifest more anxiety over aggression than boys and the masculine sex typing of physical aggression should probably result in girls manifesting more indirect aggressive responses, relative to the difference in these response modes displayed by boys.

In a previous study of sex differences in modes of aggression, Feshbach (1969) observed the reactions of pairs of 6- and 7-year-old boys and girls to the introduction of a same- and opposite-sex newcomer. While no significant differences between the sexes were observed in the expression of direct aggression, the girls obtained significantly higher indirect aggression scores. Indirect aggression toward the newcomer, as measured in the Feshbach (1969) study, was defined by rejection and exclusion of the newcomer, while physically aggressive responses, verbal threats, and hostile expressions constituted the direct aggression category. The present study is focused on indirect aggressive responses, with the object of investigating developmental consistencies in the differential reactions of the two sexes to a newcomer. In addition to employing an older age group, the present study differs from the previous investigation in the context in which the stranger is introduced and in the measures used to assess indirect aggression. Nevertheless, it is anticipated that adolescent female groups will display less friendly behaviors toward a newcomer than adolescent male groups.

While the principal impetus for this investigation stems from an interest in sex differences in modes of aggression, the data to be obtained also bear upon problems of ethnocentricity. Thus, the manner in which male and female groups react to outsiders may provide some insights into processes mediating prejudice and social distance, and into the particular significance which sex-typed attributes may have in influencing these reactions.

METHOD

SUBJECTS

The subjects in the study were seventh- and eighth-grade students, attending a predominantly middle-class white junior high school in the Los Angeles area. The sample consisted of 87 adolescents, 42 boys and 45 girls. The subjects were divided into like-sexed triads, resulting in 15 girl triads and 14 boy triads.

The first two members of the group (original group members) were selected from eighth-grade classrooms. They had been judged by their teachers to be "close friends." This judgment was made by the teachers and was subsequently verified by the children's own reports. The third member, a newcomer of the same sex, was selected from the seventh grade. The students at both age levels were average in ability, white, and from middle-class backgrounds.

PROCEDURE

During each experimental session, the subjects who had previously been categorized into friendship pairs were brought to the experimental room. They were informed that the project they were participating in was designed to provide better understanding of the methods adolescents use to solve social problems. They were then advised that they were going to solve social problems together and while there were no correct or incorrect solutions, they were ultimately to arrive at a group decision for each problem. Agreement on "one" solution by the group was emphasized.

After the experimenter read the problem to the original group member pairs, time was allotted for the subjects to answer the problem spontaneously. After a lapse of approximately 2 minutes, if no discussion was initiated, the experimenter raised facilitating questions such as "How do you think this person felt about the situation?" "What kinds of solutions can you see to this problem?" "What do you think you would do under these circumstances?" This procedure was followed for each problem presented to the original group members.

Following the presentation of the three problems the experimenter informed the original pair that she was also interested in observing the process by which an enlarged group of three members would arrive at a common conclusion. A third member, the newcomer, was then brought into the room and introduced to the original group. Two problems similar in nature to the first three, were then given to the triad to solve. Thus, the original group members participated in the discussion of five problems while the newcomers participated in the solution of two problems. The total problem-solving time for each experimental session, including both the two-person and three-person problem discussions, was approximately 25 minutes.

When the problem-solving phase of the experimental session was completed, rating scales were distributed to the triads. Each subject was then asked to evaluate and rate each of the other two group members. It was stressed that the ratings were to be based solely on impressions derived during the group discussion. Each subject independently and privately completed a 28-item rating scale for each of the other two members of the triad.

DISCUSSION PROBLEMS

The social problems used for this experiment were designed for the study with the aim of constructing realistic dilemmas with which adolescent boys and girls could readily identify. The problems were first pretested on a smaller sample of adolescents and those that evoked little or no discussion were discarded. Comparable problems were employed for boys and girls with minor changes in names and the activities involved. Two problems, illustrating those included in the study, are presented below.

> *Problem 3.* Kim, a friend of Laura's, calls up Laura to invite her to a birthday party. Since Laura isn't home, her mother accepts the birthday invitation for her. When Laura arrives home and learns about this, she is quite upset with her mother, since she and Kim just had a fight the other day and are not talking. Her mother thinks she should go.
>
> *Problem 5.* On Monday the science teacher gave an assignment to the class which should be due on Friday. Thursday evening Daniel realizes he will not be able to finish it in time to bring it to school. Daniel goes to his dad and asks him to help him because he'll never finish in time if he doesn't.

MEASURE

Rating Scale. The rating scale consisted of 28 items assessing impressions of intelligence, appearance, social desirability, social acceptance, and leadership. The possible answers ranged from "I agree very much with this statement" to "I disagree very much with this statement," the directionality of the items being balanced for favorability. Each item was weighted from one through four, with one being given to the most negative evaluation and four to the most positive. Possible total scores could then range from 28 to 112. Evidence of internal consistency is provided by the split-half reliability of .97, based on a sample of 58 adolescents.

Behavioral Interaction Measure. A tape recorder was used throughout the sessions to obtain the behavioral interaction data. The subjects were assured that only the investigator would have access to the tapes. They readily accepted this explanation and it did not appear that the presence of the tape recorder affected the spontaneous behavior in the experimental situation.

Three behavioral measures were obtained from the tape recordings for each of the 15-girl and 14-boy triads. These were:

1. Latency: Lapsed time before either of the two initial group members addressed the newcomer, and lapsed time before the newcomer spoke was determined.
2. Verbal rejection: This measure consisted of the frequency of verbal rejections of the newcomer's ideas by either original group member. In order for a rejection to be scored, a direct negation, criticism, or contradiction had to be made, for example, statements such as "That's no good." "You're wrong." "We'll stick to my idea."
3. Verbal incorporation: This measure consisted of the frequency of incorporation of the newcomer's ideas into the final decision of the group. A dichotomous incorporation-failure to incorporate judgment was made.

A sample of 16 triads, 8 girls and 8 boys, was used to determine the reliability of the rater's judgments. Two raters, who scored the protocols independently, agreed on 92% of the verbal rejection judgments. They disagreed on only 1 of the 32 incorporated into final decision judgments.

RESULTS

RATING SCALE

The original group members' impressions of each other and of the new-comer are reflected in the overall ratings presented in Table 1. As might be anticipated, the original group members, who had been selected on the basis of mutual friendship, rated each other very highly. There were no sex differences in these ratings, the mean of 98.5 for the boys being very similar to the mean of 97.5 for the girls. Both of these means are significantly higher (*t* test, $p < .001$) than the corresponding ratings of the newcomer by the original group members. The higher ratings by the origi-nal group members of each other than of the newcomer provide some empirical validation of the initial selection procedures in which teacher judgments were used as the means for determining which children were close friends. However, the newcomer's ratings of the original group mem-ber, although not significantly different from the latter's ratings of the new-comer, were close to the original group members' ratings of each other. This finding suggests that a contrast effect may also have influenced the differential judgments of the original group members.

Of central interest is the analysis of sex differences in the ratings of the newcomer by the original group members. Consistent with the primary experimental hypothesis, the mean ratings of the girls reflected a less favorable reaction to the newcomer than the mean rating of the boys. A *t* test (one-tailed) for the difference between the mean of 94.1 for the males and 88.4 for the females yields a *p* value at the .05 level. This difference is in accord with expectation.

Behavioral Interaction Measures. There were three measures taken of the interaction between the original group members and the newcomer, each designed to assess an indirect mode of expression of a negative attitude toward the newcomer. The first of these measures, latency, con-

Table 1

Sex Differences in the Personality Impression Ratings by the Original Group Member and the Newcomer

	Boys		Girls		
Ratings	M	SD	M	SD	t
Ratings by original group member of other original group member	98.4	8.7	97.5	10.4	.35
Ratings by original group members of newcomer	94.1	10.8	88.4	14.8	1.70*
Ratings by newcomer of original group member	97.3	7.9	96.5	10.6	.20

* p < .05 one-tailed test.

sisted of the time elapsing before one of the original group members addressed the newcomer. The girls took much longer than the boys before speaking to the newcomer. The median time for the girls was 73 seconds in comparison to only 22 seconds for the boys, the obtained Mann-Whitney U of 44.5 being significant at the .01 level (one-tailed). The frequency distributions for the latency scores are presented in Table 2. It is of interest that in four of the girl groups, in contrast to one of the boy groups, not a word was addressed to the newcomer, despite the fact that in all instances the newcomer spoke at some point to an original group member. From Table 2, it can be seen that, in general, the newcomers directed their remarks toward the original group members earlier than the original group members did to the newcomer. However, girl newcomers waited longer before speaking than did the newcomer boys, the median time for

Table 2
Sex Differences in Latency

Time (in sec.)	Time Elapsing Before Either Group Member Addressed Newcomer		Time Elapsing Before Newcomer Spoke to an Original Group Member	
	Boys	**Girls**	**Boys**	**Girls**
0–4			3	1
5–9	1	1	2	2
10–14	3		6	1
15–19			2	2
20–24	6	1		2
25–29	2		1	
30–34				3
35–39	1	1		2
40–44		2		1
45–49				
50–54		1		
55–59				1
60–64				
65–69				
70–74		2		
75–79				
80–84		1		
85–89				
90–94		1		
95 99				
100–104				
105–109				
110–114				
115–119		1		
Never spoke	1	4		

the girls being 23 seconds and for the boys, 11 seconds ($U = 44.5$, $p < .02$).

In order to determine whether the initial difference in response to the newcomer persisted during the experimental session, a separate analysis was made of the latency scores after the instructions for the second problem were administered. The distributions are comparable to those presented in Table 2. The girls again took much longer than the boys before addressing the newcomer, the median time for the girls being 72 seconds while the median time for the boys was 20 seconds. The obtained Mann-Whitney U of 39 was significant at the .01 level (one-tailed). The newcomer girls also took longer than the boys before addressing the older group member on the second problem, the median time for the girls being 30 seconds in comparison to 15 seconds for the boys.

The reactions to the newcomer's suggestions provided two additional interaction measures for determining the attitude of the adolescent groups to the newcomer. The first of these consisted of the frequency with which the original group members verbally rejected the newcomer's ideas. As indicated in Table 3, the number of direct verbal rejections tended to be quite low for both male and female groups, 6 of the 15 female groups and 2 of the 14 male groups explicitly rejecting one or more suggestions of the newcomer. This difference, while consistent with the previous findings, does not attain significance. The second measure consisted of the frequency with which the newcomer's ideas were incorporated into the final decision of the group. From Table 3 it can be seen that the girls were much more inclined than the boys to ignore the newcomer's ideas. Of the 15 female groups, only 4 included the newcomer's suggestions in at least one of their final decisions in comparison to 10 of the 14 male groups. This difference in distribution yields a chi-square of 4.2, significant at the .025 level (one-tailed).

DISCUSSION

The experimental results are consistent with the expectation that female friendship pairs will display more negative, rejecting attitudes to-

Table 3
Reactions to Newcomer's Suggestions

	Frequency of Verbal Rejections of Newcomer's Suggestions			Frequency of Verbal Incorporation of Suggestions into Group Decision	
Triads	**0**	**1 & 2**	**Triads**	**0**	**1 & 2**
Male	12	2	Male	4	10
Female	9	6	Female	11	4
	$\chi^2 = 1.4$			$\chi^2 = 4.2$	
	$p > .10$			$p < .05$	

Note. Calculation of χ^2 based on Yates correction.

ward a same-sex stranger than will pairs of male friends. Girls judged the newcomer less favorably than did boys, were less welcoming, and were more likely than boys to ignore the newcomer's suggestions in arriving at a group decision. Whiie the results have clearly established sex differences in the response to a newcomer, the interpretation of these data requires further clarification. The issue is whether these sex differences are a reflection of differences in hostility. The experimental operations employed in this study were explicitly designed to tap subtle, indirect manifestations of hostility and therefore are somewhat removed from more patent aggressive behaviors. Nevertheless, insofar as aggression is conceived of as a motivated sequence of behaviors resulting in the infliction of pain, then a deliberate snub and social exclusion may be functionally equivalent to a verbal insult or even to a physical blow.

At the same time, the socially rejected responses observed in this study could be mediated by variables other than hostility. For example, it might be argued that girls are more fearful of strangers and the obtained sex differences are more indicative of differences in shyness than in aggression. Although a "shyness" or "social anxiety" interpretation would account for the delay in verbally addressing the newcomer, it would not account for the failure to incorporate the newcomer's suggestions in the group decision and for the less positive attitude toward the newcomer which the girls revealed on the questionnaire. However, if one assumes that the stress of social anxiety produced the observed negative social behavior, then this interpretation becomes quite similar to an explanation which views the reactions to the newcomer as a manifestation of aggression.

Differences in social cohesiveness between male and female groups can also be offered as a possible explanation of the findings. Perhaps the difference in behavior toward the newcomer was a reflection of greater attachment by female members to their initial subgroups. However, it should be noted that the mutual ratings of the original group members for the girl groups were very similar to those of the boy groups. This finding, while not conclusive, does not support the notion that the boy and girl groups differed in cohesiveness. In order to clarify the possible role of cohesiveness, it would be informative to manipulate the degree of cohesiveness of male and female groups and to determine whether both sexes respond similarly or differentially to a newcomer under these varying conditions.

Another factor which may be contributing to the observed sex differences is the greater task orientation that has been noted in adolescent boys in contrast to the greater social orientation of adolescent girls (Douvan & Adelson, 1966). While this factor is compatible with the data bearing upon the incorporation of the newcomer's suggestions, it is less relevant to the latency and attitude findings. Nevertheless, it would be of interest to manipulate task and social orientation in subsequent studies. In addition, for primarily methodological reasons, it would be desirable to vary the sex of the experimenter. The fact that only a female experimenter was employed in the present study may have influenced some aspect of the data although it is difficult to see how it could have affected the major findings.

Although the factors mediating the experimental findings require further delineation, the data indicate that female groups are less friendly to a newcomer than male groups. This finding is consistent with those of a prior study of sex differences in response to a newcomer where a much younger age group was employed and where a free play as compared to a social problem-solving situation was used to assess reactions to the newcomer. This continuity over a wide age span suggests a stable sex difference in response to outsiders which has its roots in the early developmental history of the child. This possibility is sufficiently intriguing to justify the search for other manifestations of this trait and the investigation of its antecedents and correlates.

REFERENCES

Bennett, E. N., & Cohen, L. R. Men and women: Personality patterns and contrasts, *Genetic Psychology Monographs,* 1959, *59:* 101–155.

Berkowitz, L. Aggressive cues in aggressive behavior and hostility catharsis. *Psychological Review,* 1964, *71:* 104–122.

Buss, A. H., & Brock, T. C. Repression and guilt in relation to aggression. *Journal of Abnormal and Social Psychology,* 1963, *66:* 345–350.

Consentino, F., & Heilbrun, A. B., Jr. Anxiety correlates of sex-role identity in college students. *Psychological Reports,* 1964, *14:* 729–730.

Dollard, J., Doob, L. W., Miller, N. E., Mowrer, O. H., & Sears, R. R. *Frustration and aggression.* New Haven: Yale University Press, 1939.

Douvan, E., & Adelson, J. *The adolescent experience.* New York: Wiley, 1966.

Feshbach, N. Sex differences in children's modes of aggressive responses toward outsiders. *Merrill Palmer Quarterly,* 1969, *15:* 249–258.

Jersild, A. T., & Markey, F. V. Conflicts between pre-school children. *Child Development Monograph,* 1935, No. 21.

Kagan, J., & Moss, H. A. Personality and social development: Family and peer influences. *Review of Educational Research,* 1961, *31:* 463–474.

Maccoby, E. E. *The development of sex differences.* Stanford: Stanford University Press, 1966.

Muste, M. J., & Sharpe, D. F. Some influential factors in the determination of aggressive behavior in preschool children. *Child Development,* 1947, *18:* 11–28.

Rothaus, P., & Worchel, P. Ego-support, communication, catharsis, and hostility. *Journal of Personality,* 1964, *32:* 296–312.

Sarason, I. G., Ganzer, V. J., & Granger, J. W. Self-description of hostility and its correlates. *Journal of Personality and Social Psychology,* 1965, 1: 361–365.

Sears, R. R. Relations of early socialization experiences to aggression in middle childhood. *Journal of Abnormal and Social Psychology,* 1961, *63:* 466–492.

Wyer, R. S., Weatherley, D. A., & Terrell, G. Social role, aggression, and academic achievement, *Journal of Personality and Social Psychology,* 1965, *1:* 645–649.

the motive to avoid success and changing aspirations of college women

Matina Horner
Radcliffe College

It has been about seven years since, in an attempt to explain the major unresolved sex differences in previous research on achievement motivation, I first proposed the presence of the "motive to avoid success" as a "Psychological barrier to achievement in women." I suggested, at that time, that women are anxious about success, and that the motive to avoid success exists and receives its impetus from the expectancy held by most women that success, especially in competitive achievement situations, will be followed by negative consequences for them. Among these are social rejection and feelings of being unfeminine or inadequate as a woman.

This concept was developed within the framework of an Expectancy-Value theory of motivation which argues that the most important factors determining the arousal of one's motives and thereby the ultimate strength of one's motivation and the direction of his behavior are:

1) the *expectations* or beliefs one has regarding the nature and likelihood of the consequences of his actions and

2) the value of these consequences to him in light of his particular personality and motives.

With this in mind, it is important to emphasize the idea that to say that women have a "motive to avoid success," i.e., a disposition or tendency to become anxious about "achieving" because they anticipate or expect negative consequences because of success—is not at all the same as saying that they have a "will to fail," i.e., a motive to approach failure. Unfortunately this has become an increasingly common misinterpretation of my conceptualization of the "motive to avoid success." The presence of a "will to fail" would imply that women actively seek out failure because they anticipate or expect positive consequences from failing. Quite the contrary, I have argued that it is precisely those women who most

Reprinted from Women on Campus: 1970 a Symposium, pp. 12–23. By permission of the Center for the Continuing Education of Women, Ann Arbor, Mich.

want to achieve and who are most capable of achieving who experience the detrimental effects of a "fear of success." Their positive achievement-directed tendencies are inhibited by the presence of the motive to avoid success because of the arousal of anxiety about the negative consequences they expect will follow success. Although there may well exist such a thing as a motive to approach failure—a will to fail—it is not conceptually the same as the variable which I have called the "motive to avoid success," and should not be confused with it. Both theoretically and with regard to behavioral implications, the two are quite independent.

Unfortunately in American society even today femininity and competitive achievement continue to be viewed as two desirable but mutually exclusive ends, just as they were in 1949 when Margaret Mead pointed out that "each step forward as a successful American, regardless of sex, means a step back as a woman." Thus the active pursuit of success is hindered and the actual level of performance attained by many otherwise achievement-motivated and able young women does not reflect their true abilities. When success is likely or possible, these young women, threatened by the negative consequences they expect to follow success, become anxious, and their positive achievement strivings become thwarted.

Thus, their abilities, interests, and intellectual potential remain inhibited and unfulfilled. But, at what cost? Toward the end of this chapter we shall consider a recent analysis of some of our data which show that this lack of fulfillment does not occur without a price, a price paid in feelings of frustration, hostility, aggression, bitterness, and confusion, which are clearly manifested in the fantasy productions of these young women. In the course of our work it has become increasingly clear that once the motive to avoid success is aroused, it exerts a powerful impact on one's achievement strivings. In the initial study it was the only one of the four psychological variables assessed (i.e., the motive to achieve, to avoid failure, to affiliate with others, and resultant achievement motive) which predicted female performance. (Horner, 1968) The girls high in the motive to avoid success performed at a significantly lower level in a mixed-sex competitive achievement situation than they did subsequently in a strictly non-competitive but achievement-oriented situation, in which the only competition involved was with the task and one's internal standards of excellence.

Those low in the motive to avoid success on the other hand performed at a higher level in the competitive condition, as did most of the men in the study. The results of the study suggested very clearly that girls, especially those with a high motive to avoid success, would be least likely to develop their interests and explore their intellectual potential when competing against others, especially against men, because the expectancy of negative consequences associated with success would be greatest under such conditions. It should be pointed out that it was only after a measure of the individual differences in the strength of the motive to avoid success was developed and used in the analysis that the results for the women in this study became at all meaningful or clear.

For those who are not familiar with the way in which presence of the motive to avoid success is assessed, let me briefly summarize. (Horner, 1968, 1970) Individual differences in the strength of the motive to avoid success are determined by the presence of "fear of success imagery" in thematic stories written by subjects in response to a verbal lead connoting a high level of accomplishment, particularly in a mixed-sex competitive achievement situation. Thematic apperceptive imagery connoting "Fear of Success" is defined as that in which statements are made showing:

1) the presence of anticipation of negative *consequences* or *affect* because of the success, including fear of being socially rejected, fear of losing one's friends or one's eligibility as a date or marriage partner, and fear of becoming isolated, lonely, or unhappy as a result of success.

2) any direct or indirect expression of conflict about the success, such as doubting or wondering about one's femininity or normality, or feeling guilty and in despair about the success.

3) denial of effort or responsibility for attaining the success, sometimes using psychologically ingenious means to change the content of the cue or simply by saying "it is impossible."

4) bizarre or inappropriate responses to the cue frequently filled with hostility or confusion, as for instance in the story in which Anne is "attacked and maimed for life" for her accomplishment.

In the first study the verbal lead used to assess the presence of "Fear of Success" for women/men was: "At the end of first term finals Anne/John finds herself/himself at the top of her/his medical school class." In that study more than 65% of the 90 female stories written compared with less than 10% of the 88 male stories written contained imagery connoting Fear of Success. The significant sex differences observed in presence of fear of success imagery ($p = < .005$) have been maintained in all subsequent samples of white men and women studies with the only major change being an increase among white males in fear of success in the last two years. (Horner 1972, in press)

In our studies using black samples Herning and I have found a reversal in the presence of fear-of-success imagery, fear of success being more characteristic of the black men than of the black women tested. An interesting reversal in attitudes toward achievement occurs in our data when race role is imposed upon sex role. This is manifested in a comparison of the presence of fear-of-success imagery when both race and sex of the samples are controlled:

White Men 10%   Black Men 67%
White Women 64%   Black Women 29%

It has become quite clear from the various samples tested that one's disposition to accept success as a truly positive experience, enhancing self-esteem is by and large a function of how consistent this success is with one's internalized standards and expectations, one's stereotypes, of appropriate sex and/or race role identity and behavior. Our data show that despite a recent surge of interest in the "liberated generation" or the counterculture stressing the removal of unfair prejudices and boundaries of all sorts, conceptions of race and sex roles in particular are so deeply ingrained and historically rooted that they have remained rigid. Thus, despite recent advances in legal and educational opportunities, they psychologically bar many young men and women from taking full advantage of these changes. At any rate for most black men and white women, the attainment of success and/or leadership is seen as an unexpected event, making them the object of competitive assault or social rejection. Some examples from Black Male Stories:

> Sam is on the spot. He is "top gun" and he knows that his fellow students, intensely competitive as they are, will be out to "gun him down" academically to dethrone him.
> Sam has really booked in order to combat the "niggers ain't shit" syndrome most whitey's have. . . . A lot of white boys will jump out of H . . . C. . . . The Professors will of course make sure that Sam is not Number 1 the following term.
> Sam has found himself at the top of his class. Sam has perhaps cheated lied and finagled his way to this point.

Many theoretically important and relevant parallels exist between our samples of white women and black men which are of interest here, some of which I will return to in a latter part of the paper. Most of my comments today will, however, be directed toward understanding the impact of the motive to avoid success on the changing aspirations of college women. The data from our black samples which is very exciting and a significant part of our work on fear of success deserves to and will be treated as whole in a separate paper now in preparation. It is perhaps important to note here that we have detected an increase in fear of success among black women in the past year as a function of their involvement in the black movement.

I have argued that the motive to avoid success is a *latent,* stable, personality disposition, acquired early in life in conjunction with sex and now race role standards and sexual and/or racial identity. It was, therefore, important to begin to determine when, for whom, at what age, and under what circumstances this disposition is aroused and then serves to inhibit the achievement strivings of women. Some of our later work will be directed toward how it is acquired. It is, of course, consistent with Expectancy-Value theory to argue that the motive to avoid success is more likely to be aroused in high-achievement-oriented, high-ability women than in low-achievement-oriented, low-ability women. After all, only for those women who desire and/or can realistically expect to achieve success does the expectancy of negative consequences because of success become meaningful. These are important issues and therefore, one of the major reasons for several of the subsequent studies that have been done was simply to observe the incidence of fear of success imagery in female subjects at different ages and at different education, occupational, and abili.y levels. The incidence of the motive to avoid success has ranged from a low of 47 per cent in a 7th grade junior high school sample to a high of 86.6 per cent in two of the subsequent samples tested: first, a sample of current law school students, and second, a sample of secretaries, all of whom were very able high school graduates. In each of the college samples tested fear-of-success imagery has ranged from 60 per cent in a sample of college freshmen at a large midwestern university to 85 per cent in a sample of very high ability juniors at an outstanding eastern coed university where the emphasis on achievement is very high.

In several of these studies the content of the verbal lead used was altered so as to make the situation described more consistent and meaningful with respect to the age, educational level, and occupation of the subjects being tested. For instance, in the junior high and high school levels, the cue used was:

Sue has just found out that she has been made valedictorian of her class.

For the secretaries in the sample the cue was:

Mary's boss has been permanently transferred to the California branch of the company she works for. The board of directors has chosen Mary above many of its other junior executives to take over his highly valued position.

It is of interest to note that regardless of the specific cue used, the responses of the older, more successful women—for instance, those among our sample of present law school students and graduates compared with those of our younger college and high school students—were characterized by a concern with and an awareness of some of the *reality*-based sources of the Motive to Avoid Success and reflected the actual price one must pay for overcoming societal pressures and pursuing one's interests despite them. For example, in response to a cue about a successful female law partner came the following response from a young female attorney (a recent law school graduate):

Unmarried, probably because most men can't handle the emotional threat posed by such a bright, aggressive girl. She's attractive, well-dressed but rather hard. Comes on too strong. Has developed a defensive attitude towards men and people in general because of having to defend her right to be a lawyer. She is of course very able.

The high, if anything increasing, incidence of fear of success imagery found in our studies indicates the extent to which women have incorporated society's attitudes and then tend to evaluate themselves in terms of these attitudes which stress the idea that competition, success, competence, and intellectual achievement are basically inconsistent with femininity. The emphasis on the new freedom of women has not done away with this tendency, anymore than have the vote, trousers, cigarettes, and even similar standards of sexual behavior. If anything, the attitudes seem to be intensifying. In *The Return of the Cave Woman* Margaret Mead has pointed out that women are not using their personal potential in the general community even to the degree that society would presently allow. One might speculate about how much of this problem is attributed to the high incidence of the motive to avoid success that we have observed. There is mounting evidence in our data suggesting that many achievement-oriented American women, especially those high in the motive to avoid success, when faced with the conflict between their feminine image and developing their abilities and interests, compromise by disguising their ability and abdicating from competition in the outside world. They are convinced "that it is more important to *BE* a woman, i.e., to live through and for others, than to become some kind of specialist, therefore, most young girls, especially in college, are prepared unconsciously if not consciously to surrender chances for personal distinction so as to be fairly sure of pleasing a larger range of men." These attitudes are reflected in the high incidence of the motive to avoid success and ultimately in the significant and *increasing* absence of capable and trained American women from the mainstream of thought and achievement in the society. This withdrawal exists despite the removal of many previous legal and educational barriers and despite the presence of more opportunities for women.

In light of the terrible loss of human potential and economic resources reflected by this pattern of behavior, it seemed particularly important for us to look more intensely and critically at the factors which tend to arouse the motive to avoid success and those most effective in minimizing its influence. We therefore undertook several studies[1] at an outstanding eastern college for women, a school at which the students are chosen primarily because of their high ability, achievement, motivation, and previous success. Most of the students arrive at the school very ambitious and committed to the idea of distinguishing themselves in a future career, even if they are not exactly sure what it will be. But, as we will see from the data, by the time they are juniors, most have changed their plans toward a less ambitious, more traditionally feminine direction. Sandra Tangri, in 1969, found such a trend in her University of Michigan coeds.

The incidence of Fear of Success was 75 per cent in the first pilot sample tested, and 85 per cent in a second sample. The experimental portion of the second study is just now being completed. Thus only the admittedly limited, nonetheless interesting, data of the pilot study have been analyzed and will be discussed here in any detail.

Using a questionnaire and intensive interviews we tried to explore the elements present during the college experience, both personal and situational, which arouse the motive to avoid success. Particular attention was paid as to how this motive influences the educational and career aspirations of these bright and highly motivated young women at a time in our society when self-actualization and equality of women is drawing much public attention. All the girls in the sample were doing well and had grade points of B— or better. Nevertheless, 12 of the 16 or 75% of these girls showed evidence of high fear of success. They manifested their anxiety about success in such reported behaviors as:

1) refusing to divulge the fact that they are doing well or have received an "A," preferring instead to make their failures known. The more successful they were the less likely they were to say so. For instance, all three of the girls who had straight A averages would prefer to tell a boy that they have gotten a "C" than an "A." Most of the girls with B-s preferred to report an "A."

2) changing their majors and future career plans toward what *each of them considers to be for her (and this is important) a more traditional, appropriately feminine and less ambitious one.*

Just how important it is to attend to each individual's subjective expectations and evaluation of certain careers was clearly emphasized by the subject who changed her career goals from medicine to law because she thought:

Law school is less ambitious, it doesn't take as long . . . is more flexible in terms of marriage and children. It is *less masculine* in that it is more accepted for girls to go to law school.

The others who changed their aspirations from law school to "teaching" or "housewife" apparently do not hold the same expectations about a law career.

Several of the girls indicate that they have given up the idea of a career at all and a couple even plan to quit school. Only 2, or about 12 per cent, of the sample have in the course of their education in fact changed their plans toward a more ambitious, more traditionally masculine direction. Although several of the girls have started out majoring in the natural sciences, with the intent of pursuing a medical career, all are now, as juniors, majoring in appropriately female areas such as English, fine arts, French and history. This pattern reflects what I have at other times indicated: namely, that no one feels badly about nor seriously objects to a higher education in a woman provided the objective is to make her a more interesting and enlightened companion, wife, and/or mother. The objections, the negative consequences arise only when the objectives become more personal and career oriented, especially in non-traditional areas.

Individual differences in the motive to avoid success were very effective in predicting these patterns of behavior. Whereas more than 90 per cent of those who showed evidence of high fear of success (11 out of 12) changed their aspirations toward a more traditional direction, less than 25% of those low in fear of success did so.

A similar relationship is observed between individual differences in the motive to avoid success and responses to the question, "Are you more likely to tell your boyfriend or boys in your classes that you have gotten an A or a C?" Whereas 100 per cent of those low in fear of success would be more likely to report an A, sometimes with some explanation, only 33 per cent of those high in fear of success would do so.

Two of the factors considered as potentially the ones arousing the fear of success and thus negatively influencing the achievement strivings of these girls were the parental attitudes and those of the male peers toward appropriate sex role behavior. Many of the girls substantiated Komarovsky's argument that in the later college years girls experience a sudden reversal in what parents applaud for them. Whereas they have previously been applauded for academic success, these girls now find themselves being evaluated "in terms of some abstract standard of femininity with an emphasis on marriage as the appropriate goal for girls of this age." One says:

There is a lot of pressure from my mother to get married and not have a career. *This is one reason I am going to have a career* and wait to get married. . . . There is also some pressure from my father to get married, too.

There was, apparently, no relationship between such shifts in parental attitudes and fear of success. Nor did there appear, as you can see from that statement, to be any direct indication that parents had influenced anyone to turn away from a role-innovative type of career. If anything the influence appears to be in the opposite direction as in the above example. Some girls report being motivated for careers by the negative examples set by their mothers.

My mother is now working as a secretary, but she didn't work until now. I don't want to end up like that.

Another reason (I am going to have a career and wait to get married) is a reaction to my mother's empty life.[2]

On the other hand, the attitude of male peers toward the appropriate role of women, which they apparently do not hesitate to express, appears to be the most significant factor in arousing the motive to avoid success in these girls. The girls who showed evidence of anxiety about success and social rejection and had altered their career aspirations toward a more traditional direction were either not dating at all (interestingly enough, it was the three girls with the all A averages who were not dating at all) or were dating men who do not approve of "career women." When asked, for instance, how the boys in their lives feel about their aspirations, even the less ambitious goals, a frequent response—in fact, the most common response—was: "They laugh." Others were:

He thinks it's ridiculous for me to go to graduate school or law school.

He says I can be happy as a housewife and I just need to get a liberal arts education.

He wants a wife who will be a mother full time until the kids are grown.

I am turning more and more to the traditional role because of the attitudes of my boyfriend and his roommates. I am concerned about what they think.

This last comment is consistent with the idea that women are dependent on others for their self-esteem and have difficulty believing they can function well autonomously. This is again reflected in a statement made by one of the girls high in fear of success who is planning to leave college:

I have a lot of ideas about what I'd like to do (water sculpture presently)—but I'm waiting around for a man, and that makes me mad. I think that when I find someone I will be able to get involved in something. I need someone to respect me and what I want to do, to lend importance to what I sense is important.

The girls on the other hand who were either low in fear of success, or high in fear of success but continuing to strive for innovative careers, were either engaged to or seriously dating men who were not threatened by this success and in fact expected it of them, and provided much encouragement for them. This was reflected in such statements as:

He wants me to be intelligent. It is a source of pride *to him* that I do so well.

I would have to explain myself if I got a C. I want him to think I'm as bright as he is.

> *He* thinks it would be a good idea for me to go to law school.
> *He* feels very strongly that I should go to graduate school to get a Master's degree. He does not want to feel that he has denied me a complete education.

It is interesting to note that one of the factors distinguishing the couples in this second group from those in the first is a mutual understanding that the boy is the more intelligent of the two. "He's so much smarter . . . competition with him would be hopeless." This fact or belief seems to be sufficient to keep the motive from being aroused and affecting behavior.

In the first group there exists a tension between the two rooted in the fear that *she* is the more intelligent one. Other important factors seem to be based on how threatening the boyfriend sees her present and future success to be to *his* . . . i.e., are they in the same school, taking the same courses, planning to go to the same graduate school or to have the same career?

> He is going to medical school, too, and we take some of the same courses. I don't compete with him, but he competes with me. I usually do better than he does and this depresses him. He resents the fact that I do better.

The significance of male attitudes in determining the arousal of fear of success and its impact on behavior has been substantiated in a subsequent study in which the sex role attitudes of the male friends of the girls in the sample were actually assessed and proved to be the most significant factor accounting for the presence or absence of fear of success in the girls. We are currently trying to determine whether these male attitudes will predict to decremenal change in the performance of the girls when competing against the men compared to their own previous level of non-competitive performance.

I have already indicated that when success is likely or possible, threatened by the negative consequences they expect to follow success because it would imply a violation of sex role boundaries, young women become anxious and their positive achievement strivings and aspirations become thwarted. But at the beginning I suggested that this does not occur without a price—a price paid in feelings of frustration, hostility, aggression, etc. I'd like to briefly now consider the data reflecting this emotional cost. A comparison of the thematic apperceptive stories written by young college women differing in strength of the "motive to avoid success" in response to the cue, "Anne is sitting in a chair with a smile on her face," help make this quite evident. Whereas more than 90% of those low in fear of success wrote positive, primarily affiliative stories centering on such things as dates, engagements, forthcoming marriages as well as a few on successful achievements, less than 20% of those high in fear of success wrote stories of this type. The rest of the responses, if not bizarre, were replete with negative affiliative imagery centering on hostility toward or manipulation of others.

I think the stories speak for themselves: let me give you a few examples. Here are stories by girls low in fear of success:

1) Anne's boyfriend has just called her. Not really boyfriend—a boy she really has wanted to go out with for ages. Anne is a very goodlooking girl—but never thought Mr. X would call her.

She sees Mr. X in classes and she really thinks he is fine. She's really wanted to have a date with him for over 1 year now—and her day has finally come.

Oh boy. I'm so excited, what shall I wear. I wonder if I should buy something new to wear. Will he like me? I am so excited. Anne is very happy.

Anne will have a marvelous time on her date and hope and pray that Mr. X will take her out again.

2) Anne is happy—she's happy with the world because it is so beautiful. It's snowing, and nice outside—she's happy to be alive and this gives her a good warm feeling. Anne did well on one of her tests, likes most of her classes in college. She hopes that if she has done well in the past she will continue to in her class. She wants to go into a subject she can do well in, she wants to major in a field she's good in and likes. She doesn't want to be a flunkie. She'll go into her field, if not this one, another one which she will take next year—if everything works out, she'll be happy. She can then repay her parents for everything they've done.

3) Anne is sitting in a chair. She is very happy. Her mother walks into the room, and Anne tells her mother that her boyfriend has called, . . . they become engaged, set their wedding date.

Compare these with typical stories written by girls high in fear of success:

1) Anne is recollecting her conquest of the day. She has just stolen her ex-friend's boyfriend away, right before the high school senior prom. Anne was jealous of her friend's popularity and when they decided not to associate with each other, Anne decided to do something to really get back at her friend—take her boyfriend. Anne is thinking that she has proven herself equal to her friend socially. She wanted to hurt her and succeeded by taking the boyfriend away. Anne will lose him because he'll find out how sneaky and underhanded she is. They will go to the prom but it will end there.

2) Anne is waiting for the cab to come to take her to the Markley mixer where she wants to meet new people. She is thinking of the fun she'll have and thinking of encountering her ex–boyfriend who is president of the mixer. She had really liked her ex-boyfriend and since they broke up she really wanted to show him she can meet new boys and have fun with others besides him. She will meet another boy at the dance who showers her with his attention and she willingly and happily flaunts this boy in front of her ex-boyfriend. The new boy calls her later but she finds she doesn't really like him and only used him to show her ex-boyfriend.

3) Anne is at her father's funeral. . . . She knows it is unseemly to smile but she cannot help it. Anne is fighting to keep from laughing. Her brother Ralph pokes her in fury but she is uncontrollable. Her mother is sobbing and unaware of Anne's behavior. Anne rises dramatically and leaves the room, stopping first to pluck a carnation from the blanket of flowers on the coffin.

The differences in the two kinds of stories are, I think, very clear. One can only speculate about how much of what was expressed in fantasy is a true reflection of the actual behavior or intents of these young women, and if these responses do in fact accurately reflect their behavior, what the consequences of such behavior might be for them. One of the things that makes this a particularly interesting area to pursue is that a consistent pattern has been found in our black data, i.e., black men with low fear of success characteristically wrote stories of romance and often of success to the smile cue while high fear-of-success men wrote stories of the manipulative variety:

> He is watching a group of people argue. They are the people he hates. The people have fought against this man for some time and won. He is happy because he made them split and argue. He wants them to go on fighting.
> John is happy cause it's all over finally. He had been talking to Jean for at least two months and things had been going his way. John met her at a party and made a bet with some friends that he could really buckle her knees. . . .

In light of the high and if anything increasing incidence of the motive to avoid success in our data it seems apparent that most otherwise achievement-motivated young white women when faced with a conflict between their feminine image and expressing their competences or developing their abilities and interests adjust their behaviors to their internalized sex role stereotypes. A parallel situation seems to exist for young black men who seem to adjust their behaviors to internalized race role stereotypes. In order to feel or appear more feminine women disguise their abilities and withdraw from the mainstream of thought, non-traditional aspiration, and achievement in our society. As the data indicate however, this does not occur without a high price, a price paid by the individual in negative emotional and interpersonal consequences and by the society in a loss of valuable human and economic resources. Kai Erikson in *Wayward Puritans* (1966) has argued that "The chief ways that individuals in a group learn about the norms of that group may be from boundaries made salient by those who violate them. The cost of boundary violation may be illustrated through the isolation, chastisement or ill fortune of the deviant." Perhaps the expectation or anticipation of negative consequences because of success that we have found in our fear of success stories among both our white and black samples were realistically learned in just this way. Much work clearly remains to be done.

NOTES

1. The data in the first study were gathered and initially analyzed by Miss Molly Schwern for her junior honors project.
2. It is of interest to note here that the majority of the girls in our college samples who were high in fear of success came from middle or upper middle class homes. The fathers were successful professional or business men who were better educated than their mothers. Both parents encouraged and rewarded academic success with a high premium placed on education, factors which McClelland has shown in *The Achieving Society* lead to the development of a high motive to achieve. Only later do these girls experience the reversal in attitude discussed previously. The girls low in fear of success come from primarily lower and lower middle class homes in which the fathers have not been successful.

REFERENCES

Atkinson, J. W., and Feather, M. T. 1966. *A theory of achievement motivation.* New York: John Wiley & Sons.

Horner, M. 1968. Sex differences in achievement motivation and performance in competitive and non-competitive situations. Unpublished doctoral dissertation, University of Michigan.

Horner, M. 1970. Femininity and Successful Achievement: A Basic Inconsistency, Ch. 3 in Bardwick, Douvan, Horner, and Gutmann, *Feminine Personality and Conflict.* Belmont, Calif: Brooks/Cole.

Horner, M. 1970. The motive to avoid success and changing aspirations of college women. Unpublished, preliminary draft.

Horner, M. and Rhoem. 1968. The motive to avoid success as a function of age, occupation and progress at school. Unpublished research report.

Komarovsky, Mirra. 1959. Functional analysis of sex roles. *Amer. Soc. Rev. 15:* 508–516.

Lipinski, E. G. 1965. Sex-role conflict and achievement motivation in college women. Unpublished doctoral dissertation, University of Cincinnati.

Mead, Margaret. 1949. *Male and Female.* New York: Morrow. Also New York: Dell (Laurel Edition), 1968.

Schwenn, M. 1970. Arousal of the motive to avoid success. Unpublished junior honors paper. Harvard University.

Tangri, S. 1969. Role-innovation in occupational choice. Unpublished doctoral dissertation. University of Michigan.

maternal employment and perception of sex roles among college students

Susan R. Vogel
Mental Health Center, Brandeis University

Inge K. Broverman,   **Donald M. Broverman,**
Frank E. Clarkson
Worcester State Hospital, Worcester, Massachusetts

Paul S. Rosenkrantz
College of the Holy Cross

Numerous investigators have noted the existence of sex-role stereotypes, that is, consensual beliefs about the differing characteristics of men
and women. These sex-role stereotypes are widely held (Lunneborg, 1968;
Rosenkrantz, Vogel, Bee, Broverman, & Broverman, 1968; Seward, 1946),
persistent (Fernberger, 1948), and highly traditional (Komarovsky, 1950;
McKee & Sherriffs, 1957). Sex-role stereotypes also ascribe greater social
value to masculine than to feminine characteristics (Broverman, Broverman, Clarkson, Rosenkrantz, & Vogel, 1970; Goldberg, 1967; Kitay, 1940;
McKee & Sherriffs, 1959; Rosenkrantz et al., 1968; Sherriffs & Jarrett,
1953).

Stereotypic sex-role perceptions may be influenced by the degree of
actual sex-role differentiation in a given family or society, that is, the
greater the actual sex-role differentiation, the greater the perception of
sex-role stereotypes. Maternal employment status, in turn, may be a key
factor in determining the degree of role differentiation that occurs between
parents. If the father is employed outside the home, while the mother remains a full-time homemaker, their roles are clearly polarized for the
child. On the other hand, if both parents are employed outside the home,
their roles are more likely to be perceived as similar. A child growing
up in a family with a working mother, therefore, should experience less
parental sex-role differentiation than would a child with a nonworking
mother.

Hartley (1964) reported that the mother's employment status does, in
fact, influence a child's perception of sex-role characteristics. Daughters

of working mothers see adult men and women as sharing more in their activities than do daughters of nonworking mothers.

In the present study the authors explored the generality and persistence of this effect by examining the stereotypic sex-role perceptions of college-aged men and women with working versus nonworking mothers. It is hypothesized that individuals whose mothers have been employed perceive less difference between the masculine and feminine roles than those individuals with homemaker mothers.

METHOD

SUBJECTS

One hundred and twenty college students were used as subjects in this study; these subjects were selected from a pool of 154 subjects used in an earlier study (Rosenkrantz et al., 1968). The subjects had been asked to indicate their mother's current occupation, or, if the mother was currently unemployed, when and at what job she had previously worked. Of the original 154 subjects, there were 24 men and 23 women whose mothers had never been employed during the subject's life time (homemaker mothers). Another 35 and 38 women had mothers who were currently employed (employed mothers). The occupations of these mothers were rated according to Hollingshead (1957) and were found to be distributed in the following manner: Levels 1 and 2 (predominantly teachers, social workers, and nurses), 27 mothers; Levels 3 and 4 (predominantly secretaries, clerks, and sales women), 37 mothers; Levels 5, 6, and 7 (skilled and unskilled workers), 9 mothers. Information about the length of employment was not available. Subjects who could not be clearly classified into the homemaker or employed mother groups were eliminated from the present study.

No significant differences were found between the 47 subjects with homemaker mothers and the 73 subjects with employed mothers with respect to mother's current age and education and father's education and occupational level (Hollingshead, 1957).

ASSESSMENT OF SEX-ROLE STEREOTYPES HELD BY SUBJECTS

Instrument. Sex-role perceptions of the subjects were assessed by means of a Stereotype Questionnaire developed by the authors (Rosenkrantz et al., 1968). Briefly the instrument consists of 122 short phrases arranged in bipolar fashion with the poles separated by 60 points:

Not at all aggressive   Very aggressive
1....2....3....4....5....6....7

Subjects were instructed to mark the point along each dimension that characterized the typical adult male, that is, masculinity response. The instructions stressed that subjects should not use themselves as anchor points for the descriptions of other people. After completing the 122 items, subjects were instructed to mark the questionnaire a second time according to what they would expect the characteristics of an adult woman to be, that is, femininity response. Finally, subjects were asked to mark the questionnaire a third time describing themselves. Approximately half of the subjects were given the masculinity instruction first; the remaining subjects were given the femininity instruction first. Self instruction was always given last, in order to permit these ratings to occur explicitly within a masculine-feminine context.

Stereotypic Items. The concept of sex-role stereotype implies extensive agreement among individuals as to the characteristic differences between men and women. In the earlier study (Rosenkrantz et al., 1968), the authors found 41 items about which 75% or more of the subjects of each sex agreed as to the direction of the masculine-feminine difference. These items have been termed stereotypic items, since they represent those characteristics about which the most extreme consensus exists. For each of these stereotypic items, the difference between the means of the masculinity response and the femininity responses was statistically significant beyond the .001 level of probability.

Differentiating Items. These are 48 items about which less than 75% of subjects of each sex agreed as to the direction of the masculine-feminine difference. However, the difference between the means of the masculinity and the femininity responses of each of these items was significant beyond the .05 level of probability.

The 33 remaining items were nondifferentiating; that is, the mean masculinity and femininity scores did not differ significantly.

MALE-VALUED AND FEMALE-VALUED ITEMS

In an earlier study (Rosenkrantz et al., 1968), a different sample of college men and women was asked to indicate which pole of each item represented the more socially desirable behavior or characteristic. These ratings allowed the authors to break down both the stereotypic and the differentiating items into those items for which the masculine pole was more socially desirable (male-valued items) and those items for which the feminine pole was more socially desirable (female-valued items). There were 29 stereotypic and 25 differentiating male-valued items; the great majority of these items reflect effectiveness and competence. The remaining 12 stereotypic items and 23 differentiating items were female valued; in general, these items are concerned with emotional warmth and expressiveness.

RESULTS

Analyses of the differences between students whose mothers had been employed and those whose mothers were primarily homemakers were made separately for the stereotypic items, and for the differentiating items. Nondifferentiating items were not examined. Possible unrelated response biases of the subjects were controlled for in the following manner: For slightly more than half of the items a high score indicated the masculine pole, while for the remaining items a high score indicated the feminine pole. These latter items were reflected so that a high score indicated the masculine pole for all items. For each subject, the mean and sigma of his 366 responses (masculine, feminine, and self responses for the 122 items) were computed, and his 366 responses were then converted to sigma scores. The average masculine, feminine, and self responses were then computed for each subject across the 41 stereotypic items and across the 48 differentiating items. This resulted in 6 scores for each subject: a masculinity score (*m*), a femininity score (*f*), and a self score (*s*) for the stereotypic items and for the differentiating items.

Difference scores were also computed between each subject's *m* and *f* scores (*m-f*) for the stereotypic items and the differentiating items. These difference scores provide for a direct test of the major hypothesis of this study, that children of employed mothers perceive less *difference* between the roles of men and women than children of homemaker mothers.

Masculinity and Femininity Responses. The mean *m-f* scores, mean *m* scores, and the mean *f* scores for the subjects with working mothers were compared, using *t* tests, to the mean scores for subjects with homemaker mothers, separately for stereotypic and for differentiating items (see Table 1). As can be seen in Table 1, the major hypothesis dealing with the perception of difference between the two sex roles receives substantial support. Three of the four *m-f* difference comparisons yield significance levels of .05 or better, while the fourth *m-f* difference (men on stereotypic items) has a *p* value of .06. Thus, both men and women who are children of employed mothers perceive significantly less difference between the masculine and feminine roles, on both the stereotypic and differentiating items, than do men and women who are the children of homemaker mothers.

The expectations for the difference between groups with respect to the separate perception of the masculine and feminine roles are also largely confirmed by the data. The daughters of working mothers perceive both the masculine role and the feminine role as significantly less extreme on both the stereotypic and differentiating items than do the daughters of homemaker mothers (see Table 1). These results indicate that women whose mothers have worked perceive the masculine role as significantly less masculine, and the feminine role as significantly less feminine, than do women whose mothers have not been employed. Thus, not only is the perceived gap between masculinity and femininity significantly smaller for women whose mothers have worked, but so too, are both the masculine and feminine poles themselves defined differently by the two groups.

The comparable results for men are less consistent, but those differences that do occur are in the predicted direction, and parallel to the significant differences for women. The mean masculinity score for men with employed mothers on the stereotypic items is significantly lower than the comparable score for men with homemaker mothers, indicating that men whose mothers have worked perceive the masculine role as significantly less masculine (see Table 1). The difference is not significant, how-

Table 1

Average Masculinity and Femininity Scores for Men and Women with Employed Versus Homemaker Mothers

Score	Men with			Women with		
	Employed mothers (N = 35)	Home-maker mothers (N = 24)	t	Employed mothers (N = 38)	Home-maker mothers (N = 23)	t
	Stereotypic Items					
Masculinity	.394	.504	2.327	.482	.649	2.626*
Femininity	−.698	−.794	1.316	−.423	−.626	2.727**
Masculinity-femininity	1.092	1.298	1.990	.905	1.275	3.158**
	Differentiating Items					
Masculinity	.182	.231	1.568	.256	.369	2.026*
Femininity	−.261	−.379	2.667**	−.196	−.292	2.388*
Masculinity-femininity	.443	.610	2.581**	.452	.661	2.383*

Note. A high score indicates that the response is closer to the masculine pole, while a low score indicates that the response is closer to the feminine pole.

* $p < .05$.

** $p < .01$.

ever, between the mean masculinity scores of the two groups for the differentiating items; the mother's employment influences only the stereotypic characteristics. Just the reverse is true for the men's perception of the feminine role. Mean femininity scores for the two groups do not differ significantly on the stereotypic items but do on the differentiating items. Sons of employed mothers perceive the feminine role as less feminine than do sons of homemaker mothers (see Table 1).

In order to assess the possible differential influence of the mother's work history on the male-valued and female-valued characteristics, the comparisons described previously were repeated separately for these two dimensions within the stereotypic items and within the differentiating items. The results of these analyses for the male-valued items (competency) are presented in Table 2 and for the female-valued items (warmth and expressiveness) in Table 3.

Inspection of Table 2 reveals a striking sex difference in the perception of the competency dimension as a function of the mother's work history. For men, the mother's employment has no influence whatsoever on their perception of this dimension of the sex role. However, women with employed mothers perceive less difference between the masculine and feminine roles with respect to competency, and perceive the feminine role itself as entailing greater competency than do women with homemaker mothers. These relationships reach significance in both the stereotypic and the differentiating items (see Table 2). Women's perception of the competency dimension of the masculine role is less strongly influenced by the mother's work history. Although women with working mothers perceive the masculine role as entailing somewhat less competency than do women with homemaker mothers, this difference fails to reach the .05 level of significance (significant at the .06 level for the stereotypic items and not significant for the differentiating items; see Table 2).

Men and women also differ in their perception of the warmth–expressiveness dimension of the sex roles as a function of the mother's employment, although here it is men whose perception is more strongly influenced. Men whose mothers are employed perceive significantly less difference between the masculine and feminine roles with respect to warmth–expressiveness, on both the stereotypic and differentiating items (see Table 3). The feminine role itself is perceived as entailing somewhat less warmth–expressiveness by men with employed mothers than by men

Table 2

Male-Valued Items: Average Masculinity and Femininity Scores for Men and Women with Employed Versus Homemaker Mothers

	Men with			Women with		
	Employed Mothers	*Home-maker Mothers*		*Employed Mothers*	*Home-maker Mothers*	
Score	*(N = 35)*	*(N = 24)*	*t*	*(N = 38)*	*(N = 23)*	*t*
Stereotypic Items						
Masculinity	.638	.723	1.451	.740	.877	1.991
Femininity	−.537	−.607	.828	−.204	−.468	2.641*
Masculinity-femininity	1.175	1.330	1.377	.944	1.345	3.070**
Differentiating Items						
Masculinity	.595	.609	.223	.689	.790	1.521
Femininity	.086	.019	.955	.279	.063	2.682**
Masculinity-femininity	.509	.590	1.159	.410	.727	3.826**

Note. A high score indicates that the response is closer to the masculine pole, while a low score indicates that the response is closer to the feminine pole.

* $p < .05$.

** $p < .01$.

with homemaker mothers (this difference reaches the .05 level of significance for the differentiating items, but falls slightly short of the .05 level for the stereotypic items; see Table 3). The masculine role is perceived as entailing somewhat more warmth and expressiveness by sons of working mothers than by sons of homemaker mothers on the stereotypic items only (see Table 3).

Turning to the women's perception of the warmth dimension on the stereotypic items, the influence of the mother's work history is similar but less pronounced. On the stereotypic items, women with employed mothers perceive less of a difference between the masculine and feminine roles with respect to warmth–expressiveness, and perceive the masculine role itself as entailing a greater degree of warmth–expressiveness than do women with homemaker mothers (see Table 3). No differences occur between the groups (daughters of employed mothers versus daughters of homemaker mothers) for the differentiating items. Perception of the feminine role with respect to warmth–expressiveness does not differ significantly for the two groups.

Table 3

Female-Valued Items: Average Masculinity and Femininity Scores for Men and Women with Employed Versus Homemaker Mothers

Score	Men with			Women with		
	Employed Mothers (N = 35)	*Home-maker Mothers (N = 24)*	*t*	*Employed Mothers (N = 38)*	*Home-maker Mothers (N = 23)*	*t*
	Stereotypic Items					
Masculinity	−.195	−.021	1.887	−.128	.099	1.987
Femininity	−1.088	−1.246	1.777	−.966	−1.006	.584
Masculinity-femininity	.893	1.255	2.729**	.838	1.105	2.003*
	Differentiating Items					
Masculinity	−.265	−.179	1.102	−.214	−.087	1.054
Femininity	−.640	−.806	2.211*	−.716	−.674	.645
Masculinity-femininity	.375	.627	2.827**	.502	.587	.663

Note. A high score indicates that the response is closer to the masculine pole, while a low score indicates that the response is closer to the feminine pole.

* $p < .05$.

** $p < .01$.

Self Responses. No significant differences were found between the self responses of subjects with employed mothers compared to like responses of subjects with homemaker mothers, either for the stereotypic and differentiating items taken as a whole, or for the male-valued and female-valued items considered separately. For all cases, the self response fell between the masculinity and the femininity responses. However, since the *m-f* distance is relatively small in subjects with employed mothers, the *s* response of these subjects is closer to the opposite sex response than the *s* response of subjects with homemaker mothers, where the distance between *m* and *f* responses is significantly larger. Thus, although the self responses, as such, do not differ in these two groups, it is possible that the meaning of the self-concepts differs as a function of the different contexts in which they occur.

DISCUSSION

The results support the hypothesis that sex-role perceptions are affected by actual parental role behaviors to which children are exposed. College students whose parents have both been employed outside the home perceive significantly smaller differences between masculine and feminine sex roles than do students whose fathers have worked and whose mothers have remained at home, unemployed. Moreover, maternal employment affects perceptions of the masculine sex role, as well as the feminine role even though the fathers of both groups were uniformly employed outside the home. Perhaps the similarity of the roles of the two groups of fathers is more apparent than real. Hoffman (1963) found that in families where the mother is employed, the father participates significantly more in household tasks than in families where the mother is a full-time homemaker. This suggests that children of working mothers are exposed to the father in a somewhat different role, and possibly have closer contact with him, than children of homemaker mothers.

SEX DIFFERENCES IN RESPONSE TO MATERNAL EMPLOYMENT

Women's perceptions of the sex roles appear, in general, to be more strongly influenced by the mother's employment than are men's perceptions. Because of greater commonality of activity in the mother-daughter relationship compared to the mother-son relationship, the fact that a mother works may impinge more on girls than on boys. It is also possible that the identification process by which a girl models herself after her mother intensifies the significance of the mother's sex-role behaviors for a daughter, but not for a son.

Another sex difference appears when the effects of maternal employment on the male-valued items and female-valued items are examined separately. For each sex, maternal employment tends to "upgrade" the perception of their own sex with respect to those characteristics that are seen as socially desirable for the opposite sex. Thus, sons of employed mothers perceive men as being somewhat more warm and women less warm, as compared to sons of homemaker mothers. On the other hand, daughters of employed mothers perceive women as more competent and men as less competent as compared to daughters of homemaker mothers. It appears, then, that maternal employment exerts a positive influence on the child's perception of his own sex, by augmenting competency for girls, and emotional warmth and expressiveness for boys. Evidently the perception of those positive characteristics traditionally associated with one's own sex is much less affected by the mother's working. Boys with working mothers do not relinquish any of their own sex's positive characteristics in the area of competency, nor do they perceive women as increasing in these positive characteristics. Although girls with working mothers perceive the sexes more nearly alike with respect to emotional warmth and expressiveness, they achieve this not by sacrificing their own positive attributes (perception of the feminine role is unchanged), but by increasing the male's perceived warmth–expressiveness.

CHANGING SEX-ROLE PERCEPTIONS IN SOCIETY

The most important implication of the obtained results is the evidence they provide that the traditional conceptions of sex roles are not immutable. If individual perceptions of sex roles are subject to variation as a function of individual experience, then societal sex-role stereotypes are subject to eventual change.

That such change is called for has become increasingly clear. Rossi (1964), in her proposal for equality between the sexes, makes the claim that the traditional conceptions of masculinity and femininity are no longer either necessary or appropriate in the latter half of the twentieth-century. As these traditional conceptions now stand, they not only reflect the unequal status of the sexes, but serve to perpetuate this differential status by negatively reinforcing many socially valued behaviors for women, and a lesser number for men. For example, assertiveness, constructive aggression, and striving for achievement and excellence, all characteristics considered desirable in adults in this society, are discouraged for women; while tenderness, emotional warmth, and expressiveness, equally valued in the abstract, are not encouraged for men.

Rossi (1964) proposed a socially "androgynous" conception of sex roles, by which she means that each sex cultivates those highly valued qualities traditionally limited to the other. Sex-role conceptions held by the children of working mothers are androgynous in just this sense, that is, sons and daughters of employed mothers each perceive their own sex as sharing the positive characteristics traditionally limited to the opposite sex to a greater degree than do the children of homemaker mothers.

Presumably, the less restrictive and more congruent definitions of sex roles held by children of working mothers influence role behavior, so that the children of working mothers feel even freer than their parents to engage in overlapping role behaviors, and so achieve in their own lives a greater degree of sex-role equality.

REFERENCES

Broverman, I. K., Broverman, D. M., Clarkson, F. E., Rosenkrantz, P. S., & Vogel, S. R. Sex-role stereotypes and clinical judgments of mental health. *Journal of Consulting and Clinical Psychology,* 1970, *34:* 1–7.

Fernberger, S. W. Persistence of stereotypes concerning sex differences. *Journal of Abnormal and Social Psychology,* 1948, *43:* 97–101.

Goldberg, P. A. Misogyny and the college girl. Paper presented at the meeting of the Eastern Psychological Association, Boston, April 1967.

Hartley, R. E. A developmental view of female sex-role definition and identification. *Merrill-Palmer Quarterly,* 1964, *10:* 3–16.

Hoffman, L. W. Parental power relations and the division of household tasks. In F. I. Nye & L. W. Hoffman (Eds.), *The employed mother in America.* Chicago: Rand McNally, 1963.

Hollingshead, A. B. Two factor index of social position. New Haven, Conn.: Author, 1957. (Mimeo)

Kitay, P. M. A comparison of the sexes in their attitudes and beliefs about women. *Sociometry,* 1940, *34:* 399–407.

Komarovsky, M. Functional analysis of sex roles. *American Sociological Review,* 1950, *15:* 508–516.

Lunneborg, P. W. Stereotypic aspect in masculinity-femininity measurement. Paper presented at the meeting of the American Psychological Association, San Francisco, September 1968.

McKee, J. P., & Sherriffs, A. C. The differential evaluation of males and females. *Journal of Personality,* 1957, *25:* 356–371.

McKee, J. P., & Sherriffs, A. C. Men's and women's beliefs, ideas, and self-concepts. *American Journal of Sociology,* 1959, *64:* 356–363.

Rosenkrantz, P. S., Vogel, S. R., Bee, H., Broverman, I. K., & Broverman, D. M. Sex-role stereotypes and self-concepts in college students. *Journal of Consulting and Clinical Psychology,* 1968, *32:* 287–295.

Rossi, A. S. Equality between the sexes. In R. J. Lifton (Ed.), *The woman in America.* Boston, Mass.: Houghton Mifflin, 1964.

Seward, G. H. *Sex and the social order.* New York: McGraw-Hill, 1946.

Sherriffs, A. C., & Jarrett, R. F. Sex differences in attitudes about sex differences. *Journal of Psychology,* 1953, *35:* 161–168.

changing sexual values
and behavior

part six

It is widely recognized that significant changes in the sexual attitudes and values of adolescents have taken place during the past decade and that these changes are continuing. There is still considerable controversy, however, even among presumed experts, regarding the extent to which changing attitudes have been reflected in behavior. In the first article in this part, John Janeway Conger reviews the relevant data (most of which are very recent) and concludes that while there was probably an initial lag, attitudinal changes are increasingly reflected in the sexual behavior of contemporary adolescents. Furthermore, the *percentage changes* in recent years in premarital intercourse—from an initially lower baseline— have been greatest among middle- and upper-class young people, especially girls.

Conger cautions, however, against unwarranted generalizations, pointing out that preoccupation with group trends can obscure the fact that there is still a wide, and probably growing, diversity of sexual attitudes and behavior in different sectors of the adolescent and youth population. Such factors as age, sex, socioeconomic and educational background, race, religion, and even geographical area are all strongly related to sexual attitudes, values, and behavior. For this reason, the results of any investigation dealing with adolescent sexuality will inevitably seem exaggerated to some young people and adults and minimized to others.

He concludes that the so-called sexual revolution appears likely to continue and, while many of its results have been positive, there is a danger that a significant number of adolescents may become involved in sexual relationships that they are too young, too poorly informed, or too vulnerable emotionally to be able to handle successfully.

In the second article, Eleanore B. Luckey and Gilbert D. Nass make clear that current trends in sexual attitudes and behavior are not confined to the United States, but extend to other Western countries as well. Indeed, in most respects the attitudes and behavior are not confined to the United States, but extend to other Western countries as well. Indeed, in most respects the attitudes and behavior of college students in England, Norway, and Germany emerge as more liberal than those of students in the United States and Canada. Not surprisingly, inasmuch as this study was conducted several years earlier than some of the most recent studies referred to in Conger's article, a somewhat lower incidence of sexual experience, particularly coitus, was found for U.S. students (and presumably for students in other countries as well). However, as the investigators themselves make clear, their primary interest was not in assembling incidence statistics as such, but in examining comparative similarities and differences among countries.

In all countries surveyed, women still emerged as more conservative than men. A majority of young people in all of these countries rejected the double standard; interestingly, however, women more frequently *sup-*

ported it than men (except in the case of England). Furthermore, without exception a clear majority in all countries retained a belief in marriage as a vital part of a satisfying life. Nevertheless, despite such similarities, a number of interesting differences among countries were found. For example, sex-role differences were emphasized to a greater extent in the two North American countries than in the English and Scandinavian samples. English students emerged as most likely to have engaged in a wide variety of sexual behaviors, at younger ages, and in a more casual fashion than those of any other country; in addition, male-female differences in behavior were smallest among them. While Norwegian students, both males and females, also had a relatively high rate of premarital sexual experience, they were less likely to be "swingers" than English students, starting sexual activity later and restricting themselves to fewer partners. Canadian students generally tended to be most conservative, followed by U.S. students.

Whether the size of *relative* differences among countries found by these investigators continues to hold true currently, or whether (as seems possible in view of recent findings with U.S. students) the gap is beginning to narrow, is a matter for further research. At any rate, it appears clear that the "sexual revolution" developing among young people has not been restricted to the United States and has in fact developed further and probably faster in some other countries, such as England and Scandinavia.

There is an unfortunate tendency when examining population trends, or even trends among broad subgroups, to neglect or oversimplify the complexity of the factors influencing *individual* attitudes and behavior. There is also all too frequently a tendency to forget that sex, while expressive of sexuality, is not synonymous with it. Sexuality extends far beyond specific sexual attitudes and behaviors to one's whole conception of himself or herself as a human being and involves complex patterns of identification and ways of relating to others.

Both of these points are illustrated beautifully in E. Mavis Hetherington's study of the effects of father absence on the personality development of adolescent daughters. She compared three groups of adolescent girls: a group living at home with both parents, a group in which the father was absent due to divorce, and a group in which the father had died. While there appeared to be little disturbance in sex-typed behaviors or in preference for the female role among girls in the last two groups as a result of the father's absence, there clearly were disturbances in their ability to interact appropriately with males. Daughters of widows tended to react to males—both peers and adults—with shyness, rigidity, and withdrawal. Daughters of divorcées, though outwardly precocious, also revealed considerable anxiety and insecurity—an "overdetermined" quality—in their interactions with males, as indicated by such behaviors as nail-biting, hair-pulling, and plucking at clothes during such interactions. While daughters of widows were sexually inhibited relative to those in the intact family group, daughters of divorcées were more likely to date early and to have had sexual intercourse.

It is important to recognize that for these girls father absence affected their overall patterns of relating to the opposite sex, not simply their reactions in specifically sexual situations, and it also affected their conceptions of themselves. Thus girls without fathers felt less mastery over the course of their own lives and more generalized anxiety. As we empha-sized earlier, sex in the narrow sense of the word is only one aspect of sexuality, though obviously an important one; sexuality, in turn, is inti-mately related to one's whole conception of himself or herself as a per-son—alone and in interaction with others.

Sexual attitudes and behavior of contemporary adolescents

John Janeway Conger
University of Colorado School of Medicine

One of the more prominent aspects of the so-called youth culture of the 1960s, and apparently also one of the more enduring, has been the development of a "new sexual morality" based more on openness, honesty, and a greater concern for others in human relationships and less on conformity to institutionalized social norms (3, 4, 16, 29). This change has been manifested in a variety of ways, ranging from a reduced emphasis on ritualized "dating games" and demands for open college dormitories to greater tolerance for the sexual values and behavior of others and a desire for more and better sex education (8, 9, 10, 33, 34). For example, in one national survey of the confidential opinions of 1500 middle-class adolescent girls aged 13 to 19, 98 percent said they wanted sex taught in school (10). When asked what was currently being taught and what *should* be taught, most girls responded that such topics as the anatomy and physiology of the female reproductive system and the menstrual cycle not only should be taught, but that they *were* being covered. Most girls also felt strongly that sex education classes should deal with such philosophical or scientific issues as premarital ethics, abortion, birth control and contraception, male and female sex drives, masturbation, homosexuality, loss of virginity, impotence and frigidity, fertility, and the nature of the orgasm. In *all* of these important areas, however, less than half of the sample reported having had school instruction.

In addition, there is a growing tendency among young people to view decisions about individual sexual behavior as more a private and less a public concern (4, 8, 35). This appears to reflect, in part, a growing suspiciousness of or disenchantment with established social institutions and their proclaimed values, together with a shift among many young people in the direction of individual self-discovery and self-expression—of "doing one's thing." But it also reflects a greater emphasis on the impor-

By permission of the author.

tance of "meaningful" (i.e., genuine and sincere) interpersonal relationships, in sex as in other areas.

In the view of a majority of contemporary adolescents, the acceptability of various forms and degrees of sexual behavior, including premarital intercourse, is highly dependent on the nature of the relationship between the individuals involved (16, 20, 26, 29). Eighty per cent of adolescent boys and 72 per cent of girls in this country agree with the statement, "It's all right for young people to have sex before getting married if they are in love with each other." Seventy-five per cent of all girls maintain that "I wouldn't want to have sex with a boy unless I loved him." While only 47 per cent of boys stated this stringent a requirement, 69 per cent said, "I would not want to have sex with a girl unless I liked her as a person" (19). In contrast, most adolescents clearly oppose exploitation, pressure or force in sex, sex solely for the sake of physical enjoyment, and sex between people too young to understand what they are getting into (16, 20, 29). Nearly seventy-five per cent of all adolescents concur that "when it comes to morality in sex, the important thing is the way people treat each other, not the things they do together" (29).

Despite a growing emphasis among contemporary adolescents on openness and honesty, there is little evidence of an increased preoccupation with sex, as many parents and other adults seem to think. Indeed, it may well be that the average adolescent of today is less preoccupied and concerned with sex than prior generations of young people, including his parents when they were the same age. Greater acceptance of sex as a natural part of life may well lead to less preoccupation than anxious concern in an atmosphere of secrecy and suppression. Most contemporary adolescents (87 per cent) agree that "All in all, I think my head is pretty well together as far as sex is concerned" (29).

Furthermore, in ranking the relative importance of various goals, younger adolescent boys and girls (13 to 15) cited as most important: "Preparing myself to earn a good living when I get older," "Having fun," and "Getting along with my parents," and for younger girls, "Learning about myself." Older adolescents of both sexes (16 to 19) stressed "Learning about myself" as most important, followed by "Being independent so that I can make it on my own" and "Preparing myself to accomplish useful things." Among all age groups, "Having sex with a number of different boys (girls)" and "Making out" consistently ranked at or near the top among goals considered *least* important (29).

ARE CHANGING ATTITUDES REFLECTED IN BEHAVIOR?

Are the significant and apparently enduring changes in sexual attitudes and values among contemporary adolescents reflected in their behavior and, if so, how? At least until very recently, a number of generally recognized authorities maintained that the overall behavior of today's adolescents and youth, though more open and in some respects probably freer, did not differ strikingly from that of their parents at the same age (20, 24, 28). Conversely, other observers have asserted that although attitudinal changes may have been the more dramatic, there have also been marked changes in behavior (17, 20). What do the available data reveal?

As will become evident, the answer appears to depend on *what* behaviors one is referring to, among *which* adolescents, and *how recently.*

Although current data are admittedly incomplete, the available information indicates that there has been relatively little if any change in the past two decades in the incidence of male masturbation (1, 21, 22, 27, 29). Masturbation appears to have remained fairly stable over the years, with an estimated incidence of about 21 per cent by age 12, 82 per cent by age 15, and 92 per cent by age 20 (13, 27). However, recent data (9, 29) indicate that there has been an increase in masturbation among girls at all age levels, with incidences of *at least* 36 per cent by age 15 and 42 per cent by age 19. In contrast, only about 17 per cent of the mothers of today's adolescent girls had engaged in masturbation to orgasm by age 15, and by age 20, only about 30 per cent (12).

One might be tempted to conclude that masturbation would occur most commonly among adolescents lacking other outlets. Interestingly, however, current masturbation experience among contemporary adolescents occurs about three times as frequently among those engaged in sexual intercourse or petting to orgasm as among the sexually inexperienced (29).

Petting does appear to have increased somewhat in the past few decades, and it tends to occur slightly earlier (12, 13, 16, 20, 23, 24, 29). The major change, however, has probably been in frequency of petting, degree of intimacy of techniques involved, the frequency with which petting leads to erotic arousal or orgasm, and, certainly, frankness about this activity (2, 4, 16, 19, 28, 29).

Premarital Intercourse.   Currently, the greatest amount of public discussion (and parental and societal apprehension), as well as the most extensive data, deals with the incidence of sexual intercourse among contemporary adolescents and youth. A favorite assertion among those who have claimed there have been few *recent* changes in adolescent sexual behavior is that while there has indeed been a sexual revolution in this century, it took place, not among today's adolescents, but among their parents and grandparents. It does, in fact, appear that significant percentage increases in premarital intercourse occurred during this earlier period. For example, Kinsey's data indicate that only 2 per cent of females born before 1900 had premarital intercourse prior to age 16, 8 per cent prior to age 20, and only 14 per cent prior to age 25. In contrast, for the mothers of today's adolescents, the corresponding figures were 4 percent, 21 per cent, and 37 per cent, respectively (12, 13).

This, however, leaves unanswered the question of how the incidence of premarital intimacy among today's parents compares with that of their adolescent sons and daughters. Until very recently relevant data for such a comparison were lacking, except in the case of college students. However, in a study of a representative national sample of adolescents aged 13 to 19, published in 1973, Robert Sorenson (29) found that 44 per cent of boys and 30 per cent of girls have had sexual intercourse prior to age 16. These figures increased to 72 per cent of boys and 57 per cent of girls by age 19. When compared with females of their mother's generation in Kinsey's investigation (only 3 per cent of whom had engaged in premarital intercourse by age 16 and less than 20 per cent by age 19), this represents a very large increase, particularly at the younger age level. When compared with males of their father's generation (approximately 39 per cent of whom had engaged in premarital intercourse by age 16 and 72 per cent by age 19), contemporary adolescent boys as a whole show a much smaller change, mainly a tendency to have first intercourse at a slightly younger age. However, as will become apparent in the following section, these *overall* findings for boys obscure significant changes taking place among boys of higher socioeconomic and educational levels.

DIVERSITY OF SEXUAL ATTITUDES AND BEHAVIOR

Up to this point, our focus has been on *overall* trends in sexual attitudes and behavior among contemporary youth. Such group trends have meaning and usefulness in their own right, but they should not be allowed to distract our attention from an equally important phenomenon: the diversity of sexual attitudes and behavior in different sectors of the adolescent and youth population. There is increasing evidence that this diversity is currently marked and probably growing (5, 16, 20, 29). Such factors as age, sex, socioeconomic and educational level, race, religion, and even geographical area appear to be related to sexual attitudes, values, and behavior. For this reason, the results of almost any survey dealing with adolescent sexuality will inevitably seem exaggerated to some young people and adults and minimized to others.

What do we know about some of these variations? As we have already noted, Sorenson's recent survey (29) shows that for the first time in such studies, a majority (52 per cent) of American adolescents aged 13–19 reported having engaged in sexual intercourse. As significant as this evidence of a trend toward greater sexual freedom clearly is, it should not be allowed to obscure the complementary finding that a very substantial minority (48 per cent) of these adolescents had not as yet had such experience. Furthermore, neither of these broad groups was homogeneous. Thus, adolescents in the nonintercourse group ranged from those with virtually no sexual experience to those with a variety of experiences short of intercourse itself, including petting to orgasm.

Among the group with intercourse experience, two major subgroups emerge from the findings of Sorenson's study: *serial monogamists* and *sexual adventurers.* The former "generally does not have intercourse with another during that relationship. We say 'serial' because one such relationship is often succeeded by another" (29, *121*). The latter, on the other hand, "moves freely from one sex partner to the next and feels no obligation to be faithful to any sex partner" (29, *121*). Among nonvirgins, serial monogamy was more frequent overall, as it was among girls, older adolescents, those from the northeast and west, and those from large metropolitan areas. The total number of partners was obviously far higher among sexual adventurers, although it is interesting to note that frequency of intercourse was higher among monogamists.

Not surprisingly, the two groups tended to vary significantly in attitudes, as well as in behavior. Most monogamists believe they love and are loved by their partners, believe in openness and honesty between partners, and deny that sex is the most important thing in a love relationship—although they also expressed greater satisfaction with their sex lives. At the same time their code stresses personal freedom and the absence of commitment to marriage, despite the fact that more than half believe they will or may marry their partner eventually. Sexual adventurers, in contrast, are primarily interested in variety of experience for its own sake, do not believe that love is a necessary part of sexual relationships, and feel no particular personal responsibility for their partners, although neither do they believe in hurting others. For many adventurers, sex itself is viewed as an avenue to communication; as one young adventurer stated, "Having sex together is a good way for two people to become acquainted."

As a group, monogamists tended to be more satisfied with themselves and life in general, to get along better with parents, and to be more conventional in social, political, and religious beliefs. Despite their greater emphasis on sex as a goal in itself, female adventurers report having orgasm during intercourse less frequently than monogamists.

In general, and contrary to recent popular impressions, both the attitudes and behavior of younger adolescents still appear more *conservative* than those of older adolescents and youths (4, 6, 8, 10, 29). Younger adolescents may or may not, as some have speculated, end up less constrained by social mores than their older brothers and sisters. But the fact remains that for the great majority this is not presently the case.

Girls as a group are consistently more conservative than boys, both in attitudes and values and in behavior. In virtually all population subgroups, the incidence of all forms of intimate sexual behavior is less frequent among girls, and girls are more likely than boys to believe that partners in advanced forms of petting or intercourse should be in love, engaged, or married (9, 16, 20, 25, 29). Girls are also more likely than boys to be influenced by parental wishes and community social standards. In Sorenson's study, 80 per cent of sexual adventurers were male; in contrast, 64 per cent of serial monogamists were female. (The implication here is that a significant percentage of female monogamists were involved with males who were over 19, and hence not included in the study; the other possibility is that in some relationships the girl considered herself a monogamist but the boy did not.) The greater emphasis among girls on love as a necessary component of sexual relationships is consistent with the stronger interpersonal orientation of girls generally. The extent to which a higher level of sexual activity among boys is a function of physiological differences, cultural influences, or, as seems most likely, both, is still an unresolved question (1, 4, 17).

College youth emerge as consistently less conservative in their attitudes and values than noncollege peers of the same age. For example, in one study of American youth 17 and older (35), college youth were significantly less likely to express the view that premarital sexual relations were "not a moral issue." They were also more likely to believe that "sexual behavior should be bound by mutual feelings, not by formal ties," and they were more likely to express a desire for "more sexual freedom" than their noncollege peers.

Within the college population there appears to be considerable diversity in attitudes and values, both among geographical regions and types of schools attended—particularly in the case of girls. In general, students from the east and west coasts emerge as less conservative than those from the Midwest (16, 20, 25). In a 1969 study, more than two-thirds of midwestern students, but only about 40 per cent of eastern students (both male and female) responded affirmatively to the question, "Do you feel that ideally it is still true that a man and a girl who marry should have their first full sexual experience together?" Similarly, three-fourths of girls at midwestern schools but less than a third of those at eastern schools agreed that "coitus was reasonable 'only if married' for possible participants who would be in the 21- to 23-year age group" (20, *163*). Students at permissive, liberally oriented colleges emerge as less conservative than those at more traditional colleges (6, 16, 20). Interestingly, the only apparent exception to the tendency for girls to have more conservative attitudes and values than boys occurs among students in some highly permissive, liberal colleges (16, 20).

It is also among college youth that the greatest changes in sexual behavior have occurred since their parents' generation (4, 16, 20, 30, 31). This trend appears especially pronounced among some demographically distinguishable groups of female students. In the 1940s, Kinsey and others (12, 13, 23) found that by the age of 21 the incidence of premarital experience among college-educated persons was 49 per cent for males and 27 per cent for females. In contrast, several recent, broadly representative investigations of American college and university students of comparable ages conducted between 1967 and 1971 (9, 16, 20, 30, 31) indicate a substantial upward shift, particularly among girls. Thus, for males, obtained incidence figures in these investigations ranged from a low of 58 per cent to a high of 82 per cent; comparable percentages for females ranged from a low of 43 per cent to a high of 56 per cent. In both cases, the highest percentages were obtained in the most recent samples (9, 30, 31, 36).

Interestingly, whereas the percentage of male students engaging in premarital intercourse appeared to have reached a plateau (of about 80 per cent) by 1970, the incidence among girls was apparently still increasing in 1971: 51 per cent of female students reported having had intercourse in 1970; 56 per cent (approximately 10 per cent more) did so in 1971. Premarital relations are likely to be more frequent among those attending eastern colleges and universities than among those attending midwestern institutions (20) and among students attending private, "elite" colleges and universities.

Politically conservative youth are more conservative in sexual attitudes and values than "moderate reformers" and far more conservative than left-oriented "revolutionary" youth (4, 9, 30, 31, 34). Thus, among older adolescents *in general* (both college and noncollege), only 18 per cent of conservative youth stated they would welcome more sexual freedom, as compared with 43 per cent of moderate reformers and 80 per cent of revolutionaries (35). Similarly, nearly two-thirds of conservative youth viewed premarital sexual relations as a moral issue, compared with one-third of moderate reformers and none of the revolutionaries.

Cultural differences are clearly reflected in the variations obtained between nations in various studies (3, 11, 15, 16, 20). Canada and the United

States consistently rank lowest in incidence of premarital intercourse and England ranks highest, followed by the Scandinavian countries.[1]

Even on the basis of the limited data discussed in this essay, it appears clear that adolescent attitudes and values regarding sex *and* sexual behavior itself are changing, although the extent of the change varies widely from one segment of the youth population to another. Indeed, as in other areas of social concern, *the differences between some subgroups of youth appear wider than those between youth in general and adults in general.* There is a real and often ignored danger in generalizing too widely from specialized subgroups (e.g., a particular college campus or a particular urban high school) to youth in general. Furthermore, the greatest *relative* changes in both attitudes and behavior since their parents' generation have occurred among middle- and upper-class adolescents, particularly girls. Not surprisingly, it is among this socioeconomically favored, and probably more socially conflicted, segment of the youth population that the "youth culture" of the 1960s took root and found its sustenance.

In brief these findings, combined with general observation, do indicate an emerging new morality among contemporary adolescents. While this emerging new morality has many positive aspects—a greater emphasis on openness and honesty, mutual respect and lack of dissembling or exploitation, and a more "natural" and better-informed approach to sex—it would be a mistake to conclude that the picture is wholly unclouded. Many experienced adolescents, particularly older adolescents and youth, appear able to handle their sexual involvement and their relationships with themselves without undue stress. (Four out of five nonvirgins report getting "a lot of satisfaction" out of their sex lives; two-thirds of all nonvirgins and four out of five monogamists state that sex makes their lives more meaningful.) However, significant minorities report feelings of conflict and guilt, find themselves exploited or rejected, or discover belatedly that they have gotten in over their heads emotionally. Especially after the first experience of intercourse, girls are far more likely than boys to encounter negative feelings. While boys are most likely to report being excited, satisfied, and happy, girls most frequently report being afraid, guilty, worried, or embarrassed after their initial intercourse experience (29).

There are obviously dangers, particularly for girls, with their generally stronger affiliative needs, in assuming that sexual involvement is "okay as long as you're in love." Encouraged by such a philosophy among peers, a girl or boy may become more deeply involved emotionally than she or he can handle responsibly at a particular stage of maturity (1, 4). "An adolescent may also consciously think that his attitudes are more 'liberal' than they actually are, and involvement may lead to unanticipated feelings of guilt, anxiety, or depression" (18, *643*).

There also still remain very practical problems, such as the possibility of pregnancy. Many girls today express the opinion that "now that science has given us the [birth control] pill, we no longer have to be frightened about pregnancy. We just have to decide what is right" (4, *254*). Noble

---

[1] See pp. 231–253 of this book.—Ed.

as this sentiment may be, the facts are that only a small percentage of unmarried girls having intercourse have used the contraceptive pill to prevent pregnancy (7, 14, 29, 32); a disturbingly high percentage—between 55 and 75 per cent—have used no contraceptive device whatever, at least in their first experience; and only a minority consistently use such a device thereafter (14, 29, 36). Even among monogamists, only two-thirds reported always using contraceptive devices. Furthermore, despite talk of the pill, less than a third of female nonvirgins have used it.

Such lack of precaution against pregnancy results partly from ignorance or lack of availability of contraceptive devices. Far more often, however, it results from carelessness, impulsiveness of the moment, a magical conviction that pregnancy cannot really happen, a belief that the spontaneity of sex is impaired ("If the girl uses birth control pills or other forms of contraception, it makes it seem as if she were *planning* to have sex"), or a belief that the *other* partner has taken precautions. Furthermore, 40 per cent of all nonvirgin girls in Sorenson's study agreed that "sometimes I don't really care whether or not I get pregnant." Rather astonishingly, this investigator found that "10 per cent of all American female adolescents and 23 per cent of all nonvirgin girls report that they have been pregnant at least once" (29, *324*).

It seems unlikely that the trend toward premarital intercourse as an accepted practice, and especially toward serial monogamy as the most frequent and the most socially approved pattern among sexually experienced adolescents, will be reversed. Of all residuals of the youth culture of the 1960s, greater sexual freedom and openness appear to be the most enduring. What one must hope is that adolescents entering sexual relationships can be helped to become mature enough, informed enough, responsible enough, sure enough of their own identities and value systems, and sensitive and concerned enough about the welfare of others so that the inevitable casualties in the "sexual revolution" can be reduced to a minimum and sex as a vital part of human relationships can promote, rather than hinder, growth toward maturity and emotional fulfillment.

REFERENCES

1. Bardwick, J. *Psychology of women: A study of bio-cultural conflicts.* New York: Harper & Row, 1971.
2. Bell, R. R. Parent-child conflict in sexual values. *J. Soc. Issues,* 1966, *22:* 34–44.
3. Christenson, H. T., & Carpenter, G. R. Value-behavior discrepancies regarding premarital coitus in three Western cultures. *Am. Sociol. Rev.,* 1962, *27:* 66–74.
4. Conger, J. J. *Adolescence and youth: Psychological development in a changing world.* New York: Harper & Row, 1973.
5. Conger, J. J. A world they never knew: The family and social change. *Daedalus,* Fall 1971, 1105–1138.
6. Gallup poll, *Denver Post,* May 12, 1970.
7. Grinder, D. E., & Schmitt, S. S. Coeds and contraceptive information *J. Marriage Fam.,* 1966, *28:* 471–479.

8. Harris, L. Change, yes—upheaval, no. *Life,* January 8, 1971, 22–27.
9. Hunt, M. Sexual behavior in the 1970s, Part I. *Playboy,* October 1973, 85 ff.
10. Hunt, M. Special sex education survey. *Seventeen,* July 1970, 94 ff.
11. Karlsson, G., Karlsson, S., & Busch, K. Sexual habits and attitudes of Swedish folk high school students. Research Report No. 15. Uppsala, Sweden: Department of Sociology, Uppsala University, 1960.
12. Kinsey, A. C., Pomeroy, W. B., Martin, C. E., & Gebhard, P. H. *Sexual behavior in the human female.* Philadelphia: Saunders, 1953.
13. Kinsey, A. C., Pomeroy, W. B., & Martin, C. E. *Sexual behavior in the human male.* Philadelphia: Saunders, 1948.
14. Lake, A. Teenagers and sex: A student report. *Seventeen,* July 1967, 88.
15. Linner, B. *Sex and society in Sweden.* New York: Pantheon, 1967.
16. Luckey, E., & Nass, G. A comparison of sexual attitudes and behavior in an international sample. *J. Marriage Fam.,* 1969, *31:* 364–379.
17. Money, J., & Ehrhardt, A. A. *Man and woman, boy and girl: The differentiation and dimorphism of gender identity from conception to maturity.* Baltimore: Johns Hopkins Press, 1972.
18. Mussen, P. H., Conger, J. J., & Kagan, J. *Child development and personality.* New York: Harper & Row, 1969 (3rd ed.).
19. Packard, V. . . . and the sexual behavior reported by 2100 young adults. In V. Packard, *The sexual wilderness: The contemporary upheaval in male-female relationships.* New York: Pocket Books, 1970. Pp. 166–184.
20. Packard, V. *The sexual wilderness: The contemporary upheaval in male-female relationships.* New York: Pocket Books, 1970.
21. Pomeroy, W. B. *Boys and sex.* New York: Delacorte, 1969.
22. Pomeroy, W. B. *Girls and sex.* New York: Delacorte, 1969.
23. Reevy, W. R. Adolescent sexuality. In A. Ellis & A. Abarband (Eds.), *The encyclopedia of sexual behavior* (Vol. I). New York: Hawthorn, 1961. Pp. 52–68.
24. Reiss, I. L. How and why America's sex standards are changing. In W. Simon and J. H. Gagnon (Eds.), *The sexual scene.* Chicago: Trans-action Books, 1970. Pp. 43–57.
25. Reiss, I. L. The sexual renaissance in America. *J. Soc. Issues,* April 1966.
26. Reiss, I. L. The scaling of premarital sexual permissiveness. *J. Marriage Fam.,* 1964, *26:* 188–199.
27. Simon, W., & Gagnon, J. H. Psychosexual development. In W. Simon & J. H. Gagnon (Eds.), *The sexual scene.* Chicago: Trans-action Books, 1970. Pp. 23–41
28. Simon, W., & Gagnon, J. H. (Eds.). *The sexual scene.* Chicago: Trans-action Books, 1970.
29. Sorenson, R. C. *Adolescent sexuality in contemporary America: Personal values and sexual behavior ages 13–19.* New York: World, 1973.
30. Student survey, *Playboy,* September 1971, 118 ff.
31. Student survey, *Playboy,* September 1970, 182 ff.
32. *The report of the Commission on Obscenity and Pornography.* New York: Bantam, 1970.

33. What people think of their high schools. *Life*, 1969, *66:* 22–23.
34. Wilson, W. C. et al. *Technical report of the Commission on Obscenity and Pornography, Vol. VI: National survey.* Washington, D.C.: Government Printing Office, 1971.
35. Yankelovich, D. *Generations apart.* New York: CBS News, 1969.
36. Zelnik, M., & Kantner, J. E. Survey of female adolescent sexual behavior conducted for the Commission on Population, Washington, D.C., 1972.

a comparison of sexual attitudes and behavior in an international sample

Gilbert D. Nass

Eleanore B. Luckey
University of Connecticut

Sexual attitudes and practices of college and university youth have recently been surveyed and reported by numerous investigators. The present study includes data from the United States, Canda, England, Norway, and Germany. It should be stressed at the outset that this research was not designed to pinpoint such facts as how many men and women were having sexual outlets and how many times per week and what kind of outlets these were. The investigation purports rather to be a comparative study that suggests existing sexual attitudes and behaviors and reports similarities and differences which seem to exist between the sampled national populations.

THE SAMPLE

Unmarried, undergraduate university students from five countries were included in the sample. The United States was represented by 21 colleges and universities. These were selected with the aim of geographical distribution that would insure adequate representation of the entire country. Seven were in eastern states: a New England men's college, a private university in New York City, an Ivy League university, a state university in New England, a state college in New England, a private women's college in the northeast, and a private women's college known to have liberal parietal rules. Five were in middlewestern states: a state university, a Catholic university in a metropolitan area, a Protestant university in a non-

This study was done in collaboration with Vance Packard, who has used the findings as a basis for his book *The Sexual Wilderness*, David McKay, New York, 1968, and was presented at the Groves Conference on Marriage and the Family, Boston, 1968. The computational part of this work was carried out in the Computer Center-University of Connecticut, which is supported in part by grants GP-1819 and GJ-9 of the National Science Foundation.

Reprinted from the Journal of Marriage and the Family, 1969, 31, 364–379. By permission of the authors and the Council on Family Relations.

metropolitan area, a private coed university in a metropolitan area, and one in a non-metropolitan area. Three were in southern states: a state university, a state university in the upper south, and a private university in a metropolitan area. Finally, six were in western states: a state university in the Rocky Mountain area, a state university in the southwest and one in the northwest, a state university in California and a private one there, and a state college in the southwest.

Contained in the American sample were two all-male colleges and two all-female colleges; two were specifically church-related. Public and private, metropolitan and non-metropolitan, secular and non-secular, coeducational and sexually segregated schools were included. The varied sample was chosen to provide data suggestive of a national picture. In each school 100 students were contacted in schools that were coeducational; the population was half male and half female.

A major university was selected from each of the other countries. An equal number of men and women were chosen from each population. From the German University information was solicited from 450 individuals; each of the other foreign populations was 300. The 150 additional subjects in the German sample were included in order to compensate for using a mailed questionnaire rather than one personally handed to the subjects; it was assumed that the response rate would be lower. Choosing one university that is "typical" of any country's student population is difficult if not impossible—this being especially true in England because of the variety of university types. However, in each country the choice of a large university was made because of its diversified population both geographically and demographically.

The number of respondents was gratifying; out of a total of 3,450 solicitations there were 2,230 subjects (64.6 per cent) who responded, representing a 66.8 per cent return from the United States sample and a 61.6 per cent from the foreign universities. The return was considered gener-

Table 0
Questionnaire Distribution and Response

Sample Category	Number Distributed	Number Returned			Per Cent Returned
		Male	Female	Total	
21 United States universities	2,100	670	728	1,398	66.6
Canada	300	89	91	180	60.0
England	300	142	103	245	81.6
Germany	450	134	121	255	56.7*
Norway	300	86	66	152	50.6
Totals	3,450	1,121	1,109	2,230	64.6

*Because some of these respondents were married, they were considered not eligible for the study and were discarded. The response rate of the unmarried students was 62 per cent, and it was this number which was included in all further analyses.

ally higher than can be expected from a study of this kind and implies an adequate sample from which to generalize. It is interesting that in the North American samples more women responded than men, but in all the European samples the reverse was true. This suggests that European women may be more reluctant to discuss sexual matters than the American and that American men are more reticent than European.

In the United States only third- and fourth-year students were included in the study, but because foreign universities are not structurally comparable with American universities, the subjects were selected according to age; those between 20 and 22 were included. In all samples the ages were *very* similar; the mean for men being 21.1 years and for women, 20.9 years.

PROCEDURE

An inventory composed of 42 questions was designed so that answers could be solicited by checking or circling appropriate responses. In some instances explanatory or further comments were invited. The questionnaire was headed simply "College Checklist" and included questions on social sex roles including career roles for women, attitudes toward marriage especially with regard to sexual behavior, general views on affectional and sexual relationships, affectional and sexual experience of the respondent, and age.

The questionnaire along with a cover letter of explanation was distributed on each of the campuses, except the German, by student distributors who were supervised by a reliable assistant. Confidentiality and anonymity were assured, and stamped, addressed envelopes provided for direct return to the investigators. The German questionnaire which is the only one translated from English to the native language was *mailed* to a random sample of students. In all cases a randomly selected sample was attempted; although in schools where a goodly number of students were known to fit into a special category (for example, students living in their own apartments off campus), a special attempt was made to include some of these subjects.

There were some minor differences in questionnaries in order to keep them appropriate to the population with which they were being used. The German translation modified some of the questions, and therefore the data are not comparable; this will account for lack of German data in some categories.

RESULTS

(1) SEX ROLE DIFFERENCES

Sex roles of the male and female and whether the differences between the sexes should or should not be encouraged give clues to the attitudes youth hold with regard to their own sex and the other, whether "equality" and "sameness" is the current mode or whether sex differentiation is emphasized. Several questions were designed to approach this answer from different angles.

When asked if they thought individuals and society functioned best if male and female roles in life were different though equal, Canadian students provided the strongest approval; Norwegian students were by a considerable margin the least enthusiastic.

Coeducational living arrangements—with men and women occupying separate rooms but in the same dormitories, on the same floors, and in the same wings—were looked on with much more favor in the European schools than those in Canada and the United States. In all cases men were more disposed to these living arrangements than were women.

Table 1
Percentage Yes Responses to: "Do You Support the Idea That Individuals and Society Function Best If Male and Female Roles in Life Remain Essentially Different Though Equal?"

	Male	Female
United States	84.7	88.3
(N)	(645)	(691)
Canada	88.1	94.2
	(84)	(86)
England	68.4	65.6
	(133)	(96)
Germany	63.8	51.9
	(116)	(108)
Norway	49.4	41.9
	(77)	(62)

Table 2
Percentage Responses Favoring Coed Living Arrangements (No Separation of Sex by Floors or Wings) in Dormitories

	Male	Female
United States	35.7	26.1
	(655)	(713)
Canada	36.4	20.0
	(88)	(90)
England	66.9	62.4
	(139)	(101)
Germany	65.0	54.1
	(117)	(109)
Norway	Item not included because of prevailing dormitory practices.	

At all universities there was little support for separating the sexes in the classroom. Fifteen percent of the males and 10 per cent of the females in the United States sample indicated that they believed such separation "would produce a better environment for study." The Canadian and English response was similar, but only five per cent of the Norway students held such a belief.

The subjects were asked, "Is a four-year college education generally as essential for the personal fulfillment and life satisfaction of girls as it is for men of comparable intelligence?" As might be expected, there were decidedly more women than men who replied affirmatively. In Norway 91.8 per cent of the women and 81 per cent of the men replied affirmatively. Only two-thirds of the American men were sure. European men and women were much closer in their agreement than were the North American, and more were sure that there should be equal education. The widest discrepancy between male and female subjects was found in the United States.

Female subjects were asked if they had seriously in mind an occupational career that they would like to pursue most of the next 20 years. Many more of the English and Norwegian women had such careers in mind than those of other countries. Half or fewer of the Canadian, German, and American women planned careers, but more than three-fourths of English and Norwegian. The dilemma posed by career-marriage decisions for women was seen to exist to a considerable degree in all countries. When they were asked if they believed a good many bright girls consciously downgraded their ambitions for a career because of fear that it might hurt their chances of marriage, 71 per cent of the Canadian women agreed as compared to 57 per cent of those in the United States; although about 60 per cent of the men in each of the two countries held this position. In all countries except the United States, more women than men believed this to be true. There was a marked difference between opinions of European men, of whom only about a third thought women had to play down their ambitions in contrast with those in North America. Although the percentage of assenting women ranged from 71 to 38, the greatest difference existed between American and Canadian women. There is no ready explanation of this difference, which is inconsistent with practically all the other findings indicating the United States and Canadian populations hold similar views.

Sex role differences were generally emphasized to a greater extent in the North American countries than in the English and Scandanavian sample where men and women expect more equalization and less differentiation. European students, to a greater extent than American students, preferred both mixed-sex dormitory arrangements and classrooms. The European women planned to have careers, saw it as not interfering with marital roles, and recognized need for education. Their men agreed. Americans and Canadians tended more to see the woman's place in the home.

(2) PARENTAL INDEPENDENCE

Interesting ambiguities with regard to notions of parental independence were presented by the variation in opinions as to whether or not a strong society would be produced if social arrangements could be made that would enable all young people to be financially independent of their parents by the age of 21 regardless of whether they pursued higher education or not. England and Norway gave this idea the greatest support with about half of them agreeing to it. Germany gave it the least. Men generally favored the idea to a greater extent than women.

A related dimension, that of the parentally financed undergraduate marriage, was supported by two-fifths of the English students, both men and women. About a fourth of the Canadian and United States students supported the position; less than a fifth of Norwegian men did.

The view that young people under 21 desire more guidelines and limits received the greatest support from Canadian and United States students (men 36 per cent, women 54 per cent). Only about 20 per cent of the English supported the position, and in all countries women indicated a greater desire for guidelines than men.

Each national sample provided a different pattern in picking the category of people who should set male-female intimacy guidelines. Among persons who felt there was a need for more clearly defined standards, Canadian and American students more frequently designated "parents" and "adults" should be those to set the standards. English students favored "youthful peers" and "adults," and Norwegian students cited "parents" and "schools." "Churches" were virtually ignored by all males and were not much more frequently cited by the females.

Although no clear-cut or well-defined pattern emerged from these findings, it can be generally concluded that the English and Scandinavian youth favored greater financial and moral independence from the parental generation than the North American. However, the majority of young people in all countries rejected social arrangements which would make them financially independent of parents by age 21. They also rejected parentally financed education-marriage. Decidedly more North American than European students, and women more than men, felt guidelines and

Table 3
Percentage Responses to: "If You Feel There Is a Need for More Clearly Defined Standards Who, Under Modern Conditions, Should Have the Main Responsibility for Setting Them?"

	United States		Canada		England		Norway	
	Male	*Female*	*Male*	*Female*	*Male*	*Female*	*Male*	*Female*
Youthful peers	21.8	17.8	11.4	18.9	31.4	34.8	6.7	13.5
Parents	37.4	43.1	41.8	25.1	25.7	15.2	47.3	36.5
Schools	6.8	5.8	12.3	18.1	12.9	17.9	27.1	27.0
Churches	5.1	3.9	2.1	7.8	2.9	8.9	—	9.5
Adults	28.9	29.4	32.4	30.1	27.1	23.2	18.9	13.5
	100%	100%	100%	100%	100%	100%	100%	100%
(N)	(412)	(466)	(48)	(58)	(70)	(56)	(37)	(37)

limits were needed for sexual standards, and only in England were "youthful peers" favored over adults for determining such standards.

(3) ATTITUDES TOWARD MARRIAGE AND SEXUAL BEHAVIOR

Marriage was given a strong vote of confidence by all the samples, as the majority responded negatively to the question, "Can you visualize a happy, satisfying life for yourself that might not include marriage?" About 20 per cent more Canadian and American youth responded "no" than European. Ten per cent more of the Norwegian men than women replied negatively; this is the only response where the male percentage was higher than the female. Some of the subjects were not sure; English men more frequently indicated the "uncertain" response (31.6 per cent) than any other group. Canadian females (15.7 per cent) were less often in doubt than any other group. Twenty-nine per cent of the Norwegian females and 26.2 per cent of English females responded that they *could* be happy though unmarried, but only about 15 per cent of Canadian and American women replied in the affirmative. About a fourth of the male subjects in the United States, Norway, and England believed they could live happily though unmarried. Few Canadian subjects—either men or women—indicated they fancied an unmarried life. Again it is the European samples that have indicated a greater break with the traditional pattern.

The ideal age for marriage was fairly uniform among the universities. Males at all schools indicated about 25 as the modal choice. American women most frequently indicated an age between 21 and 23; all other national groups indicated a year or two older. In general, both men and women in all samples indicated a preference for the man to be slightly older than the woman.

The idea that a couple who marry should have their first full sexual experience together, found greatest support among Canadian and Norwegian females. The least support was by English females. The range of difference was greater between female samples. The greatest congruence between the sexes was found in the United States sample, where about one-half thought this true.

An additional specification that the sexual experience should be "only after marriage" was preferred by all female subjects when compared to male and was marked by subjects of both sexes more frequently in American universities. English men and women, and then Norwegian, marked this qualification least frequently.

In an attempt to appraise attitudes toward the double standard sex code, the question was asked:

> Do you think it is reasonable for a male who has experienced coitus elsewhere to expect that the girl he hopes to marry be chaste at the time of marriage?

A "yes" response was interpreted as potential support for the double standard. Virtually no support was given the idea by Norwegian students. American and Canadian females most strongly supported the double stan-

Table 4
**Percentage of Affirmative Responses Indicating
That Ideally a Man and Women Who Marry Should
Have Their First Full Sexual Experience Together**

	Affirmative Responses		Only After Marraige	
	Male	*Female*	*Male*	*Female*
United States	50.5	51.1	35.5	46.9
(N)	(646)	(709)	(600)	(657)
Canada	49.4	65.5	23.7	51.2
	(85)	(87)	(80)	(84)
England	37.3	29.3	20.0	28.1
	(134)	(99)	(125)	(89)
Norway	46.3	60.0	20.5	28.3
	(82)	(60)	(73)	(60)

Table 5
**Percentage Male and Female Responses to: "Do You
Think It Is Reasonable for a Male Who Has Experienced
Coitus Elsewhere to Expect That the Girl He Hopes to Marry
Be Chaste at the Time of Marriage?"**

	United States		Canada		England		Norway	
	Male	*Female*	*Male*	*Female*	*Male*	*Female*	*Male*	*Female*
Yes	21.3	35.9	20.5	32.6	15.1	10.9	1.2	6.5
No	68.4	53.4	71.1	56.2	59.7	54.5	71.8	66.1
Preposterous Anachronism	10.3	10.7	8.4	11.2	24.5	34.7	27.1	27.4
	100%	100%	100%	100%	100%	100%	100%	100%
(N)	(643)	(716)	(83)	(89)	(139)	(101)	(85)	(62)

dard position with approximately a third of them agreeing; a fifth of the men from these same two countries held this view.

The German questionnaire was modified to read:

> One often hears the opinion that it is better for a marriage if the girl is still a virgin before marriage but the man has had sexual experience beforehand. Other people say a man with sexual experience cannot expect to marry a virgin girl. With which opinion do you agree most?

Only 13.2 per cent of the men and 18.9 per cent of the women supported the double standard position. About a fourth of the women and a fifth of the men believed neither partner should have experience before marriage; two-thirds of the men and slightly more than half the women believed that both partners should have premarital experience. In all samples subjects rejected the double standard—European students more than North American. Interestingly, in all countries except England, women more frequently than men *supported* the double standard.

Also related to attitudes held toward the double standard was the inquiry (see Table 6):

> Would it trouble you to marry a person who had experienced premarital coitus with someone else before becoming seriously involved with you?

The percentage of women answering "No" was highest in the United States and lowest in Canada; the greatest percentage of men was in Norway and the lowest, in Canada. Twice as many women as men in the

Table 6
Percentage Responses to: "Would It Trouble You to Marry a Person Who Had Experienced Coitus with Someone Else Before Becoming Involved with You?"

	United States		Canada		England		Norway	
	Male	*Female*	*Male*	*Female*	*Male*	*Female*	*Male*	*Female*
Yes, seriously	16.7	9.0	15.0	12.4	10.1	6.9	2.4	6.5
Some, but not seriously	53.5	29.8	54.0	41.6	43.5	34.7	50.6	35.5
No	29.8	61.2	31.0	46.0	46.4	58.4	47.0	58.0
	100%	100%	100%	100%	100%	100%	100%	100%
(N)	(658)	(722)	(87)	(89)	(138)	(101)	(85)	(62)

Table 7
Percentage Responses to: "Do You Feel a Person Can Have Numerous Sexual Affairs and Still Bring a Deep, Enduring Emotional Commitment to the Person He or She Marries?"

	United States		Canada		England		Norway	
	Male	*Female*	*Male*	*Female*	*Male*	*Female*	*Male*	*Female*
Yes	52.1	52.9	63.2	46.7	55.7	51.0	58.8	43.5
No	14.1	18.4	13.8	20.0	9.3	18.0	15.3	24.2
Am not sure	33.8	28.7	23.0	33.3	35.0	31.0	25.9	32.3
	100%	100%	100%	100%	100%	100%	100%	100%
(N)	(657)	(717)	(87)	(90)	(140)	(100)	(85)	(62)

United States answered "No," and this represented by far the greatest discrepancy between the sexes in any one sample. As was expected, in all cases men indicated more concern than women about the chasity of their marital partner. This suggests that some male students, also primarily American and Canadian, encourage the double standard.

In all the samples both men and women subjects were approximately equally divided between those who held the opinion that an individual might have had numerous sexual affairs before marriage and still bring a deep and enduring commitment to the person he marries and those

Table 8

Percentage Responses to: "Regardless of Age (After 16) or the Stage of Formal Commitment, Do You Feel That Full Intimacy Is Appropriate If Both Persons Desire It and They Feel a Sense of Trust, Loyalty, Protectiveness, and Love?"

	United States		Canada		England		Germany		Norway	
	Male	*Female*	*Male*	*Female*	*Male*	*Female*	*Male*	*Female*	*Male*	*Female*
Yes	31.6	19.4	36.2	23.6	55.3	43.9	28.0	25.9	42.9	50.0
Only if mature	38.4	40.9	46.8	34.6	33.4	41.9	61.9	57.1	41.0	27.8
Doubt	12.1	10.6	6.4	21.8	5.2	6.0	—*	—*	12.5	5.6
Definitely not a sufficient basis	17.9	29.3	10.6	20.0	6.1	8.2	10.1	17.0	3.6	16.6
	100%	100%	100%	100%	100%	100%	100%	100%	100%	100%
(N)	(190)	(284)	(47)	(55)	(132)	(98)	(118)	(112)	(56)	(36)

* "Doubt" alternative was not on Germany questionnaire.

Table 9

✗ Age Level and Type of Relationship Viewed by *Males* as Appropriate for Considering Coitus

	Ages 14–17				18–20			
Type of Relationship	*United States*	*Canada*	*England*	*Norway*	*United States*	*Canada*	*England*	*Norway*
Only if married	67.6	80.3	28.7	55.7	33.5	38.6	9.6	17.6
Officially engaged	10.7	5.3	13.9	27.9	14.8	15.7	17.6	17.6
Tentatively engaged	6.7	3.6	7.9	6.6	15.5	15.7	15.8	35.1
Going steady	8.5	3.6	26.8	6.6	20.5	15.7	28.1	16.2
Good friends	2.1	3.6	5.9	1.6	8.1	8.6	9.6	5.4
Casually attracted	4.4	3.6	16.8	1.6	7.6	5.7	21.1	8.1
	100%	100%	100%	100%	100%	100%	100%	100%
(N)	(469)	(56)	(101)	(61)	(540)	(70)	(114)	(74)

who either did not think so or were uncertain about it. Certainly it can be said that numerous premarriage sexual partners were not seen as a serious deterrent to the marriage relationship by the majority of students in each of the samples. Sexual activity prior to marriage was viewed negatively by more females than males, and Norwegian women were the most skeptical. Except for the American sample, the difference between countries was not so great as between the two sexes of specific countries. In the United States men and women showed remarkable agreement (Table 7). It's interesting that in the United States and Canada, where there is considerably less premarital coitus (see Table 13), there are almost as many students who believe numerous sexual affairs would not interfere with marriage as in those countries where there is more premarital coitus. This would indicate that it is not fear that the experience would destroy some quality in the marriage that acts as a deterrent to premarital intercourse.

When asked the following question, "Yes" responses were high in the English and Norwegian samples; low in the American and German (see Table 8):

Regardless of age (after 16) or the stage of formal commitment, do you feel that full intimacy is appropriate if both persons desire it and they have a sense of trust, loyalty, protectiveness, and love?

In general, women subjects consistently were more reluctant to sanction such intimacy. The category receiving the greatest number of responses from all subjects in all countries was "Only if mature."

The following question was answered most frequently by all students in all countries by "Only if married" for ages prior to 18. However, gener-

Table 9 (Continued)

	21–23				24 and Over		
United States	Canada	England	Norway	United States	Canada	England	Norway
23.4	16.0	11.0	7.2	18.9	12.1	13.1	7.5
15.0	18.7	8.4	13.0	13.9	12.1	7.6	9.0
16.1	21.3	12.8	20.3	11.5	16.7	11.2	16.4
19.0	20.0	32.1	31.9	18.1	22.7	25.2	23.8
14.3	12.0	12.8	8.8	13.9	16.7	9.3	17.9
12.2	12.0	22.9	18.8	23.7	19.7	33.6	25.4
100%	100%	100%	100%	100%	100%	100%	100%
(566)	(75)	(109)	(69)	(501)	(66)	(107)	(67)

^x*Table 10*

Age Level and Type of Relationship Viewed by *Females* as Appropriate for Considering Coitus

Type of Relationship	Ages 14–17				18–20			
	United States	Canada	England	Norway	United States	Canada	England	Norway
Only if married	86.5	94.6	43.1	78.4	58.6	62.0	16.4	40.0
Officially engaged	7.7	3.6	13.8	10.8	16.7	15.5	17.8	13.3
Tentatively engaged	2.1	1.8	13.8	5.4	11.7	14.1	9.6	22.3
Going steady	2.5	0	12.3	2.7	9.7	5.6	35.6	20.0
Good friends	0.8	0	9.2	0	1.2	2.8	9.6	0
Casually attracted	0.4	0	7.8	2.7	2.1	0	11.0	4.4
	100%	100%	100%	100%	100%	100%	100%	100%
(N)	(530)	(56)	(65)	(7)	(580)	(71)	(73)	(45)

ally marriage is seen as less important as the age of the individual increases.

What kind of relationship should prevail before a male and female should consider coitus as personally and socially reasonable?

Both English men and women, more than any other nationality, indicated that "going steady" and being "casually attracted" between ages 14–17 were appropriate conditions for intercourse; English women checked the response indicating coitus was appropriate *only* in marriage substantially less frequently than did women of any other country in all age categories from 14 to 24 and over (Tables 9 and 10).

The widest gap between categories for both men and women, in all age groups, and among all nationalities was between "going steady" and "good friends." In many instances but without a discernible pattern, more male subjects considered it appropriate to have coitus with one to whom he was casually attracted than with a good friend. Women seemed to favor slightly the friend over the casual attraction. These findings undoubtedly reflect the romantic concept that being in love and being physically attracted to a sexual partner is more appropriate than is a basis of friendship.

The English were generally more acceptant than other nationalities of premarital intercourse under a variety of conditions and at younger ages. Females in all samples generally expressed considerably greater support than did the males for consideration of coitus "only if married." Canadian females, the most conservative group, gave no support for coitus outside the married or engaged relationship for ages 14–17, but 27 per cent approved when the age was 24 or over. Chronological age, which

Table 10 (Continued)

	21–23				24 and Over		
United States	Canada	England	Norway	United States	Canada	England	Norway
46.0	45.8	13.7	26.0	38.3	39.7	13.5	24.4
19.2	22.3	12.3	10.0	17.4	20.6	9.5	11.1
15.4	23.6	8.2	24.0	14.0	12.7	10.8	13.3
13.6	6.9	31.5	30.0	19.2	17.5	24.3	37.8
3.2	1.4	19.2	4.0	6.1	6.3	16.2	2.3
2.6	0	15.1	6.0	5.0	3.2	25.7	11.1
100%	100%	100%	100%	100%	100%	100%	100%
(624)	(72)	(73)	(50)	(557)	(63)	(74)	(45)

probably was judged to reflect personal maturity, was held by all subjects as an important factor in determining under what conditions coitus was appropriate.

When questioned about the opinion that a good lovemaking relationship was "almost always consummated by" mutual, simultaneous orgasm, respondents showed no national differences and no differences within the sexes. About half of the men thought it was true, about a third of the women.

By studying the opinions that were expressed toward marriage and sexual behavior, one can generally conclude that although traditional values are held to some extent in all countries, what may be called "liberal views" are also to be found in each of the national samples. European countries are more liberal than those on the North American continent. Men are less invested in marriage and less restricted in sex than women. Marriage is still an overwhelmingly popular way of life, and the age of marriage is ideally the early twenties. Indicative of a swing away from the traditional was the evidence that the double standard of sexual morals is definitely on its way out, and students are not greatly concerned about the first sexual experience being in marriage or being with the partner who eventually becomes the spouse. Even having several sexual partners before marriage was not judged particularly detrimental to the marriage. Age was viewed as a very important factor determining under what conditions coitus was appropriate; the older the individual the more freedom he had.

The English in general were seen to have the least restrictive attitudes toward sexual behavior. Norwegian women, although liberal, tended to be a good deal less liberal than their men. The Canadian sample held somewhat more conservative attitudes than the United States, but in most instances the two samples resembled each other and could be contrasted with the European samples.

(4) SEXUAL EXPERIENCE AND BEHAVIOR

When women were asked to classify the men whom they had dated in the past year into those they thought (a) would be frightened by real intimacy; (b) those who seemed content with gestures of intimacy such as a farewell embrace; (c) those who were happy enough if their hands were allowed to wander; and (d) those who were disappointed if they couldn't persuade the girl to go all the way, more American and Canadian girls marked *b* than any other response. English and Norwegian marked *d* and German marked *c* (Table 11). The contrast between Canadian and American women when compared to English women is particularly noticeable on response *d*. The North American women indicated that men were decidedly less demanding than English women reported men to be.

Canadian and United States men give a very congruent picture of their dates during the past year (Table 12). Both indicated most of their dates usually went along for fun up to the point of light petting. English male students most frequently suggested the partner resisted real intimacies unless there had been talk of love. German students most frequently indi-

Table 11
Percentage Female Responses to: "Review in Your Mind Briefly the Men You Have Dated in the Past Year. How Would You Classify Most of Them in Regard to Interest in Intimacy?"

	United States	Canada	England	Ger-many	Norway
a) I think real intimacy would frighten most of them.	13.8	11.1	13.6	15.7	14.2
b) They seem content with gestures of intimacy such as the farewell embrace.	41.5	44.4	22.2	9.6	26.2
c) If their hands can wander, that seems to keep them happy.	25.0	31.7	18.5	50.6*	28.6
d) They are disappointed if you don't want to go all the way.	16.0	12.8	44.4	24.1	31.0
e) Only dated one.	3.7	0.0	1.3	0.0	0.0
	100%	100%	100%	100%	100%
(N)	(581)	(63)	(81)	(81)	(42)

* German reworded as follows: "Most are satisfied with necking."

Table 12
**Percentage Male Responses to "Review in Your Mind the
Girls You Have Dated This Past Year. How Would You
Classify Most of Them in Regard to Interest in Intimacy?"***

	United States	Canada	England	Germany	Norway
They are pretty conservative beyond perhaps a goodnight kiss.	22.2	16.7	16.3	45.2	19.7
They will usually go along for fun up to a point of light petting.	46.6	50.6	35.0	8.9	42.1
They resist real intimacies unless there has been talk of love.	43.5	36.4	39.0	22.8	32.9
They seem happy to go as far as I want to go, short of coitus.	27.4	28.6	33.0	31.7	46.1
They seem to want to go all the way if we have a chance.	14.9	24.7	34.1	37.0	40.8
(N)	(609)	(77)	(123)	(101)	(76)

* Multiple responses were suggested in the questionnaire; therefore each figure reports that the per cent of the total N of each respective sample which agreed with that specific response.

cated their dates were pretty conservative beyond perhaps a goodnight kiss, and Norwegian men most frequently described their dates as "happy to go as far as I want to go, short of coitus."

The description that "They seem to want to go all the way if we have a chance" was marked most frequently by Norwegian students and least frequently by Canadian students. Specific behaviors of dating partners cannot be determined with any reliability by the responses of either women or men subjects or by comparing the two (Tables 11 and 12). The multiple responses of male students are especially difficult to interpret; however, the composite picture of dating behavior that does appear from the data is one of conservativism in Canada and the United States, where men and women agree that gestures of affection and light petting are modal. In contrast, more European women (especially English and Norwegian) reported that men are disappointed if "you don't want to go all the way," and more European men reported that women want to go all the way! The fact that European students do indeed engage in more sexual activity on dates was confirmed when subjects reported on their own sexual behavior.

Subjects were asked to indicate their participation in a spectrum of sexual behaviors from light embracing and holding hands to coitus

X

(Tables 13 and 14). Among the males, Canadian students generally indicated the highest frequencies of participation in the casual and light petting behavior categories, and the English students the highest in general
petting, nude embrace, and coitus. German men consistently reported the
lowest rate of involvement in all categories. The pattern of behaviors reported by American and Canadian men was strikingly similar in all categories, with Canadian men consistently reporting somewhat more conservative behavior.

   As would be expected, there is a decided drop in the number of subjects who report petting below the waist of the girl and petting below
the waist of *both* the man and the girl. Mutual genital petting behavior
is reported only slightly more frequently than coitus by men subjects of
all countries and by women in European countries; however, 15 per cent
more American and Canadian girls report mutual genital petting than re-

Table 13
**Percent of Males Reporting Experiencing Respective
Sexual Behaviors**

Type of Sexual Behavior	United States	Canada	England	Ger- many	Norway
Light embracing or fond holding of hands	98.6	98.9	93.5	93.8	93.7
Casual goodnight kissing	96.7	97.7	93.5	78.6	86.1
Deep kissing	96.0	97.7	91.9	91.1	96.2
Horizontal embrace with some petting but not undressed	89.9	92.0	85.4	68.8	93.6
Petting of girl's breast area from outside her clothing	89.9	93.2	87.0	80.4	83.5
Petting of girl's breast area with- out clothes intervening	83.4	92.0	82.8	69.6	83.5
Petting below the waist of the girl under her clothing	81.1	85.2	84.6	70.5	83.5
Petting below the waist of both man and girl, under clothing	62.9	64.8	68.3	52.7	55.1
Nude embrace	65.6	69.3	70.5	50.0	69.6
Coitus	58.2	56.8	74.8	54.5	66.7
One-night affair involving coitus; didn't date person again	29.9	21.6	43.1	17.0	32.9
Whipping or spanking before petting or other intimacy	8.2	5.7	17.1	0.9	5.1
Sex on pay-as-you-go basis	4.2	4.5	13.8	9.8	2.5
(N)	(644)	(88)	(123)	(112)	(79)

Table 14
Per Cent of Females Reporting Experiencing Respective Sexual Behaviors

Types of Sexual Behavior	United States	Canada	Eng- land	Ger- many	Norway
Light embracing or fond holding of hands	97.5	96.5	91.9	94.8	89.3
Casual goodnight kissing	96.8	91.8	93.0	74.0	75.0
Deep kissing	96.5	91.8	93.0	90.6	89.3
Horizontal embrace with some petting but not undressed	83.3	81.2	79.1	77.1	75.0
Petting of girl's breast area from outside her clothing	78.3	78.8	82.6	76.0	64.3
Petting of girl's breast area without clothes intervening	67.8	64.7	70.9	66.7	58.9
Petting below the waist of the girl girl under her clothing	61.2	64.7	70.9	63.5	53.6
Petting below the waist of both man and girl, under clothing	57.8	50.6	61.6	56.3	42.9
Nude embrace	49.6	47.6	64.0	62.1	51.8
Coitus	43.2	35.3	62.8	59.4	53.6
One-night affair involving coitus; didn't date person again	7.2	5.9	33.7	4.2	12.5
Whipping or spanking before petting or other intimacy	4.5	5.9	17.4	1.0	7.1
(N)	(688)	(85)	(86)	(96)	(56)

port coitus. Apparently a crucial point in determining whether most subjects continue to coitus or not is mutual genital petting. This is *less* true for girls in Canada and the United States than for any other group.

The reported coital participation among males in order of frequency was: England highest, followed by Norway, then the United States and Canada, and lowest Germany (Table 13). The pattern indicated by German and Norwegian men is that coitus is more frequent than mutual genital petting. All the other samples reported that for some five to eight per cent of the men, genital petting does not continue to coitus.

Men who reported involvement in whipping and spanking together with sexual intimacy were most frequently English. The second highest frequency for men was the United States sample which reported less than half the incidence of the English. German men reported the least.

English men reported the greatest patronage of prostitutes; then the German; and lowest were the Norwegian. A little more than four per cent of United States and Canadian men reported they had had sex on a pay-as-you-go-basis. It is especially interesting to note that Germany, which had the lowest coital percentage, had the second highest percentage of prostitution, and Norway which has the second highest coital involvement has the lowest prostitution reported. This leads one to conclude that quite a different set of values operate in the two countries, and that Germany maintains more of the traditional point of view and condones the double standard to a greater extent.

Women subjects in general reported less participation in all categories of sexual behavior than men did (Table 14). The highest rates for sexual behavior except for light embraces were reported by English women. Canadian, American, and German females showed similar and slightly less participation through the less intimate and the petting behaviors to the nude embrace; in these same categories the Norwegian females consistently reported the least participation. However, with the nude embrace and coitus, the international female pattern changed; a greater proportion of German and Norwegian women reported involvement and a lesser proportion of Canadian and American women. It can be assumed that petting as a prelude to coitus is more frequently the practice with European women, but with American and Canadian women it is either an end in itself or is the cutoff point of sexual activity. The order of coital frequency as indicated by women subjects is: highest, English; then Germany; Norway; and finally the United States and Canada. These data would tend to confirm the male responses which followed the same pattern except for Germany.

A third of the English women reported "one-night stands"; and although more than 20 per cent less frequently reported, the Norwegian females ranked second highest. The United States, Canada, and Germany followed in that order. Although the percentages reported by men subjects were considerably higher, the order of frequency was the same.

Table 15
Mean Ages of Males and Females at Age of First Petting Experience and of First Coitus

	First Petting Mean Age		First Coitus Mean Age	
Universities	*Males*	*Females*	*Males*	*Females*
United States	16.3	17.3	17.9	18.7
(N)	(608)	(612)	(374)	(297)
Canada	16.6	17.3	18.5	18.4
	(85)	(76)	(50)	(29)
England	15.6	15.8	17.5	17.5
	(117)	(81)	(90)	(57)
Germany	16.6	17.0	19.0	19.5
	(107)	(90)	(61)	(57)
Norway	15.6	16.5	18.4	18.8
	(73)	(50)	(53)	(29)

The one behavior category in which the female subjects reported in both a similar pattern and a similar percentage as the males within their respective sample was that of "whipping and spanking." The generally low percentage may account somewhat for this finding. Both England and Norway, which report a proportionately greater number of students engaged in these sadomasochistic practices, also rank high in coital frequency. The positive correlation of the two factors can be speculated upon, but accounting for the relationship remains for further investigation.

The ages at first petting and first coital experience are given in Table 15. The mean age for males at first petting was lowest (15.6 years) in England and Norway, eight months older in the United States, and a year older for both Canada and Germany. English females began petting earliest at age 15.6; Norwegian females almost a year later; German females at age 17; and finally Canadian and American females still four months later. English students who began petting youngest also had intercourse youngest. German and Norwegian students who were the oldest at first intercourse began petting experiences at approximately the same ages as men in other samples. United States and Canadian men and women report the shortest interval between the age at which they began petting and the age at which it was consummated in intercourse. In all cases men reported first petting at an age younger than women; except for Canadian and English men who reported first coitus at nearly the same age as Canadian and English women, men were also younger at age of first coitus.

It is interesting to note the pattern of delay between first petting and first coitus for each sample. The shortest interval is demonstrated by the Canadian and American girl. This is followed by the American man and the English man and woman. Norwegian and German men and women delay coitus for the longest intervals—all over two years—and Norwegian men wait nearly three years.

Considerable variation exists in the sample in the reported number of coital partners (Table 16). The greatest promiscuity was reported by English students, with almost three-fourths of the males reporting "several" and "many" partners; and two-thirds of the females reported in these same categories. About 58 per cent of the American male students reported "several" and "many" partners; about half the Norwegian males reported "several" and "many" partners; only a third of the German men

Table 16

Percentage Coitus-Experiencing Males and Females, by Designation of Number of Partners

Number of Partners Engaged in Coitus	United States		Canada		England		Germany		Norway	
	Male	Female	Male	Female	Male	Female	Male	Female	Male	Female
One	24.3	46.6	36.7	44.8	17.6	22.4	41.7	47.4	32.1	32.1
Two	17.9	18.8	10.2	34.5	8.8	12.1	25.0	28.1	17.0	21.4
Several	40.4	26.5	34.7	17.3	47.3	44.8	30.0	24.5	37.7	39.3
Many	17.4	8.1	18.4	3.4	26.3	20.7	3.3	0.0	13.2	7.2
	100%	100%	100%	100%	100%	100%	100%	100%	100%	100%
(N)	(374)	(298)	(49)	(29)	(91)	(58)	(60)	(57)	(53)	(28)

reported in those categories. As is to be expected, women students in all samples were less promiscuous. Nearly half of the German, American, and Canadian women reported only "one partner," and congruently, fewer of them indicated "many" and "several." Fewer than a fourth of the Canadian and German women marked these combined categories. About a third of the American women and nearly half of the Norwegian women marked these. Nearly two-thirds of the English women marked one or the other of these categories.

Alcohol was not reported as a major factor in first coital experience by many of the subjects. More English females reported they were under the influence of alcohol when they first had intercourse than any other group in the sample; even so, more than half indicated, "I and my partner had not had anything alcoholic to drink." The English had the highest rate reporting "both under the influence of alcohol"; and the German the lowest except for Norwegian women, none of whom reported the couple had been under the influence of alcohol. More Canadian youth than any other reported *no* involvement with alcohol and first coitus—about three-fourths; 68 per cent of the Norwegian men and women reported in that same category and about two-thirds of the American men and women. More English men and women reported alcohol was involved with one or the other or both partners than any other nationality.

Although there are some irregularities and unevenness of pattern, the total picture that one gains from looking at these data is a consistent one presented by the agreement of each sex and by congruent findings in each category of behavior. The English student has more sexual activity, begins younger, has more partners, has more one-night stands, more sadomasochistic experiences, and is more likely to have been influenced by alcohol at the time of the first coital experience.

North American students are less experienced and generally more conservative; the Canadian youth is somewhat less liberal than his counterpart in the United States. The Norwegian student tends to be less the "swinger" than the English. Premarital sexual experience does not start so early and is restricted to fewer partners. Although the picture of German students is not so clear, they generally occupy a place between the liberal English and Norwegian samples and the North American.

SUMMARY AND DISCUSSION

(1) SEX ROLE DIFFERENCES

Some interesting consistencies and inconsistencies are presented by the findings with regard to sex role differences when the various countries are compared. Although in the United States and Canada more students agreed that men and women were indeed different though equal, and fewer than half of the Norwegian students took this position, it was the Norwegian students who in the largest percentage indicated that a four-year college education was generally as essential for women as men. English students tended to agree with the Norwegian; and consistent with this both Norwegian and English female students expressed in greater numbers an intent to follow a career over most of the first 20 years of their out-of-college life.

The Canadian and United States students presented a different picture from the European in that more of them stressed "equality but difference," and fewer of them believed a four-year college education is necessary for women. The North American women tended to be less interested in a career. Canadian men and women more than those of any other country believed women consciously downgraded career ambitions in favor of marriage potential. The European students generally felt this was less true.

European schools favored coed living arrangements much more than North American students, but all students favored mixed classes in the classroom.

Making a broad generalization from these statistics, we could say with reliability that the European students—both men and women—indicated a greater acceptance of sexual equality of opportunity, both in the academic world and in the professional. Canadian men and women expressed ideas which to a greater extent indicated that the female's role and her preparation for it was marital rather than professional. They denied, however, that this marital role was not "equal" with the male role.

(2) PARENTAL INDEPENDENCE

English students favored independence from parents and early marriage with financial support from parents to a greater extent than students of any other nation and rejected the idea that more definite guidelines and limits for youth were needed. Both American and Canadian students were less inclined to want either earlier independence or subsidized marriage and were more inclined to think adult guidelines would be a good idea. There was virtually no support given to religious agencies as a crucial molder of guidelines or limits for youth in the realm of sexual intimacy.

One might conclude from these responses that English youth felt more competent to start and manage life on their own, given the freedom to do so.

(3) ATTITUDES TOWARD MARRIAGE AND SEXUAL BEHAVIOR

That the majority of youth the world around (or at least in this sample) still believe a satisfying life includes marriage is indicated; however, North American students were more sure of this than European. It was surprising to the investigators, however, that nearly a quarter of the samples said marriage was *not* necessary. All samples agreed that men should marry ideally at about age 25 and women at about 23.

Except in England, women more than men favored the idea that the man and woman who marry should have their first sexual experience together. Again the more conservative answers were expressed by the North American students, who preferred coital partners to be marriage partners and were more skeptical of promiscuity and its influence in marriage than were the European students.

Women students in general were more conservative (even in liberal countries) than were men. The women, as much as or more than the men, seem to perpetuate the double standard, and it was perpetuated by North

American youth more generally than European. Women are willing to accept lack of chastity on the part of the male more readily than the male accepted the lack of chastity of the female; although Norwegian students did not seem to value premarital chastity, they rejected promiscuity and the double standard of behavior. English students seem to operate most nearly on the single sex standard, and that standard was described as liberal. Again, United States and Canadian students were more conservative; they were more caught in the traditional double standard.

The majority of students in all samples agree that "maturity" should be a major criteria on which decision and choice of coital partners should be determined; English students, when compared with students from other countries, indicated that this choice can be made at an earlier age.

(4) SEXUAL EXPERIENCES AND BEHAVIOR

Reports by both men and women subjects of their sexual behavior was consistent with their attitudes. More European than North American women reported that men wanted to "go farther on dates"; more European than American men said that women were willing to go farther! Canadian and American men and women were more conservative—content with petting and necking.

North American women, contrary to European women, indicated their dates were generally content with a moderate degree of intimacy instead of disappointment if they would not go all the way. European men, contrary to North American men, indicated women dates seemed to want to go all the way when the opportunity was available.

While the investigators tried to construct patterns of sexual behavior from the responses of men and women students indicating their degree of involvement in activities which range from light embracing to coitus, it became obvious that English men and women more freely participate in a gamut of sexual activities including more genital petting, more frequent coitus, more patronage of prostitution, more sadomasochistic practices, more one-night stands. They start both petting and coitus at a younger age, have more sexual partners, and report alcohol has been a factor in initial coital experience. The general ranking of male student coital rates by countries provides the following descending order: England, Norway, United States, Canada, Germany. The order for female student coital rates was: England, Germany, Norway, United States, and Canada.

Canadian and American youth report patterns of behavior very similar to each other and are in general to be considered conservative regarding sexual behavior. German students hold the most conservative attitudes and exhibit the most restricted behavior among the European samples; Norwegian students were more liberal, and the English consistently the most liberal. Females, as one would expect, are more conservative in all countries than are the males. English women, however, hold views and behave very similarly to English men.

It can be generally concluded from looking at this mass of data that both attitudes and behavior of North American students are more conservative than those of the European. On the background of other studies done earlier, it is evident that there is an increasingly liberal attitude toward sex and generally more premarital participation.

The study gives a reliable report on sexual attitudes and behaviors held by university students in the participating countries, but it fails in that it gives little clue to the meaning or motivation associated with these. Meaning can perhaps be projected into the statistics, but so much of interpretation lies in the eye of the interpreter, that these investigators prefer to let the statistics speak for themselves as they can. The cross-cultural aspects of these data have provided a sound basis on which a comparative assessment of general trends in university students' sexual attitudes and behavior can be made. The variations that have been found suggest the need for further study to explicate and inquire into the meaning of the differential findings, as well as to continue the incorporation of research controls through cross-cultural analysis.

REFERENCES: RESEARCH ON PREMARITAL SEXUAL ATTITUDES, STANDARDS, AND BEHAVIOR

Christensen, Harold T. "Scandinavian and American Sex Norms: Some Comparisons with Sociological Implications," *Journal of Social Issues* (April 1966). 60–75.

Coleman, James. "Female Status and Premarital Sexual Codes," *American Journal of Sociology, 72:* (September, 1966).

Dedman, Jean. "The Relationship Between Religious Attitude and Attitudes Toward Premarital Sex Relations," *Marriage and Family Living* (May, 1959), 171–176.

Ehrman, Winston W. *Premarital Dating Behavior.* New York: Bantam Books, 1959.

Freeman, Harrop A., and Freeman, Ruth S. "Senior College Women: Their Sexual Standards and Activity," *Journal of National Association of Women Deans and Counselors* (Winter and Spring, 1966).

Kinsey, Alfred, *et al. Sexual Behavior in the Human Male.* Wm. Saunders Co., 1948.

———. *Sexual Behavior in the Human Female.* Wm. Saunders Co., 1953.

Kirkendall, Lester A. *Premarital Intercourse and Interpersonal Relationships.* New York: Julian Press, 1961.

Mann, W. E. "Canadian Trends in Premarital Behavior," *The Bulletin for Social Service* (December, 1967) whole issue.

Reiss, Ira L. *Premarital Sexual Standards in America.* New York: Free Press, 1960.

Robinson, Ira, *et al.* "Changes in Sexual Behavior and Attitudes of Colleges Students," *Family Life Coordinator.* (April, 1968), 119–124.

Ross, Robert T. "Measures of the Sex Behavior of College Males Compared with Kinsey's Results," *Journal of Abnormal and Social Psychology, 45:* (1950), 753–755.

Rubin, Isadore. "Changing College Sex: New Kinsey Report," *Sexology.* (June, 1968), 780–782.

Schofield. Michael. *The Sexual Behavior of Young People.* Boston: Little, Brown and Co., 1965.

effects of father absence on personality development in adolescent daughters

E. Mavis Hetherington
University of Virginia

Although the absence of a father in the preschool years has been demonstrated to affect the sex-role typing of preadolescent sons (Bach, 1946; Biller & Bahm, 1970; Hetherington, 1966; Lynn & Sawrey, 1959; Sears, 1951), few effects have been found with daughters. There has been some indication of greater dependency on the mother by girls who have limited access to their fathers (Lynn & Sawrey, 1959); however, this finding has not been reliable. For example, it is reported in a recent study by Santrock (1970) that there were no differences in preschool black girls in dependency, aggression, and femininity as a function of father absence. This lack of disruption of feminine sex-role typing is surprising in view of the evidence of the salience of the father in the sex-role typing of daughters in intact families (Hetherington, 1967; Mussen & Rutherford, 1963).

All major developmental theories of sex-role typing attribute importance to the father's role in this process. Psychoanalytic theorists emphasize the daughter's competition with the mother for the father's love as a critical factor in identification. Role theorists have suggested that because of his differential treatment of sons and daughters, the father is the most important figure in the reciprocal sex-role learning of offspring of either sex (Johnson, 1963). Social learning theorists have assumed that the daughter's acquisition of feminine behavior and of the specific skills involved in interacting with males is at least partly based on learning experiences and reinforcements received in interactions with the father (Hetherington, 1967; Mussen & Rutherford, 1963). This is reflected in the subsequent development of security and culturally appropriate responses in later heterosexual relations (Biller & Weiss, 1970). Since few effects of paternal absence on the development of daughters have been found in the preschool or elementary school years, it may be that such effects only appear at puberty when interactions with males become more frequent.

Studies of delinquent girls suggest that paternal absence may result in disruptions in heterosexual behavior. Although girls are less frequently arrested on delinquency charges than are boys (Glaser, 1965), girls who

---

The author wishes to extend her appreciation to Jan L. Deur for his assistance in the data analysis of this study.

do become delinquent are more likely than delinquent boys to be the product of a broken home (Monahan, 1957; Toby, 1957), and their delinquency is more often due to sexual misconduct (Cohen, 1955; Glaser, 1965).

It has been found that time of separation and reason for separation are important factors in determining the effects of father absence on boys. Separation before age 5 is more disruptive than later separation (Biller & Bahm, 1971; Hetherington, 1966), and a higher incidence of clinic problems (Tuckerman & Regan, 1966), delinquency (Burt, 1929), and recidivism (Nye, 1957) is associated with separation due to divorce than with separation due to death of the father.

The present study was designed to explore the effects of time of and reason for paternal separation on the behavior of father-absent adolescent girls.

METHOD

SUBJECTS

The subjects were three groups of 24 lower- and lower-middle-class, firstborn, adolescent, white girls who regularly attended a community recreation center. They ranged in age from 13 to 17 years. None of the subjects had male siblings. The first group came from intact families with both parents living in the home, the second group from families in which the father was absent due to divorce and in which the child had had minimal contact with the father following the divorce, and the third group from families in which the father was absent due to death. None of the father-absent families had any males living in the home since separation from the father occurred. There were no differences between groups on mean age or education of the subjects, occupation, education, or age of the mothers or fathers, maternal employment, religious affiliation, or number of siblings. Six daughters of divorcees, five daughters of widows, and six daughters from the intact families were only children.

PROCEDURE

The study was comprised of five sets of measures: (a) observational measures of each girl's behavior in the recreation center; (b) measures of each girl's nonverbal behavior in interacting with a male or female interviewer; (c) ratings based on an interview with the daughter; (d) ratings based on interviews with the mother; (e) scores on the California Personality Inventory Femininity Scale (Gough, 1957), the Internal-External Control Scale (Rotter, 1966), the short form of the Manifest Anxiety Scale (Bendig, 1956), and the Draw-a-Person Tests for mothers and daughters (Manchover, 1957).

Observational Procedures in the Recreation Centers. The frequency with which subjects exhibited 21 behaviors during 10 randomly sampled, 3-minute observations was recorded by two female observers. Observations were made in 1-minute units, yielding a total of 30 units. Two of the 3-

minute observations were done at a recreation center dance. Interjudge agreement ranged from 84% to 100% across the various scales. The 21 behaviors recorded were prosocial aggression; verbal aggression toward males and females separately; separate measures for male peers, female peers, male adults, and female adults of instrumental dependence; seeking praise, encouragement, and attention; and subject-initiated physical contact and nearness. In addition, presence in male, female, or neutral areas in the center and participation in masculine, feminine, or neutral activities were obtained.

Measures of masculine, feminine, and neutral areas and activities were originally standardized on 20 girls and 20 boys. The frequency with which these adolescents participated in activities or were present in a given area of the center during 20 randomly sampled, 3-minute periods was recorded. Activities and locations were classified as masculine if boys obtained significantly higher scores than girls, feminine if girls' scores were higher than boys', and neutral if there was no sex difference in frequency.

Procedure for the Assessment of Nonverbal Behavior. When the subjects were first brought into the laboratory, they participated in a 15-minute interview involving neutral content about such things as movies, school, television, etc. Half of the subjects were interviewed by male and half by female interviewers. Three interviewers of each sex were used in the study. Two observers, seated behind a one-way vision screen, recorded the frequency of nonverbal behaviors occurring in 30-second units. Thus there were thirty, 30-second observation units in the 15-minute period. The interview was tape recorded and the number of seconds of subject and experimenter speaking time and silence was calculated. Since it was necessary to control the amount of interviewer looking behavior and snice a fixed gaze was awkward, the interviewer was permitted to look down six times, for 5 seconds each, during the interview.

When the subject was initially ushered into the room by a female experimenter the interviewer was seated behind a desk with three empty chairs positioned with varying proximity to the interviewers. One chair was at the end of the desk adjacent to the interviewer, one was directly across the desk facing the interviewer, and one was across and about 3 feet down the desk from the interviewer. The subject was instructed to sit down and was permitted to select her own seat.

During the course of the interview the observers recorded eye contact when the subject was speaking, when the interviewer was speaking, and when there was silence by depressing telegraph keys which activated the pens of an Esterline-Angus multipen recorder. These procedures are described in greater detail by Exline, Gray, and Schuette (1965). The two observers agreed 96% of the time in their judgments of the subjects' visual fixations. Since eye contact is related to who is speaking, these measures were converted into proportions of eye contact relative to the amount of silence and speaking time by the interviewer and subject.

Five postural measures, adapted from those of Mehrabian (1968), were obtained: (a) shoulder orientation, in terms of 10-degree orientations away from the interviewer; (b) arm openness, as rated on a 7-point scale from 1 (arms crossed in front) to 7 (hands touching in the back); (c) leg openness on a 4-point scale from 1 (legs crossed) to 4 (legs and feet apart);

(*d*) backward lean on a 5-point scale from 1 (more than 20 degrees forward to 5 (leaning backward more than 20 degrees); and (*e*) sideways lean in 10-degree units. Interjudge reliabilities were .90 for shoulder orientation, .98 for arm openness, .94 for leg openness, .96 for backward lean, and .95 for sideways lean.

Finally, five expressive measures were recorded (Rosenfeld, 1966): smiles, positive head nods, negative head nods, gesticulations, and self-manipulations. Interrater agreement varied from 89% to 100% across these measures. These postural and expressive measures were scored only once per 30-second interval.

Daughter-Interview Measures.   When the neutral 15-minute interview was concluded, a female interviewer entered the room, the previous interviewer left, and a structured interview proceeded. These interviews were tape recorded and later rated by two judges on a series on 7-point scales. The interjudge reliabilities for these scale scores ranged from .73 to .96 with an average reliability of .82. The scales were concerned with feminine interests; female friendships; positive attitude to the feminine role; security around female peers, female adults, male peers, and male adults; perceived warmth of mother; perceived restrictiveness-permissiveness of mother; conflict with mother; closeness to mother; similarity to mother; similarity to father; positive attitude to father; warmth of father; competence of father; masculinity of father; control in family decision making of father; conflict with father before separation; disturbance at separation; close relation with any available adult male substitutes; and self-esteem. The scale for disturbance at separation was omitted in the interviews of girls from intact families. Eight of the father-absent girls, mainly those early separated, could offer no information on conflict with father before separation and six could offer no information about disturbance at separation.

Mother-Interview Measures.   Mothers were brought into the laboratory and given a structured interview by a female interviewer about child-rearing practices and attitudes toward her daughter, herself, and her spouse. Interviews were tape recorded and rated on a series of 7-point scales by two raters. Interjudge reliabilities ranged from .70 to .96 with a mean of .85. Some attempt to assess shifts in parent-child interaction over time was made by having separate ratings on 11 scales developed to assess maternal behavior before and after adolescence. This was done with the following scales: intrusiveness, overprotection, permissiveness for sexual curiosity and activity, permissiveness for aggression, punishment for sexual activity, punishment for aggression, warmth, ambivalence, psychological and physical punishment, consistency in discipline, and conflict with daughter. The interview was also rated for reinforcement of daughter for sex-appropriate behaviors, attitude toward spouse, attitude toward men, acceptance of feminine role, anxiety about female adequacy, anxiety about adequacy as a mother, happiness and fulfillment in life, happiness in marriage, frequency of contact with male adults, conflict with father preceding separation, intensity of disturbance following separation, length of disturbance following separation, support from friends and family following separation, resentment at being a single woman with a child, negative shift in self-concept following separation, child's preseparation close-ness to father, and child's disturbance at separation. The last 8 scales were given only to the divorced and widowed mothers.

Personality Measures. Following their interviews both the mother and daughter were administered the Draw-a-Person Test, the California Personality Inventory Femininity Scale, the Internal-External Control Scale, and the Bendig Short Form of the Manifest Anxiety Scale. The Femininity Scale measures femininity of interests, activities, and preferences, whereas the sex of the first figure drawn on the Draw-a-Person Test is often used as a measure of unconscious sex-role identification or orientation. The Internal-External Control Scale measures the extent to which an individual feels she has control over the reinforcements that occur in association with her behavior. The Manifest Anxiety Scale is frequently assumed to measure generalized anxiety.

RESULTS

OBSERVATIONAL MEASURES IN RECREATION CENTERS

Separate one-way analyses of variance for the three groups (father absence due to divorce, father absence due to death, and father present) were performed on the 21 observational measures. The means of variables for which significant F ratios ($p < .05$) were obtained are presented in Table 1. For significant factors in these and all subsequent analyses of variance, comparisons between means were made with two-tailed t tests,

Table 1

Group Means for Observational Variables in the Recreational Center

	Group				
	Father Absent		**Father Present**		
Observational Variable	*Divorce*	*Death*	**Present**	**F**	**p**
Instrumental dependency on female adults	3.17_a	3.17_a	1.62_b	4.00	.02
Seeking praise, encouragement, & attention from male adults	2.50_b	1.17_a	1.12_a	4.83	.01
S-initiated physical contact and nearness with male peers	3.08_b	1.71_a	1.79_a	3.03	.05
Male areas	7.75_a	2.25_b	4.71_c	7.91	.001
Female areas	11.67_a	17.42_b	14.42_a	5.37	.007

Note. All row means which do not share a common subscript differ at least at $p < .05$ with two-tailed t tests.

and, unless otherwise noted, the discussed results of these comparisons were significant at less than the .05 level.

Both father-absent groups showed more instrumental dependency on female adults than did the father-present group. Daughters of divorcees sought more attention from male adults and initiated more proxim ty seeking and physical contact with male peers than did the other girls. This seeking of contact with male peers also was supported by their greater time spent in male areas of the recreation center. In contrast, an avoidance of male areas and preference for female areas by daughters of widows was found. The groups did not differ with respect to any of the other 16 measures.

The father-absent groups were divided into girls who had lost their fathers before age 5 and those who lost them later (divorced early, $N = 14$; divorced late, $N = 10$; widowed early, $N = 13$; widowed late, $N = 11$). Two-way analyses of variance for unequal Ns, with type of father absence and age of separation as the factors, were performed on each of the observational measures of the father-absent girls. All significant findings are reported below. In addition to the previous differences reported between daughters of widows and divorcees, the results of these analyses suggest that early separation from the father has a greater effect on daughters' behavior than later separation. Means for variables associated with significant F ratios are presented in Table 2. The only significant interaction occurred on prosocial aggression where girls from divorced early families exhibited more prosocial aggression than girls from divorced late or widowed early families. Early, in contrast to late, separation

Table 2

Means for Observational Variables in the Recreation Center for Early and Late Separated Father-Absent Girls

| | Father Absent | | | |
Observational Variable	Divorced Early	Divorced Late	Death Early	Death Late
Prosocial aggression	5.14	2.60	2.15	3.54
Seeking praise, encouragement, & attention from male adults	3.14	1.60	1.46	.82
Seeking praise, encouragement, & attention from female adults	2.14	.80	2.31	1.27
S-initiated physical contact & nearness with male adults	2.28	1.50	2.69	.91
S-initiated physical contact & nearness with male peers	2.93	3.30	2.31	1.00
S-initiated physical contact & nearness with female peers	3.21	1.50	3.38	1.73
Male areas	9.14	5.80	3.23	1.09
Female areas	11.64	11.70	16.54	18.45
Female activities	12.78	18.00	15.38	16.91

is associated with greater attention seeking from both male and female adults, greater subject-initiated physical contact with male adults and female peers, more time spent in male areas and less in feminine activities.

NONVERBAL BEHAVIOR IN THE DAUGHTER'S INTERVIEW

Presented in Table 3 is the frequency with which daughters from the three groups of subjects seated themselves with varying gradations of proximity from male and female interviewers. Position 1 is the seat immediately adjacent but at right angles to the interviewer, Position 2 directly across from the interviewer, and Position 3 across and further removed from the interviewer. There were no significant differences as measured through the index of predictive association (Hays, 1963, pp. 606–609) when the interviewer was a female; however, with a male interviewer the daughters of divorcees tended to choose the most proximate seat, the girls from intact families the seat directly across the table, and the daughters of widows the most distant seat.

The means of the summed scores in 30 observational units for the remaining nonverbal measures, plus amount of silence, and subject and interviewer speaking time for the three groups with male and female interviewers are presented in Table 4. A 3 (Father Status) × 2 (Sex of Interviewer) analysis of variance was performed on each of these measures. The analyses yielded either a significant main effect or interaction on all variables with the exception of gesticulations. There was a significant main effect for father status on all variables except for interviewer speaking time and positive head nods. Sex of interviewer had a significant main effect on subject speaking time, interviewer speaking time, eye contact when the subject was speaking, positive head nods, and manipulations. Interpretation of some of these main effects must be qualified by the significant interactions associated with subject speaking time, silence,

Table 3
Position of Chair Selected with Male and Female Interviewers

	Male Interviewer			Female Interviewer		
	Father Absent		**Father Present**	**Father Absent**		**Father Present**
Position	*Divorced*	*Death*	**Present**	*Divorced*	*Death*	**Present**
1	8	0	1	1	2	1
2	3	2	8	8	7	9
3	1	10	3	3	3	2

Table 4
Mean Nonverbal Measures for Subjects with Male and Female Interviewers

	Male Interviewer			Female Interviewer		
	Father Absent		**Father**	**Father Absent**		**Father**
Nonverbal Variable	*Divorced*	*Death*	**Present**	*Divorced*	*Death*	**Present**
S speaks	619.17	463.92	601.58	614.50	632.67	624.25
Interviewer speaks	156.00	201.58	143.50	123.00	111.08	121.33
Silence	116.50	234.50	154.92	161.83	156.25	154.42
Shoulder orientation	496.67	1318.33	802.50	817.50	804.17	804.17
Arm openness	159.50	109.33	125.33	131.58	129.58	134.67
Leg openness	68.33	49.50	48.42	50.08	55.00	51.83
Backward lean	72.58	96.42	80.67	80.25	77.00	83.50
Sideways lean	434.17	300.83	399.17	407.67	400.00	402.50
Smiles	13.58	8.50	10.17	11.75	11.92	10.83
Positive head nod	7.25	4.75	6.00	7.83	8.00	6.83
Gesticulations	9.75	5.00	5.25	6.58	6.58	6.50
Manipulations	12.67	13.83	8.00	8.25	8.58	7.58
Negative head nods	2.17	2.50	2.42	2.08	2.08	2.33
Eye contact when interviewer speaking	.59	.31	.41	.44	.44	.43
Eye contact when S speaking	.68	.47	.66	.73	.67	.69
Eye contact during silence	.84	.29	.34	.34	.34	.37

shoulder orientation, arm openness, leg openness, backward lean, sideways lean, smiles, proportion of eye contact when the interviewer was speaking, and proportion of eye contact during silence. In general, few differences were found between father status groups with a female interviewer. Most differences were obtained with male interviewers and the means tended to be ordered with the divorced and widowed groups at the extremes and the intact family group in an intermediate position.

In spite of the fact that interviewers had been trained in a structured interview method, male interviewers talked more than female interviewers. This may have been because subjects talked less with male interviewers. Daughters of widows with a male interviewer spoke significantly less and were more silent than any other group of subjects. There was also a trend ($p < .06$) for daughters of divorcees to be less silent with a male than female interviewer.

Subjects in the divorced group with male interviewers tended to assume a rather sprawling open posture, often leaning slightly forward with one or both arms hooked over the back of the chair. In contrast, subjects in the widowed group sat stiffly upright or leaned backward with their back often slightly turned to the male interviewer, their hands folded or lying in their laps and their legs together. Compared to girls in any other group, daughters of widows with a male interviewer showed more shoulder orientation away from the interviewer, more backward lean, less arm openness, less sideways lean, and less eye contact during silence or when the interviewer was speaking. In contrast, daughters of divorcees with a male interviewer showed more forward lean, more arm and leg openness, more eye contact when the interviewer was speaking and during silence than did any other group of subjects. They also smiled more than did the other two groups with a male interviewer. Daughters of widows smiled less with a male than a female interviewer. It should be noted that there were no differences between means on these variables with a female interviewer.

There were more manipulations with a male interviewer than female interviewer, and manipulations were more frequent in both the father-separated groups than the intact group. There were more positive head nods and more eye contact when the subject was speaking and the interviewer was a female. Also, when the subject was speaking, there was less eye contact for daughters of widows than the other father-status groups. Although the interaction associated with this variable was not significant, an inspection of the means suggests that this finding was largely attributable to the small amount of eye contact when subjects in the widowed group were speaking to male interviewers.

Three-way analyses of variance with unequal *N*s involving type and time of separation and sex of interviewer were performed on each of these same nonverbal variables for father-separated girls only. The means for this analysis are presented in Table 5. The results associated with type of separation and sex of interviewer paralleled those of the previous analyses and are not discussed again. In addition, significant main effects for time of separation were obtained on interviewer speaking time, gesticulations, and eye contact during silence. Significant interactions between type and time of separation were obtained on backward lean, gesticulations, eye contact when the interviewer was speaking, and eye contact during silence. Triple-order interactions were obtained on subject speaking time, backward lean, sideways lean, smiles, gesticulations, eye contact when the subject was speaking, and eye contact during silence.

Interviewers spoke more with early than late separated girls. Daughters whose fathers died early talked less to a male interviewer than did any other group of girls. When the interviewer was speaking, there was less eye contact in the widowed early group than in either the divorced early or divorced late groups. The late separated daughters of widows showed less eye contact when the interviewer was speaking than did the divorced early girls. When they were speaking to a male interviewer, the girls in the early widowed group showed a smaller proportion of eye contact than did girls in any other group. Girls whose parents were divorced late looked directly when speaking to a female interviewer more often than girls whose parents were divorced early, or than did either group of late separated girls with a male interviewer. However, in talking to a male

Table 5
Means of the Nonverbal Measures for Early and Late Separated Father-Absent Girls with Male and Female Interviewers

	Father Absent Early				Father Absent Late			
	Male Interviewer		Female Interviewer		Male Interviewer		Female Interviewer	
Nonverbal Variable	*Divorced (N = 7)*	*Death (N = 7)*	*Divorced (N = 7)*	*Death (N = 6)*	*Divorced (N = 5)*	*Death (N = 5)*	*Divorced (N = 5)*	*Death (N = 6)*
S speaks	652.57	401.86	601.00	629.50	572.40	550.80	633.40	635.83
Interviewer speaks	158.00	259.57	137.71	118.33	153.20	120.40	102.40	103.83
Silence	89.43	238.57	106.14	152.17	154.40	228.80	164.20	160.33
Shoulder orientation	432.86	1340.00	864.28	801.67	586.00	1288.00	752.00	806.67
Arm openness	164.28	100.57	132.28	133.33	152.80	121.60	130.60	125.83
Leg openness	75.14	46.86	50.43	58.83	58.80	53.20	49.60	51.17
Backward lean	67.86	104.14	83.86	80.17	79.20	85.60	75.20	73.83
Sideway lean	508.57	270.00	392.87	406.66	330.00	344.00	426.00	393.33
Smiles	14.71	7.00	12.43	12.83	12.00	10.60	10.80	11.00
Positive head nod	8.43	4.14	8.00	8.33	5.60	5.60	7.60	7.67
Gesticulations	13.28	4.00	7.57	7.17	4.80	6.40	5.20	6.00
Manipulations	13.14	13.28	9.00	9.00	12.00	14.60	7.20	8.17
Negative head nods	2.28	1.71	1.71	2.17	2.00	3.60	2.60	2.00
Eye contact when interviewer speaking	.65	.26	.45	.44	.51	.39	.42	.44
Eye contact when S speaking	.77	.39	.67	.65	.55	.58	.83	.69
Eye contact during silence	.67	.28	.36	.36	.38	.31	.32	.33

interviewer, the divorced late girls showed less eye contact than the divorced early girls. During silence with a male interviewer, these divorced late girls showed more eye contact than did any other group of girls with either a male or female interviewer.

The openness and approach of the divorced early girls and inhibition of widowed early girls with a male interviewer was reflected in the differences between means in the significant triple interactions on some of the postural and gestural measures. The widowed early girls showed more backward lean with a male interviewer than did any other group of girls. In contrast, divorced early girls showed less backward lean with a male than a female interviewer.

Congruently, divorced early girls with a male interviewer showed more sideways lean than did the other three groups with a male interviewer or the divorced early group with a female interviewer. In addition, with a male interviewer, widowed early girls showed less sideways lean than did any group of subjects with a female interviewer.

The widowed early girls with a male interviewer smiled less than any other group of girls. The divorced early girls with a male interviewer not only smiled more than the widowed early girls, but also more than any late separated group except divorced with a male interviewer. In addition, they made more gesticulations than any other group.

DAUGHTER-INTERVIEW MEASURES

Separate one-way analyses of variance with father status as the factor were performed on the 22 daughter-interview variables. Significant results were obtained for the 10 variables presented in Table 6 along with the group means. Deviations of the daughters with absent fathers appeared most often in relation to feelings and interactions with males. It is interesting to note that there were no differences on variables such as feminine interests, attitudes to the feminine role, or similarity to mother and father, each of which might have been related to sex typing or identification. There also were no differences with respect to relationships with other females including the mother. All groups reported themselves as equally secure around female adults and peers, equally close to their mothers, and their mothers as equally warm and permissive. The exception to this was that daughters with divorced parents reported more conflict with their mothers.

Both daughters of widows and divorcees felt insecure around male peers and adults; however, this was manifested in different ways. The daughters of divorcees reported more, while the daughters of widows re-

Table 6

Means for Daughter Interview Measures

	Father Absent				
			Father		
Interview Variable	*Divorced*	*Death*	**Present**	**F**	**P**
Security around male peers	2.71_a	2.62_a	3.79_b	4.79	.01
Security around male adults	2.12_a	2.12_a	3.66_b	11.25	.001
Heterosexual activity	4.83_a	2.62_b	3.83_c	12.96	.001
Conflict with mothers	5.08_a	3.63_b	4.08_b	5.64	.005
Positive attitude toward father	3.08_a	4.66_b	4.21_b	7.57	.001
Father's warmth	3.33_a	4.50_b	3.87_{ab}	2.82	.06
Father's competence	3.16_a	4.75_b	4.12_b	6.65	.002
Conflict with father	4.43_a	2.25_b	3.46_c	7.03	.002
Relations with other adult males	3.29_a	3.12_a	4.54_b	5.08	.009
Self-esteem	2.87_a	3.58_{ab}	4.04_b	3.34	.04

Note. All row means which do not share a common subscript differ at least a $p < .05$ with two-tailed t tests.

ported less, heterosexual activity than any other groups. There was some evidence of more negative feelings toward the father by daughters of divorcees than by daughters of widows. Girls of divorcees reported more negative attitudes toward the fathers, more conflict with the fathers, and regarded the father as less competent than either of the other two groups of girls. Girls of widows reported having less conflict with their fathers than did either of the other groups of girls and described their fathers as warmer and more competent than did daughters of divorcees. It is interesting that both groups of father-absent daughters reported less contact with other adult males than did children from intact families. Girls from intact families frequently reported being attached to their parents' male friends. Girls from father-present homes and from widowed families showed higher self-esteem than girls from divorced families.

Separate two-way analyses involving type and time of separation were performed on the father-absent daughters' interview data. These analyses yielded little additional information except that daughters of widows reported more disturbance at loss of the father than did daughters of divorcees. The effects for type of separation paralleled those in the previous discussion and no significant age effects of interactions were obtained.

MOTHER-INTERVIEW MEASURES

Separate one-way analyses of variance for the father-status groups were performed on each rating measure of the maternal interview. The means for groups on the variables for which significant F ratios were obtained are presented in Table 7.

Divorced mothers appear to have had a negative attitude toward their ex-spouses, themselves, and life in general. Their lives and marriages had not been gratifying, and they were concerned about their adequacy as mothers. However, these mothers reported positive relationships with their daughters, and exhibited similar patterns of affection and discipline to that of the widowed and still married mothers in the preadolescent period. Most deviations followed and may have been a reaction to the daughters' adolescent behaviors. Both groups of mothers without husbands were overprotective and solicitous of their preadolescent daughters. High conflict with spouse before separation and with daughter after adolescence was found in divorced women. The lowest preadolescent conflict with the daughter was reported by the widowed group; however, there were no differences in preadolescent conflict between the divorced and intact groups. Divorcees reported themselves as being more punitive toward their daughters for sexual activity and as being inconsistent in discipline only after adolescence. This similarity in affection for their daughters, but difference in response to adolescent behavior, by widows and divorcees is reflected in the following portions of representative interviews by two mothers, the first from the widowed group, the second from the divorced group.

[Daughter's name] is almost too good. She has lots of girl friends but doesn't date much. When she's with the girls she's gay and bouncy—quite a clown but she clams up when a man comes in. Even around my brother she never says much. When boys do phone she often puts them off even though she has nothing else to do. She says she has lots of time for that later, but she's sixteen now and very pretty, and all her friends have boy friends.

That kid is going to drive me over the hill. I'm at my wits end. She was so good until the last few years then Pow! at eleven she really turned on. She went boy crazy. When she was only twelve I came home early from a movie and found her in bed with a young hood and she's been bouncing from bed to bed ever since. She doesn't seem to care who it is, she can't keep her hands off men. It isn't just boys her own age, when I have men friends here she kisses them when they come in the door and sits on their knees all in a very playful fashion but it happens to them all. Her uncle is a sixty-year-old priest and she even made a "ha ha" type pass at him. It almost scared him to death! I sometimes get so frantic I think I should turn her into the cops but I remember what a good kid she used to be and I do love her. We still have a good time together when we're alone and I'm not nagging about her being a tramp. We both like to cook and we get a lot of good laughs when we're puttering around in the kitchen. She's smart and good-looking—she should know she doesn't have to act like that.

Again, separate 2 (Type of Separation) × 2 (Age of Separation) analyses of variance were performed on ratings of separated mothers. In addition to the previously obtained differences for type of separation, early separation was found to result in greater overprotection preceding and following adolescence than does later separation. The only significant interaction was on intrusiveness following adolescence, which indicated

Table 7

Group Means for Maternal Interviewing Rating Scales

Variable	Father Absent		Father Present	F	P
	Divorced	Death			
Overprotection before adolescence	3.62_a	3.71_a	2.67_b	3.39	.04
Punishment for sexual curiosity & activity after adolescence	3.87_a	2.79_b	3.00_b	4.32	.02
Consistency after adolescence	3.54_a	4.67_b	4.67_b	4.46	.02
Conflict before adolescence	4.25_a	2.92_b	3.71_a	4.06	.02
Conflict after adolescence	4.75_a	3.46_b	3.75_b	5.55	.006
Negative attitude toward spouse	4.67_a	3.30_b	3.33_b	5.46	.006
Anxiety about adequacy as mother	4.50_a	3.83_b	3.54_b	3.30	.04
Happiness & fulfillment in life	2.75_a	3.58_b	3.75_b	2.31	.05
Happiness in marriage	2.79_a	4.75_b	4.12_b	9.36	.001
Conflict with father	4.71_a	2.67_b	3.33_b	11.84	.001

* Note. All row means which do not share a common subscript differ at least at $p < .05$ with two-tailed t tests.

that early divorced mothers were more intrusive than late divorced or early widowed mothers.

On the analyses of scales only rated for separated mothers, widowed mothers, in contrast to divorced mothers, reported greater intensity of disturbance following loss of husband, more emotional support from friends and family, and less resentment at being a woman bringing up a child alone. Many widowed mothers described having the child as "a blessing" or as "giving them something to live for."

PERSONALITY MEASURES FOR MOTHERS AND DAUGHTERS

No differences were found among groups for mothers or daughters on the number of subjects drawing a female figure first on the Draw-a-Person Test (daughters: divorced, 18; death, 19; present, 16. Mothers: divorcees, 17; widows, 19; intact, 17). One-way analyses of variance for the three father-status groups were done separately for mothers', and daughters', scores on the California Personality Inventory Femininity scale, Rotter's Internal-External Control Scale, and the Bendig Short Form of the Manifest Anxiety Scale.

Mother groups and daughter groups did not differ in their responses to the Femininity Scale. On the analyses for mothers, both divorced and widowed mothers were found to feel more externally controlled than mothers from intact families. No differences on the total Internal-External Control Scale scores were found for daughters. However, Mirels (1970) has recently factor-analyzed this scale and has concluded that it is not unidimensional but includes two factors. The first factor is comprised of items involving a felt mastery over the course of one's life, the second concerns the extent to which an individual is capable of influencing political institutions. Five items which loaded heavily on each of the factors were selected, and separate analyses of variance were performed on scores on the five personal and political control items. There were no differences between groups for either mothers or daughters on the scores on political control, but both groups of separated mothers and daughters scored lower on internalization on the personal control items than did mothers and daughters from intact families. Both groups of daughters without fathers also reported themselves as more anxious on the Manifest Anxiety Scale than daughters with the father living in the home. Divorcees were more anxious than the other two groups of mothers. No time of separation effects were found on any of the scale scores when subsequent analyses of time and type of separation were performed.

DISCUSSION

The results of this study suggest that there are different patterns of effects of father absence on the development of girls and boys. Past research indicates that in boys, separation results in disruptions in sex-role typing during the preschool years, but with increasing age and extrafamilial interaction these effects are attenuated or transformed into compensatory masculinity. In contrast, previous studies with young girls have demonstrated no effects of father separation except on occasional finding of greater dependency.

These studies in combination with the present one suggest that the effects of father absence on daughters appear during adolescence and are manifested mainly as an inability to interact appropriately with males, rather than in other deviations from appropriate sex typing or in interactions with females. There was little apparent disturbance in sex-typed behaviors or preference for the female role as assessed by observational or interview measures or the California Personality Inventory Masculinity-Femininity Scale. Father absence seems to increase dependency in girls, but this is viewed as an appropriately feminine attribute. It does not appear to be related to masculine behaviors such as aggression. Even when aggression appeared in the group of girls whose parents had been divorced early it took the form of prosocial aggression, which is a characteristically feminine form of aggressive behavior (Sears, 1961). Although these girls also scored low in female activities, this seemed to be largely attributable to their spending time in seeking proximity with male peers by hanging around the male areas of the recreation center. These girls spent so much time in the carpentry shop, basketball court, and other male areas that they had little opportunity to sew, do beadwork, or participate in female activities usually located elsewhere. During recreation center dances they spent much of their time at the boys' end of the hall around the "stag line," in contrast to the daughters of widows who stayed at the girls' end, often at the back of the group of girls. Two of the girls in the widowed group hid out in the ladies room for the entire evening of one dance. This was not because of differences in popularity between the groups of girls. When they were present in the hall the two groups of father-absent girls were asked to dance equally often. It is interesting to note that in spite of their greater time spent in male areas, daughters of divorcees did not participate in masculine activities more than the other girls. There were also no differences between groups in sex-role orientation as measured by sex of the figure drawn first on the Draw-a-Person Test, although in father-absent boys disruptions in sex-role orientation tend to be more enduring than those in sex-role preference or sex-typed behaviors.

Except for greater dependency on female adults in the recreation center, girls with absent fathers showed few deviations in relations with females. The effects of father absence on relationships with males is particularly apparent in the nonverbal measures recorded during the girls' interviews with male and female interviewers. Few group differences were found with female interviewers; however, with male interviewers, clear group differences in nonverbal communication emerged. With male interviewers, daughters of widows demonstrated relatively infrequent speech and eye contact, avoidance of proximity with the interviewer in seat selection and body orientation, and rigid postural characteristics. In contrast, daughters of divorcees again showed proximity seeking and a smiling, open, receptive manner with the male interviewer. This greater receptiveness to males by the girls whose fathers are absent because of divorce also is supported by their interview reports of earlier and more dating and sexual intercourse, in contrast to daughters of widows who report starting to date late and being sexually inhibited.

When effects of time of father separation were found, the effects of early separation were usually greater than later separation. This is in agreement with studies of the effects of father absence on sons and suggests that the first 5 years of life represent a critical period for the impact of father absence on children. This effect was most apparent in some of the nonverbal measures of communication in the daughter interview where early separation tended to increase the disparity between the behavior of the daughters of widows and divorcees. However, on the observational measures in the recreation center, time of separation tended to affect the behavior of the two groups of father-separated girls in a similar direction. It is interesting that few time of separation effects were found on interview or test measures; they emerged most frequently in observational measures.

It might be proposed that for both groups of father-absent girls the lack of opportunity for constructive interaction with a loving, attentive father has resulted in apprehension and inadequate skills in relating to males. Their tension in relating to males was supported by their reports in the interview of feelings of insecurity in interacting with male peers and male adults, and in their high rate of manipulations such as nailbiting, hair, lip, and finger pulling, and plucking at clothes and other objects while being interviewed by a male. Their general feeling of anxiety and powerlessness was also reflected in relatively high scores on the Manifest Anxiety Scale and relatively low scores on the factor dealing with a sense of personal control over the course of one's life on the Internal-External Control Scale. This may be intensified in daughters of divorced parents by their low sense of self-esteem.

If it is argued that both groups of girls were manifesting deviant behaviors in attempting to cope with their anxiety and lack of skills in relating to males, the difficult question that remains is how they developed such disparate patterns of coping mechanisms to deal with this problem.

It seems likely that differences in the behavior of the divorced and widowed mothers may have mediated differences in their daughters' behaviors. However, in relationships with their daughters, widows, divorcees, and mothers from intact families were remarkably similar in many ways. In affection, control, and discipline these mothers were similar. The differences between divorcees and the other two groups which appeared after adolescence in consistency, conflict, and punishment of the daughter for sexual activity could well have occurred as a reaction rather than a precursor to their daughter's disruptive adolescent behavior with males. However, there was less strife between widows and daughters than in any other family. All groups of mothers were equally feminine, reinforced daughters for sex-appropriate behaviors and, surprisingly, had equally positive attitudes toward men. Since these mothers were offering their daughters appropriately feminine models and rewarding them for their assumption of the feminine role, the finding that there were no disruptions in traditional measures of sex typing for the father-absent girls is compatible with expectations of social learning theorists.

The only measures on which both father-separated groups of mothers differed from those in intact families were on overprotection of the daughter before adolescence and in feeling more externally controlled. These too could be associated with loss of a husband.

It seems mainly in attitudes toward herself, her marriage, and her life that the divorcee differed from the widow. She is anxious and unhappy. Her attitude toward her spouse is hostile; her memories of her marriage and life are negative. These attitudes are reflected in the critical attitude of her daughter toward the divorced father. Although she loves her daughter she feels she has had little support from other people during her divorce and times of stress and with her difficulties in rearing a child alone. This is in marked contrast to the positive attitudes of the widows toward marriage, their lost husbands, the emotional support of friends and family at the loss of a husband, and the gratifications of having children. These attitudes are reflected in the happy memories their daughters have of their fathers.

Any explanation of the relationship between these maternal behaviors and the daughters' behavior in interacting with males is highly speculative. It may be that daughters of divorcees view their mother's separated lives as unsatisfying and feel that for happiness it is essential to secure a man. Their lack of experience in interacting with a loving father and their hostile memories of their father may cause them to be particularly apprehensive and inept in their pursuit of this goal. It might be argued that rather than being inept these girls are precociously skillful and provocative in their relationship with men. However, such things as their reported anxiety around males and the fact that they were no more popular than the other groups of girls at the recreation center dances suggests that their coping mechanisms are not effective. It may also be that life with a dissatisfied, anxious mother is difficult, and these daughters are more eager to leave home than daughters of widows living with relatively happy, secure mothers with support from the extended family. Daughters of widows with their aggrandized image of their father may also feel that no other males can compare favorably with him, or alternately may regard all males as superior and as objects of deference and apprehension.

It should be noted that the mothers in the father-separated groups are not representative of all divorcees and widows since they have not remarried. This might be more difficult for the divorcee than the widow, who reports more support by her family and even frequent closeness with her dead husband's family. The widow may have less to gain by remarriage, although both groups report an equal number of male friends and dates.

There are many questions about the effects of father absence on the development of daughters that remain unanswered. It is apparent that reasons for and age of separation, as well as current age of the daughter are important factors which must be considered in future investigations of this problem.

REFERENCES

Bach, C. R. Father-fantasies and father-typing in father-separated children. *Child Development,* 1946, *17:* 63–80.

Bendig, A. W. The development of a short form of the Manifest Anxiety Scale. *Journal of Consulting psychology,* 1956, *20:* 384.

Biller, H. B., & Bahm, R. M. Father-absence, perceived maternal behavior, and masculinity of self-concept among junior high school boys. *Developmental Psychology,* 1971, *4:* 178–181.

Biller, H. B., & Weiss, S. D. The father-daughter relationship and the personality development of the female. *Journal of Genetic Psychology,* 1970, *116:* 79–93.

Burt, C. *The young delinquent.* New York: Appleton, 1929.

Cohen, A. K. *Delinquent boys: The culture of the gang.* Glencoe, Ill.: Free Press, 1955.

Exline, R., Gray, D., & Schuette, D. Visual behavior in a dyad as affected by interview content and sex of respondent. *Journal of Personality and Social Psychology,* 1965, *1:* 201–209.

Glaser, D. Social disorganization and delinquent subcultures. In H. C. Quay (Ed.), *Juvenile delinquency.* New York: Van Nostrand, 1965.

Gough, H. G. *Manual for California Personality Inventory.* Palo Alto, Calif.: Consulting Psychologists Press, 1957.

Hays, W. L. *Statistics.* New York: Holt, Rinehart & Winston, 1963.

Hetherington, E. M. Effects of paternal absence on sex-typed behaviors in Negro and white preadolescent males. *Journal of Personality and Social Psychology,* 1966, *4:* 87–91.

Hetherington, E. M. The effects of familial variables on sex typing, on parent-child similarity, and on imitation in children. *Minnesota Symposium on Child Psychology,* 1967, *1:* 82–107.

Johnson, M. Sex role learning in the nuclear family. *Child Development,* 1963, *34:* 319–333.

Lynn, D. B., & Sawrey, W. L. The effects of father absence on Norwegian boys and girls. *Journal of Abnormal and Social Psychology,* 1959, *59:* 258–262.

Machover, K. *Personality projection in the drawing of the human figure.* Springfield, Ill.: Charles C Thomas, 1957.

Mehrabian, A. Inference of attitudes from the posture orientation and distance of a communicator. *Journal of Consulting and Clinical Psychology,* 1968, *32:* 296–308.

Mirels, H. L. Dimensions of internal versus external control. *Journal of Consulting and Clinical Psychology,* 1970, *34:* 226–228.

Monahan, T. P. Family status and the delinquent child: A reappraisal and some new findings. *Social Forces,* 1957, *35:* 250–258.

Mussen, P., & Rutherford, E. Parent-child relations and parental personality in relation to young children's sex-role preferences. *Child Development.* 1963, *34:* 489–607.

Nye, F. I. Child adjustment in broken and in unhappy unbroken homes. *Marriage and Family Living,* 1957, *19:* 356–361.

Rosenfeld, H. M. Instrumental affiliative functions of facial and gestural expressions. *Journal of Personality and Social Psychology,* 1966, *4:* 65–72.

Rotter, J. B. Generalized expectancies for internal versus external control of reinforcement. *Psychological Monographs,* 1966, *80* (1, Whole No. 609).

Santrock, J. W. Paternal absence, sex typing, and identification. *Developmental Psychology*, 1970, *2:* 264–272.

Sears, P. S. Doll play aggression in normal young children: Influence of sex, age, sibling status, father's absence. *Psychological Monographs*, 1951, *65* (6, Whole No. 323).

Sears, R. R. The relation of early socialization experiences to aggression in middle childhood. *Journal of Abnormal and Social Psychology*, 1961, *63:* 466–492.

Toby, J. The differential impact of family disorganization. *American Sociological Review*, 1957, *22:* 505–512.

Tuckman, J., Regan, R. A. Intactness of the home and behavioral problems in children. *Journal of Child Psychology and Psychiatry*, 1966, *7:* 225–233.

seven

peer influences in adolescence

part seven

Peers play an important part in psychological development at all ages, but probably particularly so during adolescence. In addition to providing opportunities to learn to interact with age-mates, regulate social behavior, and develop age-relevant skills and interests, peer relationships permit a sharing of similar problems and feelings. Such sharing may assume special importance during adolescence, when ties with parents are becoming progressively looser as greater independence from them is being achieved.

Furthermore, relationships with family members during this period of personal and social transition are often charged with conflicting emotions: dependent yearnings existing alongside independent strivings, hostility mixed with love. Parent-child conflicts over cultural values and social behavior are not uncommon. As a result, many areas of the adolescent's inner life and outward behavior are likely to become difficult to share with parents, even when the relationship is a positive one. Also, many parents do not desire—and frequently are unable—to revive the intense, shifting, and sometimes painful feelings of adolescence. Reawakening such feelings may be uncomfortable and may also endanger the arduously achieved repression of underlying impulses and feelings that appear inappropriate to an adult role. Peers, on the other hand, are all at the same stage in the life cycle and share many similar experiences.

Among the varied peer relationships of adolescence ("crowd" and clique membership, individual relationships), "friendships hold a special place and perform, at least to some extent, a special function."[1] As Elizabeth Douvan and Joseph Adelson observe in the first selection in this part, compared to other broader and more general interactions with peers, friendships typically are more intimate, involve more intense feelings (both positive and negative), and are likely to be more honest and open and less concerned with self-conscious attempts at role-playing to gain greater popularity and social acceptance. Consequently, close friends may contribute to an adolescent's development in ways the broader peer group cannot. At the same time, their very intimacy may place considerable strain on adolescent friendships, as well as on the individuals involved, especially those who are most narcissistic and demanding or least secure personally.

The nature of adolescent friendships also varies with age. Those of girls aged 11 to 13 are generally more superficial emotionally and tend to focus on social activity. Between 14 and 16, with the onset of puberty and subsequent disturbances in psychic equilibrium, "mere sharing of activity diminishes, to be replaced by a relation that is mutual, interactive, emotionally interdependent." Emotional support and understanding be-

---

[1] E. Douvan and J. Adelson, *The Adolescent Experience.* New York: Wiley, 1966, p. 661.

come central. By late adolescence the intense, sometimes desperate quality of midadolescent friendship gives way to a calmer, more modulated relationship. This happens because the girls involved are becoming more comfortable with themselves and their impulses and surer of their own identities; also, heterosexual relationships are developing at this time. In contrast to girls' friendships, those of boys are more likely to retain an emphasis on social activities with a congenial companion throughout the adolescent period and there is less emphasis on intense interpersonal intimacy.

There is a well-worn cliche that with the heightened importance of the peer group during adolescence, the young person turns away completely from his parents and becomes the captive of his peers. The implicit assumption appears to be that parental and peer influence are necessarily mutually exclusive, which is simply not the case.

In the first place, there is usually considerable overlap between parental and peer values because of commonalities in their backgrounds— social, economic, religious, educational, and geographic. In this sense, then, peers may actually serve to reinforce parental values. Second, neither parental nor peer influence is monolithic. The weight given to either will depend to a significant degree on the adolescent's appraisal of its relative value in a specific situation. For example, peer influence is more likely to be predominant in such matters as tastes in music and entertainment, fashions in clothing and language, patterns of same- and opposite-sex peer interaction, and the like; parental influence is more likely to be predominant in such areas as underlying moral and social values and understanding of the adult world.[2]

It is also important to recognize that in many instances when the peer group assumes an unusually dominant role in the lives of adolescents, it is likely to be due as much or more to poor parental relationships in the home as to the inherent attractiveness of the peer group. In the second article, Lyle E. Larson demonstrates that the relative influence of parents and peers (termed the *salience hierarchy*) during adolescence is correlated with a variety of factors, including grade level, social class, sex, the kind of situation involved, and the perceived ability and desire of parents or peers to be helpful. But by far the most important predictor of relative influence (and one that tends to be related to other predictors and to reduce their predictive value if controlled for) is what Larson calls *parent-adolescent affect,* that is, the quality of the parent-child relationship. Adolescents with positive and rewarding parental relationships (high parent-adolescent affect) were found most likely to be influenced by parents. Significantly, these adolescents were also less likely than those with poorer relationships (low affect) to see a need to differentiate between the influence of their parents and their best friends.

Not surprisingly, Larson found parental influence to be greatest at the seventh-grade level and least at the twelfth-grade level. Interestingly, it

---

[2] J. J. Conger, *Adolescence and Youth: Psychological Development in a Changing World.* New York: Harper & Row, 1973.

was also found that at the seventh-grade level the extent of parental influence was only minimally a function of the quality of the parental relationship. At later grade levels, however, where the potential impact of peer-group influence had increased significantly, parent-adolescent affect assumed markedly increased importance as a determinant of parental influence. In short, if a parent thinks that because he can influence his children at the beginning of adolescence without concerning himself with the quality of the relationship with his children and his contributions to it, he will continue to be able to do so in middle and later adolescence, then he may be making a serious mistake.

In the third article, Philip R. Costanzo demonstrates ingeniously that while adolescents generally become more conforming to peer pressures in early adolescence, there are significant individual differences in conformity at all ages. He found that adolescents scoring high on a measure of self-blame in relation to their age group's mean were more likely to behave in a conforming fashion than those low in self-blame. It might also be observed that rigid conformity to *either* peers or parents varies markedly from one adolescent to another. The more self-confident, autonomous adolescents may be able to profit from the views and learning experiences provided by both parents and peers without being strongly dependent on either or unduly troubled by parent-peer differences.[3] Ironically, the adolescent who has gained the most confidence in his own self-image as a result of the kind of democratic child rearing referred to earlier (see pp. 134–180), and who is least concerned with popularity, may find others looking to him for direction and support.

---

[3] J. J. Conger, A World They Never Knew: The Family and Social Change. *Daedalus*, Fall 1971, *100*, 1105–1138.

adolescent friendships

Joseph Adelson
Elizabeth Douvan
University of Michigan

In our society, the adolescent period sees the most intense develop-ment of friendship. There are a good many reasons for this. Erotic and aggressive drives toward family members become so intense that the youngster must have a neutral arena in which to work them out; he is in process of breaking (or recasting) his ties to the family and desperately needs the support, approval and security, as well as the norms, of a peer group. He is discovering, and trying to interpret and control, a changed body, and with it new and frightening impulses, and so requires both the example and communion of peers. He is about to crystallize an identity, and for this needs others of his generation to act as models, mirrors, help-ers, testers, foils.

All in all, it would seem that the adolescent does not choose friendship, but is driven into it. The paradox is that the very needs that drive the child will, if they are not kept in control, imperil the friendship itself. Erotic and aggressive drives, in some degree of sublimation, are the cement of adolescent peer relations. If the sublimations fail (as they often do during this time), the drives spill over into the friendship and spoil it. Adolescent friendships, as we shall see, are based to a considerable extent on narcissism, identifications, and projections. These are tricky pro-cesses. If the youngster is too narcissistic, he may be so sensitive to rejec-tion that he cannot abide friendship, or so obtuse to the needs of the other as to be unfit for it. If projection dominates the interaction, it may end in the other being seen as overdangerous. Identifications may become problematic in threatening to blur the all too tentative lineaments of ego identity. These dangers are by no means confined to the adolescent; the adult may avoid close friendships for the same reasons. But the adoles-cent, generally, will feel these dangers more acutely because of a turbu-lent intrapsychic situation, and because he has nowhere else to go. If friendship is difficult or dangerous, it is ordinarily less so than isolation, or working these things out in the family. All these circumstances join to make the adolescent friendship a tempestuous, changable affair. Best friends may change in a moment; strange partnerships may come into being. If we look back to adolescence, we may be stupefied to recall friendships with the unlikeliest, the most alien of partners, to whom we were bonded by a momentary, yet critical mutuality of needs. Even our solid and enduring adolescent friendships may turn out, if we remember them closely enough, not to have been quite so unbroken and harmonious as they first appear in retrospect. They may in fact have blown hot and cold, responsive to all the rise and fall of feeling in self and others.

If some circumstances drive the child to friendship, others give him the opportunity to use and be changed by it. There is the simple fact that he is given, nowadays, the leisure and freedom to explore friendship, free from the responsibilities of work and family which will shortly absorb so much time and energy. Society finds his labor expendable, a circumstance that produces a great many complications; it helps to produce some of the adolescent demoralizations we hear so much about. But ordinarily the adolescent's leisure and freedom from responsibility do not work out so badly. It offers him the occasion for making discoveries about himself and others. The youngster needs time, needs the sense of unlimited time, and usually he will find or make the time. Even in the overorganized segment of the middle class, where the child is likely to be hemmed in by the demands of school and official leisure, he will discover his own slow-down techniques, making sure that there is time left over for the bull session, telephone chatter and all the other (well-publicized) forms of adolescent idleness.

So we have a necessity for friendship and, ordinarily, considerable opportunity for it. Another quality of the adolescent must be noted; he enters friendship with a remarkable eagerness and capacity for change. The contrast with the latency child is an instructive one. Before adolescence the child accepts himself as he is; if he is popular or unpopular, if he has many friends or only one or none—this is the way things are; the child may sorrow over it, but he will not generally feel there is much he can do about it. He has not yet made the discovery of the tractable self. Sometime near the start of adolescence, the child develops a consciousness of the self as a social stimulus, modifiable by will and intention. He enters the world of self-help, of books and columns on manners, dating, dress, make-up, chit-chat, the world of rituals and resolutions designed to make or remake the self. He enters friendship with an eagerness to make good, and the conviction that the self can be transformed to that end.

Along with this almost conscious, almost deliberate openness to change, we have another level of openness, to which we alluded earlier, the openness to the inner states of experience; with it comes a psychic fluidity, a vulnerability to conflict, an affective lability which together give adolescent intimacies so much of their characteristic flavor. The very fragility of the defenses may at times implicate the youngster in conflict, but on the other hand (and on the whole) they permit a relation to the other which captures the deepest levels of feeling, and so bind the adolescent and friend into an immoderate and unreserved intimacy.

In the explosion of impulses that dominates the early adolescent period, we find that while a goodly share of drive energy is diverted from the family to peers, a considerable amount of it is directed to the self. The adolescent's narcissism is ubiquitous: it expresses itself in a great many obvious ways—in an excruciating self-consciousness, in the concern with clothing and appearance, in shyness, in raucous exhibitionism, in posturing, primping, preening—and in anomalies of emotion and behavior where the origin is less obvious and direct. The narcissistic orientation, as we said earlier, influences the form and function of friendship at this time. There is the well-known adolescent touchiness, a hypersensitivity to rejection which in some cases can assume almost a paranoid intensity, in the conviction that friends are talking about them, or are out to exclude, wound, and humiliate them. The youngster will put himself at the center of the peer universe; the behavior of the other is overinterpreted; casual happenings—the friend's gesture or boredom, or the passing mention of a third person—will be magnified into events of major interpersonal significance.

Even when things do not come to such a pass, the adolescent's narcissism may make his friendships far less interactive than they first appear to be. His tie to the friend may be no more than the need for a forum where, by mutual consent, each participant is allowed equal time to discourse on the self's vicissitudes. In these cases the friend is expected to offer only the mechanical responses of the listener. We also may see the role of narcissism in the choice of friend—the other is someone who is like the self, or more commonly, someone who can represent certain illusory aspects of the self. In the other, the adolescent can make objective the disavowed or prospective or half-understood qualities of the self. . . . We often find during this period an intolerance and contempt for those of a different bent of character and talent more intense than at any other stage of the life cycle. The need is to define personal identity; to accomplish this, the youngster needs the reassurance and mirroring offered by others of the same disposition.

So a pair, a trio, or larger grouping will establish itself through joint sympathies and mutual identifications. The group tendency is to define itself with considerable exclusiveness (the preoccupation with "cliques" and "snobbishness" is very strong during adolescence), the attempt being to confirm identity by insisting on homogeneity. The outside world, and especially other peers, is excluded, and more, becomes the subject of projection. We find, at this time, a tendency to strengthen ingroup ties and to reduce their inherent tendencies toward ambivalence, through ascribing to others, to the out-group, those qualities too dangerous to recognize in the self. Of course these projections often cannot be kept outside the group. If the group is large enough, a tendency will develop to exclude temporarily, or to scapegoat, particular members. There is no end to the complexities (and the tedium) of arrangements and rearrangements within the friendship group, particularly among girls: A breaks up a close tie between B and C by retelling to B something she had heard C say about B; so the displaced C will detach D from her intimacy with E and get her to join a vendetta against A and B; it is something like a da Ponte libretto.

Generally, while adolescents choose each other for friends on the basis of likeness, dissimilarity plays a greater role in the functioning of the relation than first meets the eye. Certain general qualities must be alike, social class, interests, taste, morality, but after these likenesses are established, we find that the play of interaction is conducted through differences. Adolescent friendship is based (to some extent) on complementarity (although within a framework of similarity), just as in the case of marital selection as discussed by Winch (1958). Qualities of personality must vary between friends enough to give the relation the zest, tension, and enrichment that comes out of differences.

Finally we come to the art of friendship, the winning of friends—we hesitate at this topic, since it seems to have been pre-empted by the self-help industry. Yet it is clear enough that one of the essential tasks of the adolescent period is learning friendship, learning its demands and responsibilities, its nuances and complexities. Surely, much of what goes into being a friend and being befriended is so much a part of character as to be somewhat removed from learning—warmth, grace, and integrity—these qualities and others like them are too deeply woven into the fabric of personality to be susceptible to change. Although they are not readily lost or acquired, they need to be practiced, tempered, and polished within the framework of personal relations. The child must learn, or sharpen, his discretion, tact, and sensitivity—all that goes into knowing the limits of the other's privacy, acquiring a sense of the implicit. He must learn how to get what he needs from the other, while taking into account (and serving) the other's own needs. He must come to know the tolerable limits of his own aggression, and how much hostility he is prepared to accept without endangering his self-regard; and how to stand up for his rights without guilt and without abusing the rights of the other.

These are just some parts of the interpersonal agenda of adolescence. Of course it could be said, and with some justice, that the child has been learning these things all his life. So he has, but in ways too limited to prepare him for the peculiar exigencies of adolescent friendship. The personal relations between parent and child are intrinsically hierarchical; the relations to siblings are generally ambivalent and competitive; the peer friendships of the preadolescent years are, as we shall soon see, emotionally pallid and not genuinely interactive. The child before adolescence cannot learn, from family and friends, the ego qualities he will need to master the modalities of friendship in adolescence. These relations are the result of personal choice, are interactive, equalitarian, and suffused with the child's deepest emotions. He is only partially prepared by earlier experience; he must now learn the rest himself.

Up to this point we have treated adolescent friendships in a most general fashion, highlighting those processes unique to the period as a whole. Our intention here is to examine the developmental data on girls; through it we hope to understand the forms and functions of the like-sexed friendship as it grows and changes during the adolescent years.

Our data yield clear developmental trends; changes that occur in a simple direct fashion as girls grow older. Beyond this, we find differences among the age groups which are not continuous, but point to distinctive qualities of relationship in the three stages of adolescence.

Generally, we can say the child develops, as she moves through the adolescent era, an increasing emotional investment in friendship, greater sophistication and subtlety in her conceptions about it, a growing capacity for disinterested appreciation of the friend, and greater tolerance of differences within the relationship.

PREADOLESCENCE AND EARLY ADOLESCENCE: GIRLS OF ELEVEN, TWELVE, AND THIRTEEN

It is very possible that our conception of the latency period is something of a fiction. We have fallen into the habit of seeing it as a time of life without passion. The emotions and drives, and all the conflicts they bestir, are held to disappear near age six, to be rearoused at puberty. As our knowledge of the latency period increases, we become aware that it is instinctually placid only in contrast with the Oedipal period before it and adolescence after it. It is psychodynamically more complex than we realized. Nevertheless, the contrast is impressive; we can go only so far in refining our idea of latency. Relative to what precedes and follows it, the preadolescent period is indeed low in drive and conflict; the child is absorbed in the quiet growth of ego capacities. Erikson (1950) calls it a stage of life dominated by "industry." The child begins to develop skills—reading and writing, of course, but also the myriad opportunities of a complex culture—sports and games in an infinite variety, the arts and crafts, collections and hobbies, and riddles and jokes.

It is a busy age, then; and the nature of friendship at this time reflects its busyness, its diligence, and its enriching dilletantism. The friends focus more on activity—on what they are doing together, than they do on themselves. The companion, to be sure, may be used as a point of reference—the child judging herself by the other—but there is little interest in the friend's personality as such. We see this in the fact that girls at this period can tell us so little about friendship. When we ask what a friend ought to be like, and what things make a girl popular with others, the early adolescent mentions fewer qualities than older girls do. More important, the qualities she does mention are fairly superficial ones. For example, she wants a friend to do favors for her. She wants the friend to be amiable, easy to get along with, cooperative, and fair. The friend ought not to be a crab, grouchy, mean, selfish or a showoff.

What we miss in this surfeit of adjectives is the sense that friendship can be emotionally relevant. The girl alludes to those surface qualities of the other that promote or hinder the swift and easy flow of activity. The friendship, we feel, centers on the activity rather than on the interaction itself. In this respect, the friendship is not yet relational. One wants a partner who is neither demanding nor disagreeable, whose personality will not get in the way of activity. The personality of the other is seen as a possible encumbrance to activity; later on it becomes the center of the interaction, as the girl becomes concerned with the friend's qualities in their capacity to disrupt, not the joint activity, but the friendship is still an adjunct to something else, the partnership in work and play.

The preadolescent girl is engaged in the exercise of the ego—the drives and conscience are not yet a source of concern. The child is oriented to the "real" world, to externality, rather than to the inner world. There is little preoccupation with internal qualities, either in the self or the other. The need for friendship arises out of the need to practice and extend the newly won and still growing ego resources. What the child wants is a certain degree and quality of growing room, and if there is any conflict with the family, it will probably be over this issue. The child grown in skills will demand the independence to put them to use; in some cases, the family may be too confined an arena, and a relation to friends may be needed. Most families in our society raise no objection; they may set some limit to the child's demands and the child ordinarily will accept these without fuss. Basically the youngster's emotional commitment is to the family, rather than to friends. Most of our subjects at preadolescence do not believe that they can be as close to a friend as to members of the family. They rarely report conflict with the family about friendship and the choosing of friends. Leisure time is more often spent with the family than with friends.

Boys do not have much importance yet. At least this is what we gather from what our subjects tell us; we may suspect that there is a good deal of anticipation, and no little trepidation, regarding heterosexuality—more than the girl allows herself to think there is, and far more than she will tell an interviewer. Still, as far as overt activity is concerned, friendship means the like-sexed friendship, period. The girl at this age has ordinarily not begun to date. When we put to her a hypothetical question pitting a friendship tie against the possibility of a date, she plumps for the friendship. But if the preadolescent girl does not date boys, she does play sports with them. At this age, the sexes meet on the playground, and judge each other by skill rather than sex. When sex begins to be important, there will be more distinction made between male and female activities than we find at this point. Given this lack of involvement with boys and dating, we are not surprised to find that ethical issues centering on heterosexuality do not play much part in the friendship; soon, however, the girl will be concerned with the ethics of competition for boys, and sexual morality, and the balance to be found between the ties of friendship and the demands of dating.

PUBERTY AND MIDDLE ADOLESCENCE: GIRLS OF FOURTEEN, FIFTEEN, AND SIXTEEN

The processes we discussed earlier now make their appearance. The child is swept into the erotic mysteries; the body changes and the instincts disturb the psychic equilibrium. The doubts, confusions, anxiety, and guilt evoked by the eruption of sexual urges, the incestuous and aggressive dangers in the family—these, and more, as we have said, drive the child from the family and into intimate, intense and sometimes desperate friendships. But the erotic is still too new and frightening: the child does not know enough yet, either about herself or about the opposite sex. The transition to heterosexuality is made through the like-sexed friendship.

These friendships are very different in style and purpose than those of preadolescence. At this age, our findings show, the girls are less tied to the family, spend more time with friends, and are more articulate about the nature and conditions of friendship. The mere sharing of activity diminishes, to be replaced by a relation that is mutual, interactive, emotionally interdependent; the personality of the other, and the other's response to the self become the central themes of the friendship. The girl no longer stresses the concrete and superficial qualities of the friend. It is no longer important for the friend to do favors for one, nor does popularity depend much on good manners as the younger girl is likely to tell us. When girls past puberty report on their friendships they use a vocabulary that is (relatively) abstract, differentiated, and relational. They want a friend they can confide in, someone who can offer emotional support and understanding. When they describe the popular girl, they define her as one who is able to proffer this kind of friendship—someone who is sensitive to the needs of others.

The girls of this age group are unique in some respects, that is, different from both younger and older girls. What stands out in their interviews is the stress placed on security in friendships. They want the friend to be loyal, trustworthy, and a reliable source of support in any emotional crisis. She should not be the sort of person who will abandon you, or who gossips about you behind your back.

Why so much emphasis on loyalty? We imagine that part of the reason is that the friendship is less a mutuality than it appears to be at first. The girl is less interested in the other than she thinks; what she seeks in the other is some response to, and mirroring of, the self. She needs the presence of someone who is undergoing the same trials, discoveries, and despairs. The sexual crisis, in short, is handled through identification. In this way, the girl gains some of the strength she needs to handle impulses; and through the other, she has the opportunity to learn something about her own sexuality. Through the sharing of knowledge and affects, she is relieved, to some extent, of the anxiety and guilt which accompanies the emergence of sexuality.

With so much invested in the friendship, it is no wonder that the girl is so dependent on it. To lose the friend, for the girl at this age, is to lose a part of the self; those qualities of the other that one has incorporated within the self, and those aspects of the self that one has given to the other, and with which one has identified. Intimacies, at this time, are often too symbiotic to be given up without pain. The friend who is disloyal leaves one abandoned to the impulses. Then, too, there is the fact that in leaving she takes away with her the knowledge of the girl's sexual history and fantasies. The girl is likely to feel like the woman analysand in that famous *New Yorker* cartoon, who, getting up from the couch, takes a pistol from her purse, and says: "You've done me a world of good, Doctor, but you know too much." It is this sort of feeling, no doubt, which accounts for the anxiety that the friend may gossip behind one's back.

The erotic preoccupations of this period are also reflected in the fact that our data show sexual references to be more common between fourteen and sixteen than either before or after. This group of girls is the most likely to mention sexual immorality as a cause of unpopularity and as a reason why one would not want to be friendly with some girls. In these data we see how the sexual impulses are to some extent handled by projection. Apprehensive about the strength of her own controls, the young girl may become engrossed, fascinated, and repelled by the "bad girl." The advantages of projection are too well known to need extensive treatment here. It is enough to say that by splitting female peerdom into "nice girls" and "bad girls," one is able to deposit unacceptable wishes onto the outgroup, and so reinforce one's defenses against impulse. This device also helps the girl to relieve her guilt for whatever erotic pleasures she permits herself. She will reason that her own behavior is shared by the collectivity of "nice girls," and that, in any case, her own sins pale in contrast with what she imagines are the indulgences of the "bad girl." Perhaps we ought to say here that the "bad girl" is in most cases no simple figment of fancy; in any high school of size, the girl will have the opportunity to know, at a safe distance, a number of girls who wear tight sweaters and too much makeup and who go with the wrong sort of boys. Later, when the girl has come to terms with her own sexuality, she will be able to take the girls of dubious reputation more in stride. At this age, they represent a degree of impulsivity too dangerous to be casual about.

While the erotic seems to touch everything at this age, there are of course other themes present during this most difficult period of adolescence. The girl is not only unsure of her capacity to settle sexuality; she is also confused and uncertain about personal identity and indeed about her worth as a human being. To a considerable extent, she will look to the peer group's appraisal both to define and evaluate her. It is a time when, in order to consolidate identity, confirm status, heighten self-esteem, adolescents form themselves into cliques which are, as we know, more or less exclusionist. Paradoxically, the girl in this age group gives some evidence of democratic sentiment—she tells us that she admires equalitarian manners and dislikes those who are snobbish and status-seeking. Those who live by the ingroup, as the young girl must, will also live in mortal fear of perishing by it. The girl does not view her own ingroup commitments as snobbish, but she fears a possible exclusion from the group, and so makes much of snobbism. Here we find another reason for the emphasis on security and loyalty at this age—the good friend is one who will not abandon her to social isolation.

Another source of insecurity arises from the fact that the girl ordinarily begins to date at this age. We shall discuss dating later in this chapter. Here we want to say something about its relation to the like-sexed friendship. The friend is needed as a source of guidance, comfort, and support. In the preceding section we discussed the intimate friendship in this function—how the friends share their learning, how, in recounting their experiences to each other, they become able to live vicariously, reinterpret their behavior, relieve guilt, and exercise mutual controls. At this age, too, the girl must begin to come to terms with the ethics of friendship and dating. The girl, needing friendship so desperately, wants to feel that her friend will not abandon her in favor of boys. The dating friendship, at this age, may be seen as competitive with like-sexed friendship. Another form of competition is in the possible rivalry of girls for popularity with boys. The friendship has to recognize and adjust to differential popularity. The girl who is too popular or who flaunts her popularity risks the hostility of her peers. The girl who has won popularity must learn how to accept her good fortune graciously and modestly, so that her friends can learn to temper their envy. We cannot avoid the impression that the adolescent girl is far more concerned about the opinion of girls than of boys. She wants to be popular with boys, for its effects on her appraisal by the peer group of girls.

LATE ADOLESCENCE: GIRLS OF SEVENTEEN AND EIGHTEEN

Our story has a happy ending. The desperate, feverish quality of friendship in the preceding age period now gives way to calmer, more modulated friendships. The girl has become somewhat easier about herself. She has managed to define herself and to find the basis for a personal identity. She has been able to develop fairly secure defenses against impulses and can now allow herself to discharge them in more direct experimentations in sexuality. She has learned how to handle herself with boys, and has acquired the rudiments of social skill. All of these changes relieve the pressure on the like-sexed friendship. Much of the emotional energy that has been invested in girls is now diverted to boys. As her suspiciousness of boys has dwindled, she is able to turn to them for intimacy. As she has gained skill in the dating relation, she no longer needs the friendship as a retreat, or a source of learning, or a cushion for disappointment. As identity is secured, she has fewer needs for identification-based relations with girls.

The passionate quality of friendship recedes, and it is replaced by a more equable tie to the other. By the time the girl reaches late adolescence she has developed a fairly complex understanding of friendship. This group has more to say than any other about its various functions, and what they tell us is at once more subtle and more abstract. Like early adolescent girls, they stress the confiding and sharing aspects—they want a friend with whom they can share important confidences. Yet we sense a new note in their answers—there is some indication that identifications are less prominent than before. There is now a greater emphasis on the personality and talents of the friend, a stress on what she can bring to the relation in the way of interest and stimulation. The girl becomes aware of and interested in her friend's individuality. There is a greater capacity, we imagine, to tolerate differences, and to value the friend for the ways in which she is unique. This stands in some contrast to the preceding period, where the girl, out of the need to confirm identity, might insist on a homogeneity of character, or where she could tolerate differences only when they allowed her to work out some instinctual dilemma. Now it is possible for the friendship to take on a more disinterested, neutral, playful, and diversified quality. It is no longer an apparatus for the resolution of conflict, and for that alone.

The partial solving of the sexual and identity crises brings with it a reduction of the emphases characteristic of the earlier age period. The girls make fewer references to loyalty, security, and trust when they talk about the qualities a friend should have. Needing friendship less, they are less haunted by fears of being abandoned and betrayed. There is also less of a preoccupation with sexual immorality. There seems to be a diminished use of projection, less tendency to divide girls into the good and the bad, and less concern with sexual reputation as a basis for judging, choosing, and excluding friends. Now that she can manage her sexuality, she is less fascinated by it, no longer so sensitive to it in others.

One other finding may be of some interest. When we ask younger girls what age group they prefer to be with in a social situation, they express a marked preference for older girls. We get the impression of a rush to maturity, a desire to know and grow, and a desire to share the sophistication (and the sexual secrets) of older girls. At seventeen and eighteen, this pattern ends, and we now find that girls prefer age groups which put them at the upper end of the age range. Our older girls have the advantage of greater experience and status without the burden of adult responsibility. So they seem to pause momentarily, and slow down, before they begin the transition to adulthood.

The reader may be weary of hearing that, for our knowledge of developmental processes we have had to rely on the study of girls; to those who have just joined us, let us repeat that the data on boys is limited to the 14 to 16 age group, while our interviews with girls extend from eleven to eighteen. So we cannot provide a complete comparison of male and female friendship patterns during the course of adolescence. We do, however, have enough information to know that the differences are considerable.

Before we look at our data, let us note some general differences which influence the contrasting forms of friendship for the sexes. There is the obvious fact that the girl is socialized so as to place great importance on personal relations; her life task, as wife and mother, requires her to cultivate such traits as sensitivity, warmth, tact, and empathy. The boy, to put matters oversimply, is trained toward activity and achievement; he needs to cultivate assertiveness and independence. (Of course we can easily make too much of these differences, and construct a caricature of the sexes, stressing these contrasting traits to the exclusion of all else.) Furthermore, the fear of homosexuality runs so strong among men in this country as to inhibit any display of "womanly" qualities; it also serves to frighten the man away from close ties to other men. Men fear more often than women a breakthrough of the homoerotic if they allow themsleves too great a degree of intimacy with their own sex.

There are some less obvious reasons for the different forms adolescent friendship may take in the sexes. Helene Deutsch (1944, 1945) and other psychoanalytic writers have distinguished the differing psychosexual tasks of adolescent boys and girls. The boy's problem is to sever old object ties and form new ones. The development of adult sexual impulses makes it imperative to withdraw drive cathexes from the family and divert them to new and more appropriate objects. This is, of course, the girl's problem too. The difference between them is that the boy has little trouble in understanding his own sexuality. He experiences the erotic as direct, discrete, immediate, and uncomplicated. His sexual impulses are unambiguous; the organ of sexuality is familiar. There remains much to learn, about controlling and gratifying the erotic, about heterosexuality in general, but he is not long confused about the nature of his sexuality.

The girl's sexuality is not known to her quite so simply. For the girl the erotic is diffuse, remote, ambiguous, and complex. She also has the task of controlling and gratifying impulses, but at the same time she must learn their nature. As we have indicated, she does so through intimate friendship, and through complex identifications with her own kind. Not only is the girl attuned to the interpersonal, but also she is driven to make use of it for self-understanding. The intimate friendship, then, is a resource more necessary to the girl than to the boy.

Let us try putting this another way. For the girl we can image a reticulate triad: identity, the erotic and the interpersonal. The erotic and the interpersonal are much more closely linked in women than in men. Women in our society are object-dependent; they are compliant, passive, and responsive to the fear of losing love, that is, losing the esteem of the other. The woman cannot easily separate, as many men can, her erotic feelings from her ties to another. The achievement of personal identity requires a synthesis of the erotic and the interpersonal. Each of these terms is linked to the others: to define one's identity means to know the erotic, which in turn means to know the relation between the erotic and the interpersonal.

For the boy, the definition of identity is more likely to depend on such qualities as assertiveness, autonomy, and achievement. If we imagine a triad for the boy it would be something like: identity, the erotic, and autonomy (including in the last term a number of other characteristics, such as those given above). For the boy one problem is to come to terms with authority, neither submitting to it, nor identifying with it, nor fighting it obsessively; another (and related) problem is to come to terms with assertiveness, which means that it must not be degraded into cruelty or crushed into timidity, but must be controlled, refined, and adapted into purposeful activity. The boy's sense of the erotic will reflect and be reflected by, influence and be influenced by the development of activity and autonomy. Whether sexuality is, for example, brutal, or passive, or impotent is reciprocally connected with the boy's resolution of the relation to authority. In turn, both the erotic and autonomy (again, in a broad sense) will interact with identity.

So we may say that the adolescent girl, bred to the interpersonal, must solve problems of the interpersonal, and uses interpersonal methods to do so. (In a moment, we shall present some data which indicates how important interpersonal competence is to the girl's integration and effectiveness.) For the boy, the problem at adolescence is, as we have said, the relation to authority, and all that follows from that. The boy, to some extent socialized against intimacy, is also less dependent upon intimate relations during this period. He needs to assert and maintain his independence against control by parents and by parent-surrogates. To this end he needs the gang, the band of brothers, in alliance with whom he can confirm himself as autonomous and maintain a wall of resistance to authority. Even when the boys' close friendship group is small in number, they are apt to give it a ganglike definition, for example, calling themselves "The Three Musketeers" or "The Four Horsemen." Girls, on the other hand, even when they are part of a large group of friends, tend to form into centers of intimate two- and three-somes.

While girls ordinarily show few signs of the true gang spirit, boys do have intimate friendships, based on identification, much as girls do. We have defined ideal types, rather than differences which exist invariably. Our assumption is not that the intimate friendship cannot be found among boys, but rather that it is less common, and that it does not usually achieve the depth of intimacy usual among girls.

But limitations in our data prevent us from testing this hypothesis. As we shall see in a moment the interviews show that 14- to 16-year-old boys are less involved in close friendship than girls are at the same age. Since our sample of boys does not extend into the later stages of adolescence, we have no way of knowing whether we are dealing only with a slower rate of social development (this is generally true of adolescent boys) or whether, as we believe, there is, among American males, an absolute inhibition of friendship which continues not only into late adolescence but also into adulthood as well. The slow pace of development in itself does not tell us much about the ultimate limits of friendship development.

What we do know, what the interview data make quite clear, is that boys in early adolescence are less sophisticated about friendship and less eager for intimacy than girls of the same age. The findings also suggest that the peer group collectively, the gang, is more important to the boy than to the girl, that it serves to orient and support him.

To begin with, boys are less articulate than girls about the nature and meaning of friendship. To all questions in this area, concerning the qualities a friend ought to have, and the bases for popularity and unpopularity, they give fewer answers than do girls. Neither do they count close friendship as important as the girls do. They will more often assert that a friendship can never be as close as a family relationship: 42 per cent of the boys feel this way, compared to 61 per cent of the girls the same age.

When we ask boys the criteria they use for choosing a friend, and about the sources of a boy's popularity, they name rather concrete qualities. Their answers bear a striking resemblance to those given by the preadolescent girl. They believe a friend ought to be amiable and cooperative, and in general demand little in the way of genuine interaction. They want the friend to be able to control impulses, and here they particularly have aggression in mind. They also mention excessive hostility ("he's mean, a bully, picks fights") as a major source of unpopularity. Apart from exercising a degree of control, the friend is seen as having few obligations in the relationship. Boys at this age do not emphasize, as the girls do, the affective elements in friendship. They make no demands for closeness, mutual understanding, or emotional support. There is less mention made of security, which is heavily stressed by the girls. Since the boys' friendships do not involve the deeper emotions, they are not quite so threatened by the possibility of losing the friend. The support they do ask from the friend is, again, similar to what we find among the youngest girls. They want specific, concrete supplies, rather than warmth and understanding. Their conception of the roots of popularity again reminds us of the criteria mentioned by preadolescent girls, in being specific, concrete, and fairly superficial—good looks and good manners, athletic ability, an amiable, nonaggressive disposition. There is no value placed on sensitivity or empathy; snobbishness and gossip do not figure in their evaluations of other boys. All in all, the boys show little concern with the relational aspects of friendship. Friendship for them, as for the youngest group of girls, involves a tie to a congenial companion, with whom one shares a common interest in reality oriented activities.

Our findings also give us some sense of the relative importance to boys of "gang" life, and of the role of the peer group in helping him to confront authority. Boys are more likely than girls to adduce as a cause of unpopularity the unwillingness to "go along with the crowd." In their view, the failure to conform to peer standards is a more probable basis for peer rejection than it is for girls.

Another difference is in the kind of help one expects from a friend. We have already seen that boys are nearer to the youngest girls in wanting specific, concrete supports. But we also find in the boys' answers a theme which does not get much play from girls—the expected help from a friend when in trouble or in times of crisis. Remember that our preadolescent girls wanted from their friends positive supplies in the form of favors. But boys are less receptive in orientation, and more concerned about possible conflicts with authority. They seem to anticipate being on the spot, or being in trouble. The friend is one who will support you when trouble comes. We feel sure that the trouble the boys have in mind is trouble with the adult world. Another indication of this is in the difference between the sexes as regards verbal hostility. The girls object, as we have said, to gossip, to being talked about by other girls. Here the objection is to behavior which will damage or destroy one's relation to peers. Boys however object to "tattling," that is, to the boy who breaks peer ranks to collaborate with the adult enemy. So the adolescent boy's assertive-resistant stance to adults, which we examined earlier, is also evident in his definition of friendship and peer relations. We shall look at this again when we discuss the peer group later in the chapter.

Finally, we want to consider a finding we deem to be of special importance. We have argued throughout this chapter that the interpersonal is of peculiar importance in feminine psychology, that it plays a central role in the woman's development and experience, more so than for the man. Throughout her life, she meets developmental crises through permutations of the interpersonal—the major motive is the desire for love, the major source of anxiety is the fear of losing love, the major techinque in crisis is the appeal for support and supplies from persons important to her. While the boy develops internal controls and strives to meet internal moral standards, the girl regulates her behavior to a greater degree through a sensitivity to signals from key figures in the environment. The boy, to put matters too simply, responds to guilt, the girl to shame. Just as we hypothesized that the consolidation of internal controls is related to personal integration in boys, so we anticipate that, for girls, the degree of personal integration is related to the maturation of interpersonal skills. The girl's talent in relating to objects, her techniques in attracting and holding affection, would, we felt, hold the key to her success in adaptation. Interpersonal skills, we thought, would not be nearly as critical to the boy's intergration.

To test these hypotheses, we devised a measure of interpersonal maturation. Using extreme groups, those who show relatively mature attitudes and skills in the area of friendship, and those who are strikingly immature, we compared their responses in other areas of ego development. For girls there is a clear relation between interpersonal maturation and the following variables: energy level, self-confidence, time-perspective, organization of ideas, and positive feminine identification. For boys, however, the degree of interpersonal maturation is not significantly related to energy level, self-confidence, time perspective, or self-acceptance. In short, we gather that the interpersonal mode is interwoven with the girl's personal integration, while it does not have the same degree of influence in the boy's development.

the relative influence of parent-adolescent affect in predicting the salience hierarchy among youth

Lyle E. Larson
University of Alberta

The purpose of this paper is to investigate the structure and process of social influence during adolescence. In particular, the sociocultural factors mediating and regulating the relative preferences of youth for their parents or for peers are emphasized.

The larger study, upon which this paper is based, developed as an attempt to provide some initial answers to three basic issues.[1] In the first place, a review of the available research illustrates the lack of convergence (the differences are often sharp) among the studies of the influence process. For example, peers, families, and schools are each, in various ways, seen to be *the* most significant influence on the attitudes and behaviors of youth. The literature on peer influence either characterizes youth as a small society maintaining only "threads of connection with adult society" (Coleman, 1961: 3; Schwartz and Merton, 1967) or as an age cohort that increasingly becomes age-mate-oriented with the movement from the early to late teens (Coleman, 1961; Musgrove, 1965; Bowerman and Kinch, 1959; Neiman, 1954; Rosen, 1965; Goodman, 1966). In contrast, a closer look at this research (Coleman, 1961; Bowerman and Kinch, 1959) and other studies (Brittain, 1963; Epperson, 1964; Douvan and Adelson, 1966) provides pervasive evidence for the influence of the family. Other studies have demonstrated that differing family structures, conditions, and processes have an impact on adolescent behavior (Myerhoff and Larson, 1965; Slocum, 1963; Cervantees, 1965; Clausen, 1965, 1966). Similarly, in recent literature on the influence of the school, there is the implication that the school can make or break the socializee, regardless of either parent or peer (compare with Schafer and Polk, 1967). The findings regarding peer, parent, and school predominance variously reflect exaggerated interpretations, preconceived notions of predominance, biased ques-

This is a revised version of a paper presented at the annual meetings of the National Council on Family Relations, Chicago, Illinois, October 1970.

"The Relative Influence of Parent-Adolescent Affect in Predicting the Salience Hierarchy Among Youth," by Lyle E. Larson is reprinted from The Pacific Sociological Review Volume 15, No. 1 (January 1972), pp. 83–102 by permission of the Publisher, Sage Publications, Inc.

tions, the inclusion of supportive variables, and the neglect of several fundamental dimensions.[2]

Second, both theory and research have tended to neglect the various interpenetrations and linkages within the primary and secondary sectors of the social system. Although Durkheim (1933), Parsons (1951), Buckley (1967), and others have considered the structure and process of social influence, the essential *degree* of interpenetration among the many social agents and agencies in both time and space remain unspecified. Similarly, the *relative* influence of reference groups, significant others, and other aspects of primary social influence remains unclear when one attempts to specify the competing, interacting, and linkage factors impinging on the novice.[3]

Third, it seems apparent that the increasing prevalence of delinquency, rebellion, and problems of adolescents in general commands a careful consideration of the "posture" of social influence. If the predictors of the influence posture during adolescence were known, appropriate socializing agencies would be better equipped in dealing with youth.

This paper presents the results of a test of one aspect of the above considerations: the *relative* predictive efficiency of four alternative hypotheses in explaining the "salience hierarchy" (the relative influence of parents and peers) among youth.[4]

The first approach may be called the *grade-level* approach. Stated in its simplest form—as children move into the period of adolescence, their orientations increasingly become age-mate-oriented; as adolescents move into young adulthood, they increasingly return to adult orientations (Gottlieb and Ramsey, 1964). They are said to do so for several reasons: they are expected to by parent and teacher alike, they are forced to be together through age segregation, and they share a common dilemma. The latter is typically described, with feeling, as a situation where the teenager is "betwixt and between" childhood and adulthood beseiged with opportunities and deprivations which have their roots in alien assumptions. Being in the same "boat" facilitates mutual understanding, similarity of purpose, and commonality of interest. It is with his peers that the adolescent is able to develop a sense of identity, power, belonging, and security (compare Keniston, 1960; Erickson, 1963; Friedenberg, 1963; Goodman, 1956).

As suggested in the brief review of literature above, this hypothesis is widely accepted and documented. Several questions, however, may be raised. First, are postadolescents more adult-oriented? Although greater respect for one's elders may be reacquired, adults would appear to be at least as age-mate-oriented as any other age group. Second, the assumption that the youth rejects his parents seems to be an oversimplification. The adolescent's identification with his peers may be an expansion of the social arena to include new sources of influence (Elkin and Westley, 1958). The substance of frequent interaction and similarity of perspective (or even a preference for peer associations) does not necessarily denote parental rejection any more than buying steak on Tuesday represents a rejection of hamburger. Accordingly, the question might be posed somewhat differently: are adolescents basically antiparent, aparent, or proparent/peer? Further, what characteristics might describe each of these groups?

The *goals hypothesis,* of more recent origin, holds that adolescents identify with referents that they perceive as having the desire and ability to help them achieve their goals. Referents which have either ability or desire but not both are identified with moderately. Those who are perceived to have neither the desire nor the ability to help are defined as having no influence (Gottlieb et al., 1966). In their test of this hypothesis, it was found that the greater the level of "helping" (from *no* desire and ability to *both* desire and ability) the higher the frequency of adolescent involvement with the applicable helpers.

There are three questions that might be raised with this approach. First, help with decisions about goals is not a measure of *relative* influence as much as it is *relevant* influence—i.e., the adolescent perceives that certain persons are available (with varying amounts of ability and desire) *if* needed. More important, however, is that the dimensions of ability and desire may be common commodities among the referents in the life space of the adolescent. All a referent would need, being the degree of help is ignored, is a minimum of ability and desire to qualify—for example, the adolescent could place the guidance counselor and his mediocre parent in the same category with equal ease. Second, what are the goals of adolescents and what effect do differing types of goals have on their choice of helpers? Third, to assume that adolescents initiate involvement with those who can help them would also seem to be an oversimplification. In most respects, the youth has little choice in his affiliation and interaction with his family and the school. Youth may tend to drift into relationships with peers rather than actually choosing their associates. Further, the assumption that peers are sought out for the help they can provide in choosing goals certainly has not been demonstrated.

The most productive approach thus far has been the *situational* hypothesis (Brittain, 1963, 1967–1968, 1969). In this case, the adolescent is said to follow the wishes of his parents rather than those of his peers when the context requires decisions that have futuristic implications. Conversely, when the decision involves current status and identity needs, the adolescents opt for the wishes of their peers. Brittain's research has strongly supported the assumptions that adolescents perceive peers and parents as competent guides in different areas, avoid being different from peers, avoid separation from peers, and avoid communicating with parents when they perceive parent-peer cross-pressures. Hypothetical situations creating parent-peer cross-pressures were used to measure the orientations of youth. The adolescent was forced to choose between complying with the wishes of his parents or the wishes of his peers. Likewise, these questions may be raised concerning the situational approach. First, it is difficult to assume that *hypothetical* situations measure the actual behavior of an adolescent in a real situation. Second, most situations involve more than the divergent wishes of parents and peers. Third, the situational dilemmas may not have measured the reference set (parents or peers) orientations of youth. Instead, perhaps the *choice patterns* of youth in artificial situations were measured.

Although each of the above hypotheses is more complementary than contradictory, altogether they have failed to identify an important element in the assessment of the reference set orientations of youth—the quality of the *relationship* the adolescent has with his reference sets. This approach deemphasizes the importance of goals or age level in preference to ascertaining the perceived meaning and satisfaction obtained from adolescent self-other relationships. It is suggested that the purpose, type, and the quality of the relationship the adolescent has with his parents and peers is essential in understanding and explaining the structure and process of social influence during adolescence.

When the studies noted above are considered relative to the relationship hypothesis, some striking similarities appear. In the case of peer influence, adolescents who opted for their peers did so because of what they obtained by doing so. Similarly, studies of parental influence found that adolescents who were parent-oriented were getting something particular from the relationship. Accordingly, when an adolescent identifies with a referent whom he perceives to be able and willing to help him decide on goals, there is a payoff. Although the profit margin may be small, as may be the case in opting for parents where the cross-pressures are severe, the option taken represents the adolescent's perception of greatest gain.[5] In consequence, the adolescent-reference set relationship becomes an organizing principle for explaining the salience hierarchy.

The basic proposition of the relationship approach is that the parent-adolescent and best friend-adolescent relationships are strongly related to the salience hierarchy among youth.[6] Accordingly, it is also expected that the relationship hypothesis will improve the prediction of the salience hierarchy while reducing the efficiency of the other predictors described: the grade-level, help-mate, and situational approaches. The interconnection of these four approaches in the explanation of the salience hierarchy during adolescence is the cornerstone of this paper.

METHODS

The data were obtained through the mass administration of a precoded and pretested survey instrument to all seventh, ninth, and twelfth graders in a southern Oregon city of 12,000 in November 1967. These grades were selected for two reasons. First the seventh and twelfth grades represent, respectively, the beginning of adolescence and the end of compulsory adult control. The ninth grade most nearly approximates the middle of the "settling-in" process during adolescence. Second, the three grade levels represent the most reasonable slicing points for a test of the grade-level hypothesis.

In addition to the salience hierarchy (the dependent variable) and the four predictor variables (parent-adolescent affect, reference set help, situational effect, and grade level), sex and social class are considered. Sex is included due to the wide consensus of the literature concerning the relative impact of femininity, early social development and maturity, and dependency on the role of females in society (compare with Maccoby, 1966; Udry, 1966). Based on this literature, it might be expected that females are more parent-oriented than males. Similarly, social class is included due to the known differences among family systems (for example, communication) of varying socioeconomic levels. In this case, it is expected that upper-class adolescents will be more parent-oriented than will lower-class adolescents.

The measurement of each of the four major variables is briefly described in the notes to Table 1.

Table 1
Univariate Distribution of Variables

Variable	Percentage	Frequency[a]
X_1 Sex: Females	50.8	(788)
Males	49.2	(763)
X_2 Index of Social Position:[b]		
I & II	15.7	(97)
III	25.3	(156)
IV & V	59.0	(364)
X_3 Grade Level:		
Seventh	38.9	(603)
Ninth	35.1	(545)
Twelfth	26.0	(403)
X_4 Parent-Adolescent Affect:[c]		
High	41.7	(745)
Medium	32.8	(507)
Low	25.5	(293)
X_5 Reference Set Help:[d]		
Ability and desire	49.9	(668)
Desire, no ability	41.1	(538)
Ability, no desire; neither ability nor desire	9.0	(133)
X_6 Situational Effect:[e]		
Primarily Parent Compliant	15.6	(233)
Primarily Best Friend Compliant	4.7	(70)
Situation Compliant	79.7	(1,193)
X_7 Salience Hierarchy:[f]		
Parent oriented	35.5	(549)
Parent/Best Friends oriented	39.3	(608)
Best Friends oriented	25.1	(389)

[a] No answers are eliminated. Indexes, such as the Reference Set Hierarchy, therefore have a reduced n.

[b] The measure of social class used in this study is based on the education and occupation of the father. The "two factor" index of Social Position and the occupational categories were first developed by Hollingshead (1957). Only 592 questionnaires were received from the fathers in the sample; consequently, bivariate and multivariate cross tabulations using the Index of Social Position are based on a reduced sample (592 rather than 1,542).

[c] Eleven items were used to measure the quality of the parent-adolescent relation-

Four statistical procedures are used in analyzing the data: gamma—a proportionate reduction in error measure of association; Z—a test of significance appropriate to gamma; test factor standardization—an average partial association technique which permits the control of one or more test variables (Rosenberg, 1962), and a method of assessing three-factor interaction among partial associations (Goodman, 1964).[᠊]

FINDINGS

Table 1 clearly indicates that nearly half the adolescents perceive themselves to have a *highly* satisfying relationship with their parents and nearly 75%, a satisfying relationship. Similarly, more than 90% attribute either both desire and ability or desire alone to their reference sets in helping them decide on goals. It is also apparent, however, that the situational dilemmas provide little indication of reference set priorities—that is, most adolescents responded to the nature of the situation (situation compliance) rather than to the pressures of parents or peers. Situation compliance elsewhere is seen to be a response to pressures (Berelson et al., 1954). In this study, however, the pressures are related to the content of the dilemma, not the pressures of reference sets. The adolescents' perceptions of the hierarchical pattern of influence between parents and peers, as indicated by the salience hierarchy index, indicate that a substantive percentage of youth see no reason to differentiate between their parents and peers (parents/best friend orientation). Only a minority (25%) assign greater salience to their best friends.

The intercorrelations among the seven variables are presented in Table 2. As can be seen, sex is unrelated to parent-adolescent affect and situational effect. Girls, however, more often than boys, perceive their reference sets to have both ability and desire (gamma = .23, Z = .07) but are clearly less parent-oriented than boys (gamma = −.22). The Index of

---

ship. The five items used in the creation of the Parent-Adolescent Affect Index include understanding, willingness, interest, cultural disparity, and enjoyment of family activity. They were selected on the basis of theoretical priority and the hierarchical clustering technique (Johnson, 1967).

[d] The adolescent's perception of the relative ability and desire of parents, teachers, and best friends in helping him decide on goals are combined into the index of Reference Set Help.

[e] The Index of Situational Effect is based on the effect of six differing situations on the choice patterns of youth. Each situation created a dilemma where pressures emanated from both parents and best friends. Adolescents who complied with their parents' wishes in four of the six situations were classified as parent compliant, those who complied with the wishes of their best friends as best friend compliant, and those who changed their choice as the situation changed are classified as situation compliant.

[f] Fifteen items were used to measure the salience hierarchy (the relative preferences of youth). The salience hierarchy index was created by summing the total response on five items (understanding, willingness, knowledge, communication, and control) for each individual and dividing the total by 5 to obtain a mean response. The items used in the index were selected on the basis of theoretical priority and the hierarchical clustering technique (Johnson, 1967).

Table 2
Gamma Matrix: Intercorrelations Among Sex, ISP,
Grade Level, Parent-Adolescent Affect, Reference Set Help,
Situational Effect, and the Salience Hierarchy[a]

	Symbol	X_1	X_2	X_3	X_4	X_5	X_6
Sex	X_1						
Index of Social Position	X_2	.02					
Grade level	X_3	−.05	−.04				
Parent-Adolescent Affect	X_4	.02	.24	.23[b]			
Reference Set Help	X_5	.23	.14	.05	.42[b]		
Situational Effect	X_6	.06	.02	.36[b]	.26[b]	.09	
Salience Hierarchy	X_7	−.22[b]	.16	.44[b]	.48[b]	.11	.27[b]

[a] Due to the complexity and comprehensibility of this analysis, the presentation of tables will typically be limited to correlations. The use of gamma, a proportionate reduction in error measure of order rather than category, facilitates the use of correlations rather than percentage distributors. In the case of sex and the salience hierarchy, for example, a positive correlation would indicate that females are more parent oriented than males. Note the location of categories in Table 1—both females and parent oriented adolescents appear in category one.

[b] Gamma is significant at the .05 level or greater.

Social Position is related to parent-adolescent affect: the higher the social class level, the higher the quality of parent-adolescent affect. Social class does not improve the prediction of any of the other variables. In contrast, grade emerges as a significant correlate of parent-adolescent affect, situational effect, and the salience hierarchy. In this case, seventh graders, relative to ninth and twelfth graders, perceive themselves to have a more satisfying relationship with their parents, appear to be more parent-compliant, and tend to be more parent-oriented. Similarly, parent-adolescent affect is strongly related to reference set help, situational effect, and the salience hierarchy. Finally, situational effect is strongly correlated with the salience hierarchy.

The first step in tracing the relative efficiency of each of these factors in improving the prediction of the parent-peer orientations of youth is taken in Table 3.[s] The average or standardized effect of the control variables taken as a group on the original zero-order relationship between variable X and the salience hierarchy is presented. In terms of the average effect of each predictor on the other, three variables emerge as the primary predictors of the salience hierarchy: sex, grade, and parent-adolescent affect. Situational effect appears to operate independently of the other factors. Although parent-adolescent affect has proved to be more efficient than the other predictors (in support of our expectations), it is apparent that there is considerable interaction among the predictor variables. The substance of this interaction is crucial in attempting to explain the salience hierarchy, the average effect of each variable on the other notwithstanding. Therefore, Table 4 provides the zero-order correlations for each of the

Table 3
Zero Order and Standardized Gamma Matrix: Salience Hierarchy by Sex, Grade Level, Index of Social Position, Parent-Adolescent Affect, Reference Set Hierarchy, Effect of Situations

Variables	Zero Order[a]	Standardized
Sex (PAa, RSH, ES Stdzd)[b]	—.2389[c]	—.2592[c]
Parent-Adolescent Affect (S, RSH, ES, Stdzd)	.4775[c]	.4085[c]
Reference Set Help (S, P-Aa, ES, Stdzd)	.1061	—.0095
Effect of Situations (S, P-Aa, RSH, Stdzd)	.2730[c]	.2719[c]
Grade Level (P-Aa, RSH, ES, Stdzd)	.4929[c]	.3767[c]
Parent-Adolescent Affect (G, RSH, ES, Stdzd)	.4775[c]	.3868[c]
Reference Set Help (G, P-Aa, ES, Stdzd)	.1061	—.0518
Effect of Situations (G, P-Aa, RSH, Stdzd)	.2730[c]	.1954
Index of Social Position (P-Aa, RSH, ES, Stdzd)	.1457	.0796
Parent-Adolescent Affect (ISP, RSH, ES, Stdzd)	.5020[c]	.4620[c]
Reference Set Help (ISP, P-Aa, ES, Stdzd)	.0437	—.0603
Effect of Situations (ISP, P-Aa, RSH, Stdzd)	.3028	.3087

[a] The zero order correlations in this table are slightly different than those in Table 2 because all no answers in the cross tabulations have been eliminated.

[b] The variable names are abbreviated as follows: sex = S, grade level = G, index of social position = ISP, parent-adolescent affect = PAa, reference set help = RSH, and effect of situations = ES.

[c] Gamma is significant at the .05 level or greater.

partial tables created by controlling for sex, grade, Index of Social Position, and situational effect in assessing the relationship between parent-adolescent affect and the salience hierarchy. As can be seen, the interaction test among the partials is significant for sex, grade, and situational effect. The correlations at the various social class levels and desire and ability levels do not differ significantly.

Rather than present the additional somewhat cumbersome tabulations where three or more variables are considered at one time, Figures 1–5 have been developed to graphically illustrate the actual character of the interpenetration of the predictor variables.

Figure 1 illustrates the interrelationship among sex, grade level, and parent-adolescent affect for those adolescents who assign priority to their parents (parent-oriented). Parent priority among youth decreases as grade level increases, decreases as the quality of parent-adolescent decreases, and is lower for females than it is for males. Figure 2, while illustrating similar patterns, also portrays the significance of proparent orientations (parent and parent/best-friend-oriented combined) among youth at the higher levels of parent-adolescent affect. Seventh graders are affected minimally by variant levels of satisfying parent-adolescent relationships while ninth- and twelfth-grade girls appear to be more strongly affected by *low*-quality relationships with their parents.

Table 4
Partial Correlations: Salience Hierarchy by Parent-Adolescent Affect by Sex, Grade Level, Index of Social Position, Reference Set Help, and Effect of Situations

		Correlation	
		Zero Order	Partial
Salience Hierarchy by Parent-Adolescent Affect		48[c]	
by Sex:	Females		1.47[a,c]
	Males		.51[c]
by Grade:	Seventh		.37[a,c]
	Ninth		.49[c]
	Twelfth		.49[c]
by ISP:	I & II		.55[c]
	III		.42[c]
	IV & V		.52[c]
by RSH:	Ability and desire		.44[c]
	Desire, no ability		.53[c]
	Ability, no desire; neither desire nor ability		.51[c]
by ES:	Parent-Compliant		.32[a]
	Best-Friend-Compliant		.57[b]
	Situation-Compliant		.45[c]

[a] Interaction test is significant at the .05 level or greater.
[b] Although the correlation is reasonably large, the n (70) in the case is too small for Z to be significant.
[c] Gamma is significant at the .05 level or greater.

Figure 3 permits an assessment of the assumption that social class alters the impact of sex, grade, and the relationship. In this case, it is clear that among adolescents who perceive a highly satisfying relationship with their parents, social class has little impact. However, there is a dramatic difference between males and females in the twelfth grade. Upper-class twelfth grade boys are less proparent than their female counterparts, while middle-class, twelfth-grade boys are considerably more proparent than middle-class, twelfth-grade girls. Figure 4 indicates, even so, that the patterns in the lower class are similar to those in Figure 2. It is likely that if an adequate sample were available for the upper and middle classes similar patterns would be seen.

Controlling for the effect of situations on the patterns observed above indicates that the situation has only minimal influence (see Figure 5). The patterned relationships among grade, sex, and parent-adolescent affect in their common connection to the salience hierarchy seems to indicate that hypothetical situations cannot explain the variations in the hierarchical preferences of youth. While their responses to situations varied, their orientational patterns did not.

Figure 1
Parent priority by grade level, parent-adolescent affect, and sex.

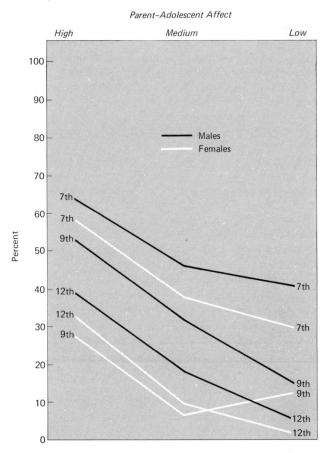

Several conclusions may be drawn from the preceding analysis:

(1) Perceived reference set help in making decisions about goals is not an important factor in the determination of the hierarchical preferences among youth when considered relative to parent-adolescent affect, grade, sex, and social class.

(2) Although those who chose the parent or best-friend-compliant options across situations are clearly more oriented to that referent, the majority of adolescents changed their choice in terms of the *content of the situation rather than their hierarchical reference set orientations.*

(3) Although the grade-level hypothesis works well in explaining the

parent priority preferences of youth (sex and parent-adolescent affect notwithstanding), grade has only a minimal impact on the *pro-parent* orientations of youth. In this sense, the preclusion of an equal-salience category for parents and peers in most research has distorted the meaning of adolescence.

(4) The relative level of parent-adolescent affect is strongly related to both parent preference and proparent priority within each grade level: the higher the degree of perceived satisfaction in the relationship, the higher the degree of parent orientation. Further, adolescents with a high degree of parent-adolescent affect see no reason to differentiate between their parents and best friends at higher grade levels. The quality of the relationship among seventh graders, however, is of minimal significance.

Figure 2
Pro-parent priority by grade level, parent-adolescent affect, and sex.

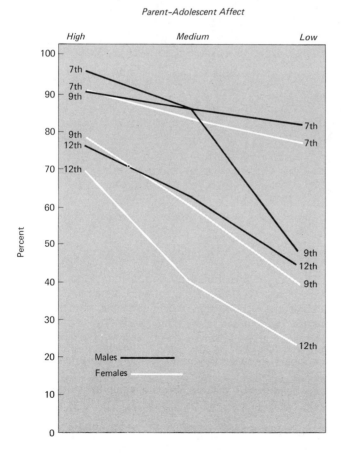

Parent–Adolescent Affect

Figure 3
Pro-parent priority by grade level, *high* parent-adolescent affect, sex, and index of social position.

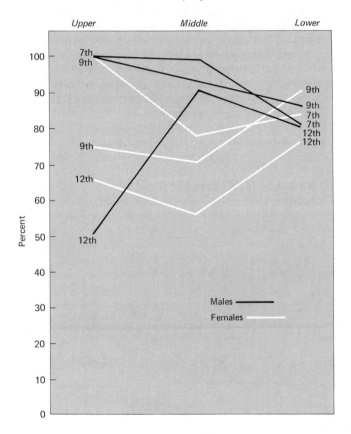

Index of Social Position by High Parent-Adolescent Affect

(5) The decrease in parent preference by increasing grade level and decreasing parent affect varies consistently for males and females: males are consistently more parent-oriented than females. This difference is most pronounced in the ninth grade. These differences are further enhanced at the lower levels of parent-adolescent affect.

(6) Social class appears to be an important variable where the level of parent-adolescent affect is not controlled (this could only be done in lower class because of the size of the sample). Under these conditions, two conclusions may be identified:

(a) In the upper class, *all* seventh- and ninth-grade boys *and* seventh-grade girls are proparent in their orientations. Twelfth-grade boys are the least proparent among their grade and sex counterparts.

(b) In the middle class, boys at *all* grade levels are considerably more proparent than girls at all grade levels.

DISCUSSION

The findings indicate that the relationship model is a useful theoretical perspective in the explanation of the salience hierarchy during adolescence.

Figure 4
Pro-parent priority by grade level, parent-adolescent affect, sex, and *lower* class.

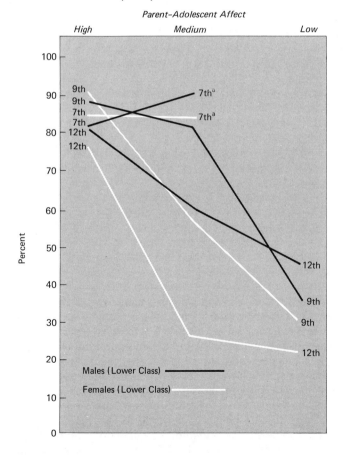

[a] The N is too small to continue the diagram at this point.

Figure 5
Pro-parent priority by grade level, changes due to effect of situations, parent-adolescent affect, and sex.

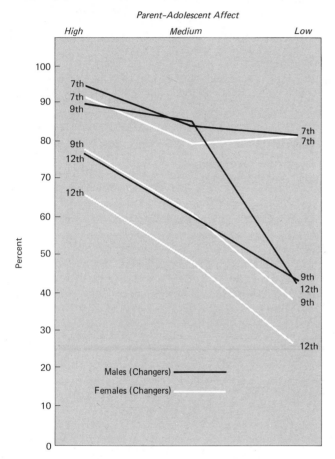

The expectation that adolescents who perceive their parents as understanding, willing to talk with them when they have a problem, fairly easy to talk to, and "in touch" will find less occasion to react against their parents and see less reason to differentiate between parental and friend societies appears to have considerable support. The overwhelming majority of those adolescents who have a high degree of parent-adolescent affect are proparent in their preferences. In contrast, when the qualities of a "good" relationship are weak or absent in the teenager's relationship with his parents, a large proportion assign priority to their best friends. Seventh graders appear to be parent-oriented, the quality of their relationship with their parents notwithstanding. Undoubtedly, they have not yet been subjected to the full impact of youth culture nor have they had the opportunity to build intensive friendships. Where the potential for parental rejection is most intense (grades nine and twelve), however, the quality of relationships with parents becomes a significant predictor.

The consistent and often substantive differences between adolescent males and females were, in part, unsuspected. Only one explanation seems immediately plausible. Boys have generally had more freedom than girls due to a more permissive parental climate. Girls are often subjected to more restrictions. In attempting to cope with the "modern girl" (free, sexual, independent), parents may be overresponding. In consequence, the adolescent girl is less responsive to enhanced parental requirements and regulations. Further research on this issue, in particular, is important.

In contrast to previous research, it has been seen that the *quality* of the adolescent's relationship with his reference sets is essential in determining the relative influence of the type and purpose of his relationships. *The degree of interpenetration of the influences of parents and best friends cannot be assessed without an evaluation of the satisfactions gained from the relationship.* In particular, just as adolescents have "good" relationships with their best friends, this paper suggests that the "goodness" of the parent-adolescent relationship should also be considered. Further, previous research clearly "loaded" the results by forcing the adolescent to choose between his parents and peers. Under these conditions, it is reasonable for the adolescent to choose his peers. Indeed, the adolescent may opt for his peers without either "violating" the essence of his parents' wishes or "hurting" the parent-youth relationship. The option to assign equal importance to both parents and friends is essential in any measurement of the hierarchical preferences of youth, particularly at the higher grade levels.

Additional research is needed on the interpenetrations and linkages among the variant aspects of social influence, on the factors that facilitate satisfying relationships between socializers and socializees, and on the sequencing of static sociocultural dimensions over time.

The contributions of this study and others which attempt to identify the independent and relative predictive efficiency of several alternative explanations, could be considerably enhanced through multivariate and path analysis techniques. Hopefully, both data and data collection procedures in related future research will be conducive to this type of analysis.

NOTES

1. This paper is based on a study conducted in November 1967, under the support of the Cooperative Research Program of the United States Office of Education, DHEW Project 7-1-105, OEG-9-070105-00350(010).
2. Coleman's (1961) findings, for example, may be questioned in several ways. First, a number of a priori judgments is apparent: the belief in the existence of a youth subculture, severe reservations about the value of athletics and girls who aspire to be movie stars or models, and a belief in the virtues of intellectualism for adolescents. Second, Coleman appeared to rely on somewhat "loaded" questions. For example, the respondents were asked to choose between their parents' disapproval, their teachers' disapproval, and "breaking with their best friends." The responses enabled Coleman to support the existence

of a youth society. When this question was rephrased and asked of another sample of adolescents (Epperson, 1964) nearly eighty per cent opted for their parents.

Similarly, even though Brittain's studies (1963, 1967–1968, 1969) are interpreted as evidence for the preponderance of peer influence, nine of his twelve situations produced a response considerably more favorable to parents than to peers.

On the other hand, the study by Slocum (1963) merely notes the possibility that the influence of the family "may be tempered by the impact of peer group standards" and then ignores the theoretical relevance of this impact.

3. Further discussion of these matters and the presentation of a theoretical model designed to reduce these ambiguities may be found in Larson (1969: 1–72).

4. The term salience hierarchy may seem to be nothing more than a semantic doubletake on the concept of reference group. In reality, the concept has particular reference to the *relative salience of reference sets.* The concept of reference set following Goodman (1965) is defined as "the cast of significant others whom the individual takes into account when he acts."

5. The cost of a particular course of action is the equivalent of the foregone value of an alternative, a familiar economic assumption. The formula is presented in Homans (1950: 597–606). One must be cautious, however, in applying an exchange model to the approach used here. The adolescent does not think only of the cost or reward to himself. He considers the cost in terms of his relationship, its nature and type.

6. It may be noted that this study focuses on the adolescent's relationships with his *best friends* rather than with peers in general. It is assumed that the stimulus "best friends" calls forth a group of persons (two or more) to whom the adolescent considers himself very close. Neither the number nor the sex of best friends is considered in this study, as these relationships are voluntary. Whether the stimulus "best friends" elicits a group of boys or a group of girls is also immaterial. The issue is that these are simply best friends. This stimulus is comparable to the others given—"most of your teachers," and "mother" and "father." The sex of the parent is important because these relationships are involuntary and primarily expressive. The adolescent's relationship with his teachers is generally not on an individual basis, as in the family, and primarily instrumental. In addition, it may be emphasized that it is unnecessary to ascertain the quality of the adolescent's relationship with his best friends. A high-quality relationship may be assumed. This assumption was tested in the pilot and conclusively confirmed.

7. It may be noted that this paper only presents the necessary tables and graphs. Many possible cross-tabulations and controls are not introduced—e.g., the effect of reference set help on the salience hierarchy controlling for grade—because the *essence* of the relationships are adequately illustrated by the tables and graphs included.

8. Due to the independent relationships among sex, grade, and social class, each of these variables is considered separately.

REFERENCES

Berelson, B. R., P. F. Lazarsfeld and W. N. McPhee
1954   Voting. Chicago: Univ. of Chicago Press.
Bowerman, C. E. and J. W. Kinch
1959   "Changes in family and peer orientation of children between the fourth and tenth grades." Social Forces 37 (February): 206–211.
Brittain, Clay V.
1963   "Adolescent choices and parent-peer cross-pressures." Amer. Soc. Rev. 28 (June): 385–391.
1967–1968   "An exploration of the bases of peer-compliance and parent-compliance in adolescence." Adolescence 2 (Winter): 445–458.
1969   "A comparison of rural and urban adolescents with respect to peer vs. parent compliance." Adolescence 13 (Spring): 59–68.
Cervantees, Lucius F.
1965   "Family background, primary relationships, and the high school dropout." J. of Marriage and Family 27 (May): 218–224.
Clausen, John A.
1956   "Family size and birth order as influences upon socialization and personality: bibliography and abstracts." Report of a work group to the committee on Socialization and Social Structure of the Social Science Research Council. (unpublished)
Clausen, John A.
1966   "Family structure, socialization and personality." Pp. 1–53 in M. L. Hoffman and L. W. Hoffman (eds.) Review of Child Development Research II. New York: Russell Sage.
Coleman, James S.
1961   The Adolescent Society. New York: Free Press.
Douvan, Elizabeth and Joseph Adelson
1966   The Adolescent Experience. New York: John Wiley.
Elkin, Frederick and William A. Westley
1958   "The myth of adolescent culture." Amer. Soc. Rev. 20 (December): 680–684.
Epperson, D.C.
1964   "A reassessment of indices of parental influence in the adolescent society." Amer. Soc. Rev. 29 (February): 93–96.
Erickson, Erik (ed.)
1963   The Challenge of Youth. Garden City, N.Y.: Doubleday Anchor.
Friedenberg, Edgar Z.
1963   Coming of Age in America: Growth and Acquiescence. New York: Random House.
Goodman, Leo A.
1964   "Simple methods for analyzing three-factor interaction in contingency tables." J. of Amer. Statistical Assn. 59 (June): 319–347.
Goodman, Norman
1965   "The adolescent's reference set." Presented at the annual meeting of the American Sociological Association.
Goodman, Paul
1956   Growing up Absurd. New York: Random House.

Gottlieb, David and Charles Ramsey
1964   The American Adolescent. New York: Dorsey.
Gottlieb, David, Jon Reeves, and Warren D. TenHouten
1966   The Emergence of Youth Societies: A Cross-Cultural Approach. New York: Free Press.
Hollingshead, August B.
1957   Two-Factor Index of Social Position. Mimeographed.
Homans, George
1950   The Human Group. New York: Harcourt, Brace & World.
Johnson, Stephen C.
1967   "Hierarchical clustering schemes." Psychometrika 32 (September): 241–254.
Keniston, Kenneth
1960   The Uncommitted: Alienated Youth in American Society. New York: Harcourt, Brace & World.
Larson, Lyle E.
1969   "The structure and process of social influence during adolescence. An Examination of the Salience Hierarchy." Ph.D. dissertation. University of Oregon.
Maccoby, Eleanor E.
1966   The Development of Sex Differences. California: Stanford Univ. Press.
Musgrove, Frank
1965   Youth and the Social Order. Bloomington: Indiana Univ. Press.
Myerhoff, Barbara G. and William R. Larson
1965   "Primary and formal aspects of family organization: group consensus, problem perception, and adolescent school success." J. of Marriage and Family 27 (May): 213–218.
Neiman, L. J.
1954   "The influence of peer groups upon attitudes toward the feminine role." Social Problems 2 (March): 104–111.
Rosen, B. C.
1965   Adolescence and Religion: The Jewish Teenager in American Society. Cambridge: Scheakman.
Rosenberg, Morris
1962   "Test factor standardization as a method of interpretation." Social Forces 41 (October): 53–61.
Schafer, Walter and Kenneth Polk
1967   "Delinquency and the schools." Pp. 222–278 in the President's Commission on Law Enforcement and Administration of Justice, Task Force Report: Juvenile Delinquency and Youth Crime. Washington, D.C.: Government Printing Office.
Schwartz, Gary and Don Merton
1967   "The language of adolescence: an anthropological approach to the youth culture." Amer. J. of Sociology 72 (March): 453–469.
Slocum, Walter L.
1963   Family Culture Patterns and Adolescent Behavior. Pullman: Washington State University.

Conformity development as a function of self-blame

Philip R. Costanzo
Duke University

In a recent study of conformity development Costanzo and Shaw (1966) found that the child's conformity to simulated peer pressure in the Asch-type situation increased with age from 7 to 12 years and thereafter decreased to age 21. Iscoe, Williams, and Harvey (1963), using a similar simulated group technique, also found a general increase in conformity from ages 7–12 and a decrease to age 15. On the basis of these studies it would seem highly tenable to posit that the peer group becomes an increasingly powerful source of social influence for the child during the period of rapid social growth between early childhood and pubescence.

Several accounts of childhood socialization have suggested that the child's gradual integration into the peer group is accompanied by a shift from the positive evaluation of parents as reference persons to the positive evaluation of peers as reference persons (Ausubel, 1958; Campbell, 1964; Stone & Church, 1968). A study by Bowerman and Kinch (1959) renders some empirical force to this proposed shift. On a combined index of identificational, associational, and normative orientations, they demonstrated that 87% of the fourth graders they tested were family oriented, while only 32% of the tested eighth graders were so oriented. These investigators also found a similar shift in orientation toward peers from the fourth to the eighth grade. The gradual decrease in conformity between adolescence and young adulthood observed by both Iscoe et al. (1964) and by Costanzo and Shaw (1966) reflects the adolescent's gradual disengagement from the peer group as a predominant source of influence. Thus, the adolescent and young adult, while still forming relatively close identifications with peer group sources, are at the same time forging an identity apart from the group. The forces of self-identification and self-confidence operate to modulate the social pressure generated by peer groups.

This article was based upon a dissertation submitted to the University of Florida in 1967. The author would like to express his thanks to Marvin E. Shaw, the chairman of his supervisory committee, for his invaluable guidance and support throughout this project.

The proposition that the peer group gradually becomes the predominant reference group for the individual between childhood and preadolescence has implications which at least partially explain the relationship between conformity and age. The peer reference group is a group by which the individual child evaluates himself, his standards, and his behavior. As the peer reference group increases in importance for the child he should tend to be more resistant to deviation from the standards which emerge from the group. Social conformity may be viewed as a consequence of the child's generalized level of resistance to deviation from group standards. With the child's increasing integration into the peer group between early childhood and pubescence, his generalized level of resistance to deviation from peer norms should increase, and hence he should be more prone to conform. As such, a measure of generalized orientation toward deviation from group norms and/or transgression against valued reference group members should be predictive of degree of conformity behavior. In the current investigation, the construct *self-blame* was used as a measure of generalized orientation toward deviation from and transgression against the peer group. The assumption underlying the use of the self-blame construct holds that the more harshly the individual evaluates his purported commission of an "offense" against a peer group member or the violation of a peer group norm, the more negatively he evaluates deviation in general, and thus the more likely it is that he will conform.

A further and related justification for the proposed relationship between self-blame and conformity can be extracted from the rather substantial body of research probing the relationship between self-esteem and conformity. In general, it has been found that low-self-esteem subjects tend to display greater conformity than subjects of moderate or high esteem (see for example, Berkowitz & Lundy, 1957; Janis, 1954; Janis & Field, 1959). The attribution of blame to self would seem to be a logical consequence of low self-esteem. That is, the individual who tends to think poorly of himself would probably tend to evaluate his actions harshly, particularly those actions which mediate negative outcomes for others or which deviate from the standards of the group. Considering degree of self-blame as an attributive consequence of degree of self-esteem, one would expect that high-self-blame subjects should show patterns of conformity behavior previously found to hold for low-self-esteem subjects.

From a developmental perspective self-esteem should be intricately linked to the growth of peer orientation. That is, with the increasing integration of the child into his peer reference group, one would expect that the child's evaluation of the importance of the peer group would increase. Thus, in the period between early childhood and pubescence, the child should gradually afford increasing esteem to his peer reference group. Correspondingly, since the group, in terms of its reference function, assumes a superordinate position in relation to the child, he should probably hold the group in relatively higher esteem than he holds himself. It is the position of this investigator that the degree of discrepancy between the child's esteem for self and his esteem for the group should be reflected in his differential evaluation of similar deviations or transgressions when they emanate from himself and when they emanate from a valued peer group member. Thus, both self-blame as an absolute measure and the difference between self-blame and other blame should be closely related to conformity. Furthermore, the relationships between both absolute and relative self-blame and conformity should be reflective of several aspects of the social-developmental process in the growth of peer relationships.

In their study of conformity development, Costanzo and Shaw used a postexperimental questioning technique to explore the possible relationship between self-blame and conformity. After each group of four age-homogeneous subjects was tested for conformity to the erroneous judgments of line stimuli, they were individually asked if they had noted a discrepancy between their own initial perceptions of the lines and those of their peers. All subjects indicated that they had, and were further asked what they felt the source of the discrepancy was. The reasons given for the discrepancies were classified as either "internal" (self-attributed reasons) or "external" (other attributed reasons). These classifications were made with 100% agreement by four graduate students in psychology. The results of this procedure demonstrated that the internal attribution of blame, like conformity, can be represented as a two-stage function of age. Just as conformity increased with age to an asymptotic point in the 11–13-year-old age group and thereafter decreased, the frequency of internal blame attribution generated a function with the same trends. Furthermore, the biserial correlation computed between conformity and internal attribution was highly significant ($r_{bis} = .87$, $p < .001$).

While these findings render strong support to the proposed relationship between self-blame and conformity, their impact is tempered by the procedure by which the measure of self-blame was extracted. That is, since the measure of blame was taken directly after the conformity manipulation, it might have been confounded by the subjects' prior tendency to conform or not to conform. The purpose of this investigation was to examine more closely the developmental and nondevelopmental relationships between self-blame and conformity through the use of independent measures of both of these behaviors. Both a relative self-blame measure (the difference between self-blame and other blame) and an absolute self-blame measure were used. The investigator felt that a measure of relative self-blame would be reflective of relative self-esteem, and furthermore was needed to discount the possible confounding of the tendency to be generally blaming with the tendency to be self-blaming that could occur with a single absolute measure of self-blame. The general prediction made was that conformity measured by a simulated group technique, and self-blame measured by a story-situation questionnarie, would be positively related both within and across age groups. More specifically, it was predicted (a) that the developmental functions of self-blame and conformity would show an initial rise in the frequency of both behaviors from 7 to 13 years and a decrease from 13 to 21 years; (b) that subjects scoring high on self-blame in relation to their age group's mean would conform more frequently than those subjects obtaining average scores, and those subjects obtaining average self-blame scores would conform more than those with low scores; (c) that the larger the difference between self-blame score and other-blame score (also obtained by a story-situation questionnaire) in the direction of self-blame, the greater the conformity.

METHOD

SUBJECTS

Four hundred and ninety males ranging in age from 7 to 21 were administered a self-blame (SB) test devised especially for this study. This initial screening sample consisted of four age groups: (a) 7–8-year-olds ($n = 86$); (b) 12–13-year-olds ($n = 130$); (c) 16–17-year-olds ($n = 128$); (d) 19–21-year-olds ($n = 146$). Those subjects ranging in age from 7 to 17 were randomly selected from the elementary, junior high, and senior high schools in Putnam County, Florida. The 19–21-year-old age group was made up of subjects randomly selected from elementary psychology courses at the University of Florida.

From this initial pool of subjects, 36 were selected at each age level on the basis of their scoring on the SB test. The 12 highest, lowest, and middle-most scorers on SB in each age group who met the criterion of average or above intelligence were chosen to participate in the conformity and other-blame (OB) portions of this study. Furthermore, a measure of social class based on the North-Hatt scale of occupations was obtained on each subject to rule out social class differences among the age groups.

EXPERIMENTAL DESIGN

A 3 × 4 factorial design was used in order to test the differences among the 4 age groups and the 3 blame groups on conformity.

Additionally, a single-factor analysis of variance with unequal n's per cell was utilized to test differences in SB attribution among the four age groups. The scores of all 490 subjects tested on the SB scale served as the dependent variable in this analysis.

MATERIALS AND APPARATUS

In order to measure SB, 12 incidents, all involving interaction or confrontation of oneself with a peer, were constructed. All of these incidents culminated in a negative or undesirable result. Eight praise-conductive incidents culminating in a positive result of peer interaction were inserted into the blame scale to avoid the negative effects that might arise from having subjects consistently blame themselves. A sample blame item used was:

> You and your friend are walking home from school. Neither of you is paying attention to where you are going. Finally, you knock into your friend and his books fall into a puddle of water and are ruined. How much are you to blame?

The answer sheet was numbered 1–20 with each number corresponding to either a self-blame or self-praise incident. Next to each number on the answer sheet there were five boxes vertically descending in size. Subjects were to indicate the amount of praise or blame they were willing to attribute to themselves for any given incident by placing a check in the appropriate size box. The largest box represented "a very lot" of praise or blame while the smallest box indicated no praise or blame at all. The same scale with self- and peer roles reversed was given to each subject participating in the conformity portion of this study in order to obtain a measure of OB.

The scales used had content validity, and split-half reliabilities were computed for each group on the SB scale. Full-test reliabilities were estimated from split-half reliabilities computed within each of the four age groups. These coefficients indicate that the test can be reliably used to estimate SB in all of the age groupings. The reliabilities obtained were: (a) Group I (7–8-year-olds)—.77; $n = 86$; (b) Group II (12–13-year-olds)—.82; $n = 130$; (c) Group III (16–17-year-olds)—.86; $n = 128$; (d) Group IV (19–21-year-olds)—.84; $n = 146$.

The apparatus used to measure conformity was the same as that used by Costanzo and Shaw (1966) and similar to the one described by Crutchfield (1955). It consisted of five booths arranged in a semicircle. The center booth was occupied by the experimenter and contained a Beseler opaque projector and master panels of lights and switches. The subjects occupied the four side booths and faced a projection screen located approximately 10 feet from each of the experimental booths to insure isolation for both subjects and experimenter.

In a slight modification of the original Crutchfield apparatus, each subject booth contained a panel of 20 lights arranged in four rows of 5 lights each. Mercury switches were located below the bottom row of lights. Each of these mercury switches, when turned on, activated one of the lights in the fourth row of the subject's response panel and an analogous light on the master response panel in the experimenter's booth. Although all subjects were instructed that the first three rows of lights would record the responses made by the other three subjects in the experimental situation, these lights were actually controlled by master switches in the experimenter's booth. This permitted identical lights to be turned on in each booth simultaneously. All responses made by subjects were recorded on the master panel in the experimenter's booth. In the present experiment, only three of the five possible response alternatives represented on the subjects' response panels were utilized.

The stimulus materials which were used in conjunction with this apparatus consisted of the simple straight line stimuli described by Asch (1951). Each stimulus card was made up of one standard line and three comparison lines. One of the three comparison lines matched the standard in length, one was longer than the standard, and another was shorter than the standard.

PROCEDURE

The initial pool of 490 male subjects drawn from all four of the age groups was administered the SB test. The scale was administered to one total age group at a time in a large classroom or auditorium in their respective schools. The experimenter introduced the scale to the subjects in each group by reading aloud the instructions provided on the face sheet of each test booklet. In the course of this introductory period the experimenter explained how to use the system of responding whereby the subjects might indicate different amounts of blame or praise by choosing an appropriate size box from the five which vertically descended in size for each item. After it was apparent that everyone understood the manner of response, the three oldest age groups were instructed to read each item carefully and to make the response that most applied to them on any given item. The youngest age group (7- and 8-year-olds) were read each item aloud because of the great variation in reading ability at this age. These younger subjects were instructed not to respond until the experimenter completed reading the incident. All subjects in all age groups appeared to understand the endorsement procedure.

Twelve subjects each from the high, medium, and low levels of SB endorsement within each age group who met the criterion of average or better intelligence were selected to participate in the conformity portion of this study, which was administered approximately 1 week after the administration of the SB scale.

The conformity portion of this study was also administered in a room at the school which the subjects were attending. When subjects reported at the time they were scheduled for, they were asked to select one of the four booths. They were also told that after they had been seated in their chosen booth there was to be no discussion among themselves. After the four subjects in any group were seated, the experimenter gave instructions pertaining to the nature of the task and the operation of the apparatus. These instructions were made as simple as possible to insure that subjects of all age levels would understand them.

After the instructions were presented, and the experimenter was assured that all subjects comprehended the task, he proceeded to administer the five preexperimental trials to ascertain the original response level of each subject and to further insure that subjects across all grades understood and were able to perform the task.

The test period consisted of 20 trials with the line stimuli. On 15 of these 20 trials the experimenter, simulating a peer majority, made erroneous judgments. Since all subjects were assigned Number 4, and erroneously believed that their peers occupying the other booths were Numbers 1, 2, and 3, they were all confronted with a unanimously wrong peer majority on 15 of the 20 experimental trials. Each individual's conformity score was the number of times his choice corresponded with the erroneous judgments of the simulated peer majority.

After the administration of the conformity portion of this study to a given age group, that age group was once again assembled and administered the OB scale.

RESULTS

Before the main findings of this study are reported, the results of some preliminary measures of social class and task competency among age groups are presented. These measures were taken in order to assure that the four age groups were equivalent with regard to social class and ability to perform the experimental task.

An analysis of variance was done in order to test the difference among the four age groups on the North-Hatt Scale of occupational prestige. Although the college age groups tended to originate from families in which the father's occupation was ranked somewhat higher than the pre-college age groups, no significant differences were found among age groups on occupational classifications ($F = 2.13$, $df = 3/140$).

A total of eight errors were made on the 720 preexperimental trials in all age groups. The errors were distributed among all four of the age groups with no predominance of error in any one age group. This performance represents a line judgment accuracy of over 98% and indicates that all subjects in all age groups could perform the task and use the apparatus with equal facility.

The results of social pressure on conformity at the different age levels are presented graphically in Figure 1. As predicted, conformity was lowest for Group I (ages 7–8), increased to an asymptotic point for Group II (ages 12–13), and decreased for Group III (ages 16–17) and Group IV (ages 19–21).

The experimenter's prediction on the development of SB was not up-held. As Figure 2 demonstrates, the tendency to attribute blame to oneself decreased with increasing age. There was a highly significant difference among the age groups on SB responsiveness ($F = 60.76$, $df = 3/486$, $p < .001$). The hypothesis that the development of SB and the development of conformity could be represented by parallel functions was not upheld. As indicated in Figures 1 and 2, the three oldest age groups displayed the downward linear trend predicted for the postadolescent groups on both SB and conformity, whereas Group I (pages 7–8) scored highest rather than lowest on SB as had been predicted.

The nonparallelism in the development of SB and conformity does not, however, contraindicate the interrelated nature of these two variables. The

Figure 1
Percentage of conformity as a function of age level ($n = 36$ per age level).

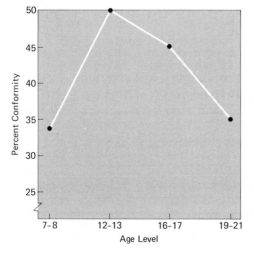

analysis of the difference among blame groups and age groups on conformity (Table 1) reveals that there were highly significant differences in conformity as a function of both age and SB intensity. Figure 3 depicts the developmental functions of conformity for high-, medium-, and low-blame groups. As SB increased, conformity likewise increased for all four age groups.

To test further the strength of the relationship between SB and conformity, correlations between these two factors were computed both within each age group and across all age groups. As indicated by Table 2, the correlation coefficients between SB and conformity within each age group ranged from .67 for Group II (ages 12–13) to .78 for Group IV (ages 19–21). It is noteworthy that when age groups were combined and a correlation computed between SB and conformity, the total correlation dropped to

Figure 2
Self-blame as a function of age level (*n* = 490).

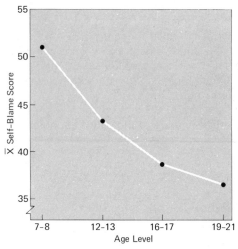

Table 1
Summary of the 3 × 4 Analysis of Variance of Conformity Responses at the Age Levels for Three Levels of Blame

Source	SS	df	MS	F
Age (A)	137.58	3	45.86	12.53*
Blaming intensity (B)	327.87	2	163.94	44.79*
A × B	8.50	6	1.47	<1
Error	483.50	132	3.66	—

* p < .001

Figure 3
Percentage of conformity as a function of age at different levels of self-blame intensity.

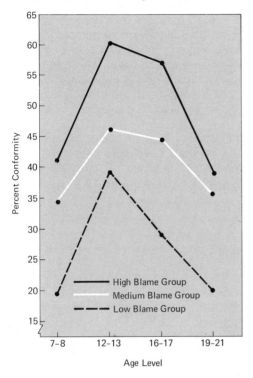

Table 2
Correlative Relationships Among Self-Blame, Other Blame, Self-Blame Minus Other Blame, and Conformity

	Age Group				
Correlation Source	*7–8*	*12–13*	*16–17*	*19–21*	*All Groups*
SB × OB	.72**	.36**	.35*	.79**	.61**
SB × C	.78**	.67**	.68**	.76**	.54**
SB-OB × C	.58**	.54**	.61**	.46*	.63**
OB × C	.68**	.19	.30	.63**	— .03**

Note. Abbreviations: SB = self-blame, OB = other blame, SB-OB = self-blame minus other blame, C = conformity.

*p < .05.

**p < .01.

.54. This drop in the strength of the relationship between SB and conformity was predominantly the result of Group I's low point scoring on conformity and their unpredicted high point scoring on SB.

The hypothesis which postulated a positive relationship between SB-OB score and conformity was tested by the correlation of these two factors both within and across age groups. Table 2 indicates that there are significant positive relationships between SB-OB and conformity within each age group. These correlations range from a low of .46 in Group IV to a high of .61 in Group III. Table 2 shows an overall correlation of .66 between SB-OB and conformity across all age groups. Figure 4 graphically depicts the development of SB-OB scoring as a function of age level. The trends of this curve are very similar to those of Figure 1 displaying conformity as a function of age level.

Additional correlations were run between OB and conformity and OB and SB. These correlations like the previous ones were computed both within the across age groups. Correlations between SB and OB within age groups varied from .35 in Group III (16–17 years) to .79 in Group IV

Figure 4
**Self-blame minus other-blame score
as a function of age level.**

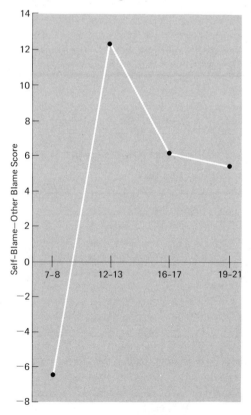

(19–21 years). These four correlations were all significant at the .05 level or better (Table 2). There was an overall, across age group correlation of .61 between SB and OB. These findings indicate that individuals are relatively consistent in their blaming tendencies whether the target person is self or other. This finding accentuates the importance of the SB-OB score as a measure of direction of blame attribution, for in using this subtraction factor, each subject can serve as his own base level for attribution of blame tendencies.

The correlations between OB and conformity within age groups varied from a low of .19 in Group III (12–13 years) to a high of .68 in Group I (7–8 years) with significant positive relationships obtaining in Groups I and IV ($r = .63$)—(see Table 2). The relationship between OB and conformity across age groups, however, yielded a coefficient of $-.03$, indicating that in a population of subjects of heterogeneous age, OB and conformity operate as orthogonal factors.

DISCUSSION

CONFORMITY DEVELOPMENT

The results of both Costanzo and Shaw (1966) and Iscoe et al. (1964) are clearly replicated by the findings of this study. The three studies taken together provide impressive support for the proposition that the suggestibility of the child to peer influence increases with age into pubescence after which the efficacy of peer influence in inducing public conformity declines with increasing age (see Figure 1). It seems reasonable to posit that the ability of the peer group to influence the child's behavior increases as a function of increases in the child's involvement with this group, and decreases with the adolescents' gradual disengagement from the peer group. Naturalistic and experimental observations of peer interactions support the notion that children become increasingly oriented to and involved with their peer group between middle childhood and pubescence (Bowerman & Kinch, 1959; Piaget, 1951). Prior to school entry the child is so enmeshed in family interaction and so guided by parental standards that the peer group is of little significance to him. On the other hand, as the child moves into late adolescence factors such as enhanced personality identity, increased social competence, and more firmly rooted social self-esteem emerge as countervailing forces against the influence of the group. The observed decrease in conformity between ages 13–21 (see Figure 1) should not be viewed as a simple reduction in the importance of the peer group, for this interpretation defies both logic and the findings of experimental investigations of adult conformity. Rather, a more likely interpretation is that the importance of self increases relative to the importance of the group. Therefore, the adolescent and young adult become more able to resist the pressures of the group.

CONFORMITY–SELF-BLAME (SB) RELATIONSHIPS

The notion that involvement with the group is a necessary precondition of conformity is by no means a unique proposal. In a recent review monograph on conformity, Kiesler and Kiesler (1969) have proposed that social influence only occurs in aggregates in which the members are cognitively or emotionally involved with one other. Studies which have manipulated the individual's involvement with the group through experimental induction have demonstrated the validity of the proposition that degree of group involvement and conforming behavior are directly related (e.g., see Deutsch & Gerard, 1955).

Earlier in this article, it was proposed that the degree to which an individual identifies with and values the group (that is, the degree to which the group serves a reference function for the individual) should be related to his avoidance of deviation from or transgression against the group. Further, insofar as transgression against the group or a member of it occurs, the more relative esteem the individual attaches to the group, the more blame the individual will attribute to himself. Since conformity and SB were both conceptualized as being rooted in the relative evaluation the individual has for himself and the peer group, it was hypothesized that these behaviors should be highly related both developmentally and nondevelopmentally.

The relationship between conformity and SB obtained in this study strongly supports the experimenter's hypotheses. The analysis of variance testing the independent effects of age and SB on conformity yielded a highly significant main effect for SB (see Table 1). Figure 3 graphically demonstrates the effect of SB on conformity. As can be noted, the three blame groups generate three separate but parallel functions of conformity development. Within each of the age groups, the greater the individual's tendency to SB, the greater his tendency to conform.

The findings were not quite so clear with regard to the developmental parallelism between SB and conformity. It was predicted that the developmental functions of conformity and SB should show initial increases from ages 7 to 13 and decreases from ages 13 to 21. While this was found to be the case with regard to SB-OB or relative SB (cf. Figures 1 and 4), the prediction was not supported with regard to absolute SB (cf. Figures 1 and 2). The 7–8-year-old age group obtained the highest mean score on absolute SB and the lowest mean score on conformity. The other three age groups, however, obtained correspondent absolute SB and conformity scores. The counterhypothetical tendency of the 7–8-year-old age group to blame themselves more than any of the other age groups might be explained by the relationship between the structure of the story-situation SB items and the 7–8-year-olds' cognitive orientation toward personal responsibility. Each of the SB incidents culminated in a negative outcome for the "other" and that outcome was to some degree (predominantly unintentionally) mediated by the "person." In the light of the young child's tendency to focus upon outcome intensity in interpreting degree of responsibility (for example, see Piaget, 1951), it is not surprising that he displays high levels of blame in response to negative outcomes. Thus, the 7–8-year-old child is less likely to use mitigating factors such as the intention of the actor in attenuating his reaction to the negative outcome produced. These considerations underline the importance of the relative SB measure as an indicator of punitive orientation toward the *actor* in distinction to punitive orientation toward the *act*.

A close comparison of Figures 1 and 4 reveals that the 7–8-year-old age group was the only one of the age groups to blame others more than themselves for the same actions, and it was that age group which obtained the lowest mean conformity score.

On the other hand, the 12–13-year-old age group was most prone to blame self more than other, and they were the highest conforming group. The oldest two age groups fell between the 7–8-year-old and 12–13-year-old group on both relative self-blame and on conforming frequency. The over-all correlation of .66 between SB-OB and conformity further substantiates the close relationship between relative blame of self over peer and conformity. The high correlations of absolute SB and conformity (see Table 2) *within* each of the age groups indicates that in a population in which there is a greater likelihood of homogeneous general punitiveness, the absolute level of SB is very significantly related to conformity (see Table 2 and Figure 3).

The foregoing findings provide impressive support for the hypothesized relationship between SB and conformity both within and across age groups. It was reasoned that both SB and conformity are mediated by the degree of the individual's involvement within the peer group. As such, both behaviors can be viewed as manifestations of the individual's identification with the peer group as a source of influence. The stronger the individual's identification with his peer group the greater the probability that he will value the peer group's attributes and behaviors more positively than his own. Further, the more intensive the child's identification with the peer group, the more negative his evaluation of deviation from or transgression against the group and its members. Using this perspective and referring to the data of this study, one might conclude that the child is most highly identified with his peers at around 12–13 years of age and least identified with his peer group in the early school years (and probably even less identified in the preschool years).

The crux of the above reasoning is that as the child experiences increasing contact with the peer group, he grows to value it with increasing positivity. As a consequence, he becomes reluctant to appear "different" than the group or to transgress against its members. The degree of discrepancy between the child's evaluation of his own transgressive actions and those of a valued peer provides a measure of the relative esteem he affords himself and the group. If one considers relative SB as a measure reflective of relative self-esteem, the findings of this study might be viewed as a further demonstration of the frequently found inverse relationship between self-esteem and conformity. However, this study raises the additional and related proposition that changes in conformity with age are at least partially mediated by changes in social self-esteem with age.

One fruitful area for further research would seem to involve the direct probing of the empirical relationships among peer involvement, relative self-esteem, and susceptibility to peer influence. In the present study, peer involvement was used solely as an explanatory concept and was inferred from age level. The development of adequate measures to assess involvement with and orientation toward peers across a wide age range might provide valuable tools for the examination of the developmental underpinnings of the self-esteem–conforming relationship.

REFERENCES

Asch, S. E. Effects of group pressure upon the modification and distortion of judgments. In H. Guetzkow (Ed.), *Groups, leadership, and men.* Pittsburgh: Carnegie Press, 1951.

Ausubel, D. P. Theory and problems of child development. New York: Grune & Stratton, 1958.

Berkowitz, L., & Lundy, R. M. Personality characteristics related to susceptibility to influence by peers or authority figures. *Journal of Personality,* 1957, *25:* 306–316.

Bowerman, C. E., & Kinch, J. W. Changes in family and peer orientation of children between the fourth and tenth grade. *Social Forces,* 1959, *37:* 206–211.

Campbell, J. D. Peer relations in childhood. In M. Hoffman & L. Hoffman (Eds.), *Review of child development research.* Vol. 1. New York: Russell Sage Foundation, 1964.

Costanzo, P. R., & Shaw, M. E. Conformity as a function of age level. *Child Development,* 1966, *37:* 967–975.

Crutchfield, R. S. Conformity and character. *American Psychologist,* 1955, *10:* 191–198.

Deutsch, M., & Gerard, H. A study of normative and informational social influences on individual judgment. *Journal of Abnormal and Social Psychology,* 1955, *51:* 629–636.

Iscoe, I., Williams, M., & Harvey, J. Modification of children's judgments by a simulated group technique: A normative developmental study. *Child Development,* 1963, *34:* 963–978.

Janis, I. L. Personality correlates of susceptibility to persuasion. *Journal of Personality,* 1954, *22:* 504–518.

Janis, I. L., & Field, P. B. Sex differences and personality factors related to persuasibility. In C. I. Hovland & I. L. Janis (Eds.), *Personality and persuasibility.* New Haven: Yale University Press, 1959.

Kiesler, C. A., & Kiesler, S. B. *Conformity.* Reading, Mass.: Addison-Wesley, 1969.

Piaget, J. *The moral judgment of the child.* Glencoe, Ill.: Free Press, 1951.

Stone, L. J., & Church, J. *Childhood and adolescence.* New York: Random House, 1968.

eight

adolescents and the schools

part eight

Adolescents, like their juniors, spend much of their time in school. In addition, many of their extracurricular activities are school centered or involve acquaintanceships made in school. Thus, it would appear that schools have a special opportunity to help adolescents (particularly early adolescents) in coping with the transitional problems of adolescence and to encourage maximum use of their newfound cognitive abilities. While some schools do serve these functions in impressive fashion, too many do not.

As Charles Silberman notes in his survey of American education, *Crisis in the Classroom,* too often the major emphasis is on "education for docility."[1] Encouragement of self-expression, intellectual curiosity, self-reliance and independent judgment, and the development of personal values all too frequently are submerged by excessive demands for order, discipline, and conformity as ends in themselves. The predictable result is likely to be apathy, boredom, or a feeling that schooling is irrelevant to personal growth and development. In the case of disadvantaged students, the situation may be even more ominous. For many of these young people, what Silberman calls "education for inequality" is added to education for docility. Confined to overcrowded, poorly equipped, sometimes physically deteriorated schools with harried, overburdened teachers, they are frequently subjected to curricula ill designed to serve their special needs and talents—and problems. Consequently, rather than being helped to gain badly needed academic skills and a sense of personal and cultural identity, they may grow less confident of themselves and their abilities and fall further behind their grade level with each passing year.

Clearly, of course, the fault in such instances does not lie solely, or in many cases even primarily, with the schools themselves. Societal neglect that brings children to school entrance ill clothed, ill housed, ill fed, and exposed from an early age to social disorganization and deterioration makes the task of motivating them and making up for prior deficiencies in cognitive development doubly difficult. As we shall see, even in the case of children and adolescents who are not victims of broader societal neglect and discrimination, lack of parental interest, disturbed family relationships, and individual psychological or cognitive problems increase the difficulty of helping to provide young people with academic motivation, appropriate skills, and a confident sense of self-worth.

While the solution to many of these problems will require a major commitment to the needs of children and adolescents thus far not evident on the part of not only the schools but society as a whole, one would at least hope that for the majority of young people the schools—specifically, in the case of adolescents, the junior and senior high schools—

---

[1] C. E. Silberman, *Crisis in the Classroom: The Remaking of American Education.* New York: Random House, 1970.

would not *add to* developmental problems. However, as Roberta Simmons, Florence Rosenberg, and Morris Rosenberg find in the first study in this part, the opposite may be the case. They confirmed that in comparison with younger children (ages 8–11), early adolescents (ages 12–14) show a significant increase in disturbances of their self-image: increased depressive affect, lowered self-esteem, increased self-consciousness, and increased feelings that others have negative or critical opinions of them. The greatest change occurs between the ages of 11 and 12.

Although these findings appear consistent with the hypothesis that the onset of puberty produces a disturbance in self-image, Simmons et al. questioned whether factors in the social environment and, in particular, entrance into junior high school, might not also be responsible for these changes. When they compared those 12-year-olds who had already entered junior high school with those who were still in elementary school, they found that disturbances in self-image were far more frequent among the former group. In their view, "Perhaps puberty does not in itself disturb the self-image but heightens vulnerability to environmental circumstances which threaten the self-concept." But if this is the case, what is it about junior high school entrance that the adolescent finds so stressful? The authors conclude that further research is needed to answer this question; but they note that the child is moving from a protected elementary school environment where he usually has one teacher and one set of classmates to a much larger, more impersonal junior high school where his teachers, classmates, and even his rooms are constantly shifting. And they raise the additional question of whether the "middle school" concept (clustering grades 4–8), now being explored in some areas, might make better developmental sense. In any case, their study provides a further indication that junior high school, rather than helping to solve the developmental problems of early adolescents, may, at least in some cases, actually increase them.

In the second article, Denise B. Kandel and Gerald S. Lesser describe the results of an investigation of the influence of parents and peers on the educational aspirations of adolescents. Contrary to some popular notions, they found that parental influence (in this case, maternal influence), even during the vulnerable adolescent period, is usually stronger than that of peers or, indeed, social-class background. Furthermore, while there is a common tendency to view parental and peer influences during adolescence as in opposition to one another, concordance between the educational influences of parents and peers is much more likely to be the case. Adolescents in agreement with their parents on their educational goals are also likely to be in agreement with their friends, particularly their closest friends, while "adolescents who disagree with their parents are also likely to disagree with their friends." Obviously, however, there are exceptions to these general findings: for example, when deviant peer-group pressures are unusually strong and homogeneous or when communication between parents and their children has broken down and parental influence is correspondingly vitiated (see pp. 275–276).

In the third article, Irving B. Weiner explores some of the individual personality factors that may significantly affect the adolescent's ability to profit from his school experience, even when the educational climate may be a generally favorable one. In the process, he emphasizes the importance not only of parents' educational goals for their children, as in the Kandel and Lesser study, but of the psychodynamic aspects of family life—in this case, maladaptive patterns of family interaction. It is his contention, based on empirical studies of underachieving adolescents and clinical experience, that the psychodynamic factors most commonly responsible for academic underachievement in adolescents (in the absence of intellectual or sociocultural handicaps) include (1) a significant amount of underlying hostility, usually toward parents, that cannot be directly expressed; (2) concerns about rivalry with parents or siblings; and (3) "a preference for passive-aggressive modes of coping with difficult situations."

The adolescent may actually seek failure, albeit unconsciously, as a way of expressing resentment toward parents. Of course, for this to succeed it is necessary for the parents to have some investment in their child's academic success. In the case of rivalry, at least two response patterns are possible. The adolescent may suffer from excessive fears of failing (in comparison to more talented siblings or parents) or, paradoxically, from fears of success (as in the case when success may provoke parental envy or threats to parental self-esteem, resulting in rejection or disapproval). In either case, the adolescent is likely to react with academically inhibiting defensive maneuvers.

While the roots of many of the problems of American junior and senior high school students may be found within the educational system itself, in many other cases they will be found elsewhere: within the individual himself, in his family background, and in the larger society—a society that is still too little concerned with the optimal psychological, intellectual, and social development of all of its young people, advantaged and disadvantaged alike.

disturbance in the self-image at adolescence

Roberta Simmons
University of Minnesota

Florence Rosenberg
The American University

Morris Rosenberg
National Institute of Mental Health

Among the most widely accepted ideas in the behavioral sciences is the theory that adolescence is a period of disturbance for the child's self-image. Hall (1904) originally characterized the age as one of "storm and stress." Erikson (1959) views it as a time of identity-crisis, in which the child struggles for a stable sense of self. Psychoanalytic theory postulates that the burgeoning sexual desires of puberty spark a resurgence of oedipal conflicts for the boy and pre-oedipal pressures for the girl (Blos, 1962, 1971; A. Freud, 1958). To establish mature cross-sexual relationships in adulthood, the child must resolve these conflicts during adolescence. In the interim, the physiological changes of puberty and the increase in sexual desire challenge the child's view of himself in fundamental ways. Both his body-image and his self-image radically change.

Sociologists (Davis, 1944) traditionally characterize adolescence as a period of physical maturity and social immaturity.[1] Because of the complexity of the present social system, the child reaches physical adulthood before he is capable of functioning well in adult social roles. Adolescence becomes extremely difficult because the new physical capabilities and new social pressures to become independent coincide with many impediments to actual independence, power, and sexual freedom.

The work of the first author is currently supported by a Research Development Award from the National Institute of Mental Health, #5-K1-MH-41, 688-03. The work was also partly supported by USPHS Grants 1-F3-MH-41, 688-01 and MH-197541-01.

[1] See Gordon (1971), Bakan (1971) and Kohlberg and Gilligan (1971) for discussions of adolescence as a social phenomenon.

The resulting status-ambiguities, that is, the unclear social definitions and expectations, have been seen as engendering a corresponding ambiguity of self-definition. In addition, the need to make major decisions about future adult roles on the basis of what he is like at present further heightens the adolescent's self-awareness and self-uncertainty (Erikson, 1959).

From society's viewpoint, these external and internal pressures to plan for a future career, to become more independent, and to establish relationships with the opposite sex, all direct the individual away from his family of origin toward the creation of a new family. In the course of adolescence he changes from a dependent being whose prime emotional attachments are to his family of origin into a person capable of embarking on an independent existence, ready to establish his most important emotional allegiances outside of his present family. With all these physical, emotional and social changes, it is small wonder that social theorists assume that this period is difficult for the child's self-image.

Yet Offer (1969), on the basis of his longitudinal study of adolescent boys from ages fourteen to eighteen, suggests that for most boys these years are not characterized by stress or turmoil. Other investigators (e.g., Grinker, 1962; Elkin and Westley, 1955; Douvan and Adelson, 1966; Weiner, 1970) also question the assumption of adolescent crisis. These studies, however, often do not deal with early adolescence; nor do they systematically measure differences in the self-image over age.

Aside from psychiatric case-histories, in fact, there is little evidence to refute or support the argument that the child's self-image changes from childhood to adolescence. (See Engel, 1959; Piers and Harris, 1964; Jorgenson and Howell, 1969.) Since most work on adolescent disturbance has been clinical in nature, several fundamental questions of the self-image remain to be answered. First, do data support the belief that the adolescent's self-image differs from that of younger children? If so, could one term this difference a "disturbance," that is, a change which would cause the child some discomfort or unhappiness? In this paper we use the word "disturbance" as a milder term than "turmoil," "storm or stress," or "crisis," so that we can encompass less severe changes. It is not meant to imply psychopathology.

Second, if there is an adolescent self-image disturbance, when does it begin? This question is crucial to the evaluation of certain theoretical notions. Erikson (1959) tells us that the adolescent must deal with the issues of a career decision and the establishment of his own family. While these concerns may be salient to the eighteen or nineteen year old, they do not concern the twelve year old. Conversely, it is the younger adolescent who is confronted with the body-image changes of puberty. This study tries to specify the onset of adolescent self-image disturbance.

Third, if there is an adolescent self-image disturbance, what is the course of its development? Do the problems appearing at the time it is precipitated continue to grow? Do they level off at a higher plane? Or do they decline as the adolescent learns to cope with them?

Finally, if it does exist, what triggers the adolescent disturbance? Typically, the onset of puberty is viewed as the trigger. But perhaps aspects of the social environment are at work.

SELF-IMAGE DIMENSIONS

In this p̃aper we adopt Gardner Murphy's (1947) view of the self as "the individual as known to the individual." So conceived, the self-image can be viewed as an attitude toward an object; and, like all attitudes, it has several dimensions (Rosenberg, 1965). We shall deal with four of these. In each case, there is reason to think that changes in these dimensions would be disturbing or uncomfortable for the individual.

The first dimension is self-consciousness; it refers to the salience of the self to the individual. As Mead (1934) posited, in an interaction the ordinary individual must take account of others' reactions to himself and his behavior. But people vary in the degree to which the self is an object of attention. Some people are more "task-oriented," i.e., more involved in the situation and less concerned with how they are doing or what others are thinking of them. For others, the self becomes so prominent that the interaction is uncomfortable. Do adolescents show more of this type of uncomfortable self-consciousness than younger children?

The second dimension of the self-image is stability. If an individual must take account of himself as an important part of a situation and if he is unsure of what he is like, then he is deprived of a basis for action and decision. Indeed, Lecky (1945) described the self-concept as "the basic axiom of one's life theory," and Brownfain (1952) showed instability to be associated with disturbance. The question is whether this stability is especially shaken during adolescence.

The third dimension is self-esteem, i.e., the individual's global positive or negative attitude toward himself. The importance of this feeling has been widely recognized. (William James, 1950; McDougall, 1908). Probably more research has been devoted to this aspect of the self-concept than to all others combined (Wylie, 1961). In part, this interest is probably attributable to the great relevance of self-esteem for emotional disturbance (Kaplan and Pokorny, 1969; Rogers, 1951; Rosenberg, 1965; Turner and Vanderlippe, 1958; Wylie, 1961, Ch. IV). Is there evidence of self-esteem disturbance during adolescence?

The final dimension deals with the "perceived self."[2] While technically not an integral part of the phenomenal self, there is both theoretical and empirical reason to believe that the perceived self has an extremely important bearing on the self-image, particularly the self-esteem. Mead's (1934) and Cooley's (1912) classic theories emphasized the importance to the individual of his perceptions of how others see him. (For empirical support, see Miyamoto and Dornbusch, 1956; Reeder, Donohue, and Biblarz, 1960; Sherwood, 1965; Manis, 1955; Helper, 1955; Rosenberg and Simmons, 1972.) Our question is whether adolescents are more likely than younger children to see others as viewing them unfavorably.

---

[2] There is no standard terminology to communicate the idea of the individual's perception of how others see and evaluate him. Different terms have been used, for example, by Cooley (1912), Miyamoto and Dornbusch (1956), Reeder, et al. (1960), and Backman, et al. (1963). For want of a better term we shall use "perceived self."

METHOD

SAMPLE

The data for this analysis were collected from public school children in grades three through twelve in Baltimore City in 1968. A random sample of 2,625 pupils distributed among twenty-five schools was drawn from the population of third to twelfth grade pupils. Each school in Baltimore City was initially stratified by two variables: (1) proportion of non-white students, and (2) median income of its census tract. Twenty-five schools falling into the appropriate intervals were randomly selected. From each school, 105 children were selected by random procedures from the central records.

Some children had withdrawn from school after the central records were compiled and were no longer available. However, we were able to interview 1,917 children, that is, 79.2 per cent of the sample children still registered in the school, or 73.0 per cent of all children originally drawn from the central records.[3] Closely reflecting the population, the present sample is 63 per cent Negro and more heavily working class than the national average. None of the findings presented here were found to be spurious when controlled for race or class.

Comparisons across ages, however, must take account of the fact that school dropouts are absent from our population of older adolescents. The fact that this study is a cross-sectional rather than panel design generally limits the conclusiveness of the findings. We cannot be certain that age differences represent actual changes, particularly in the higher school grades.

Each subject was interviewed directly after school in his school. For the elementary school children, objective background information was collected from the parents. Parents were reached either by a five to ten minute telephone interview or, when there was no telephone, by home interview. Almost all parents were extremely cooperative and in only sixty cases were we unable to locate the parent or conduct the interview.

MEASURES

Indexes were developed to measure the four aspects of the self-image discussed above. (The indicators of each measure are presented in the Appendix along with their Guttman scale coefficients.) "Self-consciousness" is based on a seven-item Guttman Scale. (Example: "If a teacher

---

[3] One school—a combined elementary and junior high school—was entered twice in the total population of schools and, by chance, was selected in both categories. It was not practicable to double the sample size of this school; hence, the responses of these thirty-five elementary school children and those of the thirty-six junior high school children were doubled in weight to better represent the total population. In our analysis, we have thus treated our sample as 1,988 children.

asked you to get up in front of the class and talk a little bit about your summer, would you be very nervous, a little nervous, or not at all nervous?") "Stability of self" is indexed by a five-item Guttman Scale. (Example: "A kid told me: 'Some days I like the way I am. Some days I do not like the way I am.' Do your feelings *change* like this?")

Since the self-esteem dimension is central, this concept was measured in two ways. First, we ascertained the individual's general, overarching feeling toward himself through a series of general questions; we call this the global measure of self-esteem. For this purpose, a six-item Guttman Scale was used. (Example: "Everybody has some things about him which are good and some things about him which are bad. Are most of the things about you good, bad, or are both about the same?")

As Murphy (1949) has observed, however, the individual's self-attitude is both general and specific. He not only has attitudes toward himself as a totality but also attitudes toward his specific qualities, such as his looks or his intelligence. A different approach to measurement, then, is to infer the individual's general self-assessment from his specific self-evaluations; we call this the specific approach. Both the global and specific indices are designed to measure general self-esteem; they are simply founded on competing rationales. In this study, the specific approach to self-esteem measurement is based on the individual's average self-assessment on the following eight characteristics: being smart, good-looking, truthful or honest, good at sports, well-behaved, hard-working in school, helpful, and good at making jokes.

While certain investigators (Miyamoto and Dornbusch, 1956) speak of "the perceived self," clearly, the individual has many perceived selves since he interacts with many types of people who evaluate him. Some of these perceived selves were investigated by our asking these children what they believed the following people thought of them: their parents, their teachers, children of the same sex, and children of the opposite sex.

RESULTS

THE DISTURBANCE

Does adolescence produce a disturbance in the child's self-picture? Table 1 clearly suggests that the emergence of self-image problems in adolescence is no myth, and that these problems occur early in adolescence. In general, self-image disturbance appears much greater in the twelve to fourteen age group than in the eight to eleven age group.

In contrast to younger children, the early adolescents (twelve to fourteen year olds) show a higher level of self-consciousness, greater instability of self-image, slightly lower global self-esteem, lower specific self-esteem, and a more negative "perceived self" (that is, they are less likely to think that parents, teachers, and peers of the same sex view them favorably). The assumption that such changes are likely to be disturbing is consistent with the fact that early adolescents also show a higher level

Table 1
Children's Self-Ratings by Age

	Age			
	Median Scores			
	8–11 *(N = 819)*[a]	*12–14* *(N = 649)*	*15+* *(N = 516)*	**Total: Median χ^2 Test**[b]
Self-consciousness (Low score = high self-consciousness	3.8***	3.0	3.2	p < .001
Stability of the self-image (Low score = high instability)	2.6***	2.1	2.3	p < .001
Self-esteem (global) (Low score = low self-esteem)	4.0	3.8***	4.4	p < .001
Self-esteem (specific) (High score = unfavorable rating)	3.6***	5.0	5.0	p < .001
Perceived self (High score = unfavorable rating)				
Perceived opinion of parents	4.8**	5.1	5.1	p < .01
Perceived opinions of teachers	3.2***	3.4	3.4	p < .001
Perceived opinions of peers of the same sex	1.6***	1.8**	2.0	p < .001
Perceived opinions of peers of opposite sex	2.4***	2.1**	2.0	p < .001
Depressive affect (High score = high depression)	2.3***	2.9	3.0	p < .001

* = p < .05 for adjacent age groups according to median χ^2 test;
** = p < .01;
*** = p < .001.

Tests between adjacent age groups are not entirely appropriate, in part, because of the nonindependence of comparisons (i.e., the 12–14 age category is compared with each of the other age groups). Since the test affords some indication of how seriously to take the observed differences, however, it is included for convenience. (See Blalock, pp. 328–34 for a discussion of this problem in the case of analysis of variance.)

[a] For missing data, total cases are reduced accordingly.
[b] Siegel (1956: 111–116, 179–184).

of depressive affect than do the younger children (Table 1).[4] The only area showing improvement in early adolescence involves the opposite sex: children see themselves as better liked by the opposite sex as they grow older.

While the early adolescents are more self-conscious and have a more unstable self-image, this self-consciousness appears to decline somewhat in later adolescence and the self-image becomes somewhat more stable. However, even in late adolescence, the subjects manifest greater self-consciousness and instability than do the eight to eleven year old children.

Only for global self-esteem is there an improvement in later adolescence marked enough for the youngsters from age fifteen up to score more favorably than the eight to eleven year olds. The older adolescents show higher global self-esteem than both the young children and the early adolescents. Earlier studies (Engel, 1959; Piers and Harris, 1964) have also shown an increase in self-esteem among senior high school students; furthermore, one of these (Piers and Harris, 1964) also demonstrated a decline in self-esteem in early adolescence as compared to childhood.

Although global self-esteem feelings decline only slightly in early adolescence, and rise conspicuously in later adolescence, this pattern is not true of self-esteem based on those specific qualities we have considered, such as intelligence, honesty, diligence and good behavior. If one simply averages the self-ratings on these qualities, he will find a relatively sharp decline between childhood and early adolescence; and this lowered self-evaluation continues into later adolescence.

While one may reasonably assume that the lowered self-evaluations of these specific qualities indicate some degree of self-image disturbance, this conclusion is not certain. For, as William James (1890) long ago noted, it is not simply a question of how favorably the individual judges himself, but also how much he has staked himself on a particular quality. For example, an adolescent may agree that he is poor at sports or is plain; but if he cares little about these qualities, he will not be disturbed by their lack. Thus only a low self-rating on a quality that is valued highly is likely to be experienced as disturbing.

To take account of self-values, we asked our respondents how much they cared about each of these qualities, i.e., how important they were to them. Table 2 deals solely with children who care "very much" about whether they are smart, good-looking, helpful, etc. It is among these children that one would expect an unfavorable self-rating on a quality to be psychologically upsetting (Rosenberg, 1965: Ch. 13).

With respect to this criterion, Table 2 indicates that the early adolescents (twelve to fourteen) have a consistently lower self-image than the younger children (eight to eleven); i.e., they are less likely to rate themselves very favorably on the qualities they consider important. In some cases, such as being "good at making jokes," the differences are minor; for others they are large. On the other hand, there is little consistent difference between early and later adolescents in this regard. The consistent

---

[4] The scale of "depressive affect" appears in the Appendix.

Table 2

Proportion Rating Selves Very Favorably on Each Characteristic Among Those Who Care "Very Much" About That Characteristic, by Age

Respondent Rates Self Very Favorably on Following Qualities	Age			Total: χ^2 Test
	8–11	*12–14*	*15 or Older*	
Smart	26%*** (547)	9% (366)	5% (244)	p < .001
Good-looking	20%* (258)	13%* (197)	6% (121)	p < .001
Truthful or honest	54%*** (527)	38% (424)	38% (320)	p < .001
Good at sports	50% (339)	46% (266)	42% (163)	p < .001
Well-behaved	46%*** (474)	31% (332)	39% (239)	p < .001
Work hard in school	71%*** (494)	50%** (373)	39% (231)	p < .001
Helpful	60%*** (506)	46% (329)	46% (225)	p < .001
Good at making jokes	49% (151)	40% (53)	46% (28)	p < .05

* = p < .05 for adjacent age groups according to χ^2 test;
** = p < .01;
*** = p < .001.

Tests between adjacent age groups are not entirely appropriate, partly because of nonindependence of comparisons. Since the test affords some indication of how seriously to take the observed difference, however, it is included for convenience.

and clear age difference appears between childhood and early adolescence, with the early adolescents less likely to say they are performing well with respect to their self-values.

It may be contended that the lower self-ratings on these qualities simply reflect the fact that adolescents are more "realistic" while the younger children tend to "inflate" their self-qualities. Other analyses of these data have shown that compared to older children, elementary school children do tend to inflate the prestige of their racial and ethnic group status and their father's occupational status (Simmons and Rosenberg, 1971; Rosenberg and Simmons, 1972). Perhaps the adolescent does become more realistic about what he is like, but this does not mean that the adjustment to reality is not distressing for him. As Blos (1962:192) has noted: "The difficulty of relinquishing the inflated self-image of childhood is usually underestimated." From the viewpoint of one's emotional state, "reality" is not the issue.

To summarize, the results show a general pattern of self-image disturbance in early adolescence. The data suggest that, compared to younger children, the early adolescent has become distinctly more self-conscious; his picture of himself has become more shaky and unstable; his global self-esteem has declined slightly; his attitude toward several specific characteristics which he values highly has become less positive; and he has increasingly come to believe that parents, teachers, and peers of the same sex view him less favorably. In view of these changes, it is not surprising that our data show early adolescents to be significantly more likely to be psychologically depressed.

The course of self-image development after twelve to fourteen is also interesting. In general, the differences between early and late adolescence are not large. There is improvement in self-consciousness, stability, and especially global self-esteem, but no improvement in assessment of specific qualities or in the perceived self. The main change occurs almost always between the eight to eleven year old children and the twelve to fourteen year old children.

ONSET OF THE DISTURBANCE

Can we be more specific about this change in the self-image from childhood to early adolescence? Does it occur gradually or suddenly? As Figure 1 shows, a noticeable difference appears between eleven year olds and twelve year olds. (Note that the eleven year old group includes children from eleven years, no months, to eleven years, eleven months; while the twelve year old group covers those from twelve years, no months to twelve years, eleven months.) Self-consciousness, instability of the self-image, low global self-esteem, and low specific self-esteem all rise relatively sharply among the twelve year olds compared to the eleven year olds, although in most cases some rise has begun earlier, particularly the year before. This movement from the eleven year old group to the twelve year old group is the only one-year period in which the children show an increase of disturbance on all these measures. In fact, on all four measures it is the largest yearly increase in disturbance up to that age. For three out of four measures, it is the largest increase between any two ages.

For almost all the dimensions considered here, disturbance continues to increase after twelve but in most cases the high point of disturbance occurs either at age twelve, thirteen, or fourteen. In fact, stability of self-image and global self-esteem seem to improve after this point, particularly in late adolescence; while disturbances in self-consciousness and in specific self-esteem seem to level off and remain at early adolescent levels. The sole area of increasing disturbance in later adolescence involves the children's perceptions of the opinions of significant others.

The course of global self-esteem development deserves special mention. We noted earlier that the self-esteem level of the twelve to fourteen year group was only slightly lower than that of the eight to eleven group. But this finding conceals an important change: the sudden dramatic decline in self-esteem among the twelve year olds (Figure 1: compare eleven and twelve year olds). But during the following year, when the children reach thirteen, global self-esteem rapidly returns to its earlier level and continues to rise in later adolescence. Later we shall see some possible reasons for this dramatic but temporary shift.

Figure 1.*

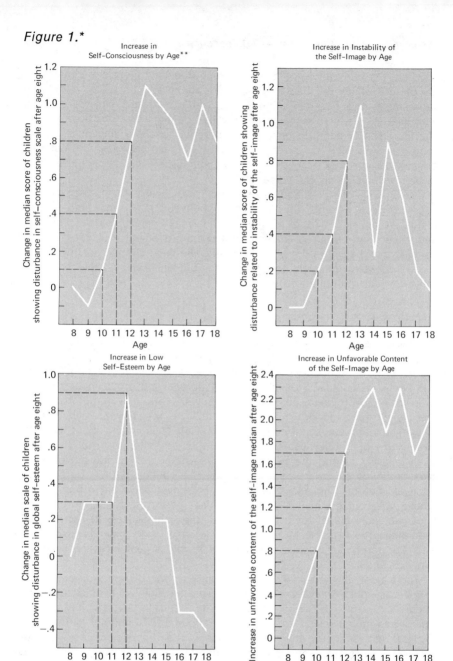

* For each scale, the median score of the eight-year old group is subtracted from the median score of each subsequent age group. If the graph line rises, then disturbance along the dimension is said to increase. The points above "O" indicate a higher level of disturbance after age 8, while the points below "O" indicate a lower level.

** The values at age 10, 11, and 12 are indicated by dotted lines. In the sample there are 98 eight–year olds, 225 nine-year olds, 263 ten-year olds, 233 eleven-year olds, 237 twelve-year olds, 213 thirteen-year olds, 199 fourteen-year olds, 150 fifteen-year olds, 162 sixteen-year olds, 130 seventeen-year olds and 56 eighteen-year olds.

Figure 2.

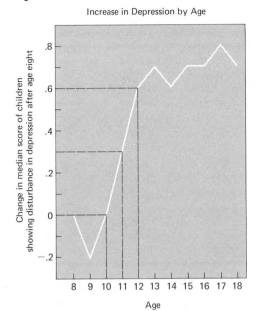

In sum, the data suggest that when they are twelve years old (that is, between their twelfth and thirteenth birthdays), children tend to experience a more marked increase in self-image disturbance. For some dimensions, this relatively sharp increase continues among those who are age thirteen. It is relevant to note that early adolescence is also characterized by a corresponding increase in feelings of depression or unhappiness, though this rise has clearly begun earlier (Figure 2). After age thirteen, there is again a general leveling off.

ENVIRONMENTAL CONTEXT

Placing the rise in self-image disturbance at some time after the twelfth birthday would seem to agree with the assumption that puberty is the chief determinant of this disturbance. But are there factors in the social environment which may also be responsible for these changes?

One important environmental change occurs for most children at this time. They generally begin their last year of elementary school (the sixth grade) when they are eleven and the first year of junior high school (the seventh grade) when they are twelve. Does the movement into junior high school itself contribute to the increase in self-image disturbance?

Obviously, one cannot examine the effects of change in environment by comparing sixth and seventh graders since one does not know whether such differences are due to the fact that the seventh graders are in junior high school or simply that they are older. It is, however, possible to disen-

Table 3
Disturbance of the Self-Image by School Context, Among Twelve-Year-Old Children

	Twelve-Year-Old Children		
Self-Image Disturbance	*In Elementary School*	*In Junior High School*	*According to χ² Analysis*
Per cent low self-esteem (global)	22% (167)	41% (59)	p < .01
Per cent low self-esteem (specific)	28% (151)	46% (57)	.10 > p > .05
Per cent high self-consciousness	27% (172)	43% (61)	p < .05
Per cent high instability of self-image	30% (158)	53% (60)	p < .01

tangle the effects of age maturation and school contexts by comparing children of the same ages.

By the spring of the school year, when our data were collected, both the sixth and seventh grades held an appreciable number of twelve year olds. If the junior high school experience were particularly stressful for the child, then the twelve year olds in junior high should show greater disturbance of their self-images than the twelve year olds in elementary school.

Table 3 dramatically supports this hypothesis. The twelve year olds In junior high school have lower global self-esteem, lower specific self-esteem, higher self-consciousness, and greater instability of self-image than their age-peers in elementary school. For example, 41 per cent of the twelve year olds in junior high school indicate low global self-esteem in contrast to only 22 per cent of those in elementary school; 43 per cent of the former manifest high self-consciousness compared to only 27 per cent of the latter. All but one of these differences are statistically significant beyond the .05 level.[5]

If these findings are valid, they certainly afford a vivid illustration of the way a social context can affect individual personality. Yet it is possible that these differences are spurious. Perhaps the sixth grade twelve year olds differ in other ways from the seventh grade twelve year olds. The sixth grade twelve year olds are more likely to have poorer grades, to be black, and to be from the lower social classes; but these factors do not appear likely to improve their self-images. In any case, controlling for these factors by means of test factor standardization (Rosenberg, 1962), we find that none of the original differences involving global self-

---

[5] One's view of the opinions of significant others, however, does not appear to be affected by movement into junior high school.

Table 4
Disturbance of the Self-Image Among Twelve-Year-Olds in the Sixth or Seventh Grade, by Race, Social Class, and Marks in School

Self-Image Disturbance	Race				Social Class				Marks in School			
	Blacks		Whites		Middle Class		Working Class		A's and B's		C's and Below	
	6th Gr.	7th Gr.	6th Gr.	7th Gr.	6th Gr.	7th Gr.	6th Gr.	7th Gr.	6th Gr.	7th Gr.	6th Gr.	7th Gr.
Per cent low self-esteem (global)	18% (106)	33% (27)	30% (61)	47% (32)	14% (21)	44% (16)	21% (119)	36% (39)	20% (49)	37% (30)	23% (104)	42% (24)
Per cent low self-esteem (specific)	33% (92)	46% (26)	19% (58)	45% (31)	48% (21)	41% (17)	26% (108)	44% (36)	17% (47)	39% (28)	29% (91)	50% (24)
Per cent high self-consciousness	28% (109)	32% (28)	27% (62)	52% (33)	24% (21)	53% (17)	29% (122)	38% (40)	22% (50)	37% (30)	29% (106)	58% (26)
Per cent high instability of the self-image	31% (104)	50% (28)	26% (53)	56% (32)	35% (20)	71% (17)	27% (112)	44% (39)	30% (47)	52% (29)	28% (96)	54% (26)

esteem, specific self-esteem, self-consciousness, or stability of self-concept, can be explained by any of these variables. Even when standardized on race, class, or marks in school, all differences between elementary school and junior high school twelve year olds remain essentially unchanged. Furthermore, Table 4 shows that in general these findings hold for blacks as well as whites, for middle class as well as working class respondents, and for students with high as well as low grades.

Does this mean that the only remaining difference between these two types of twelve year olds is the school which they attend? One other possibility involves the relative ages of these two groups in their classes. The sixth grade twelve year olds are among the oldest and biggest children in their class, while the seventh grade twelve year olds are among the youngest and least physically mature. The self-pictures of the sixth grade twelve year olds could benefit from their relative advantage, while the self-images of their seventh-grade age peers could suffer from their age-rank in their group. If so, the sixth grade twelve year olds should have more positive self-images than the younger children in their classes; while the seventh grade twelve year olds should show more disturbed self-images than the older children in their grade.

Yet Table 5 shows there is virtually no difference between the self-image ratings of eleven and twelve year olds in the sixth grade, nor is there a difference between the self-pictures of the twelve and thirteen year olds in the seventh grade.

Thus, the transition into junior high school seems to represent a significant stress along several dimensions of the child's self-image; while aging from eleven to twelve and twelve to thirteen does not in itself appear stressful. Within the same school class, age makes little difference; but within the same age group, school class makes a great difference.

One further question is whether the self-image disturbance associated

Table 5
Disturbance of the Self-Image by Age, by Grade in School

	Grade in School			
	Sixth Grade		**Seventh Grade**	
	Age 11	*Age 12*	*Age 12*	*Age 13*
Per cent low self-esteem (global)	29% (73)	24% (106)	40% (58)	36% (101)
Per cent low self-esteem (specific)	20% (69)	25% (93)	46% (56)	41% (90)
Per cent high self-consciousness	22% (76)	27% (106)	42% (60)	46% (101)
Per cent high instability of self-image	30% (76)	33% (102)	53% (59)	46% (92)

with the transition from sixth to seventh grade results from the general disturbance associated with transferring to any new school or whether it is specifically associated with entry into a junior high school. One way to examine this question is to look at those twelve year old sixth graders who have moved to their current schools this year. These children are identical with other twelve year old sixth graders in grade level but are different in being new students; conversely, they are similar to all twelve year old seventh graders in being new students, but are different in grade level.

Unfortunately, the number of twelve year olds in the sixth grade new to their schools is small; the results are thus no more than suggestive. Nevertheless, the data in Table 6 are particularly interesting. Though some differences exist between sixth graders new in the school and other sixth graders, the differences are inconsistent and would not suggest less dis-

Table 6
Self-Variables by Grade and Geographical Mobility, Among Twelve-Year-Olds Only

	Twelve-Year-Old Children		
Self-Image Disturbance	*6th Grader; Not New to School*	*6th Grader; Moved into School This Academic Year*	*7th Grader*
Self-consciousness			
High	28%	25%	42%
Medium	50	40	48
Low	22	35	10
N = 100%	(67)	(20)	(60)
Instability of self-image			
High	36%	18%	53%
Medium	49	76	41
Low	15	6	7
N = 100%	(66)	(17)	(59)
Self-esteem (global)			
Low	23%	15%	40%
Medium	27	55	36
High	50	30	24
N = 100%	(68)	(20)	(58)
Self-esteem (specific)			
Low	23%	44%	46%
Medium	51	44	30
High	26	12	23
N = 100%	(61)	(16)	(56)

turbed self-images in either group. But the findings involving junior high students are clear and consistent. The twelve year olds in junior high are considerably more likely than either sixth grade group to show disturbances of the self image, by scoring higher on self-consciousness, higher on instability of self-image and lower on global self-esteem. With regard to specific self-esteem, they are slightly higher than the sixth grade newcomer but much lower than the other sixth graders. The results as a whole suggest that a twelve year old child who moves from one elementary school to another may not find the experience as stressful as does the twelve year old who has entered a junior high school in the past year.

Note, incidentally, that the transition from junior to senior high school does not show a parallel effect on the self-image; fifteen year olds in senior high school do not show more disturbed self-images than fifteen year olds in junior high school. Why this should be so is not clear. Perhaps the difference between junior high school and elementary school is experienced as much greater than the difference between junior and senior high school.

In sum, the data indicate increased self-image disturbance associated with the transition from elementary to junior high school. The reason does not appear to be solely the age change (with its associated biological changes); for at ages roughly equivalent, the seventh graders still show greater disturbance. Nor does it simply appear to be the shock of transferring to a new school; although the number of cases is small, the newly arrived sixth graders generally show less disturbance than seventh graders and are not consistently worse off than other sixth graders (all at the same age). Furthermore, the transition from junior to senior high shows no such effect.

Perhaps puberty does not in itself disturb the self-image but heightens vulnerability to environmental circumstances which threaten the self-concept. Only further research can determine what it is about the junior high school experience that is stressful for the self-image.

SUMMARY AND DISCUSSION

This cross-sectional study has investigated several dimensions of self-image development in 1,917 urban school children in grades three through twelve. A definite disturbance of the self-image has been shown to occur in adolescence, particularly early adolescence. In some respects this disturbance appears to decline in later adolescence, while along other dimensions it persists. In many areas, a particular rise in disturbance appears to occur when the child is twelve, that is, between the twelfth and thirteenth birthdays. The rise often begins a year before, and may continue for the next year or so. Often, however, it seems to increase little, if at all, after age thirteen or fourteen.

During early adolescence, compared to the years eight to eleven, the children exhibited heightened self-consciousness, greater instability of self-image, slightly lower global self-esteem, lower opinions of themselves with regard to the qualities they valued, and a reduced conviction that their parents, teachers and peers of the same sex held favorable opinions of them. They were also more likely to show a high depressive affect.

These data agree with the findings of Offer (1969, Ch. 11), who studied a somewhat older adolescent group (fourteen to eighteen), and who reports that both parents and adolescents agreed that the greatest amount of "turmoil" in their lives occurred between ages twelve to fourteen. The finding that instability of the self-picture increases during adolescence might appear to support Erikson's (1959) views on adolescent problems of ego-identity. However, Erikson seems to place the ego-identity crisis in late adolescence; whereas our data indicate a rise in instability during early adolescence.

Our data do not completely explain the dynamic processes at work in adolescence. For example, they cannot measure the effects of hormonal and other pubertal changes on the self-image in early adolescence (see Shock, 1946; Tanner, 1971). Yet they do show, dramatically, that the child's environment appears to have a stronger effect than age-maturation on certain aspects of the self-image. One of the major reasons twelve year olds are more likely than eleven year olds to show an increase in self-image disturbance appears to be that the twelve year olds have moved into junior high school. Twelve year olds in the seventh grade are more likely to indicate disturbance on these self-image measures than are twelve year olds in the sixth grade. There are no comparable differences between eleven and twelve year olds in the sixth grade, or between twelve and thirteen year olds in the seventh grade.

Thus, movement into junior high school at puberty is a significant event for the child. He moves from a protected elementary school, where he usually has one teacher and one set of classmates, to a much larger, more impersonal junior high where his teachers, classmates, and even his rooms are constantly shifting. He moves from a setting where the teacher is a parent-surrogate, to a more impersonal environment. Here he is expected to behave more independently and more responsibly, and he must make his first career decision—whether to take an academic, commercial, or vocational course.

That a disturbance of the self-image does not occur in the move from junior to senior high school raises a question. Is this finding due to the fact that the difference between senior and junior high is quantitative and not qualitative; i.e., that the school is bigger but of similar type? Or is it that the move into a very different type of school roughly coincides with the onset of puberty, which makes the self-image of the early adolescent more vulnerable to the assaults of the junior high school environment? Our data do not answer these questions. Many of them might be answered by a study of a middle school covering the fourth to eighth grades. In such a school, one might expect a more gradual transition to departmentalization, a more gradual buildup in others' expectations for independence and responsibility. The shift would not necessarily coincide with the onset of puberty.

Knowledge about self-concept development is still pretty much an unknown land in social psychology. Our sample tells us something about what differences appear between the ages of eight and eighteen, but there is little information about development before and after these years. Whether the level or type of self-image disturbance which develops in early adolescence persists in adult life or changes in a positive or negative direction is still unknown. Nor does our study reveal the more dynamic processes of self-image change. That would require a long-term panel study. Given the importance of the self-concept to the individual, we hope that the required research will be forthcoming.

REFERENCES

Backman, Carl W., Paul F. Secord and Jerry R. Peirce
1963 "Resistance to change in the self-concept as a function of consensus among significant others." Sociometry 26 (March): 102–11.
Bakan, David
1971 "Adolescence in America: from idea to social fact." Daedalus 100 (Fall): 979–95.
Blalock, Hubert M., Jr.
1972 Social Statistics. New York: McGraw-Hill Book Company.
Blos, P.
1962 On Adolescence: A Psychoanalytic Interpretation. New York: Free Press.
Brownfain, J. D.
1952 "Stability of the self-concept as a dimension of personality." Journal of Abnormal and Social Psychology 47 (July): 597–606.
Cooley, Charles H.
1912 Human Nature and the Social Order. New York: Scribner's.
Davis, Kingsley
1944 "Adolescence and the social structure." Annals of the American Academy of Political and Social Science *236:* 8–16.
Douvan, E. and J. Adelson
1966 The Adolescent Experience. New York: John Wiley and Sons, Inc.
Elkin, F. and W. A. Westley
1955 "The myth of adolescent culture." American Sociological Review *23:* 680–3.
Engel, Mary
1959 "The stability of the self-concept in adolescence." Journal of Abnormal and Social Psychology *58:* 211–15.
Erikson, E. H.
1959 "Identity and the life cycle." Psychological Issues *I:* 1–171.
Freud, Anna
1958 "Adolescence." Psychoanalytic Study of the Child *13:* 255–78.
Gordon, Chad
1971 "Social characteristics of early adolescence." Daedalus 100 (Fall): 931–60.
Grinker, R. R., Sr., R. R. Grinker, Jr. and J. Timberlake
1962 "A study of 'mentally healthy' young males (homoclites)." American Medical Association Archives of General Psychiatry *6:* 405–53.

Hall, G. S.
1904   Adolescence: Its Psychology and Its relations to Physiology, Anthropology, Sociology, Sex, Crime, Religion and Education. New York: D. Appleton and Company.
Helper, M.
1955   "Learning theory and the self concept." Journal of Abnormal and Social Psychology 51 (September): 184–94.
James, W.
1950   The Principles of Psychology. New York: Dover (copyright, 1890 by Henry Holt and Company).
Jorgensen, E. Clay and Robert J. Howell
1969   "Changes in self, ideal-self correlations from ages 8 through 18." Journal of Social Psychology 79 (June): 63–7.
Kaplan, Howard B. and Alex D. Pokorny
1969   "Self-derogation and psychosocial adjustment." Journal of Nervous and Mental Disease 149 (November): 421–34.
Kohlberg, Lawrence and Carol Gilligan
1971   "The adolescent as a philosopher: the discovery of the self in a postconventional world." Daedalus 100 (Fall): 1051–86.
Lecky, Prescott
1945   Self-Consistency: A Theory of Personality. New York: Island Press.
McDougall, W.
1908   Introduction to Social Psychology. London: Methuen and Company.
Manis, M.
1955   "Social interaction and the self-concept." Journal of Abnormal and Social Psychology 51 (November): 362–70.
Mead, George Herbert
1934   Mind, Self and Society. Chicago: University of Chicago Press.
Miyamoto, S. Frank and Sanford Dornbusch.
1956   "A test of the symbolic interactionist hypothesis of self-conception." American Journal of Sociology 61 (March): 339–403.
Murphy, Gardner
1947   Personality. New York: Harper.
Offer, Daniel
1969   The Psychological World of the Teen-ager. New York: Basic Books, Incorporated.
Piaget, Jean
1965   The Moral Judgment of the Child. New York: The Free Press.
Piers, Ellen V. and Dale B. Harris
1964   "Age and other correlates of self-concept in children." Journal of Educational Psychology 55 (No. 2): 91–5.
Reeder, Leo G., George A. Donohue and Arturo Biblarz
1960   "Conceptions of self and others." American Journal of Sociology 66 (September): 153–9.
Rogers, Carl R.
1951   Client-centered Therapy: Its Current Practice, Implications, and Theory. Boston: Houghton-Mifflin

Rosenberg, Morris
1962 "Test factor standardization as a method of interpretation." Social Forces 41 (October): 53–61.
1965 Society and the Adolescent Self-Image. New Jersey: Princeton University Press.
Rosenberg, Morris and Roberta G. Simmons
1972 Black and White Self-Esteem: The Urban School Child. Washington, D.C.: The American Sociological Association.
Siegel, Sidney
1956 Nonparametric Statistics for the Behavioral Sciences. New York: McGraw-Hill Book Company, Incorporated.
Sherwood, John J.
1965 "Self-identity and referent others." Sociometry 28 (March): 66–81.
1967 "Increased self-evaluation as a function of ambiguous evaluations by referent others." Sociometry 30 (December): 404–9.
Shock, Nathan W.
1946 "Some physiological aspects of adolescence." Texas Reports on Biology and Medicine 4: 289–310.
Simmons, Roberta G. and Morris Rosenberg
1971 "Functions of children's perceptions of the stratification system." American Sociological Review 36 (April): 235–49.
Stone, L. J. and J. Church
1968 Childhood and Adolescence. New York: Random House.
Tanner, J. M.
1971 "Sequence, tempo, and individual variation in the growth and development of boys and girls aged twelve to sixteen." Daedalus 100 (Fall): 907–30.
Turner, R. H. and R. H. Vanderlippe
1958 "Self-ideal congruence as an index of adjustment." Journal of Abnormal and Social Psychology 57: 202–6.
Weiner, Irving B.
1970 Psychological Disturbance in Adolescence. New York: John Wiley and Sons.
Wylie, Ruth
1961 The Self-Concept: A Critical Survey of Pertinent Research Literature. Lincoln, Nebraska: University of Nebraska Press.

APPENDIX

MEASURES

Self-Consciousness Scale

Let's say some grownup or adult visitor came into class and the teacher wanted them to know who you were, so she asked you to stand up and tell them a little about yourself. Would you like that,* Would you not like it, or Wouldn't you care.

If the teacher asked you to get up in front of the class and talk a little bit about your summer, would you be . . .* Very nervous, a Little nervous, or Not at all nervous.

If you did get up in front of the class and tell them about your summer, . . .* Would you think a lot about how all the kids were looking at you, Would you think a little bit about how all the kids were looking at you, or Wouldn't you think at all about the kids looking at you.

If you were to wear the wrong kind of clothes to a party, would that bother you . . . *A lot, A little, or Not at all.

If you went to a party where you did not know most of the kids, would you wonder what they were thinking about you? . . .

*Yes, No.

Do you get nervous when someone watches you work? . . .

*Yes, No.

A young person told me: "When I'm with people I get nervous because I worry about how much they like me." Do you feel like this . . .

*Often, Sometimes, or Never.

The alternatives marked with an asterisk represent high self-consciousness. This is a Guttman scale with 89.4 per cent coefficient of reproducibility, 17.8 per cent improvement and 62.5 per cent coefficient of scalability. To validate the self-consciousness scale, we asked the interviewers to rate the child as "very nervous, somewhat nervous, or not nervous." Forty-three per cent of those students categorized as "very nervous" scored high on the self-consciousness scale, in contrast to 24 per cent of those rated as "not nervous." ($\chi^2 = 27.6769$, 4 df, p < .01). On the total scale, the cut-off point for "high self-consciousness" was obtained by trichotomizing the distribution as closely as possible and selecting the most self-conscious third. This principle was used in obtaining cut-off points for all the following scales.

Stability of Self Scale

How sure are you that you know what kind of person you really are? Are you . . . *Very sure, *Pretty sure, Not very sure, or Not at all sure.

How often do you feel mixed up about yourself, about what you are really like? . . . Often, Sometimes, or *Never.

Do you feel like this: "I know just what I'm like. I'm really sure about it." . . .

*Yes, No.

A kid told me: "Some days I like the way I am. Some days I do not like the way I am." Do your feelings *change* like this? . . .

Yes, *No.

A kid told me: "Some days I am happy with the kind of person I am, other days I am not happy with the kind of person I am." Do your feelings change like this? . . .

Yes, *No.

The alternatives marked with an asterisk represent high stability. This is a Guttman scale with 89.1 per cent coefficient of reproducibility, 20.1 per cent improvement, 64.8 per cent coefficient of scalability.

Self-Esteem Scale

Everybody has some things about him which are good and some things about him which are bad. Are more of the things about you . . . Good,*Bad, or *Both about the same.

Another kid said, "I am no good." Do you ever feel like this? (IF YES, ASK): Do you feel like this a *lot, or a *little? "I am no good."

A kid told me: "There's a lot wrong with me." Do you ever feel like this? (IF YES, ASK): Do you feel like this a *lot, or a *little? "There's a lot wrong with me."

Another kid said, "I think I am no good at all." Do you ever feel like this? (IF YES, ASK): Do you feel like this *a lot, or *a little? "I'm not much good at anything."

Another kid said, "I think I am no good at all." Do you ever feel like this? (IF YES, ASK): Do you feel like this *a lot, or *a little. "I think I am no good at all."

How happy are you with the kind of person you are? Are you . . . Very happy with the kind of person you are, Pretty happy, *A little happy, or *Not at all happy.

The responses indicated by an asterisk indicate low self-esteem. This is a Guttman scale with 90.2 per cent coefficient of reproducibility, 20.4 per cent improvement, 67.6 per cent coefficient of scalability. This scale has undergone extensive validation tests in Rosenberg and Simmons (1972, Ch. 2) for both whites and blacks. First of all, it has been validated against another measure of the same concept; that is, it appears to have trait validity. It is satisfactorily correlated with adolescents' scores on the Rosenberg measure of self-esteem which has been validated in previous research (Rosenberg, 1965). It was not possible to use the Rosenberg measure for the younger children in the sample because of its adult language; therefore, this present scale was constructed. Secondly, this scale seems to have construct validity—ten theoretical predictions were made concerning self-esteem and in all cases these predictions were confirmed using the scale. Self-esteem was shown to correlate positively with measures of depression and anxiety, with marks in school, with indicators of school leadership, and with the opinions of several significant others including parents, teachers, and friends, for all age groups. Third, the scale appears to satisfy the interchangeability criterion: it "behaves" the same way as the Rosenberg measure of self-esteem in relation to other variables. Finally, it appears to have face validity as a measure of the individual's global feelings about his own self-worth.

Content of the Self-Image

The child was given a labeled chart with four bars of different sizes and asked to rank himself on the following eight characteristics: being smart, good-looking, truthful, good at sports, well-behaved, hardworking at school, helpful, and good at making jokes. With the help of the chart he was asked: are you very (smart), pretty (smart), not very (smart), or not at all (smart). On each item, the individual was given one point for a category chosen more unfavorable than the overall median for that item. A total score was constructed by adding the points for all eight items.

Perceived Self-Image

Scales were constructed from the following items. Score values for each item are indicated in front of the appropriate category.

Parents

Would you say your mother thinks you are *1* A wonderful person, *2* A pretty nice person, *3* A little bit of a nice person, *4* or Not such a nice person.

Would you say your father thinks you are *1* A wonderful person, *2* A pretty nice person, *3* A little bit of a nice person, *4* or Not such a nice person.

Let's pretend your parents wanted to tell someone all about you. What type of person would they say you are? (The description was coded into the following three categories: *1* Only favorable and neutral remarks were made, *2* remarks were all neutral or were both favorable and unfavorable, *3* only unfavorable and neutral remarks were made.)

Teachers

Would you say your teacher thinks you are *1* A wonderful person, *2* A pretty nice person, *3* A little bit of a nice person, *4* or Not such a nice person.

What if your teachers wanted to tell someone all about you? What type of person would your teachers say you were? (The description was coded into the following three categories: *1* Only favorable and neutral remarks were made, *2* remarks were all neutral or were both favorable and unfavorable, *3* only unfavorable and neutral remarks were made.)

Peers

How much do boys like you? *1* Very much, *2* Pretty much, *3* Not very much, *4* Not at all.

How much do girls like you? *1* Very much, *2* Pretty much, *3* Not very much, *4* Not at all.

Depressive Affect

How happy would you say you are most of the time? Would you say you are . . . Very happy, Pretty happy, Not very happy, or *Not at all happy.

Would you say this: "I get a lot of fun out of life."
Yes, *No.
Would you say this: "Mostly, I think I am quite a happy person."
Yes, *No.
How happy are you today: Are you . . . Very happy, Pretty happy, Not very happy, or *Not at all happy.
A kid told me: "Other kids seem happier than I." Is this . . .
*True for you, or Not true for you.
Would you say that most of the time you are . . . Very cheerful, Pretty cheerful, Not very cheerful, or *Not cheerful at all.

In each case the starred alternative indicates high depression. This is a Guttman scale with 92.2 per cent coefficient of reproducibility, 17.8 per cent improvement, and 69.5 per cent coefficient of scalability.

parental and peer influences on educational plans of adolescents

Gerald S. Lesser
Denise B. Kandel
Harvard University

Adolescents are said to belong to a distinct adolescent subculture and to be influenced more by their peers than by their parents (Coleman, 1961). However, the extent to which the values and goals of adolescents and adults differ and the degree to which significant adults and peers actually influence the development of adolescents have not been adequately tested and specified (Berger, 1963). Most research on parental and peer influences on the educational plans of adolescents has considered one influence or the other but not both simultaneously.

Results from the frequent studies that have been concerned with the relative influences of parents and peers on the educational plans of adolescents are contradictory: McDill and Coleman (1965) and Herriott (1963) conclude that peer influences exceed parental influences; Simpson (1962) concludes that parents are more influential than peers.

In a panel study of students in their first and last years of high school, McDill and Coleman (1965) conclude that: ". . . by the end of the senior year of high school, the prestige of the adolescents in the school social system contributes more to variations in their stated college plans than does their father's or mother's education" (p. 125). However, data on the parents' actual desires for their children, also presented by McDill and

Revision of a paper presented at the Annual Meeting of the American Sociological Association, Boston, Massachusetts, August, 1968. This research was supported through the Cooperative Research Program of the Office of Education, DHEW (Project #2139, OE-4-10-069) and by the Harvard Center for Research and Development in Educational Differences (Office of Education Contract OE-5-10-239). We are grateful to our Colleagues, Gail Roberts, Robert Weiss, Richard Faust, Hans Weltzer, Reimer Jensen and Bente Cochran, for their contributions and we thank the Bureau of Applied Social Research, Columbia University, for providing technical assistance in data processing.

Coleman, indicate that even in the senior year the influence of parental desires on adolescents' plans is greater than school status.[1]

Herriott (1963) used adolescents' perceptions of the educational expectations held by eleven different types of persons as sources of data on parental and peer influences. The highest correlation was obtained between adolescents' educational aspirations and perceived expectations of a same-age friend. On the other hand, in a study of occupational aspirations of high school students, Simpson (1962) found that for both middle-class and lower-class boys, "parental influence was more strongly related to aspirations than peer influences" (p. 521). Parental influence was measured by the child's report of his parents' pressure to enter a profession. High peer influence was defined by two criteria: belonging to two or more school clubs, and mentioning at least one middle-class friend.

In their use of indirect indicators for parental or peer goals, these studies of relative influences follow the same procedures as single-influence studies. Most studies of parental influences use parental social class or education as indicators of parental educationaɬ aspirations for their children. (For review of existing studies see Haller and Butterworth, 1960; McDill and Coleman, 1965; Sewell and Shah, 1967.) However, while social class is strongly related to educational goals, parental aspirations or parental encouragement of higher education can override a lower-class background (cf. Bordua, 1960; Cohen, 1965; Ellis and Lane, 1963; Kahl, 1953; Rehberg and Westby, 1967; Sewell and Shah, 1968a and b; Strodtbeck, 1958).

Similarly, the studies of peer influences on academic achievement and aspirations have been concerned with the influence of the value climate of schools on the adolescents within these schools, and rarely with the specific plans and attitudes of the adolescent's friends (Boyle, 1966; Coleman, 1961; Coleman, *et al.*, 1966; McDill, *et al.*, 1966; Michael, 1961; Ramsøy, 1962; Turner, 1964; Wilson, 1959).

The concensus between matched pairs of adolescents in the school has been investigated in two studies which reach opposite conclusions. Alexander and Campbell (1964), in a study of male seniors in 30 high schools, conclude that "a student and his best friend tend to be similar in college plans and that the extent of similarity is greater when the choice is reciprocated" (p. 571). Haller and Butterworth (1960), in contrast, found low intra class correlations on levels of occupational and, particularly, educational aspirations in 245 pairs of 17-year-old high school boys and their best-school-friend. (For a recent reanalysis of these data in the light of a model to estimate the magnitude of peer influences, see Duncan, *et al.*, 1968.)

Our work attempts to investigate the relative influences of parents and

---

[1] The measure of influence is Coleman's "effect parameter," which also has been used in the present study. It is designed to measure the effect of one or more independent variables on a dependent variable (Coleman, 1964), using a model analogous to a factorial design in analysis of variance for quantitative data. Each difference is weighted according to the size of the sample on which it is based.

peers under differing social and cultural conditions. To overcome in part the difficulties of previous studies, we use a sample of triads in which the adolescent has been matched with his mother and his best friend in school. The indicators of educational goals are direct rather than indirect, albeit not identical for parent and peer. Furthermore, in order to establish that concordance on goals reflects the influence of mothers or of best friends upon the adolescent, we have studied concordance while holding constant certain characteristics of the social environment, such as social class or program in school, and under different types of interaction with mother and friend. Indeed, agreement between any two individuals does not necessarily reflect influence from one person to the other, since agreement by itself can result from the common social situation and not from the interaction itself (cf. Furstenberg, 1967; Hyman, 1959).[2]

Three interrelated questions are considered:

(1) What is the relative agreement, or concordance, on educational goals between the adolescent and his mother, and between the adolescent and his best-school-friend?

(2) What is the influence of common social factors, for example, social-class membership, on concordance on educational goals within dyads?

(3) What is the influence of patterns of social interaction within dyads on concordance on educational plans?

METHOD

1. SAMPLE[3]

In the spring of 1965, data were collected from all students in three high schools (N = 2327) through use of structured questionnaires. Each student was asked to name his three closest same-sex friends in school. In addition, the students' mothers were mailed self-administered structured questionnaires containing many questions identical to those in-

---

[2] Only through a longitudinal design is it possible definitely to establish the source, nature, and direction of influences. Such longitudinal data were not collected in the present study, and thus problems of interpretation exist, involving in particular reciprocity and interrelationship of influences which no statistical manipulation can resolve. For example, we cannot ascertain the extent to which adolescents influence their parents by demonstrating that they are qualified for a specific level of educational attainment, which the parents then come to accept and encourage. In dealing with friends' influence, we cannot establish the extent to which parents influence the eligible range of friends from which adolescents choose. Nor can we estimate the extent to which similarity of values and attitudes between friends is the basis for friendship rather than an outcome of friendship. We attempt to deal with some of these points in the data analysis, but in the absence of longitudinal data we stress the limitations inherent in the concept of influence as it is used throughout this paper.

[3] Data for this paper are taken from a larger cross-cultural study of adolescents and their families in the United States and Denmark. Only the data for the United States are presented here. The findings for Denmark replicate those obtained in the United States (Kandel *et al.*, 1968; Kandel and Lesser, 1969).

cluded in the students' instrument: 60% of the mothers returned completed questionnaires.[4] The schools, located in the eastern United States, included a large, lower-class urban school, a small rural school, and a regional school which draws its student body from several small adjacent communities.

Subsamples of dyads and triads were identified.

(a) Dyads (N = 1141) consisting of matched adolescent-mother pairs from intact families. These intact families represent 83% of the total matched adolescent-mother pairs.

(b) Dyads (N = 2157) consisting of all identified adolescent and best-school-friend pairs, regardless of whether or not there was a mother-match. A best-school-friend could be identified for over 90% of the adolescents.

(c) Triads (N = 1065) consisting of all adolescents from intact families who could be matched to both their mother and their best-school-friend.

The analyses are based alternatively on pairs drawn from the triads or the dyads. To compare simultaneously concordance with mother and concordance with best friend, the samples are restricted to pairs drawn from the triads. To investigate factors related to concordance, all dyads are included to maximize the number of cases. This procedure is justified by the fact that levels of concordance are almost identical among pairs from dyads and from triads. (Data not presented but available on request to authors.)

2. MEASUREMENT OF EDUCATIONAL PLANS

Students and mothers were asked parallel questions about the adolescent's educational plans. Students, and their best friends, were asked to indicate the highest level of education they expected to complete; mothers were asked: "What is the highest level of education you would like your child to complete?" An "undecided" alternative was provided the students, but not their parents. Thus, the measures used for parental and peer influences are not identical, since mothers' expectations are specifically for their child, while peers' expectations are for themselves. This point is discussed in the interpretation of the findings.

Respondents who did not answer the educational question, and adolescents who checked the alternative, "undecided," were not included in the analysis. Concordance within dyads was measured by Kendall's (1962) tau-beta.[5]

---

[4] The comparison of answers from students whose mothers replied with those of students whose mothers did not reply reveals no differences between the two groups of adolescents in socio-demographic characteristics. There is a slight tendency for responding mothers to be perceived as being more interested in educational matters.

[5] No existing statistics are completely satisfactory to measure concordance, since none gives a measure that takes into account simultaneously the absolute amount of observed agreement within pairs and the relative amount of agreement given the marginal distributions of answers.

Table 1
Concordance* on Educational Plans Between Adolescent and Mother and Between Adolescent and Best-School-Friend by Sex (Triads)

	Concordance with	
Concordance on Educational Plans	*Mother*	*Best-School-Friend*
Total sample	.504	.389
Total N	(740)	(531)
Boys	.427	.308
Total N	(357)	(245)
Girls	.532	.423
Total N	(383)	(286)

* As measured by tau-beta, all significant beyond .001 level.

RESULTS

1. CONCORDANCE ON EDUCATIONAL PLANS WITH MOTHERS AND PEERS

To assess the relative influence of parents and peers on educational plans, we examined the degree of concordance on plans among matched adolescent and mother pairs and adolescent and best-school-friend pairs in the sample of triads. The results are striking. (See Table 1.)

(a) Concordance on educational goals is highly significant both for mother and best-school-friend.

(b) Concordance is higher for mother than for best-school-friend, among both boys and girls (see Table 1).[6] When parental education is used as the indicator of parental influence, the actual degree of parental influence on the child's educational aspirations is underestimated; in our sample, the association between mothers' education and adolescents' educational aspirations (.199)[7] is much lower than the association between mothers' actual plans for their children and adolescents' educational aspirations (.504).

(c) Girls have higher levels of agreement with their mothers than boys. Thus, we are able to replicate with respect to educational goals the oft-reported finding of greater consensus among mother-daughter than mother-son pairs (Furstenberg, 1967).

Our measures of mother's and friends' influence have somewhat differ-

---

[6] "Parental" influence is, in all likelihood, even greater than is indicated by our data since we restrict ourselves to maternal desires and do not also include the father's educational aspirations for his child.

[7] The correlation with father's education is .177.

ent meanings. For the mother, we measure her aspirations for her child and assume that they are communicated to the child in the form of influencing attempts. But the mother's goal could reflect not only what she ideally would like for her child, but also her assessment of the child's ability and wishes for himself. However, we find that while maternal aspirations are based to some extent upon a realistic appraisal of their child's academic potential and achievement, the relationship is not very strong and not as strong as the association between the adolescent's own educational plans and his academic performance, such as self-reported grades, school rank in senior year, and IQ. For example, the tau-betas measuring the association between senior-year school rank and educational plans are .238 for adolescents and .104 for mothers. Among adolescents who place themselves in the lowest quartile, only 23% aspire to college as compared to 70% of their mothers. Thus, we infer that our indicator of maternal influence measures the mother's educational aspirations for her child beyond her realistic evaluation of the child's academic potential and achievement.

For the friend, we measure his aspirations for himself and assume that he influences the adolescent as an example and role model. However, peers may have one expectation for themselves while accepting the fact that their friend is not the same. While we do not know friends' educational aspirations for each other, we do have data on peers' encouragement for college plans. Adolescents were asked: "How would your close friends here at school react if you decided to attend college?" The response alternatives included: "They would encourage me," "They would discourage me," "They wouldn't care." The association (as measured by tau-beta) between this question and the adolescent's educational goals is .259 and is lower than concordance on actual educational goals within friendship pairs (.389). Thus, we believe that the use of friends' self-aspirations does not artificially lower the measured effect of friends' educational influence.

That parents influence adolescents' educational plans more than peers is illustrated further when one examines simultaneously the adolescent's aspirations, his mother's aspirations for him, and the plans of his best-school-friend. To simplify the analysis, educational plans were dichotomized into the categories of high school *versus* two-year college and over. Table 2 shows clearly, particularly for the triads in which mother and best friend hold divergent plans, that the influence of the mother is greater than that of the friend: 49% of adolescents plan to continue beyond high school when their mothers have college plans for them and their best-school-friends intend to stop at the high school level, as contrasted to 21% when their mothers have no college aspirations, even though their best-school-friends intend to go on to college. That friends have influence beyond that of the mother is shown by the increase in college plans (to 83%) when both mother and best-school-friend have college plans. As measured by Coleman's weighted effect parameter, the influence of the mother is approximately twice as high as that of the best-school-friend (.492 *versus* .288).[8]

---

[8] The greater influence of the mother as compared to the best-school-friend can also be observed in relation to future occupational goals. (Data not presented.)

Table 2
**Percent of Adolescents Planning to
Continue Their Education, by Best-
School-Friend's Educational Plans and
Mother's Educational Aspirations for
Adolescent (Triads)**

	Per Cent of Adolescents Planning to Continue Education			
	Mother's Aspirations			
Best-School-Friend's Plans	*High School*		*College*	
	%	*N*	*%*	*N*
High School	8	(88)	49	(134)
College	21	(38)	83	(267)

Weighted effect parameter of:
  Mother's aspirations   .492**
  Best-school-friend's plans .288**
  ** $p < .01$.

Far from supporting the notion that adolescents are influenced by their peers more than by their parents, these data suggest the opposite: namely, that parents are more influential than peers[9] as regards future life goals. Furthermore, far from acting at odds with parents' goals, peers seem to reinforce these goals. The majority of adolescents (57%) hold plans which are in agreement with those of their mothers *and* their friends. And adolescents who agree with their parents are also more likely to be in agreement with their peers (76%) than those who disagree with their parents (59%). In the area of future life goals, no polarization seems to exist either toward parents or peers.

Perhaps friends reinforce parental aspirations because adolescents associate with peers whose goals are congruent with parental goals. When parents have college aspirations for their children, in the majority of cases (65%), their children's best-school-friends also have college plans; when parents have high school plans, in the majority of cases (66%), their children's best-school-friends also have high school plans. These trends hold true within each social class. (Data not presented.)

---

[9] The adolescent's best-school-friend does not represent the influence of the adolescent's very best friend (who may not be in the same school with him) nor the influence of all possible peers. However, data presented later in this paper indicate that even among adolescents for whom the school friend is the very best friend overall, concordance on educational plans is lower with friend than with mother.

Table 3
Concordance* on Educational Plans Between Adolescent
and Mother and Between Adolescent and Best-School-
Friend, by Age (Dyads)

	Age				
Concordance with	14	15	16	17	18
Mother	.613	.561	.418	.542	.432
Total N	(23)	(112)	(229)	(261)	(159)
Best-School-Friend	.394	.436	.341	.315	.406
Total N	(47)	(178)	(291)	(333)	(199)

* As measured by tau-beta, all significant beyond .01 level.

Not only is parental influence on future life goals stronger than peer
influence, but it remains strong throughout the entire adolescent period
(see Table 3). The decreasing influence of parents throughout adolescence has been accepted by many sociologists (Parsons, 1942; McDill
and Coleman, 1965; Douvan and Adelson, 1966). Our data, however, do
not support this conclusion. Table 3 shows that concordance levels vary
irregularly from year to year between the ages of 14 and 18. An adolescent
at age 14 is more in agreement with his mother than he is at any other
age; from ages 15 through 18, no consistent decrease is shown, nor does
his concordance with friend show a consistent increase. These trends are
not altered when sex of the child is taken into account. (Data not
presented.)

2. CONCORDANCE: INFLUENCE OR CONVERGENCE

The levels of concordance on educational plans are high. However,
in the absence of longitudinal data, the existence of a positive correlation
between members of a dyad does not necessarily reflect the influence
of one individual by the other, since both could be subject to the same
external social influence. For instance, concordance on values between
mother-children pairs has been found not to differ from levels of concordance with nonrelated adults living in the same household (Furstenberg,
1967) or members of artificial families (Dentler and Hutchinson, 1961).
To demonstrate influence of one member of the pair upon another, it is
necessary to show that (1) agreement is not explained by a common external factor which both members experience, and (2) agreement is modified by the interaction between the two individuals; if agreement results
from the direct influence of one individual upon the other, different patterns of interaction should affect the degree of influence observed.

The very high concordance on educational plans between adolescent
and mother observed in our samples could result from the fact that adolescents and their mothers belong to the same social class and are inde-

Table 4
Concordance* on Educational Plans Between Adolescent and Mother and Between Adolescent and Best-School-Friend, by Social Class (Dyads)

Concordance with	Middle Class	Lower Class	Total
Mother	.542	.495	.495
Total N	(215)	(493)	(724)
Best-School-Friend	.418	.325	.367
Total N	(261)	(612)	(1060)

*As measured by tau-beta, all significant beyond .01 level.

pendently affected by it. Similarly, concordance between the adolescent and his best-school-friend could result from common experiences (either outside or inside the school) that lead to identical educational plans, rather than from the specific influence of one friend upon the other. In this sample, social and economic background are relatively unimportant criteria for personal choice of friends (Kandel, *et al.,* 1968); criteria such as age, or program in school, are much more important.[10] Common school experience could account for the observed agreement on educational plans between in-school friendship pairs, since school program is highly related to educational plans. The proportion of adolescents planning to go to college varies from 92% among students in the college preparatory course to 30% in the general program.

When social class[11] is held constant (see Table 4), concordance remains at a high and significant level, suggesting that agreement with mother or best-school-friend within a particular social class is not a spurious result of its independent association with social class. The cross-tabulations of mother's and adolescent's plans, which correspond to the correlations in Table 4 are striking. When mothers have college aspirations for their children, 80% of middle-class and 67% of lower-class adolescents plan to go on to college; when mothers have no college aspirations for their children, the proportion of adolescents with college plans drops to 20% and 16%, respectively, in the middle and lower class. The weighted effect parameters reflect these trends: the effect of mother's plans on adolescent aspiration is .530, as compared to .108 for social class.

These data provide strong evidence for Kahl's (1953) observation that

---

[10] The similarity (measured by tau-beta) in father's occupation of the two friends is remarkably low: .085, as compared to .539 for age or .598 for program in school. All the tau-betas are statistically significant.

parental aspiration is a more important determinant of children's educational aspirations than is social-class membership *per se*. (See also Sewell and Shah, 1968). This does not deny the importance of social class as a determining factor in educational aspirations, but our data can be interpreted to show that the impact of social class on the adolescent, to the extent that it exists, is absorbed in the nature of the maternal influence.

Although coefficients of concordance remain highly significant within each social class, there are variations among them, especially as regards friends (see Table 4). Concordance is higher with mother and in particular with best friend in the middle than in the lower class. The somewhat weaker exposure to congruent social influences of the lower-class American adolescent is illustrated further by the degree of intertriad agreement in each class. Table 5 shows that the proportion of adolescents who agree with both their mothers and friends is higher in the middle (66%) than lower class (54%). These social-class differences are explained in part by the distribution of educational plans and the relation that these plans bear to social class. The highest inter-triad agreement is observed among adolescents who choose the modal educational aspiration, that is, college: 73% of adolescents who plan to go on to college are in agreement both with their mother and their friend in contrast to 37% among those who plan to stop at the high school level. When both social class and type of plans are controlled, type of plan is a stronger correlate of inter-triad agreement than social class (see Table 5).

Table 6 examines concordance with peer, holding school program constant. As expected, school program explains more of the concordance on educational plans between friends than does social class. Within each school program, concordance is lower than for the sample as a whole, but still is significant statistically, except in the vocational program. Within each program, adolescents' plans are influenced to some extent by the plans of their school friends. For example, the proportion of students with college plans in the commercial programs increases from 25% when their

Table 5

Agreement on Educational Plans Within Triads, by Social Class and Type of Educational Plans

Proportion of Adolescents Who Agree Both With Mother and Friend	Middle Class	Lower Class
Total sample	66	54
Total N	(146)	(327)
When plan to stop at high school level	41	36
Total N	(44)	(160)
When plan to go to college	77	71
Total N	(102)	(167)

Table 6
Concordance* on Educational Plans Between Adolescent and Best-School-Friend, by Adolescent's School Program (Dyads)

Concordance with Best-School-Friend	Commercial	General	College Preparatory	Vocational	Total
Concordance	.293**	.156*	.153**	.084	.367**
Total N	(430)	(216)	(346)	(33)	(1060)

* As measured by tau-beta, * p < .05, ** p < .001.

best friend intends to stop at the high school level, to 56% when their best friend plans to go on to college.

These results suggest that concordance between adolescent and mother, and adolescent and best-school-friend, represents direct influence on the adolescent, rather than the independent influence of the shared social situation of both dyad members, as represented by social class. If this is so, factors which increase or decrease that influence must be sought in the characteristics of the interactional patterns themselves. These are examined next.

3. CONCORDANCE AND MOTHER'S INFLUENCE

A. Patterns of Family Interaction. Family variables are of particular interest in the study of parental influence because the nature of parent-child interaction is assumed to affect the degree to which parents are able to transmit their values and goals to their children. (See, for example, Clausen, 1968.) Several family variables, such as type of parental power, amount of communication, degree of closeness between parent and child, and reliance on parental advice have been suggested as facilitating transmission of values from parent to child. In our study, these family variables were related to the adolescents' *subjective* experience of parental influence, such as feeling that their opinions were close to those of their parents and preferring the opinions of parents to those of peers (Kandel, *et al.,* 1968). However, these subjective perceptions of parental influence are *not* supported by the analyses of actual influence. No consistent effect of family patterns on the actual degree of agreement between mother and adolescent on educational goals could be identified.[12]

---

[12] Using matched parent-adolescent pairs, Furstenberg (1967) also was unable to isolate any effect of family variables on concordance between parent and child in six out of seven values he considered. The one area in which he found effects was on "mobility orientation," a composite index that included several items, including educational aspirations.

These findings are difficult to interpret if they mean that parental influence takes place irrespective of the nature of the parent-child relationship. It is possible that our measures of these parent-child variables are inadequate, or that the variables are attributes of family life too general to reveal the differential influence of parents on children on a particular issue, such as educational plans. As we will now see, more specific parent-child variables do show some effect.

B. Communication About Educational Plans. The influence of the mother on the adolescent's educational plans appears when we examine the actual content of her interactions with the adolescent about these plans. Parents were not only asked about their educational aspirations for the adolescent, but also how strongly they had encouraged him (or her) to pursue education after secondary school. The mother's encouragement of higher education has a noticeable effect on the educational aspirations of her child: 82% of adolescents plan to continue their education beyond high school when the mother strongly encourages the pursuit of higher education, but only 14% when the mother reports she has advised against college attendance. (For similar findings, see, for example, Bell, 1963; Bordua, 1960; Cohen, 1965; Kahl, 1953; Sewell and Shah, 1968).

In analyzing simultaneously the effects of mother's encouragement and specific educational aspirations upon the adolescent's plans, each has an independent effect on the child's level of aspiration, with specific plans slightly stronger (.382 *versus* .302). Among mothers with college aspirations for their children, 85% of adolescents plan to continue their education when their mother also provides strong encouragement, as compared to only 53% when she does not.

Parents of different social classes vary not only in the educational goals they have for their children, but also in the encouragement they give their children to continue their education, with middle-class mothers providing more encouragement than lower-class mothers. When the mother's educational plans and strength of encouragement are controlled simultaneously, the social-class effects on the child's own plans disappear almost completely (see Table 7). Thus, the social-class differences

Table 7

Percent of Adolescents Planning to Continue Education, by Mother's College Aspiration, Maternal Encouragement, and Social Class (Dyads)

	Mothers with College Aspirations			
	Strong Encourag.		**Medium, Against**	
Per Cent of Adolescents	*Middle Class*	*Lower Class*	*Middle Class*	*Lower Class*
Planning to continue education	89%	82%	56%	50%
Total N	(122)	(196)	(48)	(153)

in adolescents' educational plans can be explained mostly by the facts that parents have different levels of aspiration and provide differential encouragement to pursue education. These parental attitudes and plans, in turn, are associated with social-class position. But for the child, the parent is clearly the link between social-class position and future life goals.

Adolescents were also asked to whom they had talked about their educational plans. The mother is mentioned as the one person most often consulted, by 85% of the adolescents. A slight tendency to be in greater agreement with the mother (.471) exists for adolescents who discuss their plans with her than those who do not (.400).

4. CONCORDANCE AND THE INFLUENCE OF BEST FRIEND

In contrast to the findings for mother, the influence of the best-school-friend on the adolescent varies according to the intensity of the friendship. Several indicators of intensity of the friendship were used: (1) whether or not the friendship choice is reciprocated, (2) how frequently the adolescent sees his friend out of school, and (3) whether the best-school-friend is also the best friend overall. Friendship pairs characterized by greater intimacy and greater frequency of contact were expected to show greater concordance. Alexander and Campbell (1964) had found that reciprocity of choice increased the similarity in college plans of high school seniors.

The results in Table 8 confirm these expectations: friends whose choice is reciprocated are in greater agreement than friends involved in unreciprocated choices; the adolescent is in greater agreement with friends he sees frequently out of school than those he sees more rarely, and, agreement is higher with school friends who are also the adolescent's very

Table 8

Concordance* on Educational Plans Between Adolescent and Best-School-Friend, by Strength of Friendship (Dyads)

Strength of Friendship	Tau-beta	N
Reciprocity of Choice		
Reciprocated	.390	(438)
Not reciprocated	.346	(622)
Frequency of Contact out of School		
More than once a week	.369	(732)
Once a week-month	.350	(213)
Never	.316	(114)
School Friend is Best Friend		
Yes	.406	(710)
No	.291	(338)

* As measured by tau-beta, all significant beyond .001 level.

best friend overall (outside school as well as in school) than with those school friends who are not.

The degree of friendship was refined further by considering simultaneously whether the choice was reciprocated *and* whether the friend in school was the best friend overall. The "very best friend" in terms of this classification, is the best friend overall whose choice is reciprocated. Concordance on educational plans with reciprocated best friends overall is higher than for any other category of friendship. However, concordance with the very best friend overall (.423) is still not as high as with the mother (.504).

SUMMARY AND CONCLUSION

These findings have relevance for several current controversies about sources of influence on adolescents' educational plans, about the process of family socialization, and about the separateness of adolescents and adults. Concordance with mother is higher than concordance with best-school-friend, even when out-of-school friendships are taken into account and the school friend is the adolescent's very best friend overall, outside or in school. Controlling for external social factors such as social class or program in school suggests that the influence of mother and friend, especially that of the mother, is intrinsic to the interaction itself. Parental desires for their children are more important direct determinants of the child's educational plans than is socioeconomic status, although the parents' aspirations themselves may be determined in great part by the parents' position in society.

While the influence of peers increases with the intimacy of the friendship, the influence of the mother appears to be remarkably independent of family structure and of the closeness of the adolescent to his mother. Thus our findings are consistent with an emerging body of data (Furstenberg, 1967) which fail to confirm many common assumptions about the role of family structure in socialization.

Regarding educational plans, the adolescent is in considerable agreement with both parents and peers. Furthermore, agreement on educational goals with parents goes together with agreement with friends, and adolescents who disagree with their parents are also likely to disagree with their friends. Thus we take exception to the "hydraulic" view taken by many investigators regarding the relative influence of adults and peers which assumes that the greater the influence of the one, the less the influence of the other. Our data lead to another view: in critical areas, interactions with peers support the values of the parents.

The assumption is commonly made that peers provide a deterrent to intellectual development and educational aspirations during adolescence (Coleman, 1961). Our own data confirm that the climate of American high schools does not appear to reward intellectual achievement in school (Kandel, *et al.*, 1968). But peers have less influence on adolescents than parents with regard to future educational goals. On this last point, the findings of a rarely quoted study by Riley, *et al.* (1961) are relevant: the self-expectations which adolescents had for themselves as adults were very close to the adolescents' perceptions of their parents' current expectations. These authors conclude that adolescents distinguish between values relevant to their current peer relationships and those relevant to the roles they will play in the future as adults. The present results suggest that it is misleading to speak of separate adolescent cultures or of general peer *versus* parental influences. The particular content area under discussion must be specified; for certain values or areas, peers may be more influential than parents; for other issues, the reverse may be true (cf. Brittain, 1963). On the issue of the adolescent's future life goals, parents have a stronger influence than peers.

REFERENCES

Alexander, C. N. and E. Q. Campbell.
  1964 "Peer influences on adolescent educational aspirations and attainments." American Sociological Review *29:* 568–575.
Bell, G. D.
  1963 "Process in the formation of adolescents' aspirations." Social Forces *42:* 179–186.
Berger, B.
  1963 "Adolescence and beyond: an essay review of three books on the problems of growing up." Social Forces *10:* 394–408.
Bordua, D. J.
  1960 "Educational aspirations and parental stress on college." Social Forces *38:* 262–269.
Boyle, R. P.
  1966 "The effect of the high school on students' aspirations." American Journal of Sociology *71:* 628–639.
Brittain, C. V.
  1963 "Adolescent choices and parent-peer cross-pressures." American Sociological Review *28:* 385–390.
Clausen, J. A. (ed.)
  1968 Socialization and Society. Boston: Little, Brown and Co.
Cohen, E. G.
  1965 "Parental factors in educational mobility." Sociology of Education *38:* 405–425.
Coleman, J. S.
  1961 The Adolescent Society. New York: Free Press.
  1964 Introduction to Mathematical Sociology. New York: Free Press.
Coleman, J. S., E. Q. Campbell, C. J. Hobson, *et al.*
  1966 Equality of Educational Opportunity. Washington: U.S. Government Printing Office.
Dentler, R. A. and J. G. Hutchinson.
  1961 "Socioeconomic status *versus* family membership status as sources of family attitude consensus." Child Development *32:* 249–254.
Douvan, E. and J. Adelson.
  1966 The Adolescent Experience. New York: Wiley.
Duncan, O. D., A. O. Haller, and A. Portes.
  1968 "Peer influences on aspirations: a reinterpretation." American Journal of Sociology *74:* 119–137.

Ellis, R. A. and C. Lane.
1963 "Structural supports for upward mobility." American Sociological Review *28:* 743–756.
Furstenberg, F. F., Jr.
1967 Transmission of Attitudes in the Family. Unpublished Ph.D. dissertation, Columbia University.
Haller, A. O. and C. E. Butterworth.
1960 "Peer influences on levels of occupational and educational aspirations." Social Forces *38:* 289–295.
Herriott, R. E.
1963 "Some social determinants of educational aspiration." Harvard Educational Review *33:* 157–177.
Hyman, H. H.
1959 Political Socialization. Glencoe, Illinois: Free Press.
Kahl, J. A.
1953 "Educational and occupational aspirations of 'common man' boys." Harvard Educational Review *23:* 186–203.
Kandel, D. B., G. S. Lesser, G. Roberts, and R. S. Weiss.
1968 Adolescents in Two Societies: Peers, School, and Family in the United States and Denmark. Final Report, Project No. 2139, Contract No. OE-4-10-069. Bureau of Research, Office of Education, U.S. Department of Health, Education, and Welfare.
Kandel, D. B. and G. S. Lesser.
1969 "Relative influences of parents and peers on the educational plans of adolescents in the United States and Denmark." Scheduled for publication in 1969 in Matthew B. Miles, *et al.* (eds.), Readings in the Social Psychology of Education. Boston: Allyn and Bacon.
Kendall, M. G.
162 Rank Correlation Methods. New York: Hafner.
McDill, E. L. and J. S. Coleman.
1965 "Family and peer influence in college plans of high school students." Sociology of Education *38:* 112–126.
McDill, E. L., E. D. Meyers and L. C. Rigsby, Jr.
1966 Sources of Educational Climates in High Schools. Final Report. The Johns Hopkins University, Contract No. OE-3-10-080, U.S. Department of Health, Education, and Welfare.
Michael, J. A.
1966 "On neighborhood context and college plans." American Sociological Review *31:* 706–707.
Parsons, T.
1942 "Age and sex in the social structure of the United States." American Sociological Review *7:* 604–616.
Ramsøy, N. R.
1962 Social Structure and College Recruitment. New York: Bureau of Applied Social Research, Columbia University.
Rehberg, R. A. and D. L. Westby.
1967 "Parental encouragement, occupation, education and family size: Artifactual or independent determinants of adolescent educational expectation?" Social Force *45:* 362–374.

Riley, M. W., J. W. Riley, and M. E. Moore.
1961 "Adolescent values and the Riesman typology: an empirical analysis." Pp. 370–386 in Seymour Lipset and Leo Lowenthal (eds.), Culture and Social Character. New York: Free Press.
Sewell, W. H., A. O. Haller and M. A. Straus.
1957 "Social status and educational and occupational aspiration." American Sociological Review 22: 67–73.
Sewell, W. H. and V. P. Shah.
1967 "Socioeconomic status, intelligence and the attainment of higher education." Sociology of Education 40: 1–23.
1968a "Parents' education and children's educational aspirations and achievements." American Sociological Review 33: 191–209.
1968b "Social class, parental encouragement, and educational aspirations." American Journal of Sociology 73: 559–572.
Simpson, R. L.
1962 "Parental influence, anticipatory socialization, and social mobility." American Sociological Review 27: 517–522.
Strodtbeck, F. L.
1958 "Family interaction, values, and achievement." Pp. 135–194 in D. C. McClelland, et al. (eds.), Talent and Society. New York: Van Nostrand.
Turner, R. H.
1964 The Social Context of Ambition. San Francisco: Chandler.
Wilson, A. B.
1959 "Residential segregation of social classes and aspirations of high school boys." American Sociological Review 24: 836–845.

psychodynamic aspects of learning disability: the passive-aggressive underachiever

Irving B. Weiner

Case Western Reserve University

The earliest formal psychodynamic formulations of learning disability were formulated by Freud (1901) in *The Psychopathology of Everyday Life,* in which he ascribed various types of forgetting and mistakes in speech, reading, and writing to unconscious psychological determinants. Psycho-analytic theorists subsequently attempted to trace otherwise inexplicable failures to learn to a number of specific underlying concerns about aggressive and sexual impulses. Thus in some cases of learning difficulty it was suggested that repression of sexual curiosity was generally inhibiting willingness to acquire knowledge; in others that the process of learning had taken on sexual connotations that had imbued it with taboo properties; and in others that defenses against aggressive urges were precluding adequate attention to subject matter with aggressive overtones, such as violence-filled novels assigned for English, dissections required for biology, the study of wars in history, or the discussion of channeling nuclear energy in physics (Blanchard, 1946; Jarvis, 1958; Liss, 1941; Sperry, Staver, & Mann, 1952).

Although such specific unconscious influences may participate in the genesis of learning difficulties that are primarily psychological in origin, available research and my own clinical experience indicate that the vast majority of achievement problems in adolescents who are not intellec-tually or socioculturally handicapped can be adequately understood in terms of maladaptive patterns of family interaction. These maladaptive patterns include (*a*) a significant amount of underlying hostility, usually toward parents, that cannot be directly expressed; (*b*) concerns about rivalry with parents and siblings that generate marked fears of failure or of success; and (*c*) a preference for passive-aggressive modes of

Portions of this paper were presented in a symposium on adolescent learning disability at the 78th Annual Convention of the American Psychological Association, Miami Beach, September 1970.

Reprinted from the Journal of School Psychology, 1971, 9, 246–251. By permis-sion of the author and Behavioral Publications, Inc.

coping with difficult situations. Learning difficulties determined by the combined impact of these psychodynamic factors constitute a fairly specific pattern of psychological disturbance that can be labeled passive-aggressive underachievement (see Weiner, 1970, pp. 265–277).

HOSTILITY

Research studies of underachieving adolescents have revealed that, in comparison with their achieving peers, they are particularly likely to be experiencing guilt and anxiety about underlying aggressive feelings and are particularly incapable of giving direct, effective expression to these negative feelings (Shaw & Brown, 1957; Shaw & Grubb, 1958; Sutherland, 1952, 1953). Other work has demonstrated that the typical source of anger in such underachieving youngsters is resentment of parental authority they perceive as restrictive and unjust (Davids & Hainsworth, 1967; Morrow & Wilson, 1961). Given his underlying anger, his difficulty in expressing it directly, and the source of his anger in his parents' behavior toward him, the passive-aggressive underachiever utilizes poor academic performance as a means of simultaneously venting his anger and retaliating against his parents.

For this means to succeed, that is, for poor academic performance to serve as an aggressive act against the parents, it is necessary that the parents have some investment in their youngster's studies. Typically in instances of psychologically determined underachievement the parents will be concerned about their youngster's school work and distressed by his academic difficulties. Furthermore, it is more often than not their concerns and expectations of him that have fomented much of his resentment.

One particular common precipitant of resentment and subsequent retaliatory underachievement is the parental imposition on a youngster of academic goals that he does not share. For example, the son of a lawyer or physician may be encouraged and expected to follow in his father's footsteps, even though he is uncertain about his career preferences or has already decided he would like to become a history teacher or an architect. A girl who is the only, oldest, or brightest child in her family may become her parents' choice to receive their support and encouragement toward a prestigious professional career, despite her own wishes to have a nonprofessional job and perhaps not even attend college. When such youngsters are unable to challenge or resist their parents' demands openly, they frequently utilize underachievement to frustrate their parents' aspirations for them, even at the price of sacrificing their own goals. Thus the would-be architect who cannot cope directly with his parents' insistence that he prepare to study law may underachieve to the point of failing to qualify for training in either profession.

RIVALRY

Passive-aggressive underachievers typically suffer from fears of failing or fears of succeeding that lead them to employ academically inhibiting defensive maneuvers. Youngsters who fear failure are inclined to set unrealistically high goals for themselves and then work only half-heartedly to attain them. This maneuver allows the underachieving student to deny any limitations he may have and to dismiss any suggestion that he has actually been a failure. He does not have to feel embarrassed at not reaching his goals, since they were so ambitious, and he can use his admittedly lackadaisical effort to justify the commonly heard claim, "I know I could get better grades any time I wanted to, but I just haven't felt like putting much time in on my school work; if I really tried I could do better."

Thus the fear-of-failure underachiever carefully hedges his bets. He rarely risks making a mistake, he consistently denies having worked hard even when he has, and he bolsters himself with false pride in how much he has been able to accomplish without having made much of an effort—"I think I did pretty well to pass, since I hardly cracked a book the whole term." This underachieving pattern is particularly likely to emerge at certain transition points in a youngster's academic career, particularly those which confront him with more difficult subject matter or more demanding academic standards than he has had to face previously. The transitions from junior high school to high school, from high school to college, and from a less to a more competitive school are especially likely to exacerbate pre-existing fears of failure and precipitate this underachieving pattern, which has been aptly described as "big-league shock" (Berger, 1961; McArthur, 1961).

With regard to intrafamilial rivalry, the underachieving youngster whose self-defeating approach to his studies reflects fear of failure is often reacting to being compared unfavorably with parents or siblings who are more able than he. The odds against his meeting this competition discourage him from making the attempt, and the greater the successes of the parent or siblings who is held up to him as an example, and the greater the family's disappointment in the underachieving youngster ("Why can't you get the marks your brother does?"), the greater his inclination to disengage from any serious pursuit of his studies.

Adolescents who fear success, on the other hand, usually have some expectation that achieving will eventually cause them more unhappiness than will any failure to realize their academic potential. This expectation typically derives from a youngster's perceptions that his parents will be so threatened by having to compete with him and so envious and resentful of his successes, especially if they exceed their own, that his attainments will evoke their disapproval and rejection. In contrast to the youngster who fears failure and is discouraged from academic effort to the extent that his own family members are successful, the fear-of-success youngster is likely to become increasingly disinterested or ineffective in his studies the more he regards his parents as unsuccessful or less able than himself (Grunebaum, Hurwitz, Prentice, & Sperry, 1962; Sperry, Staver, Reiner, & Ulrich, 1958).

The ways in which youngsters who fear success characteristically approach achievement-related situations also contrast interestingly with the coping maneuvers employed by students who are more prominently concerned with failure. As noted above, the fear-of-failure youngster tends to set very high goals and not work very hard to reach them, and by this means he escapes the anxiety of a near-miss and is in a position to convince himself and others that his attainments reflect only a small part of his true ability. The underachiever who fears success, on the other hand, publicly disparages his abilities, even when they are considerable, sets very limited, unrealistically low goals that are easily within his grasp, and makes just enough effort to reach these minimal goals and no more. Thus he carefully avoids any accomplishments that he feels might threaten his parents or dampen their affection for him.

As would be predicted from the underlying concerns of the fear-of-success underachiever, his school performance typically begins to decline when he is on the verge of surpassing his parents. A common example of this pattern of onset is the child of high school educated parents who begins during his latter high school years to do poorly in his studies or otherwise compromise his chances of getting into college. Such a situation can develop even in the context of overtly enthusiastic attitudes about college on the part of both the youngster and his parents; in such instances, the parents' communications carry the implicit message, "We've had a good life without a college education; now you're going to go away, and it will cost us all this money, and you'll get all kinds of new ideas, and we'll never be close as a family again."

PASSIVE-AGGRESSIVE BEHAVIOR

The underachiever concerned with the problems of hostility and rivalry described above typically earns low or declining grades by a passive-aggressive mode of coping with the school situation. Passive-aggressive behavior consists of purposeful inactivity, and research data demonstrate that underachievers studiously and selectively apply such inactivity to their academic tasks. In contrast to their equally intelligent but achieving peers, underachievers study less, complete assignments less promptly, and reserve their energies for extra-curricular activities (Frankel, 1960; Wilson & Morrow, 1962). Underachievers frequently display an extent of concentrated effort and achievement in sports, hobbies, or part-time jobs that contrasts markedly with their academic lassitude. Furthermore, it is not unusual for the academic underachiever to read widely and keep himself well-informed, while reading anything but material assigned in his courses and becoming informed about everything except matters he will be asked about in class discussions or on examination (see Mindani & Tutko, 1969).

Even if he should absorb knowledge relevant to his school subjects, the passive-aggressive underachiever will utilize inactivity techniques to ensure that his knowledge does not elevate his grades. He remains silent during class discussions, affecting disinterest or stupidity; he "forgets" to copy down or turn in assignments; on examinations he "overlooks" a page or a section, or he somehow misinterprets the instructions so as to disqualify many of his answers.

It is important to stress that these techniques, though purposeful, are not consciously implemented by the passive-aggressive underachiever. The underachieving youngster who is basically unmotivated to receive an education will, in the absence of any psychological disturbance, directly make his feelings known and openly resist the school's impositions on him. The passive-aggressive underachiever, on the other hand, is a youngster who otherwise would embrace and pursue academic goals but in whom underlying conflicts about hostility and rivalry, set in the context of maladaptive patterns of family interaction, are producing a psychological handicap. His passive-aggressive techniques are indirect, neurotic efforts to resolve his conflicts, and he is unlikely to be aware either of the extent to which they are undermining his grades or of their role as an aggressive act against his parents. Increasing these two areas of awareness thus turns out to be a focal point in the psychological treatment of the passive-aggressive underachiever (see Weiner, 1970, pp. 280–283).

REFERENCES

Berger, E. M. Willingness to accept limitations and college achievement. *Journal of Counseling Psychology,* 1961, 8: 140–144.

Blanchard, P. Psychoanalytic contributions to the problems of reading disabilities. *Psychoanalytic Study of the Child,* 1946, 2: 163–187.

Davids, A., & Hainsworth, P. K. Maternal attitudes about family life and child rearing as avowed by mothers and perceived by their underachieving and high-achieving sons. *Journal of Consulting Psychology,* 1967, 31: 29–37.

Frankel, E. A comparative study of achieving and underachieving high school boys of high intellectual ability. *Journal of Educational Research,* 1960, 53: 172–180.

Freud, S. (1901) *The psychopathology of everyday life.* Standard Edition, Vol. VI. London: Hogarth, 1960.

Grunebaum, M. G., Hurwitz, I., Prentice, N. M., & Sperry, B. M. Fathers of sons with primary neurotic learning inhibitions. *American Journal of Orthopsychiatry,* 1962, 32: 462–472.

Jarvis, V. Clinical observations on the visual problem in reading disability. *Psychoanalytic Study of the Child,* 1958, 13: 451–470.

Liss, E. Learning difficulties: Unresolved anxiety and resultant learning patterns. *American Journal of Orthopsychiatry,* 1941, 11: 520–524.

McArthur, C. C. Distinguishing patterns of student neuroses. In G. R. Blaine & C. C. McArthur (Eds.), *Emotional problems of the student.* New York: Appleton-Century-Crofts, 1961. Pp. 54–75.

Mondani, M. S., & Tutko, T. A. Relationship of academic underachievement to incidental learning. *Journal of Consulting and Clinical Psychology,* 1969, 33: 558–560.

Morrow, W. R., & Wilson, R. C. Family relations of bright high-achieving and under-achieving high school boys. *Child Development,* 1961, 32: 501–510.

Shaw, M. C., & Brown, D. J. Scholastic underachievement of bright college students. *Personnel and Guidance Journal,* 1957, 36: 195–199.

Shaw, M. C., & Grubb, J. Hostility and able high school under-achievers. *Journal of Counseling Psychology,* 1958, 5: 263–266.

Sperry, B. M., Staver, N., & Mann, H. E. Destructive fantasies in certain learning difficulties. *American Journal of Orthopsychiatry,* 1952, 22: 356–365.

Sperry, B. M., Staver, N., Reiner, B. S., & Ulrich, D. Renunciation and denial in learning difficulties. *American Journal of Orthopsychiatry,* 1958, *28:* 98–111.

Sutherland, B. K. The sentence-completion technique in a study of scholastic underachievement. *Journal of Counsulting Psychology,* 1952, *16:* 353–358.

Sutherland, B. K. Case studies in educational failure during adolescence. *American Journal of Orthopsychiatry,* 1953, *23:* 406–415.

Weiner, I. B. *Psychological disturbance in adolescence.* New York: Wiley, 1970.

Wilson, R. C., & Morrow, W. R. School and career adjustment of bright high-achieving and under-achieving high school boys. *Journal of Genetic Psychology,* 1962, *101:* 91–103.

nine
adolescents and the world of work

part nine

The existentialist educational writer Ramano Guardini has asserted that while adolescence may begin with the biological changes of puberty, it can end only with "practical experience in the working world."[1] Prior to such experience, many of the adolescent's views of his own capabilities and interests, and of his ability to maintain his own values and goals amid the inevitable compromises and frustrations of the "real" working world, are likely to have a highly theoretical quality. Certainly, the problem of deciding on and preparing for a vocational career represents one of the critical developmental tasks of adolescence. This has long been the case for boys and, with recent role changes for women in our society, it is becoming much more frequently the case for girls as well.

The problem of choosing a vocation has become increasingly difficult as the world in which we live has become steadily more complex and the rate of social and technological change ever more rapid. In many earlier societies—both literate and nonliterate—the range of available occupations was generally highly restricted and the young person was likely to be familiar with most of them, either through observation or apprenticeship. In today's world, however, the number and diversity of occupations appear virtually limitless; but individual adolescents (and their parents) are not likely to be familiar with the nature of most of them, the aptitudes they require, or the opportunities they present. To further complicate the matter, many jobs in our high-technology society demand highly specialized, frequently nontransferable skills. At the same time, rapid shifts in technology and in the economy generally may make many of those skills obsolete in a relatively short period of time. Clearly, one of the major problems of the 1970s in the United States and other Western countries will be that of finding appropriate employment for young people. In the case of a significant minority—particularly the economically disadvantaged or ethnically isolated—the problem may be one of finding *any* meaningful employment. The record to date has not been very encouraging and unless the problem can be resolved, both society and its youth are likely to be in serious trouble. Under such circumstances, any "revolt of the young" would be as much or more likely to come from the failure of society to provide adequate avenues for admission to the economic and social order for all of its youth as from any loudly deplored rejection by them of society and its values.

The adolescent's vocational aspirations are influenced by a variety of factors, including socioeconomic status, parental aspirations, individual psychological needs, ability, and sex and peer-group membership. Socioeconomic status helps to determine the kinds of occupations with which the young person will be familiar and hence will be likely to consider in formulating his occupational goals. Furthermore, it influences the social

[1] D. Vandenberg, Life-Phases and Values. *Educational Forum,* 1968, *32,* 296.

acceptability of particular kinds of jobs, as well as his opportunities to prepare adequately for and gain entrance into higher-status occupations.

Although working-class youth generally have lower vocational aspirations than those from middle- and upper-class backgrounds, this need not be the case. As Richard L. Simpson demonstrates in the first study in this part, working-class boys whose parents have high aspirations for them are more likely to have high aspirations themselves—educationally and vocationally—than middle-class boys whose parents do not have such aspirations. In addition, among both middle- and working-class boys, those with high aspirations were found to have a higher percentage of middle-class friends (an indication of what Simpson calls "anticipatory socialization") than those with lower aspirations. While both parents and peers affected the young person's aspiration level—particularly in the case of working-class youth—the influence of parents appeared the stronger of the two.

In the second article, Alan P. Bell explores the influence of a variety of role models on the vocational adjustment of male adolescents, both during the ninth grade and after they had been out of school for seven years age 25). Interestingly, of all the role models that Bell's subjects had available at ninth grade (e.g., father, mother, siblings, teachers, peers, adult relatives), only the father's role modeling was related to the son's vocational adjustment and behaviors ten years later. Boys who at age 15 had fathers who provided strong *and* positive role models tended to achieve higher levels of vocational adjustment than those whose fathers were either weak or nonexistent role models or who were negative models. However, the differences in vocational adjustment were generally greater when the father provided a weak or nonexistent role model than when he served as a *negative* role model. Apparently, both positive identification with *and* rejection of a parental role model can help to crystalize the adolescent's career patterns. As Bell says, "Their importance may be more similar than it has been commonly realized. Each may serve as important occasions for self-definition."

Until recently a clear preponderance of research in the area of adolescent vocational choice has been focused on boys. Although in part this differential research emphasis may have reflected a chauvinistic tendency among social scientists, as well as in society at large, it was also due in considerable measure to a traditional lack of aspiration toward long-term, highly demanding careers among girls themselves (obviously excluding the very demanding career of child rearing). With the rapidly growing interest and participation of girls in a greater diversity of vocational roles (usually in addition to traditional family roles), the research picture is also beginning to change.

In the third article, Grace K. Baruch explores two alternate hypotheses concerning the tendency of many girls and women to devalue feminine professional competence (see also Matina Horner's article, pp. 194–205). Is this tendency, where it exists, primarily a function of out-group self-prejudice," that is, do women who devalue have negative attitudes toward the career role and associate it with undesirable personal and social consequences? Or is this tendency primarily due instead to the learning of traditional feminine sex-role standards from nonworking mothers? At least among the contemporary college women in Baruch's study, it appears that the most important determinant of their attitudes toward dual roles for women—work *and* family—has been their mothers. "Whether a subject is favorable to such a pattern depends . . . upon whether her mother endorses it and, if the mother works, upon how successfully she has integrated her two roles." In brief, favorable attitudes toward career goals for women, both on the part of women themselves and probably men as well, are fostered by the existence of vocationally competent, successful, and personally satisfied models.

parental influence, anticipatory socialization, and social mobility

Richard L. Simpson
University of North Carolina

Two distinct hypotheses have been proposed to explain why some boys from working-class backgrounds aspire to middle-class occupational status while others do not. According to research by Kahl, Floud and associates, and Bordua, a working-class boy is relatively likely to seek advanced education and occupational mobility if his parents urge him to do so, and unlikely to seek mobility if his parents do not exert pressure in this direction.[1] On the other hand, studies by Beilin and Wilson suggest that anticipatory socialization into middle-class values by middle-class peers at school may be the decisive factor.[2] Beilin reports that working-class boys who plan to attend college, like middle-class boys, tend to participate heavily in organized extracurricular activities, and Turner feels

---

[1] Joseph A. Kahl, "Educational and Occupational Aspirations of 'Common-Man' Boys," *Harvard Educational Review,* 23 (Summer, 1953), pp. 186–203; Jean E. Floud (editor), A. H. Halsey, and F. M. Martin, *Social Class and Educational Opportunity,* London: Heinemann, 1956, pp. 93–95, 107–108; David J. Bordua, "Educational Aspirations and Parental Stress on College," *Social Forces,* 38 (March, 1960), pp. 262–269. See also a summary of studies in Seymour Martin Lipset and Reinhard Bendix, *Social Mobility in Industrial Society,* Berkeley and Los Angeles: University of California Press, 1959, pp. 237–240.

[2] Harry Beilin, "The Pattern of Postponability and Its Relation to Social Class Mobility," *Journal of Social Psychology,* 44 (August, 1956), pp. 33–48; Alan B. Wilson, "Residential Segregation of Social Classes and Aspirations of High School Boys," *American Sociological Review,* 24 (December, 1959), pp. 836–845.

The research reported herein was performed pursuant to a contract with the United States Office of Education, Department of Health, Education, and Welfare. The Urban Studies Program, Institute for Research in Social Science, University of North Carolina, under a grant from the Ford Foundation, provided additional support, and a grant from the University of North Carolina Research Council made possible some of the data processing. David R. Norsworthy wrote the questionnaire. Ann C. Kopyt analyzed the data while serving as a National Science Foundation undergraduate research participant. Harry J. Crockett, Jr. and Ida Harper Simpson made useful suggestions.

Reprinted from the American Sociological Review, 1962, 27, 517–522. Copyright © 1962 by the American Sociological Association. By permission.

that mobility-oriented working-class high school students should be "studied separately to discover whether or not they are incorporated into higher-level cliques. . . ."[3]

There is nothing inherently contradictory about these two hypotheses, since it is reasonable to suppose that parents and peers might independently influence the aspirations of working-class boys. However, it is also conceivable that only one of the two hypotheses might provide the true explanation for mobility aspirations, despite the evidence supporting both hypotheses when they are tested in separate studies. Conceivably the relationship between parental influence and mobility aspiration might disappear if peer group influence were controlled, or vice versa, suggesting that one of the two types of influence is more apparent than real since it has no effect unless the other type of influence is also present.

This paper will explore the effects on career aspirations of parental and peer group influences, considered separately, and will then try to see whether the relationships found are independent of each other by varying both types of influence simultaneously.

SOURCE OF DATA

The data are from questionnaires administered in 1960 to the boys in the white high schools of two southern cities. One school, in a city of about 25,000 provided 333 respondents and the other, in a city of about 60,000, provided 584 for a total of 917. All boys present in home room period on the day when the questionnaires were given filled them out—more than 90 per cent in each school. Nonresponses and unclassifiable responses to the question on occupational plans reduced the 917 respondents to 743. The respondents omitted from tabulations because of insufficient information about their occupational plans were somewhat skewed toward the lower end of the family status range, though not markedly so. Since family background is controlled in all tabulations, the sample reduction caused by their incomplete answers probably does not distort the findings appreciably. The patterns of relationship among key variables were very similar among students at the two schools; therefore both schools are combined in the analysis.

From information on the occupations of the boys' fathers and the occupations they themselves expected to enter, they were classified into four groups. *Ambitious middle-class* boys were those whose fathers' current occupations (or last occupations if the fathers were deceased) were non-manual, and who were enrolled in the college preparatory curriculum and expected to enter high-ranking professional or executive occupations, defined as those in the top two levels in Hollingshead's seven-level Index of Occupational Status.[4] *Unambitious middle-class* boys had white-collar fathers but were either not enrolled in the college preparatory curriculum,

---

[3] Beilin, *op. cit.,* p. 46; Ralph H. Turner, "Sponsored and Contest Mob'lity and the School System," *American Sociological Review,* 25 (December, 1960), pp. 855–867, quoted at p. 866.

[4] This index measures one of two components, the other being years of education completed, in Hollingshead's two-factor index of social position, whose valida-

Table 1
Percentages of Boys in Four Groups Advised to Enter
Professions by One or Both Parents

Group	Per Cent Advised to Enter Professions
1. Ambitious middle-class (N = 209)	53.1
2. Unambitious middle-class (N = 157)	21.0
3. Mobile working-class (N = 85)	43.5
4. Nonmobile working-class (N = 231)	16.0

Chi-squares, 1 d.f., one-tail tests: group 1 vs. group 2, 39.28, $p < .001$; group 3 vs. group 4, 26.21, $p < .001$; group 1 vs. group 3, 2.21, $p < .10$; group 2 vs. group 4, 1.59, $p < .15$; group 2 vs. group 3, 13.58, $p < .001$.

not planning to enter occupations in Hollingshead's top two levels, or not ambitious by either of these criteria. *Mobile working-class* boys had fathers in blue-collar occupations but were enrolled in the college preparatory curriculum and expected to enter the same high-ranking occupations as the ambitious middle-class boys. *Nonmobile working-class* boys had blue-collar fathers and failed to meet one or both of the two criteria of ambition, enrollment in the college preparatory curriculum and aspiration to enter top-ranking occupations.[5]

PARENTAL INFLUENCE

Table 1 shows the percentages of boys in the four groups who had been advised by one or both parents to enter professions. We are considering such advice as a rough indication of parental pressure toward

---

tion and utility are described in August B. Hollingshead and Fredrick C. Redlich, *Social Class and Mental Illness,* New York: Wiley, 1958, pp. 387–397. A list of illustrative occupations in the seven I. O. S. levels is given in August B. Hollingshead, "Two Factor Index of Social Position," New Haven: Yale University, 1957 (mimeographed). Only the top two I. O. S. levels were defined as indicating ambition or mobility aspiration, rather than all four white-collar levels, to compensate for the generally overoptimistic expectations which were prevalent. The requirement that the boy be enrolled in the college preparatory curriculum was made for the same reason.

[5] The mobile and nonmobile working-class boys did not differ appreciably in the percentage whose fathers held skilled as opposed to semiskilled or unskilled jobs. Therefore the differences reported later between these two groups of boys cannot be attributed to heterogeneity of class background within the blue-collar category. The ambitious middle-class boys did tend to come from higher backgrounds than the unambitious middle-class boys, and the differences between these two groups would diminish (but not come close to disappearing) if our tables controlled for fine gradations of background within the broad level which we are calling middle-class.

Table 2
Occupational Status of Fathers of Friends Cited by
Four Groups of Boys

	Status of Friends' Fathers		
Group	*All Middle-Class (Per Cent)*	*One or More of Each Class (Per Cent)*	*All Working-Class (Per Cent)*
1. Ambitious middle-class (N = 198)	57.1	39.4	3.5
2. Unambitious middle-class (N = 133)	32.3	43.6	24.1
3. Mobile working-class (N = 83)	28.9	59.0	12.1
4. Nonmobile working-class (N = 189)	5.3	54.5	40.2

Chi-squares with "all middle-class" and "one or more of each" combined, 1. d.f., one-tail tests: group 1 vs. group 2, 32.25, $p < .001$; group 3 vs. group 4, 21.15 $< .001$; group 1 vs. group 3, 7.46, $p < .01$; group 2 vs. group, 4 9.14, $p < .01$; group 2 vs. group 3, 4.71, $p < .02$.

occupational ambition which would involve, unless the father is himself professional, upward mobility. These figures give strong support to the hypothesis that parental influence is associated with mobility aspiration among working-class boys, and also with ambition among middle-class boys. Indeed, parental advice is a much better predictor of high ambition than is the boy's social class. Only 21.0 per cent of the unambitious middle-class boys and 16.0 per cent of the nonmobile working-class boys had been advised by one or both parents to enter professions; this compares with 53.1 per cent among the ambitious middle-class boys and 43.5 per cent among the mobile working-class boys.[6]

PEER GROUP MEMBERSHIP AND
ANTICIPATORY SOCIALIZATION

Following Turner's reasoning, we would predict from the "anticipatory socialization" hypothesis that among working-class boys, those with middle-class friends would more often be mobile, and that among middle-class boys, those with working-class friends would less often be ambitious. Table 2 shows that this was definitely the case. The table distributes the four groups according to their answers to a question which asked them to "describe what kind of work the fathers of three of your best

---

[6] The superiority of parental advice to social class as a predictor of ambition appears even greater if we examine the percentages in the four groups who had been advised by *both* parents to enter professions. These percentages, not shown in the table, are 6.4 per cent of the unambitious middle-class boys, 5.6 per cent of the nonmobile working-class boys, 28.7 per cent of the ambitious middle-class boys, and 24.7 per cent of the mobile working-class boys.

friends do"; the occupations they listed are classified as all middle-class (nonmanual), all working-class, or one or more of each.[7] As predicted, the ambitious middle-class and nonmobile working-class boys were at the extremes: 57.1 per cent of the ambitious middle-class boys but only 5.3 per cent of the nonmobile working-class boys mentioned only middle-class friends, while only 3.5 per cent of the former but 40.2 per cent of the latter mentioned only working-class friends. The unambitious middle-class and mobile working-class boys were intermediate and the differences between them were not clear-cut, since the mobile working-class boys were more likely to mention one or more friends of each class and the unambitious middle-class boys were more likely to mention either all middle-class or all working-class friends. However, in comparing these two intermediate groups, the unambitious middle-class boys were twice as likely (24.1% vs. 12.1%) to mention only working-class friends, but only slightly more likely (32.3% vs. 28.9%) to mention only middle-class friends. Considering the middle-class and working-class boys separately, these findings seem to give clear support to the "anticipatory socialization" hypothesis that the social class of the peer group is predictive of occupational ambition and mobility.

From the anticipatory socialization hypothesis, one would also expect mobile working-class boys to resemble ambitious middle-class boys in their extracurricular and after-school activities. Beilin's finding that those planning to attend college took part in more extracurricular activities than those not planning to attend college bears out this prediction,[8] and our data allow a further test of it. We asked the boys to list all of the "clubs and other organizations" to which they belonged. Table 3 shows that, as predicted, the mobile working-class boys approached the ambitious middle-class boys in the extent of their extracurricular participation—substantially more than the unambitious middle-class boys did and much more than the nonmobile working-class boys did. The mean numbers of clubs or organizations reported were 2.7 for ambitious middle-class boys, 1.6 for unambitious middle-class boys, 2.3 for mobile working-class boys, and 1.1 for nonmobile working-class boys.

INDEPENDENT EFFECTS

It is thus apparent that parental advice and middle-class peer group influence were both related to ambition and mobility aspiration among both middle-class and working-class boys in the two schools; and that in parental influence, peer group membership, and extracurricular activities, the mobile working-class boys resembled the ambitious middle-class boys more than the unambitious middle-class boys did. The next task is to see whether parents and peers influenced the boys' aspirations independently of each other. To test the hypothesis of independent effects, the boys were classified as "high" or "low" in the extent to which they

---

[7] The N's in Table 2 differ from those in other tables because of differing rates of nonresponse to the various questions involved.

[8] Beilin, *op. cit.*, p. 46.

Table 3
Percentages of Boys in Four Groups Belonging to
Different Numbers of Clubs

	Number of Clubs			
Group	*None or One (Per Cent)*	*2 or 3 (Per Cent)*	*4 or More (Per Cent)*	*Mean**
1. Ambitious middle-class (N = 209)	26.8	34.4	38.8	2.7
2. Unambitious middle-class (N = 157)	55.4	28.7	15.9	1.6
3. Mobile working-class (N = 85)	3.41	40.0	25.9	2.3
4. Nonmobile working-class (N = 231)	68.8	23.4	7.8	1.1

* In computing mean, "5 or more" was counted as 5.
Chi-squares with "2 or 3" and "4 or more" combined, 1 d.f., one-tail tests: group 1 vs. group 2, 30.84. $p < .001$; group 3 vs. group 4, 31.07, $p < .001$; group 1 vs. group 3, 1.57, $p < .15$; group 2 vs. group 4, 7.25. $p < .01$; group 2 vs. group 3, 10.01, $p < .01$.

had been subjected to each type of influence toward high occupational aspiration. They were defined as high in parental influence if either or both parents had recommended a professional career, and high in peer influence if they met both of two criteria: belonging to two or more clubs, and mentioning at least one middle-class friend. From this classification it was possible to define the boys as high in both types of influence, high in one but low in the other, or low in both.

Table 4 supports the hypothesis of independent effects strongly and consistently for working-class boys, and less strongly for middle-class boys. Among working-class boys, 71.4 per cent of those high in both parental and peer influence aspired to occupations in Hollingshead's top two levels, compared with only 25.6 per cent of those low in both types of influence, the boys high in one influence but low in the other being intermediate. Among middle-class boys, the rank order of the four groups in percentage aspiring to top-level occupations was the same as among working-class boys, but the differences between groups were small and statistically insignificant, with one exception: boys low in both types of influence were less than half as likely as those high in either or both influences to have high aspirations.

Table 4 also suggests that, as we have defined the two, parental influence was more strongly related to aspirations than peer influence was. Among the working-class boys high in peer influence, being high rather than low in parental influence brought the percentage of high-aspirers up from 35.7 per cent to twice this figure, 71.4 per cent; and among the working-class boys low in peer influence, high parental influence more than doubled the percentage of high-aspirers, increasing it from 25.6 per cent to 55.6 per cent. The effects of peer influence on working-class boys,

Table 4
Occupational Aspirations of Middle-Class and Working-Class Boys by Extent of Parental and Peer-Group Influence Toward Ambition

	Per Cent Aspiring to High-Status Occupations			
	Working-Class		*Middle-Class*	
Source and Extent of Influence	*(N)*	*%*	*(N)*	*%*
1. Both high	(28)	71.4	(94)	81.9
2. Parents high, peers low	(45)	55.6	(50)	78.0
3. Peers high, parents low	(70)	35.7	(109)	72.5
4. Both low	(168)	25.6	(113)	30.1

Chi-squares, 1 d.f.: *Within middle class:* group 1 vs. group 2, one-tail test, .32, $p < .35$; group 2 vs. group 3, two-tail test, .55, $p < .50$; group 3 vs. group 4, one-tail test, 39.92, $p < .001$. *Within working class:* group 1 vs. group 2, one-tail test, 1.85, $p < .10$; group 2 vs. group 3, two-tail test, 4.39, $p < .05$; group 3 vs. group 4, one-tail test, 2.48, $p < .10$. *Between classes, one-tail tests:* group 1, 1.46, $p < .15$; group 2, 5.45, $p < .01$; group 3, 23.68, $p < .001$; group 4, .69, $p < .25$.

with parental influence controlled, were substantially less than this. Among those high in parental influence, high peer influence increased the percentage of high-aspirers from 55.6 to 71.4, and among those low in parental influence, the increase due to high peer influence was from 25.6 per cent to 35.7 per cent. The seemingly greater influence of parents than of peers is also evident when we compare the percentages of high-aspirers among working-class boys high in only one type of influence. Among those high in parental influence only, 55.6 per cent were high-aspirers, but this percentage dropped to 35.7 among those high in peer influence only. Corresponding differences between the effects of parental and peer influence, though they were small and statistically unreliable, appeared among the middle-class boys.

It is also worth noting that when *both* types of influence were either high or low, they came close to nullifying the effects of class background on career aspiration. In every category of exposure to influence the middle-class boys had higher aspirations than the working-class boys, but these differences were large and statistically significant only in the two middle categories which were high in one influence but low in the other. A working-class boy who was high in either influence was more likely to be a high-aspirer than a middle-class boy who was low in both.

SUMMARY

Using questionnaire data from boys in two high schools, we have tested two alternative hypotheses concerning the factors influencing boys toward high occupational aspirations, and we have examined the simultaneous effects of the relevant variables to see whether each influences aspirations when the other is held constant. In general the findings held true among both working- and middle-class boys, and in some respects mobile working-class boys resembled ambitious middle-class boys more than unambitious middle-class boys did.

Among boys aspiring to high occupations, the percentage whose parents had advised them to enter professions was much higher than the percentage among low-aspirers. Thus the conclusion reached by Kahl, Floud and associates, and Bordua, that parental influence is a factor in the upward mobility of working-class boys, receives further confirmation and is extended to cover the ambitions of middle-class boys as well.

Mobile working-class boys were much higher than nonmobile working-class boys and somewhat higher than unambitious middle-class boys in the percentage who said that they had middle-class friends. In the number of extracurricular clubs to which they belonged, mobile working-class boys were close to ambitious middle-class boys, substantially higher than unambitious middle-class boys, and more than twice as high as nonmobile working-class boys. These findings support the hypothesis advanced by Beilin, Wilson, and Turner, that anticipatory socialization into middle-class values by middle-class peer groups helps to explain the upward mobility of working-class boys. Our findings also extend the anticipatory socialization hypothesis to cover middle-class as well as working-class boys.

A working-class boy was most likely to aspire to a high-ranking occupation if he had been influenced in this direction by both parents and peers, and least likely to be a high-aspirer if he had been subjected to neither of these influences. Among the middle-class boys, only those low in both influences differed significantly from the rest, though the direction of relationships in all cases paralleled those found among working-class boys. Of the two types of influence, that of parents appeared to have the stronger effect. Working-class boys influenced toward upward mobility by either parents or peers tended to have higher aspirations than middle-class boys not influenced toward high aspirations by either parents or peers.

role modeling of fathers in adolescence and young adulthood

Alan P. Bell.
Indiana University

Many have stressed the importance of the father-son relationship for the formation and development of the son's "personhood" and have viewed that relationship and its effect in a variety of ways. For some it is seen as the occasion for the fashioning of a son's sex-role identity—it provides him with an opportunity to observe the concrete expression of maleness in the life of his father and to accept or not that gender role for himself. Others view the impact of that relationship in even broader terms, in the evolution of a son's sense of identity which includes every aspect of his existence. According to this view, the father assumes the role of the principal socializing agent in the life of his son, determining to a large degree the son's fundamental experience of himself and of others, as well as his values and aspirations. Mowrer (1950) spoke of the father coming forward after the time in which the mother appears to be the more significant figure, "as the boy's special mentor, as his proctŏr, guide, and model." Emmerich (1959) agreed with that observation. He found fathers serving as role models more frequently than mothers in the lives of their sons. The effect of that role modeling upon a son's personal adjustment has been the object of much attention. Its relationship to certain vocational strivings on the part of sons has likewise been assessed. Flugel (1929) hypothesized that the choice of one's occupation, in many instances, is a function of the identification which a son makes with his father. Flugel's estimate of the importance of the father-son relationship in this regard is corroborated by the findings of Berdie (1943) and Crites (1962), who found that sons' vocational interests were related to their identification with their fathers. Yet, most studies which have attempted to assess the impact of fathers' role model upon sons' vocational

Based on part of a doctoral dissertation submitted to Teachers College, Columbia University. Committee members: Donald E. Super (Chairman), Allen E. Bergin, Paul E. Eiserer.

strivings and adjustments have been deficient in two general and important ways.

First, most efforts to assess the impact of fathers as role models upon their sons' behaviors have been confined to a narrow period of time. Usually attention has been given to the process of identification in childhood *or* adolescence *or* young adulthood. Clearly, what may be true of that relationship and its consequences during adolescence may not obtain during young adulthood when selections of others beyond the family as role models may surpass the father-son relationship in importance.

Second, a deficiency of much of the vocational research in this area stems from the same limited perspective afforded by studies which are not longitudinal in design. Concern with such matters as occupational choice and vocational interests without reference to the wide range of time and circumstance in which vocational behaviors occur has made it impossible to relate the findings to the broader range of career and other behaviors.

One intention of this study was to describe and to compare fathers with other key figures for the extent to which they appeared to serve as role models for their sons at two different points in time: when Ss were freshmen in high school (Grade 9) and when Ss were 7 years out of high school (Grade 19). The second intention was to determine whether or not father role modeling in adolescence and young adulthood was differentially related to sons' vocational adjustments and behaviors in young adulthood. It was believed that such an examination might provide insights into the place and importance of the father-son relationship for the vocational development and behaviors of youth.

METHOD

Typescripts of tape-recorded interviews, conducted with 142 males as part of the Career Pattern Study (Super & Overstreet, 1960), were used in the study. Two sets of interviews were available for each S. The first series took place when Ss were in the ninth grade, the second when Ss had been out of high school for 7 years (or Grade 19).

SUBJECTS

Interviews with 101 Ss were recorded and transcribed at the two periods. All Ss resided in Middletown, New York, or in its immediate vicinity during the time that the first interview was conducted. The interviews focused upon Ss' educational, vocational, and other behaviors. They were semi-structured, and each S was encouraged to speak about his leisure time, school, and family roles, his plans for the future, and his attitudes toward himself.

DEFINITIONS

Role Model. A role model was operationally defined as any person about whom S made "similarity," "imitation," or "assimilation" statements. The first kind of statement contained specific references to another person acknowledging a similarity, resemblance, or likeness (or their opposites, that is, a "negative" role model statement). The second kind of statement was a reference indicating that *S* wanted to be like (or unlike) another person. The third kind of role model statement was any specific reference to another person whose ideas, standards, or values *S* claimed to have adopted or refused to adopt.

A role model's raw score was a function of: (a) the number of different types of role model relationships (similarity and/or imitation and/or assimilation) he had with *S, (b)* their apparent importance to *S, and (c)* the number of separate thoughts or references *S* made to the role model within this context. Consideration was also given to the life-sphere (educational, occupational, or personal) in which the role modeling occurred. For example, if a statement about a person was related to the vocational enterprise ("I want to be a mechanic like my father," etc.), he was considered an occupational role model. A role model's raw score in a given sphere was then compared to scores received by every other role model of every other *S* in that sphere. This comparison resulted in the role model's assignment to a quintile status which reflected the extent to which he served as a role model: Those in the fourth and fifth quintiles were considered "most positive"; those in the third quintile, "moderate"; those in the first and second quintiles, "least positive."

Overall Role Modeling. An "overall" role-modeling score was the average of a person's role-model status in all of the spheres (educational, occupational, and personal) in which he scored at a given period. For example, a person whose quintile average as a role model to his son, while the latter was in the ninth grade, was greater than or equal to 4 was considered a most positive overall role model in the ninth grade.

RELIABILITY

Two judges read the interviews of 10 *S*s selected at random and ranked each role model in descending order of the positiveness of his role modelship in the spheres and at the time period in which he scored. A Pearsonian correlation coefficient was derived from the agreement of rankings. The coefficients ranged .80–.99.

OCCUPATIONAL CRITERIA

The *S*s' vocational adjustments and behaviors in young adulthood to which fathers' role-model scores were related were chosen for their presumed relevance and because of their already established relationships to important elements of vocational development. These criteria included the following:

1. *Attainment of school-leaving occupational goal.* Those *S*s who entered any of the occupations which they considered entering at the time

they were seniors in high school were designated as those who had attained their occupational goals.

2. *Realism of S's reasons for move.* This was defined as the extent to which the reasons which an *S* offered for leaving one job for another were remedied or lessened by the move which they made.

3. *Occupational level.* The position held by *S* at age 25 (young adulthood) was judged for occupational level using the Hamburger revision of the Warner Scale, in which "lower" scores are associated with higher occupational levels.

4. *Position success.* Each *S* was asked to rate on a 5-point scale how well he performed in each of seven aspects of his last regular position.

5. *Occupational satisfaction.* An *S*'s score was based upon the extent to which he desired to continue in his present occupation.

6. *Career satisfaction.* The *S*s were distinguished according to the degree of their satisfaction with their careers. Each *S* was asked whether or not he was satisfied with the direction his career was taking.

METHODS OF ANALYSIS

The one-way analysis of variance was used to compare the occupational behaviors of group memberships which were based upon the extent to which their fathers served as role models at a given time period. In addition, Dunn's method of contrasts was used when the analysis of variance and *F* test had shown overall significance.

RESULTS

ROLE MODEL ASSIGNMENTS AT GRADES 9 AND 19

Table 1 presents findings with respect to the number of fathers and other key figures about whom role model statements were made at the

Table 1
**Number of Role Model Assignments
at Grades 9 and 19**

Role Model	Grade 9	Grade 19
Father	98	74
Mother	79	26
Parent substitute	7	10
Sibling	42	24
Peer	8	54
Teacher	5	25
Adult relative	25	68
Other adult	9	36
Employer	0	21

Table 2
Number of Fathers, Mothers, and Nonparents Receiving
Positive or Negative Scores on the Role-Model Variables in
Grades 9 and 19

| Role Model | Grade 9 | | | | Grade 19 | | | |
Variable	F	M	NP	Total	F	M	NP	Total
Pos. educ.	20	21	11	52	5	5	14	24
Neg. educ.	9	3	12	24	6	1	9	16
Pos. occup.	81	26	43	150	49	10	110	169
Neg. occup.	80	27	9	116	42	2	17	61
Pos. personal	89	47	34	170	23	11	76	110
Neg. personal	23	19	24	66	10	4	15	29

Note. Abbreviated: F = father, M = mother, NP = nonparent.

two periods. Whereas parents, siblings, and·adult relatives were named most frequently by *S*s while they were in Grade 9, at Grade 19 they were more apt to think of their peers, teachers, adult relatives, and employers as role models.

Table 2 presents the number of fathers, mothers, and nonparents who received positive and/or negative role model scores. A father might be a positive assimilation but a negative imitation role model in the occupational sphere, for example, and therefore appear in both the positive and negative categories. While more fathers were positive than negative role models at both periods, a greater percentage became negative with the increasing age of their sons. Few mothers appeared as significant role models after Grade 9, at which period they were more positive than negative except in the occupational sphere. Nonparents emerged as increasingly more significant and positive role models at Grade 19. By that period, 58% of the positive educational role models, 65% of the positive occupational role models, and approximately 70% of the positive personal role models were nonparental.

RELATIONSHIP OF FATHER ROLE MODELING TO OCCUPATIONAL CRITERIA

Of all the role models which *S*s possessed in the ninth grade, only fathers' role modeling was related to their sons' vocational behaviors 10 years later. The *S*s who could be distinguished on the basis of their fathers' occupational and overall role model statuses in the ninth grade were found to be functioning differently at age 25.

Table 3 indicates that sons whose fathers were most positive occupational role models in Grade 9 tended to attain their occupational goals to a higher degree than those whose fathers were least positive role models.

Table 4 indicates that sons whose fathers were most positive occupational role models in Grade 9 tended to be rated higher on position success than those whose fathers were least positive, moderate, or nonscoring role models.

Table 5 shows that those Ss whose fathers were most positive overall

Table 3

Relationship of Father Occupational Role Modeling in Grade 9 to Attainment of Goal in Grade 19

Father's Rating as an		Attainment of Goal		
Occupational Role Model	*N*	*M*	*SD*	*F*
Most positive	31	1.41	.50	3.42*
Least positive	45	1.15	.36	
Moderate or no score	14	1.28	.46	

* *p* < .05.

Table 4

Relationship of Father Occupational Role Modeling in Grade 9 to Position Success in Grade 19

Father's Rating as an		Position Success		
Occupational Role Model	*N*	*M*	*SD*	*F*
Most positive	26	2.42	.57	3.34*
Least positive	47	2.06	.63	
Moderate or no score	12	2.00	.60	

* *p* < .05.

Table 5

Relationship of Father Overall Role Modeling in Grade 9 to Attainment of Goal in Grade 19

Father's Rating as an Overall		Attainment of Goal		
Role Model	*N*	*M*	*SD*	*F*
Most positive	23	1.47	.51	3.76*
Least positive	28	1.21	.41	
Moderate	39	1.17	.38	

* *p* < .05.

role models in Grade 9 tended to attain their occupational goals to a significantly higher degree than those whose fathers were moderate overall role models.

Table 6 supports the demonstrated relationship of father overall role modelship in Grade 9 to vocational behaviors in Grade 19. The Ss whose fathers were most positive overall role models in Grade 9 tended to be significantly more realistic in their job changes than those whose fathers were moderate overall role models.

Finally, Table 7 indicates that sons whose fathers were most positive overall role models in Grade 9 tended to score significantly higher in occupational satisfaction in Grade 19 than those whose fathers were moderate overall role models.

In Grade 19 the role modeling of fathers was found to be related quite differently to the occupational behaviors of sons in Grade 19. Whereas in Grade 9 the positive role modeling of fathers was related to the affective functioning of sons in Grade 19, the sons whose fathers were moderate or nonscoring role models in Grade 19 functioned most effectively at that time period.

Table 6

Relationship of Father Overall Role Modeling in Grade 9 to Realism in Grade 19

Father's Rating as an Overall Role Model	*N*	Realism		
		M	*SD*	*F*
Most positive	23	54.78	7.18	7.15**
Least positive	31	51.48	5.93	
Moderate	44	49.36	4.24	

** *p* < .01.

Table 7

Relationship of Father Overall Role Modeling in Grade 9 to Occupational Satisfaction in Grade 19

Father's Rating as an Overall Role Model	*N*	Occupational Satisfaction		
		M	*SD*	*F*
Most positive	23	3.04	1.06	5.13**
Least positive	31	2.35	.98	
Moderate	44	2.18	1.10	

** *p* < .01.

Table 8 indicates that Ss whose fathers were moderate or nonscoring occupational role models in Grade 19 scored significantly higher on occupational role models.

Table 9 shows that those Ss whose fathers were moderate or nonscoring occupational role models in Grade 19 scored significantly higher on career

Table 8

Relationship of Father Occupational Role Modeling in Grade 19 to Occupational Satisfaction in Grade 19

Father's Rating as an *Occupational Role Model*	N	Occupational Satisfaction		
		M	SD	F
Most positive	12	1.83	.38	3.59*
Least positive	35	1.62	.49	
Moderate or no score	35	1.88	.32	

*p < .05.

Table 9

Relationship of Father Occupational Role Modeling in Grade 19 to Career Satisfaction in Grade 19

Father's Rating as an *Occupational Role Model*	N	Career Satisfaction		
		M	SD	F
Most positive	16	2.43	.81	5.24**
Least positive	37	2.02	.89	
Moderate or no score	42	2.59	.66	

*p < .01.

Table 10

Relationship of Father Overall Role Modeling in Grade 19 to Occupational Level in Grade 19

Father's Rating *as an Overall* *Role Model*	N	Occupational Level		
		M	SD	F
Most positive	16	4.37	1.31	3.37*
Least positive	37	4.86	1.29	
Moderate	29	4.00	1.43	

*p < .05.

satisfaction than those whose fathers were least positive occupational role models.

Table 10 indicates that those whose fathers were moderate overall role models in Grade 19 reached a significantly higher occupational level than those whose fathers were least positive.

DISCUSSION

The findings support the thinking of those who have supposed that the role modeling of fathers has an important effect upon sons' vocational adjustment. Both the occupational and overall role modeling of fathers have been found to be related to sons' vocational behaviors. Certain aspects of that relationship which appear in the present study are worth noting.

First, it was found that significant differences in vocational adjustment existed between those whose fathers were most positive role models in Grade 9 and those whose fathers were moderate or nonscoring role models, and usually not between the former group and those whose fathers were least positive role models. This curvilinear relationship is not particularly surprising. Although the usual emphasis has been upon the possession of "positive" role models and its relationship to the formation of a sense of identity, it is possible that "negative" role models can also be helpful in the same identity strivings. It may be as important to have in one's environment those with whom one perceives a dissimilarity, whose attitudes or values one refuses to adopt, or whom one would wish not to imitate. Super, Crites, Hummel, Moser, Overstreet, and Warnath (1957) have named both identification with and rejection of role models as possible determinants of career patterns. Their importance may be more similar than it has been commonly realized. Each may serve as important occasions for self-definition.

A second finding of some interest was that father role-model categories in Grade 9 and Grade 19 were differentially related to occupational criteria in young adulthood. Whereas moderation in father role modeling at Grade 9 was found to be associated with lower scores of sons on these criteria, in Grade 19 moderation in the father-son role model relationship tended to be associated with occupational success and satisfaction on the part of their sons. It would appear that what may be appropriate with regard to the use of fathers as role models in adolescence is no longer so in young adulthood. The latter period has been thought of as involving a trend toward increased autonomy, as the giving up of internalized parents, as the opportunity for the selection of new models. It is not surprising, therefore, that this study found nonparents emerging as increasingly significant role models as the adolescent *S*s moved into young adulthood. And those *S*s whose fathers were moderate or even nonscoring role models at this period and whose statuses appeared to denote a disengagement with them on the part of their sons appeared to function more effectively in young adulthood than those *S*s whose relationship with their fathers represented a continuing and negative involvement. It may be that adolescents need their fathers as important sources of self-definition even into adolescence but must move on, in young adulthood, to new and different but important experiences of others.

SUMMARY

Research on the effects of father role modeling upon sons' vocational behaviors has usually failed to relate that experience to a broad range of career and other behaviors and to assess those differences in the modeling's effect which may depend upon whether it occurs in adolescence or in young adulthood. These deficiencies prompted the present investigation.

Using the information provided by semistructured interviews which had been conducted with Ss when they were freshmen in high school and again when they had been out of high school for 7 years, Ss' role models were identified at these periods, and the extent to which they served as role models was assessed. In addition, Ss who differed in the extent to which their fathers had served as role models in adolescence and young adulthood were compared with each other in regard to six occupational criteria.

It was found that although fathers served as the most important role models for their sons in adolescence, nonparents emerged as increasingly significant role models as sons moved into young adulthood.

It was also found that only fathers' role modelships in adolescence were predictive of sons' future occupational behaviors. Those sons whose fathers served as most positive occupational or overall role models at that time were found to function more effectively as young adults than those whose fathers were moderate or nonscoring role models. However, those whose fathers were moderate or nonscoring role models for their sons in young adulthood functioned more effectively (that is, scored higher on the occupational criteria) than those whose fathers served as least positive role models. It would appear that while it is important for fathers to serve as positive role models for their adolescent sons, such is not the case after their sons have become young adults.

REFERENCES

Berdie, R. F. Factors associated with vocational interests. *Journal of Educational Psychology,* 1943, *34:* 257–277.

Crites, J. O. Parental identification in relation to vocational interest development. *Journal of Educational Psychology,* 1962, *53:* 262–270.

Emmerich, W. Parental identification in young children. *Genetic Psychology Monographs,* 1959, *60:* 257–308.

Flugel, J. C. *The psychoanalytic study of the family.* New York: Hogarth Press, 1929.

Mowrer, O. H. Identification: A link between learning theory and psychotherapy. In, *Learning theory and personality dynamics.* New York: Ronald Press, 1950.

Super, D. E., Crites, J. O., Hummel, R. C., Moser, H. P., Overstreet, P. L., & Warnath, C. F. *Vocational development: A framework for research.* New York: Teachers College, Columbia University, 1957.

Super, D. E., & Overstreet, P. L. *The vocational maturity of ninth grade boys.* New York: Teachers College, Columbia University, 1960.

maternal influences upon college women's attitudes toward women and work

Grace K. Baruch
University of Massachusetts

Women's inability to attain work status comparable to that of men, especially with respect to achievement in the professions, has frequently been attributed to such barriers as discrimination by employers, scarcity of day-care centers, and "male chauvinism." Recent research has indicated, however, the relevance of attitudes of women themselves. In a theoretical article, Keniston and Keniston (1964) have analyzed the ambivalent, often negative, attitudes of many able women toward work and toward a dual role pattern of career and family. Tracing the origins of these attitudes to nineteenth century social realities, the authors attribute their persistence to "anachronistic images of womanliness and work, defensively reasserted by women themselves [p. 358]." Furthermore, images of femininity that exclude career commitments are transmitted from mother to daughter by the powerful process of identification. Thus, women do not unite to fight discrimination but "covertly cooperate" in their own oppression; they define the world of work as masculine.

Some empirical support for the last point of the Keniston and Keniston analysis is found in Goldberg's (1967) study of differential evaluations by college women of male and female professional competence. A set of articles from different professional disciplines was presented to two groups of subjects. Articles were identical in content for both groups but differed in the sex of the first name of the ascribed author. The results were that ratings of articles ascribed to women were consistently lower than those of male articles, regardless of the sexual association of the professional field.

Goldberg tentatively attributed the differential evaluations to antifeminism in women, comparable in dynamics to self-prejudices of other out groups, as analyzed by Allport (1958). One implication of this interpretation is that women who devalue feminine competence would be expected

Data reported here are taken from a dissertation submitted in partial fulfillment of the requirements for the PhD degree at Bryn Mawr College. The research was supported by a grant from the American Association of University Women. The author is grateful to Dean Peabody of Swarthmore College for help in arranging for subjects and to Christa Vanderbilt and Joelle Blair for conducting the interviews.

to associate negative consequences with being a professionally competent woman and to have negative attitudes toward the career role for women. Horner (1968) has attributed the "motive to avoid success," found in able women, to their anxiety over the consequences of success, in that "unusual excellence in academic intellectual or other competitive achievement becomes consciously or unconsciously equated with a loss of femininity and the possibility of social rejection becomes very real [p. 3]."

The major objective of the present study is to evaluate both the "prejudice" interpretation of Goldberg's findings and an alternate interpretation in which devaluations of feminine competence are viewed as products of a set of traditional assumptions about dimensions of the male and female sex roles that are held by women whose mothers have not worked. Vogel, Broverman, Broverman, Clarkson, and Rosenkrantz (1970) found among female college students that the tendency to stereotype and differentiate the male and female sex roles, especially on the dimension of competence, was associated with a nonworking mother; for these women competence was linked to masculinity and was not part of the feminine sex role.

The importance of studying the mother also applies with respect to the prejudice interpretation. Because of the crucial process of identification, it is the maternal model's attitudes, experiences, and problems with respect to work that are viewed as the major determinants of whether a women will associate negative consequences with a career commitment.

The specific hypothesis derived from the prejudice interpretation includes the predictions that (*a*) the tendency to devalue feminine competence is associated with a negative attitude toward career women and the dual role pattern; and (*b*) mothers of devaluers are negative and conflicted in their own attitudes and experiences with respect to the dual role pattern. (Dual role pattern and career role are used interchangeably because it is assumed that most women anticipate a domestic role in considering the career issue.) The specific hypothesis derived from the competence model interpretation is that the tendency to devalue is associated with a nonworking mother.

Determining the nature of the devaluations is important for approaching the problem of changing the status and attitudes of women; changes should be more difficult to the extent that women's self-devaluations are embedded in complex personality dynamics.

METHOD

OVERALL DESIGN

A two-stage design was used in this study. Measures of tendency to devalue feminine professional competence and of attitude to the dual role pattern were administered to a large sample of college women in a group testing session. A personal data sheet was also included to explore some related variables. From this large sample, subjects in the high and low quartiles in tendency to devalue were selected for individual interviews about relevant maternal variables. The relationship of these variables to subjects' standing on each measure was then examined. (Both because identification is assumed to take place with the child's image of the parent and for reasons of feasibility, the maternal model was studied through subjects' responses.)

SUBJECTS

For this study college students were actually the subjects of choice. First, high intellectual ability was required so that devaluations could not be attributed to realistic self-assessments. Second, all subjects had to be at the same stage of their life cycle, since women's attitudes toward work have been shown to be related to these stages (Baruch, 1967). Finally, in the college years, the career issue is salient, while realistic considerations of husband, family, and geography are of minimal influence. The subjects were students at Swarthmore College, a small coeducational liberal arts college with rigorous intellectual standards. In order to avoid revealing the focus of the study, all male as well as female students were invited to become paid volunteers, and some males were actually selected for the first stage. Only data for female subjects are reported here, however. Of 110 females, 22 served as a control group for an intended replication of Goldberg's study. There were 88 experimental subjects; complete data were received from 86. The subjects were almost entirely upper-middle-class whites; fathers of 71 experimental subjects had at least the BA degree; 68 fathers were in professional or high level business occupations. Approximately half of the subjects were freshmen, and the rest were divided almost equally among the upper three classes. The study was carried out in the fall of 1968 and the spring of 1969.

MEASURES AND PROCEDURE: FIRST STAGE

Articles Test. This test was adapted from Goldberg (1967). Articles from eight professional fields were abridged and combined in booklets; for any one article, half of the booklets had a male author's first name and half a female's. Each booklet had four male and four female articles, one from each field. As empirically determined by Goldberg, two fields had a masculine sexual association, two were feminine, and four were neutral. (Because of a plan to investigate the effect of article content on evaluations, two high-interest and two low-interest neutral articles were included.)

Seven questions followed each article, the same for all articles and subjects. The form used permitted repeated presentation of the name of the author: "With respect to its value for the general reader, what grade would you assign to Miss/Mr. X's article?" Subjects used a 12-point rating scale to grade each article for (a) value for the general reader, (b) value for the professional reader, (c) logic, (d) persuasiveness, (e) estimated professional competence of the author, (f) originality and creativity, and (g) estimated status of the author in his or her professional field. The directions described the test as one of students' ability to evaluate professional literature regardless of their knowledge of the field.

Attitude Scale. Attitude toward the dual role pattern was assessed by a Likert-type scale of 26 items, selected on the basis of pretests with another student group. Items concerned (a) the desirability of a career orientation in women, (b) the compatibility of the career and family roles, (c) the femininity of career women, and (d) women's ability to achieve intellectual excellence. Half of the statements were favorable and half unfavorable. Subjects used a 5-point rating scale to indicate degree of agreement with each item.

Personal Data Sheet. Information was obtained about the parents education and occupation, siblings, religion, college major, and college board scores. The most important item concerned maternal employment. Because women's work patterns are often irregular and intermittent, subjects were simply asked to list maternal occupation if the mother had worked regularly during any part of the preceding 6 years. This approach was based on the assumption that women tend to seek employment as their children get older. This assumption later proved incorrect. Interview data indicated that several mothers had worked when their children were young but had later given up the dual role pattern. In the second part of the study, therefore, a more detailed analysis of maternal employment was carried out.

The Articles Test was administered first and immediately collected, so that responses could not be affected by the other measures, which revealed the purposes of the study.

RESULTS OF THE FIRST STAGE

Articles Test. For the sample as a whole, no significant differences were found between mean scores given the male articles and mean scores given the female articles. These data are not presented in detail here, but they rendered further analyses of the no author group and of the effect of article content pointless. Thus, women in this sample, contrary to Goldberg's, did not devalue feminine competence.

Attitude Scale. The mean for the sample for the Attitude scale was 92.91. A subject consistently endorsing the neutral position would have received a raw score of 78 (26 items of 5 points each). Therefore, the sample as a whole indicated a favorable attitude toward the dual role pattern.

Relationship Between Devaluations and Attitude. Individual scores for the Articles Test were calculated by subtracting the mean score given the four female articles from the mean score given the male articles. These raw discrepancy scores were converted into z prime scores $(50 + 10z)$ as were raw scores from the Attitude scale. As analyzed by a Pearson product-moment correlation, there was no significant relationship between the two sets of scores ($r = .124$, $df = 84$), contrary to what was predicted from the prejudice hypothesis.

Maternal Employment. Of 86 mothers, 43 were classified as employed. The mean score for the Articles Test for subjects whose mothers worked was 51.92; for subjects whose mothers did not work it was 47.42. A one-tailed t test indicated this difference to be significant at the .025 level

($t = 2.05$). The competence model hypothesis is supported by this finding that the tendency to devalue was significantly greater among subjects with nonworking mothers.

The relationship of maternal employment to subjects' attitudes toward the dual role pattern was also examined. The mean scores for the Attitude scale for subjects whose mothers worked was 51.33; for subjects whose mothers did not work it was 49.07. This difference was not significant ($t = 1.07$); whether a mother works is not related to a subject's attitude toward the dual role pattern.

Contrary to expectation, level of maternal occupation was not related to scores for either measure, although maternal occupations ranged from clerk to physician.

Miscellaneous Variables. No relationship was found between scores for either measure and the variables of birth order and socioeconomic status. (Subjects were quite homogeneous on the latter variable.) A majority of students did not report religion or college board scores, and student unrest in the year of the study made it inadvisable to press for this information. Few subjects had selected a major field, partly because there was a high proportion of freshmen in the sample.

Selection of the Interview Sample. Subjects were ranked according to the Articles Test using the z prime scores described above. Those in the high and low quartiles in tendency to devalue ($n = 44$) were then selected for the interview sample. For the 22 subjects in the high quartile the significance of differences in their evaluations of male and female articles was tested using the Mann-Whitney U Test. Results of this analysis are presented in Table 1. For all fields but literary criticism and education,

Table 1

Mann-Whitney U Tests and Mean Scores for the Male and Female Forms of the Articles: 22 Subjects in the High Quartile

Field of Article	Mean : Female Author Form	Mean : Male Author Form	U
Linguistics	26.21	59.62	7***
City planning	32.93	52.85	11***
Nutrition	53.60	62.46	32*
Psychology	52.22	67.54	20**
Novel	58.39	52.01	43
Law	52.31	62.23	33*
Education	62.08	65.10	36
Sociology	51.31	64.82	32*

* $p < .05$, one-tailed test.
** $p < .01$, one-tailed test.
*** $p < .001$, one-tailed test.

differences were significant at the .05 level or better. The direction of differences for all questions for all pairs of articles was then evaluated by a sign test. Of 56 mean comparisons, 45 favored the male article and 10 the female; there was one tie. The sign test yielded a z of 4.58 ($p < .0005$). Thus, there is evidence that the basis of selection was meaningful.

Of 44 selected subjects, 4 had left college by the time the interviews were conducted; the remaining 40 were successfully interviewed.

MEASURES AND PROCEDURES: SECOND STAGE

Because the experimenter was familiar with the attitude scores of the subjects, interviews were conducted by two assistants. The interviews lasted approximately 45 minutes and were tape recorded. An open-ended interview schedule was developed to guide the sessions, which dealt with maternal experiences, conflicts, feelings, and attitudes concerning work and the feminine role, with fathers' attitudes in this area, and with the subjects' reactions to their mothers' choices and patterns. The major objective of the interviews was to determine, to use Keniston and Keniston's phrase, what the "lesson of the mother's life" was, for the subject's own view of the social and personal consequences of commitment to a career.

A list of all the variables rated is presented in Table 2. Not all are relevant to data reported here, but the full list indicates the nature of the interviews.

Table 2
List of All the Variables Rated in Interviews

Variable	Scale
Mother as model of dual role compatibility	3 point
Maternal commitment to work	3 point
Maternal endorsement of the dual role pattern	3 point
Mother's happiness in personal life	3 point
Maternal role conflict	2 point
Maternal satisfaction with pattern choice	2 point
Maternal interest in career-related achievement	2 point
Consistency of mother's actual and preferred pattern	2 point
Quality of subject's relationship to mother	3 point
Subject's desire for mother's pattern	3 point
Father's acceptance of career-oriented wife	3 point
Father's satisfaction in own work	3 point
Subject's desire for career	3 point
Subject's expectation of regular employment for most of adult life	2 point
Subject's identification with career oriented women	3 point
Subject's evaluation of femininity of career-oriented women	2 point
Friends' attitudes toward dual role pattern	2 point
Desire for husband favorable to career-oriented wife	3 point

After each interview the interviewer listened to the tape and then rated each variable. A 2-point, high/low scale was used where possible, but some variables proved to require a 3-point scale. The experimenter served as second rater, listening to each tape and rating the variables. Interrater reliability was exactly the same between the experimenter and each interviewer: 90.7%.

RESULTS

MATERNAL EMPLOYMENT

The maternal employment variable was reexamined for the interview sample for two reasons. First, interview data revealed that several mothers not employed during the preceding 6 years had worked regularly during the subjects' childhood. This period of employment was as relevant to this study as present or recent employment and these mothers were therefore categorized as employed. Second, the determination of what actually constituted employment proved a complicated matter. For example, a mother might give three piano lessons a week or work long hours for no pay in her husband's business. It was finally decided that to be classified as employed a mother must have worked for at least 2 years of the subject's life in paid employment of at least one-quarter time.

The mean score for the Articles Test for subjects whose mothers had worked was 53.73; for subjects whose mothers had never worked it was 41.33. Results of a one-tailed t test indicated this difference to be significant at the .005 level ($t = 3.15$). The significance of the difference in mean scores for the Attitude scale was also tested. The means were 53.32 and 47.67, respectively; the difference was not significant ($t = 1.67$).

The results again support the competence model hypothesis that tendency to devalue is associated with a nonworking mother. They further confirm that maternal employment per se has no effect upon subjects' attitudes toward the dual role pattern.

RESULTS FOR INTERVIEW VARIABLES

Results of analysis of six maternal variables are summarized in Tables 3 and 4. Three variables were analyzed by chi-square tests: (a) maternal role conflict; (b) maternal interest in career-related achievement; and (c) maternal endorsement of the dual role pattern. Analyses of variance were possible for the other three variables: (d) mother as model of dual role compatibility; (e) father's acceptance of career-oriented wife; and (f) maternal commitment to work.

There was no significant relationship between any of these variables and the tendency to devalue; attitudes and experiences with respect to work and the dual role pattern were no more negative for mothers of devaluers. Thus, there is no reason to assume that devaluers were motivated to internalize negative attitudes toward feminine professionals and to label their competence as inferior.

Table 3

Chi-Square Tests for Relevant Maternal Variables

	Articles Test[a]		Attitude Scale[b]	
Variable	χ^2	*df*	χ^2	*df*
Maternal role conflict	1.23	1	1.87	1
Maternal interest in career-related achievement	.97	1	6.51*	1
Maternal endorsement of dual role pattern	2.76	2	15.26**	2

[a] Twenty-one devaluers versus 19 nondevaluers.
[b] Twenty-one favorable versus 19 unfavorable subjects.
* $p < .01$.
** $p < .0005$.

Table 4

Analyses of Variance: Effect of Relevant Maternal Variables upon Test Scores

	Articles Test		Attitude Scale	
Variable	*F*	*df*	*F*	*df*
Mother as model of dual role compatibility	1.44	2	3.98*	2
Father's acceptance of career-oriented wife	.94	2	5.35**	2
Maternal-commitment to work	1.41	2	5.63**	2

* $p < .05$.
** $p < .01$.

The relationship between the maternal variables and subjects' attitudes toward the dual role pattern was also examined. For the chi-square tests, subjects were classified as favorable or unfavorable on the basis of whether they were above or below the mean score for the whole sample for the Attitude scale. Results for Variables *a, b,* and *c* were, respectively, 1.87 ($df = 1$, *ns*), 6.51 ($df = 1$, $p < .01$), and 15.26 ($df = 2$, $p < .0005$). Analyses of variance for Variables *d, e,* and *f* yielded *F* ratios of 3.98 ($df = 2$, $p < .05$), 5.35 ($df = 2$, $p < .01$), and 5.63 ($df = 2$, $p < .01$), respectively. Thus, significant relationships were found for all variables except maternal role conflict. That variable was faulty in design because it included as high in role conflict both mothers who work but preferred not to and mothers who did not work but desired to work. The data indicate overall that the mother's attitude toward the dual role pattern and her success with respect to it were significantly related to the subject's attitude.

DISCUSSION

Two major factors may explain the finding that the sample as a whole did not evaluate male and female competence differentially. First, 5 years elapsed between Goldberg's study and the present one, and during those years major changes occurred in social attitudes with respect to women and work. Second, the population from which Goldberg's subjects were drawn were students at a traditionally oriented women's college and may have chosen such a college for reasons related to traditional image of femininity.

With respect to those subjects who did devalue feminine competence, no support was found for the prejudice hypothesis. There was no evidence of negative attitudes toward the career role for women nor of any maternal influence that would lead the devaluers to associate negative consequences with that role and defensively to adopt antifeminism.

Results did support the competence model hypothesis that it is women whose mothers have not worked who devalue feminine competence. Career-related achievement is apparently defined as masculine by women who have not been exposed to a maternal model of work competence.

However, maternal employment was not an influence upon subjects' attitudes toward the dual role pattern. Whether a subject is favorable to such a pattern depends instead upon whether her mother endorses it and, if the mother works, upon how successfully she has integrated her two roles. Thus, if a subject's mother had worked but had also experienced negative personal consequences because of her career, the subject evaluated women's competence highly but was unfavorable to the dual role pattern.

This distinction may be important in approaching the problem of changing women's status and attitudes. One implication of this study is that, if increasing numbers of women enter the work force and attain high positions, the tendency to devalue feminine professional competence will decrease and work may even lose its masculine label. There seems no reason to assume a critical period for the effect of feminine competence model; in the present study, even recently begun maternal employment was associated with high evaluations of women's competence. Nor should it be necessary that the model be the mother. Keniston and Keniston (1964) specifically suggested that feminine competence models among college faculty could be a profound influence upon young women at an age when they are in search of new models, goals, and values. The findings also imply, however, that to be attractive the dual role pattern must be rewarding and free from serious difficulties. The importance of such facilitating devices as day care centers is clear.

Finally, just as the tendency to devalue feminine competence and attitudes about the dual role pattern proved to be independent, the social goal of improving the image of women's professional abilities can be separated from the militant advocacy of lifelong careers for all women. Because most women will ultimately need to turn to pursuits other than child rearing, it should be a matter of general concern that they evaluate themselves as capable of competence and excellence.

REFERENCES

Allport, G. W. *The nature of prejudice.* New York: Anchor, 1958.

Baruch, R. The achievement motive in women: Implications for career development. *Journal of Personality and Social Psychology,* 1967, *5:* 260–267.

Goldberg, P. Misogyny and the college girl. Paper presented at the meeting of the Eastern Psychological Association, Boston, April 1967.

Horner, M. S. A psychological barrier to achievement in women: The motive to avoid success. Paper presented at the meeting of the Midwestern Psychological Association, May 1968.

Keniston, K., & Keniston, E. An American anachronism: The image of women and work. *American Scholar,* 1964, *33:* 355–375.

Vogel, S. R., Broverman, I. K., Broverman, D. M., Clarkson, F., & Rosenkrantz, P. S. Maternal employment and perception of sex roles among college students. *Developmental Psychology,* 1970, *3:* 384–391.

ten

identity, moral development, and values

part ten

Establishing a sense of one's own identity—a definition of one's self as a person—is a central task of adolescence. Without some guiding sense of who he is and where he is headed, the adolescent faces formidable obstacles in attempting to cope with the varied demands of the adolescent period: demands for increasing independence, integration of his newfound sexual maturity, establishment of meaningful and workable relations with peers of both sexes, and deciding on his life work and personal goals.

But establishing a secure and positive ego identity is not an easy task, particularly during adolescence. It requires a perception of the self as *separate* from others (despite similarities between one's self and others and ties to them). It also requires a feeling of wholeness, of *self-consistency,* not only in the sense of internal consistency at a particular moment but also over time. One needs to have a feeling that the person he is today is similar to (though obviously not precisely the same as) the person he was yesterday. This is not a simple matter for the emerging adolescent, faced as he is with a rapidly changing physical self, new and often strange subjective feelings brought on by sexual maturation, and changing—and frequently conflicting—expectations on the part of adults and peers alike.

How successful the adolescent boy or girl will ultimately be in establishing a confident self-identity will depend in great measure on the appropriateness of prior and current parental relationships and on the way he or she is perceived and treated by society generally.

As Erik H. Erikson notes in the first selection in this part, identity formation "begins where the usefulness of identification ends. It arises from the selective repudiation and mutual assimilation of childhood identifications and their absorption in a new configuration, which in turn is dependent on the process by which a society (often through subsocieties) identifies the young individual, recognizing him as somebody who had to become the way he is and who, being the way he is, is taken for granted." While identity subsumes a variety of specific identifications, the whole is clearly greater than the sum of its parts, for these individual identifications could not, "if merely added up, result in a functioning personality."

The problem of identity cannot be separated from that of values. To maintain some stability in his conception of himself and in his internal guides to action in a complex, constantly changing world, the adolescent (or, for that matter, the adult) must be *faithful* to some values. He may have to adopt new ways of implementing these values to meet changing circumstances. But if the values are there and if they are sound, he will be able to adapt to change while remaining relatively constant in his conception of his own basic identity.

In the second article, Lawrence Kohlberg and Carol Gilligan discuss the results of their investigations of moral development. They and their colleagues found that the child's and adolescent's moral development tends to progress through an orderly series of sequential stages, and the ability to progress from one stage to the next depends on corresponding progress in cognitive development. As the adolescent enters the formal operational stage of cognitive development (see pp. 42–81), his thinking about values also becomes more abstract, complex, and characterized by "a major thrust toward autonomous moral principles which have validity and application apart from authority of the groups or persons who hold them and apart from the individual's identification with those persons or groups." At this stage many adolescents, particularly the brighter and more sophisticated, may no longer be able to accept without question the social or political beliefs of their parents. They think about moral behavior in terms of general rights and standards that have been examined and agreed on by society as a whole. As adolescence proceeds, an increasing orientation toward inner concerns with conscience may develop—away from "other directedness" and toward more "inner directedness." In some cases, the exceptional adolescent may go on to achieve what Kohlberg and Gilligan view as the "highest" stage of moral reasoning: the ability to formulate and be guided by abstract "ethical principles appealing to logical comprehensiveness, universality, and consistency."

It is well to recognize that moral development, conscience, and concern with values are not solely a result of cognitive development. Changing societal demands, intrapsychic conflicts, parent-child relationships, and other factors may all play a significant role. In the third article, Martin L. Hoffman discusses some of the findings of his research on the influence of parental absence on conscience development. In particular, he found that the absence of a father is likely to have adverse effects on a boy's conscience development. Father-absent early adolescent boys obtained lower scores than boys from intact families on measures of moral values, internal moral judgment, guilt, and acceptance of blame. Hoffman also presents evidence that these effects "may be somewhat greater than the effects of nonidentification with a father who is present, which suggests that some but not all of the effects of father absence are attributable to the lack of a paternal model."

He reasons that the findings in this study may also be due in part to changes in the mother's child-rearing behavior brought on by paternal absence. Thus, for example, he found that women without husbands appear to express less affection toward their sons than those with husbands present in the home. Finally, he found a lack of similar effects of paternal absence in the case of girls, presumably because girls are more likely to adopt their mothers as models and identify with them.

Identification and Identity

Erik H. Erikson
Harvard University

. . . The autobiographies of extraordinary (and extraordinarily self-perceptive) individuals are one source of insight into the development of identity. In order to describe the universal genetics of identity, one would wish to be able to trace its development through the life histories of "ordinary" individuals. Here I must rely on general impressions from daily life, on guidance work with mildly disturbed young people, and on my participation in one of the rare "longitudinal" studies—a source which excludes the detailed publication of biographic data. In the following genetic sketch, some repetition of what has been said previously is unavoidable.

Adolescence is the last stage of childhood. The adolescent process, however, is conclusively complete only when the individual has subordinated his childhood identifications to a new kind of identification, achieved in absorbing sociability and in competitive apprenticeship with and among his age mates. These new identifications are no longer characterized by the playfulness of childhood and the experimental zest of youth: with dire urgency they force the young individual into choices and decisions which will, with increasing immediacy, lead to commitments "for life." The task to be performed here by the young person and by his society is formidable. It necessitates, in different individuals and in different societies, great variations in the duration, intensity, and ritualization of adolescence. Societies offer, as individuals require, more or less sanctioned intermediary periods between childhood and adulthood, often characterized by a combination of prolonged immaturity and provoked precocity.

In postulating a "latency period" which precedes puberty, psychoanalysis has given recognition to some kind of psychosexual moratorium in human development—a period of delay which permits the future mate

Excerpted from Chapter IV, Identity: Youth and Crisis by Erik H. Erikson. New York: Norton, 1968, pp. 155–161. W. W. Norton & Company, Inc., and Faber and Faber Ltd. Copyright © 1968 by W. W. Norton & Company, Inc. By permission of the author and publishers.

and parent first to go to whatever "school" his culture provides and to learn the technical and social rudiments of a work situation. The libido theory, however, offers no adequate account of a second period of delay, namely, prolonged adolescence. Here the sexually matured individual is more or less retarded in his psychosexual capacity for intimacy and in the psychosocial readiness for parenthood. This period can be viewed as a *psychosocial moratorium* during which the young adult through free role experimentation may find a niche in some section of his society, a niche which is firmly defined and yet seems to be uniquely made for him.

If, in the following, we speak of the community's response to the young individual's need to be "recognized" by those around him, we mean something beyond a mere recognition of achievement; for it is of great relevance to the young individual's identity formation that he be responded to and be given function and status as a person whose gradual growth and transformation makes sense to those who begin to make sense to him. It has not been sufficiently recognized in psychoanalysis that such recognition provides an entirely indispensable support to the ego in the specific tasks of adolescing, which are: to maintain the most important ego defenses against the vastly growing intensity of impulses (now invested in a matured genital apparatus and a powerful muscle system); to learn to consolidate the most important "conflict-free" achievements in line with work opportunities; and to resynthesize all childhood identifications in some unique way and yet in concordance with the roles offered by some wider section of society—be that section the neighborhood block, an anticipated occupational field, an association of kindred minds, or perhaps (as in Shaw's case) the "mighty dead." A moratorium is a period of delay granted to somebody who is not ready to meet an obligation or forced on somebody who should give himself time. By psychosocial moratorium, then, we mean a delay of adult commitments, and yet it is not only a delay. It is a period that is characterized by a selective permissiveness on the part of society and of provocative playfulness on the part of youth, and yet it also often leads to deep, if often transitory, commitment on the part of youth, and ends in a more or less ceremonial confirmation of commitment on the part of society. Such moratoria show highly individual variations, which are especially pronounced in very gifted people (gifted for better or for worse), and there are, of course, institutional variations linked with the ways of life of cultures and subcultures.

Each society and each culture institutionalizes a certain moratorium for the majority of its young people. For the most part, these moratoria coincide with apprenticeships and adventures that are in line with the society's values. The moratorium may be a time for horse stealing and vision-quests, a time for *Wanderschaft* or work "out West" or "down under," a time for "lost youth" or academic life, a time for self-sacrifice or for pranks—and today, often a time for patienthood or delinquency. For much of juvenile delinquency, especially in its organized form, must be considered to be an attempt at the creation of a psychosocial moratorium. In fact, I would assume that some delinquency has been a relatively institutionalized moratorium for a long time in parts of our society, and that it forces itself on our awareness now only because it proves too attractive and compelling for too many youngsters at once. In addition to all this, our society seems to be in the process of incorporating psychiatric treatment as one of the few permissible moratoria for young people who otherwise would be crushed by standardization and mechanization. This we must consider carefully, for the label or diagnosis one acquires during the psychosocial moratorium is of the utmost importance for the process of identity formation.

But the moratorium does not need to be consciously experienced as such. On the contrary, the young individual may feel deeply committed and may learn only much later that what he took so seriously was only a period of transition; many "recovered" delinquents probably feel quite estranged about the "foolishness" that has passed. It is clear, however, that any experimentation with identity images means also to play with the inner fire of emotions and drives and to risk the outer danger of ending up in a social "pocket" from which there is no return. Then the moratorium has failed; the individual is defined too early, and he has committed himself because circumstances or, indeed, authorities have committed him.

Linguistically as well as psychologically, identity and identification have common roots. Is identity, then, the mere sum of earlier identifications, or is it merely an additional set of identifications?

The limited usefulness of the mechanism of identification becomes obvious at once if we consider the fact that none of the identifications of childhood (which in our patients stand out in such morbid elaboration and mutual contradiction) could, if merely added up, result in a functioning personality. True, we usually believe that the task of psychotherapy is the replacement of morbid and excessive identifications by more desirable ones. But as every cure attests, "more desirable" identifications at the same time tend to be quickly subordinated to a new, unique Gestalt which is more than the sum of its parts. The fact is that identification as a mechanism is of limited usefulness. Children at different stages of their development identify with those part aspects of people by which they themselves are most immediately affected, whether in reality or fantasy. Their identifications with parents, for example, center in certain overvalued and ill-understood body parts, capacities, and role appearances. These part aspects, furthermore, are favored not because of their social acceptability (they often are everything but the parents' most adjusted attributes) but by the nature of infantile fantasy which only gradually gives way to more realistic judgment.

In later childhood the individual is faced with a comprehensible hierarchy of roles, from the younger siblings to the grandparents and whoever else belongs to the wider family. All through childhood this gives him some kind of a set of expectations as to what he is going to be when he grows older, and very small children identify with a number of people in a number of respects and establish a kind of hierarchy of expectations which then seeks "verification" later in life. That is why cultural and historical change can prove so traumatic to identity formation: it can break up the inner consistency of a child's hierarchy of expectations.

If we consider introjection, identification, and identity formation to be the steps by which the ego grows in ever more mature interplay with the available models, the following psychosocial schedule suggests itself.

The mechanism of *introjection* (the primitive "incorporation" of another's image) depends for its integration on the satisfactory mutuality between the mothering adult(s) and the mothered child. Only the experience of such initial mutuality provides a safe pole of self-feeling from which the child can reach out for the other pole: his first love "objects."

The fate of childhood *identifications,* in turn, depends on the child's satisfactory interaction with trustworthy representatives of a meaningful hierarchy of roles as provided by the generations living together in some form of family.

Identity formation, finally, begins where the usefulness of identification ends. It arises from the selective repudiation and mutual assimilation of childhood identifications and their absorption in a new configuration, which, in turn, is dependent on the process by which a society (often through subsocieties) identifies the young individual, recognizing him as somebody who had to become the way he is and who, being the way he is, is taken for granted. The community, often not without some initial mistrust, gives such recognition with a display of surprise and pleasure in making the acquaintance of a newly emerging individual. For the community in turn feels "recognized" by the individual who cares to ask for recognition; it can, by the same token, feel deeply—and vengefully—rejected by the individual who does not seem to care.

A community's ways of *identifying* the *individual,* then, meet more or less successfully the individual's ways of identifying himself with others. If the young person is "recognized" at a critical moment as one who arouses displeasure and discomfort, the community sometimes seems to suggest to the young person that he change in ways that to him do not add up to anything "identical with himself." To the community, the desirable change is nevertheless conceived of as a mere matter of good will or of will power ("he could if he wanted to") while resistance to such change is perceived as a matter of bad will or, indeed, of inferiority, hereditary or otherwise. Thus the community often underestimates to what extent a long, intricate childhood history has restricted a youth's further choice of identity change, and also to what extent the community could, if it only would, still help to determine a youth's destiny within these choices.

All through childhood tentative crystallizations of identity take place which make the individual feel and believe (to begin with the most conscious aspect of the matter) as if he approximately knew who he was— only to find that such self-certainty ever again falls prey to the discontinuities of development itself. An example would be the discontinuity between the demands made in a given milieu on a little boy and those made on a "big boy" who, in turn, may well wonder why he was first made to believe that to be little is admirable, only to be forced to exchange this more effortless status for the special obligations of one who is "big now." Such discontinuities can, at any time, amount to a crisis and demand a decisive and strategic repatterning of action, leading to compromises which can be compensated for only by a consistently accruing sense of the practicability and feasibility of such increasing commitment. The cute, or ferocious, or good small boy who becomes a studious, or gentlemanly, or tough big boy must be able—and must be enabled—to combine both sets of values in a recognized identity which permits him, in work and play and in official and intimate behavior, to be (and to let others be) a combination of a big boy and a little boy.

The community supports such development to the extent that it permits the child, at each step, to orient himself toward a complete "life plan" with hierarchical order of roles as represented by individuals of different ages. Family, neighborhood, and school provide contact and experimental identification with younger and older children and with young and old adults. A child, in the multiplicity of successive and tentative identifications, thus begins early to build up expectations of what it will be like to be older and what it will feel like to have been younger—expectations which become part of an identity as they are, step by step, verified in decisive experiences of psychosocial "fittedness."

The final identity, then, as fixed at the end of adolescence, is superordinated to any single identification with individuals of the past: it includes all significant identifications, but it also alters them in order to make a unique and reasonably coherent whole of them. . . .

the adolescent as a philosopher: the discovery of the self in a post-conventional world

Lawrence Kohlberg   **Carol Gilligan**
Harvard University

Those whose exterior semblance doth belie
Thy Soul's immensity;
Thou best Philosopher . . .

Thou little child, yet glorious in the might
Of heaven-born freedom on thy Being's height,
Why with such earnest pains dost thou provoke,
The years to bring the inevitable yoke?
Thus blindly with thy blessedness at strife?
Full soon thy Soul shall have her earthly freight,
And customs lie upon thee with a weight
Heavy as frost, and deep almost as life!

The thought of our past years in me doth breed
Perpetual benediction; not indeed
For that which is most worthy to be blest;
Delight and liberty, the simple creed of childhood . . .
But for those obstinate questionings
Of sense and outward things,
Fallings from us, vanishings;
Blank misgivings of a creature
Moving about in worlds not realized,
High instincts before which our mortal Nature
Did tremble like a guilty thing surprised:

—Wordsworth, *Intimations of Immortality*

Reprinted by permission of Daedalus. Journal of the American Academy of Arts and Sciences, Boston, Massachusetts. "Twelve to Sixteen: Early Adolescence," Fall 1971, 100, 1051–1086.

The central themes of this essay are first, the definition of adolescence as a universal stage of development; second, the way in which the universal features of adolescence seem to be acquiring unique colorings in the present era in America; and third, the implications of these changes for education.

ADOLESCENCE AS A ROLE TRANSITION AND AS A STAGE OF DEVELOPMENT

In turn-of-the-century America, G. Stanley Hall launched developmental psychology with his discussion of adolescence as a stage of development. For the next fifty years, however, most American educators and psychologists tended to think about adolescence not as a stage but as a period in life, "the teens." The teenager was viewed as half-child, half-grown up, with a half-serious peer "culture" or "youth culture" of his own. Textbook after textbook on adolescence was written telling in statistical detail the sort of information which could be gathered from reading *Seventeen* or Harold Teen.

Even with the textbook description of the teenager, one could surmise that the central phenomenon of adolescence is the discovery of the self as something unique, uncertain, and questioning in its position in life. The discovery of the body and its sexual drive, and self-conscious uncertainty about that body, is one stock theme of adolescent psychology. The romantic concerns and hopes for the self's future has always been another element of the stock description of the adolescent. The third stock theme implied by the discovery of the self is the need for independence, for self-determination and choice, as opposed to acceptance of adult direction and control. The fourth stock theme implied by the adolescent discovery of self is adolescent egocentrism and hedonism, the adolescent focus upon events as they bear upon his self-image and as they lead to immediate experiences. (While the child is egocentric and hedonistic, he is not subjective; he focuses upon events, not upon his subjective experience of the events, as what is important.)

While the discovery of the self in the senses just listed has been a stock theme in American discussion of adolescence, it has been subordinated to another theme, the theme of adolescence as a marginal role between being a child and being grown-up. The adolescent sense of self, with its multiple possibilities, its uncertainties, and its self-consciousness has been viewed as the result of a social position in which one is seen and sees oneself, sometimes as adult, sometimes as child. In the marginal role view, the adolescent's need for independence and fantasies of the future are seen as the desire to "be grown-up," his conflicts and instabilities are seen as the conflict between the desire to be grown-up and a role and personality not yet consistent with being grown-up.

This social role view of adolescence, the adolescent as teenager, places the instability of the adolescent self against the background of a stable society. Against the background of the moods and tantrums and dreams of the American teenager lay an unquestioned acknowledgment of the stability and reality of the social order the adolescent was to enter. Underneath the hedonism and rebellion of the teenager lay the conformist. Harold Teen and Andy Hardy's first law was conformity to the norms of the peer group. Beneath this conformity to the peer group, however, was the teenager's recognition that when the chips were down about your future you listened to dear old Dad. An extreme example in reality of the American image of the teenager as cutting up while basically conforming is a group of California suburban high school seniors of the late 1950's. This group celebrated graduation by a summer of well-planned robberies. Their one concern while they engaged in their delinquent activities was that if they were detected, they would not get into the college of their choice.

Conformity to the peer culture, then, was the first theme of the American treatment of the adolescent in the fifties, of August Hollingshead's *Elmtown's Youth,* James Coleman's *Adolescent Society,* Albert K. Cohen's *Delinquent Boys.* The second theme was that this peer culture was itself determined by the realities of adult social class and mobility in which the peer culture was embedded. Whether grind, jock or hood, glamour girl, sex kitten or Plain Jane, the teenager's discovery of self led to the enactment of the stock roles of the adolescent culture. At a different level than the sociology of the teenager, American literature also presented adolescence as accepting unquestioningly the reality of adult society. Adolescence was presented as an imaginative expansion of the innocence of childhood facing the sordid but unquestionable reality of adult life. From *Huckleberry Finn* to *Catcher in the Rye,* the true American adolescent brought the child's innocence to a new awareness of adult reality, leading to a vision of the phoniness and corruption of the adult world, which was, however, unquestioned in its reality. Sherwood Anderson's story of the fourteen-year-old finding his father figure with a prostitute is titled "I Want to Know Why." While the American adolescent might be shocked by the sordid elements of adult life and might "want to know why" there was no question that he would eventually enter and accept "adult reality." Even when he wanted to know why, the American adolescent seldom questioned the American assumptions of progress and upward mobility, the assumption that society was moving ahead. Rather, he questioned the wisdom of his parents because they were old-fashioned. This questioning was itself an expression of faith in the adult society of the future. The adolescent's sense of the superiority of his values to those of his parents was an expression of the adolescent's belief in a greater closeness to the adult society of the future than his parents had; it was a faith in progress.

Today, we are aware of the possibility of a deeper questioning by the adolescent than was true at earlier times. Our image of the adolescent must accommodate to the phenomena of the counterculture, of the hippie and the revolutionary who does not believe in progress and upward mobility. Both the hippie and the New Left reject not only the *content* of adult society but its *forms.* The new radical refuses to organize as his revolutionary predecessors of the thirties did. Unlike the revolutionary of the thirties, he does not want to be grownup, to really transform and govern the adult society of the future. And beneath a questioning of social *forms* is a questioning of social *functions.* The current radical rejection of adult society seems to be the rejection of any adult society whatever, if an adult society means one including institutions of work, family, law, and government. Radicals have always questioned the social *forms* of authority, of competitive achievement, and of the nuclear privatistic family and have dreamed of a more egalitarian and communal society. The essential realities of the social *functions* of work, child rearing, and of an organized social order were never questioned, however. Since Paul Goodman's *Growing Up Absurd,* we have been aware that the reality of work and making a living has come into question. Now the new ethics of population control and the Women's Liberation Movement leads to the questioning of the supreme reality of adulthood, being a parent and having children. Finally, the reality of social order is in question. When current adolescents talk of revolution, they do not seem to mean merely that adult society is evil and is resistant to rational change. More deeply, they seem to be saying that there is no real social order to destroy anyway. Social order is a myth or illusion in the adult's mind and revolution is not the destruction of an order, whether good or bad. On the optimistic side this is the message of Charles Reich's "revolution in consciousness," the idea that the young can transform society without entering or dealing with it. On the pessimistic side, the popular versions of the counterculture reiterate the theme of *Easy Rider,* the theme that the adult culture is hostile and absurd, that it does not want you to join it but that it envies you and will destroy you in the end no matter what you do.

To summarize, all accounts of adolescence stress both the sense of questioning and the parallel discovery or search for a new self of the adolescent. Usually this questioning and search for self has been seen as the product of the adolescent's marginal role between childhood and adulthood. Usually, too, it has been assumed that there are underlying givens beneath the questioning, that whatever uncertainties the adolescent has, he wants to be a grownup. Recent experience makes real for Americans the much deeper forms of questioning which may characterize adolescence, one which is not merely a matter of roles. The potential for a deeper questioning by the adolescent is implied by the identity conflict central to Erik Erikson's psychohistorical stage theory of adolescence. It is the philosophic doubting about truth, goodness, and reality implied by J. Piaget's epistemological stage theory of adolescence. It is the doubting represented by Dostoevsky's adolescents, not Mark Twain's. Deeper doubting is still a rare phenomenon, for adolescents. Beneath most hippie exteriors is an interior more like Harold Teen than Hamlet or Raskolnikov. But theoretical understanding of adolescence as a stage must stress its ideal type potential, not its "average" manifestations.

The importance of taking adolescent questioning seriously is not only important for psychological theory, it is also central to a successful resolution of the current problems of the American high school. For education, the problem of meaning just raised is the problem of whether the high school has meaning to the adolescent. We said that American psychology placed the adolescent discovery of the self against a stable but progressive social order. It saw the discovery of self within a desire to be "grown up," however, confused or vague this image of the grownup was. The high school had a double meaning to the adolescent from this point of view. First, it was the locus of the peer culture in which he found his immediate identity, whether as grind, jock, or hood. Second, on the academic side, it was a point of connection to a place in the adult world. In most high schools these meanings still remain and the questioning of the reality of adulthood is not that deep. In others, however, it is a serious problem and high school is essentially a meaningless place. Before we can solve the problem of the felt meaninglessness of the high school, a clearer view of adolescent questioning is required. For this, we must turn to stage theory of the Erikson and Piaget variety.

THE MEANING OF THE STAGE CONCEPT—ILLUSTRATED FROM THE PRESCHOOL YEARS

To understand the universal meanings of adolescence as a stage and its implications for education, it will help to examine briefly an earlier stage and its implications for education, one more thoroughly understood than the stage of adolescence. Almost all cultures implicitly recognize two great stages or transformations in development. Adolescence, the second transformation, traditionally terminated compulsory schooling. The first transformation occurring from five to seven years of age initiated compulsory schooling.[1] This five-to-seven shift is termed the "onset of the latency period" by Freudian theory, the onset of concrete logical thought by Piaget. As embodied in educational thought, the Freudian interpretation of the five-to-seven shift implied letting the child grow, letting him work through his fantasies until he had repressed his sexual instincts and was ready to turn his energies into formal learning. This Freudian interpretation of the preschool stage suffered both from lack of confirmation by empirical research and from irrelevance to the intellectual development and everyday behavior with which the schools were concerned. When the Great Society decided to do something for the disadvantaged child, the Freudian "let him work through his oedipus complex" implications of the five-to-seven shift were dismissed as a luxury for the wealthy. Programs of preschool intellectual stimulation and academic schooling were initiated, with the expectation of long-range effects on intelligence and achievement. These programs failed to fulfill their initial hope of changing general intellectual maturity or long-range achievement.[2]

One reason they failed was because they confused specific teaching and learning with the development of new levels of thinking truly indicative of cognitive maturity. The evidence of limitations of these early education programs, together with growing positive research evidence of the existence of cognitive stages, convinced early educators of the reality of the stage transformation at the age five to seven. The stage transformation of the period five to seven is now conceived in quite a different way than in the vogue of Freudian education. In the Freudian view, the preschooler was in a stage of domination of thought by sexual and aggressive fantasies. The new stage which succeeded this was defined negatively as latency, rather than positively. Under the influence of Piaget, more recent thinking sees the preschool child's fantasy as only one aspect of the preschooler's pattern of prelogical thought. In the prelogical stage, subjective appearance is not fully distinguished from "reality"; the permanent identities of things are not differentiated from their momentary transformations. In the prelogical stage view, the preschool child's special fantasy is not the expression of an instinct later repressed but of cognitive level of thought. The decline of fantasy in the years five to seven, longitudinally documented by R. Scheffler,[3] is not a repression; it is closely related to the positive development of concrete logical patterns of thought.

The child's changed orientation to reality in the five-to-seven period is part of the development of concrete logical operations then. During this period the child develops the operations of categorical classifications, of serial ordering, addition, subtraction, and inversion of classes and relations. This development occurs in the absence of schooling in African and Taiwanese villagers in much the same way that it occurs in the American suburban child.[4]

As a concrete example, Piaget and the writers have asked children if they had had a bad dream and if they were frightened when they woke up from their bad dream.[5] Susie, aged four, said she dreamt about a giant and answered, "Yes, I was scared, my tummy was shaking and I cried and told my mommy about the giant." Asked, "Was it a real giant or was it just pretend? Did the giant just seem to be there, or was it really there?" she answered, "It was really there but it left when I woke up. I saw its footprint on the floor."

According to Piaget, Susie's response is not to be dismissed as the product of a wild imagination, but represents the young child's general failure to differentiate subjective from objective components of his experience. Children go through a regular series of steps in their understanding of dreams as subjective phenomena. The first step, achieved before five by most American middle-class children, is the recognition that dreams are not real events. The next step, achieved soon thereafter, is the realization that dreams cannot be seen by others. The third step is the notion that dreams are internal (but still material) events.

By the ages six to eight children are clearly aware that dreams are thoughts caused by themselves. To say such cognitive changes define stages implies the following things:

(1) That young children's responses represent not mere ignorance or error, but rather a spontaneous manner of thinking about the world that is qualitatively different from the way we adults think and yet has a structure of its own.

(2) The notion of different developmental structures of thought implies consistency of level of response from task to task. If a child's response represents a general structure rather than a specific learning, then the child should demonstrate the same relative structural levels in a variety of tasks.

(3) The concept of stage implies an invariance of sequence in development, a regularity of stepwise progression regardless of cultural teaching or circumstance. Cultural teaching and experience can speed up or slow down development, but it cannot change its order or sequence.

The concept of stage, then, implies that both the youngest children's conceptions of the dream as real and the school age children's view of the dream as subjective are their own; they are products of the general state of the child's cognitive development, rather than the learning of adult teachings.

Cross-cultural studies indicate the universality of the basic sequence of development of thinking about the dream, even where adult beliefs about the meaning and significance of dreams is somewhat different from our own.[6] While the stage of concrete operations is culturally universal and in a sense natural, this does not mean it is either innate or that it is inevitable and will develop regardless of environmental stimulation. In the United States, the doctrine of stages was assumed for sometime to mean that children's behavior unfolded through a series of age-specific patterns, and that these patterns and their order were wired into the organism. This indeed was the view of Gesell and Freud, and Americans misunderstood Piaget as maintaining the same thing. The implications of the Gesellian and Freudian theory for early education were clear; early teaching and stimulation would do no good since we must wait for the unfolding of the behavior, or at least the unfolding of the readiness to learn it.

In contrast, Piaget used the existence of stages to argue that basic cognitive structures are not wired in, but are general forms of equilibrium resulting from the interaction between organism and environment. If children have their own logic, adult logic or mental structure cannot be derived from innate neurological patterning because such patterning should hold also in childhood. (It is hardly plausible to view a succession of logics as an evolutionary and functional program of innate wiring.) At the same time, however, Piaget argued that stages indicate that mental structure is not merely a reflection of external physical realities or of cultural concepts of different complexities. The structure of the child's concepts in Piaget's view is not only less complex than the adult's, it is also different. The child's thought is not just a simplified version of the adult's.

Stages, or mental structures, then, are not wired into the organism though they depend upon inborn organizing tendencies. Stages are not direct reflections of the child's culture and external world, though they depend upon experience for their formation. Stages are rather the products of interactional experience between the child and the world, experience which leads to a restructuring of the child's own organization rather than to the direct imposition of the culture's pattern upon the child. While hereditary components of IQ, of the child's rate of information processing, have some influence on the rate at which the child moves through invariant cognitive sequences, experiential factors heavily influence the rate of cognitive-structural development.[7] The kind of experience which stimulates cognitive stage development is, however, very different from the direct academic teaching of information and skills which is the focus of ordinary schooling. Programs of early education which take account of cognitive stages, then, look neither like the permissive "let them grow" nursery school pattern nor like the early teaching programs popular in the sixties. They are a new form now coming into being.[8]

COGNITIVE STAGES IN ADOLESCENCE

The older children get, the more difficult it is to distinguish universal stage changes from sociocultural transitions in development. We said that the core phenomenon of adolescence as a stage was the discovery of the subjective self and subjective experience and a parallel questioning of adult cultural reality. The manifestations of this discovery, however, are heavily colored not only by historical and cultural variations, but also by previous patterns of life history of the child.

In our first section, we discussed one manifestation of the discovery of the self, the discovery of the body and its sexual drives. In part this is, of course, a biological universal, the physical growth spurt marking adolescent puberty and an accompanying qualitatively new sex drive. If there is anything which can be safely said about what is new in the minds of adolescents, it is that they, like their elders, have sex on their minds. These changes, of course, have been the focus of Freudian thinking about adolescence as a stage. If anything, however, Freudian thinking has underestimated the novel elements of sexual experience in adolescence. For the Freudian, early adolescent sexuality is the reawakening of early childhood sexuality previously latent, with a consequent resurrection of oedipal feeling. Although it is true that adolescent sexuality bears the stamp of earlier experience, it is not the resurrection of earlier sexual feelings. Adolescent sexual drive is a qualitatively new phenomenon.[9]

While sexual drives are awakened at puberty, there are vast individual and cultural variations in the extent to which they determine the adolescent's behavior and experience. Sexuality is a central concern for the self of some fourteen-year-olds; it is something deferred to the future for others. What is common for all, however, is an intensified emotionality whether experienced as sexual or not. This emotionality, too, is now experienced as a part of the self, rather than as a correlate of objective events in the world. C. Ellinwood studied the age development of the verbal experiencing and expression of emotion in projective tests and in free self-descriptions. She found that prior to adolescence (age twelve or so), emotions were experienced as objective concomitants of activities and objects. The child experienced anger because events or persons were bad; he experienced affection because persons were good or giving; he felt excitement because activities were exciting or fun. At adolescence, however, emotions are experienced as the result of states of the self rather than as the direct correlate of external events.[10]

The difference may perhaps be clarified by reference to middle-class drug experiences. Occasionally, a psychological preadolescent may take drugs, as he may drink beer or sneak cigarettes. When he does this, he does this as an activity of an exciting forbidden and grown-up variety. For the adolescent drug-taker, drugs represent rather a vehicle to certain subjective moods, feelings, and sensations. In many cases, the drug experience is a vehicle for overcoming depression, felt as an inner subjective mood. In any case, drug-taking is not an activity with an objective quality; it is a mode of activating subjective inner feelings and states. The same is true of such activities as intensive listening to music, an activity characteristically first engaged in at early adolescence (ages eleven to fourteen). The rock, folk-rock, and blues music so popular with adolescents is explicitly a presentation of subjective mood and is listened to in that spirit.

Associated with the discovery of subjective feelings and moods is the discovery of ambivalence and conflicts of feeling. If feelings are objective correlates of external good and bad events, there can be little tolerance and acceptance of feeling hate and love for the same person, of enjoying sadness and feeling sad about pleasure. Ellinwood's study documents that adolescents are consciously expressing such ambivalence, which is of course the stock in trade of the blues and folk-rock music beamed to them.

We have spoken of the adolescent discovery of subjective moods and feelings as linked to puberty. More basically, it is linked to the universal cognitive stages of Piaget. We have said that the five-to-seven transition is defined by Piaget as the transition to *abstract, reflective* thought. More exactly, it is the transition from logical inference as a set of *concrete operations* to logical inference as a set of *formal operations* or "operations upon operations." "Operations upon operations" imply that the adolescent can classify classification, that he can combine combinations, that he can relate relationships. It implies that he can think about thought, and create thought systems or "hypothetico-deductive" theories. This involves the logical construction of all possibilities—that is, the awareness of the observed as only a subset of what may be logically possible. In related fashion, it implies the hypothetico-deductive attitude, the notion that a belief or proposition is not an immediate truth but a hypothesis whose truth value consists in the truth of the concrete propositions derivable from it.

An example of the shift from concrete to formal operations may be taken from the work of E. A. Peel.[11] Peel asked children what they thought about the following event: "Only brave pilots are allowed to fly over high mountains. A fighter pilot flying over the Alps collided with an aeriel cable-way, and cut a main cable causing some cars to fall to the glacier below. Several people were killed." A child at the concrete-operational level answered: "I think that the pilot was not very good at flying. He would have been better off if he went on fighting." A formal-operational child responded: "He was either not informed of the mountain railway on his route or he was flying too low also his flying compass may have been affected by something before or after take-off this setting him off course causing collision with the cable."

The concrete-operational child assumes that if there was a collision the pilot was a bad pilot; the formal-operational child considers all the possibilities that might have caused the collision. The concrete-operational child adopts the hypothesis that seems most probable or likely to him. The formal-operational child constructs all possibilities and checks them out one by one.

As a second example, we may cite one of Piaget's tasks, systematically replicated by D. Kuhn, J. Langer, and L. Kohlberg.[12] The child is shown a pendulum whose length may vary as well as the number of weights attached. The child is asked to discover or explain what determines the speed of movement (or "period") of the pendulum. Only the formal-operational child will "isolate variables," that is, vary length holding weight constant, and so forth, and arrive at the correct solution (for example, that period is determined by length). Success at the task is unrelated to relevant verbal knowledge about science or physics, but is a function of logical level.

In fact the passage from concrete to formal operations is not an all or none phenomenon. There are one or two substages of formal operations prior to the full awareness of all possibilities just described. These substages are described in Table 1, which presents an overview of the Piaget cognitive stages. For simplifying purposes, we may say that for middle-class Americans, one stage of formal operations is reached at age ten to thirteen, while the consideration of all possibilities is reached around fifteen to sixteen. At the first formal-operational stage, children became capable of reversing relationships and ordering relationships one at a time or in chains, but not of abstract consideration of all possibilities. (They are capable of "forming the inverse of the reciprocal," in Piaget's terminology; but not of combining all relationships.) A social thinking example of failure to reverse relationships is shown in concrete-operational children's responses to the question: "What does the Golden Rule tell you to do if someone comes up on the street and hits you?" The typical answer is "hit him back, do unto others as they do unto you." The painful process of the transitional formal-operational child in response to the question is given by the following response: "Well for the Golden Rule you have to like dream that your mind leaves your body and goes into the other person, then it comes back into you and you see it like he does and you act like the way you saw it from there."[13]

We have described Piaget's stage of formal operations as a logical stage. What is of special importance for understanding adolescents, however, is not the logic of formal operations, but its epistemology, its conception of truth and reality. In the previous section we said that the child's attainment of concrete operations at age six to seven led to the differentiation of subjective and objective, appearance and reality. The differentiation at this level was one in which reality was equated with the physical and the external. We cited the child's concept of the dream, in which the unreality of the dream was equivalent to its definition as an inner mental event with no physical external correlate. The subjective and the mental are to the concrete-operational child equated with fantasies, with unrealistic replicas of external physical events. The development of formal operations leads, however, to a new view of the external and the physical. The external and the physical are only one set of many possibilities of a subjective experience. The external is no longer the real, "the objective," and the internal the "unreal." The internal may be real and the external unreal. At its extreme, adolescent thought entertains solipsism or at least the Cartesian cogito, the notion that the only thing real is the self. I asked a fifteen-year-old girl: "What is the most real thing to you?" Her unhesitating reply was "myself."

The lines from Wordsworth introducing this essay represent his own adolescent experience described by him as follows: "I was often unable to think of external things as having external existence, and I communed with all that I saw as something not apart from, but inherent in, my own material nature. Many times while going to school have I grasped at a wall or tree to recall myself from this abyss of idealism to the reality. At this time I was afraid of such processes."[14]

Wordsworth's adolescent solipsism was linked to his awakened poetic sense, to his experience of nature, and to his transcendental religiosity. It seems that for all adolescents the discovery of the subjective is a condi-

Table 1
Piaget's Eras and Stages of Logical and Cognitive Development

---

Era I (age 0–2) The era of sensorimotor intelligence

Stage 1. Reflex action.
Stage 2. Coordination of reflexes and sensorimotor repetition (primary circular reaction).
Stage 3. Activities to make interesting events in the environment reappear (secondary circular reaction).
Stage 4. Means/ends behavior and search for absent objects.
Stage 5. Experimental search for new means (tertiary circular reaction).
Stage 6. Use of imagery in insightful invention of new means and in recall of absent objects and events.

Era II (age 2–5) Symbolic, intuitive, or prelogical thought

Inference is carried on through images and symbols which do not maintain logical relations or invariances with one another. "Magical thinking" in the sense of (a) confusion of apparent or imagined events with real events and objects and (b) confusion of perceptual appearances of qualitative and quantitative change with actual change.

Era III (age 6–10) Concrete operational thought

Inferences carried on through system of classes, relations, and quantities maintaining logically invariant properties and which *refer to concrete objects*. These include such logical processes as (a) inclusion of lower-order classes in higher order classes; (b) transitive seriation (recognition that if $a > b$ and $b > c$, then $a > c$); (c) logical addition and multiplication of classes and quantities; (d) conservation of number, class membership, length, and mass under apparent change.

Substage 1. Formation of stable categorical classes.
Substage 2. Formation of quantitative and numerical relations of invariance.

Era IV (age 11 to adulthood) Formal-operational thought

Inferences through logical operations upon propositions or "operations upon operations." Reasoning about reasoning. Construction of systems of all possible relations or implications. Hypothetico-deductive isolation of variables and testing of hypotheses.

Substage 1. Formation of the inverse of the reciprocal. Capacity to form negative classes (for example, the class of all not-crows) and to see relations as simultaneously reciprocal (for example, to understand that liquid in a U-shaped tube holds an equal level because of counterbalanced pressures).

Substage 2. Capacity to order triads of propositions or relations (for example, to understand that if Bob is taller than Joe and Joe is shorter than Dick, then Joe is the shortest of the three).

Substage 3. True formal thought. Construction of all possible combinations of relations, systematic isolation of variables, and deductive hypothesis-testing.

tion for aesthetic feeling in the adult sense, for the experience of nature as a contemplative experience, and for religiosity of a mystical varity. It is probably the condition for adolescent romantic love as well. This whole constellation of experiences is called romantic because it is centered on a celebration of the self's experience as the self enters into union with the self's counterpart outside. The common view of romanticism as adolescent, then, is correct in defining the origins of romanticism in the birth of the subjective self in adolescence.

If the discovery of subjective experience and the transcendental self is one side of the new differentiation of subjective and objective made by the adolescent, the clouding and questioning of the validity of society's truths and its rightness is the other. To consider this side of adolescence we must turn from cognitive to moral stages.

Before we turn to adolescent moral thought we need to note a real difference between the development of concrete operations and the development of formal operations. There are two facts which distinguish the adolescent revolution in logical and epistemological thinking from the five-to-seven revolution in thinking. The first is that the adolescent revolution is extremely variable as to time. The second is that for many people it never occurs at all. With regard to concrete operations, some children attain clear capacity for logical reasoning at five, some at eight or nine. But all children ultimately display some clear capacity for concrete-logical reasoning.[15] This is not true for formal-operational reasoning. As an example, the percentage of 265 persons at various ages showing clear formal-operational reasoning at the pendulum task is as follows:

Age ten to fifteen: 45 per cent

Age sixteen to twenty: 53 per cent

Age twenty-one to thirty: 65 per cent

Age forty-five to fifty: 57 per cent[16]

The subjects studied were lower-middle and upper-middle-class California parents (age forty-five to fifty) and their children (age ten to thirty). The figures indicate that it is not until age twenty-one to thirty that a clear majority (65 per cent) attain formal reasoning by this criteria. They suggest that there is no further development of formal reasoning after age thirty. This means that almost 50 per cent of American adults never reach adolescence in the cognitive sense. The figures should not be taken with too greater seriousness, since various tasks requiring formal operations are of somewhat varying difficulty. In the study cited another problem, a "correlation problem," was used which was passed by even fewer members of the adult population. It is possible that easier tasks could be devised which would lead to more people displaying formal reasoning. The point, however, is that a large proportion of Americans never develop the capacity for abstract thought. Most who do, develop it in earlier adolescence (age eleven to fifteen), but some do not reach full formal reasoning until the twenties. We should note, too, that rate of attainment of formal operations is not simply a function of I.Q.: the correlations between Piaget and I.Q. measures are in the 50's. Finally, in simpler cultures—for example, villages in Turkey—full formal operations never seem to be reached at all (though it is reached by urbanized educated Turks). The high variability in age of attainment of formal operations, then, indicates that we cannot equate a cognitive stage with a definite age period. Puberty, the attainment of formal operations, and the transition from childhood to adult status are all components of adolescence variable in time and in their relations to one another.

MORAL STAGES IN ADOLESCENCE AND THEIR RELATION TO COGNITIVE STAGES

Joseph Adelson, in this volume, documents the way in which the adolescent's thinking about political society is transformed by the advent of formal-operational thought. To understand the adolescent's social thinking, however, we need to be aware not only of logical stages but also of stages of moral judgment. In our research, we have found six definite and universal stages of development in moral thought. In our longitudinal study of seventy-six American boys from preadolescence, youths were presented with hypothetical moral dilemmas, all deliberately philosophical, some of them found in medieval works of causistry.

On the basis of their reasoning about these dilemmas at a given age, each boy's stage of moral thought could be determined for each of twelve basic moral concepts, values, or issues. The six stages of moral thought are divided into three major levels, the *preconventional,* the *conventional,* and the *postconventional* or autonomous.

While the preconventional child is often "well-behaved" and is responsive to cultural labels of good and bad, he interprets these labels in terms of their physical consequences (punishment, reward, exchange of favors) or in terms of the physical power of those who enunciate the rules and labels of good and bad. This level is usually occupied in the middle class by children aged four to ten.

The second or conventional level usually becomes dominant in preadolescence. Maintaining the expectation and rules of the individual's family, group, or nation is perceived as valuable in its own right. There is concern not only with conforming to the individual's social order, but also in maintaining, supporting, and justifying this order.

The postconventional level is first evident in adolescence and is characterized by a major thrust toward autonomous moral principles which have validity and application apart from authority of the groups of persons who hold them and apart from the individual's identification with those persons or groups.

Within each of these three levels there are two discernable stages. At the preconventional level we have: Stage 1: Orientation toward punishment and unquestioning deference to superior power. The physical consequences of action regardless of their human meaning or value determine its goodness or badness. Stage 2: Right action consists of that which instrumentally satisfies one's own needs and occasionally the needs of others. Human relations are viewed in terms like those of the market place. Elements of fairness, reciprocity, and equal sharing are present, but they are always interpreted in a physical, pragmatic way. Reciprocity is a matter of "you scratch my back and I'll scratch yours," not of loyalty, gratitude, or justice.

At the conventional level we have: Stage 3: Good-boy-good-girl orientation. Good behavior is that which pleases or helps others and is approved by them. There is much conformity to stereotypical images of what is majority or "natural" behavior. Behavior is often judged by intention—"he means well" becomes important for the first time and is overused. One seeks approval by being "nice." Stage 4: Orientation toward authority, fixed rules, and the maintenance of the social order. Right behavior consists of doing one's duty, showing respect for authority, and maintaining the given social order for its own sake. One earns respect by performing dutifully.

At the postconventional level we have: Stage 5A: A social-contract orientation, generally with legalistic and utilitarian overtones. Right action tends to be defined in terms of general rights and in terms of standards which have been critically examined and agreed upon by the whole society. There is a clear awareness of the relativism of personal values and opinions and a corresponding emphasis upon procedural rules for reaching consensus. Aside from what is constitutionally agreed upon, right or wrong is a matter of personal values and opinion. The result is an emphasis upon the legal point of view, but with an emphasis upon the possibility of changing law in terms of rational considerations of social utility, rather than freezing it in the terms of Stage 4, law and order. Outside the legal realm, free agreement and contrast are the binding elements of obligation. This is the official morality of American government, and finds its ground in the thought of the writers of the Constitution. Stage 5B: Orientation to internal decisions of conscience but without clear rational or universal principles. Stage 6: Orientation toward ethical principles appealing to logical comprehensiveness, universality, and consistency. These principles are abstract and ethical (the Golden Rule, the categorical imperative); they are not concrete moral rules like the Ten Commandments. Instead, they are universal principles of justice, of the reciprocity and equality of human rights, and of respect for the dignity of human beings as individual persons.

These stages are defined by twelve basic issues of moral judgment. On one such issue, Conscience, Motive Given for Rule Obedience or Moral Action, the six stages look like this:

1. Obey rules to avoid punishment.

2. Conform to obtain rewards, have favors returned, and so on.

3. Conform to avoid disapproval, dislike by others.

4. Conform to avoid censure by legitimate authorities and resultant guilt.

5A. Conform to maintain the respect of the impartial spectator judging in terms of community welfare.

5B. Conform to avoid self-condemnation.

In another of these moral issues, the value of human life, the six stages can be defined thus:

1. The value of a human life is confused with the value of physical objects and is based on the social status or physical attributes of its possessor.

2. The value of a human life is seen as instrumental to the satisfaction of the needs of its possessor or of other persons.

3. The value of a human life is based on the empathy and affection of family members and others toward its possessor.

4. Life is conceived as sacred in terms of its place in a categorical moral or religious order of rights and duties.

5. Life is valued both in terms of its relation to community welfare and in terms of being a universal human right.

6. Belief in the sacredness of human life as representing a universal human value of respect for the individual.

We call our types "stages" because they seem to represent an invariant developmental sequence. True stages come one at a time and always in the same order.

All movement is forward in sequence and does not skip steps. Children may move through these stages at varying speeds, of course, and may be found half in and half out of a particular stage. An individual may stop at any given stage and at any age, but if he continues to move, he must move in accord with these steps. Moral reasoning of the conventional or Stage 3–4 kind never occurs before the preconventional Stage 1 and Stage 2 thought has taken place. No adult in Stage 4 has gone through Stage 6, but all Stage 6 adults have gone at least through 4.

While the evidence is not complete, our study strongly suggests that moral change fits the stage pattern just described. Figures 1 and 2 indicate the cultural universality of the sequence of stages which we found. Figure 1 presents the age trends for middle-class urban boys in the United States, Taiwan, and Mexico. At age ten in each country, the order of use of each stage is the same as the order of its difficulty or maturity. In the United States, by age sixteen the order is the reverse, from the highest to the lowest, except that Stage 6 is still little used. The results in Mexico and Taiwan are the same, except that development is a little slower. The most conspicuous feature is that at the age of sixteen, Stage 5 thinking is much more salient in the United States than in Mexico or Taiwan. Nevertheless, it is present in the other countries, so we know that this is not purely an American democratic construct.

Why should there be such a universal invariant sequence of development? In answering this question, we need first to analyze these developing social concepts in terms of their internal logical structure. At each stage, the same basic moral concept or aspect is defined, but at each higher stage this definition is more differentiated, more integrated, and more general or universal. When one's concept of human life moves from Stage 1 to Stage 2 the value of life becomes more differentiated from the value of property, more integrated (the value of life enters an organizational hierarchy where it is "higher" than property so that one steals property in order to save life) and more universalized (the life of any sentient being is valuable regardless of status or property). The same

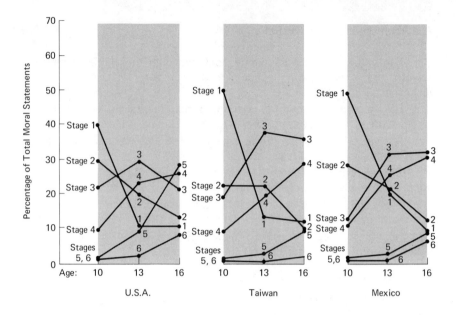

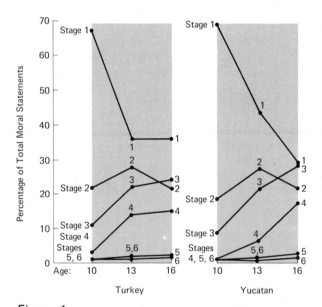

Figure 1
Middle-class urban boys in the U.S., Taiwan and Mexico. At age
10 the stages are used according to difficulty. At age 13, Stage 3
is most used by all three groups. At age 16 U.S. boys have
reversed the order of age 10 stages (with the exception of 6).
In Taiwan and Mexico, conventional (3–4) stages prevail at age 16,
with Stage 5 also little used.

Figure 2
Two isolated villages, one in Turkey, the other in Yucatan, show
similar patterns in moral thinking. There is no reversal of order,
and preconventional (1–2) thought does not gain a clear
ascendancy over conventional stages at age 16.

advance is true at each stage in the hierarchy. Each step of development, then, is a better cognitive organization than the one before it, one which takes account of everything present in the previous stage, but making new distinctions and organizing them into a more comprehensive or more equilibrated structure.

What is the relation of moral stage development in adolescence to cognitive stage development? In Piaget's and our view, both types of thought and types of valuing (or of feeling) are schemata which develop a set of general structural characteristics representing successive forms of psychological equilibrium. The equilibrium of affective and interpersonal schemata, justice or fairness, involves many of the same basic structural features as the equilibrium of cognitive schemata logicality. Justice (portrayed as balancing the scales) is a form of equilibrium between conflicting interpersonal claims, so that "in contrast to a given rule imposed upon the child from outside, the rule of justice is an imminent condition of social relationships or a low governing their equilibrium."[17]

What is being asserted, then, is not that moral judgment stages are cognitive—they are not the mere application of logic to moral problems—but that the existence of moral stages implies that normal development has a basic cognitive-structural component.

The Piagetian rationale just advanced suggests that cognitive maturity is a necessary, but not a sufficient condition for moral judgment maturity. While formal operations may be necessary for principled morality, one may be a theoretical physicist and yet not make moral judgments at the principled level.

As noted in the previous section, Kuhn, Langer, and Kohlberg found that 60 per cent of persons over sixteen had attained formal operational thinking (by their particular measures). Only 10 per cent of subjects over sixteen showed clear principled (Stages 5 and 6) thinking, but all these 10 per cent were capable of formal-operational logical thought. More generally, there is a point-to-point correspondence between Piaget logical and moral judgment stages, as indicated in Table 2. The relation is that attainment of the logical stage is a necessary but not sufficient condition for attainment of the moral stage. As we shall note in the next section, the fact that many adolescents have formal logical capacities without yet having developed the corresponding degree of moral judgment maturity is a particularly important background factor in some of the current dilemmas of adolescents.

ADOLESCENT QUESTIONING AND THE PROBLEM OF RELATIVITY OF TRUTH AND VALUE

The cornerstone of a Piagetian interpretation of adolescence is the dramatic shift in cognition from concrete to formal operations by which old conceptions of the world are restructured in terms of a new philosophy. Piaget defined the preschool child as a philosopher, revolutionizing child psychology by demonstrating that the child at each stage of development actively organizes his experience and makes sense of the physical and social world with which he interacts in terms of the classical categories and questions of philosophers concerning space, time, causality,

Table 2

Relations Between Piaget Logical Stages and Kohlberg Moral Stages (all relations are that attainment of the logical stages is necessary, but not sufficient, for attainment of the moral stage)

Logical Stage	Moral Stage	
Symbolic, intuitive thought	Stage O:	The good is what I want and like.
Concrete operations, Substage 1 Categorical classification	Stage 1:	Punishment-obedience orientation.
Concrete operations, Substage 2 Reversible concrete thought	Stage 2:	Instrumental hedonism and concrete reciprocity.
Formal operations, Substage 1 Relations involving the inverse of the reciprocal	Stage 3:	Orientation to interpersonal relations of mutuality.
Formal operations, Substage 2	Stage 4:	Maintenance of social order, fixed rules, and authority.
Formal operations, Substage 3	Stage 5A:	Social contract, utilitarian law-making perspective.
	Stage 5B:	Higher law and conscience orientation.
	Stage 6:	Universal ethical principle orientation.

reality, and so on. It is, however, only in adolescence that the child becomes a philosopher in the formal or traditional sense. This emergence of philosophic questioning has been studied most carefully in the moral realm.

The transition from preconventional to conventional morality generally occurs during the late elementary school years. The shift in adolescence from concrete to formal operations, the ability now to see the given as only a subset of the possible and to spin out the alternatives, constitutes the necessary precondition for the transition from conventional to principled moral reasoning. It is in adolescence, then, that the child has the cognitive capability for moving from a conventional to a postconventional, reflective, or philosophic view of values and society.

The rejection of conventional moral reasoning begins with the perception of relativism, the awareness that any given society's definition of right and wrong, however legitimate, is only one among many, both in fact and theory. To clarify the issue of moral relativism as perceived by an adolescent, we will consider some adolescent responses to the following dilemma:

In Europe, a woman was near death from a very bad disease, a special kind of cancer. There was one drug that the doctors thought might save her. It was a form of radium that a druggist in the same town had recently discovered. The drug was expensive to make, but the druggist was charging ten times what the drug cost him to make. He paid $200 for the radium and charged $2,000 for a small dose of the drug. The sick woman's husband, Heinz, went to everyone he knew to borrow the money, but he could only get together about $1,000 which was half of what it cost. He told the druggist that his wife was dying, and asked him to sell it cheaper or let him pay later. But the druggist said, "No, I discovered the drug and I'm going to make money from it." Heinz got desperate and broke into the man's store to steal the drug for his wife.

Should the husband have done that? Was it right or wrong? Bob, a junior in a liberal private high school, says:

> There's a million ways to look at it. Heinz had a moral decision to make. Was it worse to steal or let his wife die? In my mind I can either condemn him or condone him. In this case I think it was fine. But possibly the druggist was working on a capitalist morality of supply and demand.

I went on to ask Bob, "Would it be wrong if he did not steal it?"

> It depends on how he is oriented morally. If he thinks it's worse to steal than to let his wife die, then it would be wrong what he did. It's all relative, what I would do is steal the drug. I can't say that's right or wrong or that it's what everyone should do.

Bob started the interview by wondering if he could answer because he "questioned the whole terminology, the whole moral bag." He goes on:

> But then I'm also an incredible moralist, a real puritan in some sense and moods. My moral judgment and the way I perceive things morally changes very much when my mood changes. When I'm in a cynical mood, I take a cynical view of morals, but still whether I like it or not, I'm terribly moral in the way I look at things. But I'm not too comfortable with it.

Here are some other juniors from an upper-middle-class public high school:

> Dan: Immoral is strictly a relative term which can be applied to almost any thought on a particular subject . . . if you have a man and a woman in bed, that is immoral as opposed to if you were a Roman a few thousand years ago and you were used to orgies all the time, that would not be immoral. Things vary so when you call something immoral, it's relative to that society at that time and it varies frequently. [Are there any circumstances in which wrong in some abstract moral sense would be applicable?] Well, in that sense, the only thing I could find wrong would be when you were hurting somebody against their will.
>
> Elliot: I think one individual's set of moral values is as good as the next individual's . . . I think you have a right to believe in what you believe in, but I don't think you have a right to enforce it on other people.
>
> John: I don't think anybody should be swayed by the dictates of society. It's probably very much up to the individual all the time and there's no general principle except when the views of society seem to conflict with your views and your opportunities at the moment and it seems that the views of society

don't really have any basis as being right and in that case, most people, I think would tend to say forget it and I'll do what I want.

The high school students just quoted are, from the point of view of moral stage theory, in a transitional zone. They understand and can use conventional moral thinking, but view it as arbitrary and relative. They do not yet have any clear understanding of, or commitment to, moral principles which are universal, which have a claim to some nonrelative validity. Insofar as they see any "principles" as nonrelative, it is the principle of "do your own thing, and let others do theirs." This "principle" has a close resemblance to the "principles" characteristic of younger children's Stage 2 instrumental egoistic thinking. The following examples of a ten-year-old naïve egoist and a college student transition relativistic response are more clearly of this instrumental egoistic form.

Jimmy (American city, age 10): It depends on how much he loved his wife. He should if he does. [If he doesn't love her much?] If he wanted her to die, I don't think he should. [Would it be right to steal?] In a way it's right because he knew his wife would die if he didn't and it would be right to save her. [Does the druggist have the right to charge that much if no law?] Yes, it's his drug, look at all he's got invested in it. [Should the judge punish?] He should put him in jail for stealing and he should put the druggist in because he charged so much and the drug didn't work.

Roger (Berkeley Free Speech Movement student, age 20): He was a victim of circumstances and can only be judged by other men whose varying value and interest frameworks produce subjective decisions which are neither permanent nor absolute. The same is true of the druggist. I'd do it. As far as duty, a husband's duty is up to the husband to decide, and anybody can judge him, and he can judge anybody's judgment. If he values her life over the consequences of theft, he should do it. [Did the druggist have a right?] One can talk about rights until doomsday and never say anything. Does the lion have a right to the zebra's life when he starves? When he wants sport? Or when he will take it at will? Does he consider rights? Is man so different? [Should he be punished by the judge?] All this could be avoided if the people would organize a planned economy. I think the judge should let him go, but if he does, it will provide less incentive for the poorer people to organize.

RELATIVITY, MORAL STAGES, AND EGO IDENTITY

We first came across extreme relativist responses in some of our longitudinal subjects shortly after college entrance in the early sixties.[15] At that time, we interpreted their responses as a regression to Stage 2 thinking. Fifteen per cent of our college bound male students who were a mixture of conventional (Stage 4) and social-compact-legalist (Stage 5) thought at the end of high school, "retrogressed" to an apparent Stage 2 instrumentalist pattern in college.

In terms of behavior, everyone of our retrogressed subjects had high moral character ratings in high school, as defined by both teachers and peers. In college at least half had engaged in anticonventional acts of a more or less delinquent sort. As an example a Stage 2 Nietzschean had been the most respected high school student council president in years. In his college sophomore interview, however, he told how two days before he had stolen a gold watch from a friend at work. He had done so, he said, because his friend was just too good, too Christ-like, too trusting, and he wanted to teach him what the world was like. He felt no guilt about the stealing, he said, but he did feel frustrated. His act had failed, he said, because his trusting friend insisted he lost or mislaid the watch and simply refused to believe it had been stolen.

The forces of development which led our 20 per cent from upstanding conventional morality to Raskolnikov moral defiance eventually set them all to right. Every single one of our "retrogressors" had returned to a Stage 5 morality by age twenty-five, with more Stage 5 social-contact principle, less Stage 4 or convention, than in high school. All, too, were conventionally moral in behavior, at least as far as we can observe them. In sum, this 20 per cent was among the highest group at high school, was the lowest in college, and again among the highest at twenty-five.

In other words, moral relativism and nihilism, no matter how extensive, seemed to be a transitional attitude in the movement from conventional to principled morality.

COGNITIVE MORAL STAGES AND EGO-IDENTITY

In considering further the meaning of relativism in adolescence, it is helpful to relate logical and moral stages to Erikson's stages of ego-identity. Logical and moral stages are structures of thought through which the child moves sequentially. Erikson's stages are rather segments of the life histories of individuals; they define the central concerns of persons in a developmental period. An adolescent does not know or care that he is moving from concrete to formal thought; he knows and cares that he is having an Erikson "identity crisis."

Cognitive-developmental stages are stages of structure, not of content. The stages tell us *how* the child thinks concerning good and bad, truth, love, sex, and so forth. They do not tell us *what* he thinks about, whether he is preoccupied with morality or sex or achievement. They do not tell us what is on the adolescent's mind, but only how he thinks about what is on his mind. The dramatic changes in adolescence are not changes in structure, but changes in content. The adolescent need not know or care he is going from conventional to principled moral thinking, but he does know and care that sex is on his mind. In this sense cognitive structural stages may be contrasted with both psychosexual and Eriksonian stages.[19]

When we turn to Erikson's ego stages, we are partly dealing with a logical sequence as in logical and moral stages. Within Erikson's stages is the logical necessity that every later disposition presupposes each prior disposition, that each is a differentiation of prior dispositions. Erikson's ego stage centers around a series of forms of self-esteem (or their inverse, negative self-esteem). The first polarity trust-mistrust is one in which self and other are not differentiated. Trust is a positive feeling about self-and-other; mistrust is a negative feeling. The next polarity, autonomy versus shame, involves the self-other differentiation. Autonomy is a trust in the self (as opposed to the other); shame is a depreciation of self in the eyes of another whose status remains intact. Shame, however, is itself a failure to differentiate what one is from what one is in the eyes of the other, a differentiation implied in the sense of guilt. Similarly, initiative (I can be like him, it's all right to be or do it) is a differentiation from autonomy (I can do it). Such sequential progressive differentiations in self-esteem are involved throughout the Erikson stages. While there is an inherent logical (as opposed to biological) sequence to the Erikson ego stages, they are not hierarchical in the way cognitive stages are. Resolutions of identity problems are not also resolutions of trust or initiative problems, that is, each of the earlier problems and dispositions persists rather than being integrated into or being hierarchically dominated by the next. As a result, when we turn to Erikson's stages as defining focal concerns, we have a stage scheme which is so multidimensional as to resist empirical proof in the sense in which Piagetian stages may be proved. Ultimately the Erikson stages are "ideal-typical" in Weber's sense. They are not universal abstractions from data, but purifications and exaggerations of typical life histories. They do not predict regularities in the data, they aid in establishing historical connections in case histories. As Erikson uses his stage schema, it helps to suggest historical connections in a particular life, like Luther's. The truth of the stage schema is not in question; the truth of particular historical connections is. The stage schema helps select and illuminate these historical connections. In this sense, the stage of identity formation is not a step in an abstract but observable universal sequence, but is an ideal-typical characterization for a concrete historical period of adolescence.

As such, it need not have any exact logical relation to logical and moral stages, as they must to one another. While Erikson's stages cannot be defined, measured, or logically handled in the same sense as cognitive-developmental stages, suggestive empirical relations between ego-identity terms and moral stages are found.

M. H. Podd[20] gave an ego-identity interview to 134 male college juniors and seniors as well as the moral judgment interview. Following J. E. Marcia,[21] the identity interview covered occupational choice, religious beliefs, and political ideology. "Crisis" and "commitment" are assessed in each of these areas and serve to define each identity status. When an individual undergoes active consideration of alternative goals and values he is said to have experienced a "crisis." "Commitment" is the extent to which an individual has invested himself in his choices. The identity statuses operationally defined are: (1) identity achievement—has gone through a crisis and is committed; (2) moratorium—is in crisis with vague commitments; (3) foreclosure—has experienced no crisis but is committed to goals and values of parents or significant others; (4) identity diffusion— has no commitment regardless of crisis.

Subjects in the Podd study could be grouped into three major groups, the conventional (Stages 3 and 4), the principled (Stages 5 and 6), and the transitional. The transitional subjects could in turn be divided into two groups, those who were a combination of conventional and principled thinking and the extreme relativists who rejected conventional thought and used more instrumental egoistic ("Stage 2") modes. Two-thirds of the principled subjects had an "identity achievement" status. So too did about 40 per cent of the conventional subjects, the remainder being mainly in "identity foreclosure" (a status missing among the principled). None of the morally transitional subjects had an identity achievement status, and very few had foreclosed identity questioning.

Essentially, then, morally transitional subjects were in transition with regard to identity issues as well as moral issues. Stated slightly differently to have questioned conventional morality you must have questioned your identity as well, though you may continue to hold a conventional moral position after having done so.

The impact of the Podd study is that the relativistic questioning of conventional morality and conventional reality associated with logical and moral stage development is also central to the adolescent's identity concerns. As a corollary, morally conventional subjects have a considerable likelihood of never having an identity crisis or an identity questioning at all. Erikson's picture of an adolescent stage of identity crisis and its resolutions, then, is a picture dependent upon attainment of formal logical thought and of questioning of conventional morality. It fits best, then, the picture of adolescence in the developmentally elite and needs further elaboration for other adolescents.

HISTORICAL CHANGE IN ADOLESCENT RELATIVISM

We have linked adolescent relativism to a transition from conventional to principled morality, associated with identity crisis. This picture emerged most clearly from our longitudinal data from the late fifties and early sixties reported in the Kohlberg and Kramer article (see note 18). In this data only a small minority of college students entered a phase of moral nihilism and relativism in the transition from conventional to principled morality. Typically they attempted to construct or select an ideology of their own in this transitional phase, ideologies which ranged from Nietzschean racism to Ayn Rand objectivism to early S.D.S. New Left formulations. In these college subjects of the early sixties it was possible to see an intense identity crisis, in Erikson's terms. These college relativist-egoists were rare, and they all seemed to have been moralistic and guilt prone in high school. As part of their identity crisis, they seem to have had strong problems in freeing themselves from childhood moral expectations and guilt.

There were two universal developmental challenges to conventional morality to which these "regressors" were also responding: first, the relativity of moral expectations and opinion; second, the gap between conventional moral expectations and actual moral behavior. It is clear that these developmental challenges are universal challenges; the integration of one's moral ideology with the facts of moral diversity and inconsistency is a general "developmental task" of youth in an open society; its solution is the formation of a universal principled morality.

For our extreme relativists or amoralists, there seemed to be an additional task in the need to free themselves from their own early "rigid" morality. In Erikson's terms our retrogressors were living in a late adolescent psychosocial moratorium, in which new and nonconforming patterns of thought and behavior are tried out. Their return to morality or moral thought is the eventual confirmation of an earlier identification as one's own identity. To find a sociomoral identity requires a rebellious moratorium, because it requires liberation of initiative from the guilt from which our retrogressors suffer. At the "stage" of identity the adult conforms to his standards because he wants to, not because he anticipates crippling guilt if he does not.

By the 1970's the extreme doubt and relativism which earlier characterized only a minority of college students appears both earlier and much more pervasively. It is now sometimes found toward the end of high school.[22] In our own Harvard undergraduate course for freshmen and sophomores, about two-thirds of the students assert that there are no such things as valid moral rules or principles, no objective sense in which one thing is morally better than another. It appears that a majority rather than a minority of adolescents now are aware of relativism and of postconventional questioning, though it is still a minority who really attempt postconventional or principled solutions to these questions.

Parallel historical changes seem to have occurred in the relationship of extreme moral relativism to identity issues. Podd's findings from the *late* sixties differed from those of Kohlberg and Kramer in the *early* sixties in one important way. Kohlberg and Kramer found their extreme relativists, the Stage 2 or regressed subjects, in a condition of moratorium, in a state of "crisis" with vague and uncertain commitments. In contrast, Podd found them in a condition of identity diffusion with no sense of commitment and not necessarily a sense of crisis. In other words, extreme relativism no longer appeared to be a temporary ego-developmental maneuver of a small group of subjects in crisis, but rather to represent a more stable, less crisis-like pattern of low commitment. It seems likely to us that the psychological meaning of extreme relativism had changed in the five to ten years between the data reported by Kohlberg and Kramer (1969). Extreme relativism is no longer the struggle for independence from a strongly internal conventional morality in a period of moratorium and crisis in one's identity.

The relativistic rejection of convention, once individuality and spontaneously developed by adolescents in the course of reflecting on their own experience, is now manufactured as a cultural industry called the "counterculture." Further, the adult culture itself offers a very unsteady counter to the counterculture, particularly from the viewpoint of the adolescent to whom it offers a dwindling number of jobs and a world already overcrowded and crying out for less rather than more. It is clearly seen that one result of affluence, technology, and increased longevity has been to decrease the need of the adult community for its adolescents. Instead, it has some stake in keeping them in the youth culture since in one sense they only further threaten an already defensive adult world with fewer jobs and still more people. Thus the adults at once produce and market a counterculture and present themselves as a less than appealing alternative to it.

From the point of view of the adolescent, the counterculture has other meanings. The rejection of the conventional culture can be seen as a rebellion which can either turn into submission spelled backwards, or into the formation of principles. In our terms, the former remains conventional in form with only the content changed by being stood on its head. Although the impetus for the counterculture may have been once either principled or the expression of young people in identity crisis, the manufacture of the counterculture transforms it into yet another conventional system, although one lacking the solidity of the traditional conventional society.

While only a minority of adolescents actually have a postconventional view of morality and society, many more live in a postconventional culture or society. As a specific example, the majority of a sample of Haight-Ashbury hippies[23] emerge as mixtures of preconventional Stage 2 and conventional Stage 3 thinking. While hippie culture appears to be postconventional, it is almost entirely a mixture of Stage 2 "do your own thing" and Stage 3 "be nice, be loving" themes. The hippie culture continually questions conventional morality but on Stage 3 grounds of its being harsh and mean, or Stage 2 grounds of "Why shouldn't I have fun?" rather than in terms of its irrationality. Many hippies, then, belong to a counterculture which is largely conventional in its appeal but which lacks the solidity of traditional conventional society and is not embedded in it. As moral counterculture, the hippie culture differs primarily from the conventional culture in its extreme relativism and consequent fluidity, not in any positive forms of moral thought different from the conventional.

In most eras of the past, the adolescent went through questioning of value, meaning, and truth in a world of adults apparently oblivious to these doubts. Reflective adolescents have always considered adults as benighted for accepting conventional norms and imposing them on youth, for never doubting the truth and goodness of their world. The questioning adolescent has always seen the adult acceptance of the conventional social world as reflecting the hypocrisy, insensitivity, and dreariness of the adult. Equally, the questioning adolescent has always expected to remake the adult world nearer to his heart's desire, and at given moments in history has succeeded. What is new is the creation of a questioning culture providing half-answers to which adolescents are exposed prior to their own spontaneous questioning.

The adolescent is faced then with not one but two cultures offering alternative ideologies and ways to live. Both present resolutions to the postconventional doubt which now appears to be so pervasive. Both may be embraced in our sense conventionally for the set of answers they provide, or may be seen in principled terms, their validity as social systems resting on the principles of justice they more or less successfully embody.

IMPLICATIONS FOR EDUCATION

The extreme relativism of a considerable portion of high school adolescents provides both a threat to current educational practice and a potentiality for a new focus of education.

We said earlier that the five-to-seven shift has been traditionally represented in education by the beginning of formal schooling. The traditional education embodiment of the adolescent shift has been a different one, that of a two-track educational system dividing adolescents into two groups, an elite capable of abstract thought and hence of profiting from a liberal education and the masses who are not. At first, this division was made between the wealthy and those who went to work. As public high schools developed, the tracking system instead became that of an academic school or lycee leading to the university and a vocational school. The clearest formulation of this two-track system as based on the dawn of abstract thought was found in the British 11+ system. Based on his score on an intelligence test given at the dawn of adolescence, a child was assigned to either a grammar (academic) or a modern (vocational-commercial) high school.

The aristocratic tracking system just described rested on the assumption that the capacity for abstract thought is all or none, that it appears at a fixed age, and that it is hereditarily limited to an elite group in the population. The evidence on formal operational thought does not support these assumptions. However, when democratic secondary education ignored the existence of the adolescent cognitive shift and individual differences in their attainment, real difficulties emerged. Most recently this ignoral occurred in the wave of high school curriculum reform of the late fifties and early sixties in America, the "new math," the "new science," and the "new social studies." These curricula reforms were guided by the notion that more intellectual content could be put into high school and that this content should not be factual content and rote skills, but the basic pattern of thinking of the academic disciplines of mathematics, physics, or social science. The focus was to be upon understanding the basic logical assumptions and structure of the discipline and the use of these assumptions in reflective or critical thinking and problem-solving. Clearly the new curricula assumed formal-operational thought, rather than attempting to develop it. Partly as a result of this ignoral, some of the most enlightened proponents of the new curricula became discouraged as they saw only a subgroup of the high school population engaging with it. The solution we have proposed is that the new curricula be reformulated as tools for developing principled logical and moral thought rather than presupposing it.[24]

Experimental work by our colleagues and ourselves[27] has shown that even crude efforts based on such objectives are challenging and are successful in inducing considerable upward stage movement in thought. Hopefully, our efforts are the beginning of reformulating the "new" high school science, mathematics, social studies, and literature as approaches using "disciplines" as vehicles for the stimulation of the development of thought, rather than making young Ph.D.'s.

The difficulties and failures of the new curricula and of the general movement to democratize higher learning or liberal education, then, is not due to hereditary differences in capacity used to justify the two-track system. They represent, instead, the failure of secondary education to take developmental psychology seriously. When stage development is taken seriously by educators as an aim, real developmental change can occur through education.

In saying this, we return to the thought of John Dewey which is at the heart of a democratic educational philosophy. According to Dewey, education was the stimulation of development through stages by providing opportunities for active thought and active organization of experience.

The only solid ground of assurance that the educator is not setting up impossible artificial aims, that he is not using ineffective and perverting methods, is a clear and definite knowledge of the normal end and focus of mental action. Only knowledge of the order and connection of the stages in the development of the psychical functions can, negatively, guard against those evils, or positively, insure the full maturation and free, yet, orderly, exercises of the physical powers. Education is precisely the work of supplying the conditions which will enable the psychical functions, as they successively arise, to mature and pass into higher functions in the freest and fullest manner. This result can be secured only by a knowledge of the process of development, that is only by a knowledge of "psychology."[26]

Besides a clear focus on development, an aspect of Dewey's educational thought which needs revival is that school experience must be and represent real life experience in stimulating development. American education in the twentieth century was shaped by the victory of Thorndike over Dewey. Achievement rather than development has been its aim. But now the achieving society, the achieving individual, and even the achievement tests are seriously questioned, by adults and adolescents alike. If development rather than achievement is to be the aim of education, such development must be meaningful or real to the adolescent himself. In this sense education must be sensed by the adolescent as aiding him in his search for identity, and it must deal with life. Neither a concern with self or with life are concerns opposed to intellectuality or intellectual development. The opposition of "intellect" and "life" is itself a reflection of the two-track system in which a long period of academic education provided a moratorium for leisurely self-crystallization of an adult role identity by the elite while the masses were to acquire an early adult vocational identity, either through going to work or through commitment to a vocation in a vocational high school.

Our discussion of adolescent relativism and identity diffusion suggests that the two tracks are both breaking down and fusing. Vocational goals are evaded by relativism and counterculture questioning as are deferred goals of intellectual development. An identity crisis and questioning are no longer the prerogative of the elite, and they now occur earlier and without the background of logical and moral development they previously entailed. If the high school is to have meaning it must take account of this, which means it must take account of the adolescent's current notion of himself and his identity. Like most psychologists, most adolescents think the self has little to do with intellectual or moral development. The relativistic adolescent is content to answer "myself" to questions as to the source and basis of value and meaning. Like most psychologists he tends to equate the content of self-development with the ego, with self-awareness, with identity. The other pole of ego or self-development, however, is that of new awareness of the world and values; it is the awareness of new meanings in life.

We discussed the moral strand of ego development, which is clearly philosophical. We have also noted aesthetic, religious, metaphysical, and epistemological concepts and values born in adolescence. One side of ego development is the structure of the self-concept and the other side is the individual's concept of the true, the good, the beautiful, and the real. If education is to promote self-development, ego development must be seen as one side of an education whose other side consists of the arts and sciences as philosophically conceived. We have pointed to the need for defining the aims of teaching the arts and sciences in developmental terms. In this sense one basic aim of teaching high school science and mathematics is to stimulate the stage of principled or formal-operational logical thought, of high school social studies, the stimulation of principled moral judgment. A basic aim of teaching literature is the development of a stage or level of aesthetic comprehension, expression, judgment. Behind all of these developmental goals lie moral and philosophic dimensions of the meaning of life, which the adolescent currently questions and the school needs to confront. The adolescent is a philosopher by nature, and if not by nature, by countercultural pressure. The high school must have, and represent, a philosophy if it is to be meaningful to the adolescent. If the high school is to offer some purposes and meanings which can stand up to relativistic questioning, it must learn philosophy.

REFERENCES

1. S. H. White, "Some General Outlines of the Matrix of Developmental Changes Between Five to Seven Years," *Bulletin of the Orton Society,* 20 (1970), 41–57.
2. L. Kohlberg, "Early Education: A Cognitive-Developmental Approach," *Child Development,* 39 (December 1968), 1013–1062; A. R. Jensen, "How Much Can We Boost IQ and Scholastic Achievement?" *Harvard Educational Review,* 39 (1969), 1–123.
3. R. Scheffler, "The Development of Children's Orientations to Fantasy in the Years 5 to 7," unpublished Ph.D. dissertation, Harvard University, 1971.
4. L. Kohlberg, "Moral Education in the School," *School Review,* 74 (1966), 1–30; Kohlberg, "Early Education."
5. Kohlberg, "Moral Education in the School."
6. *Ibid.*
7. Cognitive stage maturity is different from IQ, a separate factor, though the two are correlated. (See L. Kohlberg and R. DeVries, "Relations between Piaget and Psychometric Assessments of Intelligence," in C. Lavatelli, ed., *The Natural Curriculum.* [Urbana: University of Illinois Press, 1971].) General impoverishment of organized physical and social stimulation leads to retardation in stage development. Culturally disadvantaged children tend to be somewhat retarded compared to middle-class children with the same IQ's in concrete-operational logic. Experimental intervention can to some extent accelerate cognitive development if it is based on providing experiences of cognitive conflict which stimulate the child to reorganize or rethink his patterns of cognitive ordering.
8. Kohlberg, "Early Education."
9. Kohlberg, "Moral Education in the School."
10. C. Ellinwood, "Structural Development in the Expression of Emotion by Children," unpublished Ph.D. dissertation, University of Chicago, 1969.

11. E. A. Peel, *The Psychological Basis of Education,* 2d ed. (Edinburgh and London: Oliver and Boyd, 1967).

12. D. Kuhn, J. Langer, and L. Kohlberg, "The Development of Formal-Operational Thought: Its Relation to Moral Judgment," unpublished paper, 1971.

13. Another example of transitional stage response is success on the question: "Joe is shorter than Bob, Joe is taller than Alex, who is the tallest?" The transitional child can solve this by the required reversing of relations and serial ordering of them but will fail the pendulum task.

14. Wordsworth's note to ode on *Intimations of Immortality* quoted in Lionel Trilling *The Liberal Imagination* (New York: Viking, 1941).

15. Kohlberg, "Moral Education in the School."

16. Taken from Kuhn, Langer, and Kohlberg, "The Development of Formal-Operational Thought."

17. J. Piaget, *The Moral Judgment of the Child* (Glencoe, Ill.: Free Press, 1948; originally published in 1932).

18. L. Kohlberg and R. Kramer, "Continuities and Discontinuities in Childhood and Adult Moral Development," *Human Development,* 12 (1969), 93–120.

19. J. Loevinger, "The Meaning and Measurement of Ego Development," *American Psychology* (1966), 195–206.

20. M. H. Podd, "Ego Identity Status and Morality: An Empirical Investigation of Two Developmental Concepts," unpublished Ph.D. dissertation, 1969.

21. J. E. Marcia, "Development and Validation of Ego Identity Status," *Journal of Personality and Social Psychology,* 3 (1966), 551–558.

22. C. Gilligan, L. Kohlberg, and J. Lerner, "Moral Reasoning About Sexual Dilemmas: A Developmental Approach," in L. Kohlberg and E. Turiel, eds., *Recent Research in Moral Development* (New York: Holt, Rinehart and Winston, 1972).

23. N. Haan and C. Holstein, unpublished data, 1971.

24. L. Kohlberg and A. Lockwood, "Cognitive-Developmental Psychology and Political Education: Progress in the Sixties," speech for Social Science Consortium Convention, Boulder, Colorada, 1970; L. Kohlberg and E. Turiel, "Moral Development and Moral Education," in G. Lesser, ed., *Psychology and Educational Practice* (Chicago: Scott, Foresman, 1971).

25. L. Kohlberg and M. Blatt, "The Effects of Classroom Discussion on Level of Moral Judgment," in Kohlberg and Turiel, eds., *Recent Research In Moral Development.*

26. J. Dewey, *On Education: Selected Writing,* ed. R. D. Archambault (New York: The Modern Library, republished 1964).

father absence and conscience development

Martin L. Hoffman
University of Michigan

There are many reasons for expecting the absence of a father to have an adverse effect on the child's conscience development. At the theoretical level, the father is one of the child's two major socialization agents, and for this reason alone his absence must create an enormous gap in the child's experience. The father's special role in moral development, furthermore, is suggested in both the Parsonian view that the father brings the larger society's normative standards into the home, and the Freudian view that by identifying with the father the child—at least the boy—acquires the moral standards of society as well as the motivational and control systems needed to assure adherence to them.

The empirical research is less clear in its implications. There is a growing body of evidence that the father's absence has important effects on personality development, especially for boys (see Biller, 1970, for most recent review of this research) but while some of the findings seem relevant to moral development, they do not provide a consistent picture. Thus, although father absence appears to be associated with a relative absence of doll-play aggression in young boys (Bach, 1946; Sears, 1951; Sears, Pintler, & Sears, 1946), it has also been found—primarily in lower-class samples—to relate positively to frequency of overt aggression and other antisocial behaviors in older boys (Glueck & Glueck, 1950; Gregory, 1965; Miller, 1958; Siegman, 1966). The explanation for the first set of findings has typically been that in the father's absence the child is likely to lack an aggressive role model; and the second set has typically been accounted for in terms of the compensatory or reactive masculinity of males whose primary identification is feminine because they lack a father. A more parsimonious interpretation of both sets of findings might be that fathers more typically provide models of self-control and in their disci-

This investigation was supported by Grant M-02333 from the National Institute of Mental Health and Grant HD-02258 from the National Institute of Child Health and Human Development. The author wishes to thank Lois Wladis Hoffman for her critical reading of an earlier draft of this article.

pline tend to discourage rather than encourage the expression of aggression. When such experiences are lacking, the boy develops less effective controls and is thus more likely to express aggression overtly; he need not express it in fantasy. Boys who have fathers, on the other hand, are more apt to control aggression in real life but express it in fantasy. Father absence has also been found to be associated with inability to delay gratification (Mischel, 1961), but the relevance of the delay measure to morality may be limited, since it considered only greater gains for the self in the future and did not contrast immediate gains with altruistic or prosocial future gains.

Further complicating the picture is the research on child-rearing practices and moral development in intact families. A recent study by Hoffman (in press) indicates that the boy's conscious identification with his father contributes to the acquisition of certain moral attributes; this suggests the absence of the father will have adverse effects on the son's moral development. The findings in the discipline research, however, indicate that the mother's, but not the father's, discipline is important in the child's moral internalization (Hoffman, 1970); this suggests that father's absence may have little or no effect on moral development. The notion that the effect might even be positive has been advanced by Moulton, Burnstein, Liberty, and Altucher (1966). Their view is based on the theory advanced by Henry and Short (1954) and extended by Rosen, Hoffman, and Lippitt (1957) and Hoffman (1961) that internalization of parental characteristics, as evidenced in guilt and aggression against the self, is most likely to occur when the same parent is the major source of both frustration and affection. Under these circumstances, the child is likely to inhibit aggression against the source of frustration—turning it inward—because not to do so would jeopardize the gratifications received in this affectionate relationship. In support of this view, Moulton et al. found that the affection level of the parent reported as the dominant disciplinarian relates more closely to the son's self-report of guilt than the affection level of the other parent. Extrapolating from these findings, they suggest that the absence of the father might tend to increase the extent to which affection and discipline will be focused in one parent; and when this occurs, low aggression and high guilt should be expected in the sons.

The upshot of these theories, conjectures, and research findings is that it is difficult to predict the effects of father absence on moral development, although it seems clear that any effects that do occur are likely to be more pronounced in boys than girls. The aim of this study was to throw light on these matters by making a direct comparison of the moral orientation of children with and without fathers.

METHODS

SAMPLE

This is part of a larger study of the effects of discipline and identification on moral development in intact families. The subjects were all seventh-grade white children in the Detroit metropolitan area. This age group was chosen because it is old enough to show the needed variation in moral orientation, yet young enough for parental influences to be still salient. The total pool consisted of 262 boys and 235 girls. In this group 25 boys and 28 girls were found to have no adult male living in the home for at least 6 months prior to the study. These children constituted the father-absent sample. Since this was not initially planned as a study of father absence, data about the nature of the absence, including its duration, were unfortunately not obtained.

Control Group. A control group of children from intact families, equal in size and matched closely to the father-absent group on IQ and social class, was selected from the larger pool. These controls were deemed necessary, since the previous research has reported father absence to be associated with low IQ and low socioeconomic status (Deutsch, 1960; Deutsch & Brown, 1964; Landy, Rosenberg, & Sutton-Smith, 1967; Maxwell, 1961; Sutton-Smith, Rosenberg, Landy, 1968; Miller, 1958). Scores from either the California Test of Mental Maturity or Iowa Test of Basic Skills were available for all the children. Social class was determined on the basis of the child's responses to questions about the parent's occupation and education. The distinction was basically between white-collar and blue-collar.[1] The control groups were formed by matching each child in the father-absent group with one from an intact family who was in the same social class, attended the same school, and had the same IQ decile score. Though no effort was made to control for sibling distribution, the two groups finally selected turned out to be closely matched on both sibling order and number of siblings. This was fortunate, since there is evidence (Landy et al., 1967; Sutton-Smith, et al., 1968) that sibling distribution can influence the effects of father absence on the child's cognitive development.

MORALITY INDEXES

Several moral indexes, each tapping a different aspect of the child's moral structure, were used. Three pertain to the degree to which the child's moral orientation is internalized: intensity of guilt following transgressions; use of moral judgments about others which are based on moral principles rather than external considerations; and tendency to accept responsibility for one's misdeeds. The other indexes pertain to the extent to which the subject shows consideration for others, conforms to rules, verbally accepts moral values, and expresses anger. In intact families, all but the last three have previously been found to be associated with a maternal discipline pattern which includes frequent induction (techniques pointing out the consequences of the child's behavior for others),

---

[1] The middle class was defined in terms of father's occupation being white-collar and both parents having at least a high school education; the lower class in terms of father's occupation being blue-collar and neither parent having more than a high school education. It should be noted that occupation and education data for fathers were provided by all but nine of the father-absent subjects—four boys and five girls. In these cases, the mother's occupation and education were used as the index of class.

infrequent power assertion, and frequent expressions of affection in non-discipline situations (Hoffman & Satzstein, 1967). The indexes of internal moral judgments, conformity to rules, and acceptance of moral values have also been found to relate positively to father identification in boys from intact families (Hoffman, in press).

Guilt. Two semiprojective story-completion items were used to assess the intensity of the child's guilt reaction to transgression. The child is presented with a story beginning which focuses on a basically sympathetic child of the same sex and age who has committed a transgression under conditions in which detection is unlikely. The subject's instructions are to complete the story and tell what the protagonist thinks and feels and "what happens afterwards." The assumption made is that the child identifies with the protagonist and therefore reveals his own internal (although not necessarily his overt) reactions through his completion of the story.

One story (adapted from Allinsmith, 1960) was about a child who cheats in a swimming race and wins. The other was concerned with a child who through negligence contributes to the death of a younger child. In rating the intensity of guilt, care was taken to assess first that the subject identified with the central character. If such identification was dubious, the story was not coded for guilt, nor were stories involving only external detection or concern with detection coded for guilt. All others were. For a story to receive a guilt score higher than zero there had to be evidence of a conscious self-initiated and self-critical reaction. Given this evidence, guilt intensity was rated on a scale ranging from 1 to 6. At the extreme high end were stories involving personality change in the hero, suicide, etc. In coding the stories the attempt was made to ignore differences in sheer writing style and to infer the feeling of the subject as he completed the story.

Two guilt scores were assigned to each story—one for the maximum guilt experienced by the hero, usually occurring early in the story, and the other for terminal guilt. The scores for the two stories were added to obtain an overall score for maximum guilt and one for terminal guilt.

Internal Moral Judgments. The moral judgment items consisted of several hypothetical transgressions which the children were asked to judge. These were of the type used by Kohlberg (1958) including moral judgments about persons committing various crimes, for example, stealing; choosing which of two crimes was worse, for example, one involving simple theft and the other a breach of trust; and judgments of crimes with extenuating circumstances, for example, a man who steals in order to procure a drug which he cannot afford and which is needed to save his wife's life. The subjects were first asked to indicate whether the act was right or wrong, or which was worse, and then give the reason for their choice. In coding, the reasons given were more important than the direction of the choices, and perfunctory responses were not coded at all. Responses were coded as external (e.g., "you can get put in jail for that"), internal (e.g., "Joe was worse because the man trusted him"), or indeterminate. The internal scores were summed for all items to obtain the child's internal moral judgment score.

Moral Values. Moral values were assessed by a measure in which the child rates the importance "in boys, [girls] your age" of 21 personal attributes, some of which were moral, for example, consideration for others and obedience to rules; and some of which were nonmoral, for example, leadership, popularity, achievement, and sense of humor. The child was asked first to rate the importance of each item and then to indicate which three were most important. Only the three top-ranked items were counted and these were assigned weights of 3, 2, and 1.[2] The subject's moral value score was simply the weighted sum for the moral items.

Acceptance of Blame. The measure of acceptance of blame is based on the teacher's report. The teacher is asked to check which of the following characterizes the child's reactions when he is caught doing something wrong: (a) denies he did it, (b) looks for someone else to blame or makes excuses, (c) cries, looks sad, or seems to feel bad, (d) accepts responsibility for what he has done, (e) where possible, tries on own initiative to rectify situation. In the scoring, a and b are treated as low, c as intermediate, and d and e as high on acceptance of blame. The scores range from 1 to 5.[3]

Conformity to Rules and Consideration for Others. Conformity to rules was assessed in terms of the teacher's reports of the extent to which the child (a) "behaves according to the rules . . . or breaks them" and (b) copies his classmates answers to tests. The class was divided into quartiles and scores of 1–4 for Item a and 4–1 for Item b were assigned depending on the quartile in which the child was placed. The two were summed to obtain an overall score for rule conformity.

Data about consideration for others were obtained from sociometric ratings by the children in the same classroom. Each child made three nominations for the child first, second, and third most "likely to care about the other children's feelings" and "to defend a child being made fun of by the group." The usual weights were assigned and the two scores summed.

These two indexes were deemed relevant to morality but not necessarily internalization, since they could pertain to instrumental acts for gaining approval from authority or peers.

Overt Aggression. Data about the child's aggression were based on the teacher's report of how the child "expresses anger toward other children." The categories include (a) physically attacks or threatens to . . . , (b) expresses anger verbally, (c) looks angry or sulks but says or does noth-

---

[2] The initial ratings of each item were included primarily to make sure the respondent thought about all the items in the list before ranking them.

[3] Where the teacher checked two or more reactions for a child, she also indicated which was most typical for him. The final scoring takes into account the reactions checked alone and those specified as most typical when two or more were checked. Hence a range of 1–5 is possible.

ing, (*d*) acts nervous, (*e*) turns to new constructive activity, (*f*) never seems to get angry. In the scoring, *a* and *b* are treated as high, *c* and *d* as intermediate, and *e* and *f* as low on aggression. The scoring procedure is the same as that used for "acceptance of blame," and the scores range from 1 to 5.

DATA ANALYSIS

Coding. To avoid contamination in the story-completion and moral-judgment coding, the responses of all the children in the larger pool were coded for one variable at a time. This made it impossible for the coder to build up a picture of a subject that might influence his subsequent coding of that subject's record for other variables. The intercoder reliabilities were 77% for maximum guilt, 69% for terminal guilt, and 91% for internal moral judgment. The final coding was done independently by two coders, and discrepancies were resolved in conference.

Statistics. The data were analyzed separately for boys and girls and the test of significance used throughout was the median test.

RESULTS AND DISCUSSION

The results (Table 1) provide strong support for the expectation that father absence has adverse effects on moral development in boys. Thus, father-absent boys obtained relatively low scores on all the moral indexes. The differences were significant for internal moral judgment, maxi-

Table 1

Median Differences Between Father-Absent and Father-Present Subjects on Moral Indexes

	Boys		Girls	
Moral Index	Father Absent	Father Present	Father Absent	Father Present
Maximum guilt	3.70	4.65*	4.50	5.26
Terminal guilt	2.47	2.66	2.66	3.16
Internal moral judgment	2.95	3.82*	3.65	3.54
Acceptance of blame	0.35	3.65**	3.83	3.71
Moral values	4.00	4.95*	3.60	4.50
Consideration for others	1.63	1.80	1.90	1.75
Conformity to rules	2.33	3.72**	3.83	3.93
Overt aggression	3.55*	2.65	2.65	2.45

Note. Asterisk denoting significance level is placed in higher cell (e.g., father-present boys are higher on maximum guilt than father-absent boys).
  * $p < .05$.
  ** $p < .01$.

mum guilt, acceptance of blame, moral values, and rule conformity. They were also rated by their teachers as more aggressive than father-present boys, which replicates the findings obtained in previous research with boys this age and older (Glueck & Glueck, 1950; Gregory, 1965; Miller, 1958; Siegman, 1966). In contrast to the clear-cut findings for boys, there was no consistent pattern for girls, and only one finding approached significance, that involving moral values ($p < .10$).

The next question we may ask is: What aspect of the father's absence is responsible for these effects? The possible influence of the intellectual deficit or low socioeconomic status often associated with father absence can be ruled out, since the two groups of subjects were closely equated for these variables. Another explanation which immediately comes to mind is related to the sheer absence of a paternal model as the significant factor. This seems like a reasonable explanation which might not only account for the effects of father absence on boys but also for the lack of effects on girls, since in the earlier mentioned study of intact families (Hoffman, in press) boys were overwhelmingly more likely than girls to identify with fathers ($p < .0001$), and father identification related to a number of moral indexes among boys but not girls.

Assuming that the absence of a paternal model is important, a further question is whether it is a complete answer. One way to assess this is to compare the effects of father absence with the effects of nonidentification with fathers who are present. For this purpose, we selected two groups from our larger sample of boys from intact families—one which obtained very high and another which obtained very low scores on a measure of conscious father identification. (This was the number of times father was mentioned in response to these items: "Which person do you admire or look up to the most?" "Which person do you want to be like when you grow up?" and "Which person do you take after mostly?") The two groups were the same size as the father-absent and father-present groups and controlled for IQ and social class in the same manner. The differences between the high- and low-father-identification groups on our moral indexes are presented in Table 2. Comparing this to Table 1, it appears that the effects of low identification with fathers who are present are quite similar though somewhat less pronounced than the effects of father absence (Table 2).[4] The main difference is that father absence is associated with low scores for maximum guilt and acceptance of blame, whereas low father identification is not (although its relation to acceptance of blame is in the same direction—$p < .15$). Maximum guilt and acceptance of blame, despite their limitations, are very likely our best indexes of moral internalization (which may in essence be defined as the application of standards to one's own behavior without regard to sanctions by author-

---

[4] The fact that rejecting a father who is present appears to be virtually as detrimental to moral development as not having a father, may at first seem difficult to accept. Bearing in mind the temporal limitation of our father-absence index, however, it is entirely possible that some of the boys in the father-absent group had extended and satisfactory relationships with their fathers before separation—an experience which may have been denied the low identification group.

Table 2
Median Differences Between High- and Low-Father-Identification Boys on Moral Indexes

Moral Index	High Father Identification	Low Father Identification
Maximum guilt	4.38	4.86
Terminal guilt	2.88	3.15
Internal moral judgment	3.96*	3.30
Acceptance of blame	3.53	2.80
Moral values	5.20**	3.50
Consideration for others	1.72	1.62
Conformity to rules	3.80*	3.14
Overt aggression	2.44	3.25*

* $p < .05$.
** $p < .01$.

ity) for the following reasons. First, it seems reasonable to assume that the guilt measure reflects the subject's own response to transgression, since a prerequisite for coding guilt was evidence that the subject identified with the story hero. The moral judgment measure, on the other hand, pertains to judgments of transgressions of others, and while one may "sincerely," and in that sense internally, hold the beliefs that one applies to the conduct of others, this may not indicate the reaction to one's own transgression. Similarly, the moral values index pertains to surface acceptance of moral standards and may therefore be irrelevant to internalization. Finally, the scores for aggression and rule-conformity are based on teacher ratings of behaviors which have obvious relevance to "social desirability" and may therefore reflect a pro-authority orientation rather than an internally based self-control. This is apt to be less true of acceptance of blame which, though also based on teacher ratings, involves acknowledging to authority that one has behaved in a disapproved fashion. If our argument is correct, we may tentatively conclude that whether or not the boy identifies with his father influences the degree to which he accepts moral standards, uses them as a basis for judging right and wrong, and behaves in accord with them in the presence of authority. The presence or absence of a father also bears on these matters, but in addition influences the extent to which the boy applies moral standards to his own behavior.

These differences suggest that the lack of a paternal model is not the only significant aspect of the father's absence. Another obvious factor that may be operating is the pressure the father's absence puts on the mother, which may affect her behavior toward the child. Not having a husband, for example, may result in her becoming busier and more harassed, hence impatient with the child and oriented toward immediate compliance rather than long-range character goals. As a result, she may express affection less frequently, and in her discipline use more power assertion and less induction—the pattern found in previous research to be associated with weak moral internalization (Hoffman, 1970). Furthermore, we might expect this pattern to be more pronounced with boys, who are normally more aggressive and resistant to influence than girls and may even be more so when they have no father. To test this hypothesis, we used available data for the subjects' reports of their mother's expression of affection and the discipline techniques used in several situations. These measures are described in detail elsewhere (Hoffman & Saltzstein, 1967). The findings provide partial support for the hypothesis. The boys without fathers reported that their mothers expressed less affection than boys with fathers ($p < .05$). There was no difference in the type of discipline reported, but it seems reasonable to assume that the paucity of affection would have an adverse effect on the boys' reactions in the discipline encounter. For girls, the findings were the reverse of those obtained for boys: The girls without fathers reported that their mothers express affection *more* frequently ($p < .10$). They also report less power assertion and more induction, although these findings are nonsignificant. Should this pattern of findings be replicated, it would suggest that the mother may compensate for the father's absence, but only with girls. Perhaps it is more difficult to do this with boys because of their more abrasive qualities. This stands especially if what the mother wants is ease in running the household in contrast to the girl who is more likely to help with household chores rather than make additional trouble. It is also likely that the reason for the father's absence is frequently divorce, and in these cases the mothers may carry a residue of resentment which is expressed toward their sons. As a result, a greater proportion of mother-son interactions, when there is no father, may revolve around discipline encounters, that is, there is more discipline, although the discipline is not of a different sort, and correspondingly less time is spent in affectionate interchange.

CONCLUSIONS

The findings clearly indicate that the absence of the father has adverse effects on the boy's conscience development. We have also presented evidence that these effects may be somewhat greater than the effects of nonidentification with a father who is present, which suggests that some but not all of the effects of father absence are attributable to the lack of a paternal model. That the effects may also be mediated in part by changes in the mother's child-rearing pattern is suggested by the finding that women without husbands appear to express less affection to their sons than women with husbands.

The absence of the father appears to have no discernible effect on the conscience development of girls. This is probably due mainly to the fact that girls usually identify with their mothers and not their fathers, although we have also presented evidence that mothers may compensate for their husband's absence by expressing additional affection to their daughters.

These conclusions must be qualified because of the limitations of our index of father absence, that is, we do not know its duration or how old the child was when it began. Further research, in which duration and age of child vary, is needed to find out if the effects of father absence are greater with younger than older boys, as seems to be true, for example, with respect to masculine sex-role identity (Biller, 1970). Such research may also tell us if our findings have a bearing on the origins of conscience development, or if they pertain only to the reduction in strength of an already developed conscience.

REFERENCES

Allinsmith, W. Moral standards: II. The learning of moral standards. In D. R. Miller & G. E. Swanson (Eds.), *Inner conflict and defense.* New York: Holt, 1960.

Bach, G. R. Father-fantasies and father typing in father-separated children. *Child Development,* 1946, *17:* 63–80.

Biller, H. B. Father absence and the personality development of the male child. *Developmental Psychology,* 1970, *2:* 181–201.

Deutsch, M. Minority group and class status as related to social and personality factors in scholastic achievement. *Monograph of the Society for Applied Anthropology,* 1960, *2:* 1–32.

Deutsch, M., & Brown, B. Social influences in Negro-white intelligence differences. *Journal of Social Issues,* 1964, *20:* 24–35.

Glueck, S., & Glueck, E. *Unravelling juvenile delinquency.* New York: Commonwealth Fund, 1950.

Gregory, I. Anterospective data following childhood loss of a parent: I. Delinquency and high school dropout. *Archives of General Psychiatry,* 1965, *13:* 99–109.

Henry, A. F., & Short, J. F. *Suicide and homicide.* Glencoe, Ill.: Free Press, 1954.

Hoffman, L. W. The father's role in the family and the child's peer-group adjustment. *Merrill-Palmer Quarterly,* 1961, *7:* 97–105.

Hoffman, M. L. Moral development. In P. Mussen (Ed.), *Handbook of child psychology.* New York: Wiley, 1970.

Hoffman, M. L. Identification and conscience development. *Child Development,* in press.

Hoffman, M. L., & Saltzstein, H. D. Parent discipline and the child's moral development. *Journal of Personality and Social Psychology,* 1967, *5:* 45–57.

Kohlberg, L. The development of modes of moral thinking and choice in the years 10 to 16. Unpublished doctoral dissertation, University of Chicago, 1958.

Landy, F., Rosenberg, B. G., & Sutton-Smith, B. The effect of limited father absence on the cognitive and emotional development of children. Paper presented at the meeting of the Midwestern Psychological Association, Chicago, May 1967.

Maxwell, A. E. Discrepancies between the pattern of abilities for normal and neurotic children. *Journal of Mental Science,* 1961, *107,* 300–307.

Miller, W. B. Lower-class culture as a generating milieu of gang delinquency. *Journal of Social Issues*, 1958, *14*, 5–19.

Mischel, W. Delay of gratification, need for achievement, and acquiescence in another culture. *Journal of Abnormal and Social Psychology*, 1961, *62:* 543–552.

Moulton, R. W., Burnstein, E., Liberty, P. G., & Altucher, N. Patterning of parental affection and disciplinary dominance as a determinant of guilt and sex typing. *Journal of Personality and Social Psychology*, 1966, *4:* 356–363.

Rosen, S., Hoffman, L. W., & Lippitt, R. Some effects of role reversal between parents in their relations with children. Paper presented at the Midwestern Psychological Association, Chicago, May 1957.

Sears, P. S. Doll play aggression in normal young children: Influence of sex, age, sibling status, father's absence. *Psychological Monographs*, 1951, *65* (6, Whole No. 323).

Sears, R. R., Pintler, M. H., & Sears, P. S. Effect of father separation on preschool children's doll play aggression. *Child Development*, 1946, *17:* 219–243.

Siegman, A. W. Father-absence during childhood and antisocial behavior *Journal of Abnormal Psychology*, 1966, *71:* 71–74.

Sutton-Smith, B., Rosenberg, B. G., & Landy, F. Father-absence effects in families of different sibling compositions. *Child Development*, 1968, *39:* 1213–1221.

eleven

alienation and
commitment

part eleven

It became fashionable during the turbulent decade of the 1960s to refer to young people who in one way or another did not "fit in" as being "alienated." Such labeling created the illusion that we were saying something significant about them. However, as Kenneth Keniston, long a perceptive observer of contemporary youth, points out, all that was actually being done was to imply that something was wrong and to suggest the loss or absence of a previously desirable relationship.[1] Little is actually accomplished unless we can specify further what the individual is alienated from; what, if anything, has replaced the old relationship; how the alienation is expressed (e.g., through efforts to transform society, withdrawal or despair, or efforts at self-transformation); and, finally, what the agent of alienation is (e.g., social discrimination or persecution in contrast to largely self-imposed alienation).

In the past decade significant numbers of young people—minority-group youth, poor whites, middle-class social and political activists, hippies, feminists, rural and urban commune members, followers of newly formed Eastern or fundamentalist religious groups, some delinquents, and others—could all be described as in some way alienated from previously accepted social values and life-styles. Nevertheless, there were and remain significant differences both between and within such groups in the sources of their alienation and their responses to it.

Thus much of the alienation of minorities and the poor is largely imposed from without, in the form of social and economic discrimination; in contrast, among middle- and upper-class majority youths, more subtle internal forces are likely to be at work. Even among economically disadvantaged minority youths, however, where the awareness of traditional injustice is strong and influential (particularly during adolescence), important differences in individual response may occur. For example, in the first study in this part, Glen H. Elder, Jr., notes that some urban black youths have a strong sense of solidarity with black people generally, while others do not. Furthermore, "affirmation of solidarity with black people may be coupled, on the one hand, with an outward orientation which includes advocacy of racial desegregation and integration, or, on the other, with a defensive-withdrawal attitude."

Whether a particular adolescent will be oriented primarily to his racial group as a whole, to his family, to both, or to neither (as in the case of the individualistic black adolescent primarily concerned with pursuing his own personal goals) will depend on many factors other than minority-group status alone: relative level of ability and learned skills, parental child-rearing practices, parents' achievement aspirations for their children, perceived opportunities for achievement on the part of the adoles-

---

[1] K. Keniston, *The Uncommitted: Alienated Youth in American Society.* New York: Dell, 1960.

cent himself, family socioeconomic level, and the social climate generally. Such factors will also influence whether the young person is likely to become anxious, distrustful, self-doubting, fatalistic, withdrawing, or, conversely, self-confident, emotionally secure, self-assertive, trusting, optimistic.

Fortunately, a number of recent studies indicate that increasing numbers of contemporary youths—both minority and majority—are combining specific racial or ethnic pride and cultural identification with an equally strong sense of both individual ego identity and shared participation in the human condition. Much more, however, will be required from society and from each of its members if initial progress is to be sustained and expanded.

Alienation of the poor and victims of racial or ethnic discrimination is, unfortunately, not new and in some ways at least, not difficult to appreciate. What is relatively new is the disenchantment with society and many of its values that reached a peak among many socioeconomically privileged middle- and upper-class youths during the middle and late 1960s. Many of these young people saw themselves as confronted not only by what they viewed as an immoral war in Indochina, but by a "technocratic" society in which the goals of technological "progress" and economic affluence were being relentlessly pursued without regard to the human costs or the quality of the environment. This society often appeared to them to value *things* more than *people,* achieving affluence for the few at the expense of the disenfranchised poor. In addition impersonal, highly specialized, status-oriented, hierarchical social institutions (e.g., big business, government, education, the military) were viewed as inimical to values they held strongly—including a greater emphasis on individuality and interpersonal intimacy and a lessened preoccupation with status-seeking and competitive "role-playing games."

While such general trends appeared to characterize large numbers of disenchanted middle-class youth there have obviously been differences in emphasis, as well as special concerns, among different subgroups—social and political activists, the "culturally alienated," hippies, and other "social dropouts." In recent years, particular attention has been focused on liberal or left-oriented youthful political activists. Some observers have regarded all activism and dissent, particularly student activism, as basically self-destructive and socially harmful—more a manifestation of personal maladjustment and rebellion against parents than a mature response to social pathology. Others have reached equally sweeping opposite conclusions. For them, salvaging a "sick society" depends on the efforts of dedicated youthful activists, who are not viewed as "sick," but as unusually intelligent, mature, psychologically resilient, socially effective, and identified positively with liberal parental values.

The danger of such simplistic generalizations about the personalities and motivations of *all* social dissenters is well illustrated in the second article. Jeanne H. Block was able to distinguish two groups of students seeking major societal and institutional change: those who rejected parental values and denied that their parents had exerted a positive influence on their development ("discontinuity group") and those who "attributed a positive influence to their parents and manifested little discrepancy between their own beliefs and values and those of their parents" ("continuity group"). In addition, a third group of conservative students sharing parental values ("continuous conservative group") was identified for purposes of comparison.

Despite their shared societal rejection, the two dissenting groups were found to differ significantly in personality characteristics and in the child-rearing practices of their parents. For example, the parents of continuity subjects were more comfortable in the role of parent, more concerned with developing logical and rational child-rearing procedures, more encouraging of individuation and autonomy in their children, and less likely to emphasize authoritarian control and discipline than their discontinuity counterparts. The latter appeared more tense, less consistent in their behaviors toward their children, and more preoccupied with establishing and maintaining control over them. Continuity parents also exhibited more mutual agreement between mother and father on child-rearing practices. Continuous conservative parents also showed more interparent agreement and more emphasis on a rational, orderly approach to child rearing than discontinuity parents; however, continuous continuity parents tended to be more concerned with impulse control and obedience and less concerned with encouraging individuation in their children than continuity parents of dissenters.

The results of this and other recent studies warn against making easy generalizations about alienated, dissenting, or, indeed, nondissenting young people. As Larry Kerpelman, a psychologist who has conducted extensive investigations of young activists, comments, "A variety of individuals with highly diverse talents and motivations are bound to be involved in any social movement; global descriptions are certain to be oversimplified."[2]

In the final article of this part—and of the book—Stephen M. Pittel and his colleagues address the questions, Where did all the flower children come from? and, of equal interest in the 1970s, Where have they gone? In the pursuit of answers to these questions, the investigators learned a good deal about developmental factors involved in adolescent drug use: The hippie culture that reached its culmination with the now famous "Human Be-in" in Golden Gate Park in San Francisco in the late 1960s was, among other things, clearly a drug culture. Perhaps the authors' most interesting (and also disheartening) finding is that the proclaimed happiness of the original hippies—the assertion that everything was "groovy"—though no doubt true for some, was largely a matter of self-deception for many, if not a majority. The hippies' offbeat clothes, the beads, the psychedelic designs, the flowers, the put-ons, the sometimes perceptive humor ("better living through chemistry," "kill for peace"), the frequently proclaimed (but not as frequently achieved) sexual freedom, the drug highs, and the presumed freedom from the rat race were often misleading. In their study of 250 members of the original Haight-Ashbury group, Pittel and his colleagues found that many of their

---

[2] L. C. Kerpelman, *Activists and Nonactivists: A Psychological Study of American College Students.* New York: Behavioral Publications, 1972, p. 182.

subjects were aimless, depressed, bored, or anxious; others appeared genuinely confused or physically ill. Many tended to be characterized by ego deficits, cognitive deficiencies (despite relatively high overall intelligence), and an inability "to understand, organize, or integrate the events of their lives." Despite superficially "normal" middle-class backgrounds, these young people had typically been subjected to an unusually high degree of stimulation, stress, and trauma, particularly during middle childhood. As a result of such disruptive experiences, the investigators believe that many of them were deprived of the relative freedom from turmoil during preadolescent development considered essential "for the development of ego functions needed to deal with the onslaught of adolescence."

What ultimately appears more important than the apparently limited capacity of the hippies themselves to put their proclaimed values into effective practice is the appeal that aspects of the movement have had for many young people who have remained within the system, and for many troubled adults as well. Whether we will be able to incorporate into society's value system the best of the hippies' bravely asserted, if largely unfulfilled, values (more genuine love and individual self-expression, less competitive role-playing and exploitation of others, and more true joy and wonder in living) without also adopting their inherently self-destructive aspects (reliance on drugs, narcissistic self-indulgence, social and economic parasitism, lack of discipline, and emotional immaturity as reflected in an inability to make enduring personal commitments to others and to oneself) remains a critical question for the future.

socialization and ascent in a racial minority

Glen H. Elder, Jr.
University of North Carolina, Chapel Hill

Great aspirations and achievement are frequently uncovered among the deprived by structural changes that widen opportunity and alter traditional definitions of the situation and self. To minority youth in developing societies, the promise of a new nation is the promise of an era offering improved life chances and attractive identities. Their surging, impatient mood of hopefulness strains the capacity of these nations and threatens political stability when expanded opportunity fails to satisfy rising expectations (see Gurr. 1968; Rubin, 1962).

Shortly after the U.S. Supreme Court decision in 1954 and the emergence of large-scale protests, great aspirations were found to be relatively common among black youth, closely resembling the outlook of youth in newly developing or transitional societies. In fact, their aspirations were frequently higher than those of white youth from middle-class families (Sexton, 1963). Accumulated frustrations resulting from this gap between promises and desires, on the one hand, and reality, on the other, have been viewed as a major element in the black revolts of the mid-1960s (see Davies, 1969).

The end of massive uprisings in the cities marked the rapid development of an inward focus among militant groups which emphasized the generation of consciousness of group identity, traditions, and deprivations through auxiliary socializing agents, such as black schools. In its various forms, this orientation includes commitments to racial separateness, self-defense, the socioeconomic and communal development of the black community, and the achievement of political and cultural representation

The data on which the analysis is based were obtained from a larger community study directed by Alan Wilson and supported by a grant from the National Institute of Mental Health (MH-0097).

Reprinted from Youth and Society Volume 2, No. 1 (September 1970) pp. 74–110 by permission of the Publisher, Sage Publications, Inc.

in the larger community. These commitments, as a response to survival needs in an alien setting, may diminish the life chances of the young in social institutions controlled by the majority. The circular, reinforcing effect of defensive responses and external persecution frequently produce handicaps which confirm the majority group's belief that minority youth cannot perform effectively, even in the absence of formal discrimination (see Inkeles, 1966).

The continuing deprivations and disabilities imposed on black Americans support two parental beliefs which are likely to intensify achievement frustration and racial consciousness among the young. The first is the widely held assumption that black youth must put forth extraordinary effort, relative to their white agemates, in order to surmount racial barriers and achieve a good life. This is sometimes expressed in the belief that "our children must be twice as good as white children" in order to achieve the same goals in life. The reality of this double standard and its roots in white racism are constantly impressed upon the young.

The other belief is the assumed efficacy of money and material goods as reinforcers of desirable behavior. To parents who have had very little in the way of material possessions, an economic reward may be viewed as the most effective sanction for symbolizing and upholding standards regarding their children's conduct and performance in school. In Trinidad, where the predominately rural East Indians are more deprived of political power and status than Negroes, a study (see Green, 1965: 214) of lower-class children found that East Indian parents were significantly more likely to offer material goods as rewards than Negro parents. Material rewards do appear to have positive reinforcing value on the behavior of lower-class children (Katz, 1967: 148–150), but they may also increase economic frustrations.

The implementation of both beliefs in child socialization is likely to foster a strong desire for high status and material goals under conditions which offer relatively limited prospects for their realization. Michael Smith (1965) observes that the frustrations of black parents in rural Jamica make "them want their children to pursue occupations that offer escape from a similar lot." Thus the "cycle of childhood aspiration and adult despair perpetuates itself" (Smith, 1965: 215), as the children eventually become aware of their limited access to such goals. Parental inability to implement the high aspirations conveyed to offspring, in the face of an alienating school environment, serves to broaden the disparity between desire and reality. Educational, resource, and experience deficits contribute to the minority parent's minimal knowledge of how their children should work toward desired goals, and of how to assist and motivate them (see Hess and Shipman, 1965; Baughman and Dahlstrom, 1968). "There is communicated a combination of realism and pessimism, a kind of wise weariness that may appear to belie the very educational or career goals they express for at least some of their children" (Lewis, 1965: 345). Academic difficulties may be compounded when they are dealt with by parents in a critical, punitive manner, since this practice generates hostility and emotional blocks to learning (Katz, 1967).

In this paper, we shall investigate the extent to which socialization to high-status goals and tangible reinforcements in a deprivational context contribute to a disparity between desire and reality, to frustration and nationalistic feeling among Negro boys in an industrial center on the west coast. A sample of white boys from the same community and materials on the socialization of black youth in the Caribbean will be included for comparison purposes.

SOLIDARITY WITH THE BLACK COMMUNITY

A sense of solidarity with the black community is hypothesized as most likely to arise among relatively competent black youth who are socialized to a high-status goal and envision little chance of achieving it, owing to inadequate educational preparation, academic failures, and anticipated or experienced racial barriers. A collective adaptation to achievement frustration derives from the attribution of cause to white-controlled institutions, an attribution which may explain failures in school as well as anticipated difficulties in employment, and from the realization that one's life chances are interdependent with the status and prospects of all black people. Nationalistic feeling does imply that "race is important for achievement" (Rose, 1949: 92). This response to racial domination has been identified in research on black high school students in South Africa. Upon finding ever more restrictive political barriers to the individual success of the black man, many of these youth have channelled their aspirations into the one domain which offers opportunity for autonomous action, that of "political activity in the nationalist cause" (Danziger, 1963: 39). In some cases, this adaptation to achievement frustration may be associated with and represent a defense against self-deprecation.

Affirmation of solidarity with black people may be coupled, on the one hand, with an outward orientation which includes advocacy of racial desegregation and integration, or, on the other, with a defensive-withdrawal attitude. The latter stance seems most likely to be adopted by black youth who occupy a dependent position within the minority group—indicated by low competence and a sense of powerlessness—and who perceive the larger world with suspicion and distrust. Whether reinforced by parental protectiveness or not, such dependency is likely to increase a minority child's reluctance to leave the "emotional haven" of the family (Parsons and Fox, 1952). Thus we hypothesized that the defensive-withdrawal response would be expressed in a desire to remain physically close and loyal to parents and kin.

Familistic bonds have generally been viewed as a consequence or expression of cultural and institutional imperatives. The individual is expected or required to subordinate his desires to those of his family of orientation. In familistic societies, the family is also portrayed as the individual's main source of security in a basically threatening, untrustworthy environment (Almond and Verba, 1963; Rosen, 1964). Trust is only reluctantly extended beyond the boundaries of the family group. Since suspicion and distrust are embedded in dominant-minority relations, one might expect a wider prevalence of familistic sentiment in the minority group, even with differences in member dependencies or disabilities controlled. Garigue (1960: 200) has developed this viewpoint in his hypothesis that the familistic culture of French Canada is largely a result of a "compensatory reaction against minority status in a dominant, Anglo-Saxon world." Within the minority group, individual characteristics which are disabling with respect to confident, effective participation in the larger society should increase the predisposition to withdraw.

THE SOCIALIZATION CONTEXT

Approximately 2,000 black and white boys were randomly selected for the sample from grades seven through twelve in the industrial city of Richmond, located on the eastern edge of San Francisco Bay; more than 60% of the employed males in the city held manual jobs.[1] The city's present racial composition has its origins in the economic boom created by World War II. Southern Negroes were recruited in large numbers for work in the Naval shipyards, increasing the percentage of Negro residents from one per cent in 1940 to 16% in 1950. Despite declining economic opportunities after the war, most of the immigrants remained; nearly 30% of the city's current population is Negro.

Most of the black families are located in the western flatlands area of the city, while the eastern hill sector is almost completely white. This pattern of residential segregation is reflected in the racial composition of the schools. Four of the eight junior high schools and two of the five senior high schools are mainly Caucasian (85% or more).

The depressed status of the black community is clearly shown by characteristics of the sample. Three-fourths of the Negro parents were born in the South, and most of them spent at least part of their childhood in rural areas of this region. The continuing immigration of nonwhites after World War II is indicated by the Southern birthplace of about one-fifth of the black youth. Most Negro fathers were employed in unskilled or semiskilled jobs, in contrast to a fourth of the white fathers. Father-absent families were also more prevalent in the Negro than in the white community (22 versus 9.5%). Moreover, only 18% of the Negro boys in the sample scored above the fiftieth percentile on an eighth-grade Henmon-Nelson test, as compared with two-thirds of the white boys.

DISCOVERY OF RACIAL DIFFERENCES

White-controlled institutions, perceived discrimination against Negroes, physical separation from whites, and negligible communication between the races are the everyday conditions which impinge upon the black child's socialization and life prospects in the community. It is commonly believed in the Negro community that black children are treated unfairly by white authorities. As one mother observed on school discipline, "Whenever my son gets in a fight with a Negro boy, they send both home, but if he fights with a white boy they just send him home" (Wenkert, Magney, and Neel, 1967: 41). These definitions of the situation are seldom recognized or acknowledged by members of the white community. According to a 1965 survey of adults in the city, Negroes are much more likely than whites to feel unfairly treated and dissatisfied with the work of police in their residential areas, and are more likely to claim that Negroes are discriminated against in hiring and promotion (average percentages of 57 versus 30).

Figure 1
Perception of racial discrimination and police demeanor in community by race and grade level.

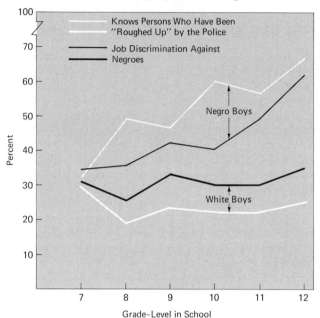

Grade-Level in School
Range in Number of Respondents: Negroes = 85–188; Whites = 207–257

These racial differences in attitude and outlook gradually emerge among children in the city as they approach adulthood. By early adolescence, black youth in the sample were more aware of job discrimination against Negroes than were white boys, a difference which is considerably larger among older boys (Figure 1). Likewise, knowledge of "rough" police treatment against persons of one's own race increases with age among Negro boys, while such experience is much less common among white youth and does not increase by age. The imprint of these perceived injustices on black children is likely to take various cognitive and emotional forms. One effect is suggested by responses to the statement, "I sometimes feel that I must be twice as good as other people to get ahead"; agreement was much more prevalent among black than among white boys of high school age (65 versus 36%). Moreover, this racial difference was greatest between boys who are most likely to achieve success, those above average in IQ. Similar racial differences were obtained on statements describing one's ability to control the environment and to plan for the future.

STATUS ASPIRATIONS AND ACHIEVEMENT TRAINING

The aspirations of black parents reflect the hope that high standards and extraordinary effort on the part of their children will effectively counter racial barriers. This hope is expressed in mobility goals which are often higher than those held by their children and by white parents of similar status (Furstenberg, 1969). When such aspirations are learned by children but are poorly implemented in parental training, they are certain to be a source of frustration.

The high achievement goals of Negro parents are very apparent in the present sample. Though considerably lower in family status than white boys, black youth were just as likely to report that their parents wanted them to attend college. About nine out of ten middle-class boys in each racial group reported this parental goal, and this proportion was not much lower among boys from unskilled and father-absent families (72%). Even if such perceptions overestimate parental aspirations, they may have real consequences in pressure to achieve and in the child's definition of the situation. No trends in parental goals by age of child were found in either racial group.

The significance of this racial similarity in parental goals is best seen within the context of the child's mental ability and family status. Since black youth were considerably lower than whites on both of these dimensions, a sizable disparity between these attributes and parental ambition is probable among the former. For the purposes of this analysis, we defined two family status groups—middle and working versus lower and low status, father-absent—and divided each group into three IQ percentile categories, 0–19, 20–39, 40+ (see note to Table 1). Low test scores in the Negro sample required these IQ categories.

Black parents appear to be more attentive to the role of education in life success than to academic skills in setting goals for their children. Their college aspirations are comparable in the perceptions of sons in all three ability groups, in contrast to a substantial variation in the white sample. The disparity between parental ambition and son's IQ is particularly large among low ability (0–19 percentile) Negro boys in both status groups. In the high-status category, for instance 90% of the least able black youth reported college aspirations on the part of their parents and 36% of their parents were described as insisting on college. These figures are considerably lower among white boys of similar status and ability (63 and 20%). Even if one assumes that IQ scores and parental goals have different meanings in each racial group, the disjuncture between these factors in the Negro sample sheds some light on the conflicting forces which impinge on the black child's performance in school. Katz (1967: 173) offers the opinion that the high aspirations of black parents "are indeed in the nature of wishful fantasies, in the sense that the parents do not know how to implement them, but the aspirations have consequences in that they somehow get conveyed to the child as expectations he is supposed to fulfill." Internalization of high parental goals among low achieving boys could produce overly harsh self-criticism, a covert response which further diminishes learning ability and increases the likelihood of negative reinforcement from parents.

PARENTAL SUPPORT FOR ACHIEVEMENT

Deficient implementation of high achievement standards has been identified in research as a major source of school failures among minority

Table 1
**Parental Educational Goals by Social Status, IQ, and Race:
Boys in Grade 8–12**

	Parental Educational Goals by Social Status and IQ[a]					
	Middle and Working IQ Percentiles			Lower and Father-Absent IQ Percentiles		
Perceived Parental Educational Goals	*0–19*	*20–39*	*40+*	*0–19*	*20–39*	*40+*
Negro						
Insists on college	36	33	35	14	15	27
Wants son to attend college	54	52	51	62	64	60
Uncertain or other	10	15	14	24	21	13
Total	100	100	100	100	100	100
	(67)	(48)	(59)	(119)	(89)	(60)
White						
Insists on college	20	22	24	12	12	20
Wants son to attend college	43	54	64	35	63	66
Uncertain or other	37	24	12	53	25	14
Total	100	100	100	100	100	100
	(35)	(68)	(491)	(40)	(59)	(147)

[a] The firm status groups were defined as follows: middle—father has at least some college and a skilled occupation; working—father has less than a college education and is employed in at least a skilled occupation—father has some college or none but is not employed in a skilled occupation; lower—father has less than a college education and is an unskilled or semiskilled worker; low-status, father-absent—father is not living at home and mother has a high school education or less. Education was included in the index because of its considerable importance as a source of Negro prestige (see Glenn, 1963).

children, a deficiency which is most probable among parents who espouse high goals for their children and yet see little hope of their fulfillment, as in the case of an academically retarded or low-IQ child. Three forms of parental support for achievement were examined in the two racial groups: supervised autonomy, interest in and demands for commendable performance in school, and the relative use of tangible and symbolic rewards in reinforcing such performance.

Through disciplined experience in self-direction and problem solving, a child may acquire the initiative, self-confidence, and skills which facilitate autonomous work in achievement situations. High standards coupled with effective supervision and discipline link self-direction with responsibility, moral boundaries, and challenging goals. In comparison to white youth, Negro boys were more likely to engage in activities beyond the sphere of parental influence and knowledge; they were not as likely to be given the opportunity to make personal decisions, and yet a majority participated in activities which were unknown to their parents.[2] Controlling for social status, we find that three-fifths of the Negro mothers of boys in junior high school were described as making all final decisions, but only one-third were reported as usually knowing the location and companions of their sons outside the household. This difference was reversed among white mothers. Fifty-eight percent were described as usually aware of son's whereabouts and associates, while less than two-fifths tended to make the final decision on matters concerning their son. Racial differences were slightly less on fathers. Both adolescent involvement in decision making and parental knowledge of a son's location and companions away from home were moderately related to social status in the two racial groups.[3]

Despite large status and aptitude differences between the two racial groups, there is a high degree of similarity in perceptions of parental achievement demands and interest among black and white boys. Approximately three out of five boys in each racial group reported that their mothers often encouraged them to do well in school, and asked them about their activities in school. Half of the fathers in each group were so described. Comparable results were obtained on parental dissatisfaction with son's effort in school. As measured by these practices and attitudes, level of parental support was positively related to family status in each racial group, and did not vary by age of son.

A sizable racial difference, however, is seen in the personal context of achievement demands, as defined by the child's IQ and family status. This is shown for mothers in Table 2 on promotion of excellence in school work and in dissatisfaction with effort (results for fathers were very similar). Negro mothers were most likely to promote good work in school and thus attempt to implement their aspirations among sons of relatively high mental ability; such implementation is least evident among low ability sons. As measured by intellectual skills, the likelihood of academic and future success seems to be influential in eliciting achievement support and pressure from Negro parents. In the white sample, on the other hand, there is relatively little variation in achiever's pressure by level of son's IQ, although it tends to be more prevalent in the high-status group among the least capable boys.

TANGIBLE AND SYMBOLIC REWARDS

Parental approval of children's academic performance may be conveyed by tangible and symbolic rewards. The former refers to money and gifts, the latter to praise, encouragement, and affection. Praise and encouragement tend to have greater lasting value in reinforcing children's behavior when compared to the effects of gifts and money. Eventually the child associates these rewards with a certain level of performance, and acquires the capacity to reinforce himself. By contrast, tangible rewards for school achievement are coupled with limitations—economic and other—which make them less available and consistent. This difference has particular significance for the minority children who display an inability to persevere in their academic effort in the absence of immediate rewards, and are rewarded primarily by gifts or money (Katz, 1967: 162).

Table 2
**Maternal Achievement Demands by Social Status,
IQ, and Race: Boys in Grades 8–12**

	Maternal Achievement Demands by Social Status and IQ of Son: Percentages					
	Middle and Working IQ Percentiles			**Lower and Father-Absent** IQ Percentiles		
Maternal Achievement Demands	*0–19*	*20–39*	*40+*	*0–19*	*20–39*	*40+*
Negro Promotes excellence[a] in schoolwork	56 (70)	72 (50)	80 (60)	55 (65)	56 (91)	60 (63)
Feels son doesn't work hard enough	51 (69)	62 (45)	68 (57)	44 (105)	42 (79)	62 (60)
White Promotes excellence[a] in schoolwork	77 (35)	57 (67)	61 (497)	60 (42)	65 (60)	58 (146)
Feels son doesn't work hard enough	57 (35)	68 (62)	57 (487)	53 (38)	59 (58)	58 (145)

[a] Percentage of boys who gave "often" as responses to "Do your parents get after you to do well in your schoolwork?"

Frequent use of tangible rewards also has the potential disadvantage of increasing the frustration of deprived children by emphasizing a resource which is in short supply.

The parents of black adolescents employed gifts and money as rewards much more freely than did the parents of white youth. Sixty per cent of the Negro boys in junior high school reported that their parents would probably or definitely give them money for a good report card, in comparison to a third of the white boys. Racial differences were also substantial in the high school group on all status levels, although money was not as frequently cited as a reward. The promise of gifts for good behavior showed similar racial variations. This reinforcement was twice as prevalent in the Negro than in the white sample (28 versus 12%) in the junior high school group). Though one could attribute this racial difference to the more severe deprivation of the black community, the data do not wholly support this interpretation. In fact, differences in tangible rewards are generally greatest between Negro and white youth in the high-status group (see Table 3). Minority status—as well as absolute economic deprivation—appears to strengthen a preference for tangible rewards in the socialization of children.

Table 3
**Parental Rewards for Good Grades by Social Status,
IQ, and Race: Boys in Grades 8–12**

	Parental Rewards for Good Grades by Social Status and IQ					
Parental	Middle and Working IQ Percentile			Lower and Father-Absent IQ Percentile		
Rewards for						
Good Grades	*0–19*	*20–39*	*40+*	*0–19*	*20–39*	*40+*
Negro						
Praise[a]	43 (70)	63 (46)	59 (58)	32 (117)	40 (88)	60 (60)
Money[b]	50 (68)	55 (47)	46 (59)	50 (118)	42 (89)	28 (61)
White						
Praise[a]	46 (35)	38 (66)	57 (493)	19 (42)	46 (59)	50 (148)
Money[b]	39 (36)	20 (67)	27 (494)	26 (42)	32 (60)	27 (147)

[a] Percentage of boys who gave "definitely" as response to "if you brought home a good report card, would your parents praise you?"
[b] Percentage of boys who gave "definitely" and "probably" as responses to "if you brought home a good report card, would your parents give you money?"

Do frequent material rewards develop a generalized external motive among deprived minority children? Are Negro children who are socialized with economic rewards likely to consider such objects as the main reason for working hard on school assignments, for completing high school, or for getting a job? One question which tapped this attitude dealt with the economic motive for working: "the only reason to have a job is for money." Black youth who said that they definitely or probably would receive money from their parents for a good report card were less likely to reject this work attitude than other boys (25 versus 49%), a difference which was relatively similar in both high- and low-status groups. The significance of economic reinforcements for intensifying frustration in a deprived context is suggested by results from a related analysis. Support for the Black Muslims was found to be strongly related to an awareness of racial discrimination and an economic motive for working. Among white boys in the sample, economic rewards for a commendable report card were related to an economic motive only in the most deprived context, in the low-status and father-absent groups, a result which is generally consistent with the notion that deprivation of a commodity increases its value.

Verbal rewards for academic performance were equally prevalent in each racial group—approximately 45% of the boys in junior and senior high school reported that they would definitely receive praise from their parents if they brought home a good report card. Parental praise was slightly related to social status in both racial groups, with an average difference of 12% between the middle-status and father-absent groups.

Bright and less competent boys experienced different types of rewards in each racial group. Parental praise for good grades was most prevalent

Table 4
Patterns of Educational Aspirations–Expectations
Among Negro and White Boys (in Grades 9–12)
by Social Status

Social Status	Number of Cases	Percentage of Negro and White Boys by Patterns of Educational Aspirations—Expectations			
		Asp. > Exp.[a]	High Asp. = Exp.	Low Asp. = Exp.	Total Percentage
Negro					
Middle	43	7	49	44	100
Working	98	18	28	54	100
Lower	148	20	25	55	100
Low, Father-Absent	63	11	25	64	100
White					
Middle	228	13	77	10	100
Working	327	20	42	38	100
Lower	207	22	30	48	100
Low, Father-Absent	39	18	28	54	100

[a] Aspiration greater than expectation represents the desire to complete college and lower educational expectations. High aspiration and similar expectation refer to the goal of a college education. Low aspiration and similar expectation refer to an educational goal which is lower than a college education.

among boys of relatively high ability, especially in the lower-status group, while monetary rewards were most common among low ability boys, black and white (Table 3). The concentration of economic rewards among the least able boys may reflect their greater responsiveness to tangible gratification and the relative ineffectiveness of verbal rewards. Tangible rewards may also serve as a substitute for personal interest among parents who are not rewarded by the successful achievements of their offspring. This interpretation seems especially relevant to Negro parents whose efforts in achievement training are dependent on the reinforcing value of their children's performance—perhaps those in the low status group.

A situation conducive to frustrated ambition is most evident among black youth in the low and middle IQ groups. The level of parental aspirations reported by these youth is similar to that experienced by more able youth, yet only in the latter group is parental support and reinforcement relatively consistent with such goals. Parental interest in school activities, encouragement of good school work, and praise for academic achievement were all more frequently reported by black adolescents of high ability. Assuming that many low-achieving boys internalized the high aspirations of their parents, barriers to achievement are likely to have produced a wide gap between desire and reality. We turn now to a consideration of conditions associated with this discrepancy and its hypothesized relation to sentiment favoring black power and solidarity.

AMBITION, REALITY, AND RACIAL-GROUP IDENTIFICATION

The proportion of black youth who wanted a college education, but expected to achieve less, increased sharply from the seventh to the twelfth grade, from 9 to 25%. This educational prospect was also held by 16% of the white boys, but it did not increase between the younger and older age groups. The age trend among blacks seems to reflect a growing awareness of barriers to their achievement—both personal and social—and contrasts with the consistently high aspirations of their parents. White youth in high school were much more likely to both desire *and* expect a college education than their Negro classmates (48 versus 27%).

Since family resources that support educational achievement favor middle-class boys, and are least available to boys in low-status, father-absent families, belief in the chance for a college education should be most common among high status boys, with low aims and expectations most characteristic of youth in the lower stratum. Boys in the intermediate groups—working and lower—appear most vulnerable to a discrepancy between college goals and lower expectations. They are not the most deprived youth in the sample, but neither do they have the advantages of higher status in access to higher education.

Table 4 presents some evidence of this curvilinear relationship between goal-means discrepancy and family status. Higher aspirations than expectations are most common among boys in the intermediate groups, and this discrepancy is the primary difference between their goal orientation and that of higher-status boys. Similar variations, though less pronounced, also appear among white boys.

It is instructive to view these racial differences in educational aspiration, and their distribution by social status, in relation to differences which were measured six to eight years earlier, a time when the dreams and hopes of black youth in the lower strata were bolstered by the promise of new opportunity. They and their parents generally expressed higher aspirations than whites of roughly similar or even higher status. The failure of this promise and the accumulation of frustrations, expressed in urban uprisings of the mid-1960s, also seem to be reflected in the more modest ambitions of Negro boys in the present study. These youth were less likely to aspire to a college education than whites, a difference which is greatest in the high-status groups.

Although we assumed that the perception of unfulfilled ambition among black youth would be associated with average ability, limited parental support for achievement, and high parental goals, a different picture emerges from the data. It is the combination of high parental aspirations *and* pressure to achieve among boys who are neither the least nor the most able that is most predictive of frustrated ambition. Seventy per cent of the boys with this educational prospect reported that mother usually got after them to do well in school, in contrast to 63 and 45% of the boys with college and lower expectations. Comparable differences were obtained on father's encouragement of good work in school, on parental dissatisfaction with academic performance, and on more general measures of parental concern in socialization, such as supervision of son's activities away from home. The average IQ percentile of the discrepant group is 29, as against 38 and 23 for the high and low expectation groups.

Frustration is most evident in the responses of boys who aspired to a college education but anticipated little chance of its fulfillment (Table 5). These boys were not more aware of explicit racial barriers than boys with low aspirations and expectations, but they tended to show greater interest in school and concern about what their teachers thought of them. Their expectations and desires regarding marriage and employment were relatively consistent with the belief that college might not be possible. This is particularly evident on their occupational perspective; the perceptions of these boys closely match those of youth with similar educational expectations. For example, they resembled boys with low expectations on likelihood of uncertainty in getting the job they wanted, of positive sentiments toward a low-status job, and of low-status expectations for the first job after completion of formal schooling and military obligations. To a large percentage of these youth, the achievement of a high-status job is a long-term and unlikely proposition at best. In view of the discrepancy between their desires and reality, it is not surprising that they tend to be higher than the other two groups on generalized anxiety regarding the future, discouragement, and self-disparagement. It is important to note, however, that they stand more apart from other boys in the sample on worries concerning the future than on feelings of worthlessness.

Low-status parents are not well equipped to offer useful information and guidance to their ambitious sons, as a result of their limited educational and occupational experience, and these boys are generally less inclined to rely upon parental advice than are boys from high-status families. This discrimination on appropriate reference individuals for upward mobility is illustrated by the comments of an academically successful Negro boy from a lower-class family in Trinidad. "My parents are not up-to-date people. I think it wise that I should let you know that I have never discussed my intentions with my parents or anyone else except now, and I don't have any intentions of doing so with them either" (Rubin and Zavalloni, 1969: ch. 5). In the present sample, the percentage of black youth who frequently discussed future plans with mother was relatively small in the low-status group (about 24%), and did not vary by level of educational aspiration. Such conversations were more common among boys from high-status families, and were also related to their aspiration level. Frequent discussions were most prevalent among black youth who were high on both aspirations and expectations (61%), followed by boys in the discrepant and low aspiration–expectation groups (53 versus 35%). Discussions with Negro fathers occurred less frequently than with mothers, although differences between the educational groups were similar.[1]

Table 5
Negro Boy's Perceptions (Grades 9–12) of Racial Oppression, Parental Goals, School Achievement, and Self, by Patterns of Educational Aspirations– Expectations

Orientations	Percentages of Negro Boys by Educational Aspirations–Expectations		
	Asp. > Exp.	*High Asp. = Exp.*	*Low Asp. = Exp.*
Racial Oppression	n = 59[a]	n = 110	n = 203
1. Racial discrimination may prevent me from getting the job I want	72	68	69
2. I know people who have been roughed up by the police	63	49	58
Parents			
3. Parents want son to achieve professional or managerial-type job	55	71	37
4. Parents want me to aim for goals which I think are of little value; agree, undecided	47	36	54
School			
5. Like school	48	63	36
6. Stayed away from school to do other things	39	39	53
7. Cares a lot about what teachers think of him	55	49	34
Dating and Marriage			
8. Started dating at age 16, 17, or 18	46	54	38
9. Wants to get married at age 21 or later	42	53	36
Occupational Achievement			
10. I am completely or pretty sure that I will get the job I want	45	63	45
11. Would strongly dislike becoming a truck driver	23	36	23
12. Expects to achieve high status job (professional or managerial) after completion of schooling or military	28	48	20
13. Eventually *wants* to achieve high-status job	51	62	32
14. Eventually *expects* to achieve high-status job	41	56	30
Self-Evaluation			
15. I often feel discouraged	51	35	37
16. At times I think I am no good at all	41	30	32
17. Generalized anxiety toward future[b]	56	25	36

[a] Minimum number of cases for all items.
[b] Generalized anxiety toward future was measured by a summation of scores on six items: "Are you worried about knowing (1) what your real interests are?"; (2) what you will do after school?"; (3) what work you are best suited for?"; (4) whether you should go to college?"; (5) how much ability you really have?"; (6) how you can learn a trade?" Very worried was scored 2; somewhat worried, 1; and not worried, 0. The above percentages represent scores of nine or more on a scale ranging from 0–14.

GREATER SUPPORT FOR BLACK SOLIDARITY

If identification with the black community is strengthened when ambition is frustrated by anticipated racial barriers, it should be least common among black youth who firmly believe in their own chance to achieve mobility through education. The expectation of successful status placement reinforces individualism in social ascent and contradicts the belief that race is a major factor in achievement. To measure sentiment toward black solidarity or power, we used three interrelated items which describe strategies for the achievement of goals advocated by black power organizations: "Get all Negroes to take the same stand on racial issues"; "Black leadership of Negro organizations, but allow whites to be members"; and "Negroes should strike back if attacked." On each item, strongly agree was scored 2, agree, 1; and undecided or disagree, 0. On the resulting summated index, with values ranging from 0 to 6, scores of three or more were defined as support for black solidarity.

The relation between the anticipated frustration of educational ambition and support for black solidarity generally corresponds with our expectations. In grades nine through twelve, approval of black solidarity was most prevalent among Negro boys who anticipated unfulfilled goals (61%), followed by youth with relatively low aspirations and expectations (44%), and then by boys who expected to achieve a college education (29%—$\bar{X}$ = 10.0, 2df., <.01). The substantial popularity of black solidarity among boys who did not aspire or expect to achieve a college education may reflect an adaptation in the preceding years to anticipated barriers which produced lower goals. Available evidence indicates that black power youth in this group were more inclined than their counterparts in the discrepant group to reject culturally approved means to achieve valued goals. Estrangement from school, suspension from school, one or more juvenile offenses, rejection of the legitimacy of normative constraints, and negative sentiment toward residence in a racially integrated neighborhood were all more characteristic of boys in the low aspiration–expectation group who affirmed the collective interests of the black community.

Blocked educational achievement is clearly only one of the many potential sources of identification with the black community (socialization, intergroup conflict, and the like), as suggested by the prevalence of this sentiment among boys who expect to achieve high goals; but its effects are expressed through student actions in universities and high schools. In addition to issues centering on black studies, revolts among black students have stemmed in part from the alienation and hostility of students who find themselves poorly prepared for university standards. A common response to this problem is the demand that all entrance and evaluative criteria be eliminated for minority youth.

In the English-speaking Caribbean, serious deficiencies in educational opportunities and quality on the secondary level, limited economic opportunities, and the lofty aspirations of Negro youth, both personal and nationalistic, have generated increasing support for local black power movements. On the island of Trinidad, which achieved independence from Great Britain in 1962 and has been governed by Negro leadership since

1956, studies (Rubin and Zavalloni, 1969) conducted on the eve of independence disclosed extraordinarily high aspirations among bright Negro and East Indian youth from the lower class. The end of British rule marked the beginning of an anticipated golden era for many of the young, unconstrained by formidable economic, social, and educational problems of the new nation (*Caribbean Monthly Bulletin*, 1964; 1965; 1966; 1967; *The New York Times,* 1969; 1970). A former official of the now defunct West Indian Federation recalled the general "feeling that once 'we' took over everything was going to work out well, as if there was something magic about a black government. But we took over the problems that the British were glad to get rid of. Black is beautiful, yes, but it represents no magic formula for solving a host of economic problems." The per capita income of the islands was high in 1960, relative to other islands, but it did not increase or keep pace with the aspirations of the young. By 1968, a third of the employable under the age of thirty-five were jobless, while the average high school graduate generally obtained his first job after the age of twenty. The scarcity of jobs markedly increased the importance of education as a route to economic security, and enlarged sources of frustration in the educational system—a shortage of places on the secondary and university level, poor quality teaching, and a curriculum heavily biased toward the content and structure of British grammar education. In 1969–70, jobs were available for only one-sixth of the high school graduates.

ESCALATION OF BLACK POWER ACTIVITY

In line with Davies' (1969) J-curve theory of revolutions, increased awareness of these and other deprivational conditions represents a major force behind the current black power movement on the island. As protests, demonstrations, and bombings increased during the early months of 1970, the government's public definition of the situation changed from "the hooliganism of a small minority" to outward acknowledgement of the serious internal threat posed by the unrest and strife, as expressed in its prohibition of a planned march in Port of Spain (April 1970), arrests of four leaders, and police enforcement of the ban. This action provoked a general uprising in the city and mutiny among black power advocates in the Armed Forces, resulting in the most serious national crisis in the nation's young history.

Recruits to the black power movement, among the brightest youths on the island, are described as angry, frustrated students and the unemployed who are acutely aware of their dismal future under an "uncaring" black government which has clothed itself in the white man's garments. As one leader who is a likely Prime Minister put it, "all current West Indian government officials are charlatans who run the plantation for whites and fail to use political power for the good of their people. Black power must be the fact of making government work effectively for people of both African and East Indian descent, and our society cannot move forward without seeing to the needs of both races. We must make it stop catering to the interests of Canada, the United Kingdom, and the United States at the expense of its citizens." The movement has projected a broad appeal for support, with special emphasis on the involvement of "black Indian brothers" and unionists, and is oriented toward the development of black awareness, responsive black leadership, and black control of the economy. White exploitation through control of the nation's resources and industries (oil, natural gas, sugar, and tourism) is the major target of the movement. The long-term consequences of the black power movement are partially contingent on its effectiveness in gaining support and cooperation from the East Indians.⁵

The currrent escalation of unrest and protest on the predominantly black island of Jamaica was anticipated by a study (Smith, 1965: 220) in the mid-1950s which disclosed a large disparity between the goals and realistic prospects of rural youth. On the basis of these findings, Smith envisioned a crisis of national proportions unless substantial reforms were made in the opportunity structure. The initial features of this crisis have recently emerged in the form of a highly militant, black power movement. One of the spokesmen for this movement is the son of Marcus Garvey, the founder of African nationalism. In Garvey's view, Jamaican black power vigorously opposes the present situation of a few black leaders (prime minister and governor general) and an economic structure "where the white man is at the top and a huge black mass is submerged in inferiority, like the hidden portion of an Iceberg." To contain the movement, Jamaican authorities have used repressive methods, Including the banning of black militants from other countries and censorship of black power materials (censorship of "subversive" materials has also been employed by Trinidad authorities).

Mass communications have been instrumental in spreading the black power message from the politicized in urban areas to the countryside, and it is through the media, as well as the overseas education of black leaders, that the black liberation movement in the United States has entered the consciousness and ideas of the deprived West Indian. In ideology, rhetoric, and personal dress, there is considerable resemblance between black power activists of the Caribbean and the United States. There are also important parallels in the roots of the black movement in the two areas. However, West Indian blacks (including the East Indians) have a substantial demographic advantage, as the largest population group, over their counterparts in the United States.

DEPRIVATION, DEPENDENCY, AND FAMILISTIC SENTIMENT

In its relation to anticipated failure in status achievement, familistic sentiment among Negro youth may resemble support for black solidarity, but there are important differences in the hypothesized origins of these reference group orientations. While a strong attachment to the family discourages, and is inversely related to individualistic achievement, as numerous studies (Kahl, 1965) have shown, this tie is more likely to develop from social conditioning than from the anticipation of blocked mobility opportunities in adolescence. Black youth who are reluctant to leave the family are apt to be those who feel least capable of competing and achieving in a society controlled by whites—those who are relatively low in measured intelligence and lack a sense of mastery over their destiny.

Familistic attitudes among black adolescents were completely unrelated to support for black solidarity, but they were slightly more prevalent among boys who did not aspire to a college education than among youth with higher aspirations. The measure of familism used in the analysis was constructed from two interrelated items: "Nothing is worth moving away from one's parents" and "Even when I get married, my main loyalty will still be to my mother and father." For both items, strongly agree was scored 3; agree, 2; undecided, 1; and disagree, 0. On this index, familistic sentiment is considerably more prevalent among Negro boys than among whites. Fifty-eight per cent of the Negro boys (grades 9–12) had scores of three or more, in comparison to 30% of the white boys. As a point of comparison, it is of interest to note that these attitudes are nearly as prevalent among Negro youth in the sample as they are among boys in the familistic culture of Brazil, according to a recent study by Rosen (1964).

Can this racial difference be explained by the powerlessness of minority status and the relative security or protection offered by the black family, or is it primarily a consequence of the more prevalent personal disabilities among black youth which encourage withdrawal from perceived dangers in a predominantly white society. The minority child's departure from the family represents an act of faith in his personal competence and in the trustworthiness and receptivity of the larger society. Since minority status and incompetence undermine this faith, they represent potential sources of primary attachment to the family of orientation.

Although Negro families in the sample are markedly lower in socioeconomic status than white families, this difference does not account for the greater prevalence of familistic sentiment among black youth. In high- and low-status families, these boys were nearly twice as likely as white boys to feel emotionally attached to their families. Dependence or incompetence, on the other hand, is related to familistic attitudes in both racial groups. Racial differences on intelligence and familism are interrelated, as shown in Table 6. A much larger proportion of black than of white boys had IQ scores below the 29th percentile, but in each racial group the percentage who gave priority to family ties is identical. However, moderate racial differences do appear among brighter boys.

Table 6
**Familistic Sentiment Among Negro and White Boys
(Grades 9–12) by IQ**

	Familistic Sentiment by Race and IQ: Percentage	
IQ Percentiles	*Negro*	*White*
0–19	68 (101)	67 (52)
20–39	55 (82)	47 (92)
40–59	46 (50)	34 (142)
60–79	30 (27)	28 (189)
80+		20 (192)
	tau$_c$ = .23, <.001	tau$_c$ = .23, <.001

Minority status and relatively low ability are conducive to a sense of fatalism, and this outlook was more prevalent among black than among white boys. A third of the black youth in grades nine through twelve agreed that "what is going to happen will happen regardless of what I do" and that "a person should live for today and let tomorrow take care of itself," in comparison to 14% of the white boys.[6] A fatalistic perspective was more strongly associated with familism among Negro boys than among whites (Tau$_c$ = .26 versus .07). However, even among black youth, fatalism contributes very little to the prediction of familistic sentiment beyond the effect of IQ, since low test scores and fatalism are interrelated.

The effect of low ability on family attachment may be strengthened by parental protectiveness toward less assertive and competent offspring. Studies have found a relationship between these parental patterns and adolescent reactions to the extrafamilial world—apprehension, anxiety, and distrust (see Pinner, 1965)—which could reinforce family ties.

The reference individuals chosen by youth are likely to be influenced by their sense of attachment to the family. Interpersonal trust is an essential precondition for emulation and this attitude is not likely to extend beyond the family among familistic boys. Accordingly, we expected parents to be more attractive than age-mates as behavior models among boys with familistic attitudes, with the reverse pattern of identification occurring most often among emotionally independent youth. In both racial groups, the degree of familistic sentiment was found to be moderately correlated with a desire to emulate mother and father (av. Tau$_c$ = .14 < .05). Selection of best friends as models, on the other hand, was negatively associated with familism, but only among Negro boys was the relationship statistically significant (Tau$_c$ = .17 < .01). Since subordination of self to the family discourages mobility, it is noteworthy that familistic boys in each racial group were inclined to reject the idea that a "person should leave home after he gets out of school" (av. Tau$_c$ = .16 < .01).

GROUP ORIENTATIONS, ATTITUDES, AND SOCIAL ASCENT

Familistic sentiment is frequently associated with a world view in which the external milieu is stereotyped as untrustworthy, dangerous, and exploitive. Among youth in a racial minority, we might expect familistic sentiment to be associated with aspects of this world view, and perhaps with antiwhite attitudes as well. Since sensitivity to white domination is generaly linked with racial identification, rejection of whites seems most probable among black youth who are identified with both their family and racial group.

The relative independence of familism and black solidarity among Negro boys permitted the construction of four types of group orientations, defined by high or low scores on each index; communal, racial, familistic, and individualistic. A *communal* orientation was defined by scores of three or more on both the familism and black solidarity indexes. The *familistic* and *racial* orientations represent scores of three or more on identification with the family or minority. Minimal attachment to either group represents an *individualistic* orientation. Individualistic boys had the highest average IQ percentile (38), followed by the racially oriented ($\overline{X} = 34$), and the remaining two groups ($\overline{X}$'s $= 25$). Table 7 shows a comparison of boys in each group on perspectives toward other people and the world at large, on interracial contact and attitudes, and on deviance and achievement.

A perception of the world as untrustworthy, friendless, and ruled by self-interest is most prevalent among black youth who are identified with both the family and racial group. The distrust and alienation of communally oriented boys appears to be directed mainly toward white society, while familistic youth display greater social distance and indifference toward their own people. The latter are less apt to associate with blacks, and relatively few approve of strategies for improving the collective status of Negroes. Questions more specifically directed toward trust and cooperation in the black community would probably show even sharper differences in the targets of distrust selected by these two groups of boys.

The belief that negative attitudes toward whites or separatism is an inevitable correlate of racial group identification is challenged by the data presented in Table 7. It is familism rather than racial identification per se which is associated with personal disinterest in residential integration. Thus among the supporters of black power, boys who reject dependency on their family of orientation are just as receptive to residential integration as youth who are not oriented toward either their family or racial group.

Despite the opportunistic attitude of many boys in the communal group, there is surprisingly little difference between them and other boys in recorded delinquency and educational prospects in each of the four orientation groups. This is particularly evident among boys who are oriented toward either their racial group or family. The largest percentage of boys with frustrated ambition appears among the racially oriented, and yet they are less apt to have committed an offense than boys in the familistic group.

Although racial group identification stems in part from blocked mobility, it is not necessarily incompatible or in conflict with social ascent through education and the occupational system, or with a desire for racial integration. Conflict does occur when such identification is combined with a primary attachment to the family, but this effect is due largely to the latter condition. Whether favorable to black solidarity or not, familistic youth displays considerable reluctance to leave the family in late adolescence and relatively few are receptive to the idea of living in a racially integrated neighborhood. Since these youth are relatively low in both verbal skills and mastery, an important step toward the promotion of achievement would involve the reduction of these deficiencies in a context of equal opportunity. This strategy centers on a fundamental task of socialization in a modern society, that of developing the resources which enable children to leave their family of origin and establish an independent identity. As an infantile form of identification in adolescence, familism is symptomatic of failure in this task.

Development of capacities for competent independence differs markedly from the primary strategy which has been employed to assimilate minority children, that of reworking their identity in the image of the dominant group. By assaulting group identity, schools and other social

Table 7

**Attitudes and Behavior of Negro Boys (Grades 9–12)
by Typology of Group Orientations**

	Percentages of Negro Boys (Grades 9–12) by Typology of Group Orientations			
Attitudes	Com-munal	Racial	Fami-listic	Individ-ualistic
Perspective Toward World	n = 76[a]	n = 51	n = 79	n = 86
1. If you don't watch yourself, people will take advantage: strongly agree	37	28	21	12
2. What is lacking in the world is the old kind of friendship: strongly agree	36	11	15	15
3. Everyone is out for himself: agree	55	42	36	34
4. It is allright to get around the law if you can get away with it: agree	40	20	21	24
5. Fatalistic: 0–1 scores on index	35	22	51	19
Interracial Contact and Attitudes				
6. All of friends are Negro	31	21	13	17
7. Primary interaction with Negro peers[b]	85	70	60	57
8. Likes white people	34	40	43	43
9. Interracial contact[c]	42	51	45	40
10. Would you like to live in an integrated neighborhood	28	54	23	48
11. Whites should be forced to open their neighborhoods to Negroes: strongly agree	49	55	20	21
12. Conditions should be improved in Negro community: strongly agree	56	57	19	38
Deviance and Educational Goals				
13. Delinquency: One or more offences (from official police files)	55	50	63	47
14. Educational Aspirations-Expectations				
Asp. < Exp.	20	28	18	10
High Asp. = Exp.	18	24	33	36
Low Asp = Exp.	62	46	48	54

[a] Minimal number of cases across all items.

[b] The percentage of Negro boys who answered "often" to the following questions: "Have you ever eaten with a Negro?"; "Have you ever danced with a Negro?"; and "Have you ever gone to a party where most of the people were Negro?"

[c] The three questions listed in footnote b were also asked in reference to contact with whites. The percentage of Negro boys with interracial contact was defined by scores of three or more on an index constructed from the above items. For each item, often was scored 2, sometimes 1, and never 0.

agencies have frequently generated the very circumstances which strengthen the protective and separatist influence of the family in the life of minority children—alienation, incompetence, and fatalism.

SUMMARY

Historically, rejection through persecution, isolation, and barriers to achievement has been a primary source of ingroup feeling among members of a minority. In the present context of widespread mobilization and race consciousness, we hypothesized that identification with the collective interests of the black community would be most prevalent among relatively able Negro boys who are socialized to success goals which are found to be inaccessible, largely as a consequence of external barriers. The likelihood of this frustration is increased by Negro parents who promote high aspirations but are unable to implement them effectively through training and available resources. The belief that one's ability and opportunities are equal to the task of goal attainment tends to nurture a desire for achievement through individual effort.

In addition to, or instead of, a commitment to racial solidarity and power, some youth—primarily those who lack competence and a sense of mastery—may turn inward to the family protection and security. In a white-controlled society, a black child's willingness to leave the family in late adolescence is likely to be contingent on skills appropriate to future achievement, on self-confidence, and on the perceived receptivity of the larger society.

These determinants of racial group and family identifications were investigated in a sample of black youth from an industrial community on the west coast of the United States. For comparative purposes, we included a sample of white boys from the same community and materials on the life opportunities and racial ideology of Negro youth on English-speaking islands in the Caribbean. The Negro boys in the study came from lower status families than their white classmates, and were significantly lower in IQ. The main findings of the analysis are summarized below.

(1) Awareness of unjust treatment by the police, racial discrimination in employment, and restricted life prospects increased among black youth from early adolescence to the last year of high school. In the white sample, perception of these aspects of the black child's experience showed little change by age.

(2) Black youth reported high parental aspirations concerning a college education which were equal to those reported by whites, even though the latter were appreciably higher on both family status and measured intelligence. Perceived level of parental aspiration varied more strongly by family status and son's IQ in the white than in the black sample. Thus the greatest disparity between parental aspiration and prospects for such achievement occurred among low-status Negro boys in the low-ability group.

(3) Within this aspirational context, three child-rearing practices relevant to achievement socialization were compared in the two racial groups: supervised autonomy, parental interest in commendable academic performance and dissatisfaction with present level of effort, and rewards, tangible and symbolic. With social status controlled, Negro parents were more frequently described as making final decisions involving their son and as not knowing his location and companions when away from the household. Second, the perceived level of parental achievement demands and interest was similar in each racial group, although sizable differences emerged when comparisons were made with IQ and status subgroups. Promotion of excellence in school work and dissatisfaction with effort were directly related to IQ among Negro boys, especially in the high-status group. No substantial variation by these factors was obtained in the white sample. Thirdly, money was used more frequently by Negro parents than by whites to reward academic performance with the largest racial difference occurring among less able youth from high- and low-status families. Frequent use of praise did not vary by race, and was directly related to family status and son's IQ in both racial groups.

(4) From early to late adolescence, black youth became aware of racial barriers to achievement and of their inability to realize chosen educational goals. In the twelfth grade, nearly a third anticipated failure in achieving their goal of a college education. A similar discrepancy was also found among a much smaller percentage of white boys, but this perception did not increase or decrease by age. Consistent with their more favorable opportunities, white youth in high school were much more likely than blacks to feel optimistic toward their prospects for a college education. This expectation increased by family status within each racial group, with frustrated ambition most prevalent among boys who were neither highest nor lowest in family status.

(5) Negro boys who did not expect to achieve their goal of a college education differed in three additional respects from others in their racial group. First, they were not as bright on the average as boys with college expectations, but neither were they as low in IQ as boys who neither aspired to nor expected a college education. Secondly, they were more likely than other boys to report parental pressure to achieve in school, dissatisfaction with effort, and close supervision of their activities. And thirdly, they were more apt to feel discouraged and anxious about future roles. Boys in the discrepant group resembled youth with low educational expectations and aspirations on uncertainty regarding achievement of their preferred job, on positive sentiment toward a low-status job, on low-status occupational expectations, and on disinterest in parental goals. The anticipation of racial barriers was equally common among all boys in the sample.

(6) Support for black solidarity was most prevalent among boys who did not expect to achieve their goal of a college education, followed by youth who neither desired nor expected to attain this goal, with the lowest degree of support among boys who expected to complete four years of college. The anticipation of frustration in educational and occupational achievement also appears to be a major factor in the growth of a black power movement in the Caribbean.

(7) The second type of reference group attitude, familistic sentiment, was substantially more common among black than among white boys, a difference which is partially explained by the greater prevalence of low ability and fatalism with a primary allegiance to parents and a desire to remain physically close to the family. Familistic youth generally preferred parents more than peers as behavior models and were likely to disapprove of the idea that young people should leave home after completing high school.

(8) Boys who were identified with both the family and racial group were most likely to perceive the world as untrustworthy, friendless, and ruled by self-interest. They displayed greater acceptance of their own people and tended to score lower on fatalism than boys who were only familistic. Although ingroup attachments may engender outgroup hostility, such as racial antipathy, only familistic sentiment was negatively correlated with the desire to live in a racially integrated community.

These findings direct attention to three sources of deprivation and frustration among minority children in a multiracial, industrial society: (1) socialization and structures which strengthen the adolescent's primordial dependence on the family of origin by failing to equip him with the skills and confidence to function independently; (2) socialization which transmits high and often unrealistic aspirations but fails to develop the necessary skills or provide external resources for such achievement; and, most importantly, (3) the external discriminatory barriers which exclude minority children from achievement opportunities. While the latter two conditions are common knowledge, the origins and consequences of familistic attachments deserve greater attention. Withdrawal to the family inhibits use of available opportunity, while strengthening the hand of racial subordination and social dependency.

NOTES

1. The secondary school population of the community was stratified by race, sex, school, and grade level. Since Negro youth and boys in each racial group were of primary interest to the study, they were disproportionately sampled: 85% of the Negro boys, 60% of the Negro girls, 30% of the non-Negro boys, and 12% of the non-Negro girls (Oriental, Caucasian, and others). This procedure produced a stratified probability sample of 5,545 students.

Completed questionnaires were obtained from approximately three-fourths of the students in the probability sample. Teachers administered the questionnaire in three parts, each of which took approximately fifty minutes; in most of the schools the sections were administered on three consecutive days. Validation tests of the questionnaire data were conducted by interviewing a small number of students in the sample and their parents. An analysis of sample bias resulting from this attrition disclosed small but consistent differences between the students who completed the questionnaire and those who did not; the former were slightly better students.

When the proportion of the population in each substratum—race/sex categories by grade and school—is identical, the sample statistics are direct, unbiased estimates of population parameters. To achieve this end, the proportion of responding in each of the four race/sex categories was calculated. Cases were then randomly duplicated in those substrata whose response rate dropped below that of their race/sex category and randomly discarded from those substrata whose rate exceeded that for the race/sex category. In this entire sample, only 193 cases were deleted and 171 randomly added. For the purpose of comparing Negro and white boys, a small number of Mexican-American and Oriental respondents were omitted from the sample.

2. Low self-direction in decision making was measured by either of the following responses to the question, "How are most decisions made between you and your mother/father?": "She/he tells me what to do" and "We talk about it, but she/he decides." A high level of supervision was measured by "usually" responses to each of the following questions: "Does your mother/father know where you are when you are away from home?"

3. Among intact families, there is no evidence that Negro mothers were relatively more influential in conjugal decision making on child-rearing matters than white mothers. Controlling for social status, we find that 35 and 16% of the Negro fathers and mothers were described as more influential in setting disciplinary policy. This compares with 41 and 15% among white youth. Moderate racial differences do appear, however, on the administration of discipline. With social status controlled, we find the predominant involvement of mothers slightly greater in the black sample (19 versus 33%).

4. In the white sample, this sex difference was reversed. Frequent discussions were more common with father than with mother, especially in the high status group.

5. Race relations and its political implications have been a taboo subject to the nonracialism policy of the English-speaking islands. At a time when racial tensions were still largely covert, Vera Rubin (1962) introduced her essay, "Culture, politics, and race relations" with the following statement. "The candid discussion of relating race relations and politics may seem contrary to the national interests of emerging nations, but it would seem essential to bring this emotion-laden area under objective scrutiny in order to understand the political problems of welding a multi-cultural, multi-racial society into a homogeneous nation" (p. 433). However, this problem is completely ignored in her

recent report of a youth study in Trinidad, even though relevant data were available from the survey and the contrast between great aspirations and contemporary socioeconomic conditions called for an analysis (see Rubin and Zavalloni, 1969). The neglect is perhaps symptomatic of the critical political situation on the island.

6. Agree responses on each of these items were scored 0, undecided 1, disagree 2, and strongly disagree 3. Scores on the summated index range from 0 to 6.

7. According to research on Negroes and East Indians in Trinidad, the communal orientation would appear to be most prevalent among culture conscious East Indian adolescents. Through isolation on the island, rural East Indians have maintained strong cultural ties to the homeland and to the kinship unit. The young tend to express their personal and social goals in terms of "their own people," rather than in terms of the national community. In contrast, Negro youth from the lower class are most likely to perceive a high degree of unity among personal group, and national goals (see Rubin and Zavalloni, 1969).

REFERENCES

Almond, G. A. and S. Verba (1963) The Civic Culture. Princeton: Princeton Univ. Press.

Campbell, A. and H. Schuman (1968) "Racial attitudes in fifteen American cities," pp. 1–67 in The National Advisory Commission on Civil Disorders: Supplemental Studies, Washington, D.C.: Government Printing Office.

Danziger, K. (1963) "The psychological future of an oppressed group." Social Forces 42 (October): 31–40.

Davies, J. C. (1969) "The J-curve of rising and declining satisfaction as a cause of some great revolutions and a contained rebellion," pp. 690–730 in H. D. Graham and T. R. Gurr (eds.) Violence in America: Historical and Comparative Perspectives. New York: Bantam.

Furstenberg, F. F. (1969) "The transmission of attitudes in the family." Unpublished.

Garique, P. (1960) "The French-Canadian family," pp. 181–200 in M. Wade (ed.) Canadian Dualism. Toronto: Univ. of Toronto Press.

Gillespie, J. M. and G. W. Allport (1955) Youth's Outlook on the Future: A Cross-National Study. New York: Doubleday.

Glenn, N. D. (1963) "Negro prestige criteria: a case study in the bases of prestige." Amer. J. of Sociology 68 (May): 645–657.

Green, H. (1965) "Values of Negro and East Indian children in Trinidad." Social and Economic Studies *14:* 204–224.

Gurr, T. R. (1968) "Psychological factors in civil strife." World Politics 20 (January): 245–278.

Hess, R. and V. Shipman (1965) "Early experience and the socialization of cognitive modes in children." Child Development *36:* 869–886.

Inkeles, A. (1966) "Social structure and the socialization of competence." Harvard Educational Rev. 36 (Summer): 265–283.

Kahl, J. A. (1965) "Some measurements of achievement orientations." Amer. J. of Sociology 70: 669–681.

Katz, I. (1967) "The socialization of academic motivation in minority group children," pp. 133–191 in D. LeVine (ed.) Nebraska Symposium on Motivation. Lincoln: Univ. of Nebraska Press.

Kerr, M. (1951) Personality and Conflict in Jamaica. London: Liverpool Univ. Press.

Lewis, H. (1965) "Child rearing among low-income families," pp. 342–353 in L. A. Ferman, J. L. Kornbluh, and A. Haber (eds.) Poverty in America. Ann Arbor: Univ. of Michigan Press.

Parsons, T. and R. Fox (1952) "Illness, therapy, and the modern urban American family." J. of Social Issues 8: 31–44.

Pinner, F. H. (1965) "Parental overprotection and political distrust." Annals of the Amer. Academy of Pol. and Social Science 361 (September): 58–70.

Rose, A. (1949) The Negro's Morale: Group Identification and Protest. Minneapolis: Univ. of Minneapolis Press.

Rosen, B. C. (1964) "The achievement syndrome and economic growth in Brazil." Social Forces 42: 341–354.

Rubin, V. (1962) "Culture, Politics, and race relations." Social and Economic Studies 11: 433–455.

———— and M. Zavalloni (1969) We Wish to Be Looked Upon. New York: Teachers College Press.

Sexton, P. (1963) "Negro career expectations." Merrill-Palmer Q. 9: 303–316.

Smith, M. G. (1965) The Plural Society in the British West Indies. Berkeley: Univ. of Calif. Press.

Wenkert, R., J. Magney, and A. Neel (1967) Two Weeks of Racial Crisis in Richmond, California, Berkeley: Survey Research Center.

Generational continuity and discontinuity in the understanding of societal rejection

Jeanne H. Block
University of California, Berkeley

Investigators and observers of the student movement concur in finding rejection of societal values at the core of youthful dissent. However, interpretations diverge regarding the motivational basis underlying such contemporary social protest. The present study identifies two differently motivated kinds of societal rejections and explores empirically their respective antecedents and psychological concomitants.

One interpretation of student protest and activism is based on psychoanalytic theory. Although they elaborate the essential thesis differently, Feuer (1969), Bettelheim (1969), and Rubinstein and Levitt (1969) coalesce in ascribing radical student protest to unresolved Oedipal conflicts wherein the adolescent is rebelling against the parent, either directly or symbolically. These observers of the contemporary student scene agree about the origins of rebellion (unresolved Oedipal conflicts compounded

An earlier version of this paper was presented to the Foundations' Fund for Research in Psychiatry Conference on "Adaptation to Change," Puerto Rico, June 1968. The research on which this paper draws was supported by grants to the Institute of Human Development from the Rosenberg Foundation and the Foundations' Fund for Research in Psychiatry and by Research Scientist Development Award K2-MH-20,870-02 to the author by the National Institute of Mental Health. The Research Committee of the University of California, Berkeley, provided funds to Robert Somers that made data collection for the 1967 study possible. All of these funds are gratefully acknowledged. I wish to thank my colleagues, Norma Haan, M. Brewster Smith, and Robert Somers for permitting me to employ some of the data we have collected jointly. The final manuscript has profited from the thoughtful and judicious editing of my husband, Jack Block.

by permissive child rearing), the focus of social protest (on the institutional surrogates for the parent), and the psychopathological implications of social rejection so motivated (little legitimacy is accorded student protests addressed to society and its institutions).

Another understanding of student social protest is represented in the studies of Flacks (1967), Keniston (1968, 1969), Block, Haan, and Smith (1969), and Smith, Haan, and Block (1970). The findings of these investigators have shown that parents of student activists are themselves politically both liberal and active and socialize their young in ways that predispose them to political–social involvement. The convergence of parent and child value systems indicates that identification with, rather than rebellion against, the parent can be a motivating factor in protest activities. The findings supporting this socialization hypothesis suggest that, although the origins of social protest are manifold, a central component for many activists involves rational processes applied in critical examination of contemporary society and a moral commitment to societal change. Both this rationality and this moral commitment may be encouraged by socialization processes emphasizing individuation, authenticity, and humanitarian values (Block, Haan, & Smith, 1968; Haan, Smith & Block, 1968). According to the socialization-toward-involvement interpretation, the focus of student protest is primarily against particular societal institutions and values rather than primarily against the parents. There is the additional implication in this view that some degree of legitimacy attends the moral protests of the young, which are directed against dehumanizing institutional practices and special societal values.

The two types of societal rejection represented by these contrasted interpretations can be readily operationalized and comparatively evaluated. Students seeking societal and institutional change must first be identified. Then, this subset of students must be further subdivided into those who reject their parents as well as the larger society (the discontinuous individuals) versus those who identify with their parents, although fundamentally critical of the broader society (the continuous individuals). Clearly, these two types of societal rejection have different implications for the quality of personal development, the nature of consequent political–societal protest, and the response of societal institutions. To explore the basis for these two routes to societal disaffection, the present inquiry was undertaken.

Three primary comparisons were developed. First, samples of discontinuous and continuous individuals were compared to ascertain their differences with respect to their self-percepts, their ego ideals or value systems, and their views of their upbringing. Second, the *parents* of two additional samples of discontinuous and continuous individuals were compared with respect to their child-rearing orientations to replicate and to extend relationships found between socialization practices and generational discontinuity or continuity. Third, a sample of continuous conservatives—college students conservative in their political outlook and also in political agreement with their parents—was identified so that the child-rearing attitudes of their parents could be studied to clarify some questions raised by earlier comparisons.

STUDY I: THE SELF-PERCEPTS AND EGO IDEALS
OF CONTINUOUS VERSUS DISCONTINUOUS STUDENTS

METHOD

Selection of Comparison Groups. The subject pool contained 1,051 subjects from the University of California, Berkeley, and San Francisco State College, representing a broad spectrum of political ideologies and socioeconomic and educational levels, as well as different orientations on political–social issues. The subjects were studied in 1964. Details of data collection and sample constitution may be found in Smith et al. (1970). From this pool of subjects, two groups of subjects with different patterns of rebellion were selected on the basis of their questionnaire responses: (a) those rejecting both their parents and society and (b) those rejecting society but basically identifying with their parents.

The criterion for rejection of traditional societal values was based on the subject's self-rating on an 8-point continuum of political orientation, which ranged from extreme conservatism (1) to radicalism (8). The subjects who rated themselves as *liberal-radical* or *radical* (Steps 7 or 8, positions one standard deviation or more above the mean of the total sample) were considered to have rejected traditional societal values. Using this criterion, 147 subjects were identified.

The subjects meeting this first criterion were then evaluated with respect to their rejection or acceptance of parental values. Six scores reflecting agreement with or influence by the parents were available for each subject: (a) the agreement of the subject with the political party preference of the mother; (b) the agreement of the subject with the political party preference of the father; (c) a composite score reflecting agreement of the subject with his mother on six political–social and personal issues (e.g., civil rights, student demonstration, religion); (d) a composite score reflecting agreement of the subject with his father on these six political–social and personal issues; (e) a composite score reflecting the subject's judgment of his mother's influence on his personal, ethical, and political development; and (f) a composite score reflecting the subject's judgment of his father's influence on his personal, ethical, and political development.

A subject was identified as rejecting parental values when (a) there was a discrepancy of 4 or more points (on the 8-point continuum) between the subject's self-related radicalism or liberal radicalism and his rating of the ideological position of his mother and of his father (i.e., *both* parents were viewed as moderate conservatives or more extreme conservatives), and (b) the subject manifested low agreement with and influence by his mother and his father (scores one standard deviation or more below the agreement and influence means of the total sample). Thus, the young people meeting these criteria rejected their parents' political and value orientations and, more important, denied a positive influence of their parents on their developing personalities. These subjects are designated the *discontinuity* group to emphasize their estrangement from their parents' values as well as those held by society at large. Twenty-five males and 15 females met these selection criteria.

A subject was identified as *accepting* parental values if the discrepancy between his political positions and that of each of his parents did not exceed 3 points on the rating scale (the mean discrepancy proved to be 1.24 and typically, these parents were viewed as liberals) and, also, the scores on the agreement and influence indexes for both parents exceeded the means characterizing the total sample. The subjects meeting these criteria attributed a positive influence to their parents and manifested little discrepancy between their own beliefs and values and those of their parents. They are designated as the *continuity* group, which includes 37 males and 22 females.

Forty-eight subjects who were radical or liberal-radical in their political persuasions failed to obtain scores on the parental agreement and parental influence dimensions that qualified them for the continuity and discontinuity groups. These subjects were not included in the subsequent analyses.

RESULTS

The findings to be reported are based on three data sources available from a more extensive study of student activism (Block et al., 1968; Block, Haan, & Smith, 1969; Haan, et al., 1968; Smith, Haan, & Block, 1970). Specifically, each subject contributed descriptions of both his perceived self and ideal self using a 63-item adjective *Q* set. For each *Q* item, the differences between the two comparison groups was evaluated by the use of *t* tests. The sexes were analyzed separately because of the expectation that the psychology of radicalism in men can differ from the psychology of radicalism in women.

Self-Descriptions. With respect to the self-characterizations of these young people as reflected by adjective *Q* descriptions, the male continuity individuals describe themselves, comparatively, as somewhat less *unconventional* ($p \leq .05$) and as more *responsible* ($p \leq .01$), *masculine* ($p \leq .05$), *orderly* ($p \leq .05$), and *practical* ($p \leq .10$) than their counterparts in the discontinuity group, for whom *amusing* ($p \leq .10$) and *creative* ($p \leq .10$) were distinguishing adjectives.

The women in the continuity group characterized themselves, comparatively, as having *vitality* ($p \leq .05$) and *confidence* ($p \leq .05$) and as being significantly more *independent* ($p \leq .01$), *assertive* ($p \leq .01$), *talkative* ($p \leq .05$), *informed* ($p \leq .05$), *perceptive* ($p \leq .10$), and *responsible* ($p \leq .10$). The discontinuity young women, alienated from both societal and parental values, appear to be troubled, insecure, and anxious girls, as shown by the differentiating adjectives, *rebellious* ($p \leq .01$), *doubting* ($p \leq .05$), *shy* ($p \leq .05$), *self-denying* ($p \leq .05$) *stubborn* ($p \leq .05$), *needs approval* ($p \leq .10$), and *worrying* ($p \leq .10$).

Ideal-Self Descriptions. In the context of rejection of traditional societal values, young continuity people, who have a mutually respecting relationship with their parents, assert values for themselves that might be considered comparatively "straight," while the students in the discontinuity group proclaim a "counterculture" orientation. These conclusions derive from the value implications of the ideal-self description that the subjects conveyed. In their ideal-self descriptions, the male continuity subjects comparatively emphasize the values of *foresight* ($p \leq .05$), of being *self-controlled* ($p \leq .05$), *critical* ($p \leq .05$), and *argumentative* ($p \leq .05$). The females in the continuity group place greater value on being *logical* ($p \leq .01$), *considerate* ($p \leq .05$), and *foresightful* ($p \leq .05$).

By contrast, the distinguishing adjectives for the women in the discontinuity group reveal a concern for *adventurousness* ($p \leq .05$), keeping one's cool (*aloof and uninvolved* $p \leq .05$, *calm* $p \leq .05$, *reserved and shy* $p \leq .05$), and *being free and not "hung-up"* ($p \leq .10$). This constellation of adjectives suggests that the discontinuity women zealously aspire to an interpersonal independence. The men in the discontinuity group, on the other hand, expressed ideals that are both more classically feminine and consonant with the nominal ethic of the love-generation community: they aspire to being *genuine and authentic* ($p \leq .01$), *creative* ($p \leq .05$), *artistic* ($p \leq .10$), *playful* ($p \leq .10$), and *loving* ($p \leq .10$).

These results suggest an interesting reversal of emphasis in the sex roles sought by discontinuity subjects: the discontinuity women project ideal-self-images that seem typically more masculine, while the discontinuity males place greater emphasis on achieving qualities conventionally viewed as feminine.

Perceptions of Parental Child-Rearing Values. Socialization antecedents associated with different political–social orientations were assessed by the students' retrospective descriptions, using the Child-Rearing Practices Report (CRPR; Block, 1964), a 91-item *Q* set focusing on the parental values and practices by which they had been reared. Descriptions of both maternal and paternal child-rearing values were obtained. Obviously, these data can involve some degree of distortion and rationalization and are imperfect registries of the actual child-rearing behaviors of the parents. However, they are valid indicators of the perceptions or understandings held by the subjects of the ways in which they were reared, and, as such, they are interesting in their own right. Because the perceptions of the more alienated discontinuity group might involve some post hoc rationalized justification for their current estrangement from their parents, thus affecting the meaning of the child-rearing findings, the analysis of CRPR data from the actual parents of the discontinuity and continuity students, reported in the next section, becomes especially relevant.

Tables 1 and 2 present the differences in the socialization practices experienced by the two groups, as reflected in the CRPR. The CRPR analyses were done separately and combined for the sexes. Since the results were generally equivalent for the sexes, only the results of the combined analyses were presented to save space. The items reported are all significant at or beyond the .01 level (34% of the items for the mothers and 44% of the items for the fathers were significant at or beyond the .05 level).

With respect to both mothers and fathers, a consistent pattern emerges.

Table 1
Student Q-Sort Descriptions of Mothers' Child-Rearing Attitudes Significantly Differentiating Continuity and Discontinuity Groups at or Beyond the .01 Level

CRPR Item	Continuity Group Mean (n = 55)	Dis-continuity Group Mean (n = 36)	t Ratio
My mother:			
Respected my opinions	5.78	4.33	3.87
Didn't think young children should see each other naked	2.73	3.64	3.01
Wished my father were more interested in his children	3.20	4.31	2.67
Kept me away from families who had different ideas or values	1.71	3.31	5.37
Encouraged me to wonder and think about life	5.04	3.19	4.92
Felt I should have time to think and daydream	4.85	3.78	2.74
Let me make decisions myself	5.87	4.50	3.62
Talked it over and reasoned with me when I misbehaved	4.89	3.64	3.13
Gave me a good many responsibilities	4.58	3.06	3.96
Thought children had to take chances as they grew up	5.13	3.89	3.03
Encouraged me to be curious	5.55	3.72	5.15
Explained things by using the supernatural	1.85	3.58	4.37
Expected me to be grateful	4.58	5.81	3.44
Let me know when she was angry with me	5.69	4.58	3.24
Let me know how much she sacrificed for me	3.27	4.92	3.70
Let me know how ashamed and disappointed she was when I misbehaved	3.09	4.42	3.42
Encouraged me to be independent	4.82	3.64	2.65
Found it interesting to be with her children	5.00	3.69	3.76
Controlled me by warning of all the bad things that could happen	2.51	4.17	4.14

Note. The Q items are in somewhat abbreviated form. Seven categories of response were used, with "7" indicating items most characteristic and "1" indicating items least characteristic. Means in italics are more characteristic.

Table 2
Student Q-Sort Descriptions of Fathers' Child-Rearing Attitudes Significantly Differentiating Continuity and Discontinuity Groups at or Beyond the .01 Level

CRPR Item	Continuity Group Mean (n = 50)	Dis- continuity Group Mean (n = 34)	t Ratio
My father:			
Respected my opinions	5.88	4.12	4.75
Helped when I was being teased	3.96	2.91	3.37
Gave me comfort when I was upset	4.70	3.41	3.10
Kept me away from families who had different ideas and values	1.70	3.26	5.15
Thought children should be seen and not heard	2.06	3.68	4.05
Encouraged me to wonder and think about life	5.96	3.50	7.11
Felt I should have time to think and daydream	4.98	3.32	4.57
Let me make decisions myself	6.16	5.03	3.36
Felt I was a bit of a disappointment	2.52	4.00	3.37
Was easygoing and relaxed	4.90	3.65	2.78
Talked it over and reasoned with me when I misbehaved	5.10	3.71	3.36
Gave me a good many responsibilities	4.80	3.76	2.68
Thought children had to take chances as they grew up	5.92	4.68	3.74
Encouraged me to be curious	5.92	4.03	5.36
Let me know he appreciated my efforts	5.74	4.59	2.93
Dreaded answering my questions about sex	3.08	4.38	3.38
Wanted me to make a good impression on others	4.84	5.97	3.90
Found it interesting to be with his children	4.76	3.53	2.90
Instructed me not to get dirty while I was playing	1.94	2.79	2.90
Controlled me by warning of all the bad things that could happen	2.50	3.53	2.94
Didn't want me looked upon as difficult	3.48	4.68	2.92

Note. The Q items are in somewhat abbreviated form. Seven categories of response were used, with "7" indicating items most characteristic and "1" indicating items least characteristic. Means in italics are more characteristic.

The parents of the continuity group were described as encouraging of reflection, of curiosity, and of questioning. They appeared to find greater satisfaction in their parental roles, to respect the child's opinions, and to be interested in and appreciative of his accomplishments. The individuation of the child was emphasized, according to the perceptions of these young people, in that they were helped by their parents to develop a sense of autonomy. It is interesting to note that young people in the continuity group were not "permissively" reared—a term that has unfortunately been misinterpreted to mean license, indulgence, and freedom from limits. Rather, the parents could be described as "responsibly responsive." They appeared to have clear expectations for their children, and they encouraged maturity, responsibility, and independence. The misbehaviors of the child were neither ignored nor indulged, but instead were acknowledged and discussed with the child. Students in the continuity group are further distinguished by the emphasis in their families on rationality. They were encouraged by both parents to confront dilemmas and to arrive at their own conclusions. The response to wrongdoing was rational discussion rather than physical punishment.

Young people rebelling against both parental and societal values present a different picture. The parents of subjects in the discontinuity group were described as emphasizing appearances and being concerned about the impression others might have of their children. The child-rearing regime was described as suppressive and unresponsive to even the legitimate needs of the child. Socialization appeared to be concerned with attempts to circumscribe the children's thinking, reactions, and behaviors. Guilt and anxiety arousal were relied upon as mechanisms of control, according to the CRPR descriptions of the discontinuity group. Although there is the possibility of a retrospective rationalization of their alienation by the young people in the discontinuity group, the quality of child rearing ascribed to the parents by their children is consistent with the relatively more conservative political philosophy known, by virtue of selection criteria, to be held by these parents. Further, the child-rearing characteristics attributed to their parents by the discontinuity students are in accord with the child-rearing orientations of the actual parents of the discontinuity individuals, which will be reported later.

Because it was anticipated that continuity would be facilitated when the child-rearing values of both mother and father were congruent, the similarity of the child-rearing orientations of parent pairs as perceived by their child was evaluated by correlating the CRPR Q descriptions of mother and father to develop an index of agreement. The mean agreement score for the continuity group ($r = .546$) was significantly higher than the mean agreement for the discontinuity group ($r = .351$), a difference significant beyond the .001 level (one-tailed test).

STUDY II: THE CHILD-REARING ORIENTATIONS OF PARENTS OF CONTINUOUS AND DISCONTINUOUS STUDENTS

Because of the possibility that the students' perceptions of parental child-rearing values might be affected by self-serving distortions, particularly on the part of the more alienated discontinuity group, it seemed desirable to evaluate this alternative by undertaking a second study that would focus on students' parents.

METHOD

Selection of Comparison Groups. In 1967, the CRPR and an attitude questionnaire were mailed to the 536 available parents of a randomly selected sample of 322 Berkeley undergraduates, participating in a study conducted by Robert Somers. Sixty-six percent of the parents completed the test materials. The questions that were asked of the students and of their parents corresponded closely with the questions that were included in the 1964 study; thus, it again was possible to classify subjects with respect to the continuity–discontinuity categories, using criteria similar to those used earlier. However, the selection criteria, while similar in nature, were necessarily less stringent in the present study for two reasons: (*a*) The available subject pool from which extremes could be selected was smaller (1,051 subjects in 1964 and only 322 subjects in 1967), and (*b*) in the 1964 study, an explicit strategy involved the oversampling of activist students, who were more likely to be radical in the political commitments, while subjects in the 1967 study were a randomly selected sample. Since there were fewer students at the extremes, it was necessary to relax the selection criteria to achieve comparison samples of a statistically useful size, a compromise that results in less separation of the 1967 continuity and discontinuity groups, making statistical tests more conservative.

All students rating themselves as politically radical, liberal-radical, or, unlike the 1964 study, liberal (Steps 8, 7, and 6 of the continuum) were identified (the *N* proved to be 95). The further criteria applied for inclusion in the discontinuity group were (*a*) the existence of a discrepancy of 3 points or more (not 4 points or more, as in the 1964 sample) between the student's rating of his political preferences, and the ratings by his parents of their political preferences, and (*b*) the overall index of agreement between parent and child on such contemporary issues as the Vietnam war, legalization of marijuana, civil rights, patterns of dress, etc., was below the mean agreement (not one sigma below as in the 1964 sample) characterizing the total sample.

The criteria applied for inclusion in the continuity group were as follows: (*a*) There was a discrepancy of no greater than 1 point between the student's rating of his political preference and the ratings by his parents of their political preferences (the average discrepancy proved to be .54), and (*b*) the overall index of agreement between student and parent exceeded the mean of the total sample. No data reflecting parental influence on the students were available, and this consideration, used previously, could not be invoked.

Applying these criteria to this pool of students, 13 women and 15 men were included in the continuity group, 8 women and 9 men were placed in the discontinuity group, and 23 women and 27 men either could not be classified or had parents who did not participate.

In contrasting the discontinuity and the continuity groups in the two samples, the typical discontinuity or continuity student in the 1964 sample

Table 3

Mothers' CRPR Self-Descriptions Significantly Differentiating the Continuity (C), Discontinuity (D), and Conservative Continuity (CC) Groups

CRPR Item	Continuity Group Mean (n = 30)	Discontinuity Group Mean (n = 22)	t Ratio C vs. D	Conservative Continuity Mean (n = 27)	t Ratio CC vs. C	t Ratio CC vs. D
I encourage my child always to do his best	6.13b	6.14	—	6.69a	2.67**	1.94
I often feel angry with my child	3.57a	2.59b	1.87	2.65	1.87	—
I punish my child by isolation	3.45	3.50a	—	2.50b	2.03*	1.81
I watch closely what and when my child eats	4.53a	3.91	—	3.73b	1.97	—
I wish my husband were more involved with the children	2.27b	3.32a	2.43*	2.69	—	—
I try to stop my child from playing rough games where he might get hurt	3.67a	3.36	—	2.88b	1.68	—
I think it is good practice for a child to perform before others	3.57	3.50b	—	4.19a	1.72	1.69
I gain some of my greatest satisfactions from my child	5.47b	6.14a	1.76	5.96	—	—
I encourage my child to wonder and think about life	5.97a	5.59	—	5.15b	2.18*	—
I teach my child that punishment will "find" him	2.67b	3.55a	1.96	3.19	—	—
I don't allow my child to get angry with me	2.57	3.00a	—	2.11b	—	2.32*
I give up some of my own interests for my child	4.47	4.32b	—	5.04a	—	1.69
I have never caught my child lying	3.27	3.64b	—	2.54b	—	2.21*
I talk it over and reason with my child when he misbehaves	5.27b	5.54	—	6.15a	2.82**	1.83
I have strict, well-established rules for my child	3.23	3.14b	—	4.08a	1.81	1.72
I encourage my child to be curious	5.93	6.14a	—	5.50b	—	1.68
I sometimes feel I am too involved with my child	3.57	3.73a	—	2.77b	1.78	2.03*
I believe children should be weaned early	3.13a	2.36b	1.72	3.00	—	—
I believe in early toilet training	3.40	2.86b	—	4.19a	—	2.66*
I sometimes use the supernatural in explaining things to my child	3.00	3.59a	—	2.65a	—	1.79
I encourage my child to talk about his troubles	6.50a	5.82b	2.27*	6.31	—	—
I dread answering my child's questions about sex	2.07b	2.77b	1.91	2.54	—	—
I think my child should be encouraged to do better than others	3.30b	3.59	—	4.08a	2.02*	—
I punish my child by taking away his privileges	4.10	3.36b	—	4.69a	—	3.13**
I give my child extra privileges when he behaves well	4.27a	3.45b	1.92	4.19	—	1.90
I sometimes tease and make fun of my child	2.97	2.00b	2.27*	3.08a	—	2.37*
I teach my child that he is responsible for what happens to him	4.67b	5.50a	1.74	4.69	—	1.72
There is a good bit of conflict between my child and me	2.60a	2.05	—	1.34b	2.97**	1.95
I do not allow my child to question my decisions	2.13	2.95a	2.13*	2.08b	—	2.11*
I feel it is good for my child to play competitive games	4.80b	5.64	2.56*	5.88a	3.66**	—

Table 3 (Continued)

CRPR Item	Con-tinuity Group Mean (n = 30)	Discon-tinuity Group Mean (n = 22)	t Ratio C vs. D	Conser-vative Con-tinuity Mean (n = 26)	t Ratio CC vs. C	t Ratio CC vs. D
I let my child know how ashamed and disappointed I feel when he misbehaves	4.00	3.95[b]	—	4.77[a]	1.89	1.76
I want my child to make a good impression on others	5.17	4.82[b]	—	5.54[a]	—	1.84
I encourage my child to be independent	6.20[a]	5.82	—	5.61[b]	1.77	—
I think it is important for my child to play outside in fresh air	5.10[b]	5.41	—	5.96[a]	2.75**	—
I believe it is unwise to let my child play without supervision	3.27[b]	4.45[a]	3.01**	3.46	—	2.12*

Note. The Q items are in somewhat abbreviated form. Seven categories of response were used, with "7" indicating the most characteristic and "1" indicating the least characteristic.
[a] Means that are most characteristic.
[b] Means that are least characteristic.
* $p \leq .05$.
** $p \leq .01$.

defined himself as a radical, with only a sprinkling of liberal-radicals in the group (mean ratings are 7.90 and 7.64 for the discontinuity and the continuity groups); the 1967 discontinuity and continuity groups contained liberals and liberal-radicals in about even numbers, with only a few radicals present (mean ratings are 6.75 and 6.40 for the discontinuity and continuity groups). The mean agreement scores of the 1964 discontinuity and continuity groups were separated by more than two standard deviations, while the 1967 discontinuity and continuity groups were separated by less than one standard deviation. These restrictions of range characterizing the 1967 sample unfortunately attenuate the comparisons to be reported.

RESULTS

Before comparing the parents of the continuity and the discontinuity groups with respect to their socialization values and practices, their comparability was assessed with respect to educational achievement and occupational status, indexes that could influence socialization attitudes and confound the interpretation of results. No differences even approaching significance were found between the parents of the continuity and the discontinuity groups with respect to either of these indexes; the parents of the discontinuity group were slightly better educated, while the occupational status of the parents of the continuity group was somewhat higher.

Tables 3 and 4, present the CRPR terms, reliably differentiating between the parents of the discontinuity students and the parents of the continuity students. The results are reported for the sexes combined in order to simplify presentation, since sex-separated analyses reveal generally equivalent orientations in the parents of male and female children classified in a like manner.

Table 4
Fathers' CRPR Self-Descriptions Significantly Differentiating the Continuity (C), Discontinuity (D), and Conservative Continuity (CC) Groups

CRPR Item	Continuity Group Mean (n = 28)	Discontinuity Group Mean (n = 17)	t Ratio C vs. D	Conservative Continuity Group Mean (n = 24)	t Ratio CC vs. C	t Ratio CC vs. D
I respect my child's opinions	6.46ᵃ	5.76	2.20*	5.58ᵇ	2.52*	—
I help my child when he is being teased	4.48ᵃ	3.41ᵇ	2.38*	4.21	—	1.78
I expect my child to handle his problems by himself	3.14	4.06ᵃ	1.94	2.79ᵇ	—	2.29*
I don't think young children of different sexes should see each other naked	2 89ᵇ	4.00ᵃ	2.04*	3.21	—	—
I think physical punishment is the best method of discipline	1.78ᵇ	2.82	2.52*	3.33ᵃ	3.54**	—
I think it is good practice for my child to perform before others	3.71ᵇ	5.00ᵃ	2.84**	4.00	—	1.83
I express affection by hugging, kissing, and holding my child	4.11	4.35ᵃ	—	3.33ᵇ	—	2.66*
I encourage my child to wonder and think about life	6.11ᵃ	5.47	—	4.71ᵇ	3.57**	—
I find it difficult to punish my child	5.25ᵃ	4.59	—	3.83ᵇ	2.88**	—
I don't allow my child to say bad things about his teachers	2.93ᵇ	4.12	2.57*	4.13ᵃ	3.14**	—
I am easy going and relaxed with my child	4.86ᵃ	3.71ᵇ	2.29*	4.42	—	—
I give up some of my own interests for my child	5.25	4.41ᵇ	2.02*	5.42ᵃ	—	2.20*
I tend to spoil my child	4.64ᵃ	3.41ᵇ	1.92	3.92	—	—
I have never caught my child lying	3.00ᵇ	4.35ᵃ	2.04*	4.12	2.05*	—
I have strict, well-established rules for my child	2.79ᵇ	3.00	—	3.71ᵃ	1.85	—
I expect my child to be grateful	2.71ᵇ	4.59ᵃ	3.79**	3.96	2.51*	—
I sometimes feel I am too involved with my child	2.93ᵃ	2.82	—	2.21ᵇ	1.80	—
I believe in early toilet training	3.21ᵇ	3.59	—	4.25ᵃ	2.34*	—
I think praising a child when he is good gets better results than punishing bad behavior	5.79ᵃ	4.88ᵇ	1.77	5.21	1.92	—
I don't think children should have secrets from their parents	2.82ᵇ	4.24ᵃ	3.10**	3.00	—	2.34*
I try to keep my child from fighting	4.93ᵃ	3.53ᵇ	3.05**	3.83	2.23*	—
I dread answering my child's questions about sex	2.43ᵇ	2.82	—	3.29ᵃ	1.68	—
I punish my child by taking away his privileges	4.07	3.53ᵇ	—	4.83ᵃ	—	2.62*
I believe my child should be aware of all my sacrifices	1.96ᵇ	2.35	—	3.13ᵃ	2.72**	—
I sometimes tease and make fun of my child	2.93	3.29ᵃ	—	2.00ᵇ	1.77	2.22*
There is a good deal of conflict between my child and me	2.32	2.94ᵃ	—	1.92ᵇ	—	1.80
I don't allow my child to question my decisions	2.18ᵇ	2.71	—	3.04ᵃ	2.17*	—
I feel it is good for my child to play competitive games	5.14	5.12ᵇ	—	5.88ᵃ	2.08*	—
I like to have some time to myself away from my child	5.00ᵃ	4.94	—	4.25ᵇ	1.72	—
I let my child know how ashamed and disappointed I feel when he misbehaves	3.68	3.47ᵇ	—	4.37ᵃ	—	1.83

Table 4 (Continued)

CRPR Item	Continuity Group Mean (n = 28)	Discontinuity Group Mean (n = 17)	t Ratio C vs. D	Conservative Continuity Group Mean (n = 24)	t Ratio CC vs. C	t Ratio CC vs. D
I want my child to make a good impression on others	4.86b	5.65a	1.77	5.21	—	—
I find it interesting to be with my child for long periods	4.57a	4.35	—	3.71a	1.98	—
I think jealousy and quarreling between siblings should be punished	3.14b	3.65	—	4.21b	2.39*	—
I think children should learn early not to cry	2.07b	2.53	—	2.91a	2.23*	—
I don't think a child should be given sex information until he can understand everything	2.54b	3.23	—	3.54a	2.24*	—
I enjoy seeing my child eating well and enjoying his food	5.68a	4.82b	1.83	5.29	—	—
I don't allow my child to tease and play tricks on others	4.39	3.71b	—	4.58a	—	1.95

Note. The Q items are in somewhat abbreviated form. Seven categories of response were used, with "7" indicating the most characteristic and "1" indicating the least characteristic.
a Means that are most characteristic.
b Means that are least characteristic.
*p < .05.
**p < .01.

Comparing to content of the distinguishing items, the parents of the discontinuity students appeared to be more concerned with conventional values than were the parents of the continuity group. Competition and the importance of maintaining a good impression were given greater emphasis by the discontinuity parents. Further, the discontinuity parents appeared to be more authoritarian, restrictive, and suppressive in their socialization practices, as shown by their more frequent endorsement of items reflecting physical punishment and the "thou shalt nots" of child training. Children were not allowed to question decisions, to be critical of their teachers, to have secrets from their parents, or to play unsupervised. Finally, there is some suggestion of greater anxiety among the parents of the discontinuity students with respect to adequacy in the parental role. They indicated greater concern about coping with the sexual development of their children, demanded gratitude and appreciation from their children, and tended to require that their children assume the responsibility for solving their own problems. The earlier noted tendency of parents to use anxiety and guilt-arousing mechanisms of control were reproduced here in items reflecting gratitude and the invocation of threats of punishments from an impersonal, unpredictable, but implacable source. The results for the discontinuity parents seem to cohere with those of the earlier study.

Turning now to the descriptions of child-rearing practices provided by the parents of the continuity students, the results are somewhat more equivocal, particularly on the part of the continuity mothers. These parents appeared to have relationships with their children that both respected the child and encouraged his individuality, as witnessed by items valuing the child's opinions, encouraging discussion of problems with the child, and accepting the child's privacy needs. Interactions between mother and child also were described more candidly, since the continuity mothers were freer in admitting, or denied less vehemently, their negative feelings and their less exemplary socialization practices. Although the continuity parents described themselves as somewhat more indulgent and protective, they also were demanding of their children; the mothers believed in early weaning, and the continuity fathers expected their children to assume household and family responsibilities and were significantly more concerned with the control of aggressive behaviors than were fathers of the discontinuity group. The 1967 child-rearing descriptions by parents did not emphasize the importance of encouraging reflectivity, curiosity, and introspection as was true of the continuity students' perceptions of parental practices.

As before, the agreement between parent pairs in their child-rearing attitudes was evaluated by correlating their respective CRPR Q descriptions. The findings replicate those of the 1964 study based on perceptions of parental agreement. Again, the parents of the continuity individuals displayed greater agreement in their orientations toward child rearing ($r = .552$) than did the parents of the discontinuity individuals ($r = .450$), a difference significant beyond the .025 level (one-tailed test).

Considering the CRPR results for both the 1964 and 1967 studies, there seems to be a good deal of consistency in the relationships observed, despite the different contexts of application and the differences in sampling constraints. Unlike the 1964 study, wherein the unflattering portrayal of the discontinuity parents conceivably could be interpreted as a retrospective justification by the discontinuity subjects for their alienation from parents, the 1967 study, employing the parents of the discontinuity individuals, cannot be so interpreted. Indeed, in the latter study, one would expect the parents of the discontinuity subjects to justify, retrospectively, their estrangement from their children by portraying their socialization practices more positively in an attempt to minimize their responsibility for the subsequent alienation of their children. In this case, distortion in the more positive direction would make significant differences between the continuity and discontinuity parents more difficult to achieve.

On the basis of both studies, the constellation of significant items suggests that continuity parents experienced greater comfort in their parental roles, were more candid, and encouraged the individuation of their children, placing less emphasis on authoritarian control and discipline per se. Greater congruence of parental child-rearing philosophies also characterized the continuity parents in both studies. The discontinuity parents, on the other hand, appeared more tense in the parent–child relationshp and were more concerned with establishing and maintaining control over their children. The parents were in less agreement about their child-rearing values, which must result in inconsistent feedback to the child. Viewed in this light, the alienation of the discontinuity students may represent an attempt to escape excessive demands and intrusive, authoritarian controls imposed by inconsistent parents who often disagree with each other about their child-rearing attitudes.[1]

STUDY III: UNCONFOUNDING IDEOLOGY AND GENERATIONAL CONTINUITY

To further understand the forces of socialization influencing the continuity and discontinuity individuals, whose parents differ widely in their political (and social) orientations, a third group of students was identified from the 1967 subject pool that shares with the continuity group a continuity across generational boundaries and that shares with the discontinuity group the conservative political affiliation of their parents. This group, the *continuous conservative* group, was composed of students whose self-rated political position placed them in the conservative or moderate categories (of the 8-point political continuum) and whose self-rated ideological position did not deviate more than one step from the ratings by their parents on the same political continuum. These parents are slightly more conservative than their children and are similar in their degree of political conservatism to the parents of the discontinuity individuals. Twenty-eight subjects (18 males and 10 females) were identified by these criteria. Of this group, further information revealed their acceptance of the societal status quo, since 26 had not engaged in student demonstrations; the remaining two subjects had actively opposed student demonstrations.[2]

The CRPR Q descriptions of the parents of the continuous conservative students were contrasted with those of the parents of the continuity individuals, to identify the items differentiating parents holding conservative versus liberal political positions where their children have identified with parental ideology in each case. The CRPR Q descriptions of the parents of the continuous conservative students were also compared with those of the parents of the discontinuity individuals, to identify the items differentiating parents who rear children identifying with them from parents rearing children who have become disaffiliated where political ideology is held constant (at a conservative position).

The results of these comparisons are also included in Tables 3 and 4 in the last two columns. The results are reported for the sexes combined to save space, since the results are not importantly associated with gender.

---

[1] Although discontinuity parents disagree with each other in terms of their child-rearing attitudes, it is important to note that they did not manifest greater disagreement in the political–social sphere. When mothers' and fathers' ratings of endorsement are compared on 12 political–social dimensions (attitudes about student protests, drugs, effectiveness of Black Power, etc.), the mean standardized agreement scores were 49.4 and 49.0 for parents in the continuity and discontinuity groups, respectively, and 48.8 for the continuous conservative group (see below).

[2] No liberal discontinuity types could be found in the subject pool, an observation supporting the findings of Middleton and Putney (1963), who also noted that conversion to a conservative political ideology by young people reared in a liberal political tradition is a rare phenomenon.

SOCIALIZATION DIFFERENCES ASSOCIATED WITH CONSERVATIVE VERSUS RADICAL-LIBERAL IDEOLOGY

The child-rearing values of the continuous conservative group appear consistent with the conservative political attitudes characterizing the group. Contrasted against the liberal parents of the continuity students, the continuous conservative parents emphasized discipline and self-control in child upbringing. Fathers in the continuous conservative group described themselves as more authoritarian with their children, emphasized power and status differences between parent and child, encouraged the suppression of impulse and affect, and encouraged guilt. Mothers in the continuous conservative group appeared more concerned with competition and achievement.

Parents in the continuity group diverged from the continuous conservative parents in being less concerned with the schematizing of experiences and the suppression of impulse. Rather, these parents fostered introspection and encouraged their children to confront experience. The salient items suggest that the liberal parents of the continuity individuals emphasize the child's individuation, are candid in their interaction with the child, are less concerned with obedience, and place less emphasis on impulse control in areas other than aggression, where they are the most restrictive.

The socialization items differentiating the two continuity groups suggest that both power assertion (authoritarianism) and concern with the schematizing of experience are related to parental ideology; however, neither of these dimensions appears to be associated necessarily with alienation from parents, since parents placing high on these dimensions as well as those placing low both have adolescent young who manifest generational continuity. The average agreement score for parents of the continuous conservative students was .516, and it did not differ significantly from the continuity group mean.

SOCIALIZATION DIFFERENCES ASSOCIATED WITH ACCEPTANCE VERSUS REJECTION OF PARENTS

Comparisons of the two ideologically conservative groups of parents who differ with respect to the generational continuity–discontinuity shown by their children suggest that the child-rearing orientations of the parents of the discontinuity students are less coherent than those of the parents of the continuous conservative students. Mothers in the discontinuity group described themselves as overly involved with their children, they insisted that their children were always truthful, and they did not press for early training. Conjointly, these mothers emphasized authoritarian control—they forbade their children to question their decisions, they did not allow the expression of anger, and they felt most strongly that children should not be left to play without adult supervision. In contrast, mothers in the continuous conservative group appeared consistent, clear, and certain in their maternal roles—they were more accepting of anger, they had well-defined expectations for their children, and they dealt with transgressions.

The fathers in the discontinuity group characterized their relationships with their children as relatively more ambivalent and conflicted. They described themselves as wanting their children to handle their own problems but, also, as not wanting their children to have secrets from them. They ascribed less salience to items reflecting responsible parenthood (providing direction, limits, guidance, and support), while emphasizing physical interactions with their children. In contrast, the fathers in the continuous conservative group appeared more conscientious, helpful, and consistent in their parental roles.

In searching for patterns of child rearing that may be associated with adolescent rejection of parental values, the data suggest that acceptance of the child and conscientious, consistent, rational parenthood are more critical qualities or emphases than the degree of control imposed on the child. The child-rearing orientations of parents in the discontinuity group are, comparatively, less coherent and less rational. The discontinuity mothers tended to be permissive in some areas and demanded submission and compliance in others, while the discontinuity fathers were less conscientious and consistent in their paternal roles. The data on parental agreement also tended to reflect the greater inconsistency of the discontinuity parents, since the average agreement score for the discontinuity parents (.450) was lower than that of the continuous conservative parents (.516), a difference significant at the .07 level (one-tailed test).

DISCUSSION

The results of this study are in accord with the observations of other investigators who have concerned themselves with generational continuities and discontinuities. Watts and Whittaker (1968) concluded that the different styles of life characteristic of Berkeley activists and Berkeley "street people" were critically determined by the extent to which the intellectual, religious, political, and social values of the parents are relevant to and incorporated by the young. From his assessment of radical and militant youth, Leibert (1969) developed a typology in which he distinguished between "idealistic" and "nihilistic" radicals. He found that clear discontinuities in the moral and political value systems between parents and adolescents were associated with "nihilistic" radicalism and poor ego integration, while the values of the more integrated "idealistic" radicals had a strong similarity to those of their families. Leibert's conclusions fit well with the findings reported here. Finally, these results are consistent with Keniston's findings (1965, 1968) where uncommitted, alienated youth were found to be estranged from their families and to have rejected parental value systems, while committed young radicals were found to hold values similar to their parents and to evidence considerable identification with their parents.

Clearly, the findings surrounding the continuity group challenge the monolithic interpretations of student activism offered by Feuer (1969) and Rubinstein and Levitt (1969), wherein protest is seen as a universal, intemperate expression of Oedipal rebellion. The results of the present study further document the heterogeneity of the left and argue against a single, simplistic theory of political–social protest, equally applicable to all critics of contemporary society. Parental acceptance of, and even impulsion toward, radical social action is chracteristic of the continuity subjects in whom identification, rather than rebellion, appears to be the child–parent leitmotif.

We must note, however, that it is possible to view the findings for the discontinuous individuals, who have come to their political–social commitments in the absence of a liberal family tradition and without parental encouragement, as offering some support for the Oedipal thesis. The conflict attributed to the parent–child relationship, the rejection of parental values, and the tendency toward sex-role reversal suggested by the self-descriptions of the discontinuity group all can be fitted to an interpretation in terms of unresolved Oedipal conflicts. But alternative explanations of the discontinuity subjects are possible as well, since generational discontinuities cannot be taken as prima facie evidence of Oedipal rebellion. In any event, the heterogeneities found to characterize societal rejections clearly challenge attempts to ascribe protest to a single, universal cause.

The data further suggest that rebellion against parental values, as distinct from rebellion against societal views, may be viewed as a reaction of the young adult to the absence of consistency and coherence in his parents' child-rearing philosophies. Loevinger (1959) suggested that the battle between the generations is never more vicious than when parental reactions to a child are an expression of unmodulated impulse rather than determined by reason. She proposed that any parent-held theory of child rearing, even a theory that might fail to pass the muster of psychologists, is better than no theory at all, because it provides the child with a parental example of the principle of self-regulation for the welfare of another. Loevinger suggests that it is the socializing *intention* of the parent more than the *kind* of socializing that civilizes the child. The data tend to support her observations, since the child-rearing attitudes of the parents of the discontinuity subjects appear to be less guided by principle and to be more determined by parental conflicts and anxieties. Although the value systems reflected in the socialization practices of parents of the continuity and continuous conservative subjects diverge, each appears to have articulated and coherent notions about what is important in child rearing.

The greater intraparent consistency that appears to characterize both the continuity and the continuous conservative groups is reflected in greater interparent consistency as well, since there tends to be greater agreement between the parents about child-rearing values for both the continuity and the continuous conservative groups than for parents in the discontinuity group. It is interesting that agreement or disagreement between parents, with respect to political–social views, is not necessarily related to adolescent acceptance or rejection of parental values as noted above, perhaps because ideological differences between parents are manifested relatively abstractly and impersonally. Indeed, differences in parental political attitudes may contribute to an enriched intellectual environment for the developing child. Differences in socialization values, however, center upon the child who consequently can be buffeted by his disagreeing parents and be torn in his loyalties. Agreement between parents with respect to child-rearing values, on the other hand, adds to the overall consistency of the child's socialization experiences, reduces contradictory feedback, and contributes to the child's sense of coherence and predictability in his environment.

It has long been recognized that some degree of continuity across generational boundaries is essential to personality integration. Erikson (1965) suggested, "To enter history, each generation of youth must find an identity *consonant with its own childhood* and consonant with an ideological promise in the perceptible historical process [italics added, p. 24]." Continuity establishes some basis for communication and allows for ego-syntonic ways of negotiating conflicts. The continuity subjects appear to be finding a way to maintain the integrity of their own contemporaneously defined but historically influenced value positions—to be achieving a clearer sense of identity—without the need to reject their parents or to sacrifice familial ties.

Finally, we must note that the data from the studies reported here were gathered in an earlier political age, a time when protest was generally peaceful and demonstrators were generally good-natured and somewhat optimistic about the usefulness of their efforts. It may well be that the significance of our findings for the current political area is modified appreciably by the recent widespread view within the Left that political change will come too slowly to prevent societal disaster. Although our data cannot speak directly to the present, some extrapolations seem possible.

The discontinuity group is composed of radical, restless, searching young people centrally concerned with issues of personal expressiveness. Their political radicalism seems more a manifestation of a personal orientation toward immediacy than a considered and sustained commitment to social change. Accordingly, they would come quickly to accept the view that societal change is not feasible when the system does not respond immediately and their goals are frustrated. Two alternative behavioral consequences can be anticipated for the discontinuous individuals when their disenchantments are reinforced by an unresponsive society. They can seek their gratifications in the nonpolitical realm by "dropping out," or they can aggress against the source of their political frustration by violent means. It seems likely that the continuous individuals will be less pulled by either of these two alternatives. Unfortunately, research documentation of these conjectures may be long in coming, because research participation by today's Left is becoming more difficult to achieve.

REFERENCES

Bettleheim, B. Obsolete youth. *Encounter,* 1969, *23:* 29–42.

Block, J. H. *The Child-Rearing Practices Report.* Berkeley: Institute of Human Development, University of California, 1965. (Mimeo)

Block, J. H. Haan, N., & Smith, M. B. Activism and apathy in contemporary adolescents. In J. F. Adams (Ed.), *Understanding adolescence: Current development in adolescent psychology.* Boston: Allyn & Bacon, 1968.

Block, J. H., Haan, N., & Smith, M. B. Socialization correlates of student activism. *Journal of Social Issues,* 1969, *25:* 143–177.

Erikson, E. Youth: Fidelity and diversity. In E. Erikson (Ed.), *The challenge of youth.* Garden City, N.Y.: Doubleday, 1965.

Feuer, L. *The conflict of generations: The character and significance of student movements.* New York: Basic Books, 1969.

Flacks, R. The liberated generation: An exploration of the roots of student protest. *Journal of Social Issues,* 1967, *23:* 52–75.

Haan, N., Smith, M. B., & Block, J. The moral reasoning of young adults: Political–social behavior, family background, and personality correlates. *Journal of Personality and Social Psychology,* 1968, *10:* 183–201.

Keniston, K. *The uncommitted: Alienated youth in American society.* New York: Harcourt, Brace & World, 1965.

Keniston, K. *Young radicals: Notes on committed youth.* New York: Harcourt, Brace & World, 1968.

Keniston, K. The other end of the Oedipus complex. Paper presented at the annual meeting of the American Orthopsychiatric Association, New York City, March 1969.

Leibert, R. S. Towards a conceptual model of radical and militant youth: A study of Columbia undergraduates. Paper presented at the annual meeting of the Association for Psychoanalytic Medicine, New York City, April 1969.

Loevinger, J. Patterns of parenthood as theories of learning. *Journal of Abnormal and Social Psychology,* 1959, *59:* 148–150.

Middleton, R., & Putney, S. Student rebellion against parental political beliefs. *Social Forces,* 1963, *41:* 377–383.

Rubinstein, B., & Levitt, M. The student revolt: Totem and taboo revisited. Paper presented at the annual meeting of the American Orthopsychiatric Association, New York City, March 1969.

Smith, M. B., Haan, N., & Block, J. H. Social-psychological aspects of student activism. *Youth and Society,* 1970, *1:* 261–288.

Watts, W. A., Lynch, S., & Whittaker, D. Profile of a nonconformist youth culture: A study of the Berkeley non-students, *Sociology of Education,* 1968, *41:* 178–200.

developmental factors in adolescent drug use: a study of psychedelic drug users

**Stephen M. Pittel,   Victor Calef,   Roy B. Gryler,
Linda Hilles,   Ricardo Hofer,   Phyllis Kempner**
Mount Zion Hospital and Medical Center, San Francisco

This paper is concerned with the backgrounds and developmental histories of a group of approximately 250 volunteer subjects who identify themselves with the hippie community of San Francisco. Although many of them entered the hippie culture after the 1967 "summer of love" which first attracted thousands of young people to the Haight-Ashbury neighborhood, as a group these subjects are quite comparable to the stereotype of the original "flower children." Unlike the "street people" and "hard" drug users who have come to dominate the public image of the Haight-Ashbury today, these subjects exhibit most of the characteristics of dress, personal appearance, values, attitudes, and patterns of drug use of the early hippie population. A comparison of the biographical characteristics and MMPI profiles of these subjects with a group of hippies drawn from the original residents of the neighborhood failed to show any significant differences between the groups (Kendall and Pittel, 1971). Even though they do not share the naive Utopianism of the early hippies, and are forced to live in a less idyllic setting than might have been found a few years ago, we have good reason to believe that they are representative of those young people who first drew our attention to the hippie phenomenon.

This research was supported largely through NIMH grant MH. 15737 to Robert S. Wallerstein, M.D., and Stephen M. Pittel, Ph.D., for studies on "Psychosocial Factors in Drug Abuse." Additional support has been provided by the Chapman Research Foundation and by Mount Zion Hospital and Medical Center. This paper was presented at the meetings of the American Academy of Child Psychiatry, Denver, Colorado, October 17, 1970.

Reprinted from the Journal of the American Academy of Child Psychiatry, 1971, 10, 640–660. Copyright © 1971 by the American Academy of Child Psychiatry. By permission.

All of the subjects are volunteers who are paid one dollar per hour for their participation. Initially, subjects were recruited in the Haight-Ashbury neighborhood by research assistants or were referred to us by various community agencies. After the first few weeks, however, most of our new subjects were referred to us by friends who had come to us previously. Although we do not offer any services to subjects, our success in obtaining their initial cooperation and in maintaining contact with a large majority of them for two to three years suggests that their participation is not motivated by payment alone. Relatively few of them have approached us directly for referrals to treatment or other services, but most of them welcome the opportunity to talk about themselves and to enter into a quasi-therapeutic interaction with mental health professionals.

Ninety-five per cent of these subjects are between 18 and 26 years old, with a mean age of 22 years for males and 20 years for females. Initial use of marijuana and hashish began for most of them at about 17, although some of the younger subjects began the use of these drugs as early as age 11. Use of LSD, mescaline, peyote, and other potent psychedelic drugs began for most of them within a year after starting to use cannabis, and most of them became committed to the drug subculture at about the time of their first psychedelic drug use.

On the average, both males and females have used, at least on an experimental basis, 13 psychoactive drugs; 25 per cent of them have used between 18 and 29 different drugs. In addition to the psychedelics, the drugs most typically tried by them include amphetamines, barbiturates, alcohol, cocaine, codeine, and amyl nitrite. At the time of our first contact few of them had even experimented with the use of heroin, and the great majority of them showed a clear preference for marijuana and psychedelic drugs over all others. The modal pattern of drug use for these subjects includes the daily use of marijuana or hashish coupled with the less frequent use of LSD, mescaline, and other psychedelics. At the time of their initial assessment, psychedelic drug use varied from one or more times a week for a few subjects to monthly or less frequent use for the majority. As most of them have also used psychedelics more heavily for periods ranging from a few weeks to two or more years, typically at the beginning of their involvement in the drug culture, a conservative estimate would place the average number of psychedelic experiences for the group between 75 and 100. Some of them have had more than 300 psychedelic "trips."

In previous papers based on our observations of these young drug users we have described certain characteristic impairments in their current psychological functioning (Calef et al., 1970; Pittel, 1969; Pittel and Hofer, 1971). Impairments in the capacity for object relations, cognitive functioning, impulse and affect control, and particularly in the ability to integrate and synthesize experience have been found to varying extents in most of these subjects. While it is equally true that the great majority of these subjects also manifest signs of neurotic, psychotic, or character pathology, we have specifically avoided discussing them in such terms because they do not exhibit the characteristic degree of organization and patterning of symptoms diagnostic of these clinical syndromes.

In this paper we shall present data from questionnaires, life history interviews, psychiatric examinations, and written autobiographical material describing the background and psychological development of these subjects. From this material we shall attempt to formulate a model to account for their current mental status and for their involvement in the drug culture.

METHODOLOGICAL ISSUES

In attempting to reconstruct the psychological development or our subjects from the information available to us, we are beset by a host of pitfalls. Even though we are reasonably sure that they have not consciously falsified their accounts, many of our subjects have extremely poor recall of their childhood, and few can provide us with more than sketchy impressions of their histories, often including the recent years of their adolescence. Some of our subjects, for example, begin their written autobiographies with an account of their first experiences with psychedelic drugs which, for them, marks the beginning of their current existence. Some subjects claim an almost total amnesia for the first decade or more of their lives, and detailed information can be obtained from them only through painstaking inquiry.

To complicate matters further, these subjects are striking in their lack of psychological-mindedness. Even those with relatively rich stores of childhood memories tend to relate historical details with little recognition of either causal or chronological sequences; they are unable to provide much assistance to the interviewer attempting to reconstruct a meaningful portrait of their development. Finally, it is almost impossible to assess the nature or extent of retrospective falsification which results from their involvement in a deviant culture or to determine the distortions which might occur as a function of their extensive drug use.

While these methodological problems introduce many sources of potential bias to our data, we have attempted to compensate for them by focusing attention only on those developmental characteristics which are shared by the great majority of our subjects. Wherever possible, we have checked the validity of our observations through school transcripts, medical and psychiatric records, and other documentary sources which we have collected routinely. In some cases we have had contact with the subjects' parents, teachers, or family friends who have consented, with the subjects' permission, to provide us with additional background information.

Without exception the information obtained from these sources has corroborated the retrospective accounts or our subjects. Additional evidence for the validity of their accounts may be inferred from the convergence of our findings with those obtained by other investigators working with similar samples (e.g., Cohen, 1970; Holmes, 1970; Barron et al., 1970; Zaks et al., 1970). Therefore, despite the pitfulls inherent in this type of research, particularly with this group of subjects, it seems unlikely that we have been led too far astray in our search for the developmental antecedents of their current involvement in the drug culture.

FAMILY BACKGROUND

In most essentials our findings regarding the family backgrounds of these subjects are in close agreement with other published studies of psychedelic drug users (see Berg [1969] for a review of representative studies). They come primarily from middle- and upper-middle-class families with reported annual incomes averaging between $13,000 and $15,000 for the entire sample. Both they and their parents have had a median of at least one year of college education, with approximately 30 per cent of their fathers and 25 per cent of their mothers having obtained at least a bachelor's degree.

Over 90 per cent of their fathers are employed in occupations ranging from skilled worker through professionals and executives, and almost 50 per cent of them were employed in administrative, managerial, or semi-professional positions. Approximately 40 per cent of their mothers had been employed part- or full-time while the subjects were children, the majority of them in clerical, semiprofessional, or teaching positions.

Other demographic data are consistent with their traditional American middle-class family background. Most of them (67 per cent) come from major urban or suburban centers of population, such as New York, Boston, Chicago, Denver, Los Angeles, and San Francisco; relatively few of them are from the South, Southwest, or Northwest. Approximately half of them were raised as Protestants, 25 per cent as Catholic and 15 per cent as Jewish. Their parents belong to an average of two clubs or social organizations and have no more than one or two interests outside of their work or family. Virtually all of the subjects rate their parents as political moderates, or as being slightly right or slightly left of center.

To supplement the purely statistical picture of their familial background obtained through questionnaire measures, we turn next to a composite portrait of parental traits and behaviors as viewed by their children. The data summarized here were obtained separately for male and female subjects who were asked to rank order a series of cards bearing descriptive statements about parental traits and practices (Block, 1965) according to their assessment of how characteristic or uncharacteristic these statements are in describing their mothers and fathers. The following are items ranked as most and least characteristic of *both* parents by both male and female subjects.[1]

Items ranked most characteristic of both parents

enjoyed seeing me eat well and liking my food
let me know when he was angry
encouraged me always to do my best
wanted to make a good impression on others
taught me that I was responsible for what happened to me

---

[1] Items ranked most or least characteristic of only one parent are not included here.

expected a great deal of me
felt it was important for me to play outdoors and get lots of fresh air.

Items ranked least characteristic of both parents

expected me not to get dirty while I was playing
taught me at an early age not to cry
thought it unwise to let children play a lot by themselves without supervision from grownups
did not want me to try things if he thought I might fail
used to punish me by putting me off somewhere by myself for a while
sometimes explained things to me by talking about supernatural forces
and beings
did not allow me to say bad things about my teachers.

The impression of their parents given in these data is not inconsistent with their typically conventional backgrounds. Their parents are seen as having high expectations for them, encouraging their achievement, showing concern about their well-being, and even as being tolerant of their independence and right of self-expression. While independence and achievement pressures are more evident than expressions of warmth and understanding, their parental image is considerably more positive than might be expected among those who so strongly reject their heritage of middle-class values.

The picture that emerges from examination of either these or the demographic data suggests that we are dealing with a group that is neither socially deviant nor one which has been traditionally characterized by their heavy use of drugs. Clearly, this is not the familial background which we associate with the young heroin user (Chein et al., 1964), the young alcoholic (Rosenberg, 1969), or with the traditional adolescent delinquent (Hathaway and Monachesi, 1963). Rather, it corresponds more closely to the background of the middle-class American student (Offer et al., 1969), or perhaps more appropriately to that of student activists of 5 or 6 years ago (Keniston, 1968b).

INTELLIGENCE AND EDUCATION

In a review of trends in college drug use Keniston (1968a) notes the the incidence of psychedelic drug use is strongly related to the "intellectual climate [of academic institutions.] . . . the highest rates [of drug use] are found at small, progressive, liberal arts colleges with a nonvocational orientation, a high faculty-student ratio, high student intellectual caliber as measured by College Boards, close student-faculty relationships, and a great value placed on the academic independence, intellectual interests, and personal freedom of students" (p. 98). Keniston also suggests that within any college, psychedelic drug users are more likely to be found "in the most intellectual, humanistic and introspective' fields . . . such as music, literature, drama, the arts and psychology" (p. 99) and that they will tend to have higher grades than nondrug users.

Whether there is a causal relationship between psychedelic drugs and intellectual values or ability is a moot point. Nevertheless, it is clear that a great number of bright and talented young people have been attracted to this type of drug. This is neither a recent phenomenon nor one limited to the young; intelligent and articulate writers, including Havelock Ellis (1902) and William James (1916), were taken with this type of drug at the turn of the century, and Aldous Huxley (1954), Allan Watts (1962) and Timothy Leary (1968) have renewed the intellectual's interest in psychedelics in recent years.

It is, therefore, not surprising that our subjects are characterized by high intelligence and often by superior educational achievement. As reported in a previous paper (Calef et al., 1970), the median full-scale IQ score for a sample of 40 subjects tested on the Wechsler Adult Intelligence Scale was 119,[2] despite our finding that virtually all of the tested subjects were functioning below their intellectual capacity. We have also observed that the majority of our subjects place a great premium on their intellectual functioning, and they are more likely to become anxious during intelligence testing than in any other assessment procedure.

Similarly, from subjects' self-reports and from academic transcripts we have evidence that shows the educational performance of this group to be well above average, particularly in grade school. High school and college grades tend to become progressively worse,[3] reflecting, at least in part, their dissatisfaction with educational institutions. Yet despite the gradual deterioration of their academic work, a majority of those who ultimately "dropped out" of school (65 per cent of the entire sample) did so while maintaining average or above-average grades (cf. Hirsch and Keniston, 1970). It is also noteworthy that approximately 55 per cent of our subjects report that they would like to return to school at some future date to continue their education. Although they do not all expect to follow through on these plans in the near future, some indication of their commitment to intellectual values is given by their often reluctant acknowledgment that the "establishment" may still be able to provide them with some benefits (Pittel et al., 1970).

Although the intellectual potential of these subjects is generally above average, it is necessary to differentiate between two quite dissimilar subgroups within the total sample. While the differences between these groups are not at all limited to their intellectual capacities or academic achievements, it is here that they most clearly diverge. First are those subjects who show a superior intellectual endowment and who appear

---

[2] A median IQ of 118 was obtained for an additional sample of 45 subjects from (group) intelligence test scores entered in their grade and high school transcripts. If highest rather than average scores are used to estimate the IQ of subjects with more than one test result, the median score for the sample is 122.

[3] This finding obtains only when grade point averages are traced for individual subjects through their academic career. Those with higher grades tend to become progressively worse prior to their "dropping out," while those with lower grades do not show such a dramatic decline. Using data for the entire sample we find that approximately 50 per cent of the subjects maintain A or B averages in both high school and college.

to be characterized by unusually intense sensitivity and mental activity. These subjects have excelled typically in grade school and beyond, and many of them have shown from early childhood signs of unusual intellectual or other talents. The following abstract from our case records is illustrative of such subjects.

David is a 23-year-old, single, white male, who has recently graduated from college as a sociology major. His father is a physician in private practice; his mother is unemployed but has numerous hobbies, such as arts and crafts, pottery, and gardening. His earliest memory is of his mother teaching him to play solitaire, which he described as a "friendly and helpful" gesture. He also recalled an early fantasy of having magical friends with whom he would imagine building boats and doing "organized things on paper."

He was precocious intellectually in grade school and recalls that there was a "real pecking order" among his peers, with much competition over who was most superior. Although he preferred to stay home and read, his mother forced him to play with other children. He became engrossed in chemistry when he was 10 years old and then in mathematics a few years later. He began learning calculus in the 9th grade and he writes, "from then until high school graduation, chemistry and mathematics were unequivocally, securely beautiful in my eyes and I studied them avidly." These interests, along with a fascination with "great" literature, philosophy, and history, led him to become an "intellectual snob," but he nonetheless became active in numerous high school clubs and extracurricular activities, including the debating team and the NAACP. He also served as editor for his school paper.

He scored at the 99th percentile in four of six areas in the National Merit Scholarship competition, receiving scores at the 92nd and 85th percentiles on those remaining. In college his interests shifted from mathematics and chemistry to the study of "social-economic-political problems," which he saw as the "only remaining hope for relieving the suffering of humanity." During the last two years of college, his grades dropped for the first time since beginning school, from an A to a B minus average. He comments on this: "I studied and studied, but the college system of overstudy caused serious brain damage and I turned off on all intellectual pursuits."

In addition to their intellectual accomplishments, some of these gifted subjects have shown talents in writing, poetry, music, painting, and crafts, even in early childhood. Others have distinguished themselves in more novel ways as, for example, one subject who attained a Master rating as a chess player while in junior high school, another who performed as a mnemonist for the amusement of his family and later to make extra money while in school, and one who reported his accomplishments as a "poet, writer, photographer, former actor, leathersmith, grease monkey, professional barker, circus rigger, trapeze artist, coffee-house manager, and priest." This subject failed to mention in his autobiography his brief careers as a pornographer, chef, and maitre d'hôtel which he modestly disclosed at a subsequent interview.

In contrast to these unusually bright or gifted subjects, the remainder of this sample are not distinguished by any particular intellectual characteristics. Most of them are above average in intelligence, performed well in school, and had interests and hobbies typical of most children. Others are noteworthy for having had difficulties in school, or for their lack of special interests. However, what characterizes these subjects is that they had not manifested any truly superior abilities in early childhood. Thus, this second group is more heterogeneous in intelligence and achievement-than the former, and it includes by far the greater proportion of our subject population.

PSYCHOLOGICAL DEVELOPMENT

To understand some of the factors which led these adolescents and young adults to their current life style it is necessary to look beyond questionnaire and objective test results to the richer and more complex data of the clinical method. It is here that two central features of the background of each of our subjects emerge, and we can begin to see the basis of their use and commitment to psychedelic drugs.

The first of two themes shared by these subjects is that of loneliness and a profound sense of isolation from others. Most of these subjects report problems in forming meaningful, intimate, and lasting relationships from early childhood, and almost all of them attribute their isolation to a sense of being "special" or "different." It is more a feeling of uniqueness than mere loneliness which characterizes these subjects and which distinguishes them from other normal or disturbed adolescents (cf. Keniston, 1968b).

The early social isolation and subsequent difficulties in forming adequate relationships based on the experience of being "different" may be traced to a wide variety of personal and social causes. For some of the more gifted subjects it appears to result from their intellectual precocity and the richness of their sensory-perceptual experience. These subjects are unable to communicate the quality of their experience to others and are unable to achieve any consensual validation of their perception of reality. In contrast to most other subjects, whose isolation tends to stem from environmental deprivations or personal inadequacies, these gifted subjects place a high premium on the qualities which make them unique. They typically deny feeling lonely in early childhood, and most of them believe that their isolation from others was self-imposed.

Even among those who do not suffer from any embarrassment of riches, there are some who value positively the attributes which led them to feel apart from others. One subject, for example, was raised as the only child in a religious commune in New England, and was taught by her elders that she possessed unique spiritual gifts. Although she reports that children in a public school she attended approached her with some apprehension, she claims that it was her greater religious awareness which made her unwilling to befriend them. Another example of a positively valued isolation is that of one of the three black subjects in our sample, whose parents attempted to protect him from the influences of an urban ghetto by teaching him to play the piano beginning at age 3. Throughout most of his preadolescent years this subject was immersed in musical study and had few dealings with any youngsters. He particularly shunned contact with his peers and he believed himself to be superior to other people, especially blacks, because of his musical interests.

At the other end of the spectrum are those who have suffered throughout their lives by their inability to find friendship and who view themselves more as stigmatized than as superior. Again, within this group there exist numerous bases for the feeling of being an outcast. Some subjects attribute their childhood isolation to chronic illness or to other infirmities which led to their being scorned and rejected. Others place the onus upon their physical appearance, claiming that they were too fat, too skinny, too tall, or too puny to be accepted as equals by any peer group. Still others report that their upwardly mobile parents placed them among peers with high status while failing to provide them with adequate training, experience, clothing, or other signs of affluence to make them acceptable.

One case illustrative of this type of social isolation is that of Jennifer, an attractive young lady whose long red hair, green eyes, and freckled compexion clearly mark her Irish origins. Jennifer was adopted as an infant by Jewish immigrant parents who owned and operated an Oriental gift shop in the Catskill Mountains.

Jennifer was told by her parents that she had been adopted, and her mother made quite a point of impressing upon her that she was "chosen" and "special." Throughout her childhood she was encouraged to forget her natural parents who, the mother claimed, were both dead. Nonetheless, Jennifer frequently wondered about her natural parents and created elaborate fantasies which focused on them.

She imagined herself as a princess from a fantasy island who would one day meet a strange woman who looked like her, would turn out to be her mother, and would take her to a special place where they belonged. Later in childhood, she began to have preternatural fantasies of being a changeling or a fairy child who would turn out to be "someone special."

She describes difficulties in making friends from the beginning of school. "I had nothing. I didn't think I was pretty. I was chubby and had red hair. The red hair set me off from other people, it was bizarre and different." Although she got good grades, she continued to feel isolated in school, and spent much of her time daydreaming. Her mother felt that her social isolation was her own fault since she was not aggressive enough. She then began to think that her mother as well as her classmates were making fun of her. She could not understand how she might be accepted by those whose appearance was so unlike her own.

Summarizing these experiences in her autobiography, she writes: "The primary impact of this raising period was an incredibly lousy self-image which, in spite of 3 years of psychiatry, 4 years of drugs, 5 of education, and 5 away from parents, I have been unable to shake. . . . And so I find myself in the Haight-Ashbury, land of the losers. To me, the most extraordinary thing about our subculture . . . is that almost all of us were losers or felt ourselves to be . . . in whatever 'real' world we lived in before, in whatever sense was important to us."

A second major theme in the histories of our subjects is their exposure to an unusually high degree of stimulation, stress, and trauma throughout their childhood and early adolescence. What particularly characterizes their accounts of childhood (and may explain some of their difficulty in recalling childhood events and chronologies) is their sense of living amidst great confusion, chaos, and disorganization, and their inability to escape for even brief periods to a calmer and more benign environment. The image they create of their childhood belies the placidity of their middle-class origins; none of our clinical staff had had experience with histories as sad or disturbing as those given by these subjects.

The following longer case history illustrates the quality of the stresses characteristic of the childhood and adolescence of our subjects.

Sally is an 18-year-old, single, white, Jewish female. She and her 2-year-older brother were born in Boston, and were raised in a number of wealthy suburbs along the East Coast. She was described as she appeared for a psychiatric interview as "a very young-appearing, not especially attractive girl, with a heavy face, thick lips, a big nose, and big brown eyes. Her face usually had a sad, morose look, but she smiled occasionally with pleasant humor. She had longish brown hair and wore little-girl clothes—a red dress, knee socks, low shoes, and a short jacket. She wore no makeup or jewelry."

Her earliest memory is of standing in her front yard watching another little girl walk by. They both stared at each other, as if they wanted to make friends. She thinks that this memory might indicate that she felt lonely as a child. Her next memory, at age 5, is of part of her finger being almost severed when her brother turned the wheel of a bicycle as she was playing with its chain. She recalls screaming, without feeling any pain, as if she were standing outside of herself. She also recalls an early memory of her mother wiping blood from a gash in her leg, caused by her falling over a pile of bricks.

Sally describes her mother as a quiet person who "wanted a happy, harmonious home life," and says that much of her early childhood was secure and comfortable. Yet she recalls that there were always a lot of visitors, parties, activities, and excitement around the house. She describes her father as being restless and energetic, having many outside interests and little ability to remain content without going somewhere or doing something. Her father was a successful businessman who as a hobby designed and built all of the homes in which they lived.

She had few friends in grade school and spent most of her time playing at home alone, while her brother was out with his friends. She sensed that something was wrong between her parents and was unhappy much of the time because of this. Also, her brother was continually getting into trouble at school and in the neighborhood for his mischievous behavior. Her brother was struck by a car when he was 7, causing severe neurological motor damage resulting in uncontrollable shaking and spasms in his left arm. After the brother's accident he became even more demanding of the family's attention and frequently disrupted the household by getting into some sort of trouble. Sally recalls being frightened and upset by her brother's misbehavior. She also could not understand why her brother had become so cruel and mean to her after his accident; previously she had seen him as her protector.

Twice, between the ages of 7 and 11, the family moved to satisfy the father's wanderlust. During those years the tension in the family increased, her father driving himself to greater achievements and becoming more irritable, her brother becoming chronically angry and depressed, and her mother making futile attempts to quell her husband's often violent attacks on their troublesome son. Finally, the parents were divorced when Sally was 11.

She then lived alone with her mother, who seemed to her always tired and depressed. Her brother had been sent to the Devereux School, where he continued to be a troublemaker and was often threatened with expulsion. For the next 3 years she did well in school and began to make a few friends, but she became obese and had no personal involvement with boys. During these years, each of her parents attempted to turn her against the other. Her father promised her things in exchange for information, while her mother accused her former husband of lying and insincerity.

During a summer vacation while the brother was home from boarding school, her mother left the house determined to meet and make peace with her husband. Later that day she committed suicide by taking an overdose of sleeping pills. Without explaining the reason for his visit, the father took both children out to dinner and the theater that evening, and only afterwards told them their mother was dead.

Sally went to live with her father, but after a relatively tranquil 6 months in which she grew to love him for his cheerful and easy manner and affluent life style, they began to fight violently about their family history. The father accused her of driving her mother to suicide, of failing to be more understanding of both him and his wife, and for bringing about all of the troubles of the family. She says about this: "He said things that could never be forgiven. He made me feel terrible . . . like it was all my fault. He tried to make me feel guilty. I felt like I was going crazy . . . maybe he was right."

She ran away from her father's home and was subsequently placed in a residential treatment center where she says she was happy for a time. Eventually, she began to speak with her father again, after being told by her social worker that he might be in need of help.

When she was 16 her brother, who had begun to use drugs heavily, wrote to her saying he had taken an overdose of heroin and would be dead by the following day. She rushed to his apartment, where she found him dead. She cried for a few minutes, rode a streetcar to the beach where she met some friends, and then stayed and talked with them for the rest of the evening, as if nothing had happened.

Sally first used marijuana shortly after running away from her father. She states that she enjoyed being stoned because it made her feel relaxed and good. Her first experience with a stronger psychedelic drug, peyote, took place a few months after her brother's death, and she says of her first peyote experience, "I felt very relaxed and peaceful. I felt as if I were in a fairy tale. I was fascinated by explosive, fantastic, and colorful patterns. This organic drug described to me all the peace that rests on this earth."

This fragment from one of our case histories is not unique as an illustration of some of the extreme pressures to which these subjects are exposed; virtually any of our case reports might have been selected for presentation here, with little change in emphasis or sense of tragedy. Nor was this case presented in full. More recent events in this subject's life, from her entry into the drug subculture to the present, suggest that her use of drugs, and her commitment to a life-style radically different from that of her parents, have exposed her to a further series of painful events and relationships, and have brought her no closer to the attainment of peace or harmony. In our most recent follow-up contact with this subject, who is now 20 years old, employed full-time, and who now describes herself as having reentered the "straight" society, she describes her current use of barbiturates: "Reds make me feel slow and mellow and highly sexual . . . there is no unpleasantness. The only thing I regret is that I cannot enjoy this more often . . . the drug doesn't last but two hours."

THEORETICAL CONSIDERATIONS

Before suggesting a hypothetical reconstruction of the developmental factors which contribute to the use of psychedelic drugs in this sample of adolescents and young adults, let us summarize briefly the evidence we have presented. We have found that these subjects come from a respectable and privileged stratum of society and that they typically are bright or even superior in intellectual endowment; that, despite considerable success in academic and other achievements through most of their early years, they have become alienated from the values of their parents and have chosen, in adolescence, a life style based largely on the use of mind-altering drugs. We have found, also, that they have had great difficulties in forming and maintaining adequate relationships with others, and that they have thought of themselves as being "different" from other people, perhaps as a means of tolerating their profound psychological isolation. For some of them the inability to form relationships may result from the inadequacy of their early familial experiences. For others, it seems more a function of the hypertrophy of intellectual and sensory-perceptual mechanisms, which makes it difficult for them to find any basis for peer group affiliation.

Throughout their lives they have been subjected to a series of familial and other pressures, often of a traumatic nature, which have created for them a world of chaos and confusion from which they could find no respite. The psychological consequences of these childhood events frequently became intensified in early adolescence, and it is then that many of them suffer most acutely from their isolation and sense of separateness. At this point in their development a number of behavioral and psychological problems may arise. These include rather typical adjustment problems, rebellion against parental authority, delinquency, etc., as well as a full spectrum of more severe neurotic or psychotic disturbances. In response to the difficulties they are experiencing, these subjects may, at this time, begin to experiment with drugs and to modify their life style to that of the hippie culture. For some the process is gradual; for others a complete change in expressed values and behavior may occur following their first use of psychedelic drugs, as in a religious conversion experience.

At the time of their initial assessment at the Haight-Ashbury Research

Project these subjects show certain characteristic impairments in ego functioning; they do not exhibit the stable symptomatic pictures of neurotic, psychotic, or character pathology. It should be added that the absence of clearly defined and well-organized pathology is apparent even in those who had previously manifested specific forms of character pathology or mental illness.

In general, these observations and findings are quite consistent with the clinical portraits of the young drug user sketched by Frosch (1970), Hartmann (1969), and Wieder and Kaplan (1969), as well as those derived from a number of psychological assessment studies (e.g., Holmes, 1970; Smart and Jones, 1970). However, in contrast to most other theorists, our reconstruction of the psychological factors which contribute to the use of psychedelic drugs does not rest on a model of intrapsychic conflict. Rather, we believe that the great majority of our subjects suffer from deficits in ego function which either antedate or overshadow the contributions of conflict to their psychological development. To put it differently, we agree with most theorists that the young drug user turns to psychedelic and other drugs to avoid painful affects and in an effort to deal with personal and developmental crises. Yet, we believe that the anxiety of the drug user results more from his lack of ego structures and his inability to integrate and synthesize experience than from the libidinal and aggressive conflicts associated with the oedipal situation. Indeed, it is possible that these subjects lack even that degree of ego organization required for the formation of symptoms. While continued reliance on drugs to achieve a respite from anxiety may lead to even greater impairment in the capacity for integration and synthesis, impaired ego functioning is seen more as the basis for drug use than as its consequence (Calef et al., 1970).

From a developmental standpoint we hypothesize that the ego formation of our subjects has suffered from major assaults dating from early childhood. Both those whose difficulties are largely the product of familial stresses and those who are the victims of an excessive burden of sensory input and mental activity manifest early impairments in the capacity for object relations and in the control of impulses and affects. Corresponding to these impairments is a relative failure in the internalization of stable object representations and of representations of the self, the latter giving rise to their perception of themselves as outcasts or freaks.[4]

Subjected to a series of additional stresses throughout childhood and adolescence, many of these subjects develop further impairments in reality testing, judgment, attention, concentration, and many other ego functions. Those gifted subjects whose background often are more benign in

---

[4] It is significant in understanding the subcultural bond which unites young drug users and contributes to their sense of belonging with one another that they refer to themselves as "freaks" without giving this a pejorative meaning (cf. Einhorn, 1970). It is probable that they have always thought of themselves in this way and have used the strength of their numbers and shared drug use to negate its usual connotation. Goffman (1963) describes other stigmatized individuals whose disabilities lead them to form groups to aid in compensating for their "spoiled identities."

terms of familial and environmental stresses tend to manifest fewer impairments in cognitive functions during most of childhood. Rather, it is during adolescence that these subjects begin to exhibit their failure to cope with the ever-increasing amount and complexity of their inner and outer stimulation.

Although the characterization of the childhood of our subjects is little more than a preliminary sketch, it is intended to call attention to what may be the central determinant in their development and in their attraction to the psychedelic cult. We are referring here to the inability of these subjects to understand, organize, or integrate the events of their lives. This phenomenon may be described also as a relative absence of enduring ego structures, including those which might lead to symptom formation, to deal with developmental and environmental stresses they cannot otherwise manage (cf. Calef et al., 1970; Pittel, 1969; Pittel and Hofer, 1971).

To the extent that we are correct in attributing the ego impairments of the young drug user to the disorganization and chaos of their backgrounds, our attention should be focused more on the severity, frequency, and rate of traumatic and stressful events such as separations, deaths, seductions, betrayals, and disappointments than on their actual or symbolic meaning. We must assign great significance to the more or less continuous occurrence of these disruptive experiences through childhood and adolescence, rather than focusing on the events of the first few years of life. It is our impression that these subjects have never experienced even the relative moratorium from stress that theory assigns to the latency period.

As Blos (1962), Bernfeld (1935), and others (e.g., Sarnoff, 1971) have suggested, this period of relative freedom from turmoil is essential for the development of ego functions needed to deal with the onslaught of adolescence. It is here that we believe our subjects suffer most critically from their inability to escape being bombarded by excessive stimulation, and that they lose their final opportunity to develop necessary integrative and synthetic functions. While it may have little more than metaphoric significance, it is striking to us how closely descriptions of the harmony and peace achieved through the psychedelic experience correspond to an idealized picture of the latency period. It is not inconceivable that the psychedelic cult is made up of those who have been robbed of this essential part of childhood and that they have chosen to seek childlike freedom through the use of drugs.

To these theoretical suggestions we must add some cautionary notes. As the incidence of illicit drug use has increased in recent years to include both a great number and a broad cross-section of individuals, and to encompass a wide variety of drugs and myriad patterns of use, the possibility of formulating any general theory of drug abuse has rapidly diminished. Until patterns of drug use and abuse become stabilized within various groups of individuals, and investigators learn to identify these patterns and specify the characteristics of those who employ them, theory based on one set of observation will have little relevance to other situations. Further, as social, cultural, economic, and political forces continue to change, perhaps even more rapidly than they have in the past, it will become increasingly difficult to rely on psychological explanations of drug use.

As Alvin Toffler (1970) has suggested in his recent book, *Future Shock,* our generation and those which follow must learn to cope with anxieties unknown until recently, anxieties which result from the impermanence of all social structures and institutions and from the overwhelming complexity of our daily lives.

The young drug users we have studied may be but the first victims of an accelerative thrust which threatens the existence of all structures, including those of the psychic apparatus. If psychological isolation and a relative inability to integrate and synthesize experiences are likely consequences of the growing technological and cultural changes in our society, the choice of a chemoplastic adaptation may well be the normative expectation for those who will reach adolescence in years to come.

REFERENCES

Barron, S. P., Lowinger, P., & Ebner, E. (1970), A clinical examination of chronic LSD use in the community. *Compreh. Psychiat., 11:* 69–79.

Berg, D. F. (1969), Extent of illicit drug use: a compilation of studies, surveys and polls. Unpublished manuscript, Bureau of Narcotics and Dangerous Drugs, U.S. Department of Justice.

Bernfeld, S. (1935), Über die enfache männliche Pubertät. *Z. psychoanal. Päd., 9:* 360–379.

Block, J. (1965), The child-rearing practices report. Institute of Human Development, University of California, Berkeley (mimeographed).

Blos, P. (1962), *On Adolescence.* New York: Free Press of Glencoe.

Calef, V., Gryler, R. B., Hilles, L., Hofer, R., Kempner, P., Pittel, S. M., & Wallerstein, R. S. (1970), Impairments of ego functions in psychedelic drug users. Paper presented at the Conference on Drug Use and Drug Subcultures, Asilomar, Calif.

Chein, I., Gerard, D. L., Lee, R. S., & Rosenfeld, E. (1964), *The Road to H: Narcotics, Delinquency, and Social Policy.* New York: Basic Books.

Cohen, M. (1970), Psychological and social characteristics of psychiatrically hospitalized drug users. Paper presented at the Conference on Drug Use and Drug Subcultures, Asilomar, Calif.

Einhorn, I. (1970), From data collection to pattern recognition: the sociology of the now. In: *Psychedelics,* ed. B. Aaronson & H. Osmond. Garden City: Doubleday.

Ellis, H. (1902), Mescal: a study of a divine plant, *Pop. Sci. Mon., 61:* 52–71.

Frosch, W. A. (1970), The drug abuser's chosen drug. Paper presented at the Conference on Drug Use and Drug Subcultures, Asilomar, Calif.

Goffman, E. (1963), *Stigma: Notes on the Management of Spoiled Identity.* Englewood Cliffs, N.J.: Prentice-Hall.

Hathaway, S. R. & Monachesi, E. D. (1963), *Adolescent Personality and Behavior: MMPI Patterns of Normal, Delinquent, Dropout, and Other Outcomes.* Minneapolis: University of Minnesota Press.

Hartmann, D. (1969), A study of drug-taking adolescents. *The Psychoanalytic Study of the Child, 24:* 384–398. New York: International Universities Press.

Hirsch, S. J. & Keniston, K. (1970), Psychosocial issues in talented college dropouts. *Psychiatry, 33:* 1–20.

Holmes, D. (1970), Characteristics of hippies in the East Village of New York. Paper presented at the Conference on Drug Use and Drug Subcultures, Asilomar, Calif.

Huxley, A. (1954), *The Doors of Perception* and *Heaven and Hell.* New York: Harper & Row.

James, W. (1916), *Varieties of Religious Experience.* New York: Longmans, Green.

Kendall, R. F. & Pittel, S. M. (1971), Three portraits of the young drug user: comparison of MMPI group profiles. *Psychedelic Drugs, 3:* 63–66.

Keniston, K. (1968a), Heads and seekers: drugs on campus, counter-cultures and American society. *Amer. Schol., 38:* 97–112.

———— (1968b), *Young Radicals: Notes on Committed Youth.* New York: Harcourt, Brace & World.

Leary, T. (1968), *High Priest.* New York: World Publishing.

Offer, D., Sabshin, M., & Offer, J. L. (1969), *The Psychological World of the Teenager.* New York: Basic Books.

Pittel, S. M. (1969), Psychological effects of psychedelic drugs: preliminary observations and hypotheses. Paper presented at meetings of the Western Psychological Association, Vancouver, B. C.

———— & Hofer, R. (1971), The transition to amphetamine abuse. In: *Current Concepts of Amphetamine Abuse,* ed. E. A. Ellinwood. Washington, D.C.: Government Printing Office (in press).

———— Wallach, A., & Wilner, N. (1970), Utopians, mystics and skeptics: ideologies of young drug users (unpublished manuscript).

Rosenberg, C. M. (1969), Young alcoholics. *Brit. J. Psychiat., 115:* 181–188.

Sarnoff, C. A. (1971), Ego structure in latency. *Psychoanal. Quart., 40:* 387–414.

Smart, R. G. & Jones, D. (1970), Illicit LSD users: their personality characteristics and psychopathology. *J. Abnorm. Psychol., 75:* 286–292.

Toffler, A. (1970), *Future Shock.* New York: Random House.

Watts, A. W. (1962), *The Joyous Cosmology.* New York: Vintage Books.

Wieder, H. & Kaplan, E. H. (1969), Drug use in adolescents: psychodynamic meaning and pharmacogenic effect. *The Psychoanalytic Study of the Child, 24:* 399–431. New York: International Universities Press.

Zaks, M. S., Hughes, P., Jaffe, J., & Dolkart, M. B. (1970), Characteristics of "Yippies" attending the 1968 Democratic National Convention. Paper presented at the Conference on Drug Use and Drug Subcultures, Asilomar, Calif.